Market-driven Management

Strategic and Operational Marketing

Jean-Jacques Lambin

*Professor of Market-driven Management at
Università degli Studi di Milano-Bicocca*

www.macmillan-press.co.uk/business/lambin

First published 2000 by
MACMILLAN PRESS LTD
Houndmills, Basingstoke, Hampshire RG21 6XS
and London
Companies and representatives
throughout the world

ISBN 0–333–79318–8 hardcover
ISBN 0–333–79319–6 paperback

A catalogue record for this book is available
from the British Library.

This book is printed on paper suitable for recycling and
made from fully managed and sustained forest sources.

10 9 8 7 6 5 4 3 2 1
09 08 07 06 05 04 03 02 01 00

Editing and origination by
Aardvark Editorial, Mendham, Suffolk

Printed and bound in Great Britain
by Antony Rowe Ltd, Chippenham, Wiltshire

To Daisy, Sophie and Lara

Contents

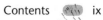

part four

Market-driven Management Decisions 459

part five

Ten Case Studies in Market-driven Management 699

List of figures

List of tables

List of exhibits

Preface

Why a New Textbook on Marketing?

This book is the second edition of the author's *Strategic Marketing Management* book published in 1997 by McGraw-Hill. The book has been extensively revised and has expanded the market orientation concept introduced in the 1997 edition, not only in the field of strategic marketing but also in operational marketing. This is why the title of the book has been changed to: *Market-driven Management: Strategic and Operational Marketing*.

Why yet another textbook on marketing? In other words, what distinctive qualities does this new book claim to offer? This question, central in strategic marketing, is just as relevant for an author as it is for an innovative firm.

The first objective is to close a cultural gap. In Europe, the marketing-textbook market is largely dominated by American writers and I feel that there is a need for a text presenting the European perspective in English. In North America, the slogan *What is good for business is good for society* is largely undisputed and, to my knowledge, there are few radicals among North-American marketing academicians or practitioners questioning the premises underlying the marketing discipline. Elsewhere, and in particular in European societies exposed to other social and political currents, this is not as obvious and the role of marketing is always controversial and often seriously challenged by different social groups. A first objective of this book is, therefore, to clarify the ideological foundations of marketing and to explain its role as a key determinant in a democratic economic system. This objective is particularly important for Eastern European countries who have recently chosen the road to a market economy.

The second objective of the book, and particularly of this new edition, is to introduce the concept of *market orientation* as a substitute for the traditional *marketing concept* of the 4Ps popularised by the US business schools. This is more than just a semantic issue. The marketing concept tends to be more concerned with the American view of the functional role of marketing in co-ordinating and managing the four Ps to make a firm more responsive to meeting customers' needs. The market orientation-concept, by contrast, (a) de-emphasises the functional roles of marketing departments, (b) enlarges the market definition to the key market actors (distributors, competitors, prescribers and the macro-marketing environment) as well as customers, and (c) states that developing market relations and enhancing customer value is the responsibility of everyone in the organisation. This necessary change of emphasis, at the start of the third millennium, is motivated by the increased complexity of the competitive environment which is becoming global, deregulated, and deeply modified by the information technology revolution.

The third objective of this book is to introduce upfront the strategic dimension of the market-orientation concept, while the most popular introductory marketing text-books tend to treat marketing management as a stand-alone business function and to overlook the hidden part of the marketing iceberg – the strategic choices on which market-driven management decisions must be based. Similarly, most strategic marketing texts examine strategic decisions that are made at the corporate level but devote only scant attention to how these decisions are implemented at the opera-tional level for individual brands or products. My objective in writing this book is to propose a broader treatment of marketing integrating both its dimensions, strategic and operational. Marketing is both a business philosophy and an action-oriented process. Too often, the tendency among practitioners and the general public is to reduce marketing to its active dimension and to overlook the underlying business philosophy without which marketing is simply a set of short-term selling tools.

Structure of the Book

The overall structure of the book is summarised at the beginning of each of the five parts and comprises fifteen chapters in total.

Part one is devoted to the analysis of *the changing role of marketing* in the European market. Chapter 1 introduces a distinction between operational marketing (the action dimension) and strategic marketing (the analytic and philosophy dimension). In the new European macro-marketing environment (Chapter 2), marketing is confronted with challenging new roles and priorities which require a reinforcement of strategic marketing and the adoption of a market orientation within the entire organisation. The pro-active firm must evolve from marketing management to market-driven management. This chapter is central in the book and provides a full development of the market-orientation concept and is also a measurement instrument.

The objective of part two is to analyse *the customer's purchase and response behaviour*, whether an individual or an organisation. Strategic marketing is, to begin with, the analysis of customers' needs and purchase behaviour (Chapter 3). From a marketing point of view, the customer's choice behaviour is not searching for a product as such, but a solution to his or her problem (Chapter 3). The role of the marketing informa-tion system (Chapter 4) is essential to gain qualified knowledge to understand and predict the customer's behaviour and response (Chapter 5).

Part three analyses the specific tasks to be performed by *strategic marketing*. The role of strategic marketing is to follow the evolution of the firm's *reference market* and to identify various potential product-markets or segments on the basis of an analysis of the needs which must be met (Chapter 6). Once the potential product-markets are identified, the *attractiveness* of the economic opportunities must be evaluated. The appeal of a product-market is quantitatively measured by the notion of market poten-tial and dynamically measured by its economic life or its life cycle (Chapter 7). For any given firm, the appeal of a product-market depends on its *competitiveness*, in other words, on its capacity to meet buyers' needs better than its rivals can. This competi-tiveness will exist as long as the firm holds a competitive advantage, either because it can differentiate itself from its rivals due to sustainable distinctive qualities, or because of higher productivity putting it at a cost advantage (Chapter 8). On the basis of this strategic audit, the market-driven firm can formulate an appropriate *marketing strategy* for each business unit included in its product portfolio (Chapter 9). The strategic *marketing plan* describes objectives, positioning, tactics and budgets for each business unit of the company's portfolio in a given period and geographical zone (Chapter 10).

Part four is devoted to *operational marketing* and to the implementation issues of strategic marketing decisions and comprises the new product decisions (Chapter 11), distribution channel decisions (Chapter 12), pricing decisions (Chapter 13), marketing communication decisions (Chapter 14) and media advertising decisions (Chapter 15).

Finally, part five presents 10 case studies illustrating strategic and operational marketing decisions. The cases are very short and lend themselves to class discussion without extensive advance preparation.

Distinctive Features

This text offers full coverage of both strategic and operational marketing. In addition, it has the following distinctive characteristics:

- it discusses the ideological foundations of marketing and its role in the turbulent environment of today's market economy;
- it introduces the concept of market orientation as a substitute for the traditional marketing concept;
- it analyses the structure of needs of both the individual consumer and of the business-to-business customer;
- it integrates important theoretical concepts such as buyer behaviour theory, attitude models, information theory and stresses the application of this conceptual material to the realities of marketing;
- it provides an integrated treatment of consumer and business-to-business marketing underlining practical differences and conceptual similarities;
- it offers thorough coverage of macro- and micro-segmentation analyses illustrated by numerous examples taken from the European scene;
- it provides an overview of marketing research methods and particularly of survey research;
- it gives a general overview of the most popular market response measures provided by marketing research, devoid of all technical development;
- it integrates international and global marketing throughout the text rather than relegating it to a single chapter;
- it contains a section devoted to the distributor's strategic marketing; a topic often neglected in marketing textbooks;
- it raises the issues of responsible marketing;
- it devotes several sections to e-commerce and its potential for marketing management;
- it is illustrated with numerous real life examples and up-to-date European data and statistics.

⬤ Why a European Perspective?

Another claim of this book is to present to the reader a *European perspective* in strategic marketing. The question that comes readily to mind is then, *is European marketing really different from, let's say, American or Japanese ways of marketing*? I strongly believe that significant differences do exist, not so much in terms of concepts or methods, but rather in terms of priorities, complexity and business philosophy. Three factors explain these differences:

⬤ the challenge of European market integration,
⬤ European cultural diversity and pluralism,
⬤ the social accountability of European society.

European countries are confronted with a formidable challenge – the idea of unifying the European market by removing all non-tariff barriers that have existed in some countries for centuries. At a business level, European companies are analysing the impact of this market transformation, redefining their reference market, reassessing their competitiveness and determining appropriate strategies and organisational structure. The launching of the single currency (the euro) creates an entirely new European context, where sound strategic thinking and analysis is becoming more than ever a priority preoccupation, not only for multinational firms, but for small and medium-sized companies as well.

The European market is highly fragmented, both in terms of culture and consumer habits. The elimination of all barriers between European countries will create a borderless single market but not, however, a homogeneous single market. Cultural differences and variations in consumer attitudes across Europe will remain, even if European firms have the possibility of executing a common marketing programme throughout Europe. Thus European firms will have to cope with this cultural complexity and find adaptable solutions. A level of standardisation of consumer behaviour similar to the one observed in the US market will never be reached in Europe. The capacity to respect this diversity and to discover supranational segments will be a key factor for success.

European public authorities are more concerned than American authorities with the protection and integration of individual, family and social values in economic life and public policy. The European firm has to cope with more severe societal constraints than the American firm. The slogan – *the business of business is business* – largely accepted until recently by the business community, is no longer true and the European firm cannot remain immune from societal interference and accountability. These societal constraints are the expressions of new needs in society and come from public policy regulations, EU directives, green consumerists or environmentalists. They encourage companies to widen the traditional marketing concept and to develop an increased consciousness of fallout generated by their marketing activity. In today's European socio-economic context, this greater societal sensitivity makes the concept of accountable *market-driven management* particularly relevant.

Finally, this book offers a European perspective, with the vast majority of examples and case histories being drawn from the European scene. It is also well illustrated with up-to-date European data and statistics.

⬤ How to Use this Book: Two in One

This book provides full coverage of both strategic and operational marketing but contains much more material than strictly required for a first level marketing course. In fact, the book has been successfully used at two levels – in an introductory course and also in more advanced marketing courses. A 'roadmap' is briefly presented here to help the user of the book.

In a *Marketing 1* course, (for example, *Strategic Marketing or Market-driven Strategy*), I would recommend the following sequence: Start with Chapter 1 (marketing concept); skip or cover lightly Chapter 2 (market-orientation concept); cover Chapter 3 (customer behaviour); cover Chapter 6 (segmentation); Chapter 7 (market attractiveness); Chapter 8 (company competitiveness); Chapter 9 (strategy formulation) and Chapter 10 (strategic marketing plan).

In a *Marketing 2* course (for example, *Operational Marketing or Market-driven Management*), assign Chapter 1 as reading; cover Chapter 2 (market-orientation concept); assign Chapter 3 as reading; cover Chapter 4 (market research) and Chapter 5 (customer response behaviour); skip Chapters 6, 7, 8 and 9. Cover Chapter 10 (marketing plan); Chapter 11 (new product decisions); Chapter 12 (distribution channel decisions); Chapter 13 (pricing decisions); Chapter 14 (communication mix decisions) and Chapter 15 (advertising decisions).

The main merit of this sequence – strategic and operational marketing – is to avoid duplication and repetition as is the case with the marketing principles and marketing management sequence adopted by many American textbooks.

Marketing 1 Strategic Marketing (or Market-driven Strategy)	**Marketing 2** Operational Marketing (or Market-driven Management)
Cover extensively Chapter 1	Assign Chapter 1 as a reading
Make a rapid overview of Chapter 2	Cover extensively Chapter 2
Cover extensively Chapter 3	Assign Chapter 3 as a reading
Skip Chapters 4 and 5	Cover extensively Chapters 4 and 5
Cover extensively Chapters 6, 7, 8 and 9	Use Chapters 6, 7, 8 and 9 as reference reading
Make a rapid overview of Chapter 10	Cover extensively Chapters 11, 12, 13, 14 and 15
Skip Chapters 11, 12, 13, 14 and 15	Use Chapter 10 as a reference for a comprehensive case discussion

⬤ Ancillary Material

An instructor's resource manual will be available on line and in hard copy format. For each chapter of the book, a PowerPoint slide presentation is available together with the more representative tables and figures that cover the major concepts of the chapter. The instructor's manual has a teaching note for each case as well as the solutions to the quantitative problems presented at the end of each chapter.

A student resource centre website is also available for students or instructors who would like to communicate with the author. The student website will list articles related to new developments in both strategic and operational marketing and will also publish facts and figures (taking the form of exhibits) illustrating European and global marketing strategies.

Acknowledgements

This book is a revision of the fourth edition of the French book Le marketing stratégique (Paris, Ediscience International, 1998). This second English edition is the outcome of several years of research, teaching and consulting in Europe. This experience, the exchange of ideas and discussions with business professionals at various executive seminars or during consulting assignments, has done much to further my knowledge of the marketing process.

Several people have directly or indirectly contributed at various stages to the development of this new edition, and in particular my colleagues from the marketing unit at my former university, the Institut d'Administration et de Gestion (IAG): Chantal de Moerloose, Ruben Chumpitaz, Frederic Bielen, Isabelle Schuiling and Claudine Laperche. A word of gratitude also to colleagues Paul Pellemans from Louvain, Carlo Gallucci from ESADE, Valentin Dunayevsky and Boris Lifliandchik from the Leti-Lovanium International School of Management of Saint Petersburg, Jaime Rivera from Carlos Tercero University (Spain) and Silvio Brondoni from the Università degli Studi di Milano. Last but not least, I am grateful to my students, captive customers, but nevertheless very attentive and demanding, who helped me to improve this text over the years. Personal thanks to each of them.

JEAN-JACQUES LAMBIN
Bousval

part one

The Changing Role of Marketing

STRUCTURE OF THE BOOK

PART ONE The Changing Role of Marketing

The role of marketing in the firm and in a marketing economy	From marketing to market-driven management
CHAPTER ONE	CHAPTER TWO

PART TWO Understanding Customer Behaviour

The customer choice behaviour	The marketing information system
CHAPTER THREE	CHAPTER FOUR

The customer's response behaviour
CHAPTER FIVE

PART THREE Market-driven Strategy Development

Needs analysis through market segmentation
CHAPTER SIX

Market attractiveness analysis	Competitiveness analysis
CHAPTER SEVEN	CHAPTER EIGHT

Formulating a market strategy
CHAPTER NINE

The strategic marketing plan
CHAPTER TEN

PART FOUR Market-driven Management Decisions

Market-driven new product decisions	Market-driven distribution decisions	Market-driven pricing decisions	Market-driven communication decisions	Market-driven advertising decisions
CHAPTER ELEVEN	CHAPTER TWELVE	CHAPTER THIRTEEN	CHAPTER FOURTEEN	CHAPTER FIFTEEN

PART FIVE Ten Case Studies in Market-driven Management

1. **The Lander Company** *W.J. Stanton*
2. **The WILO Corporation** *R. Köhler*
3. **TV: Cold Bath for French Cinema** *A. Riding*
4. **Ecover** *D. Develter*
5. **Volvo Truck Belgium** *J.J. Lambin*
6. **The Petro-equipment Company** *J.J. Lambin*
7. **Sierra Plastics Company** *W.J. Stanton*
8. **Tissex** *G. Marion*
9. **Newfood** *G.S. Day et al.*
10. **SAS: Meeting Customer Expectations** *D.L. Kurtz and K.E. Clow*

chapter one

The role of marketing in the firm and in a market economy

Marketing is both a business philosophy and an action-oriented process. This first chapter aims to describe the *system of thought*, to clarify the ideological foundations of marketing and their main implications regarding the firm's operations and organisation. As an *active process*, marketing fulfils a number of tasks necessary to the smooth functioning of a market economy. A second objective of this chapter is to describe these tasks, the importance and complexity of which have evolved with changes in technology, economics, competitiveness and the international environment. Within this framework, we shall examine the implications of these environmental changes, for the management of the firm, and particularly for the marketing function.

Chapter learning objectives

When you have read this chapter, you should be able to understand:

1. the theoretical and ideological foundations of marketing;
2. the difference between 'operational' and 'strategic' marketing;
3. the role of marketing in the firm in relation with the other functions;
4. the tasks performed by marketing in a market economy;
5. the steps in implementing marketing in the firm's organisation;
6. the limitations of the traditional marketing concept.

The Ideological Foundations of Marketing

The term *marketing*, which has even entered the non-English vocabulary, is a word heavily loaded, debased and often misunderstood, not only by its detractors, but also by its proponents. Three popular meanings recur regularly.

- Marketing is advertising, promotion and hard selling, in other words a set of particularly aggressive *selling instruments*, used to penetrate existing markets. In this first, very mercantile sense of the word, marketing is viewed as mainly applicable to mass consumer markets and much less to more sophisticated sectors, such as high technology, financial services, public administration, social and cultural services.

- Marketing is a set of *market analysis tools*, such as sales forecasting methods, simulation models and market research studies, used to develop a prospective and more scientific approach to needs and demand analysis. Such methods, often complex and costly, are often considered to be only available to large enterprises, and not to small and medium-sized ones. The image projected is often that of unnecessarily sophisticated tools, entailing high costs and little practical value.

- Marketing is the hype, *the architect of the consumer society*; that is, a market system where individuals are commercially exploited by sellers. It is necessary to create new needs continuously, in order to sell more and more. Consumers become alienated from the seller, just as workers have become alienated from the employer.

Behind these somewhat oversimplified views there are three characteristic dimensions to the concept of marketing (see Table 1.1):

- an *action* dimension (the conquest of markets),
- an *analysis* dimension (the understanding of markets) and
- a *culture* dimension (a state of mind).

More often than not, the tendency is to reduce marketing to its action dimension – that is, to a series of sales techniques (operational marketing) – and to underestimate its analytic dimension (strategic marketing).

Table 1.1   The market orientation concept in theory

Components	Activities	Organisational position
Analysis	The strategic brain	The business units
Action	The commercial arm	The marketing function
Culture	A business philosophy	The corporation

Implicit in this vision of the role of marketing is the idea that marketing and advertising are omnipotent, that they are capable of making the market accept anything through powerful methods of communication. Such hard selling methods would often be devised independently of any desire to satisfy the real needs of buyers. The focus is on the needs of the seller, that is to achieve a sale.

The myth of the power of marketing is a persistent theme despite the fact that there exists abundant proof to the contrary. For example, the high proportion (more than 50 per cent) of new products and brands that fail bears witness to the capacity of the market's resistance to the allegedly seductive powers of marketers.

The principle of customer sovereignty

Although this misunderstanding goes very deep, the *theory* or ideology which is the basis of marketing is totally different. The philosophy at the root of marketing – what may be called the marketing concept – rests in fact on a *theory of individual choice* through *the principle of consumer sovereignty*. In this framework, marketing is no more than the social expression of the principles advocated by classical economists, at the turn of the eighteenth century, and translated into operational rules of management. These principles, which were set forth by Adam Smith (1776), form the basis of the market economy and can be summarised as follows:

> Society's well-being is the outcome, not so much of altruistic behaviour, but rather of the matching, through voluntary and competitive exchange, of the buyer and seller's self-interest.

Starting from the principle that the pursuit of personal interest is an unfailing tendency in most human beings – which might be morally regrettable but remains a fact – Adam Smith suggested accepting people as they are, but developing a system that would make egocentric individuals contribute to the common good despite themselves. This is then the system of voluntary and competitive exchange, administered by the *invisible hand*, or the selfish pursuit of personal interests which in the end serves the interests of all.

Although in modern economics this basic principle has been amended with regard to social (solidarity) and societal (external effects, collective goods, Government regulations) issues, it nevertheless remains the main principle driving the economic activity of a successful firm operating in a freely competitive market. Furthermore, it is now clearer than ever before, that those countries that rejected Adam Smith's ideas are now discovering, to their cost, that they have regressed economically. The turmoil in Eastern Europe and the growth of emerging economies having adopted the market economy system (through deregulation and privatisation) give a clear illustration of this.

At the root of the market economy, we find four central ideas. These ideas seem simple, but have major implications regarding the philosophical approach to the market:

● Individuals strive for *rewarding experiences*; it is the pursuit of one's self-interest that drives individuals to produce and to work. This search is the engine of growth, of individual development, and eventually determines the overall well-being.

● *Individual choice* determines what is rewarding. This varies according to tastes, culture, values, and so on. Apart from respecting the ethical, moral and social rules imposed by society, no other judgement is implied as to the value or the triviality of this choice, or what might be regarded as 'true' or 'false' needs. The system is *pluralistic* and respects the diversity of tastes and preferences.

● It is through *free and competitive exchange* that individuals and the organisations they deal with will best realise their objectives. When exchange is free, it only takes place if its terms generate utility for both parties; when it is competitive, the risk of producers abusing their market power is limited (Friedman and Friedman, 1980).

● The mechanisms of the market economy are based on the principle of individual freedom, and more particularly on the *principle of consumer sovereignty*. The moral foundation of the system rests on the recognition of the fact that individuals are responsible for their own actions and can decide what is or is not good for them.

The fields of marketing

Marketing is rooted in these four principles. This gives rise to a philosophy of action valid for any organisation serving the needs of a group of buyers. The areas of marketing can be subdivided into three main fields:

● *Consumer marketing*, where transactions are between companies and end-consumers, individuals or households;
● *Business marketing* (or business-to-business marketing), where the two parties in the exchange process are organisations;
● *Social marketing,* which covers the field of activity of non-profit organisations such as museums, universities, and so on.

This approach implies that all activity within the organisation must have the satisfaction of its customers' needs as its main objective. Given that this is the best way of achieving its own goals of growth and profitability. It is not altruism, but the organisation's self-interest that dictates this course of action.

Such is the ideology on which marketing is based. One can imagine that there may be a large gap between what marketing claims to be and what it is in reality. Flaws come readily to mind. Nevertheless, the successful firm must pursue the ideal of marketing. It may be a myth, but it is a *driving myth*, which must continuously guide the activities of the firm.

The two faces of marketing

The application of this philosophy of action assumes a twofold approach on the part of the firm, as shown in Figure 1.1:

● The objectives of *strategic marketing* typically include: a systematic and continuous analysis of the needs and requirements of key customer groups and the design and production of a product or service package that will enable the company to serve selected groups or segments more effectively than its competition. In serving these objectives, a firm is ensured a sustainable competitive advantage.

Figure 1.1   The two faces of marketing

● The role of *operational marketing* involves the organisation of distribution, sales and communication policies in order to inform potential buyers and to promote the distinctive qualities of the product while reducing the information costs.

These objectives, which are quite complementary, are implemented by the firm's branding policy, a key instrument for the application of the marketing concept in a market economy. We therefore propose the following definition of marketing:

Marketing is a social process, geared towards satisfying the needs and wants of individuals and organisations, through the creation of free competitive exchange of products and services that generate values to the buyer.

The three key concepts in this definition are need, product and exchange. The notion of *need* calls into question the motivations and behaviour of the customer, the individual consumer or the organisational client; *product* or service refers to the producers' response to market expectations; and *exchange* directs attention to the market and the mechanisms that ensure the interplay of demand and supply.

● **The Role of Marketing in the Firm**

The term 'marketing' – literally the process of delivering to the market – does not express the inherent duality of this process very well and emphasises the 'active' side of marketing more than the 'analytic' side. (As an aside, we may point out that to avoid the ambiguity – and the use of an English word in the common vocabulary – the French Academy (l'Académie Française) coined the terms *la mercatique* and *le marchéage* to illustrate these two facets of marketing. In practice, however, these terms are seldom used by the French business community.) The terms strategic and operational marketing are therefore used in practice.

Operational marketing

Operational marketing is an *action-oriented process* which is extended over a short- to medium-term planning horizon and targets existing markets or segments. It is the classical commercial process of achieving a target market share through the use of *tactical means* related to the product, distribution (place), price and communication (promotion) decisions (the 'four Ps', or the 'marketing mix', as they are called in the

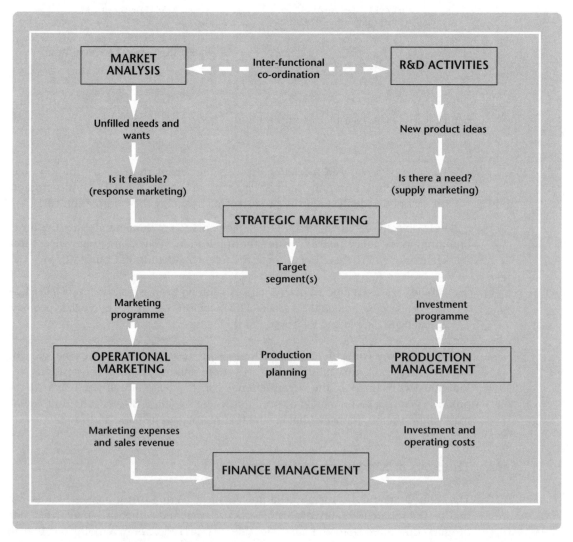

Figure 1.2   The role of marketing in the firm

professional jargon). The operational marketing plan describes objectives, positioning, tactics and budgets for each brand of the company's portfolio in a given period and geographical zone.

The economic role that marketing plays in the operation of the firm is shown in Figure 1.2. The main relationships between the four major managerial functions: (research and development, operations, marketing and finance) are illustrated.

The main task of operational marketing is to generate sales revenues, that is the target turnover. This means to 'sell' and to obtain purchase orders by using the most efficient sales methods while at the same time minimising costs. The objective of realising a particular sales volume translates into a manufacturing programme as far as the operations department is concerned, and a programme of storage and physical distribution for the sales department. Operational marketing is therefore a determining factor which directly influences the short-term profitability of the firm.

The vigour of operational marketing is a decisive factor in the performance of the firm, especially in those markets where competition is fierce. Every product, even those of superior quality, must have a price acceptable to the market, be available in the network of distribution adapted to the purchasing habits of the targeted customers, and be supported by some form of communication which promotes the product and enhances its distinctive qualities. It is rare to find market situations where demand exceeds supply or where the firm is well known by potential users or where competition is non-existent.

There are many examples of promising products that have failed to prevail in the market due to insufficient commercial support. This is particularly the case in firms where the 'engineering' spirit predominates, whereby it is believed that a good quality product can gain recognition by itself, and the firm lacks the humility to adapt to the needs of customers.

> Latin culture is especially susceptible to this attitude. Mercury was the god of merchants as well as of thieves and Christ expelled the tradesmen from the Temple; as a result, selling and advertising are still often viewed as shameful diseases. (Pirot 1987, p. 87)

Operational marketing is the most dramatic and the most visible aspect of the discipline of marketing, particularly because of the important role played by advertising and promotional activities. Some firms – banks for example (see Kotler 1997, p. 30) – have embarked on marketing through advertising. In contrast, some other firms – like many producers of industrial goods – have for a long time tended to believe that marketing does not apply to their business, thus implicitly linking marketing to advertising.

Table 1.2   Contrasting operational and strategic marketing

Operational marketing	Strategic marketing
Action-oriented	Analysis-oriented
Existing opportunities	New opportunities
Non-product variables	Product-market variables
Stable environment	Dynamic environment
Reactive behaviour	Pro-active behaviour
Day-to-day management	Longer-range management
Marketing department	Cross-functional organisation

Operational marketing is therefore the firm's *commercial arm* without which even the best strategic plan cannot lead to satisfactory results. However, it is also clear that without solid strategic options, there can be no ultimately profitable operational marketing. Dynamism without thought is merely unnecessary risk. No matter how powerful an operational marketing plan, it cannot create demand where there is no need, just as it cannot keep alive activities doomed to disappear. Hence, in order to be profitable, operational marketing must be founded upon a strategic design, which is itself based on the needs of the market and its expected evolution.

Strategic marketing

Strategic marketing is, to begin with, the analysis of the *needs* of individuals and organisations. From the marketing viewpoint, the buyer is not seeking a product as such, but after the *solution to a problem* which the product or the service might provide. This solution may be obtained via different technologies which are themselves continually changing. The role of strategic marketing is to follow the evolution of the *reference market* and to identify various existing or potential *product markets or segments* on the basis of an analysis of the diversity of needs to be met.

Once the product markets are identified, they represent economic opportunities whose *attractiveness* needs to be evaluated. The appeal of a product market is quantitatively measured by the notion of the *potential market*, and dynamically measured by its economic life, or its *life cycle*. For a given firm, the appeal of a product market depends on its own *competitiveness*, in other words on its capacity to meet buyers' needs better than its rivals. This competitiveness will exist as long as the firm holds a *competitive advantage*, either because it can differentiate itself from its rivals due to sustainable distinctive qualities, or because of higher productivity, putting it at a cost advantage.

Figure 1.2 shows the various stages of strategic marketing in relation to the firm's other major functions. Irrespective of whether a product is *market-pull* or *company-push* (or technology-push), it has to undergo the process of strategic marketing to evaluate its economic and financial viability. The interface between research and development, operations and strategic marketing plays a decisive role in this respect. The choice of the product market that results from this confrontation is of crucial importance in determining production capacity and investment decisions, and hence is vital to the equilibrium of the firm's overall financial structure.

The role of strategic marketing is therefore (a) to lead the firm towards existing opportunities or (b) to create attractive opportunities, that is, opportunities which are adapted to its resources and know-how and which offer a *potential for growth and profitability*. The process of strategic marketing has a medium- to long-term horizon; its task is to specify the firm's *mission*, define objectives, elaborate a development strategy and ensure a balanced structure of the product portfolio. By way of summary, the contrasting roles of operational and of strategic marketing are presented in Table 1.2.

This job of reflection and strategic planning is very different from operational marketing and requires different talents in the individuals who exercise it. Nevertheless, the two roles are closely complementary, as illustrated by Table 1.2, in the sense that the design of a strategic plan must be carried out in close relation to operational marketing. Operational marketing emphasises non-product variables (distribution, pricing, advertising and promotion), while strategic marketing tends to emphasise

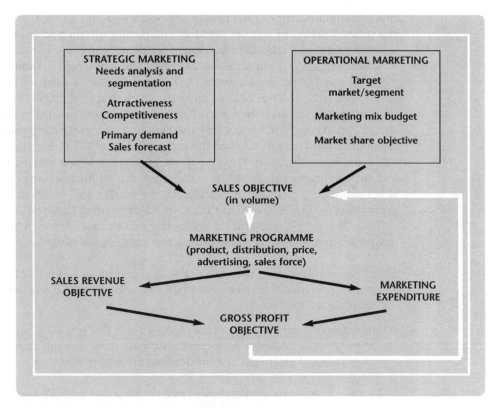

Figure 1.3 The integrated marketing process

the ability to provide a product with superior value at a competitive cost. Strategic marketing leads to the choice of product markets to be exploited in order of priority and the forecast of primary demand in each of these product markets. Operational marketing, on the other hand, sets out market share objectives to reach in the target product market, as well as the marketing budgets necessary for their realisation.

As shown in Figure 1.3, the comparison of the market share objective and primary demand forecast in each product market makes it possible to develop a *sales objective* first in volume and then in terms of turnover, given the chosen pricing policy. The *expected gross profit* is obtained after deducting direct manufacturing costs, possible fixed costs for specific structures, marketing expenditure attributed to the sales force, and advertising and promotion as allowed for in the marketing budget. This gross profit is the contribution of the product market to the firm; it must cover overhead costs and leave a net profit. The content and structure of the marketing plan are described in detail in Chapter 10.

Response versus supply marketing

As illustrated in Figure 1.2, innovations or new product ideas can have two very distinct origins: the market or the firm. If the new product idea comes from the market as a result, for example, of a market research study having identified unfilled (or poorly filled) needs or wants, the innovation is *market-pull*. The market observation is communicated to R&D people who will try to find an appropriate response to this unfilled need. The role of operational marketing will then be to promote the new solution proposed to the identified target segment.

Another origin of an innovation, more frequently observed in industrial or hi-tech markets, may be the laboratory or R&D people who, as a result of fundamental or applied research, discover or develop a new product, a new process or a new organisational system to meet better existing or latent needs. In this case, the role of strategic marketing will be to verify the existence of a potentially profitable market segment and to assess its size and the success factors of the innovation which is here a *company-push innovation*. The role of operational marketing may be more complex and challenging because its role is to create the market for a product or service which is not explicitly demanded or expected by the market and which may require from potential customers a change in their consuming or using habits.

Thus, in strategic marketing, a distinction can be made between two distinct but complementary approaches: *response marketing* and *supply marketing*.

- In *response marketing*, the objective is to *find needs or wants and to fill them*. The goal of operational marketing is to develop a latent or existing demand; innovations are market-pull.

- In *supply or creative marketing*, the objective is to *find new ways to fill existing needs or wants*. The objective is to create new markets through technology and/or organisational creativity. The innovations are supply-push.

In affluent economies, where most needs and wants are well met and where the majority of existing markets are stagnant, supply marketing has an important role to play to create new market opportunities in the future. As Akio Morita, Sony's leader, puts it:

> Our plan is to lead the public with new products rather than ask them what kind of products they want. The public does not know what is possible, but we do. So instead of doing a lot of market research, we refine our thinking on a product and its use and try to create a market for it by educating and communicating with the public. (quoted by Schendler,1992)

Thus, the objective of strategic marketing is not only (a) to listen to customers and then to respond to their articulated needs, but also (b) to lead customers where they want to go, even if they do not know it yet. Thus the role of marketing in the firm can be summarised in the following terms:

> The role of marketing in a firm operating in a market economy is to generate a 'profit' by designing and promoting 'added-value solutions' to people's and organisations' 'problems'.

The word 'designing' refers to strategic marketing and the word 'promoting' to operational marketing.

The Role of Marketing in a Market Economy

In a market economy, the role of marketing is to *organise free and competitive exchange* so as to ensure efficient matching of supply and demand of goods and services. This matching is not spontaneous and requires *liaison activities* at two levels:

● Organisation of *exchange*, in other words the physical flow of goods between the manufacturing and the consumption sites.
● Organisation of *communication*, in other words the flow of information to precede, accompany and follow exchange in order to ensure efficient meeting of supply and demand.

The role of marketing in society is therefore to *organise exchange and communication between sellers and buyers*. This definition emphasises the tasks and functions of marketing, irrespective of the purpose of the process of exchange. As such, it applies to both commercial and to non-profit-making activities, and in general to any situation where free exchange takes place between an organisation and the users of the products and services it offers.

Organisation of exchange transactions

The organisation of the exchange of goods and services is the responsibility of the distribution process, whose task is to move goods from a state of production to a state of consumption. This flow of products to the consumption state creates three types of utility, thus giving distribution a higher value added.

● *State utility* The set of all material transformations putting goods in a consumable state: these are operations such as fragmenting, packaging, sorting, and so on.
● *Place utility* Spatial transformations, such as transport, geographical allocation, and so on, which contribute to putting goods at the disposal of users at places of utilisation, transformation or consumption.
● *Time utility* Temporal transformations, such as storage, which make goods available at the time chosen by the user.

It is these various functions that make manufactured goods accessible and available to the targeted customers, and thus allow the actual matching of supply and demand.

Historically, these tasks of distribution have mainly been performed by autonomous intermediaries, such as sales agents, wholesalers, retailers and industrial distributors, in other words by what is called the *distribution sector*. Some functions of the distribution process have been integrated, for instance on the manufacturing side (direct marketing), on the consumption side (consumers' co-operatives), and on the distribution side (supermarkets, chainstores, and so on).

Furthermore, some vertical marketing systems have been developed which group together independent firms involved at various stages of the production and/or distribution process. This is done in order to co-ordinate their commercial activities, to realise economies in operating costs and thus to reinforce their impact on the market. Examples include voluntary chains, retailer co-operatives and franchise organisations. In many sectors, vertical marketing systems tend to supplant the very fragmented traditional distribution channels. They form one of the most significant developments in the tertiary sector, which has helped to intensify the competitive struggle between various forms of distribution and to improve the productivity of distribution significantly.

The value added of distribution is measured by the *distribution margin,* which is the difference between the price paid to the producer by the first buyer and the price paid by the ultimate user or consumer of the product. The distribution margin may therefore include the margins of one or many distributors; for example those of the wholesalers and the retailers. Therefore, the distributive margin remunerates the functions performed by the intermediaries. In the consumer goods sector, it is estimated that the cost of exchange, covering the whole range of tasks performed by distribution, is about 40 per cent of the retail price. The cost of distribution represents a significant part of the price paid by the buyer in all sectors of activity.

Organisation of communication flows

The merging of the various practical conditions for exchange is not sufficient to ensure efficient adjustment of demand and supply. For exchange of goods to take place, potential buyers must be equally aware and informed of the existence of goods

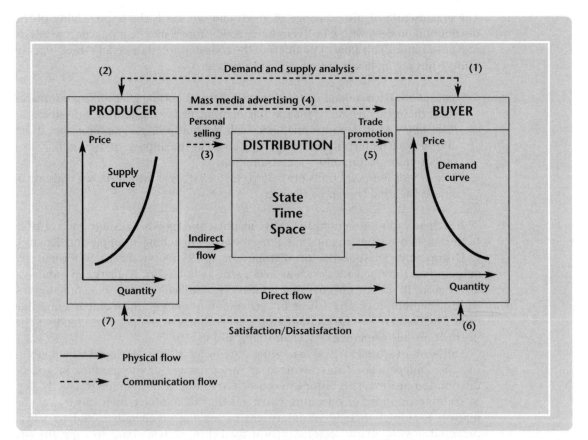

Figure 1.4　The role of marketing in a market economy

or of the combination of alternative attributes likely to meet their needs. Communication activities are aimed at accumulating knowledge for manufacturers, distributors and buyers. As shown in Figure 1.4, it is possible to distinguish seven different flows of communication in a typical market.

1. Before investing, the collection of information is initiated by the producer in order to identify the buyers' needs and wants which constitute an attractive opportunity for him or her. This is typically the role of *market research* prior to an investment decision.

2. Similarly, the potential buyer (mostly industrial) initiates a study of the possibilities offered by suppliers and invitations to tender (sourcing research).

3. After production, the manufacturer's communication programme oriented towards distribution – *a push strategy* – with the objective of obtaining product referencing and the co-operation of distributors with regards to selling space, promotion and price.

4. The manufacturer initiates collection of information on all forms of brand advertising or direct selling activities aimed at making end-buyers aware of the existence of the brand's distinctive qualities: *a pull strategy*;

5. Activities of promotion and communication prompted by distributors aimed at creating store loyalty, building traffic through promotional activities, supporting proprietary brands, informing about sales terms, and so on.

6. After utilisation or consumption of goods, the measurement of *satisfaction or dissatisfaction*, through surveys or consumer panels, carried out by the marketer so as to enable the firm to adjust supply to buyers' reactions.

7. After utilisation or consumption of goods, *claims* and evaluations through comparative testing transmitted spontaneously by buyers, acting alone or in organised groups (consumerism).

In small markets, communication takes place spontaneously between the various parties of the exchange process. In large markets, there is a significant physical and psychological gap between the parties, and communication needs to be specifically organised.

Marketing as a factor of business democracy

Marketing, and specifically strategic marketing, has an important role to play in a market economy, not only because it contributes to an efficient matching between demand and supply, but also because it triggers a virtuous circle of economic development, as illustrated in Figure 1.5. The steps of this development process are the following:

● Strategic marketing helps identify poorly satisfied or unmet market needs and stimulates the development of new or improved products.

● Operational marketing designs a dynamic marketing programme to create and/or develop market demand for these new products.

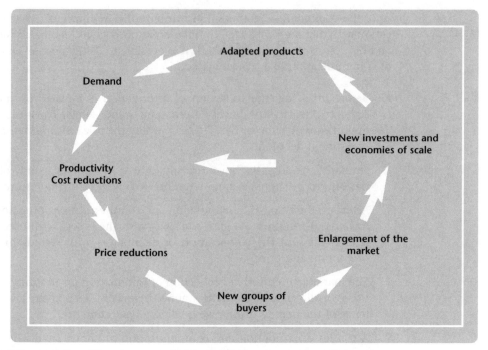

Figure 1.5　The virtuous circle of development triggered by strategic marketing

● This increased demand generates cost decreases which make possible price reductions, thereby opening the market to new groups of buyers.

● The resulting enlargement of the market requires new investments in production capacity which generate economies of scale and stimulate further efforts in R&D to create new generations of products.

Strategic marketing contributes to the development of a business democracy because (a) it starts with the analysis of consumers' expectations, (b) it guides investment and production decisions on the basis of anticipated market needs, (c) it is respectful of the diversity of tastes and preferences by segmenting markets and developing adapted products and (d) it stimulates innovation and entrepreneurship (see Exhibit 1.1).

As already underlined, reality is not always in line with theory. The market orientation business philosophy has been progressively accepted and implemented by firms in Western economies.

● **The Changing Priority Role of Marketing**

Viewed from the standpoint of the organisation of communication and exchange in a market economy, it is clear that, in spite of its current prominence, marketing is not a new activity, given that it covers tasks which have always existed and have always been taken care of one way or another in any system based on free exchange. Even in an autarky, founded on the most elementary form of exchange – barter – there are

Exhibit 1.1

The Praising of Mercantilism

Once again I am reminded of the wretchedness of my solitude. Where I am concerned, to sow and reap is good: the evil sets in when I grind and knead and bake, for then I am working only for myself. The American colonist need have no misgivings about making bread; he will sell the bread, and the money he stores in his chest represents the saving of time and work. But I in my solitude am deprived of the benefits of money, although I have no lack of it.

Today I can measure the folly and malice of those who affect to despise money, that divine institution. Money spiritualises all that it touches by endowing it with a quality that is both rational (measurable) and universal, since property reckoned in terms of money is accessible to all men. Venality is one of the cardinal virtues. The venal man suppresses his murderous and anti-social instincts – honour, selfpride, patriotism, political ambition, religion, fanaticism, racialism – in favour of his need to co-operate with others, his love of fruitful exchange, his sense of human solidarity. The term Golden Age should be taken literally, and I see now that mankind would swiftly achieve it were its affairs wholly in the hands of venal men. Alas, it is nearly always high-minded men who make history, and so the flames destroy everything and blood flows in torrents; The plump merchants of Venice afford us an example of the luxurious happiness possible in a state governed solely by the law of lucre, whereas the emaciated wolves of the Spanish Inquisition show us the infamies of which men are capable when they have lost the love of material well-being. The Huns would soon have checked their advance if they had known how to profit by the riches they have acquired. Encumbered with their gains, they would have stayed to enjoy them, and life would have resumed its course. But they were disinterested savages. They despised gold. They rushed onward, burning as they went.

Source: Tournier (1969, pp. 61–2).

flows of exchange and communication, but their manifestation is spontaneous and neither requires the allocation of specific resources, nor any form of organisation to ensure their functioning.

It is the complexity of the technological, economic and competitive environment that has gradually led firms first to create and then to reinforce the marketing function. Hence it is interesting to follow the history of this evolution in order to understand better the present role of marketing. One can distinguish three stages, each characterised by different priority marketing objectives: passive marketing, operational (or organisational) marketing and strategic (or active) marketing.

Passive marketing: product orientation

Passive marketing is a form of organisation prevalent in an economic environment characterised by the existence of a potentially important market, but where *supply is scarce,* with insufficient available production capacity to meet the market's needs.

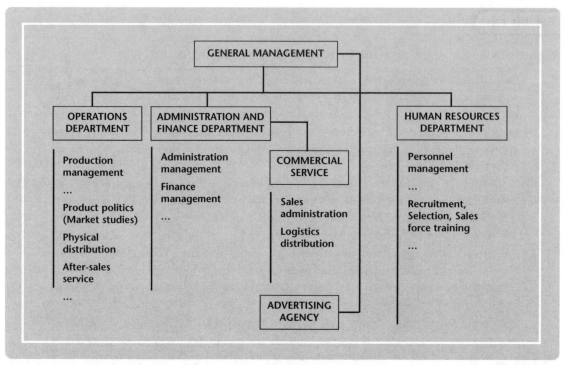

Figure 1.6   Typical organisation of a product-oriented company

Demand is therefore higher than supply. Passive marketing, to work, also implies that needs are known and stable and that technological innovation in the reference market proceeds at a slow pace.

> This type of economic situation was observed, for instance, at the beginning of the century during the industrial revolution, and more recently in the period immediately after the Second World War. This environment continues to prevail in many developing countries at present and particularly in Eastern Europe.

It is clear that in a situation characterised by scarce supply, marketing has a limited and passive role. Given that needs are known, strategic marketing is performed naturally, operational marketing is reduced to organising the flow of manufactured goods, and promotional activity is rendered superfluous, given that the firm cannot supply the market as it would have liked. Contacts with the market are often limited to the first echelon, that is the first buyer of the product, who is usually an intermediary, wholesaler or industrial distributor. There is therefore little contact with final demand and market research is infrequent. This state of affairs is also reflected in the organisation of the firm, which is dominated by the operations function, with the development of production capacity and improvement of productivity as the main priorities. Marketing is there to sell what has already been produced.

When a firm adopts the 'product concept' it is, in general, structurally organised with the following characteristics (see Figure 1.6):

- A *functional disequilibrium* in the sense that, in the organisational chart, marketing does not occupy the same hierarchical level as the other functions, such as operations, finance or personnel.

- The first level of marketing is *commercial service*, in charge of sales administration and in contact with the first buyer in the distributive chain, not necessarily with the end-user.

- The product decisions are made by operations management; selling prices and sales forecasts are the responsibility of the financial department. There is typically a *dispersion of responsibilities* as far as the marketing instruments are concerned (the four Ps).

This kind of organisation fosters the development of the *product concept* based on the implicit assumption that the firm knows what is good for the buyer and the latter shares this conviction. Moreover, the managers of such firms are often convinced that they are producing a superior good and tend to take it for granted that buyers will continue to want their products. They tend to have an *inside-in perspective*, where the emphasis is placed on internal constraints and preoccupations and not on the customer's requirements or expectations. Such a viewpoint – typical of a bureaucratic organisation – is therefore completely opposed to the idea of the buyer who views a product as a solution to a problem.

This state of mind is conceivable in an environment where demand exceeds supply, where buyers prepared to buy any kind of product if they can find it. In reality, such market conditions are exceptional, and when they prevail they are temporary. The danger of the product concept is that it makes the firm myopic in its outlook and does not encourage a proactive behaviour, that is one that will anticipate a change in the environment and prepare itself accordingly.

Passive marketing is a form of marketing organisation which is no longer suitable for the environment facing the majority of firms in industrialised countries today. The product concept nevertheless persists in some firms, mainly among industrial firms or financial services firms, such as insurance companies. The lack of market orientation is a major cause of many bankruptcies. It is also the dominant state of mind observed among Eastern European firms, which have found themselves suddenly confronted with the formidable challenge of the market and of competition.

Thus in a product-oriented company, the dominant business philosophy can be summarised in the following terms:

The key to business success is producing quality goods and services at a reasonable cost. Good products and services sell themselves. If possible, products and services should be standardised to keep costs down.

Until recently, the product concept also dominated in developing countries, mainly among experts of economic development. But even there marketing can play an active role and contribute towards economic development, to the extent however that such methods are now adapted to situations which are totally different from industrialised countries. On this topic, see the excellent doctoral dissertation of Mbwinga Bila (1995).

Operational marketing: sales orientation

Operational marketing puts the emphasis on the *selling concept*. In Western European countries this approach to management was progressively adopted by firms in the consumer goods industry during the 1950s, when demand was expanding rapidly and production capacity was available. On the other hand, although these markets were in full growth, the distributive system was often deficient and unproductive.

The following changes in the economy are the cause of this new approach to marketing management:

● The appearance of *new forms of distribution*, mainly self-service, has helped to modify the productivity of conventional distribution networks which were not adapted to the requirements of mass distribution.

● The *geographical widening of markets*, and the resulting physical and psychological gap between producers and consumers, have made it increasingly necessary to resort to means of communication such as mass media advertising.

● The development of *branding policies*, a requirement for self-service selling and a way for the firm to control its final demand.

The priority objective of marketing at this stage is to create an efficient commercial organisation. The role of marketing becomes less passive. Now the task is to *find and organise markets for the products made*. At this stage, most firms concentrate on the needs of the central core of the market, with products which satisfy the needs of the majority of buyers. Markets are therefore weakly segmented and strategic decisions

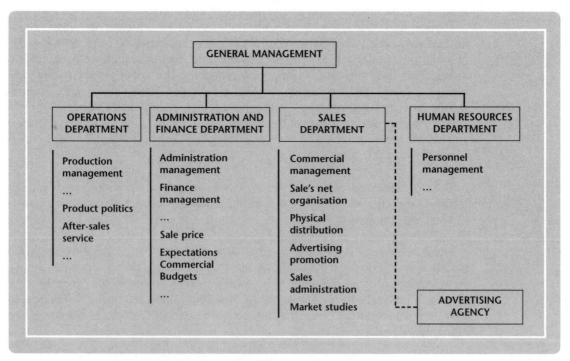

Figure 1.7   Typical organisation of sales-oriented company

regarding product policy remain the responsibility of the operations department. The main function of marketing is to organise the efficient distribution of products and to manage all tasks that fall under this process of commercialisation.

As far as the organisational structure is concerned, these changes in priorities translate into the creation of a *sales or a commercial department*, and one can observe a readjustment of functions (see Figure 1.7). These sales departments are given the task of setting up a sales network, organising physical distribution, advertising and promotion. They also manage market research programmes, which are beginning to manifest their importance, for example in analysing buying habits, the effectiveness of advertising and the impact of branding and packaging policies, and so on.

The selling concept

The *selling concept* is a characteristic often present in organisational marketing. Its implicit assumptions are as follows:

● Consumers naturally tend to resist buying 'unsought products'.
● Consumers can be pushed to buy more by using different means of sales stimulation.
● The firm must create a powerful sales department and use substantial promotional means to attract and keep customers.

Thus, within the firm, marketing people tend to have an *inside-out perspective*, and to give priority to the company's objectives over the customer's post-purchase satisfaction. The underlying assumption is that good selling is always 'salesperson-driven'.

Some industries which make products not naturally sought by buyers, such as life insurance or control instruments, have developed hard selling techniques, which have become popularised through various writings on the 'Art of Selling'. Furthermore, when there is extra capacity in a sector, it is not unusual to see firms wanting to liquidate their stocks employing these methods by aggressively using television commercials, direct mail, newspaper advertisements, and so on. It is therefore not surprising to see that the public at large, as well as some firms, tends to equate marketing with hard selling or even forced selling.

Thus, in a sales-oriented company, the dominant business philosophy can be summarised in the following terms:

> The key to business success lies in persuading potential customers to buy your goods and services through advertising, personal selling or other means. Potential customers must be informed and convinced of the benefits of the products.

The risk of manipulative or wild marketing

Operational marketing has encouraged the development of the selling concept, which implies a degree of *commercial aggressiveness*, with the implicit assumption that the market can absorb everything, if enough pressure is applied. Judging by the high growth rate of private consumption and the level of household equipment purchased during the immediate post-war period, this selling policy did prove to be efficient.

However, the efficiency of the selling concept must be evaluated by keeping in mind the situation at the time, that is a fundamentally expanding market, weakly

Exhibit 1.2

Some Examples of Wild Marketing Practices

- Sales of defective or dangerous products.
- Exaggeration of the product's content through the use of flashy packaging design.
- Resorting to fraudulent practices with regard to price and delivery policies.
- Resorting to promotional techniques which exploit impulsive buyer behaviour.
- Advertisements which exaggerate the product's attributes and the promises that these attributes represent.
- Advertisements which exploit the agonies and anxieties of individuals.
- Enticing people to over-consume using hard selling methods.

In the long run, 'wild marketing' is self-destructive for a company or for a brand and goes against its best interests.

differentiated products, and consumers who were less experienced as buyers. The risk run by the selling concept is to consider this commercial approach as being valid in any situation and to confuse it with the marketing concept. Levitt (1960, p. 48) compares the two concepts as follows:

> Selling focuses on the needs of the seller, marketing on the needs of the buyer. Selling is preoccupied with the seller's need to convert his product into cash; marketing with the idea of satisfying the needs of the customer by means of the product and the whole cluster of things associated with creating, delivering and finally consuming it.

An over-enthusiastic use of advertising and selling can lead to *manipulative marketing or wild marketing*, which tries to mould demand to the requirements of supply rather than adapt supply to the expectations of demand. Exhibit 1.2 gives some examples of commercial practices which can be classified as wild marketing.

The excesses of wild marketing have led to the birth of a countervailing power in the form of consumers' organisations, initiated by consumers, and in the form of legislation which increasingly reinforces the protection of consumers' legal rights prompted by public authorities. Self-discipline adopted by companies and the adoption of rules of ethics have also contributed to the development of ethical behaviour. It is clear today that 'wild marketing' is self-destructive for a company or for a brand and goes against its best long-term interest.

Strategic marketing: marketing orientation

The temptation is great to confine the marketing concept to operational marketing particularly when markets are fast growing and when the size of the untapped market potential is large. The necessity to adopt the marketing concept and to integrate the strategic dimension of marketing is perceived when markets reach maturity, segmentation and positioning strategies become key issues, competition intensifies and the pace of technological innovation accelerates. In this environment, the role of marketing is not simply to exploit an existing market through mass marketing techniques. The priority objectives are to detect new segments or niches having a growth potential, to develop new product concepts, to diversify the firm's product portfolio, to find a sustainable competitive advantage and to design a marketing strategy for each business unit. The *analysis* component of the marketing concept becomes the critical management skill. Its role is to select solid strategic options on which more efficient operational marketing programmes will be based. At this stage, a marketing-oriented firm has an *outside-in perspective.*

The integration of the marketing concept has taken place at different periods according to sectors depending on the development stage reached by the market. The firms operating in the *fast moving consumer goods* (FMCG) sectors, were among the first to adopt the strategic dimension of the marketing concept. Other sectors, like the computer and the petroleum industries, suddenly exposed in the 1990s to a structural slowing down of demand, have discovered more recently the necessity to become more marketing-driven.

The phase of active marketing is characterised by the development and/or the reinforcement of the role of strategic marketing and by the adoption of a customer orientation within the firm. Three factors are at the root of this evolution:

- Maturity of markets and the progressive *saturation* of the needs of the core market.
- Acceleration in the rate at which *technological progress* diffuses and penetrates.
- Increased *internationalisation* of markets as a result of the progressive lifting of barriers to international trade.

We will examine these three factors of change successively, as well as their implications for the marketing function in the firm.

Saturation of the core market

The rapid expansion of the economy during the 1960s led to a saturation of demand for products corresponding to the basic needs of the market, and this evolution is a second significant change which has contributed once again to the modification of the role of marketing in the firm. This change manifested itself with the appearance of a potential demand for products adapted more specifically to the needs of distinct groups of consumers and buyers. This evolution, which appeared at different times in different sectors, leads to market *fragmentation* and strategies of *segmentation.* As an example, let us examine the following fictitious case.

> A firm is contemplating the launching of a new aperitif in the market and is wondering about the preference of potential consumers as to the degree of bitterness of the aperitif. Various tests are organised showing that the majority of consumers prefer a medium level of bitterness, as shown in the preference distribution of Figure 1.8.

The tests also show that some consumers, fewer in number, prefer a higher degree of bitterness and others a lower degree of bitterness. A situation of *diffused preferences* is typical of a latent market and the firm must decide how to position its product with respect to this dominant feature.

The natural tendency is to follow the *majority rule* and develop a product at a medium level (say level 4) of a significant product characteristic, so as to correspond

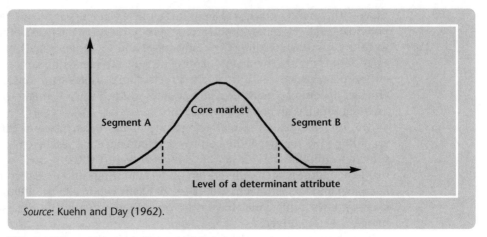

Source: Kuehn and Day (1962).

Figure 1.8　The majority rule fallacy

to the preferences of the core of the market and thus minimise total dissatisfaction and fulfil the expectations of the greatest number. The pioneering firm thus finds access to the most important potential market and also benefits from economies of scale in production and distribution. At this stage, the firm will be exercising operational marketing to penetrate the market as rapidly as possible.

Market choices will therefore crystallise over products designed to meet the expectations of the majority. Peripheral preferences will not be met and this group of consumers will have to accept compromises. If successful, the pioneer will soon be followed by many imitators and the situation will progressively lead towards the 'majority fallacy', whereby all competing brands are clustered at the same medium level of the relevant product characteristic.

The *strategic marketing* stage appears when the needs of the core market are saturated as a result of this situation, where a large number of competitors are making similar offers. At this stage it becomes worthwhile to rediscover the neglected differences in preferences and pay attention to the peripheral segments by launching products specially conceived to meet their needs.

In the example above, the latecomer on the market, analysing consumers' preferences, makes the same observations as before. However, by launching one very smooth (level 2) and simultaneously one very bitter aperitif (level 6), the alert firm can hope to gain a total market share well over what it would gain if it launched a similar product (a 'me too') to the existing ones at level 4, where all the competing brands are clustered.

These segments are certainly smaller, but nevertheless they constitute an unexploited potential, given that these consumers have never found a product in the market corresponding to their real preferences. The firm will adopt a *segmentation strategy* (based here on taste) and the market will subdivide into segments which correspond to the differentiated products. This stage, called the *segmentation stage*, requires a finer understanding from the firm of the market and of the benefits sought by different groups of buyers.

At this maturity stage of the market, product policy must therefore be increasingly based on the analysis of needs and the services expected from products. In industrialised economies, most markets adequately meet basic needs. Finding growing segments is not an easy task, but requires a deep understanding of markets, needs, users and the use of products. This knowledge can only be achieved by strengthening the 'analytic' aspect of marketing, that is by using strategic marketing and by adopting a customer orientation.

Technological progress

One of the significant features of the period between the Marshall Plan (1947) and the creation of OPEC (1973) is the extraordinary diffusion of technological progress, which penetrated and influenced most industrial sectors within a few years. As a result, we saw, during 30 years of continuous growth, a real explosion of new products and new industries, both quantitatively and qualitatively. A large number of products that we use daily today did not exist a short while ago.

> According to the Nielsen Company, 100 new products are launched every day on the sole French food market, that is about 37,000 new products per year. (Boisdevésy, 1996, p .61)

The diffusion of technological progress results from acceleration, generalisation and systematic approach in scientific research.

- The diffusion of *technological progress is accelerated*; we mean that we observe an increasing rate of innovation and a shorter time frame required to pass from development to commercial exploitation on a large scale.

This evolution implies a shorter technological life of products and hence the time available for recovering R&D costs. Table 1.3. illustrates this point in the computer market sector.

Table 1.3 The shortening of the product life cycle: an example: the computer market

Development phases	Average duration (months)			
	1981	1984	1988	1991
R&D	24	20	18	8
Market research	9	7	4	2
Expected life	88	48	24	12

Source: Dataquest, April,1992, SVM 25.

- The spread of *technological progress is generalised* throughout sectors, firms and countries. Few sectors have been sheltered from technological innovations, some of which are, as Schumpeter (1949) put it, 'destructive', that is, they menace or eliminate existing industries.

Basic sectors such as steel, leather, textiles, paper, have always been threatened by substitutes coming from industries which are technologically very distant. This evolution calls for a closer scrutiny of the technological and competitive environment.

● The spread of *technological progress is systematic*, in the sense that, unlike the days when scientific research was carried out by more or less isolated individuals, it has now become institutionalised in firms, universities and private or public specialised centres. Governments play a significant role in this domain, by allocating important resources to help scientific and industrial research.

Technological innovation no longer depends on the chance of inventions. An innovation is the outcome of a concerted and planned effort, which itself is directed by some theoretical representations. There is continuity in the elaboration of theoretical tools, which is the job of fundamental research, and the implementation of methods that can be directly used in the production of goods and services. Research itself is planned according to tested methods and in terms of objectives laid out in advance.

This technological evolution has a direct bearing on product policy and forces the firm, for example, to review the structure of its product portfolio at a much faster rate than before. Therefore, this increased dependence on the technological environment requires a strengthening of the role to be played by market analysis and environment monitoring.

At Hewlett-Packard, for instance, more than 50 per cent of the turnover is generated by products launched into the market during the last three years and more than 500 projects of new product are currently in the process of development. (House and Price, 1991)

This increased dependence on the technological environment calls for a reinforcement of the market monitoring system within the organisation.

Internationalisation of markets

The period now referred to as the 'Golden Sixties' corresponds to the beginning of the internationalisation of markets, a process which has continued up to the 1990s. At the European level, internationalisation took the form of the creation of the Common Market; at the world level it took the form of GATT (General Agreement on Tariffs and Trade) and the resulting progressive liberalisation of trade, the end of the Cold War and the expansion of East–West trade. All these factors contributed to the widening markets, and, in general, to the intensification of competition and the reappraisal of established competitive positions.

To the various stages of international development there often correspond specific forms of organisation at the international level which reflect different views of international marketing. Keegan (1989) suggests the following typology:

● *Domestic organisation.* The firm is focused on its domestic market, and exporting is viewed as an opportunistic activity. This type of organisation is frequently in the 'passive marketing' stage as described above.

● *International organisation.* Internationalisation takes place more actively, but at this stage the firm's orientation is still focused on the home market, which is considered as the primary area of opportunity. The *ethnocentric* company, unconsciously, if not explicitly and consciously, operates on the assumption that home country methods, approaches, people, practices and values are superior to those found elsewhere in the world. Attention is mostly centred on similarities with the home country market. The product strategy at this stage is a 'market extension' strategy, that is products that have been designed for the home country market are 'extended' into markets around the world.

⬤ *Multidomestic organisation*. After a certain period of time, the company discovers that the difference in markets demands adaptation of its marketing in order to succeed. The focus of the firm is now multinational (as opposed to home country) and its orientation is *polycentric*. The polycentric orientation is based on the assumption that markets around the world are so different and unique that the only way to succeed is to adapt to the unique and different aspect of each national market. The product strategy is adaptation, that is to change or adapt products to meet local differences and practices. Each country is managed as if it were an independent entity.

⬤ *Global organisation*. A global market is one that can be reached with the same basic appeal and message and with the same basic product. Both the product and the advertising and promotion may require adaptation to local customs and practices, as illustrated in Table 7.10. The *geocentric* orientation of the global corporation is based on the assumption that markets around the world are both similar and different, and that it is possible to develop a global strategy that recognises similarities which transcend national differences while adapting to local differences as well. The basic notion of a world strategy can therefore be summarised as follows: *think globally and act locally*. This last stage is at the moment taking shape in the world and in particular in the European economy. It implies important changes in the logic of strategic marketing.

In the European and in the world economies, this internationalisation process took place during the Golden Sixties. This process also required a reinforcement of the analytical capabilities of the firm to successfully enter foreign markets.

Organisation of the marketing function

The three groups of changes we have just examined all imply a consolidation of strategic marketing in the firm. As far as the organisation of the firm with an 'active marketing' orientation is concerned, the significant change will be in regard to *product decisions*, which will henceforth be the responsibility of the marketing department in close liaison with the R&D department and the manufacturing department. This means that in actual practice, strategic marketing regulates product policy and decides whether products are economically viable. The idea for new products may come from anywhere: manufacturing, R&D, or any other source, but it must first pass through the test of strategic marketing before adoption and manufacturing.

Firms which have adopted the marketing concept will have a marketing department (see Figure 1.9) whose responsibilities will comprise all the tasks that flow from operational marketing and strategic marketing, including the choice of product markets. At this stage, the market-oriented firm has an *outside-in perspective* and places priority emphasis on customers' expectations as a starting point for its product policy.

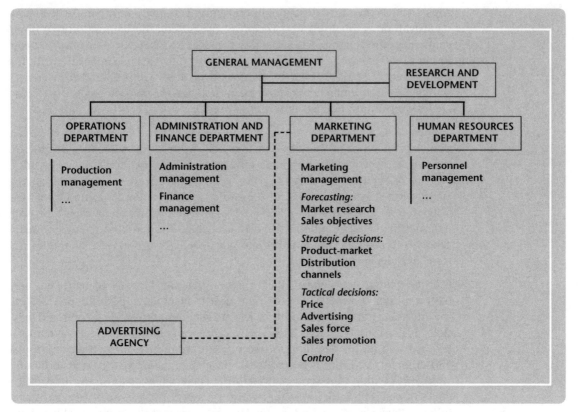

Figure 1.9   Typical organisation of a marketing-oriented company

In a marketing-oriented firm, the role of the seller has changed and is very different from the one observed in sales-oriented companies (see for example, Miller and Heiman, 1987; Dupont, 1994). The marketing concept has replaced and reversed the logic of the selling concept. As stated by the General Electric Company shortly after the Second World War,

> Rather than making what you have always made, then trying to sell it, find out what will sell, then try to make it.

In this framework, the role of the seller becomes less one of 'trying to sell' as one of 'helping to buy'. The process of selling initially bases itself on the needs of the buyer. This kind of commercial attitude can only be practical in an organisation where the marketing orientation dominates. To quote Drucker (1973, p. 86),

> There will always, one can assume, be need for some selling. But the aim of marketing is to make selling superfluous. The aim of marketing is to know and understand the customer so well that the product or service fits him and sells itself. Ideally, marketing should result in a customer who is ready to buy. All that should be needed then is to make the product or service available.

This ideal situation will only rarely be achieved, but it is important to remember that such is the objective of the marketing theory discussed earlier.

In a *marketing-oriented company*, the dominant business philiosophy can be summarised in the following terms:

> The key to business success is to integrate all company activities and personnel towards satisfying customers, while providing satisfactory profits to the firm. The firm should find out what benefits customers want and then provide these benefits through goods and services.

To achieve this objective, the marketing department has an important role to play.

The product or brand management system

From an organisational viewpoint, the implementation of the marketing concept has been achieved by the creation of powerful marketing departments (see Figure 1.10) in charge of both strategic and operational marketing. *Brand and product management* play a key role in these organisational structures. A brand manager is concerned with the strategic issues such as R&D and product innovation, branding policies and communication, business analysis and forecasting. His or her task is also to organise a dialogue with the other functions within the firm and to co-ordinate and control all the operations or activities related to the brand. A separate sales department is respon-

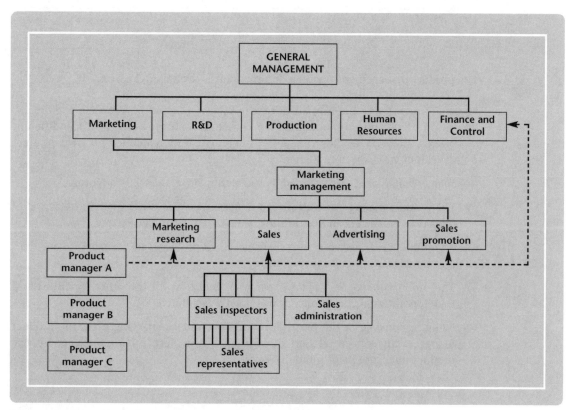

Figure 1.10   The traditional marketing department

sible for the sales tasks and for getting products on to retailers' shelves. This system, adopted by most consumer goods companies and also by many industrial firms, contributed to establishing manufacturers' brand dominance in the market.

According to a survey conducted in France (Kueviakoe, 1996), the responsibilities of a typical brand or product manager would be the ones presented in Table 1.4, in their order of importance.

Inspection of Table 1.4 suggests that most of these responsibilities pertain more to operational than to strategic marketing. In principle, the product manager is supposed to be responsible for the medium–long-term development of the product, while sales people are responsible for the implementation of the marketing plan in the short term, under the leadership of the marketing manager.

Table 1.4   Main responsibilities of product managers: a survey

To co-ordinate all activities related to the product	To order marketing research studies
To prepare the marketing plan	To brief market research companies
To fix the sales price	To design and decide on packaging
To estimate the unit cost	To choose the advertising platform
To prepare the marketing budget	To monitor laws and regulations
To compare actual and expected sales	To train the sales force
To propose promotional actions	To prepare the contracts and agreements
To assist the sales force	

Source: Kueviakoe (1996, p. 81).

The product management organisation introduces several advantages:

● The presence of a brand manager creates *dynamism and emulation* in the organisation by designating individuals in charge of the development of the different brands. He behaves more like an entrepreneur responsible for his own product development (a minipresident).

● *Smaller brands* are less neglected, because they have a product advocate.

● The product manager is well placed *to harmonise and co-ordinate* all the activities related to his own brand or product, thereby increasing efficiency.

● The product manager can *react more quickly* to problems in the marketplace than a committee of functional specialists.

● The product manager is a *single point of contact* for all the other functions and therefore internal communication is greatly facilitated.

● Being responsible or the preparation of the annual marketing plan, the product manager can concentrate on developing a *cost-effective marketing mix* for the product to ensure its profitability.

● In charge of the medium–long-term development of the product, the product manager can initiate product improvements in co-operation with R&D people to take advantage of *new market opportunities*.

But a price has to be paid for these advantages. Among the *problems and difficulties* generated by a product management organisation, let us consider the following points:

● The product management system is based on the principle of *decentralisation and delegation*, and this implies a clear political accord between the managing director and the marketing manager.

● The product manager has a *staff position* and as such does not necessarily have enough authority to carry out his responsibilities effectively. He or she has to rely on persuasion to get the co-operation of advertising, sales, manufacturing and other departments. The function is demanding and requires diplomatic skills.

● The product management system is *costly* and implies a duplication of contacts between the sales force, the functional specialists and the product managers.

● Product managers are generally junior people who normally manage their brand for only a short time. This *short-term involvement* induces them to give priority to short-term operational marketing activities, at the expense of longer term strategic thinking.

In this structure, it is up to the marketing manager to deal with these potential conflicts between the product managers, the sales force and the other functional departments and to delineate clearly the limits of the product managers' role and responsibility. Product managers report directly to the marketing manager who can therefore devote time and effort to strategic issues in close liaison with the managing director

Limitations of the traditional marketing concept

The implicit assumption at the root of the marketing concept is that *satisfying buyers' needs* is the prime objective of the firm, not because of altruism, but because it is the best way for the firm to achieve its own profit and/or growth objectives. There is nothing particularly sophisticated about the marketing concept as argued by Ames and Hlavacek (1989, p. 30). In today's competitive environment, no one really argues with the importance of strategic marketing. In fact it would probably be hard to find anyone to argue against the idea that gearing all activities of a business to be responsive to customer or user needs is not only sensible, but the only way to run a business. Despite this general agreement, many companies are simply paying lip service to the concept and are not particularly happy with what marketing has done to them. Understanding the marketing concept is one thing; following through with the commitment to implementing this philosophy of action is quite another.

In practice, the marketing concept is integrated differently in the firms – as illustrated in Table 1.5 – even if most claim to be inspired by it. In fact, as we mentioned earlier, the marketing concept is an *ideal* to be reached, rarely fully realised, but one that should nevertheless guide all the activities of the firm.

Table 1.5 The changing role of marketing

Marketing in practice	Marketing in theory		
	Action	Analysis	Culture
Passive marketing	–	–	–
Operational marketing	YES	–	–
Strategic marketing	YES	YES	–
Market-driven management	YES	YES	YES

As in the case of the product concept and the selling concept, the marketing concept has its own limitations, of which one should be aware. Three major limitations or questions are usually raised against the traditional marketing concept:

1. When referring to needs satisfaction, does marketing refer to short-term or to long-term satisfaction? Should marketing be concerned with the well-being of buyers?

    We are confronted here with a basic issue which is raised more and more frequently in industrialised economies, where social aspirations have shifted from quantity to 'quality' of life. In this end of century's social environment, the firm is expected to behave as a good citizen and to assume social accountability as well as to maintain affluence. Thus, the traditional marketing concept must evolve towards the *accountable* or societal marketing concept (Kotler, 1997).

2. Is the marketing objective of individual needs' satisfaction made at the expense of social needs? Is the social cost of consumption a cost neglected by traditional marketing?

    This second question is the result of the public's awareness of the scarcity of non-renewable resources and of the impact of consumption on the environment, which until recently was viewed as a free public good. In advanced economies, the socio-ecological view of consumption 'from cradle to grave' is a largely accepted vision which induces firms to redesign their product concepts in a green perspective. Thus, the traditional marketing orientation must evolve towards the green marketing concept.

3. Does an over-enthusiastic adoption of the marketing concept lead the firm to put too much emphasis on products in high demand, or market-pull, at the expense of products yet unknown but pushed by technology?

    A marketing strategy exclusively guided by market wishes inevitably tends to favour minor and less revolutionary innovations than those proposed by the laboratory. Such innovations, which correspond to needs felt and expressed by the market, are by this token less risky and are therefore seen as more attractive to the firm. On the other hand, a strategy based on technological advance is more likely to lead to a breakthrough innovation and hence ensure that the firm has a long-term competitive advantage which is more difficult to catch up with. Many *breakthrough innovations* in fact originate from the laboratory (or from the firm) and not from the market. It is therefore important to maintain a balance between these two strategies of product development: 'technology or company-push' and 'market-pull'.

These three questions call for a new evolution of the role of marketing within the firm. At the beginning of the new millennium, the ongoing change in alert companies is the move from a marketing orientation towards a market orientation, which places the emphasis on the *culture* dimension, in addition to its *action* and *analysis*.

Chapter summary

Marketing is both a business philosophy and an action-oriented process. One can identify three components in the marketing concept: action, analysis and culture (principle of consumer sovereignty). The ideological foundations of marketing are deeply rooted in the principles which govern the functioning of a market economy. Within the firm, marketing's function is twofold: (a) to create opportunities or to lead the firm towards market opportunities adapted to its resources and know-how and which offer a potential for profit and growth (strategic marketing): (b) to be the firm's commercial arm for achieving a targeted market share through the use of tactical means related to product, distribution, price and communication decisions (operational marketing). The role of marketing in society is to organise exchange and communication between sellers and buyers, thereby assuming an efficient matching of supply and demand. This role is of an increased complexity in modern economies and determines the productivity of the entire market system. The priority role of marketing has evolved with the complexity of the economic, technological and competitive environment. In current marketing practice, one can identify three levels of implementation of the marketing concept: passive marketing, operational marketing and strategic marketing. Each of these business philosophies has its own limitations. To remain competitive in the environment of the twenty-first century, excellent companies are going one step further today and are moving from a marketing-oriented to a market-oriented culture.

QUESTIONS AND PROBLEMS

1. 'Marketing is both a business philosophy and an action-oriented process which is valid for every organisation in contact with its constituency of users.' Select a non-profit organisation (university, hospital, museum, and so on) and discuss this proposition by reference to Figures 1.2 and 1.4. As a support for your analysis, read Sheth (1993).

2. Is marketing applicable in a firm operating in a developing country? How would you describe the priority objectives of strategic marketing in this type of environment? What would be the relative importance of each marketing instrument (the four Ps)?

3. Compare and contrast marketing orientation, sales orientation and product orientation. What are the organisational implications for each of these three business philosophies?

4. Referring to your personal experience as a consumer, give examples of wild marketing practices. Which remedies would you suggest to deter companies from using these practices?

5. You have to audit the marketing function of a firm operating in a high-tech industrial market. To assess the degree of customer orientation of this firm, prepare a set of questions to be discussed with the general management of the firm.

6. How would you proceed to introduce strategic marketing in a small or medium-sized company which has limited financial and human resources?

Bibliography

Ames, B.C. and Hlavacek, J.D. (1989) *Market Driven Management*, Homewood IL, Dow Jones-Irwin.

Boisdevésy, J.C. (1996) *Le marketing relationnel*, Paris, Les Editions d'Organisation.

Dupont, C. (1994), *La négociation*, 4th edn, Paris, Dalloz.

Drucker, P. (1973) *Management, Tasks, Responsibilities and Practices*, New York, Harper & Row.

Friedman, R. and M. (1980) *Free to Choose*, New York, Avon Brooks Science Institute.

House, C.H. and Price, R.L. (1991) The Return Map; Tracking Product Teams, *Harvard Business Review*, **69**, January–February, pp. 92–100.

Keegan, W.J. (1989) *Global Marketing Management*, 4th edn, Englewood Cliffs NJ, Prentice Hall.

Kotler, P. (1997) *Marketing Management*, 9th edn, Englewood Cliffs NJ, Prentice Hall.

Kuehn, A.A. and Day, R.L. (1962) Strategy of Product Quality, *Harvard Business Review*, **40**, November–December, pp. 100–10.

Kueviakoe, D. (1996) Entre grande stabilité et faible autorité: la position du chef de produit dans les entreprises, *Revue Française du Marketing*, No. 156, pp. 79–91.

Levitt, Th. (1960) Marketing Myopia, *Harvard Business Review*, **38**, July–August, pp. 24–47.

Mbwinga Bila, R. (1995) *Déterminants et stratégie de compétitivité industrielle en Afrique Subsaharienne*, Louvain-la-Neuve, Academia.

Miller, R.B. and Heiman, S.E. (1987) *Conceptual Selling*, Berkeley CA, Heiman-Miller.

Pirot, R. (1987) Plaute, ancêtre du marketing, *Revue Française du Marketing*, No. 114, pp. 83–8.

Schendler, B.R. (1992) How Sony Keeps the Magic Going, *Fortune*, February.

Schumpeter, J.A. (1949) The Theory of Economic Development, Cambridge MA, Harvard University Press.

Sheth, J. (1993) User-oriented Marketing for Non Profit Organizations, in: Hammack, D.C. and Young, D.R. (eds.), *Nonprofit Organisations in a Market Economy*, San Francisco CA, Jossey-Bass.

Smith, A. (1776) *The Wealth of Nations*, London, Methuen.

Tournier, M. (1969) *Friday*, Baltimore, MD, The Johns Hopkins University Press.

chapter two

From marketing to market-driven management

In recent years, the concept of market orientation has received increased attention both from the business and the academic communities. This revival of interest in the concept can be attributed, among others, to three geopolitical drivers. First, the wave of deregulation and of privatisation which, worldwide, liberates markets, dismantles monopolies and is forcing former state-owned enterprises to dramatically change their business culture. Second, in Western Europe, the process of economic integration triggered by the creation of the European single market and the Monetary Union induces firms to redefine their strategic options in an enlarged and more competitive environment. Last but not least, the adoption of the market economy system by the former Communist bloc, including countries like China and Vietnam which are trying to find an original road towards a state-led market economy.

In this new context, it is important for the dynamic firm to have a good understanding of the managerial implications of the market orientation business philosophy and to have at its disposal reliable managerial instruments for both diagnosing the present state of a business and establishing the most appropriate course of action for its future development. Launched in 1988 by Shapiro (1988), this debate is not purely academic, since it questions the traditional organisational mode of the marketing function within the firm, and more particularly the functional structures described in the preceding chapter. These structures are currently being abandoned by many companies for interfunctional organisation modes which facilitate the dissemination of the market culture within the firm at all levels and across all functions.

In this chapter, we shall review the most important changes observed in the macro-marketing environment which call for a reinforcement of the market orientation of the firm to meet the challenges of the new millennium. We shall also propose a definition and a measurement instrument of the market orientation concept, and conclude with a description of the new marketing function.

Chapter learning objectives

When you have read this chapter, you should be able to understand:

1. the major changes of the European macro-marketing environment;
2. the expectations and the behaviour of the new consumer;
3. the challenge of the environmentalism movement for the firm;
4. the 'accountable' marketing concept and its ethical implications;
5. the impact of the globalisation of the European and world economies;
6. the market orientation concept and its managerial implications.

● **The New Macro-marketing Environment**

The underlying causes of the new challenges to be faced at the end of this century in Western Europe can be traced to several changes due to structural modifications of technology, the economy and markets, coupled with a realignment of social priorities. Today, at the end of the 1990s, change continues at a pace which makes it safe to predict that the current escalation of turbulence will persist in the years to come. Everyday events are there to confirm this feeling. The development of privatisation and deregulation policies with the change of corporate culture it implied; the painful adaptation of the market economy system, not only in Eastern and Central Europe, but also in countries like China and Vietnam; the launching of the single currency in Europe and the resulting increase of price transparency and of competition. These changes in the firm's macro-marketing environment are all examples of major modifications, which in turn generate socio-cultural changes. In this section, we shall review the implications of these changes on marketing.

Table 2.1   Average yearly GDP growth rate

Periods	Europe 15	United States	Japan
1960–1973	4.7	3.9	9.6
1973–1979	2.5	2.5	3.6
1979–1990	2.3	2.4	4.1
1991–1995	1.5	2.5	1.3
1996	1.8	3.4	3.9
1997	2.7	3.9	0.8
1998	2.8	3.5	−2.6
1999	2.2	1.5	0.2

Source: OECD (1998).

The new European economy

Since 1973, Western Europe has had a GDP growth (in real terms) of about 2 per cent against 4.7 per cent, in average, before 1973 (see Table 2.1). The OECD forecast for the year 2000 is around 2 per cent. At the end of this century, the European economic situation is dominated by the creation of the European Monetary Union (EMU) and by the introduction of the euro, which should create a new dynamic and stimulate growth.

At the eve of the launch of the euro as cash money, the overall economic and competitive situation of the European economy can be summarised by the following facts:

● *Slowed down growth*, hardly over 1.5 per cent per year of the GDP (in real terms) from 1991 to 1995, compared to more than 4.7 per cent on average over the period 1960–73. The growth rate is expected to be around 2.5 per cent in 1998.

● Despite spectacular economic growth since 1960, Europe's standard of living is still 25 per cent lower than the USA and about 15 per cent lower than Japan.

● Even if the creation of the European Union has contributed to a reduction in the disparities among countries within the EU, differences in standard of living remain in a 1 to 3 ratio in 1995, against a 1 to 4 ratio in 1960.

● The *unemployment rate*, which had only reached about 3 per cent of the active population in 1973, went up to 10 per cent in 1983 in the seven largest industrial countries. In 1998, it was still around 10 per cent in OECD Europe, with the exception of the Netherlands and of the United Kingdom.

● Double-digit *inflation* occurred in the European Community from 1973 to 1980, and has then fallen to below 3 per cent since 1993.

● *Budget deficits* are today well under control around 3 per cent as a result of the Maastricht Treaty.

● *The commercial influence* of the European Community countries has weakened. This can be witnessed in the decline of the share of exports (excluding intra-Community trade) of 2.5 per cent between 1987 and 1993, from 41.3 per cent to 38.8 per cent.

● The *launch of the euro*, as deposit money in January 1999 and as cash money in January 2002, should create a new dynamic (see Exhibit 2.1). The European single currency will increase price transparency, reduce transaction costs and eliminate exchange risks. According to economists, this should contribute to stimulate competition and economic growth.

In the twenty-first century, European firms will operate in a much more difficult economic environment. The profound changes in the economy imply very rapid and harsh penalties for management errors, as witnessed by the spectacular rise in the number of firms going bankrupt.

Exhibit 2.1

The Expected Benefits of the European Single Currency

- On 1 January, 1999, the conversion rates of each of the 11 European currencies to the euro have been irrevocably fixed and the euro has become a currency in its own right. The conversion rate of 1:1 between the ECU and euro has also been confirmed. The changeover process from the national currencies to the euro will be completed on 1 July, 2002. During the transitional period, each enterprise has a choice between two approaches: to make a complete 'once-for-all' changeover on 1 January, 2002; or to use the euro for some operations during the transitional period.
- Thanks to the euro, the European single market will no longer be disturbed by so-called 'competitive devaluations', that is not justified from an economic viewpoint.
- The expected benefits of the European single currency are: increased price transparency between EU countries and increased competition – Elimination of foreign exchange transaction costs – Elimination of foreign exchange risks – Simplification of accounting systems for the international firm – Alternative to the US dollar as international currency in international trade.
- The challenges facing enterprises will be the following: To prepare a detailed changeover plan – To establish a price list in euros – To be prepared for a dual pricing display during the transitional period – To deal with price disparities observed in Euroland – To review the positioning of their brands country by country – To assess the risk of parallel imports.

Technological Innovation

Increasingly, firms are confronted with *innovation competition*, based on technical progress, which is used more and more as an offensive weapon to conquer markets. The effect of *creative destruction*, in the Schumpeter sense (1949), is well known. What is new is its acceleration and geographical generalisation and, in industrialised economies, the development of the service sector as the main provider of growth and employment.

The growth rate of an economy is closely related to the number of innovations – technological or organisational – and the number of new industries or service activities that can be created with these innovations. Unfortunately, new technologies and innovations do not appear at regular intervals. In the absence of important innovations, an economy can stagnate. This was the case during the early 1980s in Western economies and especially in Europe. Industries that have served basic needs have reached saturation. These industries did not necessarily decline, but their growth rate slowed down. New industries, mainly service industries, emerged that cater to the affluent consumer in the form of luxury goods, recreation, travel and services. In addition, high-technology sectors have also developed, which constitute highways towards economic expansion. These growing markets are the stakes for which the world is engaged in a competitive battle at the eve of the third millennium. (Little, 1998).

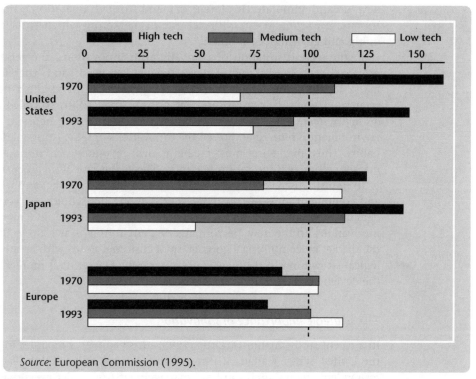

Source: European Commission (1995).

Figure 2.1   Low-tech Europe. Ratio of country exports as a percentage of total manufacturing exports to the OECD average

The data of Figure 2.1. compare the relative positions of the USA, Japan and Europe from 1970 to 1993, in terms of shares of exports of high-, medium- or low-tech products. This chart highlights the two following points:

- in the high-tech sectors (where the added value is the highest), the USA has the highest share (in decline since 1970), followed by Japan (increasing since 1970) and by Europe (in stagnation);

- in the low-tech sectors (where the value added is the lowest), the largest share which used to be Japan is now Europe.

Thus, it appears that the European competitive position has deteriorated during the last twenty years.

The concept of discontinuous innovation

Concerning technological innovations, the degree of risk will vary according to the origin of the new product (or service) idea. In Chapter 1 a distinction was made between a *market-pull innovation*, that is one that directly meets observed needs, and a *technology or company-push innovation*, that is one that results from research, creativity and technological opportunities. In the first case, needs are expressed and primary demand is a latent demand; the role of marketing is to develop and stimulate this latent demand through operational marketing. This is *response marketing*, the traditional role of marketing which still prevails in developing and growing economies.

In the second situation of company-push innovations, the products or services proposed are often ahead of expressed market needs and, therefore, the role of marketing is more complex here, since primary demand must be created (from scratch). Thus, the innovation creates the market. With so-called *discontinuous or disruptive innovations*, the market boundaries are not well defined, the competitive environment is blurred and often the innovations upset existing market practices and habits. Thus, marketing must create its own favourable environment and strategic marketing has an important role to play. This is the case of *supply or creative marketing*.

In industrialised economies, where basic needs are well met and where penetration and equipment rates of consumer goods among households are very high, primary demand stagnates and the growth potential comes more and more from creative innovations. In the new macro-marketing environment, it is up to the firm to create the market by combining a good grasp of customer needs with creativity and technological know-how. In this new context, strategic marketing is more vital than ever for the development of the firm.

The strategic importance of innovation

In a recent study, Arthur D. Little (1998) surveyed 669 companies in 10 industries in the United States, Canada, Latin America, Europe and the Asia–Pacific region. The respondents represented top-level management from chief executive officers (CEOs) and chief technology officers to business unit leaders, as well as functional management from R&D to marketing.

One of the key findings of the survey is that companies have shifted from a predominantly cost-cutting posture to a more strategic focus on innovation and are giving high strategic priority to innovations. Eighty-four per cent of the respondents agree that, in the present environment, *innovation is a much more critical business success factor than it was just five years ago*. In fact, innovation is stealing the spotlight from the more traditional restructuring and downsizing priorities, with a focus on growth. However, despite the renewed importance of innovation, less than 25 per cent of the responding companies were happy with their current performance in innovation.

The study also assessed the three primary types of innovation across regions and industries around the world:

- *Product/service innovation.* The creative development and commercialisation of radically new products and services, often grounded on new technology and linked to unmet customer needs.

- *Process innovation.* The development of new ways of producing products or delivering services that lead to advantages on costs, quality, or timeless on delivery.

- *Business innovation.* The development of new businesses and new ways of conducting business that provide unbeatable competitive advantage.

The survey also underlines the importance of *cross-functional teams* to further the development of the innovation process across the enterprise, for example moving people regularly between laboratories and business units, to ensure that researchers fully understand the needs of the marketplace.

The socio-cultural changes

In recent years significant socio-demographic changes have been observed in industrialised countries. Among these changes are:

● declining birth rate,
● increase in life expectancy,
● increasing number of working women,
● postponement of the age of marriage,
● increasing divorce rate,
● increasing numbers of single-parent families,
● Increase in number of dual-income households,
● increase in number of unemployed or early retired people,
● increasing number of ethnic groups intra- or extra-EU.

These changes all have direct implications on the demand structure and on consumer purchase behaviour. They create new market segments and new requirements in existing segments. Examples are:

● the *senior citizens* (over 65) segment for banking services, recreational activities, medical care, and so on.
● the segment of *single-adult households*, that is the unmarried, divorced, widowed or single-parent families;
● the *dual-income households* having higher discretionary income, also called the 'DINKS' (double income no kids)
● the segment of *working women* for all time-saving goods and services, like microwave ovens, catalogue shopping, easy-to-prepare foods, fast-food restaurants, and so on.

These segments constitute new opportunities requiring the adaptation of the traditional mass marketing approach which should be replaced by a *mass-customisation approach*.

The new consumer

The mass marketing era lifted the aspirations of consumers from the materialistic needs of comfort and safety to a drive for new values. Satisfaction of 'good living' needs coupled with growth in discretionary income have changed consumer demand patterns. Having 'filled their bellies', as Ansoff put it (1984, p. 7), individuals begin to aspire to higher levels of personal satisfaction. They become increasingly discriminating in their demand for more customised services and complete information about their purchases, as well as for post-sales responsibility from the manufacturer and for ecologically friendly products. For many consumers, shopping is no longer viewed as fun or recreational, but rather as a tedious task to be performed as economically and efficiently as possible. Time, stimulation, pleasure and change are the new dominating values.

According to a survey conducted by CREDOC in France, a majority of people within the active population would prefer more leisure time than more money. This majority group has increased in size by 10 per cent in two years and belongs mainly to the two-thirds of well-to-do and well-educated people.

In Western Europe, the purchase behaviour of the new consumer can be characterised as follows:

⬤ *A feeling of power.* Consumers behave in markets where supply is plethoric (more than 100 so-called 'new products' per day in the food sector in France), where competition is very strong, not only among brands but also between manufacturers and mass distributors, and where a large variety of information sources are organised for the consumer. Moreover, the consumerist movement is powerful, well-organised and listened to. All these factors show that the balance of power is in favour consumers who are quite of aware of this fact.

⬤ *A professional purchase behaviour.* Well educated and experienced, consumers behave as smart shoppers. Being informed about the products and being able to compare, they choose independently of brands, advertising, stores and salespersons' recommendations. It means finding the best value for money. From passive consumers they become more active or *'consum'actors'* (Ochs, 1991). Treated as partners by large distribution firms, they claim to influence product policies. To ask for advice, to grumble, to complain, to suggest, or to congratulate, European consumers no longer hesitate to call the firm directly, as evidenced by the growing success of consumer services with the firms (see Exhibit 2.2).

⬤ *The 'satisfaction–delight–loyalty' relationship.* New consumers hold the firm responsible in case of dissatisfaction and, if not happy with the way their complaint has been handled, not only will they not buy again, but they will also talk a lot about their deception to friends or business relations. Thus a dissatisfied customer is a lost customer, a damaging effect in zero-growth markets, where replacing a lost customer by a new one is particularly difficult and costly. Moreover, research results show that simply giving what is expected is not enough to keep a customer loyal. The objective should be to give more than expected, to have *delighted customers.*

⬤ *Emergence of new expectations.* Today's consumers do not accept the mass marketing practices of the 1970s and 1980s targeted to an average consumer. They want to be listened to, heard, understood and respected. They are looking for an answer to their problem at a fair price. Their choices are opportunistic, luxury or low end, depending on the consumption situation. But in any case, the new consumers want transparency on prices, product characteristics and attributes, and so on. Moreover, they want an ethical consumption and refuse to have guilty feelings because of their purchases or through brand advertising.

If these characteristics are observed in each EU country, large disparities still exist within Europe as illustrated by the data of Table 2.2, and one can hardly speak of a European consumer. The data of Table 2.2. measuring consumer opinion on economic and financial conditions (consumer confidence indicator) show that large differences exist among countries and over time. In Table 2.2., three countries emerge as particularly optimistic in 1999: Ireland, the Netherlands and Finland.

Exhibit 2.2

The Growing Success of Consumer Affairs Departments

- Since the early 1990s, consumer affairs departments entirely focused on consumer relationships have been growing fast and raise an increasingly keen interest.
- In France, more than two hundred consumer affairs departments were identified in 1997, from less than one hundred five years ago. Surprisingly, they receive an increasing number of letters and telephone calls from consumers, up to a point that this can be considered as a real societal phenomenon.
- In 1996, the customer service unit of Nestlé established 180,000 contacts with consumers of its brands, twice as many as it did five years ago.
- This year, Danone expects queries from about 200,000 consumers.
- In 1996, more than 15,000 customers called or wrote to Colgate–Palmolive, against 12,000 the previous year.
- At Avis, the car rental company, which has had a consumer affairs department since 1991, 126,000 letters and calls are received each year.

Source: Le Monde, 12 February 1997.

Table 2.2 The European consumer confidence indicator

Countries	Average 87/96	Maximum 87/91	Minimum 91/95	1994	1995	1996	1997	1998	1999 (May)
Belgium	−11	5	−30	−15	−14	−23	−22	−6	−1
Denmark	−3	2	−10	8	9	4	9	3	−4
Germany	−12	5	−30	−15	−9	−21	−19	−7	−4
Greece	−25	−8	−36	−22	−31	−27	−26	−29	−18
Spain	−14	3	−38	−25	−20	−14	−3	5	6
France	−18	−7	−29	−17	−17	−28	−20	−10	−6
Ireland	−8	−2	−27	−1	4	11	18	17	19
Italy	−16	0	−36	−21	−21	−25	−22	−11	−15
The Netherlands	−3	11	−21	−7	4	3	17	22	16
Austria	–	–	–	–	–	−15	−12	−3	0
Portugal	−12	6	−31	–	–	−18	−10	−5	−6
Finland	−1	9	−13	9	11	9	15	15	14
Sweden	–	–	–	–	–	−7	1	6	6
UK	−12	7	−25	−12	−10	−5	4	0	2
Europe	−13	−3	−26	−16	−13	−17	−11	−4	−3

Source: European Economy (1999).

The consumerist movement

The evolution of the consumption environment and of consumer purchase behaviour has contributed to the development of the consumerist movement. Born during the 1970s on a defensive mode, the consumerist movement has changed today to the extent that many of its causes have been met by firms either through legislation or by self-regulation, namely through the creation of an in-company consumer affairs department.

Consumerism was born out of the growing consciousness of the excesses of operational marketing, or the practice of wild marketing (see Exhibit 1.2) which attempts to mould demand to meet supply requirements rather than adapt supply to demand expectations. Consumerism is the consequence of the relative failure of the marketing concept. As stated by Drucker (1980, p. 85), *'consumerism is the shame of marketing'*.

The main arguments of the consumerist critique are as follows:

⬤ Marketing tries to satisfy consumers' *short-term needs* at the expense of their *long-term well-being*.
⬤ Products are developed in order to *favour the profit objective* of the firm rather than the objective of satisfying needs.
⬤ Marketing favours the *symbolic value* of products (affective and emotional values) at the expense of their functional value.
⬤ There is a fundamental *imbalance* between buyers' and sellers' legal rights.

It is important to emphasise that consumerism does not fundamentally question the marketing concept, but rather demands its full application (see Exhibit 2.3). In fact, the consumerist movement reveals a phenomenon of *'socialisation'* or of *'unionisation' of demand*, similar to the workers' movement at the beginning of the century. This is an important fact for the firm, as it confronts ever more involved consumers who react to its actions in an organised manner and who are better informed thanks, among others, to consumer associations.

In the past, business has fought the consumer movement bitterly, resisting its charges and responding with its own accusations. If the consumer movement is moving from ideology to ethics as a basis for action, business's old pattern of response will become less and less appropriate. Today, the business community tends to regard the consumer movement as an early warning system for impending trouble rather than as the unappeasable enemy of the past.

Exhibit 2.3

Examples of Consumerist Issues

Truth in lending	Open dating
Unit pricing	Truth in advertising
Ingredient labelling	Product safety
Nutritional labelling	Comparative testing

Exhibit 2.4

Economic Analysis of Environmentalism

- In 1972, the Meadow report of the Club of Rome called the attention of the economic and social world to the limits of economic growth, the risk of exhausting non-renewable resources, the destruction of the environment and the uncontrolled growth of waste. This new awareness led public authorities and political movements to listen to the recommendations made by economists.

- To the economist, the environment is part of the economy and the best way to protect the environment is to assign a price to its use instead of considering it as a free public good, in contrast with the other goods found in a market economy.

- If there is no market price, consumers and manufacturers are motivated to use the environment as a 'free reservoir' even if the social costs generated by their polluting behaviour are high, since these costs are not assessed by the market. Thus, those generating these social costs do not pay them and are not held responsible for the costs involved in their elimination.

- The solution proposed by the economists is to set a price on the use of the environment. This price should be equal to the sum of the total social costs generated by pollution as they are evaluated by the polluted parties. Given this price, polluters would use the environment only to the extent the expected benefits of this use are higher than the price they would have to pay. This way, the polluters would assume the social cost of pollution. This is the idea behind the principle 'who pollutes pays'.

- The economic instruments used to set a price to the use of the environment generally take the form of a direct tax on the polluting activities, either in a prevention (eco-taxes) or in a repairing (eco-fees) perspective.

Due to its countervailing power, consumerism has undoubtedly contributed to the *improvement of the ethical level of marketing practice*. It forms a pressure group that firms can hardly ignore. For more about the history of consumerism, see Aaker and Day (1982).

Environmentalism and green marketing

The *environmentalist movement* reflects the new awareness of the scarcity of natural resources and reveals a change of outlook regarding consumption. Environmentalists question the impact of consumption and of marketing on the environment, as summarised in Exhibit 2.4. The reasoning is as follows:

Each consumption has positive and negative utilities. By insisting on increasing consumption quantitatively, marketing is instrumental in neglecting the impact of negative consequences. These negative consequences have a high social cost, which is also a neglected cost. Given the scarcity of resources, it is necessary to allow explicitly for the social cost of consumption.

The data of Table 2.3 illustrate the relevance of the environmentalist reasoning in the personal transportation sector.

In contrast with consumerists, environmentalists do not accept the principle of consumer sovereignty if the application of this principle leads to the destruction of the environment. They feel that the aim of the economic system should not be the satisfaction of the consumer as such, but rather the *improvement in the quality of life*. Their main concern is to protect and enhance people's living environment. The environmentalist movement has had a great impact in many industries and is undoubtedly a factor which is deeply affecting economic and industrial life.

Only few years ago, the idea of paying taxes to collect and recycle packages and solid waste was unthinkable. Today it is common practice in most countries of Western Europe to have government-sponsored programmes designed to focus on pollution control. These programmes are financed by *eco-fees* paid by manufacturers per package used to cover the cost of collection, selection processing and recycling of waste. The *eco-taxes system* adopted in Belgium, embraced the concept of pollution prevention and is targeted directly to the end-user to induce him or her to use environmentally sound products.

Table 2.3 Socio-economic costs of personal transportation modes

Personal transportation modes	Indirect social costs*			Total	Ratio
	Accidents	Noise	Pollution		
Cars (petrol)	1017.0	55	213	1285.0	36.4
Cars (diesel)	1017.0	55	75	1147.0	32.5
Buses	95.0	11	148	254.0	7.2
Electric trains	2.3	33	0	35.3	1.0
Diesel trains	2.3	33	44	79.3	2.2

*In Belgian francs per 1000 travellers kilometres (that is 1 traveller over 1000 km or 20 travellers over 50 km); traffic jam costs not included. The last column shows the ratio of each transportation mode. The train has an indirect social cost of 1 franc and the petrol-driven car has a cost of BF36.4. *Source: Le Soir*, Brussels, 16 December, 1987.

The life cycle inventory model

Two fundamentally different approaches have evolved in assessing what constitutes an 'environmentally friendly' product. The first, the *incremental approach*, is one in which any environmental improvement to a product, however minor, is considered valid and can be labelled as 'environmentally friendly'. The second, the *'cradle to grave' approach*, also called the *life cycle inventory approach*, is one in which the total impact on the environment must be evaluated before the product can be labelled 'environmentally friendly'.

> Life cycle inventory (LCI) is a process that quantifies the use of energy, resources and emission to the environment associated with a product throughout its life cycle. It accounts for the environmental impact of raw materials procurement, manufacturing and production, packaging, distribution and in-use characteristics straight through to after-use and disposal. (Ottman 1993, p. 104)

Table 2.4 highlights the results of an LCI study commissioned by Procter & Gamble comparing the relative environmental impacts of cloth versus paper disposable nappies.

Obviously these two approaches, incremental versus life cycle, are very different viewpoints difficult to reconcile. Not surprisingly, businesses usually take the incremental approach while environmental groups prefer the *'cradle to grave'* approach (see Figure 2.2).

Table 2.4 Example of life cycle inventory: cloth versus disposable nappies

	Cloth	Disposable
Raw material consumption (lb)	3.6	25.3
Water consumption (gal)	144	23.6
Energy consumption (BTUs)	78.890	23.920
Air emission (lb)	0.860	0.093
Water pollution (lb)	0.117	0.012
Solid waste(lb)	0.24	22.18

Source: Ottman (1993, p. 105); *The New York Times,* 14 July, 1990.

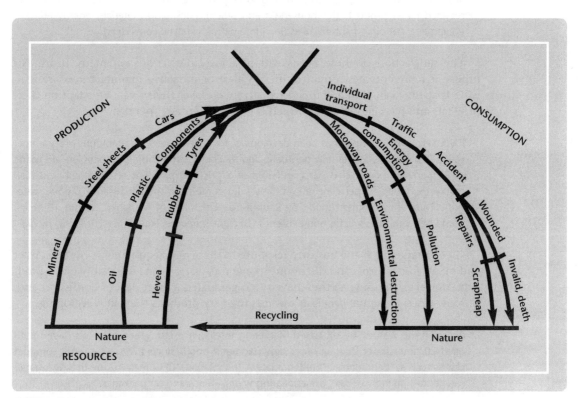

Figure 2.2 The socio-ecological vision of consumption life cycle inventory: from cradle to grave

The environmental concern is the expression of new needs within society. It is not a fad or a protest trend, like the hippies in the late 1960s and early 1970s. It is a way of life which has and will spread throughout all levels of society. Satisfaction of these societal needs will certainly imply new constraints for many firms; for other firms, these new needs constitute an emerging market with new opportunities such as anti-pollution products, environmentally sound products, energy-saving products, recycled products, and so on. Two examples of companies having successfully taken advantage of the environmental concern are the Body Shop Company, a speciality retail chain of natural cosmetics and toiletries, and Ecover, a firm which manufactures an all-natural, concentrated laundry detergent and line of household cleaners.

Green marketing

One impact of the environmentalist movement is the emergence of a new breed of consumerists, the *green consumerists*. Green consumerists have realised that it is possible to change what they consume in a way which benefits the environment and themselves. As a result, green consumerism is putting pressure on distributors and manufacturers to switch to food products and household goods that are healthier and environmentally friendly. They also put pressure on governments to act. Areas that seem likely to develop modified products which are environmentally safe are:

> Personal hygiene, household cleaning products (phosphate-free), food items (organic farming), recycling (paper, glass, tin, and so on), toiletries and cosmetics (CFC-free sprays), recycled paper products (for household and office), packaging materials, energy efficient equipment, petrol and automobiles (lead-free petrol, catalytic converters).

The satisfaction of these needs will pose new restrictions on many firms. For others, it represents new opportunities as alert or proactive manufacturers are realising that they can gain a competitive advantage over their rivals by adapting their products and packages in a way which is environmentally friendly.

> Rank Xerox, for example, has been developing, for several years, an ambitious programme, called Renaissance, for reusing photocopying machine parts. These photocopiers are made of 80 per cent of recycled parts and sold at a price 20 per cent of that for brand new machines. Today 40 per cent of company sales come from the Renaissance product category. Thus, the comment made by Rank Xerox Environment Manager: 'within 10 years, brand new products will be non-existent'. (*La Libre Entreprise*, November 20, 1993, p. 27)

Green marketing is the industry response to these new requirements of the market and many corporations and distributors have hurried to create ostensibly green products. However, in doing so they have often generated a great deal of confusion and, in some cases, an actual backlash towards the very products they are developing.

> According to a study by UK-based Marketing Intelligence Ltd, green products have multiplied 20 times faster than all other new packaged goods since 1986. As a result, product claims such as 'degradable', 'biodegradable', 'recyclable', 'CFC-free', 'ozone-friendly', 'environmentally friendly or safe' are appearing widely in ads and on packages.

These terms are often used by marketers in positioning their products and then disputed by environmentalists. Because of claims and counter-claims many consumers became confused, sceptical and questioning. This situation was created by the different approaches taken to assess 'environmentally friendly' products, the incremental or the life cycle approach.

Green consumerists argue that the lack of objective and uniform standards as to the meaning of green labels has left the environmentally conscious buyer uncertain and sceptical about green marketing in general. Green advertising campaigns are viewed as merely attention-getting devices for *'companies trying to hitchhike on the green bandwagon'*. It is clear that a 'going green' policy should cover the entire manufacturing process and not just the advertising of the end product. As discussed in Chapter 11 of this book, a going green policy should start at the stage of the product concept design, in the laboratory with R&D people and not with advertising people. Firms that position themselves as 'environmentally friendly' must be in a position to prove their environmental credentials. Thus companies adopting the incremental approach face the possibility of attacks by environmental groups who prefer the cradle-to-grave approach.

The first challenge facing the firm is to define what constitutes *'green'* in its specific product category. According to Ottman (1993, p. 49), green products are typically durable, non-toxic, made from recycled materials and minimally packaged. Of course there are no completely green products, for they all use up energy and resources and create waste and pollution during their manufacture, distribution, consumption and after-use and disposal. So *green is relative, describing those products with less impact on the environment than alternatives.* The McDonald's restaurants' case summarised in Exhibit 2.5. illustrates the complexity of environmental issues and the lack of agreement upon methods to measure the precise environmental impacts of a product against alternatives.

Firms that position themselves as 'environmentally friendly', particularly consumer product companies, should consider adopting a 'cradle-to-grave' approach in assessing the environmental impact of their products. Through this environmental audit, the firm can better assess the risk of scrutiny and possible attack by environmentalists. Seeking assistance and advice of environmentalist groups can also sensitise the firm to their concerns. Another benefit is that the firm gains expertise in a complex evolving area that is likely to become an important source of competitive advantage in the future.

To clarify the situation, national governments are introducing special product labels – *eco-labels* – to identify environmentally sound products for consumers and to encourage industry to design goods meeting these requirements. West Germany was the first country to introduce (in 1978) its official eco-labelling scheme (Blue Angel). These labels are criticised today by environmentalists because they are not based on a complete life cycle analysis. It seems that a European eco-label will progressively replace the national eco-labels.

The revolution in the food retail sector

In the performance of the tasks of exchange and communication described in Figure 1.1., the initiative was until recently on the suppliers' side who, specifically in the fast moving consumer goods (FMCG) sector, have developed dynamic branding policies

Exhibit 2.5

The McDonald's Restaurants' Case

A good example illustrating the complexity of environmental issues is the McDonald's restaurants' case. Late in 1990, the decision was made to wrap hamburgers in waxed papers instead of polystyrene foam. This decision was made in response to considerable consumer pressure (boycott, sit-ins, and so on) and publicity based on the impression that foam boxes were bad for the environment. Consider however the following:

■ Polystyrene foam containers satisfy health regulations, keep the food warm, but are made from non-renewable fossil fuels, are rarely recycled, and usually end up in rubbish dumps where they remain intact for generations.

■ Paper wrappers are made from renewable forest resources, are theoretically *decompostable*, but are made in an energy-intensive industry notorious for releasing toxic chemicals into the environment, they are not recycled and also end up in rubbish dumps, where they also remain for long period of time.

■ One environmental group has calculated that foam containers consume 70 per cent more energy, produce 70 per cent more air pollution and 80 per cent more water pollution than the paper wrappers. Another environmental group claims these calculations ignored the issue of whether toxic chemicals produced by making the foam were better or worse than those from paper production.

McDonald's had researched the foam box issue three years previously and concluded that the boxes actually were more recyclable than paper. However, the real issue facing McDonald's was not the use of polystyrene; it was that the clam shell container had become a public symbol of a wasteful society.

Source: McDougall (1993, pp. 80–1).

supported by strong *pull communication* strategies targeted to the end-consumer. Branding policy has always been a key factor in the marketing strategy of suppliers.

A significant change of the last ten years, in Europe and in the United States as well, is the growing power of the retailers. From passive intermediaries in the channel, retailers are now active marketers developing new store concepts and own-label brands designed for well-targeted segments. They are now directly competing with manufacturers' brands; they have the power to dictate terms to their suppliers and to push their brands off the shelves if they are not leaders in their product category. Several factors explain this shift of power from manufacturers to retailers:

● The high *concentration rate* of retailers, specifically in the FMCG sector: in the UK, Netherlands, Belgium and Germany, approximately 50 per cent of the market is accounted for by the top 10 retailers.

● The creation, at the European level, of powerful *purchasing centres* which give retailers a strong bargaining power over suppliers.

● The development of *computerised systems* for recording sales at retail checkouts which not only gives retailers full market information but which also has important logistics implications for the optimisation of the grocery supply chain, minimising inventory levels and optimising product availability.

● The adoption by retailers of sophisticated *store brand policies* targeted to segments often neglected by manufacturers and the growth of private labels.

● The emergence of a new breed of retailers, the *hard discounters*, who in warehouse stores, charge very low prices on their own private brands while excluding suppliers' brands from their shelves.

These new developments, which will be reviewed in a more detailed way in Chapter 12, considerably modify European grocery retailing and its power relationship with suppliers. They reinforce the necessity of strong strategic analysis on the suppliers' and the distributors' sides.

● The Emergence of Accountable Marketing

The consumerist and environmentalist movements have forced some marketing theoreticians to widen their classical marketing concept in a way that puts the emphasis on the necessity to develop an increased consciousness within the firm of the socio-cultural side-effects of its economic and especially its marketing activity. Thus Kotler (1997) proposed the adoption of the *societal marketing concept*:

> The societal marketing concept holds that the organisation's task is to determine the needs, wants and interests of target markets and to deliver the desired satisfactions more effectively and efficiently than competitors in a way that preserves and enhances the consumer's and the society's well-being. (Kotler, 1997, p. 27)

This concept is based on three implicit assumptions:

● Consumers' wishes do not always coincide with their long-term interests or those of the public at large.

● Consumers prefer organisations that show real concern for their satisfaction and well-being as well as the collective well-being.

● The most important task of the organisation is to adapt itself to the target markets in such a way as to generate not only satisfaction, but also individual and collective well-being, in order to attract and keep customers.

Two key ideas distinguish the concept of societal marketing from that of the classical marketing concept: (a) marketing must be concerned with the *well-being of buyers* and not simply with the satisfaction of their short-term needs; (b) the firm must pay attention to the side-effects of its economic and industrial activity in order to ensure the *long-term well-being of society as a whole* and not only that of individual consumers. By adopting this wider outlook, the firm will better achieve its own growth and profit objectives.

Ethical marketing

The firm embracing the accountable marketing concept has to define clearly the rules of ethics it intends to follow in its relationships with the market. If, in recent years, one has observed improved marketing conduct, it is largely due to strong counter-vailing powers, like the consumerist and environmentalist movements, which in a way forced companies to improve their ethical conduct. Nothing is more convincing than the fear of punishment to induce good citizen behaviour. The accountable firm must go beyond this and publicly confirm its commitment to promote ethical decisions and to create a corporate culture conducive to ethical behaviour.

In business, marketing is the most visible functional area because of its interface with the different market players: consumers, distributors, competitors and public opinion. Advertising and selling activities are the most noticeable and close to the public view and, therefore, it is not surprising that marketing is the subject of considerable societal analysis and scrutiny. Marketers, more than any other functional managers, are likely to be confronted with ethical dilemmas at some point in their careers. We believe that marketing managers need guidance from their firm to deal with ethically troublesome issues. This should not prevent managers forming their own personal philosophy.

The costs of non-ethical conduct

An ethical dilemma occurs when a manager is confronted with *a decision that involves the trade-off between lowering one's personal values in exchange for increased organisational or personal profit.* In other words, marketers sometimes feel compelled to do things that they feel ought not to be done to achieve some organisational objectives, like increased sales, market share or short-term profit. The firm should attempt to foster ethical decisions, not only because it is simply the proper thing to do, but also because it is its well-understood self-interest in the long term, since non-ethical behaviour can generate significant psychological, personal, organisational and societal costs (Laczniak and Murphy, 1993):

- *Psychological costs* supported by the conscience of the individual who has intentionally violated an ethical rule.

- *Personal costs.* When unethical actions become known, the outcome for the manager who engaged in the transgression is a reprimand or job termination. Even when superiors concede privately that organisational pressures may have contributed to a manager's unethical action, they will never admit this publicly. Unethical managers believing that their companies will support them are typically mistaken.

- *Organisational costs.* Substantial costs, like legal penalties or loss of goodwill, can result for the firm when ethical transgressions by a company become public. Two cases in point are the Nestlé powder milk infant formula promoted in less developed countries and the Drexel Burnham with the junk bonds trading.

● *External costs.* More difficult to assess, those societal costs may be very important: excess economic costs, wastefulness and pollution costs that have to be assumed by the taxpayer or by the state.

More generally, unethical actions can undermine the functioning of a free market economy where the efficient firm, and not the dishonest one, is supposed to be rewarded. Also, unethical marketing practices damage the trust in the existing free market system among the general public and may generate, from public authorities, authoritarian regulations ill-adapted to the market. Consumers today expect an ethical behaviour from the firm in its exchange relationship, fair relationships with its employees and commitment *vis-à-vis* the major societal issues. In the present socio-cultural environment, companies are expected to have a good citizenship behaviour and the consumer wants to share values with the firm through his or her consumption choices.

Models of ethical behaviour

To what extent are firms attempting to balance the drive for profits with ethical considerations? Reidenbach and Robin (1991) have identified five types of organisational ethical behaviours forming a hierarchy, from the lowest to the highest level of corporate moral development:

● *Stage 1: Amoral.* It is the lowest level. Owners and managers are the only important stakeholders. The prevailing philosophy is to maximise profit at almost any cost.

● *Stage 2: Legalistic.* Being ethical means simply obeying the law. The only obligations that a firm of this type recognises are legal obligations.

● *Stage 3: Responsive.* The firms having reached this level begin to develop some ethical concern. They recognise that a good relationship with the community is important. The responsive firm usually behaves ethically, if only for self-serving reasons.

● *Stage 4: Emerging ethical.* These firms make explicit recognition that the cost of being ethical may sometimes involve a trade-off with profits. Concern for values is explicitly mentioned in the corporate mission statement or in a code of ethics.

● *Stage 5: Developed ethical.* The organisations have clearly articulated value statements communicated, accepted and implemented by everyone in the organisation. These companies are at the peak of the ethical hierarchy.

In Western Europe, according to Bloon *et al.* (1994), most companies have reached stage 3 of the hierarchy. The number of companies at stages 4 and 5 is growing however.

Ideas for ethical action

How do we decide what constitutes the best ethical resolution of an issue? Laczniak and Murphy (1993, p. 49) suggest proceeding through a sequence of questions that tests whether the contemplated action is ethical or has possible ethical consequences. These questions are presented in Exhibit 2.6.

Exhibit 2.6

How to Improve Ethical Reasoning

1. The legal test: Does the contemplated action violate the law?
2. The duties test: Is this action contrary to widely accepted moral obligations such as: fidelity, gratitude, justice, non-maleficence, beneficence?
3. The special obligation test: Does the proposed action violate any other special obligation that stems from the type of marketing organisation at focus? (pharmaceutical firms, toy manufacturers and so on.)
4. The motive test: Is the intent of the contemplated action harmful?
5. The utilitarian test: Is there a satisfactory alternative action that produces equal or greater benefits to the parties affected than the proposed action?
6. The rights test: Does the contemplated action infringe upon property rights, privacy rights, or the inalienable rights of the consumer (such as the right to information, the right to be heard, the right to choice and the right to remedy)?
7. The justice test: Does the proposed action leave another person or group less well-off?

Source: Laczniak and Murphy (1993, p. 49).

The main difficulty in implementing this test to a specific situation is to resolve the conflicts of interest that may exist among the different stakeholders of the firm.

> For example, there is fiduciary responsibility on the part of managers to render stockholders a fair return. At times, this might involve taking steps that are clearly counterproductive to another stakeholder group, such as employees. The judgmental difficulty then comes in deciding which of the two duties take precedence. (Laczniak and Murphy, 1993, p. 50)

Corporate citizenship behaviour

Firms are rapidly embracing the accountable market orientation concept, as suggested by the increasing number of companies adopting a code of ethics, in which they define ethical rules concerning their products and services, the information they deliver and the type of relationships they want to maintain with their clients, their employees, their shareholders, and so on, and with society at large as well. The reasons for the adoption of a corporate citizenship behaviour can be summarised as follows:

● Any firm needs a healthy and prosperous environment to reach its own development objectives.
● One shall not build economic progress out of a social disaster.
● The welfare state, and the social and fiscal solutions it implies, has clearly reached its limits, both on qualitative and financial grounds.
● Rather than paying more taxes, the civilian society should wake up and commit itself, where it has the appropriate skills and resources.

The domains of activity where the firm has the know-how and the resources are varied. Potential objectives could be:

● To develop the economic and industrial fabric of a region.
● To stimulate and maintain the employment rate.
● To participate in the education process.
● To protect the physical environment.
● To participate in the social life of the community.
● To fight against social exclusion.

An interesting example of this claimed behaviour is given by the code of ethics published in the international daily press by La Lyonnaise des Eaux. Also revealing is the fact that the Davos World Economic Forum has adopted as the theme of the 1999 meeting the concept of *Responsible Globality*, which explicitly refers to a world economy without losers.

The accountable marketing concept

As a result of these economic and socio-cultural changes, the *accountable marketing* concept is gaining wider acceptance among firms. Four elements are central in this new concept:

● The objective of short-term satisfaction is replaced by the objective of the well-being of customers.
● The social cost of consumption must be internalised in the operating cost of products and services.
● The firm should internally define rules of ethical conduct.
● Market orientation becomes the focus of the entire organisation and should not be confined to the sole marketing function.

As discussed at the end of this chapter, these changes have implications for the way the marketing function must be organised in a market-oriented company.

● The New International Environment

The end of the 1990s is characterised by the completion of the process of internationalisation of the world economy through *globalisation*. In a growing number of activities, the geographic reference market is no longer a country or a continent, but the large industrialised countries, that is the Triad market. Competitive advantage must now exist at this level.

The issue of globalisation

Competition is now global for a whole series of activities. This is obvious in the case of products of global 'nature', such as high-technology equipment (aerospace, aviation, telecommunications, and so on) or raw materials (basic products, and so on). It is less so in the case of 'universal' consumer goods, whether durable or non-durable (hi-fi, video, cameras, drinks, hamburgers, jeans, and so on), and even less so in the case of services (credit cards, tourism, rentals, data banks, advisory services, recruitment, and so on).

> The industrialised countries, comprising Europe, North America and Japan -the Triad – form the natural reference market for firms operating in global sectors. This market includes more than 700 million inhabitants. However, this represents only 15 per cent of the world population, but two thirds of gross world production and about 85 per cent of world discretionary purchasing power. (Ohmae, 1987, p. 10)

Competitive advantage must be defined at the Triad level. It is not enough just to do well at home any more; the firm must also perform well internationally in order to get a *leverage effect*. We can cite many reasons for the globalisation of competition (Ohmae 1987, pp. 10–14):

● The 700 million consumers begin to form a *more homogeneous market* as a result of communication, transport and travelling. The progressive uniformity in needs and wants is favourable to the development of a potential market for 'global products', which is very attractive to firms because of economies of scale in production, distribution, advertising, and so on.

● *Diffusion of technical progress* has become so fast that it is necessary to introduce an innovation in the three large Triad markets simultaneously. A delay in one of the markets exposes the firm to the possibility of being beaten by a rival who can launch a similar product and thus achieve a dominant position, which is difficult to overturn.

● The *development cost* of some equipment goods is so high that it can only be recovered at the world level.

● *Transnational segments* emerge within the Triad which constitute attractive opportunities for the international firm.

To these major trends in the world economy one must add the European single market which, as discussed above, every day becomes more a reality.

Internationalisation is not a new phenomenon for marketing; it has been developing since the end of the Second World War. What is new is the *interdependence of markets* as a result of globalisation. Markets are no longer considered as separate entities, but more and more as a single market. We shall examine here the implications of the globalisation of competition for the firm's marketing management.

The standardisation–customisation dilemma

Every firm must face the question of knowing how to organise itself in order to confront the global market in such a way as to maintain a sustainable competitive advantage. When approaching this question, two very distinct attitudes may be adopted: one which promotes the standardisation of marketing activity in all markets, thus giving priority to internal performance objectives, and another which, in contrast, gives priority to *customisation* of products, thus marketing specific needs of different markets.

A *customisation strategy* pinpoints existing differences between markets and does this in the spirit of the marketing concept. Three groups of factors help to differentiate markets:

● Differences in *buyer behaviour*, not only in terms of socio-demographics, income or living conditions, but especially in terms of consumption, habits, customs, culture, and so on.

● Differences in *market organisation*, including the structure of distribution networks, the availability of media, regulations, climatic conditions, means of transportation, and so on.

● Differences in *competitive environment*, in terms of the degree of concentration of competition, the presence of domestic rivals, the competitive climate, and so on.

It is clear that there are important differences among markets and that these differences will persist in the future. These differences will have implications for the marketing strategy to be adopted.

Believers in *the standardisation strategy* underline the advantages that can result from a strategy based on what is similar between markets rather than what differentiates them. The *standardisation thesis*, upheld by Buzzell (1968), Levitt (1983) and Ohmae (1987), is based on three hypotheses:

● World needs will become *homogenised* thanks to technology, transportation and communication.

● Consumers are prepared to forgo specific preferences in order to benefit from products with *lower prices* and good quality.

● Standardisation resulting from homogenisation of world markets brings about *economies of scale*, thus reducing the cost.

To support his thesis, Levitt mentions examples of products with high profiles such as: McDonald's, Coca-Cola, Pepsi, Revlon, Kodak, Sony, Levi's, and so on, in addition to high-technology products which are naturally universal.

A false dilemma?

If homogenisation of needs is indeed real, this does not mean that standardisation is the only alternative open to the global firm. Levitt (1983) reduces global marketing to a standardisation strategy. Three sets of counter-arguments can be put forth, however, which alter Levitt's arguments substantially:

1. Although it is true that needs are becoming homogenised throughout the world, we are only talking about 'segments', which are found in all Triad countries, with the same expectations and with slight variations. Parallel to these world segments, we also observe a '*demassification*', or a 'personalisation of consumption' giving rise to segments which are more and more specialised and which vary greatly between countries because of the greater importance of cultural and regional values.

2. There is no evidence to show that consumers are becoming universally more sensitive to prices. Products such as Cartier watches, Louis Vuitton bags, Hermès scarves or Canon cameras, which are recognised as global products, are great commercial successes; but they are not particularly known for low prices.

3. It is no longer true that economies of scale go hand in hand with frantic standardisation. New production technologies have now taken industry out of the Taylor era of large manufacturing chains which produced a single product at high speed. There are now new flexible workshops with instantaneous command change and lagged differentiation techniques, which can retain the advantages of standardisation while at the same time being able to customise according to personalised requirements.

The problem of technical norms, however, remains a major handicap for standardisation. In Europe, each country still has its own particular norms which force firms to manufacture many variations of the same product. The 'crude' theory of standardisation is therefore very doubtful and many authors have already discussed its limitations.

In reality, the dilemma of standardisation versus customisation is a false one, in the sense that it poses the question of internationalisation as 'all or nothing'. As suggested by Takeuchi and Porter (1986), the real question is how to reconcile the two approaches. One can concentrate on the similarities that exist between markets, which will probably develop more and more, without forgetting their differences and the corresponding need to customise. Most cases of international blunders are the outcome of a lack of cultural sensitivity and acknowledgement of values and attitudes, which means that a successful strategy in one country may prove to be bad in another.

Typology of international environments

The necessity for the firm to adopt a global approach in international marketing is dependent upon the characteristics of its market environment. Goshal and Nohria (1993) suggest analysing the international environment by reference to two dimensions:

1. *Local forces* like local customers, tastes, purchasing habits, governments and regulatory agencies which create strong needs for *local responsiveness and adaptation.*

2. *Global forces* like economies of scale, uniform customer demands, worldwide competition, product uniformity which are powerful incentives for *global integration and standardisation.*

For each of these two dimensions, Goshal and Nohria (1993) identify two levels (weak and strong) and broadly distinguish four environmental conditions faced by multinational companies, as illustrated in Figure 2.3:

● The environment is *global* when forces for global integration are strong and local responsiveness weak. In such markets, structural uniformity in the organisation is best suited to these conditions. It is the situation observed in many high-technology markets where local forces are non-existent and inoperative. The trend is towards standardisation and centralisation of responsibilities. (See Exhibit 2.7.)

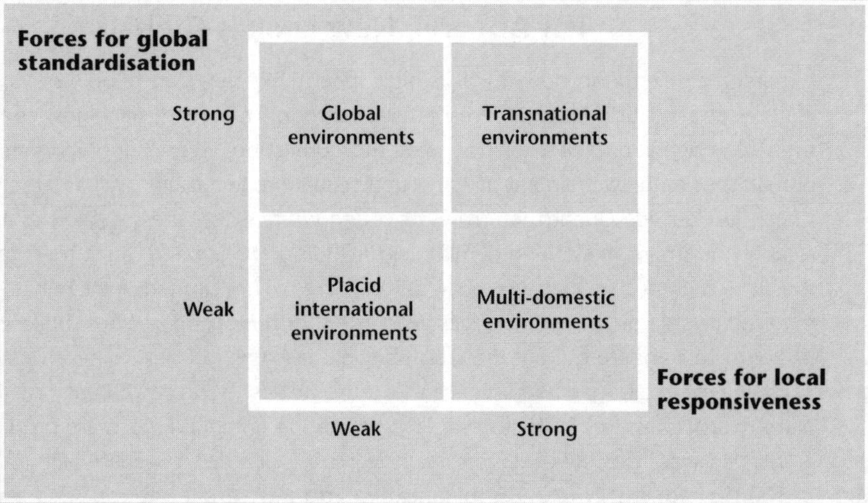

Source: Adapted from Goshal and Nohria (1993).

Figure 2.3 Typology of international environments

⬤ In the *multinational (or multidomestic)* environment, in contrast, the forces for national responsiveness are strong and the forces for global integration weak. In this type of market, adaptation to local conditions is a key success factor and companies tend to adopt different governance modes to fit each local context. Many food companies fall into this category, where taste and culinary habits are important determinants of preferences and of purchase behaviour.

⬤ In the *placid international environment* both forces are weak. The business of producing cement is an example:

Cement products are highly standardised and distribution systems are similar across countries. Thus demands for local responsiveness are weak. However, the trade-offs between the economics of cement production and transport costs are such that global integration is not attractive. (Goshal and Nohria, 1993, p. 26)

⬤ In the *transnational* environment both forces, local and global, are strong. It is the most complex situation where some degree of standardisation and centralisation is necessary, while maintaining the capacity to respond to local situations is also required:

It is the case for example of a brand like Carlsberg, which has all the characteristics of a global brand. Distributed in 130 countries throughout the world, its taste, logo and bottle design are identical. Nevertheless, the 'beer culture' is very different from one country to another, even within Europe. Thus a transnational organisation combining centralisation and local (or regional) adaptation is better suited to this brand.

Exhibit 2.7

For Apparel, New Look is Global

Apparel manufacturing now involves high-speed links between people of vastly different cultures and political systems, who interact through facsimile machines, computers and even high-definition television to meet the conflicting, ever-changing demands of the human species for the raiment of status and seduction. In a clean, well-lit factory in Foshan, China, just outside Guangzhou, rows of young women sew dresses, blouses and skirts for a variety of American clothing companies, including The Limited, the largest retail chain in the United States, with more than 3200 stores. The Limited, which has consistently reported double-digit sales increases even in sluggish retailing seasons, built its success on its ability to translate quickly the latest catwalk fashions into less expensive merchandise. The Limited's mass merchandisers can take the newest trend from Paris or New York and place cheaper versions in its stores weeks before the original designs are produced.

Mr du Mont, executive vice president of Mast industries, the manufacturing subsidiary of The Limited said: 'within 60 minutes of a customer order, we can send a visual representation of the style, shown on the store's favourite model, to Hong Kong. It comes out in ink-jet printers with a quality similar to a lithograph you might frame and put on your wall. And we can do it in about 16 million colours. Mast strives for a turnaround time of 1000 hours for recognising and delivering a new style. The turnaround – about 41 days – represents the period between a merchant saying: 'I need 10,000 of these', and the clothing being delivered to the store.

Source: Hochswender (1996).

Another example is the case of Volvo Truck (Lambin and Hiller, 1990). Trucks are designed upfront for the world market and are identical with few minor adaptations. But a key success factor in any market remains the role played by the local dealer who is in charge of after-sales service and of the warranty. A highly centralised organisation would not suit this market environment.

The global marketing concept

Compared to the multidomestic approach, the global approach differs in these three basic ways:

- The global approach looks for *similarities* between markets. The multidomestic approach ignores similarities.
- The global approach actively seeks *homogeneity* in products, image and advertising messages.
- The global approach asks: *Should this product be for the world market?* The multidomestic approach relying solely on local autonomy, never asks the question.

Globalisation requires many internal modifications as well. By design, globalisation calls for more centralised decision making. For several years, the popular slogan 'think global, act local' has been thought to describe the strategy of the global firm. Faced with the internationalisation of markets, the transnational or the global firm should:

● *think globally in its strategic marketing*
● *act locally in its operational marketing*

Global marketing would imply a two-stage process. At the *first level*, global thinking would imply the search for transnational segments of customers over a wider geographical market, no matter how narrow these new segments may be. The firm would then develop products targeted to these transnational segments. Their total market representation on the regional and international scale may constitute an important volume capable of generating economies of scale for the company. Globalisation in this sense would apply essentially to the product concept and not necessarily to the other tools of marketing, such as communication, price and distribution, which would remain customised to local characteristics (Quelch and Hoff, 1986). Thus, customisation would constitute the *second level* of consideration.

> 'Windows', 'Word', 'Excel' and other popular software products of Microsoft can serve as examples of global products adapted to local conditions. They exist in a multitude of national versions; in addition there exists even a special English version for Central and Eastern Europe. (*Business Central Europe*, 1994, No. 9, p. 10)

This traditional vision of transnational marketing is criticised by several international companies because the slogan 'think global, act local' suggests that a firm has the capability to develop product concepts independently of local needs analysis and then to impose those products on the rest of the world by means of heavy communication. This is the reason why Procter & Gamble decided to place its international action under the slogan 'think global and local' (Cerfontaine, 1994), thereby underlining that product development should be conceived simultaneously on the local and global levels. Thus, we have here a four-stage process:

● analyse local needs in a given country,
● globalise the product concept developed locally,
● customise the product to each local environment,
● use operational marketing to implement the chosen strategy.

As far as marketing management is concerned, the most important implication of globalisation is the necessity for the firm to define its geographic reference market as the Triad countries and to elaborate active or defensive strategic options which take the new interdependence of markets into account.

It is important to realise that the global marketing concept concerns all firms and not only large international firms. The small or medium size firm operating in a global market must also be internationalised in such a way as to confront other competitors through a defensive tactic.

● The Concept of Market Orientation

We have seen in this chapter that, during the 1990s, the macro-marketing environment of the firm has changed dramatically. Powerful drivers of market orientation are at work with privatisation policy, deregulation of the economy, the process of economic integration and of globalisation of the world economy. What was the overall performance of the traditional marketing function in its confrontation with the above changes?

The shortcomings of traditional marketing

The main reproaches or criticisms about traditional marketing's performance are the following:

● To have confined market orientation to the marketing department, thereby preventing the development of a market culture within the organisation.
● To be a big spender and to have failed to develop objective and quantified measures to judge its own overall performance.
● To have privileged tactical marketing instruments over strategic ones, by giving precedence to advertising and promotions over product innovations.
● To be risk-adverse by placing more emphasis on minor market-pull innovations over more revolutionary (but more risky) technology-push innovations.
● To have responded to environmentalism by green advertising unsupported by prior product redesign, thereby undermining the credibility of green marketing.
● To have neglected the 'fewer frills, low price' segments, thereby opening the door to private labels development.
● To have created confrontational rather than collaborative relationships with large retailers and to lose the battle of the brand in several product categories.
● To lose contact with the new consumer and to have failed to develop a long-term relationship with the customer base.

Today, an increasing number of firms believe that the marketing function must reinvent itself in a way which reinforces the *overall market orientation* of the firm. Thus the problem is not with marketing, but rather with the marketing function. In the new competitive environment, marketing has become too important to be left to the marketing function alone.

The cost of a weak market orientation

The absence of a strong market orientation culture may have significant impact on the competitiveness of the firm. Several potential problems may arise:

● *Environment monitoring.* If the marketing function is the only one in charge of managing the interface between the firm and its environment, is there not a risk to see the announced changes underestimated by the other functions within the organisation? Has marketing enough credibility and enough weight to induce major changes within the firm? For example, it is surprising to see how the chemical industry was caught unprepared, when new legislation suddenly imposed

severe restrictions on non-recyclable plastic bottles, while this environn.
issue had been a much debated question for more than twenty years.

● *The links between R&D and innovations.* If the market orientation is confine
within the marketing department, the dialogue between R&D and strategic
marketing will be more difficult and the link between inventions and innovations
weaker. As a consequence, R&D activities will give rise to fewer successful imple-
mentations of inventions. According to a recent European study, it seems that
fundamental research in Western Europe is indeed less productive than in the US
and in Japan. An analysis of the metallurgic sector in Belgium confirmed this
observation (Theys, 1994).

● *New product development process.* Developing a new product is typically a cross-
functional effort which involves not only the marketing department, but all other
functions as well. In companies where the dominant culture is not the market orientation, new product development processes are generally sequential and the project
is passed from one specialist to another. This process ends up with a desirable 'target
price' reflecting the successive internal costs and which becomes the market price
suggested to (or imposed upon) sales personnel. In a market-driven company, on the
other hand, it is the *'acceptable market price'* which is identified upfront and which
becomes the constraint to be met by R&D and production people. The success rate
of new products is much higher in this second case (Cooper, 1993).

● *Competitive advantage and the value chain.* The definition of a sustainable competitive advantage is a major responsibility of strategic marketing. As shown by
Porter (1980), the value chain is a basic tool for diagnosing competitive advantage
and finding ways to create and sustain it. Thus, a firm must define its competitive
advantage by reference to the different value activities – primary and support –
that are performed. Each of these value activities, and not only the marketing
activities, can contribute to a firm's relative cost position and create a basis for
differentiation. If the firm is not market-oriented, it is not easy to induce the non-
marketing activities to participate in the search for a sustainable competitive
advantage. The risk is then to base competitive positioning on minor points of
differentiation of low added value to the buyer.

● *Financial implication of sales promotions.* A good indicator of performance for the
marketing department is an increase in sales revenue which, in non-expandable
markets, implies a market share increase. An easy but short-sighted way to
achieve this objective is to embark on trade promotions and coupon offers which
are in fact a *disguised form of price cutting.* These promotional actions, because of
their effectiveness, generate strong retaliatory actions from competition who
respond by more promotions or coupon offers. This escalation leads to a situation
of almost permanent promotions which eventually undermine brand loyalty and
profitability. As a result of this 'marketing myopia', marketing activities are under
increasing challenge and control from the finance department which questions
the wisdom of this type of action.

● *Transactional versus relationship marketing.* Finding new customers is traditionally
an important objective of transactional marketing which is mostly interested in
immediate sales results. In mature markets, this objective loses relevance and
cultivating the existing customer base becomes the priority goal. In business-to-

business marketing, the repeat purchase rate of satisfied customers is around 90 to 95 per cent (Goderis, 1998) and therefore, attracting new customers is viewed as an intermediate objective. Relationship marketing tries to create and maintain a long-term mutually profitable relationship with customers. This customer satisfaction objective, however, is not just the responsibility of the marketing function, but again of all other functions participating in the process of value creation for the customer. Thus, the customer satisfaction objective must be shared by everyone in the organisation.

In conclusion, it appears that the lack of market orientation of a given firm may seriously undermine its capacity to meet the challenges of the new macro-marketing environment. The next step is to define, in operational terms, what it really means to be market-oriented.

Marketing or market orientation?

A complicating factor is that in the professional literature and in business quarters as well, the terms 'market orientation' and 'marketing orientation' are often used interchangeably (Shapiro, 1988):

- The *marketing orientation concept* tends to be concerned more with the American view of the marketing concept, especially marketing's functional role in co-ordinating and managing the four Ps to make a firm more responsive to meeting customers' needs.

- The *market orientation concept*, in contrast, de-emphasizes the functional roles of marketing departments, enlarges the market definition to the key market actors (and not only to the customer) and states that developing customer relations and enhancing customer value is the responsibility of everyone in the organisation.

In this book, we promote the term 'market orientation' to emphasise the importance of the *'culture'* component of the concept in contrast with the *'action'* component. Two questions have to be examined now: (a) Who are the key market actors and (b) how to develop a reliable measure of market orientation?

The market actors: the general case

In recent years, there has been increasing attention given to market orientation as a business philosophy within academic literature. For a review, see Gray *et al.* (1998) and also Morgan and Strong (1998). The most significant contributions come from Kohli and Jaworski (1990) who have provided a conceptual definition of the construct and from Narver and Slater (1990) who examined the relationship between market orientation and business profitability empirically. For European evidence, see the work of Rivera (1995), Fritz (1996), Lambin (1996) and Pitt *et al.* (1996).

In contrast with previous works, Narver and Slater (1990) have enlarged the marketing concept by defining the market orientation by reference to three components: customer orientation, competitor orientation and interfunctional co-ordination. So, for these authors, the construct of 'market orientation' is broader than the traditional concept of 'customer orientation'. In this book, we go a step further by proposing that market orientation is a business philosophy involving *all participants in the market and all levels within the organisation* (Lambin, 1996).

Thus, as illustrated in Figure 2.4, in the general case we define market orientation in terms of five market participants or market players: customers, distributors, competitors, prescribers and the macro-marketing environment.

The basic hypothesis is that market-oriented firms allocate human and material resources (a) to collect information about the expectations and behaviours of the different market participants. This information is then used (b) to design market-oriented action plans which are implemented (c) by involving all levels of the organisation. Thus, to build a valid measure of market orientation two sets of indicators will be defined for each of the four market participants: *analysis* and *action* indicators, and one set of indicators for measuring the level of *interfunctional co-ordination*. In short, the conceptual definition of market orientation used here is very similar to the existing definitions proposed by Kohli and Jaworski (1990) and by Narver and Slater (1990). The difference with these approaches rests on a broader definition of the market participants.

For each of these five components, we have identified a set of indicators with the objective (1) of deriving a valid measure of market orientation for each component and (2) of analysing their relationships with various measures of business performance. These indicators are presented in the questionnaire of Appendix 1. Other grids are available in the literature. See, for example Kohli *et al.*(1993) and also Gray *et al.* (1998).

Customer orientation

Customer satisfaction is the central element of market orientation and is at the core of the traditional marketing concept. It implies the commitment to understand customer needs, to create value for the customer and to anticipate new customers' problems. Let us note, however, that the customer may be close to or remote from the

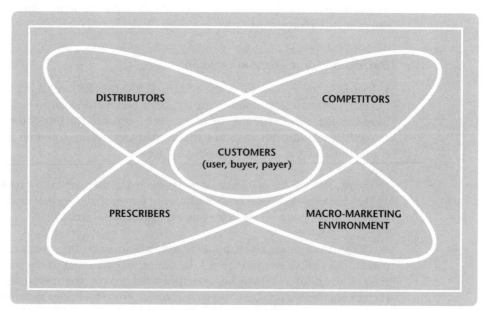

Figure 2.4   The key market actors – the general case

firm depending on the type of organisation: consumer goods or industrial goods companies. Industrial firms generally operate within an industrial chain and in this case, the end-customer (or indirect customer) may be different from the direct customer and be situated at the end of the chain. Being customer-oriented involves taking actions based on market intelligence, not only on direct customers, but on indirect customers as well. Also, in analysing customer behaviour, and as discussed in the following chapter, it important to establish a distinction between the three roles of a customer in a transaction: user, payer or buyer (Sheth *et al.*, 1999).

In a customer orientation, the product (or service) is viewed in the customer's perspective and is defined as a *solution to a problem*. This is, for example, the new strategy adopted by IBM who, in its mission statement, describes its offer as *'computer-based solutions to managerial problems'*; (and not hardware and software). Similarly the company Automatic Systems is selling *'solutions to access control problems'* (and not gates and doors). The adoption of the *solution-to-a-problem* approach has an impact on the way to define the other components of the marketing mix in the buyer's perspective:

- *Distribution:* convenient and easy access to the solution sought by the buyer.
- *Price:* total cost (and not only the tag price) supported by the buyer to get the solution sought.
- *Advertising:* information communicated to the buyer on the distinctive qualities claimed for the proposed solutions.
- *Selling:* negotiation, or the search for the solution best adapted to the customer needs and mutually profitable.

The level of end-customer orientation can be measured through the two sets of indicators presented in the questionnaire of Appendix 2.1 (at the end of this chapter). The *analysis indicators* are chosen to verify whether the firm has allocated human and material resources to collect market intelligence on key facts about end-customers. Similarly, the *action indicators* are selected to describe the actual behaviour adopted by the firm *vis-à-vis* end-customers.

Distributors' or resellers' orientation

The struggle for the control of the end-market has always been a major issue both for manufacturers and distributors. In the food sector, for many years, manufacturers have succeeded in restricting the role of distributors to the physical tasks of distribution. Their relationship was more that of partners having common interests, even if conflicting interests were inevitably also present.

> The retailer looks for maximum return on space and contribution to overall retailer image. The supplier seeks maximum shelf space, trial for new (unproved) products and preference over competitors. It is easy to see where the potential for conflicts lie.

The shift of power from suppliers to distributors in some sectors, and in particular in the FMCG sector, requires the adoption of a much more proactive strategy *vis-à-vis* distributors. Today, as underlined above, key changes in the environment include increasing retailer concentration, the growth of internationally based retail buying groups and the growing use of information technology by European food retailers. While suppliers would like to see retailers as partners, it is clear that retailers tend to see their relationships with manufacturers more in terms of competition than co-operation.

As shown in Table 2.5, the level of competition or co-operation is influenced by the market structure which determines the power of prospective partners in a market. With the exception of the situation where both levels of concentration are weak (see cell 3), manufacturers have to explicitly define an appropriate relationship marketing strategy *vis-à-vis* distributors.

Table 2.5 Market structure and manufacturers'–distributors' relationships

Concentration rate among distributors	Concentration rate among manufacturers	
	Low	High
High	Distributors' domination (1)	Mutual interdependence (2)
Low	Relative independence (3)	Manufacturers' domination (4)

In the food sector, the level of concentration of mass retailers is very high in several countries of Western Europe and the situation is clearly that described in cell 1 (see Table 2.5). Today, even powerful brand manufacturers need the co-operation of retailers more than retailers need powerful brands in their mix, even if the development of electronic commerce may change the balance of power in the years to come. Thus, in the current market situation many brand manufacturers tend to become more *retailer-driven* to avoid the risk of being delisted and design retailer-driven marketing programmes by raising questions like: *how can we reduce the costs of our distributors? Can we eliminate their inventory costs, improve their cash flow, support their store positioning strategy, and so on?*

> In the USA, the Nabisco Company is very explicit and communicates the following message to large retail chains. 'Nabisco does not use your money to cover inventory costs; we maintain your stock, we supply in function of sales development and in general, our products are already sold before you are invited to pay. The turnaround of our biscuits is two times higher than that of the other manufacturers and the profitability is very good. (*Belgian Business & Industry*, September 1995, p. 55)

This strategic option is particularly relevant in the contexts of cells 1 and 2 (Table 2.5). Thus, *trade marketing* is simply the application of the marketing concept to distributors, who are no longer viewed as partners but as *customers* in their own right. In order to manage this relationship with retailers, manufacturers will have to develop an in-depth understanding of their generic needs (see Exhibit 2.8), their desired store image and the perceived importance of a particular product category for the chain store's positioning. A good understanding of the objectives and constraints of the intermediate customer is a perequisite for the development of a successful relationship marketing strategy.

To go further on this topic, see Corstjens and Corstjens (1996).

Exhibit 2.8

Generic Needs of Distributors

1. **Freedom to price and promote the merchandise**: freedom to price their merchandise in line with their own goal and interests; freedom from pressure to implement supplier-designed promotions.

2. **Adequate trade margins**: when selling at the manufacturer's suggested price trade, discount from the list price adequate to cover costs operation and to generate a profit.

3. **Protection from undue competition**: selling the merchandise to too many other resellers; selling the merchandise to off-price resellers; engaging itself in direct selling to end-users.

4. **Support from manufacturers**: training, advertising and promotion, merchandising, information on new developments on the market.

5. **Efficient order fulfilment**: minimise their inventory carrying costs; to avoid stockouts through joint management of inventory flows (see below EDI and EWR).

Source: Sheth J. *et al.* (1999, pp. 663–8).

To measure the level of market orientation of a firm towards its distributors, we have identified the two sets of indicators (analysis and action) presented in the questionnaire in Appendix 2.1 at the end of this chapter.

Competitors' orientation

Competitors, be they direct and/or substitute competitors, are key market participants and the attitude to be adopted towards competition is central in any strategy formulation, since it will serve as the basis for defining competitive advantage. The objective is to set out a strategy based on a realistic assessment of the forces at work and to determine the most appropriate means of achieving defined objectives. Competitors' orientation includes all the activities involved in acquiring and disseminating information about competitors in the target market.

The firm's autonomy is influenced by two kinds of factors: the sector's competitive structure and the importance of the product's perceived value for customers. Table 2.6 presents these two factors, each at two levels of intensity. With the exception of the situation of perfect competition depicted in cell 4, an explicit account of competitors' position and behaviour is required in the most frequently observed common market situations.

In saturated or stagnant markets, the aggressiveness of the competitive struggle tends to increase and a key objective is to counter rivals' actions. In this competitive climate, the destruction of the adversary often becomes the primary preoccupation. The risk of a strategy based only on *warfare marketing* (Ries and Trout, 1986) however, is that too much energy is devoted to driving rivals away at the risk of losing sight of the objective of satisfying buyers' needs. A proper balance between customers' and competitors' orientations is therefore essential and a market orientation, as described in this chapter, tends to facilitate the implementation of this objective. To measure the level of competitors' orientation, we have identified the two sets of indicators summarised in the third section of the questionnaire of Appendix 2.1.

Table 2.6 Competitive environments and autonomy in strategy formulation

Market power: perceived value of the product	Number of competitors	
	Low	High
High	Monopoly or differentiated oligopoly (1)	Monopolistic competition (2)
Low	Undifferentiated oligopoly (3)	Perfect competition (4)

Source: Lambin (1996).

Prescribers' orientation

In many markets, in addition to the traditional market actors – customers, distributors and competitors – other individuals or organisations can play important roles in *advising, recommending or prescribing brands*, companies, products or services to customers or to distributors. The most obvious example is the pharmaceutical market where doctors exert a key influence on the success of a drug and are viewed by pharmaceutical companies as the most important market player or *intermediate customer*, even if they are not actually users, buyers or payers.

> A similar role is assumed in the home building market by architects, who are important influencers for many construction pieces of equipment, like window frames, glass, heating systems, and so on. Similarly for independent designers in the furniture market or in the 'haute couture' or fashion markets.

In *business-to-business markets*, the role of prescribers is often taken by engineering companies, experts or consulting firms who recommend certain equipment and publish shortlists of products meeting the required specifications. To be considered by potential buyers, you have to be on the 'shortlist'. This is current practice in official public tenders.

A prescriber orientation implies that the firm identifies the key prescribers or opinion leaders, assesses the nature of their role and needs in the purchase decision process and develops a specific communication programme to inform them, to motivate them and to obtain their support.

The macro-marketing environment

Within any reference market, macro-environmental trends – demographic, economic, political/legal, technology and socio-cultural – bear on the market's future develop-

Exhibit 2.9

Components of the Macro-marketing Environment

Socio-cultural

Population, demography, income distribution, social mobility, changes in lifestyles, attitude vis-à-vis labour and leisure, consumerism, education level, social organisation, linguisitic development

Technology

Government support for R&D, specialisation of industrial research efforts, innovation intensity, speed of technology transfer, rate of obsolescence

Economy

Business fluctuations, GDP growth, interest rates, monetary circulation, inflation, unemployment, disposable income, savings, energy cost and availability, economic integration, deregulations

Ecology

Ecology movement, green marketing development, life cycle inventory, strength of political support, eco-taxes and eco-fees, waste management

Political/legal

Anti-trust legislation, envrionmental protection laws, fiscal legislation, foreign trade regulations, employment support, economic and trading blocs, deregulation and privatisation laws, government stability, and so on

ment (see Exhibit 2.9). These external factors can provide productive opportunities or severe limitations for the company's products. The market-oriented firm must develop a environment monitoring system to help it to anticipate these changes or to facilitate and accelerate the adoption of corrective actions.

It is fashionable to downplay the usefulness of planning systems. Experiences with such largely unforeseen upheavals as the stock market crash of 1987, the East European revolution, or the Asian crisis of 1997, and so on have revealed the shortcomings and the limitations of planning systems which are too rigid. Just because a strategy must be developed and implemented under turbulent and uncertain conditions is not a sufficient reason for abandoning the discipline of structured planning. Planning is necessary for the functioning of the firm. What is important in a turbulent environment, however, is to keep enough *flexibility in the system* and to systematically explore worst or extreme cases, through the scenario method, risk and contingency planning and crisis recovery plans. Thus, the macro-marketing environment is typically a moderating variable.

To verify the existence of a flexible environment monitoring system, as shown in Appendix 2.1, we shall use the following two sets of indicators. The *information indicators* would be the following:

⬤ Development of an environment monitoring system.
⬤ Identification of vulnerability and risk factors.
⬤ Availability of early warning indicators.

As *action indicators* we would have the following items:

● Involvement in professional networks.
● Active lobbying practices.
● Use of the scenario method in strategic planning.
● Existence of crisis recovery plans.

The levels of market orientation

In the majority of markets, four market participants (excluding prescribers here) are active players in the reference market. The different levels of market orientation are presented in Table 2.7.

In the general case, that is where the four market participants are active, the firm must be fully market oriented and should integrate the four orientations in its business practice. Thus, we define as market-oriented, *a firm which is customer, distributor, prescriber, competitor and macro-environment oriented and which maintains a good balance between the four types of orientation through interfunctional co-ordination.*

Table 2.7   The different levels of market orientation

Extent of Market Orientation				Customers (K)	Competitors (C)	Distributors (D)	Prescribers (P)
K	–	–	–	yes	no	no	no
K	C	–	–	yes	yes	no	no
K	–	D	–	yes	no	yes	no
K	–	–	P	yes	no	no	yes
K	C	D	–	yes	yes	yes	no
K	C	–	P	yes	yes	no	yes
K	–	D	P	yes	no	yes	yes
K	**C**	**D**	**P**	**yes**	**yes**	**yes**	**yes**

Interfunctional co-ordination

The key idea here is to consider that market orientation is the business of everyone and not only of marketing people. Masiello (1988) gives four reasons why many companies are not spontaneously market-oriented:

● Functional areas do not understand the concept of being market-driven.
● Most employees do not know how to translate their classical functional responsibilities into market/customer responsive actions.
● Most functions do not understand the role of other functions.
● Employees in each functional area do not give meaningful input to the market orientation of the company (Masiello,1988).

In addition to these organisational problems, Webster (1994) suggests two other factors. *First,* managers in other functions have other constituencies than customers (shareholders, suppliers, personnel, scientists) that must be served and satisfied and the trade-offs between these potentially conflicting interests must be co-ordinated and managed. *Second*, managers in other functions may honestly believe that they are putting the customer's interest first when they look at things from their own internal company perspective and it is easy for them to refuse to be guided by the information provided by the marketing department alone.

Thus, dissemination of market information, both formally and informally, inter-functionally prepared decisions, co-ordination of activities, regular contacts with customers are the key remedies to use in order to instil a sense of market orientation regardless of functional boundaries. The indicators used (see Appendix 2.1) to measure the extent of interfunctional co-ordination could be among the following:

- Formal and informal dissemination of market information at all levels.
- Direct interaction with customers at all levels of the firm.
- Interdepartmental meetings to discuss market trends.
- Concerted elaboration of the marketing strategy.
- Measure of the contribution of each function to the customer's satisfaction.

Interfunctional co-ordination is viewed here as an *organisational factor*, which will facilitate the involvement of all levels in the firm's organisation and will create the market orientation culture (see Figure 2.5). Interfunctional co-ordination allows for communication and exchange between the different departments that are dealing or confronted with some or all of the four *market stakeholders*. Without interfunctional co-ordination, the market orientation process could be dominated by a single preoc-cupation (competitors or distributors) which would reduce the potential business performance. Thus, interfunctional co-ordination is viewed as a *mediating variable*, to the extent that it accounts for the relationship between market orientation and busi-ness performance.

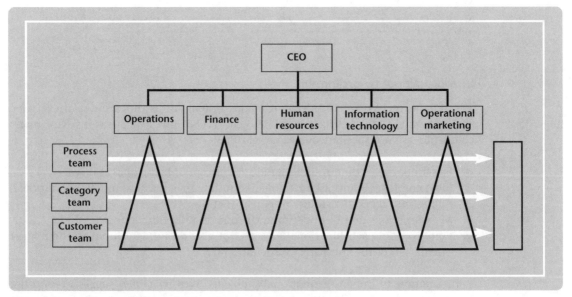

Figure 2.5   Organisation of a market-oriented company

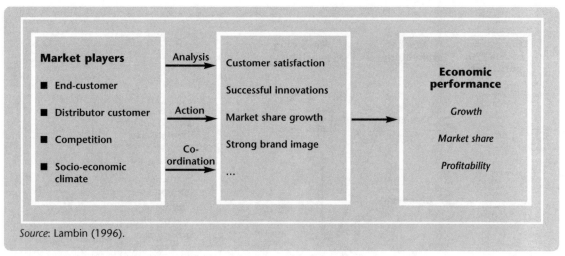

Source: Lambin (1996).

Figure 2.6 Hypothetical relationship between market orientation and economic performance

By way of conclusion of this analysis, it appears that the market orientation concept covers a field which is much broader than the traditional domain of marketing management, since it includes the organisational culture and climate that most effectively encourages the behaviours that are necessary for the successful implementation of a market orientation.

Market orientation and economic performance

As stated above, marketing theory suggests that there is a relationship between market orientation intensity and economic performance. Thus, the hypothesis is: *a firm which becomes more market-oriented will, in the long term, improve its economic and competitive performance.* Several theoretical and empirical observations support this proposition (see Figure 2.6):

⬤ Market-oriented companies have a large number of satisfied customers and therefore a higher rate of repeat purchase (Lash, 1990; Goderis, 1998) and lower selling costs (Dwyer *et al.*, 1987).

⬤ A market-oriented firm gives faster response to changing needs by launching new or improved products, thereby maintaining a good balance between growth and profit objectives in its product portfolio (Cooper, 1993).

⬤ A market-oriented firm brings more value to customers and therefore has a lower price sensitivity and higher market acceptable prices (Nagle, 1987).

⬤ A market-oriented firm is in a better position to identify a sustainable competitive advantage and to increase or defend its market share (Porter, 1985).

These conditions, when met, directly or indirectly, contribute to the firm's long-term economic performance. Various indicators of economic performance can be

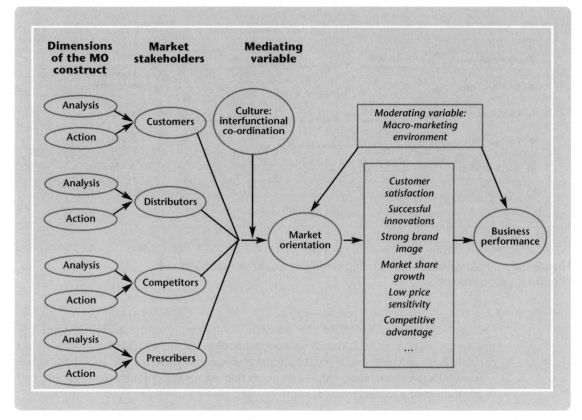

Figure 2.7   The construct of market orientation

used: return on capital, sales or market share growth, success rate of new products, and so on.

Measuring market orientation

The basic hypothesis is that market-oriented firms allocate human and material resources (a) to collect information about the expectations and behaviour of the different market participants. This information is then used (b) to design market-oriented action plans which are implemented (c) by involving all levels of the organisation. Thus, to build a valid measure of market orientation two sets of indicators will be defined for each of the four market participants: *analysis* and *action* indicators, and one set of indicators for measuring the level of *interfunctional co-ordination*.

For each of these five components, we have identified a set of indicators with the objective of deriving a valid measure for each component and of analysing their relationships with various measures of business performance. These indicators are summarised in Appendix 2.1. These indicators are presented there in general terms and they must be adapted in each case to reflect the characteristics of a specific sector. The general model tested is presented in Figure 2.7.

● Reinventing the Marketing Organisation

The developments in the macro-marketing environment and the wide adoption of a market orientation at all levels of the firm have had several implications for the marketing function. *First,* the brand management system so successfully adopted by many companies during the last thirty years seems, today, unable to face the complex challenges of the new environment. As put by George *et al.* (1994) from the McKinsey company,

> Brand managers (today) are not really mini general managers (as they were supposed to be). They are usually too junior, too inexperienced and too narrowly centred on marketing to provide the cross functional leadership and strategic thinking required to navigate through today's complex marketing landscape. They are too removed from the sources of value added (which are not just advertising based), too overwhelmed with day-to-day tasks (like developing trade promotions in packaged goods, or staying on stock plan and taking mark-downs in retailing) and too focused on implementing quick-fix solutions that will get them promoted in 18 months. (George *et al.,* 1994, p. 46)

Second, as the market orientation concept becomes more and more accepted and increasingly implemented across all functions within the firm, namely as a result of the 'total quality' movement often initiated by operations management, the specific role of marketing as a separate function is coming under questioning and has to be reassessed. There is accumulating evidence that the new macro-marketing environment is forcing many companies to review the role to be played by the traditional marketing department in the corporation. Several dramatic organisational changes are reported in the professional literature and in the economic press (see for instance, *The Economist,* 9 April 1994) which confirm this evolution and for example,

> the abolition of chief marketing executive posts and the closure of marketing departments by major international companies like Unilever, Elida Gibbs and Pillsbury (Grand Metropolitan), AT&T and their replacement by business groups, customer development teams, customer focus teams, multidisciplinary teams and category rather than brand management. (Piercy and Cravens, 1995, p .12)

Towards cross-functional organisations

According to George *et al.* (1994), tomorrow's marketing organisations will be organised around two roles, integrators and specialists, linked together through teams and processes rather than functional or business unit structures:

● *Integrators (or process managers)* will play the critical role of guiding activities across the firm's entire value chain; identifying which market segments to compete in and which levers to pull to maximise long-term profitability. They will be charged with tearing down the walls that divide function from function and with leading cross-functional teams to execute these strategies. Typically, they will be responsible for marketing strategy development (see Part 3 of this book). Integrators can be responsible for a distinct end-user segment (consumer integrators) or specific

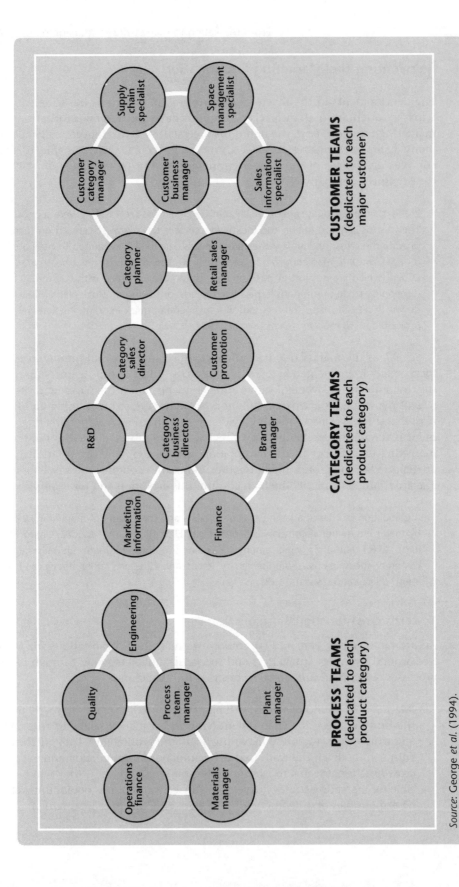

PROCESS TEAMS
(dedicated to each product category)

Operations finance

Quality

Materials manager

Process team manager

Engineering

Plant manager

CATEGORY TEAMS
(dedicated to each product category)

Marketing information

R&D

Category business director

Finance

Category sales director

Brand manager

Customer promotion

CUSTOMER TEAMS
(dedicated to each major customer)

Customer category manager

Category planner

Customer business manager

Retail sales manager

Supply chain specialist

Space management specialist

Sales information specialist

Source: George et al. (1994).

Figure 2.8 Managing through teams at Kraft

Exhibit 2.10

Evolution of the Priority Role of Marketing

Passive marketing	The firm is product-oriented and has an inside-in perspective
Operational marketing	The firm is sales-oriented and has an inside-out perspective
Strategic marketing	The firm is customer-oriented and has an outside-in perspective
Market-driven management	The firm is market-oriented and has a societal perspective
Global market-driven management	The firm is world market-oriented and has a transnational perspective

group of business customers like giant retailers (customer integrator) or be responsible for a process, like new product development (process integrators).

● *Specialists* will provide the technical and specialised skills required to successfully implement the marketing strategy in the different disciplines such as marketing research, business intelligence, pricing strategy, advertising, promotion, direct marketing, and so on. The trend will also be towards subcontracting to outside specialists marketing activities such as market research and analysis, database management, and even the execution of some operational marketing tasks.

In the new organisational context, the fifth component of market orientation – *interfunctional co-ordination* – is particularly important because it implies the involvement of all levels in the firm's organisation. The key idea here is to consider that market orientation is the business of everyone and not only of the marketing people.

The new priorities of the marketing function

The evolution of the changing priority role of marketing is summarised in Exhibit 2.10. The environmental changes mentioned above all imply a reinforcement of the market orientation for companies operating in highly industrialised markets. Companies need to review their strategic options in order to face the new challenges presented by the economic, competitive and socio-cultural environment and by the internationalisation of the world economy.

One can identify eight new priorities implied by the adoption of a market-driven business philosophy:

1. *Market-driven Management*. Successful implementation of a market-driven business philosophy requires cross-functional co-ordination and a corporate culture which encourages the adoption of a strong market orientation at all levels of the organisation.

2. *Customised Marketing.* In affluent societies, sophisticated and powerful customers expect to find tailor-made solutions to their problems and it is up to the firm to meet these expectations through direct response segmentation and interactive communication.

3. *Green Marketing.* Environmentalism is the expression of a new societal need revealing deep changes of outlook regarding consumption. Green marketing should start in the laboratory at the stage of the product concept design, a responsibility which goes far beyond just the marketing function.

4. *Trade Marketing.* There is a shift of power in the marketing channels, particularly in the field of FMCG. New types of relationships must be developed between suppliers and distributors who should be viewed as customers in their own right.

5. *Competition Orientation.* In stagnant and mature markets, the capacity to anticipate competitors' actions and to outfox rivals is a key factor of success. This capacity implies the existence of a competition monitoring system.

6. *Development of Foresighting Systems.* In a turbulent environment, traditional sales forecasting methods are ineffective and the firm must develop organisational flexibility and contingency planning systems.

7. *Global Marketing.* There is a growing interdependence among the countries of the Triad where the industrial and cultural fabric becomes more homogeneous. Supranational segments appear which constitute market opportunities for the firm.

8. *Accountable Marketing.* New social needs are emerging in society which call for more responsible behaviour. Firms are beginning to show concern for both the individual and the collective well-being of society, instead of simply satisfying short-term needs.

In the following chapters, we shall examine the *'how to?'* issues raised by these new priorities.

Chapter summary

The macro-marketing environment of the firm has changed dramatically during the 1990s. A key change is the acceleration and the generalisation of the technological progress which shorten product life cycles and force companies to renew their product portfolio faster than previously. The internationalisation of the world economy, the creation of the European Single Market, the opening of Eastern Europe and the appearance of new competitors are critical challenges which also imply redeployment and/or restructuring of current activities. In affluent societies, consumers are better educated and more demanding and mass marketing techniques are coming of age. Customised marketing is the new market expectation. New societal needs also emerge, advocated by the consumerism and environmentalism movements, which call for the firm's greater sensitivity to the socio-cultural fallout of its economic action. Green marketing based on eco-designed products and accountable marketing based on corporate ethical behaviour are the appropriate industry responses. At the international level, the growing interdependence of markets raises the issue of standardisation versus customisation. To remain competitive, the adoption of global or transnational marketing is the appropriate strategy in market environments where local forces are weak. All these environmental changes call for a reinforcement of the level of the firm's market orientation. In today's turbulent environment, market orientation is too important to be left to the marketing department alone. The market culture should be diffused at all levels within the organisation through interfunctional co-ordination. In this new context, marketing is more important than ever but the marketing department as a separate function is being critically questioned and should reinvent itself. Marketing should be viewed as a process integrating the different functions and not a separate entity within the organisation. In the current macro-marketing environment new priorities emerge for the firm.

QUESTIONS AND PROBLEMS

1. Which factors explain the development of global marketing?
2. What are the strategies and/or policies to be adopted by firms operating exclusively in their domestic market, to reinforce their competitiveness within the enlarged European market?
3. Does the growing environmental concern represent a threat or an opportunity for the firm? How would you proceed to answer this question in your own company?
4. Are you personally in favour of the legal application of the 'Who pollutes pays' principle? Compare the marketing and social impact of eco-taxes versus eco-fees.
5. Assuming that you are in favour of the accountable marketing concept, to what extent will this state of mind, new for your company, affect your marketing strategy and your practices regarding product, distribution, communication and pricing policies?
6. Is green marketing the right answer from the firm to meet society's environmental concern? Examine what green marketing means for each component of the marketing mix.
7. What difference(s) do you see between the following three business philosophies: 'marketing orientation', 'customer orientation' and 'market orientation'?
8. Select a company you know well and measure its level of market orientation, using the indicators presented in the questionnaire below. Construct an aggregate score of market orientation and a separate score for the 'analysis', 'action' and 'interfunctional co-ordination' components. Interpret the results and formulate recommendations.

Appendix 2.1

● **Introducing the Questionnaire**
(Please read carefully)

In the questionnaire presented hereafter, you will find 40 propositions describing the behaviour of a firm in its relationship with the market. Could you indicate *to what extent each proposition provides a good description of the actual behaviour of your own firm*, referring to the last three years of the firm's business life.

If your Company has several and very different Strategic Business Units (SBUs), select the most representative one and refer only to this SBU in evaluating the propositions. If the SBU operates in a consumer market, the end-customer is the consumer; in business-to-business markets, you should refer to the direct customer.

The rating scale has 10 positions, going from 0 to 10. A score of 0/10 means that you, *personally*, totally disagree with this description; a score of 10/10 means that you fully agree with the proposed description. The intermediate scores are there to qualify your judgement. Don't hesitate to use the full range of available scores, as shown on top of the questionnaire's first page. Please write the adopted score in the right column of the questionnaire and *evaluate all the propositions presented*, keeping in mind that there are no good or bad answers, only *your perceptions* of a state of affairs.

Regarding the last six questions (22 to 27) pertaining to the environment and to the firm's performance, the rating scale has five positions, each of them supported by a verbal label. Could you indicate which label best describes your overall opinion and write in the right column the corresponding score.

PROFILE OF THE RESPONDENT

Enterprise:
Type of industrial activity:
Number of persons employed:
Position of the respondent in the firm:
Department:
Number of years in the firm:

THANK YOU FOR YOUR CO-OPERATION

Disagreement/Agreement Scale

0/10	1/10	2/10	3/10	4/10	5/10	6/10	7/10	8/10	9/10	10/10

Strongly					Neither					Strongly
disagree					agree or disagree					agree
Pas du tout d'accord					*Avis neutre*					*Tout-à-fait d'accord*

INTERFUNCTIONAL CO-ORDINATION   *Coordination interfonctionnelle*

1. We encourage direct contact with customers at all company levels and functions.
   Nous encourageons les contacts directs avec les clients dans toutes les fonctions et niveaux de l'entreprise.

2. Market information (on consumers, competition, distributors, and so on) is diffused systematically to all departments within the firm.
   L'information relative au marché (clients, concurrents, distributeurs) est diffusée systématiquement au sein de tous les départements de l'entreprise.

3. Market strategies are developed in concertation with several departments.
   Les stratégies de marché sont développées en concertation avec plusieurs départements.

4. We regularly organise meetings between several departments to analyse market information.
   Nous organisons régulièrement des réunions interdépartementales pour analyser les informations du marché.

MACRO-ENVIRONMENT   *Macro-environnement*

5. We know well the technological changes that could have a substantial impact on our industrial activity.
   Nous connaissons bien les changements technologiques susceptibles d'avoir un impact sur notre activité industrielle.

6. We are aware of the ecological side effects of our industrial activities.
   Nous sommes conscients des retombées écologiques de notre activité industrielle.

7. We have identified leading indicators to monitor major changes in the technological and socio-economic environment.
   Nous disposons d'indicateurs à l'avance pour surveiller les principaux changements de l'environnement technologique et socio-économique.

8. We take actions to minimise the negative ecological impact of our products and of our industrial activity.
   Nous agissons en vue de minimiser l'impact écologique négatif de nos produits ou de notre activité industrielle.

COMPETITORS   *Concurrents*

9. We systematically analyse the strengths and weaknesses of our direct competitors.   *Nous analysons systématiquement les forces et les faiblesses de nos concurrents directs.*
10. We systematically analyse the threats coming from substitute products.   *Nous analysons systématiquement les menaces de produits substituts.*
11. We analyse the best practice of competition to improve the quality of our own offers.   *Nous analysons les meilleurs pratiques de nos concurrents pour améliorer la qualité de notre offre.*
12. We are fast to respond to competitors' actions directed at our end-customers.   *Nous répondons rapidement aux actions de nos concurrents visant nos clients finaux.*

INDEPENDENT DISTRIBUTORS   *Distributeurs independants*

13. We systematically examine current and emerging needs of our distributors.   *Nous analysons systématiquement les besoins actuels et nouveaux de nos distributeurs.*
14. We regularly measure the level of satisfaction/dissatisfaction of our distributors and their image of our company.   *Nous mesurons régulièrement le niveau de satisfaction/insatisfaction de nos distributeurs et l'image qu'ils ont de notre société.*
15. We regularly analyse the compatibility of our strategy with the objectives of our distributors.   *Nous analysons régulièrement la compatibilité de notre stratégie avec les objectifs de nos distributeurs.*
16. Our managers are personally committed in the firm's contacts with our distributors.   *Nos dirigeants sont impliqués personnellement dans les contacts avec les distributeurs.*

END-CUSTOMERS   *Clients finaux* or **DIRECT CUSTOMERS**   *Clients directs*

17. We systematically analyse our customers' current and future needs.   *Nous analysons systématiquement les besoins présents et futurs de nos clients.*
18. We regularly examine the factors influencing the buying process of our customers.   *Nous analysons régulièrement les facteurs influençant le processus d'achat de nos clients.*
19. We regularly measure the level of our customers' satisfaction/dissatisfaction.   *Nous mesurons régulièrement le niveau de satisfaction/insatisfaction de nos clients.*
20. We periodically measure our customers' perceived image of our brand(s) or company.   *Nous mesurons périodiquement l'image de marque de nos produits ou de notre entreprise auprès de nos clients.*

21. Over to the *last three years*, market-driven management in our company is a business philosophy which was understood, accepted and well implemented at all levels and across all departments.

Au cours des trois dernières années, l'orientation marché (market-driven management) a été une philosophie de gestion comprise, acceptée et mise en œuvre à tous les niveaux et dans tous les départements de notre entreprise.

PRESCRIBERS (if appropriate)   *Prescripteurs (si approprié)*

22. We systematically analyse current and future needs of the prescribers operating in our market.

Nous analysons systématiquement les besoins présents et futurs des prescripteurs opérant dans notre marché.

23. We regularly examine the influence and the role played by prescribers *vis-à-vis* our direct customers.

Nous analysons régulièrement le rôle et le degré d'influence des prescipteurs sur nos clients directs.

24. We regularly organise information and/or training sessions for prescribers about the characteristics of our products.

Nous organisons régulièrement à l'intention des prescripteurs des actions de formation et/ou d'information sur nos produits.

25. We periodically measure the perceived image of our brand(s) or company among key prescribers.

Nous mesurons périodiquement l'image de marque de nos produits ou de notre entreprise auprès des prescripteurs les plus importants.

MARKET POWER OF DISTRIBUTORS   *Le pouvoir de marché des distributeurs*

26. In the market under study, over the *last three years*, how strong was the market power of the distributors?

Dans le marché étudié, au cours des trois dernières années, quel était le pouvoir de marché des distributeurs?

Very weak (1)	Weak (2)	Moderate (3)	Strong (4)	Very strong (5)
Très faible (1)	*Faible (2)*	*Modéré (3)*	*Fort (4)*	*Très fort (5)*

AGGRESSIVENESS OF THE COMPETITIVE ENVIRONMENT   *L'aggressivité du climat concurrentiel*

27. In the market under study, over the *last three years*, how aggressive was the competitive environment?

Dans le marché étudié, au cours des trois dernières années, comment était le climat concurrentiel?

Very placid (1)	Placid (2)	Moderate (3)	Aggressive (4)	Very aggressive (5)
Très calme (1)	*Calme (2)*	*Modéré (3)*	*Agressif (4)*	*Très agressif (5)*

TURBULENCE OF THE SOCIO-ECONOMIC ENVIRONMENT *Le degré de turbulence de l'environnement socio-économique*

28. In the market under study, over the *last three years*, how turbulent was the socio-economic environment?

Dans le marché étudié, au cours des trois dernières années, quel était le degré de turbulence de l'environnement socio-économique?

Very placid (1)	Placid (2)	Moderate (3)	Turbulent (4)	Very Turbulent (5)
Très calme (1)	*Calme (2)*	*Modéré (3)*	*Turbulent (4)*	*Très turbulent (5)*

TURBULENCE OF THE TECHNOLOGICAL ENVIRONMENT *Le rythme du changement technologique*

29. Over the *last three years*, what was the pace of the technological change?

Au cours des trois dernières années, quel était le rythme du changement technologique?

Very placid (1)	Placid (2)	Moderate (3)	Fast changing (4)	Very fast changing (5)
Très lent (1)	*Lent (2)*	*Modéré (3)*	*Rapide (4)*	*Très rapide (5)*

TURBULENCE OF THE ECOLOGICAL ENVIRONMENT *La pression du mouvement écologique*

30. Over the *last three years*, how strong was the pressure of ecology in your reference market?

Au cours des trois dernières années, quelle était la pression du mouvement écologique?

Very weak (1)	Weak (2)	Moderate (3)	Strong (4)	Very Strong (5)
Très faible (1)	*Faible (2)*	*Modéré (3)*	*Forte (4)*	*Très Forte (5)*

PRESENT PERFORMANCE OF THE COMPANY *Performance de votre entreprise*

31. (a) Referring to the *current 18 months*, rate the *overall* performance of your firm compared to your direct competitor(s):

(a) *En se basant sur les 18 derniers mois, comment se caractérise, de manière générale, la performance de votre entreprise par rapport à votre (vos) concurrent(s) direct(s):*

(b) More specifically, how does your firm perform in terms of:

(b) *Et, plus spécifiquement, comment se caractérise-t-elle en termes de:*

– sales revenue growth
– *croissance du chiffre d'affaire*

– market share gain
– *gain de part de marché*

– profitability
– *rentabilité*

– innovation
– *innovation*

Much worse (1)	Worse (2)	Equal (3)	Better (4)	Much better (5)
Très inférieure (1)	*Inférieure (2)*	*Egale (3)*	*Supérieure (4)*	*Très supérieure (5)*

COMMENTS:

Bibliography

Aaker, D.A. and Day, G.S. (1982) *Consumerism: Search for the Consumer Interest*, 4th edn, New York, The Free Press.

Ansoff, H.I. (1984) *Implanting Strategic Management*, Englewood Cliffs NJ, Prentice Hall.

Bloon, H., Calori, R. and de Woot, P. (1981) *EuroManagement: A New Style for the Global Market*, London, Kogan Page.

Brady, J. and Davis, I. (1993) Marketing in Midlife Crisis, *The McKinsey Quarterly*, No. 2, pp. 17–28.

Buzzell, R.D. (1968) Can you Standardize Multinational Marketing?, *Harvard Business Review*, **46**, November–December.

Cerfontaine, B. (1994) Le marketing global chez Procter & Gamble, Conference given at IAG, Louvain-la-Neuve, March.

Cooper, R.G. (1993) *Winning at New Products*, Reading MA, Addison Wesley.

Corstjens, J. and Corstjens, M. (1996) *Store Wars*, New York, John Wiley & Sons.

Drucker, P. (1980) *Managing in Turbulent Times*, New York, Harper & Row.

Dwyer, F.R., Schurr, P.H. and Sejo, O.H. (1987) Developing Buyer–seller Relationships, *Journal of Marketing*, **51**, April, pp. 11–27.

European Commission (1995) *Green Book on Innovation*, Bulletin of the European Union, Supplement 5/95.

European Commission (1997) *The Competitiveness of European Industry*, Luxembourg, Office des Publications des Communautés Européennes.

European Economy (1997) Supplement B, *Business and Consumer Survey Results*, No. 11, November.

European Economy (1999) Supplement B, *Business and Consumer Survey Results*, No. 6, June.

Fritz, W. (1996) Market Orientation and Corporate Success: Findings from Germany, *European Journal of Marketing*, **30**(8): 59–74.

George, M., Freeling, A. and Court, D. (1994) Reinventing the Marketing Organisation, *The McKinsey Quarterly*, No. 4, pp. 43–62.

Goderis, J.P. (1998) Barrier Marketing: From Customer Satisfaction to Customer Loyalty, *CEMS Business Review*, **2**(4): 285–94.

Goshal, S. and Nohria, N. (1993) Horses for Courses: Organisational Forms for Multinational Corporations, *Sloan Management Review*, Winter, pp. 23–35.

Gray, B., Matear, S., Boshoff, C. and Matheson, P. (1998) Developing a Better Measure of Market Orientation, *European Journal of Marketing*, **32**(9–10): 864–903.

Hochswender, W. (1996) *The New York Times* (date unknown).

Kohli, A.K. and Jaworski, B.J. (1990) Market Orientation: The Construct, Research Propositions and Managerial Implications, *The Journal of Marketing*, **4**, April, pp. 1–18.

Kohli, A.K., Jaworski, B.J. and Kumar, A. (1993) MARKOR: A Measure of Market Orientation, *Journal of Marketing Research*, **30**, April, pp. 467–77.

Kotler, P. (1997) *Marketing Management*, 9th edn, Englewood Cliffs NJ, Prentice Hall.

Laczniak, G.R. and Murphy, P.E. (1993), *Ethical Marketing Decisions*, Boston MA, Allyn and Bacon.

Lambin, J.J. (1996) The Misunderstanding About Marketing, *CEMS Business Review*, **1**(1): 37–56.

Lambin, J.J., and Chumpitaz, R. (1999), Market Orientation and Business Performance: Methodological Issue and New Empirical Evidence, unpublished working paper, IAG, Louvain-la-Neuve, March.

Lambin, J.J. and Hiller, T.B. (1990) Volvo Trucks in Europe, in: Kerin, R.A. and Peterson, R.A. (1993) *Strategic Marketing Problems*, Boston MA, Allyn & Bacon.

Lash, M.L. (1990) *The Complete Guide to Customer Service*, New York, John Wiley & Sons.

Levitt, T. (1983) The Globalization of Markets, *Harvard Business Review*, **61**, May–June, pp. 92–102.

Little, A.D. (1998), *Findings of the Arthur D. Little Global Survey on Innovation*. Boston MA, A.D. Little.

Masiello, T. (1988) Developing Market Responsiveness Throughout Your Company, *Industrial Marketing Management*, No. 17, pp. 85–93.

McDougall, G.H.G. (1993) The Green Moverment in Canada: Implications for Marketing Strategy, *Journal of International Consumer Marketing*, **5**(3): 69–87.

Morgan, R.E. and Strong, C.A. (1998) Market Orientation and Dimensions of Strategic Orientation, *European Journal of Marketing*, **32**(11–12): 885–903.

Nagle, T.T. (1987) *The Strategy and Tactics of Pricing*, Englewood Cliffs NJ, Prentice Hall.

Narver, J.C. and Slater, S.F. (1990) The Effect of a Market Orientation on Business Profitability, *The Journal of Marketing*, **54**, October, pp. 20–35.

Ochs, P. (1998) *Le Marketing de l'Offre*, Paris, Economica.

OECD (1998) *OECD Economic Outlook*, December.

Ohmae, K. (1987) The Triad World View, *The Journal of Business Strategy*, **7**(4): pp. 8–19.

Ottman, J.A. (1993) *Green Marketing: Challenges and Opportunities for the New Marketing Age*, Lincolnwood IL, NTC Business Books.

Piercy, N.F. and Cravens, D.W. (1995) The Network Paradigm and the Marketing Organization, *European Journal of Marketing*, **29**(3): 7–34.

Pitt, L., Caruana, A. and Berthon, P.R. (1996) Market Orientation and Business Performance: Some European Evidence, *International Marketing Review*, **13**(1): 5–18.

Porter, M.E. (1980) *Competitive Strategy*, New York, The Free Press.

Porter, M.E. (1985) *Competitive Advantage*, New York, The Free Press.

Quelch, J.A. and Hoff, E.J. (1986) Customizing Global Marketing, *Harvard Business Review*, **64**, May–June, pp. 59–68.

Reidenbach, R.E. and Robin, P. (1991) A Conceptual Model of Corporate Moral Development, *Journal of Business Ethics*, April.

Ries, A. and Trout, J. (1986) *Warfare Marketing*, New York, McGraw-Hill.

Rivera, J. (1995) 'L'orientation-marché': une stratégie concurrentielle performante, Doctoral dissertation, IAG, Louvain-la-Neuve, Belgium.

Schumpeter, J.A. (1949) *The Theory of Economic Development*, Cambridge MA, Harvard University Press.

Shapiro, B.P. (1988) What the Hell Is Market-oriented?, *Harvard Business Review*, **66**, November–December, pp. 119–125.

Sheth, J., Mittal, B. and Newman, B.I. (1999) *Customer Behavior, Consumer Behavior and Beyond*, Fort Worth TX, Dryden Press.

Takeuchi, H. and Porter, M.E. (1986) Three Roles of International Marketing in Global Strategy, in: *Competition in Global Industries*, Boston MA, Harvard Business School Press.

Theys, F. (1994) Succès et échec de l'innovation dans l'IFME, unpublished working paper, IAG, Louvain-la-Neuve, Belgium.

Webster, F.E. (1994) *Market-driven Management*, New York, John Wiley & Sons.

Webster, F.E. (1997) The Future Role of Marketing in the Organisation, in: Lehman, D.R. and Jocz, K.E. (eds), *Reflections on the Futures of Marketing*, Cambridge MA, Marketing Science Institute.

part two

Understanding Customer Behaviour

STRUCTURE OF THE BOOK

PART ONE The Changing Role of Marketing

The role of marketing in the firm and in a marketing economy
CHAPTER ONE

From marketing to market-driven management
CHAPTER TWO

PART TWO Understanding Customer Behaviour

The customer choice behaviour
CHAPTER THREE

The marketing information system
CHAPTER FOUR

The customer's response behaviour
CHAPTER FIVE

PART THREE Market-driven Strategy Development

Needs analysis through market segmentation
CHAPTER SIX

Market attractiveness analysis
CHAPTER SEVEN

Competitiveness analysis
CHAPTER EIGHT

Formulating a market strategy
CHAPTER NINE

The strategic marketing plan
CHAPTER TEN

PART FOUR Market-driven Management Decisions

Market-driven new product decisions
CHAPTER ELEVEN

Market-driven distribution decisions
CHAPTER TWELVE

Market-driven pricing decisions
CHAPTER THIRTEEN

Market-driven communication decisions
CHAPTER FOURTEEN

Market-driven advertising decisions
CHAPTER FIFTEEN

PART FIVE Ten Case Studies in Market-driven Management

1. The Lander Company *W.J. Stanton*
2. The WILO Corporation *R. Köhler*
3. TV: Cold Bath for French Cinema *A. Riding*
4. Ecover *D. Develter*
5. Volvo Truck Belgium *J.J. Lambin*
6. The Petro-equipment Company *J.J. Lambin*
7. Sierra Plastics Company *W.J. Stanton*
8. Tissex *G. Marion*
9. Newfood *G.S. Day et al.*
10. SAS: Meeting Customer Expectations *D.L. Kurtz and K.E. Clow*

chapter three

The customer choice behaviour

The satisfaction of buyers' needs is at the heart of a market economy and of marketing. This chapter aims to make clear such basic conceptions of the needs theory as generic versus derived needs and absolute versus relative needs, needs classification and needs hierarchy. We shall also discuss the possibility of saturation in relation to different kinds of needs. The importance of strategic marketing in adapting firms to the constant development in needs satisfaction will be pointed out. We shall also examine the main positions of economics and marketing theoreticians concerning the role marketing plays in creating or intensifying needs. Then we shall turn to psychology and in particular to the contributions experimental psychology has made in the study of human motivation. Finally, we shall analyse the motivation of the organisational or business-to-business customer which must be examined within a totally different framework from that of individual consumers.

Chapter learning objectives

When you have read this chapter, you should be able to understand:

1. the nature and the diversity of individual needs;
2. the concept of value as the motivational force of the individual buyer;
3. the difference between consumer and business marketing;
4. the main characteristics of the demand for industrial goods;
5. the nature of organisational buying.

Human Needs in Economic Theory

The notion of need is a term that creates endless polemic because it contains elements of subjective judgement based sometimes on morality or ideology. Beyond the vital minimum that everyone accepts – but which no one tries to define – is it really necessary to vary one's food to satisfy taste, to travel out of curiosity or to have different hobbies? We must admit that, at least as far as consumer markets are concerned, these questions are not irrelevant, especially in view of the following facts: (a) the uninterrupted arrival of new products and brands on the market; (b) the continuous and spectacular presence of advertising in increasingly varied forms; and (c) the relative stability of the level of consumer satisfaction, despite the undisputed improvement in standard of living. These facts then raise the following questions:

- Do all these new products and brands really correspond to pre-existing needs?
- Would producers accept such high advertising expenditures if consumers were not allowing themselves to be influenced?
- Is the growth and economic development that marketing claims to encourage useful in the long term?

Economic theory does not help to answer these questions. Economists believe it is not part of their discipline to worry about what motivates an action, or to enter into an introspection, which is always difficult, or especially to formulate a value judgement. It is useless to say that man strives for pleasure and avoids pain; it suffices to see that this indeed is the essence of the 'want to use' to justify its utility. The driving force, economic or otherwise, that makes an individual take an economic action, is outside the scope of economics; only the results are important. The wish to be satisfied is the only acknowledged cause of behaviour.

A need must be felt before a choice is made, which means that the scale of preferences logically precedes effective choices. If an individual is intellectually adult and reasonable, it should be possible to predict the person's behaviour, which results from rational calculation.

> The consumption choices of an individual which express his needs can be described a priori completely, without experimentation and on the condition that a rational behaviour, summarised by five axioms called the axioms of rationality, can be assumed. (Jacquemin and Tulkens, 1988, p. 50)

The economic theory of consumer behaviour is therefore limited to the analysis of the logical implications of the hypothesis of man's rationality. The problem of motivation is totally avoided, since economists believe that *the real behaviour of the consumer reflects his or her preferences and inversely that the consumer's preferences are revealed by his or her behaviour.*

The weakness of the basic assumptions in economics have been underlined on many occasions. In economic theory, the concept of *rationality* is defined as equivalent to the concept of *coherence*. However, the predictive value of coherence conditions depends mainly on the existence of well-known and stable preferences in the mind of the decider. But this is far from being satisfied if the original motivations are ignored, poorly known or simplified to the extreme, as is the case in economic models. How can we then be surprised by the observed difference between the 'economic person' and the 'real person'? We should nevertheless mention that, over the last few years, many serious efforts have been made to enrich the abstract psychology of the economic person and to come closer to the real person. Some examples are the works of Katona (1951), Abbott (1955), Becker (1965) and Lancaster (1966).

Generic versus derived needs

According to the dictionary, *a need is a requirement of nature or of social life*. This definition distinguishes two kinds of needs: *innate needs*, which are natural, generic or inherent in nature or in the organism, and *derived (or acquired) needs* which are cultural and social and depend on experience, environmental conditions and the evolution of society.

In the frame of strategic marketing analysis it is practical to view generic needs as *problems* of potential buyers who try to solve them by acquiring different products or services (this problem solving approach will be discussed in Chapter 4). If we take this view, then, following Abbott (1955, p. 40) we can define a *derived need* as a particular technological response (the product) to the generic need, as well as being the object of desire.

> For example, the car is a derived need with respect to the generic need of autonomous individual means of transportation. The same is true of the personal computer with respect to the need to process information.

A generic need cannot be saturated; saturation relates only to derived needs, in other words to the dominant technological response at the time. At a given point, one may detect a tendency towards the saturation of the derived need, because of increased consumption of the good at a particular stage in its *life cycle*. The marginal utility of the derived need tends to diminish. But the basic problems (of transportation, communication, protection, and so on) do not disappear, which means that generic need remains insatiable. Thanks to the impulse given by technological progress, the generic need it simply evolves towards higher levels due to the arrival of improved products and therefore new derived needs.

The production of goods for the satisfaction of generic needs will therefore be incessantly subject to the stimulus of its own evolution. The latter will encourage the arrival of new products on the market which are more suitable to satisfying the new level of needs. These derived needs will be saturated in their turn and be replaced by new, more developed, products. The phenomenon of relative saturation brought about by technological progress, which is the basis of the model of product life cycle discussed later on in this book, is observed for most goods and at two levels: first, in the improvement of technological performance of products themselves (more economical cars, more powerful computers, and so on); and second, in the pure and simple substitution of a particular technological answer by another with higher performance (compact disc replacing long-playing records, fax replacing telex, and so on). The latter form of innovation, or *destructive innovation*, is becoming ever more important due to the generalisation of technological progress in all sectors, as mentioned before.

Furthermore, it seems that the move to a product which is hierarchically superior tends to increase the marginal utility yet again. The decline of the marginal utility is thus interspersed with sudden peaks. Goods are often desired for their novelty features and the privilege of owning them, even if little is added to their performance.

Therefore, the distinction between generic and derived needs makes it clear that, although there can be no general saturation, it is perfectly possible to detect sectoral saturation. An important role for *strategic marketing* is thus to encourage the firm to adapt to this observed development in needs satisfaction. In this framework, it is better for the firm to define its mission by reference to generic rather than derived needs, given that the latter are satiable while the former are not. These are the basics of the *market orientation concept* described in the previous chapter.

Absolute versus relative needs

Going further into analysis of derived needs, Keynes discovered that saturation is possible only for a certain part of them. In fact, Keynes had established an important distinction between

> those needs which are absolute in the sense that we feel them whatever the situation of our fellow human beings may be, and those which are relative in the sense that we feel them only if their satisfaction lifts us above, make us feel superior to our fellows. (Keynes 1936, p. 365)

Absolute needs are satiable, while relative needs are not. Relative needs are insatiable, because the higher the general level, the more these needs tend to surpass that level. In such conditions, producing to satisfy relative needs is tantamount to developing them. This is how individuals, even when they have in absolute terms enjoyed net improvements in their standard of living, often tend to think that their situation has deteriorated if those who normally serve as the yardstick have improved more relative to them. Cotta (1980, p. 17) writes, *'others' luxury becomes one's own necessity'.* The distance between reality and the level of aspiration tends to move continuously with growing dissatisfaction.

The distinction between absolute and relative needs is in fact far from being as clear-cut as one might at first think. One could say, for example, that anything essential to survival is infinitely more important that any other consumption. This idea is inexact.

> To live is certainly an important objective for each of us, but suicide exists. Heroic acts too. More generally, every consumer, in his day to day search for satisfaction of various needs, takes risks that put his life in danger either immediately or in the long run. Smoking, overeating, driving, working too hard or not looking after one's health properly, travelling: these are all activities that one should avoid if survival is placed above all else. (Rosa, 1977, p. 161)

Needs of a psycho-sociological origin may be felt just as strongly as the most elementary needs. For example, being deprived of intimacy and attention may provoke death or serious deficiencies in psychic and social functioning in the more extreme cases.

Despite a lack of clarity, the distinction between absolute and relative needs remains interesting in two respects. On the one hand, it shows that relative needs can be just as demanding as absolute needs. On the other, it brings to the fore the existence of a dialectic of relative needs which leads to the observation of the general *impossibility of saturation*. Even the tendency towards material comfort cannot objectively define a state of satisfaction. When an individual reaches a predefined level, he or she can then catch a glimpse of a new stage of possible improvement.

Needs, wants and demand

Though the notions of generic and derived needs seem productive and easy to understand, somewhat different terminology is also employed. For example, Kotler (1997, p. 9) establishes a distinction between needs, wants and demand. He defines need as *'a state of felt deprivation of some basic satisfaction'*. This essentially coincides with the definition of a generic need.

Wants are specific satisfiers of deeper needs. While generic needs are stable and few, wants are many, changing and continually influenced by social forces. It is clear that wants are just another name for derived needs. Wants become *potential demands* for specific products when backed by an ability and willingness to buy.

As suggested by Hamel and Prahalad (1994), understanding customer needs and wants is not always a simple task and it is useful to estabish a distinction between articulated and unarticulated needs which themselves can be further subdivided in sub-categories.

Articulated needs

⬤ Stated needs *(what the customer says)*
⬤ Unstated needs *(what the customer expects)*
⬤ Imaginary needs *(what the customer dreams of)*

Unarticulated needs

⬤ Real needs *(the well-being of the customer)*
⬤ Unconscious needs *(what unconsciously motivates the customer)*

As illustrated in Figure 3.1, responding only to the customer's articulated needs may be misleading, leaving interesting opportunities unexploited. The objective of strategic marketing is to provide customers with an appropriate solution based on a good understanding of their real needs, *be they articulated or not*.

'False' needs versus 'true' needs

The distinction between needs, wants and demand is important, but the needs–wants relationship remains rather controversial. For example, Attali and Guillaume (1974) reject the described relationship between needs and wants. In direct opposition to Kotler's view, they believe that *needs are generated by wants*, things that have become normalised. They include things which no longer give pleasure, but that would be unacceptable to do without because they fall in the domain of the normal (Attali and Guillaume, 1974, p. 144). It is the dynamics of wants that explains the accumulation of needs.

Taking into account this controversy, the use of terms *generic and derived needs* seems preferable. However the interesting point about the analysis above is possibly the fact that it puts forth the cultural and social origin of our needs.

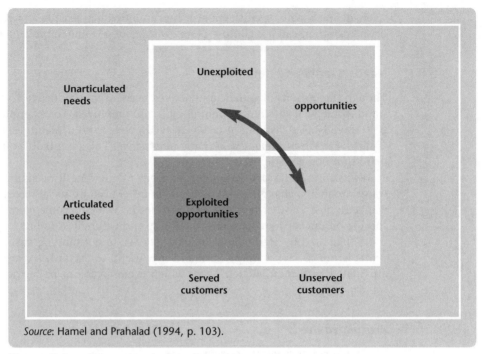

Source: Hamel and Prahalad (1994, p. 103).

Figure 3.1　Beyond articulated needs

Marketing and the creation of needs

The criticism frequently levelled at modern marketing is that it has changed the market into a mechanism that creates needs rather than satisfies them. As we already know, the answer to this criticism given by economists is incomplete: they content themselves with the assumption that what consumers choose suits them, and they are unable to explain the real nature of consumption phenomena. But for strategic marketing the role society as a whole and marketing in particular play in creating needs is an important issue. It cannot be evaded because it is diametrically opposed to the classical analysis of consumer sovereignty, which is the keystone of the market economy.

We can now answer this question drawing on results of analysis of the needs structure described above. One can easily imagine a generic need that corresponds to each of the tendencies governing the life of individuals, these tendencies being necessarily limited in number. Such generic need is therefore related to human nature and hence not created by society or by marketing; it exists before demand, whether latent or expressed. Marketing however can exacerbate needs, even if they existed before. Nevertheless it is true that a great majority of our needs are cultural by origin. Hence there is a *dialectic of needs*, caused by the social and cultural environment and by technological development. Like all other social forces, marketing contributes to this dialectic.

According to Kotler (1997, p. 5) marketing tries to influence wants (or derived needs) and demands by making the product attractive, affordable and easily available.

Marketers, along with other influences in society, influence wants. They suggest to consumers that a Cadillac would satisfy a person's need for social status. Marketers do not create the need for social status but try to point out how a particular good would satisfy that need. (Kotler, 1997 p .4)

If we admit that marketing creates or, more precisely, participates in creation of at least some of derived needs, a much more serious problem arises: what social role – positive or negative – does marketing play in the modern society? This problem was and still is in the focus of interest of marketing theoreticians.

One of the extreme views was put forward by Attali and Guillaume (1974). They believe that producers exploit the dynamics of wants to find markets allowing them to preserve their economic power.

> If social demand, which dialectically results from needs, wants and social supply, is so restricted by the constraints of the productive system, shouldn't the political control of the production of needs logically precede that of production? (Attali and Guillaume, 1974, p. 146)

This viewpoint is obviously contrary to that of orthodox economists. Rosa (1977) notes that this analysis makes the implicit assumption that there are *real* needs and *'false'* needs and that the false needs are created by society and by the producer.

> In this school of thought, there is a fundamentally unequal exchange relationship between a dominated consumer and a dominant producer; society corrupts the individual by creating artificial wants in order to better subjugate and alienate him. The conclusion that follows is simple; it suffices to make the 'good' political choice to get 'good' structures which will necessarily develop the flourishing and expression of 'real' needs. (Rosa, 1977, p. 176)

This analysis, which was widespread among so-called 'left intellectuals' in Europe at one stage, has one important weakness, in that it never indicates how to distinguish true needs from false needs. Given that the vast majority of our present wants are indeed of a cultural origin, where should we draw the line, and especially who will be the enlightened dictator of consumption? Clearly it is very difficult to answer these questions objectively.

> to substitute the disputed sovereignty of the consumer for the questionable sovereignty of a bureaucrat or of an intellectual can only create more problems than it can ever hope to resolve. (Rosa, 1977, p. 159)

It should also be added that the hypothesis of consumer impotence is daily rejected by facts such as the figures available on the rates of failure of new products; more than one in two products fails to enter the market successfully. The discretionary power of the consumer is a reality and firms know it well. We must therefore recognise that the debate of 'true' versus 'false' needs is in the first place an ideological debate. Economists refuse to enter this debate because they know it cannot be reconciled with a scientific approach.

To conclude this overview of economists' and marketing theoreticians' points of view, let us bear in mind the following propositions:

1. The economist is not concerned with the problem of motivation. There are only wants and preferences. The real question, as far as he is concerned, is to know whether or not the consumer has *autonomy of action and decision* and whether his preferences have some stability or if on the contrary they are malleable (Rosa, 1977, p. 162).

2. The problem is not to know whether there are true or false needs, because it is impossible to establish the distinction objectively on the one hand, and economists refuse to make a judgement on the frivolity of choices on the other. They consider the *structure of preferences as given.*

3. It is true that a great majority of our needs are cultural by origin. Hence there is a *dialectic of needs*, caused by the social and cultural environment and by technological development. Like all other social forces, marketing contributes to this dialectic.

4. The relative nature of many needs means that the wish to acquire superior products has a particular life of its own. *There can therefore be no general saturation.* Saturation is alien to the nature of relative needs. Their objectives are almost unlimited. By satisfying them, they become activated rather than fulfilled.

5. *Technological progress* and the resulting constant renewal of products also lead to a hypothesis of impossibility of saturating generic needs, to the extent that innovations make it possible to meet these needs more and more effectively.

To be able to distinguish between necessary needs and superfluous needs, one ought to define what should be the organic and social life of individuals and know the structure of their motivation. We therefore need to turn to theories of human motivation in order to make some progress.

● Motivation of the Individual Customer

Economists, as we saw, make no distinction between what consumers choose and what suits them, and never consider the process of needs formation. What do individuals seek in their quest for well-being and how does this state of well-being come about? These two questions are never tackled by economic theory. Yet it is clear that a more thorough analysis of consumer behaviour and the structure of their motivation would make it easier to understand the links that both economists and marketing try to establish between supply and demand. Experimental psychology has made enlightening contributions in this field and helps us discover a whole range of general motivational orientations that determine various individual behaviours. This section is based on the works of Hebb (1955), Duffy (1957), Berlyne (1960), Scitovsky (1976) and Nuttin (1980).

The 'stimulus–response' theory

A central preoccupation of the theory of motivation has been to study why the organism moves into a state of activity. Motivation here becomes *energy mobilisation*. Originally, experimental psychology was mostly interested in needs and drives of a purely physiological nature, such as hunger, thirst, sex, and so on. In this scheme, called the *'stimulus–response theory'* (or S–R theory) the stimulus is considered as the active starting point of the organism's reaction. One then speaks of *homeostasis*, which is a mechanism whereby a disorder creates an urge giving rise to activity which restores equilibrium and thus removes the urge. In this framework, the organism is basically assumed to be reactive: in other words, it responds in specific ways to stimuli. This more or less repudiates the problem of motivation. Inactivity is supposedly the natural state of the individual.

We observe, however, that the human organism does not always react to the stimulus presented by its surroundings. Furthermore, it is a common occurrence to find individuals embarking on activities that disrupt equilibrium and setting up states of tension which would be hard to explain if one believed the S–R theory. This theory reduces the mechanism of motivation to a process of reducing tension and practically ignores *the ascending phase of motivation*, that is, the process by which new tensions or conflicts are worked out. However, this type of behaviour is frequently observed, especially in affluent societies, where basic needs are mostly met. A need, seen as a homeostatic need, cannot totally explain individual behaviour.

> More mysterious than the process of discharge is the process that can be called recharging; and more central than the reduction of tension is the act by which man seeks increased responsibilities, takes bigger risks and finds himself new challenges. (Nuttin, 1980, p .201)

Today, experimental psychology emphasises more and more the spontaneous activity of the nervous system and considers behavioural activity to be tied to the organism's being, just as much as physiological activity is.

The concept of arousal

Motivation theorists nowadays tend to explain behaviour in a new way, particularly because of the fact that neurophysiologists have considerably improved their knowledge of the way the brain functions and now have a completely different viewpoint. Hebb (1955, p. 246), for instance, formulates a hypothesis which is based, not on reactivity, but on the natural activity of the nervous system. Contrary to the beliefs held until then, the brain does not have to be excited from outside in order to be active and to discharge. It is not physiologically inert and its natural activity constitutes a system of self-motivation. Hebb, and also Duffy (1957, p. 267), put forth the idea that the general state of motivation can be equated with arousal, or the activity emanating from the reticular formation of the brain stem. Activity level depends on the degree of organic energy mobilised, that is on the variation in the level of arousal and vigilance. The level of arousal is measured by the variations in electric current controlled with an electroencephalogram (EEG); these variations show up as waves in the EEG; the faster the electric discharge of neurones, the higher the level of arousal and the higher the frequency of oscillations in the EEG, measured in periods per second.

Scitovsky (1976) underlines the importance of the concept of arousal in understanding the reasons for a given behaviour.

> A high arousal is associated with vigilance and quick response; it makes the senses more sensitive to stimuli, increases the brain's capacity to process information, readies the muscles for action, and so shortens the total reaction time that elapses between an incoming sensa-

tion and the response through action. It makes you feel excited, emotional, anxious and tense. On the other hand, when you feel slow, less than vigilant, lax and drowsy, you are in a state of low arousal. (Scitovsky, 1976, p. 19)

The increased level of arousal increases the organism's state of vigilance, thus providing favourable ground for the cerebral mechanism of stimulus–response to function rapidly and directly. The psychological measures of the level of arousal therefore provide a direct measure of the *motivational and emotional (drive) force* of a given situation for the individual (Duffy, 1957, p. 267). Also, this description of the concept of arousal suggests the existence of a continuum in the individual's level of activation.

Well-being and the optimal level of arousal

It is clear that the level of arousal has a great influence on the feeling of well-being or discomfort felt in general by people, and consequently bears on the determination of their behaviour. Excessive stimulation provokes tension, anxiety, nervousness, worry, frenzy, even panic; on the other hand stimulation which is too weak, or non-existent, brings about boredom, or a certain degree of displeasure, and creates the desire for a bigger stimulation. A job which is too simple or too monotonous can become painful if one is forced to pursue it without interruption over a long time. In fact, psychologists (Hebb, 1955, p. 250) accept that there is an *optimal level of arousal and stimulation*, optimal in the sense that it creates a feeling of comfort and well-being. Deviations below the optimum provoke a feeling of weariness, and deviations above the optimum provoke a sensation of fatigue and anxiety. Experimental observations show that, on the whole, individuals try to maintain an intermediary level of activation (Berlyne, 1960, p. 194).

We can identify here a first aspect of the general direction of motivation in individuals: *ensure comfort and prevent discomfort*. This motivation implies, on the one hand, the *reduction of tensions*, which satisfies various corporal and mental needs and reduces the level of arousal, which may be too high; on the other hand, it implies a *battle against boredom*, a behaviour which looks for stimulation and thus increases the level of arousal, which might be too low. These two types of behaviour have one thing in common; both try to fill up a gap and to *ensure a 'negative good'*, that is to stop pain, inconvenience and discomfort (Scitovskiy, 1976, p. 69).

For economists, the reduction of arousal and tension is particularly important because as far as they are concerned almost all human activity, including consumption, is based on this process. We find here the notion of need defined by economists as simply a state of deficiency. However, the other type of behaviour, that is the raising of a level of arousal which is too low, is ignored by economists. This is commonly observed in more affluent economies, where prosperity has largely eliminated discomfort due to tension, but where the search for stimulation, novelty and change is becoming ever more important.

The new consumer is also a dreamer. He buys a product, certainly to use it, but even more for the magic it offers him as premium. (Séguéla, 1982, p. 50)

In some situations, finding sufficient stimulation to combat boredom can be a matter of life or death. This is true for old people for example. It is also well known that longevity is strongly related to having been able to keep a satisfying job late in life.

The need for stimulation

Berlyne's work in this area is interesting, especially because it is based on solid experimental ground. Berlyne (1960) shows that novelty (meaning anything surprising, different from past events and from what one expected) attracts attention and has a stimulating effect.

> Novelty stimulates and pleases especially when it creates surprisingness, change, ambiguity, incongruity, blurredness and power to induce uncertainty. (Berlyne, 1960, p .290)

It is as if the incongruence of the new event produces a dynamic effect which sets in motion exploratory actions. It must, however, be made clear that the new and surprising is attractive only up to a limited degree, beyond which it becomes disturbing and frightening. Attractiveness first increases, then diminishes with the degree of newness and surprisingness. This relationship takes the shape of an inverted U-curve, known as *the Wundt curve* (Berlyne, 1960), shown in Figure 3.2. What is not new or surprising enough is boring, and what is too new is bewildering. An intermediate degree of newness seems to be the most pleasing.

The stimulation provoked by the collative properties of goods forms an important source of satisfaction for individuals. Much of the activity of marketers, such as new product policies, segmentation and positioning, communication and promotion, focuses on meeting this expectation. For better or for worse, goods act as stimuli over the nervous system, a little bit like toys for children. The intelligence of a child can become stagnant with lack of adequate toys. In the same manner, an adult deprived of all the stimuli, provided notably by the consumer society, can be overcome with boredom, depression and alienation.

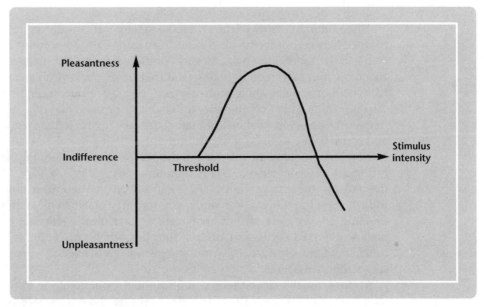

Figure 3.2　The Wundt curve

> Many people feel younger when they purchase a brand new car and associate the age of their car with that of their own body. Thus buying a new car takes on symbolic proportions by representing physical rejuvenation. (Valaskakis *et al.*, 1978, p. 167)

Therefore, the organism needs a continuous stream of stimuli and different experiences, just as it needs air and food. *Human beings need to need.* This basic motivation, as well as the more obvious motivation of reducing tensions, explains a large variety of individual behaviour which can only elude the deductions made by economists. The theory of 'novelty seeking' provides an explanation for consumers' actions, which introduce change, variety and novelty into their lifestyle.

The need for pleasure

The sensation of comfort or discomfort is related to the level of arousal and depends on the latter's situation with respect to the optimum. Experimental psychologists have now proven that pleasure exists as a phenomenon different from absence of suffering or presence of comfort. The sensation of pleasure begins with variations in the level of arousal, in particular when a level of arousal which is too low or too high is approaching its optimum (Berlyne, 1960, p. 187).

Two sources of pleasure can be identified: one results from the satisfaction of a need and the resulting reduction in tension; the other comes from the stimulation itself. *Satisfaction of a need* is pleasant in itself and drives the organism to pursue its activity to the point of satiation and even beyond.

> In very poor communities, families often plunge into debt for the sake of a funeral feast or a wedding celebration. Such behaviour horrifies economists of the not-so-poor countries... Yet the very universality of the custom of feasting among the poor people of so many different cultures is evidence that the pleasures of a good meal for those who seldom taste one are very great and weigh heavily against the biological needs of survival. (Scitovsky, 1976, p. 66)

The economic theory of the rational behaviour of consumers implies a judicious balance between different needs and does not take into account pleasure, which can lead the individual to an allocation different from that predicted by economic theory. It is in fact frequently observed that people behave so as to have full satisfaction from time to time, and they properly space out the moments or periods during which they completely fulfil their wants. This type of behaviour is frequently observed in industrialised countries, in the leisure sector for example, and in particular in holiday expenditure.

Note that the pleasure inherent in the satisfaction of a need implies that discomfort must precede pleasure. This common-sense rule is a very old one; it was debated by the ancient Greeks. Psychiatrists call it the *law of hedonic contrast*. It follows from the rule that too much comfort may preclude pleasure (a child who is nibbling all day long cannot appreciate a good meal). This fact can explain the malaise observed at times in affluent societies, when satisfaction of needs does not bring about any pleasure. By eliminating simple joys, excessive comfort forces us to seek strong sensations.

At this stage the second source of pleasure, the one resulting from the *stimulation itself*, comes into its own. Here the object of the need is not to make up for a shortage, but to contribute to the development of the individual. To quote Nuttin (1980), this is the *ascending phase of motivation*; a phase in which new tensions and discordance are established, giving individuals the *will to progress and surpass themselves*. This is Maslow's self-actualisation need. People take pleasure in excitement. They get more satisfaction out of the struggle of reaching an objective than they get when they actually reach it. Once individuals have passed the moment of triumph, they almost regret having reached their goal. Most people then give themselves an even more distant objective, probably because they prefer to act and fight rather than passively observe their success (Nuttin, 1980, p. 201). In this way, individuals force their environment to stimulate them or to continue to stimulate them.

The pleasure of this type of stimulation results from the temporary tension it creates. Such pleasure is more constant than the pleasure of comfort and outlasts it, because this stimulation leaves more room for imagination and creativity to the individual.

> the object of this stimulation is almost unlimited. By meeting them, tension goes up rather than down. Thus the tendency persists eyond the point where the objective is reached. (Nuttin, 1980, p. 202)

Here, we are now talking about *insatiable needs*. It is in the nature of *self-development* needs to know neither the saturation nor the periodicity of homeostatic needs.

> We see here what pleasure is and its relation to comfort: the former is the variation of the latter. If happiness is simply comfort, then it depends on the intensity of satisfied wants. Pleasure is complete when the want is a little or much more satisfied than it was. If happiness is not comfort but pleasure, then it is condemned to only live some privileged moments, prolonged with the help of memory. (Cotta, 1980, pp. 11–12)

From the psychologist's point of view, seeking pleasure is an important factor in human behaviour, and it is a fundamental motivational force which must be taken into account in any analysis of individual buying behaviour.

Determinants of the individual's well-being

An overview of the major contributions of experimental psychology to the study of human motivation finally arrives at a much wider understanding of the notion of need. We started from the point of view of economists, for whom need is essentially a 'state of shortage' revealed by the buying behaviour, without any explanation of the origin or the nature of motivations at the root of this state of deficiency. The absence of theory about motivations leads economists to make normative recommendations which have as much value as their starting assumptions, but which have little to do with actual observed behaviour.

Research by psychologists makes it possible to retain three general motivational directions, which can explain a large variety of behaviours and which appear to be factors that explain the individual's general well-being. These determinants can be regrouped as *comfort, pleasure and stimulation*. Figure 3.3 explains diagrammatically the relations between these three determinants on the one hand, and their relation to individual well-being on the other.

The *three motivational forces*, determining individual well-being, can be briefly described as follows:

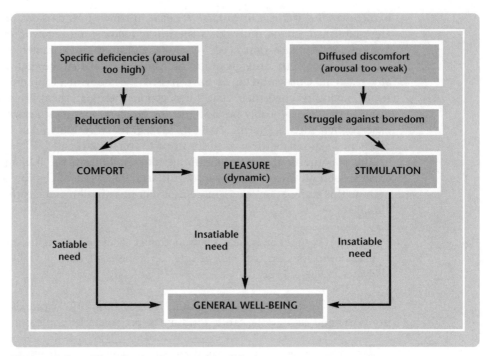

Figure 3.3   The determinants of well-being

● The search for *comfort*, which results from two kinds of behaviour: one that reduces tensions by satisfying homeostatic needs; and one that struggles against boredom with the help of stimuli such as novelty, change, incongruity, uncertainty, risk, and so on.

● The search for *pleasure*, which also results from two sources: pleasure inherent in the reduction of tensions and pleasure obtained from stimuli.

● The search for *stimulation*, not only as a means to combat boredom, but as a goal in itself, without any other objective in mind but the tension it arouses, generating pleasure and creating the opportunity of development and actualisation for the individual.

The search for comfort aims to make up for a deficiency and thus to ensure a *defensive good*; pleasure and stimulation aim to ensure a *creative good*.

By relying on this description of the major motivational forces we are in a better position to answer the questions facing marketing mentioned at the beginning of this chapter. The increased use of marketing – which takes the form of products being continually renewed, more and more subtle differentiation, sophisticated perceptual positioning, advertising suggesting elaborate lifestyles, and so on – in reality only responds to the rise in needs of pleasure and stimulation observed in richer societies, where basic needs are well met, but where, on the other hand, needs such as novelty, surprise, complexity and risk have become vital necessities.

The need to try varied experiences, to live different lifestyles, and the possibility to try new products and to have new sources of satisfaction form an important subject matter in this type of society. This search is endless, because there is no possible saturation in this type of need.

Some philosophers advocate rising above all wants in order to escape this endless escalation, which, far from bringing internal peace, causes worry and creates an infernal cycle. The wise Hindu Sarna Lakshman writes:

> Desire tells us: get this and then you will be happy. We believe it and we try to acquire the relevant object. If we don't get it, or if we don't get enough, we suffer. If we get it, then desire immediately suggests another objective, and we don't even see that we have been fooled. (quoted by Boirel, 1977)

These philosophers are advocating the *ideal of ataraxy*, that is the absence of turmoil as a result of the extinction of desire. The alternative to this extreme solution is *creative consumption*, that is, consumption that encourages ascending motivations of progress, self-actualisation and excellence. If it is true that 'man prefers hunting to the catch', as Pascal said, then want, as being the driving force of activity, can be the first cause of satisfaction brought about by creative consumption.

The Multidimensional Structure of Needs

The contributions of motivation theory help us to identify more general *motivational orientations* in human beings. These orientations govern a large variety of individual behaviour. These disciplinary contributions, however, provide only a general description of the needs structure, with little attempt at operationalisation and no explicit reference to buying behaviour. Moreover, they tend to focus on one dimension of behaviour (economic, social, psychological, and so on) and do not propose a comprehensive framework which integrates the concepts used in each contributing discipline. The question is to know *what are the values sought* by the buyer and how to translate these values in products and services adapted to the buyers' expectations. Several attempts have been made to develop a comprehensive list of the needs sought.

Typologies of human needs

Well-being means having a product or service to satisfy each need, so a natural approach is to develop a list of needs and to compare it with available goods. The word *'goods'* here has a special meaning. They are not only physical entities or services, but may be abstract, social or psychological entities, such as love, prestige, and so on. The seminal works of Murray (1938), Maslow (1943), Rokeach (1973) and Sheth *et al.* (1991) are representatives of this approach.

Murray's Inventory of Human Needs

Murray calls a need a hypothetical construct because it is of a physiochemical nature that is unknown. It resides in the brain and is thus in a position to control all significant behaviour. In Murray's words:

A need is a hypothetical construct that stands for a force in the brain region that organises and directs mind and body behaviour so as to maintain the organism in its most desirable state. (Murray, 1938, p. 123)

Murray gives a rather systematic inventory, classifying individuals' needs into four dimensions: *primary (viscerogenic) and secondary (psychogenic)* needs, according to whether they are of physiological origin or not; *positive and negative* needs, depending on whether the individual is attracted by the object or not; *manifest or latent* needs, according to whether the need drives to a real or imaginary behaviour; and *conscious or unconscious* needs, according to whether or not they drive the individual to take introspective steps. Murray lists 37 needs covering these categories.

Murray believes that all people possess the same needs, but he recognised that the expression of them will differ from one person to another because of differences in personality and in environmental factors. Needs could be provoked by either internal or external stimuli, and they could be weak or strong at any particular time. Needs exist in three different states: (1) refractory, in which no incentive will arouse it; (2) inducible, in which a need is inactive but susceptible to excitation; and (3) active, in which the need is determining the behaviour of the organism (Murray, 1938, pp. 85–6). Thus, marketing activities could have a direct impact on inducible needs.

Exhibit 3.1

Maslow's Hierarchy of Needs

PHYSIOLOGICAL NEEDS

These are fundamental; once satisfied, they cease to be determinant factors of motivation and no longer influence behaviour.

SAFETY NEEDS

Physical safety, preservation of the physical structure of the organism, psychological safety, conservation of the psychic structure of personality. Need for own identity, to feel in charge of one's destiny.

SOCIAL NEEDS

People are social animals and feel the need to fit into a group, to associate with their fellows, they feel the need to love and be loved. Mutual help, belonging and sense of community are also social needs.

SELF-ESTEEM NEEDS

Self-esteem, personal dignity, confidence in oneself and one's own competence. The feeling that one's objectives are valid. The esteem that others feel for us. The need for recognition, to be respected, to have a social status.

SELF-ACTUALISATION NEEDS

Those needs are at the top of the scale of human needs, and include self-realisation and development; the need of people to surpass themselves; to use all their capacities and push their limits; and to give a meaning to things and find their *raison d'être*.

Source: Maslow (1943).

Maslow's need hierarchy

Maslow (1943) adopts a similar approach, grouping fundamental needs into five categories: physiological, safety, social, esteem and self-actualisation needs. Exhibit 3.1 describes these needs. Maslow's analysis, however, goes further and is not limited to a simple classification. Maslow postulates the existence of a *hierarchy of needs*, which depends on the individual's state of development.

According to Maslow, there is an *order of priorities* in needs, in the sense that we begin to try to satisfy dominant needs before going on to the next category. Once the needs of a lower order have been satisfied, they allow needs of the higher order to become motivators and influence our behaviour. There is a progressive abatement in the intensity of needs already met and an increasing intensity of needs of a higher order not yet satisfied. As illustrated in Figure 3.4, we observe an evolution of the structure of needs depending on the individual's development as he or she goes from an overall objective of survival or living standard towards more qualitative objectives regarding lifestyle or quality of life.

Maslow's analysis is interesting because it puts forth not only the *multidimensional structure* of needs, but also the fact that needs have different degrees of intensity in different individuals. In reality, there is always some coexistence of these categories of needs, with one category or another becoming more important according to the individual, or according to the circumstances of one particular individual.

Products to be developed for satisfying needs must therefore be planned accordingly. A good or product may have more than one role or function beyond just the basic one. Individuals use goods not only for practical reasons, but also to communicate with their environment, to show who they are, to demonstrate their feelings, and so on. It is important for marketing to be aware of the role played by goods and brands, not simply for their functional value, but also for their emotional or symbolic values. We shall see later in this chapter that the multidimensional structure of needs also exists with the organisational customer.

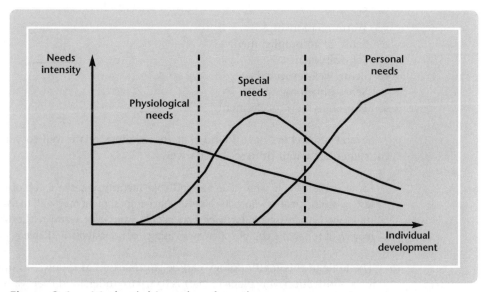

Figure 3.4   Maslow's hierarchy of needs

Rokeach's list of values

Human values research stresses the important goals which most people seek. Values are closely linked to human needs, but exist at a more realistic level. They are the *mental representations of underlying needs*, not only of individual needs but also of societal and institutional needs. In other words, values are our ideas about what is desirable.

> A value is an enduring belief that a specific mode of conduct or end-state of existence is personally or socially preferable to an opposite or converse mode of conduct or end-state of existence. A value-system is an enduring organisation of beliefs concerning preferable modes of conduct or end-states of existence along a continuum of relative importance. (Rokeach, 1973, p. 5)

There are two types of values: (1) terminal and (2) instrumental. Terminal (or end-state) values are beliefs we have about the goals or end-states for which we strive (for example happiness, wisdom, and so on). Instrumental (or means) values refer to beliefs about desirable ways of behaving to help us attain the terminal values (for example, behaving honestly or accepting responsibility).

Since values are transmitted through cultures, most people in a given society will possess the same values, but to different degrees. The relative importance of each value will therefore be different from one individual to another and these differences can be used as market segmentation criteria, as shown in Chapter 6 of this book. The prominence of different values can also change over time. Rokeach postulates that the total number of values that a person possesses is relatively small. In his empirical work, Rokeach identifies eighteen terminal and instrumental values (Rokeach, 1973, p. 28).

In recent years, researchers have been working to develop a shortlist of values that can be measured in a reliable manner. Kahle (1983) has identified eight summary terminal values:

- Self-respect
- Security
- Warm relationships
- Sense of accomplishment
- Self-fulfilment
- Being well-respected
- Sense of belonging
- Fun/enjoyment/excitement

Several researchers have found that these values relate well to various aspects of consumer behaviour or to social change.

> For example, people who value fun and enjoyment may desire a cup of coffee for its rich taste, whereas people who value a sense of accomplishment may wish to use coffee as a mild stimulant to increase productivity; and people who value warm relationships with others may want to share a cup of coffee as an aspect of a social ritual. (Kahle *et al.*, 1988)

The logic of this methodology can be summarised as follows: to understand individuals' motivation, one place to start is to try to understand their values, particularly with products that involve consumer value. Also, an understanding of the way values are changing in a given society will facilitate the development of effective strategies for dealing with the dynamics of societal change.

The means–end chain model

The work of Maslow (1943) and Rokeach (1973) have shown values to be a powerful force in governing the behaviour of individuals in all aspects of their lives. Their use in marketing research is interesting, both from an analytical and predictive point of view, to relate consumers' behaviour to their values. Such is the objective of the means–end chain (MEC) concept developed by Gutman (1982) and by Reynolds and Gutman (1988).

> For example, knowing that consumers want to look well dressed doesn't tell us much about their values level consideration, unless we know why they want to look that way, that is their 'desired end-state'. Is it a purely functional objective, a desire to seduce a partner, the search for novelty and stimulation, a concern for integration in a social or professional group, or simply a personal accomplishment objective?

The MEC model attempts to explain how consumers select products that will be instrumental in helping them achieve their desired consequences, which in turn move consumers towards their valued end-states. The *means* are the purchased products or services, while the *ends* are the desired terminal values proposed by Rokeach and viewed as desirable end-states of existence sought by individuals through their consumption behaviour. As illustrated by Figure 3.5, a conceptual representation of the chain which is divided into three parts: (a) the product attributes (tangibles and intangibles); (b) the consequences (physiological or psycho-sociological) resulting from the consumption behaviour accruing directly or indirectly to the consumer, and (c) the terminal or instrumental values.

For uncovering means and ends hierarchies as described above, Reynolds and Gutman (1988) have developed an in-depth interviewing and analysis methodology, called the *laddering technique*, which involves a tailored individual interviewing format with the goal of determining the links between the key perceptual elements across the range of attributes, consequences and values. Interpretation of this type information permits an understanding of consumers' underlying personal motivation with respect to a given product class. This is more the field of qualitative or in-depth research. To go further on this topic, see Reynolds and Gutman (1988), Valette-Florence (1994) and Pellemans (1998).

The Sheth–Newman–Gross theory of consumption values

Applying the concept of 'value' to buying behaviour, Sheth, Newman and Gross (1991, pp. 18–25) describe market choice as a multidimensional phenomenon involving multiples values: functional, social, emotional, epistemic and conditional. They define these values as follows:

● *Functional Value*. The perceived utility acquired by an alternative as the result of its ability to perform its functional, utilitarian or physical purposes. Alternatives

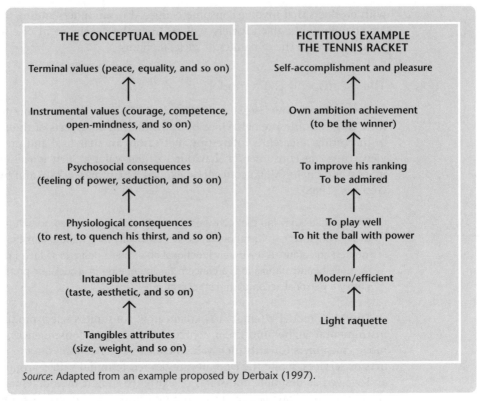

Source: Adapted from an example proposed by Derbaix (1997).

Figure 3.5   The means–end chain model

acquire functional value through the possession of salient functional, utilitarian or physical attributes.

- *Social Value*. The perceived utility acquired by an alternative as a result of its association with one or more social groups. Alternatives acquire social value through association with positively or negatively stereotyped demographic, socio-economic and cultural ethnic groups.

- *Emotional Value*. The perceived utility acquired by an alternative as a result of its ability to arouse feelings or affective states. Alternatives acquire emotional value when associated with specific feelings or when they facilitate or perpetuate feelings.

- *Epistemic Value*. The perceived utility acquired by an alternative as a result of its ability to arouse curiosity, provide novelty and/or satisfy a desire for knowledge. Alternatives acquire epistemic value through the capacity to provide something new or different.

- *Conditional Value*. The perceived utility acquired by an alternative as a result of the specific situation or the context faced by the choice-maker. Alternatives acquire conditional value in the presence of antecedent physical or social contingencies that enhance their functional or social value, but do not otherwise possess this value.

These five values make *differential contributions* to specific market choices in the sense that some values can contribute more than others. Those values are also *independent*. They relate additively and contribute incrementally to choice. Although it is desirable to maximise all five values, users are often willing to accept less of one value to obtain more of another. That is why buyers are willing to trade off less salient values in order to maximise those that are most salient (Sheth *et al.*, 1991, p. 12).

Considerable overlaps are observed, when comparing these summary values with the different need categories proposed by diverse disciplines. The functional value corresponds to the general motivation for comfort in Murray's viscerogenic needs and in Maslow's safety and physiological needs. The social and emotional functions correspond with Maslow's social needs of belongingness and love, with Rokeach's values of 'social recognition' and 'true friendship' and with the more general motivation for stimulation. The epistemic value is similar to Maslow's need for 'self-actualisation', to Rokeach's values 'exciting life' and 'pleasure' and also to the general need for stimulation and pleasure. Previous contributions did not include the conditional value construct, which is particularly well adapted to the situation of buying behaviour. In addition, Sheth *et al.* (1991; see Chapter 5) have operationalised their theory by developing a generic questionnaire and a standardised procedure for adapting the analysis to any specific market situation.

The *'value' approach* provides the market analyst with a simple but comprehensive framework for analysing the need structure of the individual buyer and for segmenting markets. The five summary values proposed by Sheth–Newman–Gross theory will be used in the following section to define the concept of the multi-attribute product.

The product as a package of benefits

We have seen that, from a buyer's point of view, a product or a brand can be defined as a *'bundle of attributes'* which provides the buyer with the functional value or 'core service' specific to that class of product, as well as a set of secondary values or utilities which may be necessary or added (see Figure 3.6). These additional services differentiate the brands and may have a determining influence on buyers' preferences. Here, we will first discuss the different elements of this bundle and then conclude with a formal model of this notion.

The core service

The core service provided by a brand corresponds to *the functional value of its class of product*; it is the basic and generic benefit provided by each of the brands in a given product category.

> For a compressor, the core service is the production of compressed air; for a toothpaste, dental hygiene; for a watch, it will be time measurement; for an airline company, the transportation from Paris to New York; for wallpaper, home decoration, and so on.

As underlined earlier, the core service defines the reference market in generic terms by providing an answer to the question: *'What business are we in?'* The rationale is the following:

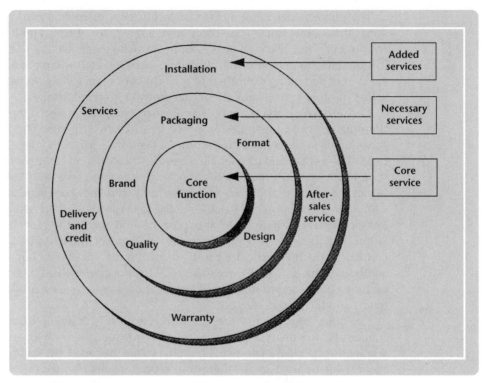

Figure 3.6   The product as a package of benefits

- The buyer is not looking for a product as such, but for the core service it provides.
- The buyer can get the same core service from technologically different products.
- Technologies are moving and changing rapidly and profoundly, whereas the needs to which the core service responds, remain stable.

Levitt (1980) states that in order to avoid the risk of myopia, it is in the firm's best interest to define its *reference market* with respect to the core service provided, rather than to a particular technology. This allows the consumer to identify the alternative solutions likely to be considered when they are confronted with a choice problem.

All brands in the same reference market provide the buyer with the same core service in a way that tends to become uniform, given that competition and the diffusion of technological progress balance out technological performance. Consequently, in a significant number of markets, the core service by itself is no longer a determining factor in the buyer's decisions. The way in which the core service is provided or delivered becomes more of a deciding factor.

The peripheral services

In addition to the basic functional utility, a brand provides a series of other *utilities or peripheral services*, which are secondary compared to the core service, but which may prove to be decisive when competing brands tend to have even performances. These peripheral services may be of two kinds: 'necessary' services and 'added' services.

Necessary services identify with the mode of production of the core service (fuel efficiency, roominess, noise, and so on) and all that normally accompanies the core service (packaging, delivery, payment terms, after-sales service and so on).

For example, Atlas-Copco 'oil-free' compressors produce compressed air which is totally free of oil particles; Epson printers are particularly quiet; Japanese cars are well-known for their reliability; Apple microcomputers are very user-friendly; Bang and Olufsen products have an outstanding design; Swatch has a large variety of designs, and so on.

Added services are utilities unrelated to the core service, which the brand provides as extras. Hence they constitute an important source of differentiation.

For instance, Singapore Airlines offers a frequent flyers programme 'Privileged Passenger Service' (PPS) that is especially attractive; some makes of cars include radio equipment in their basic price; some credit cards give the right to preferential conditions in five star hotels; and so on.

These peripheral services themselves, whether necessary or added, form attributes which *generate satisfaction for the buyer*. These attributes may differ greatly according to the brand and can thus be used as choice criteria. Furthermore, one can imagine that different buyers attach different degrees of importance to the presence of some attributes. Thus, a brand can be defined as a bundle of attributes which produces the core service plus the peripheral services, necessary or added, whose importance and performance can be differently perceived by potential buyers (see Exhibit 3.2).

Note that any brand has at least one unique feature (generally more than one), which is simply its brand name. The buyer's global perception of a brand is commonly referred to as *the brand image*.

The Individual Customer's Purchase Behaviour

From the marketing point of view, buying behaviour covers all activity preceding, accompanying and following purchase decisions. The individual or the organisation actively takes part in the decisions in order to make choices in a systematic way, as opposed to random or stochastic selections. The purchasing behaviour is seen as a *process of problem solving*.

A rational approach to problem solving

All possible steps that may have something to do with the resolution of the problem are therefore part of the buying process. They can be grouped into five stages:

- Problem recognition
- Information search
- Evaluation of alternatives
- Purchase decision
- Post-purchase behaviour

Exhibit 3.2

Levitt's Concept of a Product

Levitt establishes a distinction between the generic, the expected, the augmented and the potential product. A distinction very close to the concept of bundle of attributes.

The *generic product*, or the main benefit provided by a product; its core service or basic functional value.

The *expected product* represents the customer's minimal expectations which normally comes with the generic product (delivery modes, invoicing terms, service, image).

The *augmented product* includes what is offered in addition to what the customer thinks he needs or has become accustomed to expect.

The *potential product* consists of everything potentially feasible to attract and hold customers. It refers to what may remain to be done.

Source: Levitt (1980).

This view of an active buyer is in total contrast with that of the passive buyer who is dominated by the unconscious and is defenceless against the selling activities of the firm and advertisers. The complexity of the decision process varies, however, with the type of buying decisions and with the risk implied by the choice.

In this framework, purchasing behaviour is neither erratic nor conditioned by the environment. It is rational in the sense of *the principle of limited rationality*, which means within the bounds of individuals' cognitive and learning capacities. The implicit assumptions are:

● Consumers make choices after *deliberation*, the extent of which depends on the importance of the perceived risk.
● Choices are based on *anticipation of future data* and not only on short-term observations.
● Choices are also guided by the *principle of generalised scarcity* according to which any human acts. Any decision has an opportunity cost.

We live in an environment where everything is scarce: not only money and goods, but also information and especially time, our scarcest resource because it is perfectly inextensible (Becker, 1965).

This approach is called a *'rational approach to problem solving'*. The use of the term 'rational' is not in contrast with the term 'emotional', which implies a value judgement on the quality of the choice. The steps undertaken are considered to be rational as long as they are *'consistent'* with the set objectives, whatever these objectives may be.

For example, an individual, for whom the social value or status effect is important, is prepared to pay more for a product with the same quality. Such action is considered to be rational because the behaviour is consistent.

In other words, as long as information about the objective is sought, critically analysed and processed, behaviour is rational within the limits of the gathered information and the cognitive capability of the individual. This, however, does not exclude the existence of another 'better' choice.

We are using here the notion of 'consistency' which is so dear to economists, with a fundamental difference. The consumer is *consistent with respect to his or her own set of axioms*, and not with respect to a set of axioms defined with no reference to a specific situational context or preferences structure. Rational behaviour does not exclude *impulsive behaviour*. As long as the latter is adopted deliberately, either for the simple pleasure of acting impulsively, or for the excitement of being confronted with unexpected consequences, the behaviour is said to be rational.

Rationality here implies no more than the adoption of a kind of systematic choice procedure. This could be defined as the coherent use of a set of principles forming the basis of choice. When choice is made at random, behaviour is unpredictable and erratic, and analysis is impossible. Marketing accepts the existence of the latter type of behaviour, but believes that it is not representative of actual behaviour observed in most real-life situations.

This concept of consistency of behaviour makes it possible to reconcile different disciplinary approaches (economic, psychological, sociological) in the study of buying behaviour. *Marketing is interested in the real person*, the individual with all his or her diversity, as illustrated by the list of values described in the previous chapter. Actual choices are influenced by several values, but the individual or the organisation may very well accept a sub-optimal level of functional value, for example, in order to maximise social or epistemic value. This type of choice will be termed 'rational' because it is consistent with the personal set of values prevailing in the specific choice situation (conditional value).

Importance of the perceived risk

Not every purchase decision requires a systematic information search. The complexity of the approach to problem solving depends on the importance of the *perceived risk* associated with the purchase, in other words, on the uncertainty about the scope of the consequences of a particular choice. There are six kinds of risk or unfavourable consequences normally perceived by the buyer (Jacoby and Kaplan, 1972):

- A *functional risk,* if the product characteristics or attributes are not in conformance with prior expectations.

- A *financial loss*, when the product is faulty and needs replacement or repair at one's own expense.

- A *loss of time*, due to hours of making complaints, returning to distributors, repairs, and so on.

- A *physical risk*, due to the consumption or use of products potentially harmful to one's health or the environment.

- A *social risk,* if the brand purchased conveys a social image which does not correspond to the true personality of the customer.

- A *psychological risk*, when a bad purchase leads to loss of self-esteem or creates general dissatisfaction.

Market research shows that buyers develop strategies and ways of reducing risk that enable them to act with relative confidence and ease in situations where their information is inadequate and the consequences of their actions are incalculable (Bauer, 1960, p. 120).

To reduce the perceived risk before the purchase decision, the buyer can use various forms of information, such as personal sources (family, neighbours, friends), commercial sources (advertising, salespersons, catalogues), public sources (comparative tests, official publications) and experimental sources (product trials, inspection). The higher the perceived risk, the more extensive the information search will be.

The customer's involvement

In recent years, the concept of *consumer involvement* has received considerable attention in the marketing literature. Involvement can be defined as:

> a state of energy (arousal) that a person experiences in regard to a consumption-related activity. (Wilkie, 1994, p. 164)

Thus involvement implies attention to something because it is somehow relevant or perceived as risky. High involvement requires high levels of prior deliberation and strong feelings, while low involvement will occur when consumers invest less energy in their thoughts and feelings. The concept of involvement, which overlaps somewhat with Howard and Sheth's classification of problem-solving situations above, is useful for analysing consumer behaviour at different levels of involvement and for deciding on the type of communication strategy to adopt in each situation.

The three roles of the customer

Any marketplace transaction requires at least three customer roles: (1) buying (that is selecting) a product or service; (2) paying for it, and (3) using or consuming it. Thus, a customer can be a buyer, a payer or a user/consumer (Sheth *et al.*, 1999):

- The *user* is the person who actually consumes or uses the product or receives the benefits of the service.
- The *payer* is the person who finances the purchase.
- Finally, the *buyer* is the person who participates in the procurement of the product from the marketplace.

Each of these roles may be carried out by the same person (for example the housewife) or an organisational unit (for example the purchase department) or by different persons or departments. As underlined by Sheth *et al.* (1999, p. 6),

> The person who pays for the product or service is not always the one who is going to use it. Nor is the person who uses it always the person who purchases it. Any of the three customer roles (user, payer or buyer) makes a person a customer.

It is therefore important in any market situation to know the possible ways in which customers divide their roles among themselves in order to adapt the marketing efforts to the type of role specialisation. Four types of role specialisation can be identified.

User is buyer and payer

Most consumer products purchased for personal use fall into this category, like clothing, watches, sporting goods, haircuts, and so on. A single person combines all three roles. This is the traditional domain of consumer analysis, even if the same concentration of roles can also be observed in business markets for small business owners.

User is neither payer nor buyer

Here the user is different from both the payer and the buyer, a situation met in consumer markets for a whole range of products purchased by the housewife for her household or children's use. Similarly, in business-to-business markets, the purchasing department is buying and paying for many products like office furniture and equipment, consumable products for employees who are using the goods, while not associated in the buying decision. As we shall see in the next section, in business-to-business markets, for high perceived risks buying decisions, the purchasing process is more complex and the role specialisation less clearly defined.

User is buyer but not payer

In some situations, the user may be the buyer but not the payer for the product or service. All purchasing decisions made on expense accounts fall into this category. Also, the services offered within the framework of insurance coverage or social security programmes are not paid by the user who is nevertheless the buyer. For example, in many companies, a large variety of health plans are offered from which employees choose. Although the employee will be the buyer and the user, he is not paying. The risk of over-consumption is often observed in this type of situations.

User is payer but not buyer

In some cases, the user is payer but not the buyer. For example, in business-to-business markets, an external agent may be retained to purchase equipment, raw materials or supplies for a company which uses and pays for them. In the financial markets, stockbrokers act as agents for clients.

When a single customer embodies all the roles, the firm will use a different strategy than when different people are user, payer and buyer.

The different problem-solving approaches

Three types of approach to problem solving can be distinguished, routine response behaviour, and limited and extensive problem-solving behaviours (Howard and Sheth, 1969):

- *Extensive problem solving* is adopted when the value of information and/or the perceived risk are high. For example, this happens in situations where the buyer is confronted with an unfamiliar brand in an unfamiliar product class. The choice criteria by which alternatives are assessed will be weak or non-existent and an intensive information search will be necessary to identify the relevant criteria.

● *Limited problem solving* applies to the situation of a buyer confronted with a new, unfamiliar brand in a familiar product class, usually where existing brands do not provide an adequate level of satisfaction. Choice criteria already exist, but there will still be a certain amount of search and evaluation prior to purchase.

● Finally, *routine response behaviour* is observed in the case where the consumer has accumulated enough experience and knowledge and has definite preferences about one or more familiar brands within a familiar product category. Here the process of choice is simplified and repetitive, with little or no prior information search. Under this situation of low involvement, considerable consumer inertia and/or brand loyalty would be expected.

Note that routine response behaviour is also observed for low-cost, frequently purchased items, be they familiar to the buyer or not. For this product category, the best information comes from buying the product, because the cost of experimenting is low. If there is dissatisfaction, the consumer will simply not rebuy the brand at the next purchase occasion. Given the low cost of error, there is no need to search diligently for information. The fields of consumer behaviour analysis are summarised in Figure 3.7.

The cost of information

An individual facing a problem of choice, undertakes the search for information mainly to reduce uncertainty about available alternatives, their relative values and the terms and conditions of purchase. We can classify the various costs incurred by this information search into three categories:

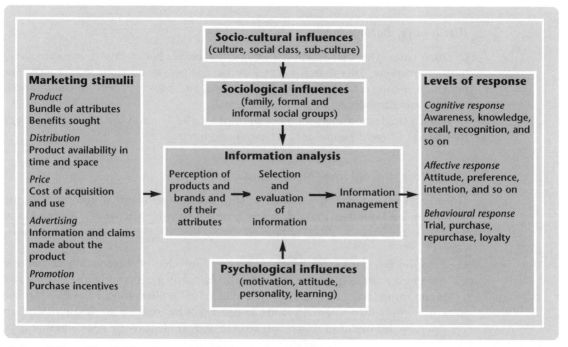

Figure 3.7   The fields of customer behaviour analysis

- *Inspection costs*, implied by studying different markets and defining the range of possibilities (including substitutes) that the buyer could include in the set being contemplated.

- *Perception costs*, borne in view of identifying the relevant characteristics of goods included in the choice set, as well as the terms of exchange (places of purchase, price, guarantee, and so on).

- *Evaluation costs*, resulting from the evaluation of how much the sought attributes are present and how authentic the market signals are about the quality of goods.

These costs are mainly in the form of time spent. But the cost of time – measured by its opportunity cost – varies from individual to individual; it also varies with factors of circumstance. For example, the cost of time is not the same during holidays as it is during a period of work. Therefore, it is not always in the consumer's interest to prolong the information search beyond a certain level. The extent of searching efforts will also vary with the degree of perceived risk in the buying decision under consideration.

The sources of information

The cost of perceiving attributes varies with the observable nature of products attributes and benefits. Nelson (1970, p. 214) establishes a distinction between *search goods* (having observable external qualities), *experience goods* (having verifiable internal qualities) and *credence goods* (having unverifiable internal qualities). For the first category of goods, the product attributes can easily be checked before purchase by simple inspection; these are products like clothing, furniture and toys for which the choice criteria can easily be verified with little cost. For experience goods, however, the most important characteristics are only revealed with use, after purchase. Examples of this type of products are books, medicines, cars and computers. For this type of product, perception costs can be very high for a single individual, and even higher for credence goods (like professional services). But the efficiency of surveying can be improved by using different sources of information, which have various degrees of reliability:

- Information sources *dominated by the producer*, in other words advertising, opinions and advice given by sellers and distributors, displays and brochures. The advantage of this kind of information is that it is free and easily accessible. The information is, however, incomplete and biased, in the sense that it emphasises the positive qualities of the product and tends to overshadow others.

- Personal information sources, *dominated by consumers*; this is information communicated by friends, neighbours, opinion leaders or what is better known as 'word of mouth'. This kind of information is often well adapted to the needs of the future buyer. Its reliability obviously depends on that of the person transmitting the information.

- Information sources which are *neutral*, such as articles published in newspapers and reviews specialising in housing, furnishing, hunting, audio-visual products and automobiles. Such publications often provide a lot of information at a relatively low cost. This category also includes publications such as official reports or reports of specialised agencies, laboratory tests and comparative tests initiated by consumer associations. The advantage of this source of information is its objectivity, its factual nature and the competence of the opinions reported.

It is worth underlining here the specific role played by *consumer associations*. In a situation where the perception of the attributes of a product is particularly costly, it is in the interest of the individual consumer to regroup with other consumers in order to proceed with a thorough analysis which would be impossible for an individual alone. This is a form of unionisation of consumers, which constitutes a countervailing force *vis-à-vis* the firm, and has the reduction of the cost of information to the consumer as its main objective.

The value of advertising information

The amount of information contained in advertising is an important societal issue and advertising's informational function lends some legitimacy to advertising in a market economy. The information categories or 'cues' present in advertisements are listed in Table 3.1.

Table 3.1 Advertising information content categories

1. Price: What does the product cost? What is the value retention capability?	8. Nutrition: Are specific data given concerning the nutritional content of the product or is a direct comparison made with other products?
2. Quality: What are the product's characteristics that distinguish it from competing products?	9. Packaging: What package is the product available in which makes it more desirable than alternatives?
3. Performance: What does the product do and how well does it do what it is designed to do in comparison to alternative purchases?	10. Warranties: What post-purchase assurances accompany the product?
4. Components: What does the product comprise? What ingredients does it contain?	11. Safety: What safety features are available on a particular product compared to alternatives?
5. Availability: Where can the product be purchased? When will the product be available for purchase?	12. Independent research: Are results of research gathered by an independent research firm presented?
6. Special offers: What limited-time non-price deals are available with a particular purchase?	13. Company research: Are data gathered by a company to compare its product with a competitor's presented?
7. Taste: Is evidence presented that taste is perceived as superior by a sample of potential customers?	14. New ideas: Is a totally new concept introduced during the commercial? Are its advantages presented?

Source: Adapted from Resnik and Stern (1977).

In a meta-analysis conducted by Abernethy and Frank (1996) across 118 data sets (for a total of 91,438 ads), the mean number of cues was 2.04. More than 84 per cent of the ads had at least one cue, 58 per cent had two or more cues and 33 per cent had three or more cues. The type of information most commonly presented is performance, which appeared in 43 per cent of the ads studied. Other common types of information are availability (37 per cent), components (33 per cent), price (25 per cent), quality (19 per cent) and special offers (13 per cent). It is interesting to note that ads from developed and developing countries had relatively similar number of cues: on average, 2.08 and 1.92 respectively.

Given that advertising information is an information source dominated by the producer, it does not have the same value as other sources of information in the eyes of the consumer. It is indeed a *sales appeal*, which generates information designed to emphasise the positive aspects of the product. However, as far as the consumer is concerned, the utility of this type of information is twofold:

- on the one hand, the consumer can *get to know the distinctive qualities claimed* by the producer and to see whether what the product 'promises' corresponds to what the consumer is seeking;

- on the other hand, it helps him *save personal time*, since the information reaches him or her without the consumer having to collect it.

Lepage (1982, p. 53), underlines the fact that the important point for the consumers is that the efficiency of the advertising message intended to reach them should be higher than it would have cost them to collect the same information by other means, for example by displacing themselves. These two services performed by advertising have the effect of helping the consumer to perceive opportunities of choice and of new potential forms of satisfaction at a minimum cost (Kirzner, 1973).

Motivation of the Business-to-business Customer

So far, our analysis has concerned only the needs and motivations of the individual as a customer. But a large part of commercial activity, in any economy, is made up of transactions between organisations, or business-to-business. This includes firms selling equipment, goods, intermediary products, raw materials, and so on to other firms using these products in their own manufacturing process. Although the principles governing marketing are just as pertinent for firms selling industrial goods as for firms selling consumer goods, the concrete manner in which these principles are implemented may appear very different.

Specificities of business-to-business markets

The main differences between consumer and business-to-business marketing can be regrouped into three categories according to whether they relate to demand, to the profile of the organisational customer and to the characteristics of the industrial products or services.

The demand for industrial goods

The industrial or organisational demand is a *derived demand*, that is, a demand expressed by an organisation which uses the products purchased in its own manufacturing process, in order to meet either the demand of other organisations or the demand of the end-user. Thus, industrial demand is part of a chain – *a supply chain* – which depends on a downstream demand and is ultimately 'derived' from the demand of consumer goods. Industrial demand, and particularly capital equipment demand, is *highly fluctuating* and reacts strongly to small variations in final demand (the acceleration principle). Industrial demand is often *price inelastic*, in so far as the product represents a small fraction of its costs or constitutes a key component, perhaps made to exact specifications, which has no substitute.

The organisational customer

The industrial firm faces *multiple customers:* its direct customers and the customers of its direct customers also participating in the supply chain. At each level of the supply chain, the organisational customer has a *collegiate structure*: a group of individuals, the buying centre, who exercise different functions and roles and have distinct competencies and motivations. The organisational customer is a *professional buyer,* technically competent; the purchase decision involves a degree of normalisation not found in consumer purchasing. Thus, the problem-solving approach in business-to-business markets is in general extensive.

Product characteristics

The products sought are generally *well defined* by the customer who knows what is wanted; specifications are clearly defined and the supplier has little room for manoeuvring. Industrial products enter into the manufacturing process of the industrial customer and thus have a *strategic, if not vital, importance*. Industrial products often have a very *large number of different uses*, unlike consumer goods which are almost inevitably for a specific use.

The structure of the industrial supply chain

The demand for an industrial good is even more specially complex to analyse because thewhen a product is at the start of the transformation chain, far from the final demand on which it nevertheless depends. Thus it faces many echelons of successive demand, each with differentiated needs structures.

The notion of an *industrial chain* goes beyond a list of names by branch or by sector and makes the conventional division of the economy into primary, secondary and tertiary sectors out of date. An industrial chain consists of all the stages of production, from raw materials to satisfying the final need of the consumer, irrespective of whether this final need concerns a product or a service. There is a hierarchy of industries which are either clients or suppliers of a given firm according to whether they are upstream or downstream. The strategic force of an industrial client depends, among other things, on his ability to anticipate and control the end market of the chain in which it participates.

The following list describes the structure of a typical industrial demand (see Figure 3.8). Clearly the chain of demands may be much longer and more complex in some cases. Without claiming this to be an exhaustive list, the following distinctions can be established:

- *First transformation*. Demand is for processed materials that are transformed into semi-finished goods, for instance, steel bars, sheets, chemicals, leather, and so on.

- *Final transformation*. Demand is for primary products which will be transformed into more elaborate processed products. For example, transformation of raw sheet metal into rust-proof sheet metal, either plated or pre-painted. Bekaert transforms raw steel into wires of different diameters.

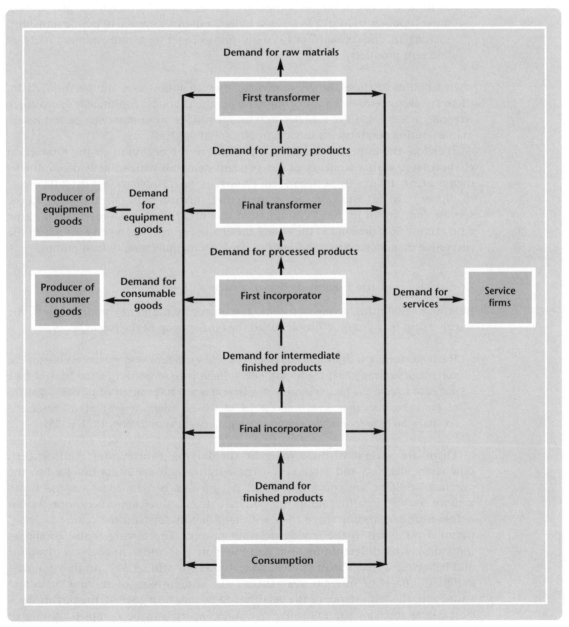

Figure 3.8   Typical structure of an industrial supply chain

● *First incorporation*. Demand is for finished goods used to manufacture more complex products which are themselves components of other products. For example, pre-painted sheet metal is used to manufacture radiators; wires are used to manufacture radial tyres.

● *Final incorporation*. Demand is for finished products incorporated in manufacturing finished products for final demand, for example, tyres and batteries, spark plugs, TV tubes, automobile windscreens, and so on.

● *Assemblers*. Demand is for a large variety of products which will be put together to form systems or large compounds. For example, radiators are placed with other products to form a heating system. Similarly, a system of public transport, such as an underground rail system, brings together a tremendous variety of different products.

In addition to these successive demands which follow one another in a chain, there are also lateral demands of capital equipment goods, consumable items (fuel, wrapping materials, office supplies, and so on) and services (maintenance and repair, manufacturing and business services, professional services).

Therefore the industrial firm in the position of the beginning of the production chain is faced with a sequence of independent demands which finally determine its own demand. It faces two categories of clients: its *direct customers and the customers of its customers*. In order to apply active marketing, the firm must take into account the specific demands of its direct customers, of the intermediary customers and of those who express final demand at the end of the chain. Figure 3.9 gives an example of the successive customers, direct and indirect, facing a manufacturer of heat pumps.

Composition of the buying decision centre

In an industrial firm, buying decisions, and especially the more important ones, are mostly taken by a group of people called the *buying group* or the *buying centre*.

> The buying centre is defined as consisting of those individuals who interact for the specific purpose of accomplishing the buying task... These persons interact on the basis of their particular roles in the buying process. The buying group is characterised by both a pattern of communication (interaction) and a set of shared values (norms) which direct and constrain the behaviour of the individual within it. (Webster and Wind, 1972, p. 35)

There are several distinct roles in the buying centre: users, influencers, purchasers, deciders and gatekeepers. These individuals are either involved in the purchase itself or are concerned about its possible consequences on the firm's activity, and thus participate in the purchase decision-making process one way or another. Understanding those roles will help one understand the nature of interpersonal influence in the buying decision process. The buying centre comprises individuals with different functions and therefore with different goals, motivations and behaviours. Hence many purchase decisions are conflicting, and they follow a complex process of internal negotiation. The composition of the buying centre varies with the importance of the decisions to be made. In general, the buying decision centre includes the following five roles, which can be occupied by one or several individuals:

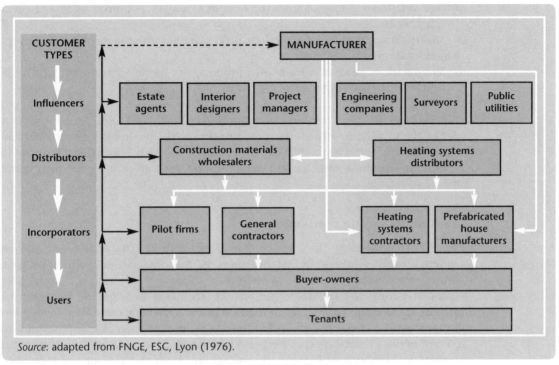

Figure 3.9   Vertical structure of the domestic heat pump market

Source: adapted from FNGE, ESC, Lyon (1976).

⬤ *Purchasers* have formal authority and responsibility for selecting alternative brands and suppliers and for determining the terms of purchase and negotiating contracts. This is usually done by the purchasing manager.

⬤ *Users* are the persons who use the product: the production engineer or the workers. The users can formulate specific purchase requirements or refuse to work with some materials. Generally speaking, users are better placed for evaluating the performance of purchased goods and services.

⬤ *Influencers* do not necessarily have buying authority but can influence the outcome of a decision by defining criteria which constrain the choices that can be considered. R&D personnel, design, engineering and consultants, and so on typically belong to this category.

⬤ *Deciders* have formal authority and responsibility to determine the final selection of brands or vendors. There is generally an upper limit on the financial commitment that they can make, reserving larger decisions for other members of the organisation, for instance the board of directors.

⬤ *Gatekeepers* are group members who control the flow of information into the group and who can exercise indirect influence on the buying process.

The composition of the buying centre will vary with the complexity and the degree of uncertainty of decisions in the firm. One can distinguish three kinds of situation:

● *New task*: the purchase of a new product in a new class of products for the client organisation.
● *Modified rebuy*: problem and product are known, but some elements of the buyers' specifications are modified.
● *Straight rebuy*: purchase of a known product, not modified and with which the firm has extensive experience.

In the first two cases the buying centre intervenes totally. One can see that it is vital for the supplier to identify all those involved in the purchasing process, because it must identify the targets of its communication policy. It is equally important to understand how these participants interact among themselves and what their dominant motivation is.

Needs of the buying decision centre

The industrial customer is therefore identified with the 'buying centre' which comprises persons from different functions in the organisation, who thus have distinct personal and organisational motivations. The notion of need in industry goes beyond the conventional idea of rational choice based only on the quality–price criterion. Choices are rational, as in the case of the individual consumer, in so far as all motivations and constraints with a bearing on purchase decisions are taken into account: personal motivations, interpersonal relations, economic and organisational constraints, environmental pressures, and so on. As in the case of the individual consumer, need therefore has a multidimensional structure. The *overall need of an industrial customer* can be described with reference to at least five values:

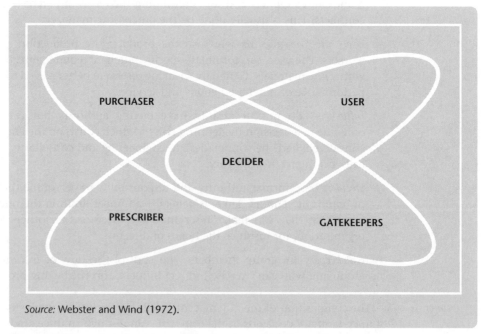

Source: Webster and Wind (1972).

Figure 3.10   Composition of the buying decision centre

⬤ *Technology*: product specifications, state-of-the-art technology, up-to-date and constant quality, just-in-time delivery, and so on.
⬤ *Finance*: price competitiveness, transfer costs, installation and maintenance costs, payment terms, delivery reliability, and so on.
⬤ *Assistance*: after-sales service, help with installation and operation, technical assistance and servicing, and so on.
⬤ *Information*: communication, qualified sales personnel, priority access to new products, training, business intelligence, and so on.
⬤ *Strategy*: reciprocal relations, compatibility of organisational forms, brand or company reputation, and so on.

The examples presented in Exhibit 3.3 and in Table 3.2 illustrate the multidimensional nature of the industrial customer's need.

We note that the determinants of well-being for the industrial client are of a very different nature from those governing the well-being of the individual consumer. The structure of motivations of the industrial customer is both more complex and simpler. It is more complex because it involves an organisation and different individuals operating in the organisation; it is simpler because the main motivations are more objective and thus easier to identify. However, despite the real differences that exist between the two areas, the basic ideas of the market orientation concept have the same relevance in the industrial market as they have in the consumer market: *to adjust supply to the overall need of the customer*.

Table 3.2   Evaluation of a supplier in an industrial market

Macro-attributes (and weight)		Key Sub-attributes	Internal Metrics
Equipment	30	Reliability Easy to use Features/Functions	% repair call % calls for help Function performance test
Sales	30	Knowledge Response Follow-up	Supervisor observations % proposals made on time % follow-up made
Installation	10	Delivery interval Does not break Installed when promised	Average order interval % repair reports % installed on due date
Repair	15	No repeat trouble Fixed fast Kept informed	% repeat reports Average speed of repair % customers informed
Billing	15	Accuracy: no surprises Resolve on first call Easy to understand	% billings inquiries % resolved on first call % billings inquiries
Total	100	–	–

Source: Adapted from: Kordupleski *et al.* (1993).

Exhibit 3.3

The Needs of an Industrial Customer: an Example

The statement from the purchase manager: 'No, we won't work with this supplier any more, they are not reliable', may have different meanings:

- The quality of their products is not constant (technical value).
- Their prices are whimsical (financial value).
- They were supposed to have repaired a machine two months ago (assistance value).
- They have promised to send one of their engineers to tell us about new products being developed; we have called many times and they still haven't done it (information value).
- They treat us as insignificant (psycho-sociological value).

Source: Valla (1980, p. 25).

If this principle is not implemented, the penalty in the industrial market is probably paid more rapidly because of the buyer's professionalism and the fact that needs are more clearly defined.

The industrial buying process

The analysis of the buying process basically consists of identifying the specific roles played by each member of the buying centre at different stages of the decision-making process, their choice criteria, their perceptions of the performance of products or firms in the market, the weight given to each point of view, and so on.

As in the case of the buying decision of the individual consumer, the industrial buying process can be divided into several stages. As illustrated in Table 3.3., Webster and Wind (1972, p. 80) suggest six phases in the process:

- Anticipation and identification of need.
- Determination of specifications and scheduling the purchase.
- Search for buying alternatives.
- Evaluation of alternative buying actions.
- Selection of suppliers.
- Performance control and appraisal.

This is typically the same sequence as that observed in the case of an extensive problem-solving approach.

Clearly, the decision of an industrial client does not always follow this process. The complexity of the decision and its degree of risk or novelty determine how formal the buying process will be. Furthermore, the decision-making and organisational processes can also vary according to the firm, both in terms of its size and its fields of activity.

Table 3.3   Decision stages and roles of the buying decision centre

Stages in the buying process	Composition of the buying centre				
	User	Influencer	Buyer	Decider	Gatekeeper
Identification of needs	*				*
Establishing specifications	*	*			*
Identifying alternatives			*		*
Evaluating alternatives	*	*	*	*	*
Selecting the supplier			*	*	*
Evaluation of performances	*				

Source: Webster and Wind (1972).

One can imagine that the roles of the members of the buying centre are different at each stage of the decision-making process. The analysis of the buying process must answer the following questions:

● Who is a major participant in the decision-making process of buying a given industrial product?
● Who are the key influencers intervening in the process?
● What is the level of their influence?
● What evaluation criteria does each decision participant use?
● What is the weight given to each criterion?

This information is usually collected by survey. It helps to clarify the issue, particularly when it comes to training salespeople by helping them to understand the mechanism of the industrial buying process better.

Valla (1980, p. 27) underlines the fact that training sales people to understand this type of analysis particularly helps them to:

● understand better the buyer's role as well as the system of motivations and constraints within which the buyer operates;

● go beyond mere contact with the purchaser by identifying other possible communication targets within the industrial client's organisation;

● determine better when is the best moment to directly intervene *vis-à-vis* appropriate targets in order to increase efficiency of contacts;

● be in a better position to take advantage of opportunities when they present themselves, due to broader relations with all members of the buying centre.

We shall see in Chapter 7 that the way the buying centre functions is an important segmentation criterion in industrial markets.

Chapter summary

The satisfaction of customers' needs is at the heart of a market economy, yet it is popular in some quarters to claim that marketing creates needs. The notion of need generates controversy because it contains value judgement based on morality or ideology. Apart from the ethical or social rules imposed by society, marketing is pluralist and respects the diversity of tastes and preferences. The distinction between absolute and relative needs brings to the fore the existence of a dialectic of relative needs which leads to the general impossibility of saturation. Similarly, the distinction between generic and derived needs shows that saturation does not relate to generic needs but only to derived needs, that is the dominant technological response at the time. Experimental psychology has proposed a range of motivational orientations. Particularly useful are the conceptual frameworks proposed by the stimulus–response theory, Maslow's need hierarchy and the Sheth–Gross–Newman theory of consumption values. If the principles governing organisational or business-to-business marketing are the same as for consumer marketing, two major differences do exist. First, the industrial customer is represented by a group of individuals, called the buying centre, who exercise different functions and have distinct motivations. Second, the industrial firm is faced with a supply chain made up of interdependent firms which eventually determine its own demand, called derived demand. Thus the industrial firm faces two categories of clients: its direct customers and the customers of its customers. Second, the industrial customer is represented by a group of individuals, called the buying decision centre, who exercise different functions and have distinct motivations. Understanding of the needs and of the role played by each member of the buying centre in the buying decision process, at each stage of the chain, is a key input for the development of marketing strategy.

QUESTIONS AND PROBLEMS

1. What are the implications of Galbraith's criticism of marketing as the creator of artificial needs? Analyse this theory using a concrete example based on your personal experience as consumer.
2. By reference to typology as proposed by either Maslow or Sheth, Newman and Gross, explain the success of products such as Coca-Cola, Club Med, Swatch. Choose a product to illustrate your answer.
3. Describe and compare the structure of the needs of an individual consumer and those of an industrial customer. Identify the main similarities and differences resulting from the complex structure of an industrial customer's need.
4. Describe the needs of each member of a buying decision centre in a company which produces high-tech goods.
5. Is it possible to imagine a point of complete saturation of consumption?

Bibliography

Abbott, L. (1955) *Quality and Competition*, New York, John Wiley & Sons.

Abernethy, A.M. and Frank, G.R. (1996) The Information Content of Advertising: A Meta-analysis, *Journal of Advertising*, **25**(2).

Attali, J. and Guillaume, M. (1974) *L'anti-économique*, Paris, Presses Universitaires de France.

Bauer, R.A. (1960) Consumer Behavior as Risk Taking, in: Hancock A.S. (ed.), *Proceedings, Fall Conference of the American Marketing Association*, June, pp. 389–98.

Becker, G.S. (1965) A Theory of the Allocation of Time, *The Economic Journal*, September, pp. 494–517.

Berlyne, D.E. (1960) *Conflict, Arousal and Curiosity*, New York, McGraw-Hill.

Boirel, M. (1977) *Comment vivre sans tension?* Brussels, Marabout.

Cotta, A. (1980) *La société ludique*, Paris, Grasset.

Derbaix, C. (1997) *Analyse du comportement du consommateur*, Notes de cours, FUCAM.

Duffy, E. (1957), The Psychological Significance of the Concept of Arousal and Activation, *The Psychological Review*, **64**, September, pp. 265–75.

Gutman, J. (1982) A Mean-End Chain Model on Consumer Categorization Processes, *Journal of Marketing*, **46**, Spring, pp. 60–72.

Hamel, G. and Prahalad, C.K. (1994) *Competing for the Future*, Boston MA, Harvard University Press

Hebb, D.O. (1955) Drives and the C.N.S. (Conceptual Nervous System), *The Psychological Review*, **62**, July, pp. 243–54.

Howard, J.A. and Sheth, J.N. (1969) *The Theory of Buyer Behavior*, New York, John Wiley & Sons.

Jacoby, J. and Kaplan, L.B. (1972) *The Components of Perceived Risk*, in: Venkatesan, V. (ed.) Proceedings, 3rd Annual Conference, Association for Consumer Research.

Jacquemin, A. and Tulkens, H. (1988) *Fondements d'économie politique*, 2nd edn, Brussels, De Boeck-Weesmael.

Kahle, L.R. (ed.) (1983) *Social Values and Social Change: Adaptation to Life in America*, New York, Praeger.

Kahle, L.R., Poulos, B. and Sukhdial, A. (1988) Changes in Social Values in the United States During the Past Decade, *Journal of Advertising Research*, February–March, pp. 35–41.

Katona, G. (1951) *Psychological Analysis of Economic Behavior*, New York, McGraw-Hill.

Keynes, J.M. (1936) Essays in Persuasion – Economic Possibilities for our Grandchildren, *The Collected Writings of J.M. Keynes*, (Vol. 9), London, Macmillan.

Kirzner, I.M. (1973) *Competition and Entreneurship*, Chicago IL, Chicago University Press.

Kordupleski, R.E., Rust, R.T. and Zahorik, A.J. (1993) Marketing: The Missing Dimension in Quality Management, *California Management Review*, Spring.

Kotler, P. (1997) *Marketing Management*, 9th edn, Englewood Cliffs NJ, Prentice Hall.

Lancaster, K.J. (1966) A New Approach to Consumer Theory, *The Journal of Political Economy*, **74**, April, pp. 132–57.

Lepage, H. (1982) *Vive le commerce*, Paris, Dunod, Collection L'œil économique.

Levitt, T. (1980) Marketing Success through Differentiation – of Anything, *Harvard Business Review*, January–February,

Maslow, H. (1943) A Theory of Human Motivation, *The Psychological Review*, **50**, pp. 370–96.

Murray, H.A. (1938) *Explorations in Personality*, New York, Oxford University Press.

Nelson, D. (1970) Information and Consumer Behavior, *The Journal of Political Economy*, **78**, March–April, pp. 311–29.

Nuttin, J. (1980) *Théorie de la motivation humaine*, Paris, Presses Universitaires de France.

Pellemans, P. (1998) *Le marketing qualitatif*, Brussels, De Boeck Université.

Planchon, A. (1974) *Saturation de la consommation*, Paris, Mame, Collection Repères-Economie.

Resnik, A. and Stern, B.L. (1977) An Analysis of Information Content in Television Advertising, *Journal of Marketing*, **50**, April.

Reynolds, T.J. and Gutman, J. (1988) Laddering Theory, Method, Analysis, and Interpretation, *Journal of Advertising Research*, February–March, pp. 11–31.

Rokeach, M.O. (1973) *The Nature of Human Values*, New York, The Free Press.

Rosa, J.J. (1977) Vrais et faux besoins, in: Rosa, J.J. and Aftalion, F. (eds), *L'économique retrouvé*, Paris, Economica.

Scitovsky, T. (1976) *The Joyless Economy*, Oxford, Oxford University Press.

Séguéla, J. (1982) *Hollywood lave plus blanc*, Paris, Flammarion.

Sheth, J.N., Newman, B.I. and Gross, B.L. (1991) *Consumption Values and Market Choices: Theory and Applications*, Cincinnati OH, South Western Publishing Company.

Sheth, J., Mittal, B. and Newman, B.I. (1999) *Customer Behavior, Consumer Behavior and Beyond*, Fort Worth TX, Dryden Press.

Valaskakis, K. *et al.* (1978) *La société de conservation*, Montreal, Les éditions Quinze.

Valette-Florence, P. (1994) Introduction à l'analyse des chaînages cognitifs, *Recherche et Applications en Marketing*, **9**(1): 93–117.

Valla, J.P. (1980) Le comportêment des groupes d'achat, in: *L'action marketing des entreprises industrielles*, Paris, Collection Adetem, pp. 22–38.

Webster, F.E. and Wind, Y. (1972) *Organizational Buying Behavior*, Englewood Cliffs NJ, Prentice Hall.

Wilkie, W.L. (1994) *Consumer Behavior*, 3rd edn, New York, John Wiley & Sons.

Wundt, O. (1874) in: Berlyne, D.E. (1960) *Conflict, Arousal and Curiosity*, New York, McGraw-Hill.

chapter four

The marketing information system

The central problem confronting a market-oriented organisation is how to monitor the needs of the marketplace and of the macro-marketing environment in order to anticipate the future. In response to this need for information, the concept of a formalised *market information system* (MIS) has emerged to acquire and to distribute market data within the organisation, thereby facilitating market-oriented decisions. The objective of an MIS is to integrate marketing data (internal accounting data, salespeople's reports, marketing services data, marketing research studies and so on) into a continuous information flow for marketing decision making. Within an MIS, *marketing research* has mainly an *ad hoc* data-gathering and analysis function to perform. Marketing research can supply information regarding many aspects of the marketplace. In this chapter, we shall review the main components of an MIS, in placing more emphasis on the tasks and methods of marketing research.

Chapter learning objectives

After reading this chapter, you should be able to understand:

1. the importance of market information in a market-driven company;

2. the structure of a market information system;

3. why marketing research must be scientifically conducted;

4. the differences between exploratory, descriptive and causal research;

5. the characteristics of the main primary data collection methods;

6. the potential of the new methods of causal research.

Structure of a Market Information System

Few managers are happy with the type of market information they receive. The usual complaints are:

- Available information is very often not relevant to decision needs.
- There is too much information to be used effectively.
- Information is spread throughout the firm and difficult to locate.
- Key information arrives too late to be useful or is destroyed.
- Some managers may withhold information from other functions.
- The reliability and accuracy of information are difficult to verify.

The role of an MIS is to study information needs carefully, to design an information system to meet these needs, to centralise the information available and to organise its dissemination throughout the organisation. An MIS has been defined as follows:

> A marketing information system is a continuing and interacting structure of people, equipment and procedures to gather, sort, analyse, evaluate and distribute pertinent, timely and accurate information for use by marketing decision makers to improve their marketing planning, implementation and control. (Kotler 1997, p. 110)

The structure of an MIS is described in Figure 4.1. The figure shows the macro-marketing environment to be monitored by management. These flows of information are captured and analysed through three subsystems of data collection: the internal accounting system, the business intelligence system and the marketing research system. A fourth subsystem – the analytical market system, which is in charge of the data processing and transfer of information to management, as aids to under-standing, decision and control – will be discussed in the following chapter.

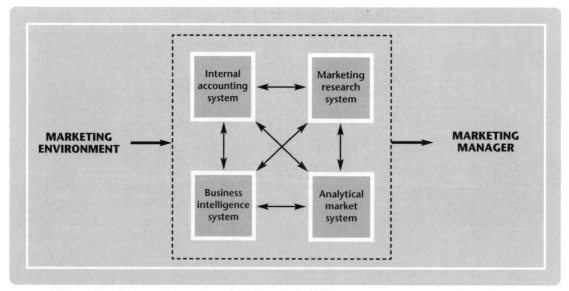

Figure 4.1   Structure of a market information system

Thus, viewed in this perspective, marketing research appears as only one component of an MIS. Marketing research's role is clear and confined to a specific decision problem, while the role of an MIS is much broader and is organised on a permanent basis. Let use briefly examine the tasks and content of the three subsystems.

The internal accounting system

All organisations collect internal data as part of their normal operations. These data, which are collected for purposes other than research, are called *internal secondary data*. Sales data are recorded within the 'order–shipping–billing' cycle. Cost data are recorded, sales reports are submitted by sales representatives and dealers, advertising and promotion activities are recorded, R&D and manufacturing reports are made. These are but a few of the data sources available for research in a modern organisation. Sales records should allow for classification by type of customer, payment procedure, product line, sales territory, time period and so forth.

By way of illustration, a monthly sales statement classified by product, customer group, and sales territory will permit the following analyses:

● Comparison of year-to-date sales in volume and value.
● Analysis of the product mix structure of the total turnover.
● Analysis of the concentration rate of the turnover per customer.
● Evaluation of the sales efficiency by comparing territory sales, number of sales calls, average revenue per sales call and so forth.
● Analysis of the market penetration per territory by reference to buying power indices.

Many companies do not collect and maintain sales and cost data in sufficient detail to be used for research purposes. These data, stored and processed by the market analytical subsystem, should constitute a database of time series useful, namely, for forecasting purposes. The types of analyses to be conducted are, for example:

● Graphic analyses to identify trends, seasonality patterns and growth rates.
● Short-term sales forecasts based on endogenous sales forecasting techniques, such as exponential smoothing.
● Correlation analyses between sales and key explanatory factors such as distribution rates, advertising share of voice, relative price.
● Multi-variables or multi-equation econometric models.

These forecasting techniques will be discussed in more detail in Chapter 8.

The generalised use of computers has greatly facilitated the development of internal accounting systems. A certain number of attributes should be met in designing a reporting system:

● *Timeliness:* the information must be available when needed and not reported too late.
● *Flexibility:* the information must be available in varied formats and detail such that the specific information needs of alternative decision situations can be served.

● *Inclusiveness:* the reporting system must cover the entire range of information needs, while avoiding the risk of information overload.

● *Accuracy:* the level of accuracy should fit the needs of the decision situation, and the information should not be presented in too much detail.

● *Convenience:* the information must be easily accessible to the decision-maker and presented in a clear and usable manner.

Data from the internal accounting system originate within the organisation and are available at minimal cost. They constitute the backbone of the MIS. As illustrated by Figure 4.2, the sources of information used by firms are multiple and varied. It is interesting to note in this particular example that the most important source of information are the customers themselves.

The business intelligence system

The data provided by the internal accounting system must be complemented by information about the macro-marketing environment and about competition. It is the role of the business intelligence subsystem to gather information about developments in the environment, to enable management to monitor the strengths and weaknesses of the firm's competitive position. A detailed description of the type of information to collect is presented in Chapter 11.

Several methods can be used to collect business intelligence information: the casual method, the use of the salesforce, the establishment of information centres or the purchase of data from syndicated services:

● The *casual method* is the informal search for information carried on by managers on their own through reading newspapers and trade publications, talking to suppliers, distributors, customers, or by participating in professional meetings, trade shows, and so on.

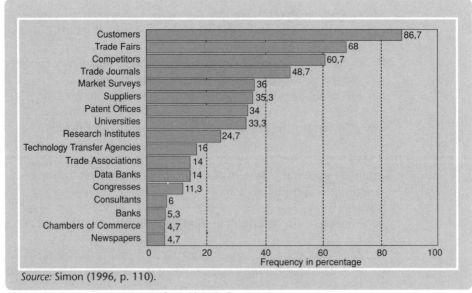

Source: Simon (1996, p. 110).

Figure 4.2   Importance of market information sources

- The *sales force* is often in good position to provide data regarding many aspects of the market situation and to spot new market developments or new competitive actions. Sales representatives should be trained and motivated to report market information.

- Some companies have established *information or documentation centres* where the staff systematically scans and analyses major trade industrial or professional publications. For example, much can be learned about competition through reading competitors' published reports. Newsletters or bulletins are then published and disseminated within the company.

- Most companies also purchase *syndicated data* from outside firms, which collect and sell standardised data about market shares, retail prices, advertising expenditures, promotions, and so on.

Besides internal accounting information and market intelligence, marketing management also requires studies on specific problems or opportunities, such as a product concept test, a brand image study or a sales forecast for a particular country or region. It is the role of marketing research to conduct these types of focused studies.

The Marketing Research System

The role of marketing research is to provide market information data that will help management to adopt and implement a market orientation. Its role can be defined in the following terms:

> Marketing research involves the diagnosis of information needs and the selection of relevant interrelated variables about which valid and reliable information is gathered, recorded and analysed. (Zaltman and Burger, 1975, p. 3)

According to this definition, marketing research has four distinctive functions to perform:

- The *diagnosis of an information need*, which supposes a good interactive relationship between the decider and the market analyst.
- The *selection of the variables* to be measured, which implies the capacity to translate a decision problem into empirically testable research questions.
- The responsibility of the *internal and external validity* of the collected information, which implies a good command of the research methodology.
- The *transfer of information* to management as an aid to understanding, decision and control.

The role of the market analyst is not confined, therefore, to the technical aspects linked to the execution of a research project. He or she has to participate actively in the research problem definition, the design of the research plan and the interpretation and exploitation of the research results.

Managerial usefulness of marketing research

Marketing research has its usefulness for strategic and operational marketing decisions. Three types of objectives can be identified:

● *Understanding aid:* to discover, describe, analyse, measure and forecast market factors and demand.
● *Decision aid:* to identify the most appropriate marketing instruments and strategies and determine their optimal level of intervention.
● *Control aid:* to assess the performance of the marketing programmes and evaluate results.

The first objective is more directly linked to strategic marketing decisions and has an important creative component: to discover new opportunities and/or untapped market potential. The other two objectives are felt more directly by operational marketing people.

Marketing research often has important implications for functions other than marketing. For example, research results on the changing mood of the market *vis-à-vis* ecology may induce R&D and production staff to develop environmentally sound products. Similarly, sales forecasting is a key input for financial analysis and for distribution planning and logistics.

A key question for a manager faced with a decision problem is to decide whether or not a specific marketing research study should be conducted. Several factors must be considered in examining this question:

1. *Time constraint.* Marketing research takes time, and in many instances decisions have to be taken rapidly even if the information is incomplete. The time factor is crucial and the urgency of the situation often precludes the use of research. This factor reinforces the importance of the MIS, which is a permanent information system.

2. *Availability of data.* In many instances, management already possesses enough information and a sound decision may be made without further research. This type of situation will occur when the firm has a well-managed permanent MIS. Sometimes, marketing research is nevertheless undertaken to prevent the criticism of ill-prepared decisions. Marketing research here takes the form of an insurance that will be useful if the decision taken happens to be the wrong one.

3. *Value to the firm.* The value of marketing research will depend on the nature of the managerial decision to be made. For many routine decisions, the cost of a wrong decision is minimal and substantial marketing research expenditures are difficult to justify. Thus, before conducting a research, managers should ask themselves: *'Will the information gained by marketing research improve the quality of the marketing decision to an extent large enough to warrant the expenditure?'* In many cases even a modest marketing research study may substantially improve the quality of managerial decisions.

Frequently, marketing research projects are not directly linked to a particular decision but are purely exploratory. The objective is then to improve the understanding of a market or to search for opportunities in a new unknown market. This type of research is likely to improve the choice of strategic options by the firm.

Marketing research and the scientific method

If nobody questions today that management is much more of an art than a science, it is important to state clearly that marketing research must be scientific. It is important because marketing research has to deal with *accredited (or certified) knowledge*, and without accredited knowledge good management decisions cannot be made (Zaltman and Burger, 1975, p. 7). The implication of this statement is that the scientist attempts to uncover objective 'truths'. Because management is primarily interested in making decisions based on accurate and unbiased data, it is clear that the market researcher must follow a scientific procedure in order for data to be collected and analysed properly.

The rules of the scientific method are designed to provide, among others, two types of validity, internal and external:

- *Internal validity* is concerned with the question of whether the observed effects of a marketing stimulus (price, advertising message, promotion, and so on) could have been caused by variables other than the factor under study. Is the relationship established without ambiguity? Without internal validity the experiment is confounded and the causal structure is not established.

- *External validity* is concerned with the generalisability of experimental results. To what populations, geographic areas, treatment variables can the measured effects be projected?

This problem of scientific reliability is fundamental because, on the basis of marketing research results, management will make highly risky decisions, such as the launch of a new product, modification of a price or adoption of a specific advertising theme.

Characteristics of scientific knowledge

The understanding of the main features of science is essential to performing marketing research scientifically, and therefore we shall now briefly review the main features of the scientific method (Zaltman and Burger, 1975, pp. 26–30):

1. *Scientific knowledge is factual.* Science starts by establishing facts and seeks to describe and explain them. Established facts are empirical data obtained with the aid of theories and, in turn, help to clarify theories.

2. *Science goes beyond facts.* The market analyst should not confine his or her work to facts that are easily observed and already in existence. Thus qualitative research is an integrated part of the research process. The market analyst may want to find new facts, but new facts should be authentic and lend themselves to empirical verification or falsification.

3. *Scientific knowledge is verifiable (or falsifiable).* Scientific knowledge must be testable empirically through observational or experimental experiences. This is one of the basic rules of a science. It must be possible to demonstrate that a given proposition or theory is false. The scientist can only say: *'I have a theory which I have objectively tested with data and the data are consistent with my theory.'*

4. *Science is analytic.* The market researcher tries to decompose the buying decision process into its basic parts to determine the mechanisms which account for the way the process functions. After analysing the component parts separately and also in their interrelationships, the market researcher is then able to determine how the whole decision process emerges. An illustration of this analytic process is given in the next chapter in the discussion of the concept of attitude.

5. *Scientific knowledge is clear and precise.* Scientific knowledge strives for precision, accuracy and reduction of error although it is almost impossible to achieve these completely. The researcher attempts to reach these objectives by stating questions with maximal clarity, giving unambiguous definitions to concepts and measures and recording observations as completely and in as much detail as possible.

6. *Scientific knowledge is communicable.* Research must be in principle communicable – that is, it must be sufficiently complete in its reporting of methodologies used and sufficiently precise in the presentation of its results to enable another researcher to duplicate the study for independent verification or to determine if replication is desirable.

7. *Scientific knowledge is general.* The market researcher should place individual facts into general patterns, which should be applicable to a wide variety of phenomena. This provides generalisations that can guide marketing decisions. The market analyst is concerned with learning not just what an individual buyer does, but rather what that buyer does that others are also likely to do in the same situation.

The manager–researcher interface

The managerial value of marketing research is largely determined by the quality of the interface between the market analyst responsible for the research project and the decision-maker who has to use the research results. In many instances, market researchers are not sufficiently management-oriented and many managers are not sufficiently research-oriented. To overcome this difficulty of communication, the manager and the researcher's responsibilities should be clearly defined and accepted by both parties.

The *user of the research* should keep the market researcher informed on:

● The precise problem faced by the firm and the way that a decision is going to be made.
● The background of the problem and its environment.
● All limitations on costs and time for doing the study and on the courses of action that the company can realistically consider.
● What data will be provided by the firm and where to obtain it.
● Any changes in the situation that arise as the study is under way.

Similarly, the *responsibilities of the researcher* are:

● Being honest and clear regarding the meaning and any limitations of the expected findings.
● Being of maximum help in presenting and explaining the conclusions and aiding the decision-maker's application.

⬤ Demanding that the decision-maker provide the information needed to plan and conduct the study.

⬤ Insisting that valid and full reporting be made of the findings.

⬤ Refusing to distort or abridge them on behalf of the user's biases and prejudices.

In reporting research findings some researchers fail to recognise that their role is advisory; they are not being asked to make the decision for management. Similarly, some managers operate as if the researcher is clairvoyant regarding the nature of the decision situation and the information needed to reduce the decision uncertainty. Consequently, many research projects are not decision-oriented because of the manager's poor communication skills.

Stages in the research process

Systematic inquiry requires careful planning in an orderly investigation. Marketing research, like other forms of scientific research, is a sequence of interrelated activities. The five stages of the research process are presented in Figure 4.3.

1. *Problem definition.* The first step in research calls for the manager (the user of the research result) and the market analyst (the researcher) to define the problem carefully and to agree on the research objective. In marketing research, the old adage, *'a problem well defined is a problem half solved'* is worth remembering. Another way to express the same idea would be: *'if you don't know what you are looking for, you won't find it'*. Thus, at this stage a working interface 'decider–analyst' is essential and the research objective should state, in terms as precise as possible, the information needed to improve the decision to be made.

2. *Research design.* The research design is a master plan specifying the methods and procedures for collecting and analysing the needed information. It is a framework

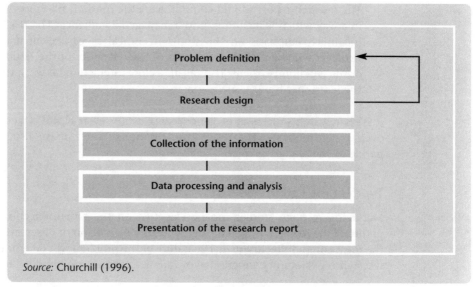

Source: Churchill (1996).

Figure 4.3   The stages of a research process

for the research plan of action. This is typically the responsibility of the market analyst. The research plan should be designed professionally and specify the hypotheses and the research questions, the sources of information, the research instrument (focus groups, survey or experimentation), the sampling methodology, the schedule and the cost of the research. The decider should approve the research plan to ensure that the information collected is appropriate for solving his or her decision problem.

3. *Collection of the information.* Once the research design is approved, the process of gathering the information from respondents may begin. In many cases, the data collection phase is subcontracted to a specialised market research company. Data collection methods are rapidly changing under the impact of telecommunications and computers. Telephone interviews combined with data-entry terminals, computer-assisted interviews, interactive terminals in shopping malls, fax interviews, electronic cash registers using the universal product code (UPC) are new techniques which accelerate the data-gathering process and also eliminate the risks of errors. There are generally two phases in data collection: pre-testing and the main study. The pre-test phase, based on a small subsample, is used to determine whether the data-gathering plan for the main study is appropriate.

4. *Data processing and analysis.* Once the data have been collected, they must be converted into a format that will answer the manager's questions. This stage implies editing the data, coding, tabulating and developing one-way or two-way frequency distributions. These tasks are also generally subcontracted to specialised agencies and strict controls should be made on the rules and procedures adopted. Statistical analysis techniques will be used to summarise the data, to present them in a more meaningful way, to facilitate the interpretation or to help discover new findings or relationships. Advanced multivariate statistical analyses should be used only if they are relevant for the purpose of the study.

5. *Presentation of the research report.* The final stage in the research process is that of interpreting the information and making conclusions for managerial decisions. The research report should communicate the research findings effectively, that is in a way which is meaningful to a managerial audience. The risk here is to place too much emphasis on the study's technical aspects, even if any responsible manager will want to be convinced of the reliability of the results, otherwise he or she will not use them. Thus again a close interaction between the manager and the researcher is a key success factor.

This research process is of general application even if the stages of the process overlap continuously. The relative importance of each phase also varies with the nature of the market research.

Types of marketing research

Marketing research studies can be classified on the basis of techniques or of the nature of the research problem. Surveys, experimentation or observational studies are the most common techniques. The nature of the problem will determine whether the research is exploratory, descriptive or causal. Examples are provided in Table 4.1.

Table 4.1 Types of marketing research problems

Exploratory research	Descriptive research	Causal research
Sales of brand A are declining and we do not know why.	What kinds of people buy our brand? Who buys the brand of our direct competitor?	Do buyers prefer our product in an 'eco-design' package?
Would the market be interested in our new product idea?	What should be the target segment for our new product?	Which of the two advertising themes is more effective?

Source: adapted from Churchill (1996).

● *Exploratory research* is conducted to clarify the nature of a problem, to gain better understanding of a market situation, to discover ideas and insights and to provide directions for any further research needed. It is not intended to provide conclusive evidence from which to determine a particular course of action. The methods used are desk research and qualitative studies.

● *Descriptive research* seeks to determine answers to 'who', 'what', 'when', 'where' and 'how' questions. Descriptive research is concerned with determining frequency with which something occurs or the relationship between two variables. Unlike exploratory research, descriptive studies are based on some previous understanding of the nature of the research problem. Descriptive information is often all that is needed to solve a marketing problem. The methods used are typically secondary data, observation and communication. Most marketing research studies are of this type.

● *Causal research* is the most ambitious form of research and is concerned with determining cause-and-effect relationships. In causal studies, it is typical to have an expectation of the relationship, which is to be explained, such as predicting the influence of price, packaging and advertising. Causal studies usually take the form of controlled experiments.

In principle, exploratory and descriptive research precede cause-and-effect relationship studies and are often seen as preliminary steps, as illustrated in Figure 4.4. But other sequences may also exist. For example, if a causal hypothesis is discovered, the analyst might need another exploratory or descriptive study. In the following sections, we shall analyse in more detail the objectives and the methods used in these three types of market research studies.

Exploratory Research Studies

Marketing research is of an exploratory type when the emphasis is placed on gaining insights and ideas rather than on formally testing hypotheses derived from theory or from previous research studies. This type of study is very popular among firms, because of its low cost, speed, flexibility and emphasis on creativity and on the generation of ideas.

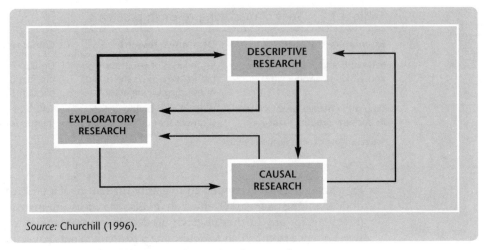

Source: Churchill (1996).

Figure 4.4   The different sequences of research

Objectives of exploratory research

The need for exploratory research typically arises when the firm is confronted with ill-defined problems such as: *'sales of brand X are declining and we do not know why'* or *'would people be interested in our idea for a new product?'* In these two examples, the analyst could guess a large number of possible answers. Since it is impractical to test them all, exploratory research will be used to find the most likely explanation(s) that will then be tested empirically. Thus, the main objectives of exploratory research are the following:

● To give a rapid examination of the threats of a problem or the potential of an opportunity.
● To formulate a poorly defined problem for more precise investigation.
● To generate hypotheses or conjectural statements about the problem.
● To collect and analyse readily available information.
● To establish priorities for further research.
● To increase the analyst's familiarity with a problem or with a market.
● To clarify a concept.

In general, exploratory research is appropriate to any problem about which little is known.

Hypothesis development

Exploratory research is particularly useful at the first stage of the research process at the problem formulation phase, to translate the research problem into specific research objectives. The objective is to develop testable hypotheses. Hypotheses state what we are looking for; they anticipate the possible answers to the research problem and add a considerable degree of specificity. Normally there will be several competing hypotheses, either specified or implied.

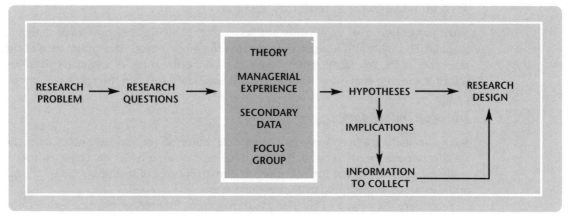

Figure 4.5   The process of hypothesis development

How does the analyst generate hypotheses? The process of hypothesis development is illustrated in Figure 4.5. Four main sources of information can be identified:

1.   theory from such disciplines as economics, psychology, sociology or marketing;
2.   management experience with related problems,
3.   the use of secondary data (see below), or
4.   exploratory research when both theory and experience are lacking.

After an exploratory research, the market analyst should know which type of data to collect in order to verify or falsify the competing explanations. An example is presented in Table 4.2. concerning the low level of market penetration of cable TV in some regions. The exploratory study has identified seven possible explanations (or hypotheses). The derived research objectives clearly indicate the type of data required to verify these tentative explanations.

Table 4.2   From a research problem to research questions

Research problem: *Why is the penetration rate of cable TV in private homes far below average in several geographic areas?*

Hypotheses	Research questions
1. Good TV reception is available without cable.	■ What is the quality of TV reception without cable?
2. Residents are illegally connecting their sets to the cable network.	■ Is it technically possible to be illegally connected?
3. There is a very transient population in these regions.	■ What is the mobility rate in these regions?
4. Residents have had poor experience with cable services.	■ What is the corporate image of the cable company in the regions?
5. The price is too high given the level of income in the region.	■ How different are income statistics among regions?
6. The sales force coverage has been inadequate.	■ How active was the sales force in the regions?
7. A large part of the residents are in age or social class groups that watch little TV.	■ Analyse demographic and social class statistics per region.

Techniques used for exploratory research

Since the objective of exploratory studies is to find new ideas, no formal design is required. Flexibility and ingenuity characterise the investigation. The imagination of the researcher is the key factor. The techniques used are the study of secondary data, key informant survey, analysis of related cases and qualitative research through focus groups.

Use of secondary data

Secondary data are previously published data collected for purposes other than the specific research needs at hand. Primary data, on the other hand, are collected specifically for purposes of the investigation. The main sources of secondary data, internal and external, are presented in Figure 4.6.

Secondary data can be classified as coming from internal or external sources, the former being available within the organisation and the latter originating from outside. Internal data are centralised in the internal accounting system described in the first section of this chapter. External data come from an array of sources such as government publications, trade association data, books, bulletins, reports and periodicals. Data from these sources are available at minimal cost or free in libraries. External sources not available in a library are usually standardised marketing data, which are expensive to acquire. These syndicated data sources are consumer panels, wholesale data, media and audience data, and so on.

To start with, secondary data are the most logical thing to work on and their usefulness should not be underestimated. The primary *advantage* of secondary data is that it is always faster and less expensive to obtain them than to acquire primary data. Also they may include information not otherwise available to the researcher. For example, truck and car registrations are secondary data published by the car registration administration. A competent market analyst should be familiar with the basic sources pertaining to the market studied.

Secondary data, however, present a certain number of *disadvantages* and the market analyst should examine their relevance thoroughly. The most common problems associated with secondary data are: (1) outdated information, (2) variation in definition of terms, (3) different units of measurement. Another shortcoming is that the user has no control over the accuracy of secondary data. Research conducted by other persons may be biased to support the vested interest of the source. Also, the user of secondary data must critically assess the data and the research design to determine if the research methodology was correctly implemented. The following rules should be followed in the use of secondary data:

1. Always use the primary source of secondary data and not secondary sources that secured the data from the original source.

2. Assess the accuracy of secondary data by carefully identifying the purpose of the publication.

3. Examine the overall quality of the methodology; a primary source should provide a detailed description of how the data were collected, including definitions, collection forms, sampling and so forth.

The above is not to say that such data cannot be used by the analyst. Rather, it is simply to suggest that such data should be viewed more critically.

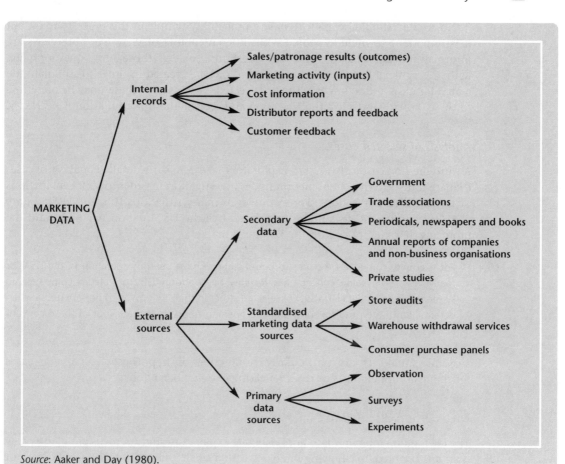

Source: Aaker and Day (1980).

Figure 4.6   Sources of marketing data

Key informants survey

After having explored secondary sources, additional insights and ideas can be gained by talking with individuals having special knowledge and experience regarding the problem under investigation. These knowledgeable persons may be 'players' or 'experts'. By 'players' we mean anyone participating in the market situation, such as the personnel within the firm, wholesalers, retailers, suppliers or consumers. By 'experts' we mean anyone having privileged information due to their function, such as civil servants, economists, sociologists, R&D personnel, members of a professional organisation and so forth.

> For example, a publisher of children's books [who is] investigating a sales decrease gained valuable insights by talking with librarians and schoolteachers. These discussions indicated that an increased use of library facilities, both public and school, coincided with the product's decline in sales. These increases were, in turn, attributed to a very sizeable increase in library holdings of children's books resulting from federal legislation that provided money for this purpose. (Churchill, 1996, p. 78)

No attempt should be made to have a probability sample in this type of survey, but it is important to include people with different points of view. The interviews are informal and do not use structured questions, such as those on a questionnaire. Rather, very flexible and free-flowing situations are created in order to stimulate the search for ideas and to uncover the unexpected. Various hypotheses may be presented to these individuals to test their reaction and see whether reformulation is necessary.

Analysis of selected cases

A third method currently used in exploratory research is the detailed analysis of cases that are similar to the phenomenon under investigation in order to seek explanations or to gain ideas for actions. For example, in many situations the United States are ahead of Europe and it is interesting to analyse the US situation to understand the problems that might occur in the European market.

> For example, convenience stores in petrol stations have been in operation in the USA for many years. The same concept has recently been adopted by petroleum companies in Western Europe. A detailed study of selected stores in the USA proved to be very useful when determining the types of assortment, the opening hours, and the layout of these convenience stores.

Some situations are particularly productive of hypotheses – namely, cases reflecting abrupt changes or cases reflecting extreme behaviour.

Focus group discussions

The focus group interview is a more elaborate exploratory study. A focus group interview is an unstructured, free-flowing interview with a small group of 8 to 12 people. It is not a rigidly constructed question-and-answer session but a flexible format discussion of a brand, an advertisement or a new product concept. A focus group functions as follows:

> The group meets at a location at a predesignated time; it consists of an interviewer or moderator and 8 to 12 participants; the moderator introduces the topic and encourages group members to discuss the subject among themselves; focus groups allow people to discuss their true feelings, anxieties and frustrations as well as the depth of their conviction.

The primary advantages of focus group interviews are that they are relatively rapid, easy to execute and inexpensive. In an emergency situation three or four group sessions can be conducted, organised and reported on in less than a week. From the first discussion the analyst invariably learns a great deal. The second interview produces more, but less is new. Usually, in the third and fourth sessions, much of what is said has been heard before and there is little to be gained from continuing. By way of illustration, the result of a group discussion about coffee consumption is presented in Exhibit 4.1.

In addition to the advantage of time, Wells (1974, pp. 133–4) underlines the following *advantages* for group interviews:

● The group interview is a superb mechanism for generating hypotheses when little is known about the problem under study.

● The group method drastically reduces the distance between the respondent who produces research information and the client who uses it.

● Another advantage of the group interview technique is its flexibility, by contrast with survey interviewers who work from a rigid question schedule.

● The group interview has the ability to handle contingencies of consumer behaviour of the type: 'if… otherwise', an answer unlikely to emerge in a survey.

● In a group discussion respondents stimulate one another and more information is spontaneously obtained than in individual interviews.

● Finally in a group interview study, the findings emerge in a form that most people fully understand.

The *limitations* of focus group interviews are important and should not be underestimated:

● The respondents are not representative of the target population given their number and the recruiting procedure. Thus, the external validity of the results is necessarily limited.

● The interpretation of the results is typically judgemental and highly dependent on the personality of the analyst. Given the absence of a structured questionnaire and the wealth of disparate comments usually obtained, the analyst can always find something which agrees with his or her view of the problem The importance of this bias is difficult to measure, however.

● The risk always exists to see one participant dominating the session and to provoke negative reactions from the other members of the group.

● Evaluations by means of group interviews tend to be conservative. It favours ideas that are easy to explain and understand and, therefore, not very new.

● Very disturbing is the unethical practice of some market research firms specialising in focus groups to recruit 'professional respondents' to make the session go well.

Despite these limitations, focus group interviews are very popular, particularly among advertising agencies. A more recent development in the field of qualitative research is the use of interpretation models such as the Freudian or the Jungian models (Pellemans, 1999). The risk here is to privilege one scheme of interpretation. To avoid this trap, several interpretation models should be used simultaneously and their results confronted.

Projective techniques

Respondents are often reluctant or embarrassed to discuss their feelings but may be more likely to give a true answer (consciously or unconsciously) if the question is disguised. A projective technique is an indirect means of questioning that enables respondents to 'project' their beliefs or feelings into a third person when exposed to an unstructured stimulus. Projective techniques are currently used in clinical and personality tests. The theory behind such a technique is that when a person is asked to structure or organise an essentially unstructured or ambiguous situation he can do so only by calling upon and revealing his own personality or attitudinal structure.

The Results of a Group Discussion: Motivations for Coffee Consumption in Belgium

1. Time and space structure

Coffee gives a certain rhythm to your day; it is a ritual, which punctuates the different parts of a day: morning, morning break, mealtime, after a meal, evening, weekend, afternoon break, and so on. Each moment has its own identity, typical to its environment and conditions for the expected satisfaction for consumption.

2. Social function

Offering a cup of coffee is a typical sign of hospitality. A cup of coffee relaxes and welcomes, develops a feeling of harmony, a certain atmosphere. Coffee brings people together, is the excuse for bringing people together.

3. Sensorial function

Coffee is satisfying to the individual himself or herself, catering as much to the emotions as to the senses. The sense of smell, taste, the appearance and the warmth of coffee are all involved.

4. Function as a stimulant

Coffee supposedly acts as both a physical and psychological stimulant. Even a restorative, curative function is attributed to coffee; it picks you up; it is an affective, emotional comforting tonic.

Source: MDA Consulting Group, Brussels.

> The more unstructured and ambiguous a stimulus, the more a subject can and will project his emotions, needs, motives, attitudes and values. (Kerlinger 1973, p. 515)

The most common projective techniques in marketing research are picture–story association, sentence completion, word association, role-playing. On this topic see Kassarjian (1974).

Limitations of exploratory research

Exploratory research cannot take the place of quantitative, conclusive research. Nevertheless, there is great temptation among many managers to accept small sample exploratory results as sufficient for their purpose because they are so compelling in their reality. The dangers of uncritical acceptance of the unstructured output from a focus group or a brief series of informal interviews are twofold:

● First, the results are not representative of what would be found in the population and, hence, cannot be projected.
● Second, there is typically a great deal of ambiguity owing to the moderator's interpretation of the results.

In fact, the greatest danger of using exploratory research to evaluate an alternative advertising copy strategy, a new product concept and so on, is not that a poor idea will be marketed, because successive steps of research will prevent that; the real danger is that a good idea with promise may be rejected because of findings at the exploratory stage. In other situations, where everything looks positive in the exploratory stage, there is the temptation to market the product without further research (Adler, 1979).

In view of these pitfalls, these methods should be used strictly for insights into the reality of the buyer's perspective and to suggest hypotheses for further research.

Descriptive Research Studies

Descriptive studies, as their name suggests, are designed to describe the characteristics of a given situation or of a given population. Descriptive studies differ from exploratory studies in the rigour with which they are designed. Exploratory studies are characterised by flexibility. Descriptive studies attempt to obtain a complete and accurate description of a situation. Formal design is required to ensure that the description covers all phases desired and that the information collected is reliable. The most popular technique used in descriptive research is the survey.

Objectives of descriptive studies

Descriptive research encompasses a vast array of research objectives. The purpose is to provide a graph of some aspect of the market at a point of time or to monitor an activity over time. The objectives of descriptive studies are:

- To describe the organisation, the distribution channels or the competitive structure of a specific market or segment.
- To estimate the proportion and the socio-demographic profile of a specified population which behaves in a certain way.
- To predict the level of primary demand over the next five years in a given market using heuristic or extrapolating sales forecasting methods.
- To describe the buying behaviour of certain groups of consumers.
- To describe the way buyers perceive and evaluate the attributes of given brands against competing brands.
- To describe the evolution of lifestyles among specific segments of the population.

Descriptive research should be based on some previous understanding and knowledge of the problem in order to determine with precision the data collection procedure. As illustrated in the previous section, it should rest on one or more specific hypotheses. Three conditions must be met before beginning a descriptive research:

1. One or several hypotheses or conjectural statements derived from the research questions to guide the data collection.
2. A clear specification of the 'who', 'what', 'when', 'where', 'why' and 'how' of the research.
3. A specification of the method used to collect the information: communication or observation.
4. A specification of the information to collect is presented in Exhibit 4.2.

Two types of descriptive studies can be identified; longitudinal and cross-sectional. *Cross-sectional studies* involve a sample from the population of interest and a number of characteristics of the sample members are measured once at a single point of time. *Longitudinal studies* involve panels; they provide repeated measurement over time, either on the same variables (panels) or on different variables (omnibus panels). The sample members in a panel are measured repeatedly, as contrasted to the one-time measurement in a cross-sectional study. The most common form of cross-sectional study is the sample survey.

Primary data collection methods

In Figure 4.6 a distinction was made between three methods of primary data collection: observation, communication and experimentation. Experimentation differs from the other methods in terms of degree of control over the research situation. Experimentation is the method typically used in causal research and its characteristics will be discussed in the next section. The observation and the communication methods are used for cross-sectional and longitudinal studies.

Observation methods

Scientific observation is the systematic process of recording the behavioural pattern of people, objects and occurrences without questioning or communicating with them. The market analyst using the observation method of data collection witnesses and records information as events occur or compiles evidence from records of past events. At least five kinds of phenomena can be observed:

- Physical actions and evidence, such as purchases, store locations and layout, posted prices, shelf space and display, promotions.
- Temporal patterns, such as shopping or driving time.
- Spatial relations and locations, such as traffic counts or shopping patterns.
- Expressive behaviour, such as eye movement or levels of emotional arousal.
- Published records, such as analysis of advertisements or newspaper articles.

The most important advantage of the observational method is its *unobtrusive nature* since communication with the respondent is not necessary. The 'observer' may be a person or the data may be gathered using some mechanical device such as a traffic counter, TV audiometers placed in homes to record and observe behaviour, or optical scanners in supermarkets to record sales and purchase behaviour. Observational data are typically more objective and accurate than communication data.

Technological systems such as the universal product code (UPC) have had a major impact on mechanical observations, and UPC consumer panels now provide companies with quick, accurate and dynamic data about how their products are selling, who is buying them and the factors that affect purchase.

Despite their advantages, observation methods have one crucial limitation; they cannot observe motives, attitudes, preferences and intentions. Thus, they can be used only to secure primary behavioural data.

Exhibit 4.2

Specification of the Information to Collect

A firm is considering the launching of new food product to be purchased by medium–high income family housewives. The questions which must be examined before the beginning of the field work are:

- *Who?*   Who is the target person? The buyer, the user, the prescriber?
- *What?*   Which characteristics to measure: the socio-demographic profile, the attitude, preferences, purchasing habits, and so on?
- *When?*   When to ask? Before or at the purchasing time, after the use of the product, how long after, and so on?
- *Where?*   At the purchasing place, at home, at the working place, and so on?
- *Why?*   What is the purpose of the study, what use will be made of the results?
- *How?*   How to proceed? Face-to-face interview, telephone, mail, and so on.

The answers to these questions are not obvious. The results of the exploratory study should be useful to reduce the sources of uncertainty.

Communication methods

Communication involves questioning respondents to secure the desired information, using a data collection instrument called a questionnaire. The questions may be oral or in writing and the responses may also be given in either form. There are three methods of collecting survey data: personal interviewing, telephone interviewing and mail or self-administered questionnaires:

1. *Personal interviewing.* This method is well suited for complex product concepts requiring extensive explanations or for new products. Information is sought in face-to-face question-and-answer sessions between an interviewer and a respondent. The interviewer usually has a questionnaire as a guide, although it is possible to use visual aids. Answers are generally recorded during the interview. Personal interviews get a high response rate, but are also more costly to administer than the other forms. The presence of an interviewer may also influence the subjects' responses.

2. *Telephone interviewing.* This is best suited for well-defined basic product concepts or specific product features. Questioning is done over the telephone. The information sought is well-defined, non-confidential in nature and limited in amount. The method has the advantage of speed in data collection and lower costs per interview. However, some telephone numbers are not listed in directories, and this causes problems in obtaining a representative sample. Absence of face-to-face contact and inability to use visual materials are other limitations.

3. *Mail questionnaires*. These are used to broaden the base of an investigation. They are most effective when well-defined concepts are involved and specific limited answers are required. They are generally less expensive than telephone and personal interviews, but they also have a much lower response rate. Several methods can be used to encourage a higher response rate. Questionnaires by mail must be more structured than others.

A comparison of the advantages and disadvantages of these three methods is made in Table 4.3. Each method of data collection has its own merits. Often these methods can be used in combination; for example, the telephone can be used to introduce the topic and to secure co-operation from the respondent. If the attitude is positive, the questionnaire is then sent by mail with a covering letter. Through this procedure, reasons for refusal can be obtained and follow-up calls can be made to secure the needed response.

Questionnaire design

Good questionnaire design is the key to obtaining good survey results. A questionnaire is simply a set of questions selected to generate the data necessary for accomplishing a research project's objective. Developing questionnaires may appear to be simple, especially to those who have never designed one.

> A good questionnaire appears as easy to compose, as does a good poem. The end product should look as if effortlessly written by an inspired child, but it is usually the result of long, painstaking work. (Erdos, 1970)

The function of the questionnaire is that of measurement. The questionnaire is the main channel through which data are obtained from respondents and transferred to researchers, who in turn will transfer this certified knowledge to managers for decision making. This channel has a dual communication role: (a) it must communicate to the respondent what the researcher is asking for, and (b) it must communicate to the researcher what the respondent has to say. The accuracy of data gathered through questionnaires will be greatly influenced by the amount of distortion or 'noise' that occurs in the two types of communication. A sloppy questionnaire can lead to a great deal of distortion in the communication from researcher to respondents, and vice versa.

> To assume that people will understand the questions is a common error. People simply may not know what is being asked. They may be unaware of the product or topic of interest; they may confuse the subject with something else, or the question may not mean the same thing to everyone interviewed. Respondents may refuse to answer personal questions. Most of these problems may be minimised if a skilled researcher composes the questionnaire. (Zikmund, 1986, p. 371)

Figure 4.7 shows that the questionnaire is at the interface of the four participants in any survey:

● The *decider*, who requires specific information to solve a decision problem.
● The *market analyst*, whose role is to translate the research problem into research questions.

Table 4.3   Comparison of survey methods

TYPE	ADVANTAGES	DISADVANTAGES
Personal Interview	1. Allows interviewer to gain additional information from his own observation. 2. Better control over the sequence of questions. 3. Allows more detailed information to be gathered. 4. Usually get a higher percentage of completed answers, since interviewer is there to explain exactly what is wanted. 5. Can use visual aids (for example, tables, charts, samples and prototypes) to demonstrate concepts. 6. Allows in-depth exploration of product attributes and how to solve problems. 7. Is flexible to allow interviewer to adjust questions to respondent's greatest interests. 8. Personal contact often stimulates greater co-operation and interest by respondents.	1. Can be costly when compared to other methods, especially when wide geographic areas must be covered. 2. Interviewer bias can seriously cause misleading responses and misrecording of answers. 3. Requires detailed supervision of data collection process. 4. Time-consuming to train interviewers and to obtain data. 5. May distract respondents if interviewer is talking and writing answers at the same time. 6. Different approaches by different interviewers makes it difficult to standardise conduct of survey.
Telephone Survey	1. Fast (for example, quicker than personal or mail). 2. Inexpensive (for example, cost of an equal number of personal interviews would be substantially greater). 3. Easier to call back again if respondent is busy at the time. 4. Usually has only a small response bias because of closed-ended questions. 5. Has wide geographical reach.	1. Limited to number published in telephone directory. 2. Can usually obtain only a small amount of information. 3. Can usually provide only limited classification data. 4. Difficult to obtain motivational and attitudinal information. 5. Difficult for highly technical products or capital goods. 6. Can become expensive if long-distance calls are involved.
Mail Survey	1. Can get wide distribution at a relatively low cost per completed interview. 2. Helps avoid possible interviewer bias; absence of interviewer may lead to a more candid reply. 3. Can reach remote places (for example, drilling engineer on site in Saudi Arabia). 4. Unless his name is requested, the respondent remains anonymous and, therefore may give confidential information that otherwise would be withheld. 5. Respondent may be more inclined to answer since he can do so at his leisure.	1. Accurate, up-to-date mailing lists are not always available to ensure successful distribution. 2. As many as 80–90 per cent may not return questionnaires. Respondents generally have stronger feelings about the subject than non-respondents do. 3. Questionnaire length is limited. 4. Inability to ensure these questions are understood fully and answers are properly recorded. 5. It is difficult to lead respondents through questions one at the time since the respondent can read the entire questionnaire before answering. 6. Time-consuming. 7. Troublesome with certain highly technical products.

Source: adapted from Chase and Barasch (1977).

- The *interviewer*, who has to collect reliable information from respondents.
- The *respondents*, who have to agree to communicate the information sought.

One important characteristic of a good questionnaire is its degree of standardisation – a condition required ensuring that the answers obtained from different respondents and through different interviewers are indeed comparable and therefore lend themselves to statistical analysis.

Questionnaire design procedure

Although there are no rules for developing a flawless questionnaire, the collective experience of numerous researchers offers a broad set of guidelines for minimising the likelihood and the severity of data validity problems in designing questionnaires. On this topic, an excellent reference remains Boyd and Westfall (1972). A seven-step procedure is proposed to assist the design of a questionnaire.

Step 1: Determine the information required. Since the questionnaire is the link between the information needs and the data to be collected, the researcher must have a *detailed listing of the information needs* as well as a clear identification of the respondent group. This step is normally the result of exploratory research and of the hypothesis development phases. The different forms of market response described in the preceding chapter will help the analyst to identify the concepts to be measured.

Step 2: Determine the type of questionnaire to be used. Data collection can be made by personal interview, mail or telephone. The choice among these alternatives is largely determined by the type of information to be obtained. It is necessary to decide on the *type of questionnaire* at this point since the content and wording of the questions, the length of the questionnaire and the sequence of questions will all be influenced by this decision. A decision to use conjoint analysis, for example, would preclude the use of a telephone interview. Thus, at this stage the market analysis must specify precisely how the primary data needed will be collected and also the type of analysis to be made with the data.

Step 3: Determine the content of individual questions. Once the information needed is known and the data collection method decided, the researcher is ready to begin formulating the questions. Several points should be reviewed systematically once the content of questions is determined:

- *Is the question necessary?* Avoid including interesting questions, which are not directly related to the information needed.

- *Are several questions needed instead of one?* Some questions may have two or more elements and if these are left in one question, interpretation becomes impossible. This is typically the case for the 'why' question.

- *Does the respondent have the information requested?* Three sub-questions can be examined: (1) is the point raised within the respondent's experience? (2) can the respondent remember the information? (3) Will the respondent have to do a lot of work to get the information?

- *Will respondents give the information?* Even though they know the answer, respondents will sometimes not answer questions because (1) they are unable to phrase their answer or (2) because they do not want to answer.

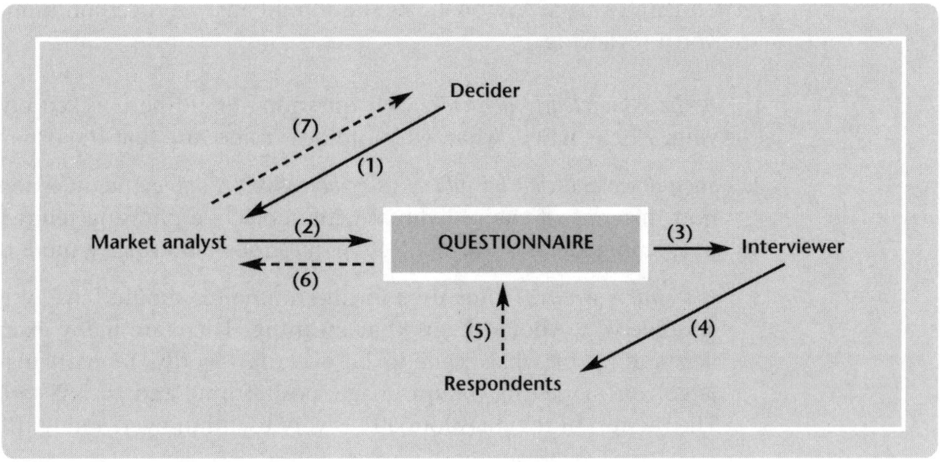

Figure 4.7   The key role of the questionnaire in a survey

Step 4: Determine the type of question to use. In forming the actual questions, the researcher has the choice between three major types of questions:

⬤ *An open-ended question* requires the respondents to provide their own answers to the question.

⬤ A *multiple-choice question* requires the respondent to choose an answer from a list provided with the question. The respondent may be asked to choose one or more of the alternatives presented.

⬤ A *dichotomous question* is an extreme form of the multiple-choice question which allows the respondent only two responses, such as yes–no, agree–disagree and so on.

Examples of questions are presented in Appendix 4.1.

In a multiple-choice question, when the proposed answers are ranked, the objective is not simply to identify a category as in a *nominal scale*, but rather to 'measure' a level of agreement, a degree of importance or a level of preference. Two types of scale can be used: an *ordinal scale* where the numbers possess the property of rank order or an *interval scale* which has all the properties of an ordinal scale and, in addition, the differences between scale values can be meaningfully interpreted. The distinction is important because the permissible mathematical operations are different with each type of scale. In practice, responses to questions on importance or preference are frequently assumed to form an interval scale.

Different scales are currently used. The most common are the *Likert scale* with descriptor labels attached to each category, the *semantic differential scale* using bipolar adjectives and the *constant sum scale*, where the respondent is instructed to allocate a given sum among two or more attributes on the basis of their importance to that respondent. This is the procedure used in Chapter 6 to measure a multi-attribute model (see Table 6.3) through the compositional method.

Step 5: Decide the wording of questions. The problem at this stage is to phrase the questions in a way that (1) the respondent can easily understand and (2) does not give the respondent a clue as to how he or she should answer. A certain number of questions are worth reviewing.

1. *Is the issue clearly defined?* Each question should be checked on the six points: who, where, when, what, why and how to be sure that the issue is clear.

2. *Should the question be subjective or objective?* A subjective question puts the question in terms of the individual while objective phrasing tends to refer to what people in general think. Subjective questions tend to give more reliable results.

3. *Use simple words.* Words used in questionnaires should have only one meaning, and everyone should know that meaning. There are many examples of misunderstanding of what seem to be everyday words. In particular, the technical jargon of marketing (brand image, positioning, and so on) should be avoided. The pre-test of the questionnaire is very useful in overcoming this difficulty.

4. *Avoid ambiguous questions.* Ambiguous questions mean different things to different people. Indefinite words as *often, occasionally, frequently, many, good, fair, poor* and so on may have many different meaning. For example, *frequent reading* of *The Economist* may be six or seven issues a year for one person and twice a year for another.

5. *Avoid leading or one-sided questions.* A leading question is one that may steer respondents towards a certain answer. One-sided questions present only one aspect of an issue. A question should be constructed in as neutral a way as possible, by avoiding the name of a brand or a company or by presenting all the sides of an issue.

6. *Avoid double-barrelled questions.* A double-barrelled question is one that calls for two responses and thereby creates confusion for the respondents. In this case, two questions instead of one are necessary.

7. *Use split-ballot wherever possible.* There is no wording that is the only correct one for a question. When there are two wordings from which to choose, but no basis on which to select one in preference to the other, one wording can be adopted on half of the questionnaires and the other on the other half.

Step 6: Decide the sequence of questions. There are generally three major sections in a questionnaire: (1) the basic information sought; (2) the socio-demographic information useful in obtaining the profile of the respondent and (3) the identification sections to be used by the interviewer. The general rule is to put the sections in that order: the body of the questionnaire in first position and the socio-demographic questions at the end, unless they serve as filter questions to qualify respondents for the survey. The researcher should also pay attention to the following points:

1. *Use simple and interesting opening questions.* If the opening questions are interesting, simple to comprehend and easy to answer, the respondent's co-operation will be gained.

2. *Use the funnel approach.* The funnel approach involves beginning with a very general question on a topic and gradually leading up to a narrowly focused question on the same topic.

3. *Arrange questions in logical order.* The order should be logical to the respondent. Sudden changes in subject confuse the respondent and cause indecision.

4. *Place difficult or sensitive questions near the end.* Sensitive questions should be relegated towards the end of the questionnaire, once the respondent has become involved in the study.

A mail questionnaire raises specific sequence problems since it must sell itself. It is particularly important that the opening questions capture the respondent's interest. Questions should then proceed in logical order. In a mail questionnaire, it is not possible, however, to take advantage of sequence position in the same way as in personal interviews since it is the respondent who will decide the order of response. The layout and physical attractiveness are particularly important for a self-administered questionnaire.

Step 7: Pre-test the questionnaire. Before a questionnaire is ready for the field it needs to be pre-tested under field conditions. Pre-testing involves administering the questionnaire to a limited number of potential respondents selected on a convenience basis but not too divergent from the target population. It is not necessary, however, to have a statistical sample for pre-testing. The pre-testing process allows the researcher to determine if the respondents have any difficulty in understanding the questionnaire or if there are ambiguous or biased questions. Tabulating the results of the pre-test is also very useful to ensure that all the needed information will be obtained.

Sampling methods

Once the market analyst has developed and tested the questionnaire, the next question is the selection of the respondents from whom the information will be collected. One way to do this would be to collect information from each member of the target population through a *census*. Another way would be to select a fraction of the population by taking a *sample* of respondents. The census approach is frequently adopted in industrial market research studies when the target population has a total size of 100 to 300 units. In most situations, however, the population sizes are large and the cost and time required to contact each member of the population would be prohibitively high. Thus, sampling can be defined as follows:

> Sampling is the selection of a fraction of the target population for the ultimate purpose of being able to draw general conclusions about the entire target population.

Sampling techniques can be divided into two broad categories of probability and non-probability samples:

- *In a probability sample,* an objective selection procedure is used and each member of the population has a known, non-zero chance of being included in the sample.

- *In a non-probability sample,* the selection procedure used is subjective and the probability of selection for each population unit is unknown.

These two sample selection procedures have their own merits. The main superiority of probability sampling is that there are appropriate statistical techniques for measuring random sampling error, while in non-probability samples the tools of statistical inference cannot be legitimately employed. If, as a general rule, a probability sample should be preferred, there are situations where non-probability samples are useful, namely because they are less costly and easier to organise.

Probability samples

The different types of probability samples are simple random samples, stratified samples (proportionate or disproportionate), cluster samples and multi-stage area samples:

- *A simple random sample* is a sampling procedure that assures that each element of the population will have not only a known but also an *equal chance* of being included in the sample. Different drawing procedures exist (random number, systematic sampling), which all presuppose the existence of a list of the population members.

- *In a stratified sample* the target population is subdivided into mutually exclusive groups – based on criteria such as size, income or age – and random samples are drawn from each group, called a 'stratum'. In a proportionate stratified sample the total sample is allocated among the strata in proportion to the size of each stratum, while in a disproportionate stratified sample, the total sample is allocated on the basis of relative variability observed in each stratum.

- *In a cluster sample*, the target population is divided into mutually exclusive subgroups called clusters instead of strata, and a random sample of the subgroups is then selected. Thus, each subgroup must be a small-scale model (or a miniature population) of the total population. The difference between stratified and cluster sampling is illustrated in Figure 4.8.

- *Multi-stage area sampling* involves two or more steps that combine some of the probability techniques of cluster sampling. Instead of picking all the units from the randomly chosen clusters (or area), only a sample of units is randomly picked from each of them; the selected subclusters themselves can be subsampled. The main advantage of multi-stage area sampling is to permit probability samples to be drawn even when a current list of population is unavailable.

In general, probability sampling methods will be more time-consuming and expensive than non-probability sampling methods because (1) they require an accurate specification of the population and an enumeration of the units of the population and (2) because the selection procedure of the sample units must be precisely followed.

Non-probability samples

Three types of non-probability sampling can be identified: convenience, judgemental and quota:

- *Convenience sampling* refers to a sampling procedure of obtaining the respondents who are most conveniently available for the market analyst.

● *Judgemental sampling* is a procedure in which the market analyst exerts some effort in selecting a sample of respondents that he or she feels most appropriate for the research objectives.

● *Quota sampling* resembles stratified random sampling and convenience sampling. The interviewer finds and interviews a prescribed number of people in each of several categories. The sample units are selected on a subjective rather than a probabilistic basis.

In general, the choice between probability and non-probability sampling involves a trade-off between the capability to generalise the sample results to the target population with a known degree of accuracy and lower time/cost requirements.

Errors in survey research

One of the main responsibilities of the market analyst in charge of a survey is to estimate the overall accuracy and reliability of the survey results. The total error associated with a survey can be subdivided into two broad categories: sampling error and non-sampling error, also called systematic bias. The different sources of error, sampling and non-sampling, are described in Figure 4.9.

The size of the sampling error can be reduced by increasing the sample size or by improving the design of the sampling procedure. More difficult to control are the

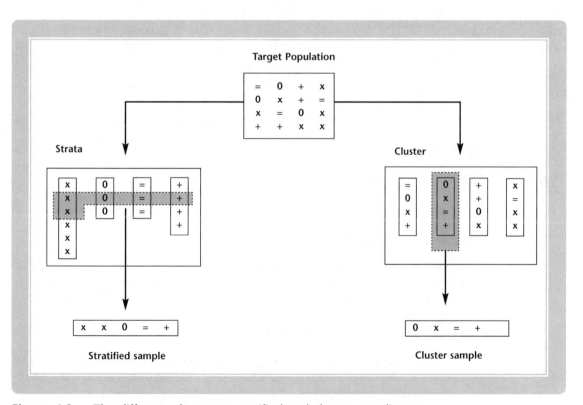

Figure 4.8 The difference between stratified and cluster sampling

non-sampling errors, which arise from a multitude of factors, such as poor question-naire construction, ill-trained interviewers, errors from respondents or errors in coding responses. The best way to minimise non-sampling errors is to have a strict control over the entire process of primary data gathering, coding and analysis. If the survey research is subcontracted to a market research company, the market analyst should give precise instructions and closely supervise the fieldwork.

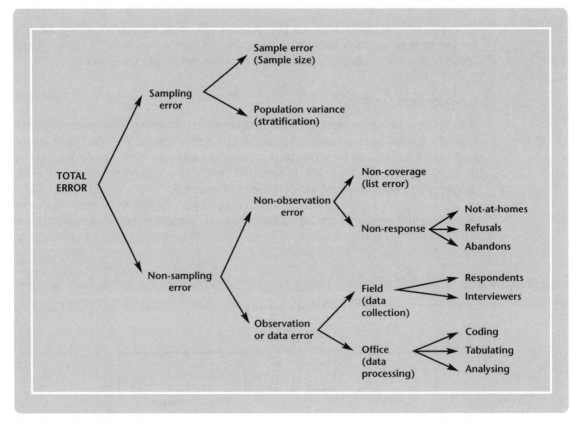

Figure 4.9   Total error in survey research

Data analysis to knowledge

Once data have been collected, emphasis in the research process turns to analysis. The raw data collected in the field must be transformed into information that will help to answer the questions raised by the decider. The transformation of raw data into information and to knowledge is achieved in several steps: data conversion, descriptive analysis and inferential analysis:

⬤ *Data conversion* implies data editing, coding, storing and tabulating, in order to obtain an organised collection of data records (called a data set or data bank) which lends itself to analysis.

● *Descriptive analysis* gives an initial idea about the nature of the data; it involves obtaining appropriate measures of central tendency and of dispersion of the data for all variables, frequency distribution, cross-tabulations, graphic representations and so forth. Multivariate techniques like factorial analysis can also be used to summarise data.

● *Inferential analysis* aims at exploring the extent and nature of possible associations between pairs of variables, to test hypotheses about the target population or to examine the statistical significance of differences.

Attitude and brand (or corporate) image measurement is an important application of surveys and will be discussed in Chapter 6. Several multivariate data analysis methods presented there are based on survey data. These methods are used to extract meaningful information from primary data. The most popular ones are: simple and regression analysis, discriminant analysis, factorial analysis, multi-dimensional scaling and cluster analysis. For an overview of applications and problems of these techniques, see Hair *et al.* (1992).

● Causal Research Studies

The use of a two-way table to uncover a relationship between two variables is common practice in descriptive research. A frequent temptation when a two-way table shows evidence of a statistically significant relationship, especially if one variable is presumed to influence the other (as in regression analysis) is to view this result as conclusive evidence of a causal relationship. This temptation should be resisted unless the empirical evidence stems from an experiment in which the other variables that may influence the response variable were controlled. A *causal research design* is required to establish the existence of a causal link. A descriptive study can only suggest the existence of a causal link. The basic tool used in causal studies is the controlled experiment.

Objectives of causal studies

In descriptive studies it is impossible to separate entirely the effect of a given variable from the effect of other variables. Causal studies overcome this difficulty by organising the data-gathering procedure in such way as to permit unambiguous interpretation. Causal studies have three distinct, although very complementary, research objectives:

● To establish the direction and the intensity of a *causal link* between one or several action variables and one response variable.
● To measure in quantitative terms the *rate of influence* of an action variable on a response variable.
● To generate *predictions* of a response variable for different levels of the action variables.

These three objectives can be dissociated and several causal studies have the sole objective of establishing a cause-and-effect relationship in order to gain a better understanding of the phenomenon under study. In these cases, no quantitative estimates of the influence rate are sought.

Three rather intuitive types of evidence are relevant for evaluating causal relationships:

● Evidence that the action variable *precedes* the response variable.
● Evidence that a strong *association* exists between an action and an observed outcome.
● Evidence that the influence of *other possible causal factors* has been eliminated or controlled.

This last condition is particularly demanding and requires that all extraneous variables be controlled in order to ensure that the experiment has not been confused. The most important *threats to internal validity* in an experiment are briefly described here:

● *History:* event external to the experiment that affects the responses of the people involved in the experiment.

● *Maturation:* changes in the respondents that are a consequence of time, such as ageing, getting hungry or getting tired.

● *Testing effect:* awareness of being in a test which can sensitise and bias respondents.

● *Before-measure effect*: the before-measure effect can also sensitise and bias respondents, therefore influencing both the after-observation and the respondent's reaction to the experiment treatment.

● *Instrumentation:* the measuring instrument may change, for example, when there are many observers or interviewers.

● *Mortality:* respondents may drop out of the experiment.

● *Selection bias:* an experimental group may be systematically different in some relevant way from the target population.

An experimental design is specifically constructed by the market analyst to ensure that these extraneous factors are eliminated or controlled.

Experimentation defined

Experimentation is a scientific investigation in which the researcher manipulates and controls one or more action variables and observes the response variable(s) for variation concomitant to the manipulation of the action variable. *Treatments* are the action variables that are manipulated and whose effects are measured. The *test units* are the entities, respondents or physical units to whom the treatments are presented and whose response is measured.

An *experimental design* involves the specification of (a) the treatments that are to be manipulated, (b) the test units to be used, (c) the response variable to be measured and (d) the procedure for dealing with extraneous variables.

Two types of experimentation can be distinguished:

● In a *laboratory experiment* in which the researcher creates a situation with the desired conditions (a trailer set up as a store or a survey situation) and then manipulates some variables while controlling others.

● A *field experiment* is organised in a realistic or natural situation (in-store test), although it too involves the manipulation of one or more action variables under carefully controlled conditions.

In general, field experiments are superior to laboratory experiments in terms of external validity.

Types of experimental design

In a typical experiment two groups of respondents (or stores) are selected in such a way that the groups have similar characteristics as far as the purpose of the study is concerned. The causal factor or the treatment (for example, advertising A) is introduced into one of the two groups, called the *experimental group*. No such factor is introduced in the other group, called the *control group*. If sales increase withi. the experimental group but not in the control group, it is inferred that the hypothes.ɔ is tenable, that is that advertising caused the sales increase. If no sales increase occurs in the experimental group, or if sales increase to the same extent in the control group, it is inferred that the hypothesis is not tenable (Boyd and Westfall, 1956, p. 82).

Within this general pattern, experimental designs vary in the manner in which experimental and control groups are selected and the degree of control that is exercised over the extraneous factors that affect the results. To illustrate this, two pre-experimental designs and two true experimental designs will be discussed briefly.

The 'one shot' case study. A single group of test units is exposed to treatment (X) and then an 'after' measurement (O) is then taken on the response variable. Thus we have

$$X \ O$$

This is not a true experimental design and it is clearly impossible to draw any meaningful conclusions from it. The observed level of O may be the result of many uncontrollable factors and in the absence of pre-treatment observation, it is impossible to conclude.

The one group 'before–after' design. In this design a 'before' measurement is made in addition to the 'after' measurement. Thus, we have

$$O_1 \ X \ O_2$$

The difference between the 'after' and 'before' measurements ($X_2 - X_1$) would be assumed to be the effect of the treatment (X). This assumption is questionable, however, because the difference between the 'after' and the 'before' measurements could very well be a measure of the treatment *plus* the changes caused by all the uncontrolled factors, such as history, maturation, testing effect and so on.

The 'before–after' design with control group. A true experiment is one where the researcher is able to eliminate all extraneous factors as competitive hypotheses to the treatment. An experimental and a control group are selected in such way that they are interchangeable for purposes of the experiment. The control group is measured at the same time as the experimental group, but no treatment is introduced. Thus, we have

$$\textit{Experimental group: } O_1 \ X \ O_2$$
$$\textit{Control group: } \quad\ \ O_3 \qquad O_4$$

Thus, the difference between the 'after' and the 'before' measurements of the control group $(O_4 - O_3)$ is the result of uncontrolled variables. The difference between the 'after' and 'before' measurements of the experimental group $(O_2 - O_1)$ is the result of the treatment *plus* the result of the same uncontrollable events affecting the control group. The effect of the treatment alone is obtained by subtracting the difference in the two measurements of the control group from the two measurements of the experimental group.

$$True\ treatment\ effect = [O_1 - O_2] - [O_4 - O_3]$$

All potential destroyers of internal validity are controlled by this design, except the testing effect in the experimental group, which is not eliminated.

Thus, when the 'before' measurement is made in an undisguised way – for example, by interviewing respondents – the *interactive testing effect* is likely to be present and cannot be separated from the treatment effect. If the collection of the data is made without the knowledge of the individuals involved, this design is appropriate. In the other cases, a way to escape the problem of the testing effect is the 'after-only with control group' design.

'After-only with control group' design. In this design, the experimental and the control groups are selected in such a way as to be equivalent. No 'before' measurement is made in either group and the treatment is introduced in one of the groups selected as the experimental group.

$$X\ O_1$$
$$O_2$$

The effect of the treatment is determined by computing the difference between the two 'after' measurements $(O_2 - O_1)$. In this design, uncontrollable factors influence both the control and the experimental groups and there is no testing effect because no pre-measurements are made. The only weakness of this design is its *static nature*, which does not permit an analysis of the process of change as in the 'before–after' design. A classic example of application of this design is the 'Instant Nescafe study' summarised in Table 4.4.

> The objective of the study was to determine the image of the housewife who uses instant coffee. Two comparable groups of housewives were shown similar shopping lists and asked to describe the housewife who prepared the list. On the list shown to the control group, one item was Maxwell House Coffee, a well-known drip grinds coffee brand. On the list shown the experimental group, the item was replaced by Nescafé Instant Coffee, a relatively new concept at the time. The results measured were the percentages of the respondents who described the shopping list author as having various characteristics. The effect of the treatment (Nescafé Instant Coffee user) was the difference in the percentage ascribing each characteristic to the 'instant coffee woman' from the percentage ascribing the same characteristics to the 'drip grind' woman. (Boyd and Westfall, 1972, p. 96)

The results of this experiment, a replication of a study conducted by Mason Haire in 1950 – are summarised in Table 4.4. A chi-square test shows that there are no significant differences between characteristics ascribed to the Maxwell shopper and those for the Nescafé shopper (Webster and von Pechmann, 1970, pp. 61–3).

A fundamental principle is implicitly assumed to be applicabl
design: the market analyst does not care what extraneous factors a
as they operate equally on all experimental and control groups. Thus *ran*
test units and of the groups and random allocation of the treat
groups are key conditions of validity.

Table 4.4   Results of the instant coffee experiment

Measurements	Experimental group		Control group	
Before measurement	No		No	
Treatment variable	Instant coffee (Nescafé)		Drip grind coffee (Maxwell)	
After measurements	Lazy	18%	Lazy	10%
	Thrifty	36%	Thrifty	55%
	Spendthrift	23%	Spendthrift	5%
	Bad wife	18%	Bad wife	5%

Source: Webster and von Pechmann (1970, p. 62).

With the development of scanner systems in supermarkets, the organisation of marketing experiments is greatly facilitated today.

Conjoint analysis

Conjoint analysis is a multivariate technique used specifically to understand how consumers develop preferences for products or services and to formulate predictions about market attitude *vis-à-vis* new product concepts. The method is based on the *multi-attribute product concept* (see Chapter 3), that is on the premise that consumers evaluate the value or utility of a product/service idea, by combining the separate amounts of utility provided by each attribute. The power of the method is to provide an explanatory model of consumers' preferences, which can then be used to define the product concept constituting the optimum combination of attribute levels. In a more precise way, a conjoint analysis brings answers to the following questions:

- For the respondent, what is the *partial utility* (or the part worth) of each level of each attribute used to define the product/service?
- What is the *relative importance* (weight) of each attribute in the overall evaluation of the product concept?
- How do compare the *total utilities* of several concepts representing different bundles of attributes?
- What kind of *trade-off or arbitrage* are potential consumers willing to make between levels of attributes?
- What is the *share of preferences* of potential buyers for the different product concepts investigated?

This method of preference analysis, as any research method, has some limitations. It is difficult to apply, (a) when the attributes are totally new to consumers,

(b) when the number of attributes to consider to have a realistic description of the product concept are too large and (c) when the cognitive capacities of the respondents are weak.

The premises of conjoint analysis

The conjoint analysis method is based on a set of assumptions or hypotheses that will be summarised here:

1. The buyer perceives a product or service as a *bundle of attributes* or characteristics, each being represented at a specific level. The level of each attribute generates the benefit(s) sought.

2. When a potential buyer evaluates a product, she (or he) mentally associates a value (or a utility) to each attribute level; these values, which are called *partial utilities*, reflect her (or his) personal value system.

3. To determine the *total utility* of the product, the buyer mentally combines the amounts of utility provided by each attribute at various levels.

4. The rule used in combining attributes to produce an evaluation of the total utility of the product/service is a *compensatory rule*. As will be discussed in Chapter 5, this means that the buyer, in evaluating the whole bundle, mentally offsets weak scores on one attribute by high scores on another to make his final judgement.

The method, which is also called *trade-off analysis*, is based on the arbitrage principle by which the respondent must consider both the 'good' and the 'bad' characteristics of the product to form his final preference. Is the buyer ready to sacrifice one attribute (for example price or weight) to gain more satisfaction on another (for example luxury design or power)? This type of arbitrage will be used to estimate the value of the partial utilities. To compare the different product concepts, the researcher must select a measure of preference: the non-metric rank-ordering method (that is rank-ordering the product concepts from most to least preferred); or the metric rating method (that is a 1 to 10 scale).

Identification of the attributes

Perhaps the most important decision an analyst makes in conjoint analysis is selecting the attributes to characterise the product/service. This first step implies a good knowledge of the decision criteria used by buyers and also of their determinants. This type of information can be obtained through exploratory research, focus group studies, descriptive research or through experts' judgements, such as distributors, prescribers, and so on. It is essential that the selected attributes or characteristics meet the following conditions:

1. To define the *total worth of the concept*, considering both positive and negative attributes.
2. To select all the *determinant choice criteria*, which best differentiate between the products. Some factors may be important but not discriminating criteria.
3. To be *independent factors*, that is not redundant; the presence of one does imply necessarily the presence of another.

4. To be *actionable attributes* and not 'fuzzy' attributes; the factors and levels of the factors must be capable of being put into practice.

The total number of factors should not be too high. Adding attributes directly affects the statistical efficiency and reliability by increasing the number of parameters to estimate. Good results have been obtained with a maximum of 7 attributes. Also, increasing the number of levels very rapidly increases the number of distinct concepts to be compared and evaluated by the respondents, with the risk of information overload.

> In a conjoint analysis for cleaning products conducted by Green and Wind (1975), 5 attributes or characteristics were retained, of which 3 (brand name, packaging and price) were at 3 levels each and 2 ('Good Housekeeping' seal and guarantee) at 2 levels (yes or no). In total, in a complete factorial design, one would have (3 × 3 × 3 × 2 × 2) = 108 distinct product concepts to compare and to rank. Clearly a mission impossible. In fact, using a fractional factorial design, only 18 concept comparisons are required.

In practice, if the full profile method is used, it is advisable not to present more than 20 concepts to the respondents. The ideal number is between 15 and 20. Beyond this number the non-response rate, due to fatigue or boredom, becomes very high.

Fractional factorial design

In reality, as experimentation theory shows, it is not necessary to adopt a complete factorial design with all possible combinations to estimate the main effects of the attributes and their first-order interactions. It is quite feasible to design a fractional factorial design, while still maintaining orthogonality (that is absence of correlation) among the partial utilities estimates.

Table 4.5 Example of Latin square design

	B1	B2	B3	B4
TN1	P1	P2	P3	P4
TN2	P2	P3	P4	P1
TN3	P3	P4	P1	P2
TN4	P4	P1	P2	P3

B = brand; TN = tar and nicotine; P = price.

When the number of levels is the same for each attribute, the experimental design is symmetrical and one can adopt a *'Latin square'*, a *'Greco-Latin square'* or a *'hyper Greco-Latin' square* design, when the number of attributes is 3, 4 or 5 respectively.

> For example, in a price elasticity experiment in the blended cigarettes segment, three attributes at 4 levels each were considered; the brand (B), the content in tar (T) and nicotine (N) and the price (P). In a full factorial design, we would have 64 (4 × 4 × 4) distinct product concepts. By adopting a Latin square design, the number of concepts to evaluate is reduced to 16, as shown in Table 4.5.

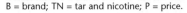

Each product concept is described on a profile card. The tasks of the respondents are to rank the 16 cards by order of preference, from the most (or least) to the least (or most) preferred.

When there is no symmetry, that is when the number of levels is different attribute by attribute, one can still augment the number of repetitions to make it symmetrical. In a study of the impact of different public information campaigns concerning ozone destruction, Frutsaert (1989) has measured hair spray users' attitudes *vis-à-vis* aerosols. The attributes considered were: brand: (L'Oréal, Garnier, Gillette and Riem); price: (50, 100, 150 and 200BF; types of packaging: spray or aerosol.

We have here three attributes of which two have four levels and one two levels only, thus in total we have 32 ($4 \times 4 \times 2$) distinct product concepts. A Latin square design requires the same number of levels for each attribute. To make the design symmetrical, the two levels of the attribute 'packaging' were 'repeated', while respecting the orthogonality condition. In doing so, we obtain 16 different product concepts with more observations on the attribute 'packaging' which is precisely the main preoccupation of the study.

When the design is not symmetrical and the number of attributes is higher, other experimental designs can be adopted. These designs are described in the literature and in particular in Addelman (1962).

Preference data collection methods

To collect the preference data, two methods exist: the full-profile and the paired comparison methods.

The most popular method is the *full-profile* presentation, principally because of its ability to reduce the number of comparisons through the use of fractional factorial designs. In this approach, each product concept is described separately, most often on a profile card. This approach elicits fewer judgements and the judgements can be either ranked or rated. Among its advantages are:

- a more realistic description achieved by defining levels of each attribute in the product concept,
- a more explicit portrayal of the trade-offs among all attributes,
- a situation which is very close to the actual purchase behaviour.

The main limitation is the risk of fatigue due to information overload when the number of concepts to rank or to rate is large, even if a fractional factorial design is used, a problem which is avoided by using the paired comparison method.

In the *paired comparison method*, the respondent does not have to rank the n concepts simultaneously, but only two by two. In this method, $n(n - 1)/2$ paired comparisons of concepts will have to be done successively. Generally, this method makes the task of the respondent longer but easier. The analyst will then have to regroup the paired comparisons in a single evaluation.

Estimating partial utilities

The options available in terms of estimation techniques have increased dramatically in recent years, more particularly in conjunction with the use of the adaptive conjoint technique. Rank-order evaluations require a modified form of variance analysis specifically designed for ordinal data. Among the most popular and best known computer programs are MONANOVA and LINMAP. If a metric measure of preference is obtained (for example rating rather than rankings), multiple regression methods with dummy variables (0.1) can be used, as illustrated as follows.

Table 4.6 Example of data bank used in a conjoint analysis

Concepts	Rank (y)	Explanatory variables (x)							
		K	M2	M3	M4	P2	P3	P4	C2
1	–	1	0	0	0	1	0	0	1
2	–	1	1	0	0	1	0	0	1
3	–	1	0	1	0	1	0	0	0
4	–	1	0	0	1	1	0	0	0
5	–	1	0	0	0	0	1	0	1
6	–	1	1	0	0	0	1	0	0
7	–	1	0	1	0	0	1	0	0
8	–	1	0	0	1	0	1	0	1
9	–	1	0	0	0	0	0	1	0
10	–	1	1	0	0	0	0	1	0
11	–	1	0	1	0	0	0	1	1
12	–	1	0	0	1	0	0	1	1
13	–	1	0	0	0	0	0	0	0
14	–	1	1	0	0	0	0	0	1
15	–	1	0	1	0	0	0	0	1
16	–	1	0	0	1	0	0	0	0
Repetitions	–		4	4	4	4	4	4	8

* Reference concept: M = L'Oréal; P = 200BF; C = aerosol.

When metric measures of preference are obtained, a multiple regression model must be built, where the dependent variable is the rating, or sometimes the rank from 1 to n. The levels of the attributes are the independent variables expressed in a dummy form (0,1), 0 meaning the absence of a level and 1 its presence. In the general case, each level has its own separate partial utility. Other more restrictive model specifications can be adopted: the linear model with a single coefficient or the quadratic form also called the ideal point model.

In the above hairspray example, the regression model to be estimated by least squares is described in Table 4.6. In this particular case, the reference product concept is represented by the following combination: 'M = L'Oréal; P = 200BF; C = aerosol'. In the rank column (y), the preference ranking given by the respondent will be indicated, from 16 for the most preferred to 1 for the least preferred. For each respondent, we will thus obtain one regression equation depicting his personal utility function.

The usual statistical tests (R2 and F-test) can be used to assess the reliability of the statistical results and to test the null hypothesis of no association between the dependent variable and the different explanatory variables. Similarly, the Student t-test will be used to test the statistical significance of the regression coefficients. By way of illustration, let us analyse the utility function of one respondent; the estimated regression equation is as follows:

$$\text{Rank} = 3.50 \quad -3.25M2 \quad -3.50M3 \quad -4.25M4 \quad +3.25P2 \quad +2.25P3 \quad +1.50P4 \quad +8.0C2$$
$$(5.0) \qquad (3.0) \qquad (3.2) \qquad (3.9) \qquad (3.0) \qquad (2.1) \qquad (1.4) \qquad (10.4)$$
$$R2 = 0.94 \qquad\qquad F\text{-test} =$$

First of all, one observes that the overall statistical fit is very good. The null hypothesis can be safely rejected, since the observed value of the F-test is clearly higher than its critical value at the 5 per cent confidence level. Similarly, all the t-Student (except one: P4), are higher than their limit values at the 10 per cent confidence interval. The constant term (3.50) gives the rank of the reference product concept (L'Oréal, aerosol, 200BF). The part worth gives the marginal gain or loss in ranks for each change in the package of attributes.

The results are presented in the form of utility curves, as shown in Figure 4.10. They give the following information regarding the value system of that particular respondent:

1. The first three coefficients measure the utility (or value) associated with the brand names: Garnier, Gillette and Groupe Riem. Since the signs are negative, one observes that these three brands are less positively evaluated than the reference brand which is l'Oréal.

2. The next three coefficients measure the price sensitivity: since the reference price is the highest (200BF), the utility increases as the price decreases from 200 to 50 (+3.25), from 200 to 100 (+2.25) and from 200 to 150BF (+1.50). Thus, as expected, the price elasticity is negative.

3. Finally, this particular respondent is very sensitive to the type of packaging and his (or her) satisfaction highly increases (+8) when the aerosol is replaced by the spray.

A last interesting piece of information is given by the *importance rate* given by the respondent(s) to each attribute or product characteristic. The range gives the importance rate, that is, the absolute difference observed between the highest and the lowest utility given to each characteristic. In this example, these values are presented in Table 4.7. The *relative importance* is obtained by dividing the range by the sum of the observed differences (here 15.5). For this respondent, the most important attribute is the packaging, then the brand name and finally the price.

Table 4.7 Measuring the relative importance of attributes

Attributes	Range	Relative importance (%)
Brand Name	0 – (–4.25) = 4.25	27.4
Price	0 – (–3.25) = 3.25	21.0
Design	0 – (8) = 8	51.6
Total	15.5	100.0

The next problem is to interpret the results for the entire sample of respondents. Two approaches can be adopted. First, one can calculate the average value of all the partial utilities observed for each attribute. This method, which has the merit of simplicity, implies however a loss of information since it boils down to assuming homogeneity of preferences within the target population. A second method, based on *cluster analysis*, will try to regroup respondents in segments homogeneous in terms of their preferences. This method is currently used in benefit segmentation (see Chapter 6).

Structural equations modelling

Data analysis methods have made considerable progress during the last decade and these techniques, called *second generation data analysis methods*, or structural equation modelling (SEM), have the capacity to examine a series of dependence relationships simultaneously, while standard multivariate techniques can examine only a single relationship at a time. In reality, the market analyst is often faced with a set of inter-related questions. For example, in a study aiming at measuring the performance of a store, the following interrelated questions have to be examined:

- What variables determine a store's image?

- How does that *image* combined with other variables (proximity, assortment) affect purchase decisions and *satisfaction* at the store?

- How does satisfaction with the store result in long-term *loyalty* to the store?

- How does loyalty to the store affect *visit frequency and exclusivity*?

- How does visit frequency and exclusivity determine the store *profitability*?

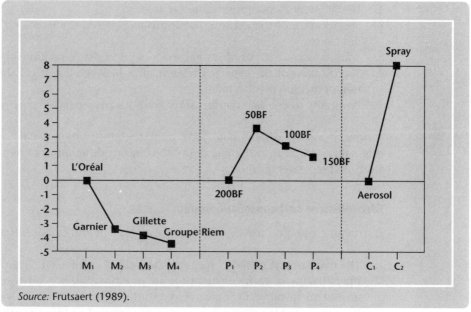

Source: Frutsaert (1989).

Figure 4.10 Partial utilities for one respondent

As illustrated in Figure 4.11, we have here a series of dependence relationships where one dependent variable (store image) becomes an independent variable (among others) in subsequent dependence relationship (satisfaction) which in turn 'explains' another dependent variable (loyalty), and so on. Until the 1980s, none of the multivariate techniques allowed us to address these questions with a single comprehensive method. For a review of these methods, see Hair *et al.* (1992) and Croutsche (1997).

The concept of a latent variable

A distinctive feature of SEM is the use of latent variables. A latent variable is construct or a concept that cannot be measured directly, but can be represented or measured by one or more indicators or observable variables.

> Income and education are observable factors, which can be viewed as indicators of the non-observable construct: social status.

Similarly, in the above example, store image, satisfaction, loyalty and performance are typical examples of latent variables that can be measured by a set of indicators, as shown in the following chapter.

> The firm's performance is also a latent variable that can be measured indirectly by the return on investment (ROI), by sales or market share growth, or by the success rate of new products, and so on.

These latent variables are interrelated and can be used to describe the construct as illustrated in Figure 4.11.

The main features of SEM can be summarised as follows (Croutsche 1997, p. 355):

1. Use of latent or non-observable variables.
2. Specification of the existing relationships between the latent variables and their indicators.
3. Simultaneous analysis of several series of dependence relationships.
4. Specification of the expected relationships between latent variables and integration of measurement errors.
5. Possibility to conduct confirmatory analyses and not only exploratory analyses.

Several aspects differentiate SEM from traditional multivariate techniques. The originality of SEM is in the possibility to combine different existing methods, which were used separately before.

Measurement and causal submodels

A structural equation model combines measurement and causal submodels:

1. The *measurement submodel* specifies the indicators for each construct and assesses the reliability of each construct for use in estimating the causal relationship. The measurement submodel operates as a confirmatory factorial analysis. A theoretical structure is proposed *a priori* between the observed and latent variables and tested.

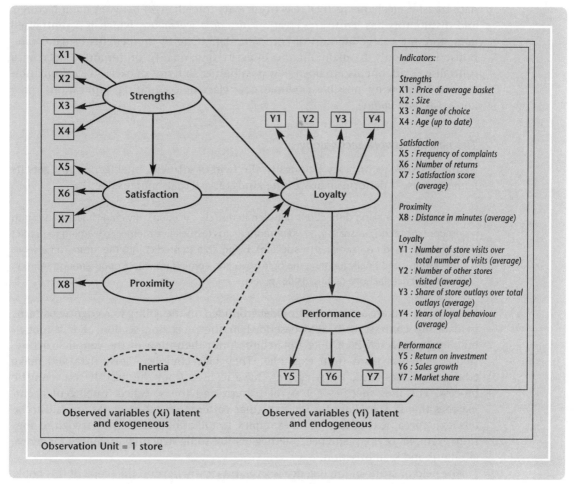

Figure 4.11   Measuring the performance of a store brand name

2. The *causal submodel* specifies the relationships between the latent variables as in any simultaneous equation model. Complex interrelated causal relationships can be represented.

Thus, the market analyst has a data bank and proposes a causal model based on theory or past experience. Two matrices are created: one based on the existing observations, the other on the basis of theory. If the two matrices are not too different, the data confirm the *a priori* model; in the opposite case, the theoretical model is rejected.

Much software has been developed to implement SEM, of which LISREL, EQS and AMOS are the most popular. The use of this software requires, however, a large data bank to give sufficiently stable and accurate results.

Intelligent expert systems

The development of centralised marketing information systems, the generalisation of bar-code data from checkouts in supermarkets and the adoption of electronic data-transfer mechanisms (EDI, electronic data interchange) between manufacturers and distributors has led to the creation of a *data warehouse,* which is a centralised data store for a large amount of corporate data. One of the benefits of data warehouse is not only to maintain the integrity and quality of corporate data by a centralised staff, but also to open new possibilities in terms of executive information systems by making possible a whole new class of computing applications, now known as *data mining.*

The neural network technology

Neural network technology belongs to the field of artificial intelligence and gets its name because it performs many of the kinds of task that humans do.

> These include making distinctions between items (classification), dividing similar things into groups (clustering), associating two or more things (associative memory), learning to predict outcomes based on examples (modelling), being able to predict into the future (time series forecasting), and finally juggling multiple goals and coming up with a good-enough solution (constraint satisfaction) (Gibus, 1966, p. 41).

Neural networks are a computing model grounded on the ability to recognise patterns in data. By contrast with SEM described in the preceding section, it is a model-building approach which does not require prior definition of the causal structure. Neural networks learn from examples. They take complex, noisy data and make educated guesses based on what they have learned from the past. It is a heuristic process. The user specifies a type of pattern and the so-called 'intelligent agent' searches the data, looking for the particular pattern. Neural networks are said to be *intelligent*, because they learn from examples, just like children learn to recognise dogs from examples of dogs, and because they exhibit some structural capability for generalisations and memorisation.

The field of artificial intelligence is vast and clearly beyond the scope of this book, but its potential for market research is considerable. To go further on this topic and for a description of how neural networks can be applied to business problems, see the excellent book by Gibus (1996).

Marketing applications of the neural network technology

At present, the most commonly used applications of neural networks are the areas of micro marketing, risk management and fraud detection. An example of micro marketing is given by the US giant retail chain Wal-Mart, a frequent user of *market basket analysis* through this technology to find associations between products. This information is then used to determine product affinities and suggest promotion that can maximise profits.

> In trawling through some historical data and analysing it, the manager of a large US retailer noticed a distinct correlation between the sales of nappies and beer, just after work hours, which was particularly marked on a Friday. Further research confirmed the explanation: the man of the family was stopping off on his way home to pick up nappies for the baby – and a six-pack for himself. The retailer responded by merchandising nappies closer to the beer section and was rewarded by an increase in sales of both items. (Gooding, 1995, p. 25)

Other applications of the neural network technology are found in micro-segmentation and in risk management, particularly in the personal credit and the private insurance sectors.

In insurance, for example, it has long been recognised that female drivers are a lower risk than their male counterparts and can be offered cheaper car insurance premiums. Data mining is used to find further subsegments of female drivers with different price and risk profiles; instead of providing a standard premium to women in the same age category, insurers can now price differently in order to retain their most profitable customers or encourage customers who are likely to be unprofitable to go elsewhere.

A third popular domain of application is fraud detection as used by the credit card company Visa International. In concept neural networks are extremely simple. People tend to have patterns of buying. They tend to spend within certain limits, buy certain types of goods, and acquire new things at a fairly predictable rate. Neural networks are designed to identify behaviours which do not fit these patterns. The expert system uses 30 to 35 different parameters and routinely analyses millions of transactions every day from around the world to detect patterns which appear fraudulent and send the scores to the card-issuing banks several times a day. It is then up to the local bank to decide whether or not to contact customers.

An example of an established fraud pattern is as follows: a credit card is used to pay for petrol at a service station and that transaction is followed by the purchase in rapid succession of a series of large price-tag consumer electronics. The purchasing pattern would alert the neural network to possible fraud, immediately signalling the likelihood of a credit card theft by a criminal intent on using up all remaining credit as quickly as possible.

The field of information technology is changing fast with the increasing use of microcomputers, the proliferation of mobile phones and the explosion of the Internet. Information technology really does have the potential to make marketing management more effective because it enables organisations to build powerful personal relationships with their customers, to understand better their needs and to respond faster to their expectations. For an introduction to the subject, see O'Connor and Galvin (1997).

Chapter summary

A market-oriented firm has to develop a market information system to monitor changes in the macro-marketing environment. The role of marketing research is to provide market information data that will help management to implement a market-oriented strategy. Marketing research has to provide management with accredited (or certified) knowledge and, for this reason, has strictly to follow the rules of scientific method. The development of a research project implies a sequence of interrelated activities, which ensures a systematic and orderly investigation process. Three types of marketing research can be identified: exploratory, descriptive and causal studies. The objective of exploratory research is to generate hypotheses and to translate the research problem into research objectives. The techniques of exploratory research are: use of secondary data, key informant surveys, analysis of selected cases and focus group discussions. Group discussions, also called qualitative research, are particularly useful, but they should be used strictly to suggest hypotheses for further research and not as conclusive evidence. Descriptive studies attempt to obtain a complete, quantitative and accurate description of a situation and must follow a precise methodology. The techniques used are observation and communication. The most popular communication method is by far the survey method through personal, telephone or mail interviewing. Good questionnaire design is the key to obtaining good survey results and a seven-step procedure is proposed to help in designing a questionnaire. Sampling techniques can be divided into two categories: probability and non-probability samples. These two sampling techniques have their own merits. The two sources of error in survey research are sampling and non-sampling errors. To minimise non-sampling error the market analyst should have strict control over the entire data-gathering process. Causal research is used to establish the existence of a causal link between an action and a response variable. An experimentation is a scientific investigation in which the researcher manipulates and controls one or more action variables and observes the response variable for variation concomitant to the manipulation of the action variable. Different types of experimental designs exist which vary in the way the analyst controls extraneous factors.

QUESTIONS AND PROBLEMS

1. State (a) the complaints that managers typically have against marketing researchers and (b) the complaints that marketing researchers typically have against managers.
2. What is the difference between external and internal validity and which research procedure(s) will contribute towards an improvement in the validity of both?
3. Why is it important to determine research hypotheses before undertaking survey research?
4. What is the basic difference between exploratory and conclusive research?
5. Compare and contrast quantitative and qualitative research in terms of the following: (a) the purpose of the research, (b) the data collection methods used, (c) the analysis procedure, and (d) how the findings can be used by marketing managers.
6. What are the general advantages and disadvantages associated with obtaining information by questioning or by observation?
7. What distinguishes a probability sample from a non-probability sample? Compare the merits and weaknesses of these two sampling procedures.
8. What are (a) an ambiguous question, (b) a leading question and (c) a double-barrelled question?
9. What are the main types of true experimental designs? What are the key issues or problems associated with each of these designs?

Appendix 4.1

● Examples of Questions

1. **Open-ended question, unaided awareness**
   Which magazines do you know?
   − . . . .   − . . . .   − . . . .
   − . . . .   − . . . .   − . . . .

2. **Closed question: dichotomous: aided awareness**
   Here is a list of different magazines, which one(s) do you know?

Magazine A	YES/NO
Magazine B	YES/NO
Magazine C	YES/NO
Magazine D	YES/NO
Magazine E	YES/NO

3. **Closed question: multiple choice: qualified awareness**
   To what extent do you know the following magazines?

	Don't know	Know by name only	I read them regularly
	....	....	....
	....	....	....
	....	....	....
	....	....	....
	....	....	....

4. **Agreement/disagreement scale: Likert itemised rating scale**
   Please indicate the amount of agreement/disagreement concerning the following statement: *The following three magazines give well-documented and objective information*

	Strongly disagree (1)	Disagree (2)	Neither agree or disagree (3)	Agree (4)	Strongly agree (5)
A					
B					
C					

5. **Osgood rating scale with bipolar adjectives**
   How adequate is the coverage of *contemporary* issues in the following three magazines:

	Very poor coverage (−3)	(−2)	(−1)	(0)	(+1)	(+2)	Very good coverage (+3)
A							
B							
C							

6. **Importance scales**
   In selecting a magazine, how important is the presence of TV programmes?

Not at all important (1)	Not very important (2)	Somewhat important (3)	Very important (4)	Extremely important (5)

Very poor (1)	Fair (2)	Good (3)	Very good (4)	Excellent (5)

7. Constant-sum scale: evaluation of the relative importance of an attitude

Divide 100 points among each the following toothpaste characteristics according to how important each characteristic is to you when selecting a brand of toothpaste.

Cavity protection   ...
Breath freshening   ...
Taste and colour   ...
                         100

8. Evaluation scale: rating some attribute

How would you rate the attribute 'clear editorial presentation' of Magazine A?

Very poor	Fair	Good	Very good	Excellent
(1)	(2)	(3)	(4)	(5)

9. Preference scale

Divide 100 points among each of the following brands according to your preference for the brand.

Brand A: ...
Brand B: ...
Brand C: ...

10. Two-by-two comparison: preferences

Among the following 'pairs' of brands, which one do you prefer?

A ...   or   B ...
A ...   or   C ...
B ...   or   C ...

11. Triad of preferences

Among the following magazines: Brand A, Brand B, Brand C,
Which one would you prefer to buy?   ....

If the one you prefer is not available, which
one would you then prefer to buy?   ....

And if none of these first two preferred
brands is available, which one would you buy?   ....

12. Purchase intentions

How likely is it that you will purchase a compact disc player within the next three months?

I definitely will not buy	I probably will not buy	I might buy	I probably will buy	I definitely will buy
(1)	(2)	(3)	(4)	(5)

13. Probability of purchase

How likely is it that you will buy a new car within the next 12 months?

0	10	20	30	40	50	60	70	80	90	100
Absolutely no chance		Slight probability						Strong possibility		Absolutely certain

14. Measure of the behavioural component of an attitude (action tendency)

How likely is it that *you would* pay a 5 per cent premium price to purchase an environmentally friendly brand in this particular product category?

Extremely unlikely	Very unlikely	Somewhat likely	Likely, 50-50	Somewhat likely	Very likely	Extremely likely
(1)	(2)	(3)	(4)	(5)	(6)	(7)

Appendix 4.2

● **Selected Reviews and Journals Useful in Marketing Research**

AMA Educator's Proceedings Conference
The Academy of Management Journal
The Academy of Management Review
L'Actualité Economique
American Council of Consumer Interest
American Economic Review
Applied Economics
Bank Marketing
BBL Bulletin Financier
Business Horizon
Business Marketing
Business and Society Review
Business Strategy Review
Business Week
Cahiers Economiques de Bruxelles
California Management Review
Cambridge Journal of Economics
Comité Belge de la Distribution (dossiers CBD)
Communication Research
Décisions marketing
Distribution d'Aujourd'hui
The Economist
European Business Forum
European Economic Review
European Journal of Marketing
European Management Journal
L'Expansion-Management Review
Fortune
Futuribles
G-Bulletin
Gestion 2000
Harvard Business Review
IBM Journal of Research Development
Industrial Journal of Distribution & Logistic Management
Industrial Journal of Research in Marketing
Industrial Marketing Management
Industrial Relations Journal
Interfaces
InternationalJournal of Advertising
International Journal of Research in Marketing
International Journal of Retail & Distribution Management
International Journal of Strategic Management
International Marketing Research
International Marketing eview
Journal of the Academy of Marketing Science
Journal of Advertising
Journal of Advertising Research
Journal of Business
Journal of Business Administration
Journal of Business Ethics
Journal of Business Research
Journal of Consumer Affairs

Journal of Consumer Marketing
Journal of Consumer Research
Journal of Economic & Business
Journal of Environmental Economics & Management
Journal of Euro-marketing
Journal of Forecasting
Journal of Global Marketing
Journal of Industrial Economics
Journal of International Consumer Marketing
Journal of International Marketing
Journal of Management
Journal of Management Studies
Journal of Macromarketing
Journal of Marketing
Journal of Marketing Management
Journal of Marketing Education
Journal of the Market Research Society
Journal of Marketing Channels
Journal of Marketing Research
Journal of Personal Selling and Sales Management
Journal of Product Innovation Management
Journal of Retailing
Journal of Sales & Marketing Management
Journal of Services Marketing
Journal of Travel and Tourism Marketing
KB Bulletin hebdomadaire
Kobe University Economic Review
Libres Services Actualités
Long Range Planning
Management International Review
Management Science
Marketing in Europe (*The Economist Intelligence Unit*)
Marketing Letters: a Journal of Research in Marketing
Marketing News
Marketing Research
Marketing and Research Today (ESOMAR)
Marketing Science
Media Marketing
The McKinsey Quarterly
Psychology and Marketing
Recherche et applications en marketing
Recherche Economique de Louvain
Revue Française de Gestion
Revue Française du Marketing
Sales and Marketing Management Review
Service Industry Journal
Sloan Management Review
Strategic Management Journal
Stratégie
Test Achats

Bibliography

Aaker, D.A. and Day, G.S. (1980) *Marketing Research*, 2nd edn, New York, John Wiley & Sons.

Addelman, S. (1962) Symmetrical and Asymmetrical Fractional Factorial Plans, *Technometrics*, **4**, February, pp. 47–58.

Adler, L. (1979) To Learn What's on the Consumers' Mind, Try Focus Group Interviews, *Sales and Marketing Management*, April 9, pp. 76–80.

Assadi, D., (1998) *Intelligence économique sur Internet*, Paris, Publi-Union Editions.

Boyd, H.W. and Westfall, R. (1956,1972) *Marketing Research: Text and Cases*, Homewood IL, Irwin.

Chase, C. and Barash, K.L. (1977) *Marketing Problem Solver*, 2nd edn, Radnor, PA, Chilton.

Churchill, G.A. (1996), *Marketing Research, Methodological Foundations*, 6th edn, Chicago IL, Dryden Press.

Croutsche, J.J. (1997) *Pratique de l'analyse des données*, Paris, Editions ESKA.

Erdos, P.L. (1970) *Professional Mail Surveys*, New York, McGraw-Hill.

Ferber, R. (ed.) (1974) *Handbook of Marketing Research*, New York, McGraw-Hill.

Gibus, J.J. (1996) *Data Mining with Neural Networks: Solving Business Problems from Application Development to Decision Support*, New York, McGraw-Hill.

Gooding, C. (1995) Boosting Sales with the Information Warehouse, *Financial Times*, 1 March.

Hair, J., Anderson, R.E., Tatham, R.L. and Black, W.C. (1992) *Multivariate Data Analysis*, 3rd edn, New York, Macmillan.

Kassarjian, H.H. (1974) Projective Methods, in: Ferber, R. (ed.), *Handbook of Marketing Research*, New York, McGraw-Hill.

Kerlinger, F.N. (1973) *Foundations of Behavioural Research*, London, Holt Rinehart & Winston.

Kotler, P. (1991) *Marketing Management*, 7th edn, Englewood Cliffs NJ, Prentice Hall.

Lambin, J.J. (1990) *La recherche marketing: analyser, mesurer prévoir*, Paris, Ediscience International.

O'Connor, J. and Galvin, E. (1997) *Marketing and Information Technology*, London, Pitman.

Pellemans, P. (1999), *Recherche qualitative en marketing: une perspective psychologique*, Brussels, De Boeck Université.

Simon, H. (1996) *Hidden Champions*, Boston, MA, Harvard Business School Press.

Valette-Florence, P. (1988) Spécificités et apports des méthodes d'analyse multivariée de la deuxième génération, *Recherche et Applications en Marketing*, 3(4).

Webster, F.E. and von Pechmann, F. (1970) A Replication of the Shopping List Study, *Journal of Marketing*, **34**, April, pp. 61–77.

Wells, W.D. (1974) Group Interviewing, in: Ferber, R. (ed.), *Handbook of Marketing Research*, New York, McGraw-Hill.

Zaltman, G. and Burger, P.C. (1975) *Marketing Research: Fundamentals and Dynamics*, Hinsdale IL, Dryden Press.

chapter five

The customer's response behaviour

The purpose of this chapter is to analyse how potential buyers choose and how they respond to marketing stimuli used by producers as part of their product, distribution, pricing and communication policy. The information collected or received by buyers during their purchasing process helps them to identify the relevant characteristics in goods and to evaluate different products or brands in their evoked set. As a result of this evaluation phase, buyers rank their preferences and decide whether or not to buy, unless situation factors intervene. Having sampled the purchased brands, buyers feel either satisfied or dissatisfied. This feeling will determine their after-purchase behaviour. This process of preference formation is analysed in its entirety by marketing researchers and this enables the firm to adapt its offerings more effectively to market expectations. In this chapter, we shall review the main concepts and methods used to anticipate and measure market response.

Chapter learning objectives

When you have read this chapter, you should be able to understand:

1. the ways buyers respond to the marketing stimuli used by the firm;

2. the difference between cognitive, affective and behavioural response;

3. the various paths of response observed among buyers;

4. the different measures of the cognitive, affective and behavioural response;

5. the post-purchase behaviour of the buyers;

6. the behaviour of dissatisfied customers;

7. the brand equity concept.

The Levels of Market Response

One can identify different ways in which potential buyers respond to perceived information and producer stimuli. Here, *'response'* means *all mental or physical activity caused by a stimulus*. A response is not necessarily manifested in external actions, but may be simply mental.

Economic theory is only interested in the act of purchase *per se* and not in the overall behavioural process, which leads to purchase. From the economist's point of view, as we saw earlier, preferences are revealed by behaviour and consumers' response is the same as the demand expressed by the market in terms of quantities sold. In reality, market demand defined in this way is an 'ex-post' or historical observation, often of little practical value to the decision-maker. Market analysts hope to retrace and understand the process followed by the buyer so as to intervene in that process in a better informed manner and to be able to measure the effectiveness of marketing actions. Therefore, response behaviour is a much broader notion to the marketer than it is to the economist.

The 'learn–feel–do' hierarchy

The various response levels of the buyer can be classified into three categories: *cognitive response,* which relates to retained information and knowledge, *affective response,* which concerns attitude and the evaluation system and *behavioural (or conative) response,* which describes action: not only the act of purchasing, but also after-purchase *behaviour.* Table 5.1 describes the main measures currently used for each response level.

Table 5.1   Key measures of market response

- **COGNITIVE RESPONSE**
  Saliency – Awareness – Recall – Recognition – Knowledge –
  Perceived Similarity
- **AFFECTIVE RESPONSE**
  Consideration Set – Importance – Determinance – Performance –
  Attitude – Preference – Intention to Buy
- **BEHAVIOURAL RESPONSE**
  Fact-finding behaviour – Trial purchase – Repeat purchase – Brand
  repertoire – Share of category requirement (exclusivity) – Brand
  loyalty – Satisfaction/dissatisfaction

It has been postulated by practitioners in communication that these three response levels follow a sequence and that the individual, like the organisation, reaches the three stages successively and in this order: cognitive (learn) – affective (feel) – behavioural (do). We then have a *learning process* which is observed in practice when the buyer is heavily involved by his or her purchase decision, for example when the perceived risk (Bauer, 1960) or the brand sensitivity (Kapferer and Laurent, 1983) is high.

The learning response model was originally developed to measure advertising effectiveness (Lavidge and Steiner, 1961) and later extended to include the process of adoption of new products (Rogers, 1962). Palda (1966) has shown that this model is not always applicable and that uncertainty remains as to the causal links and direction existing between the intervening variables. Moreover, the learning process hypothesis implies a well thought out buying process, observed only when the buyer is heavily involved in his purchase decision. Psycho-sociologists have also shown that other sequences exist and are observed, for example, when there is *minimal involvement* (Krugman, 1965), or when there is *cognitive dissonance* (Festinger, 1957).

Although the learning process hypothesis is not generally applicable, the *'learn–feel–do'* model remains valuable in structuring the information collected on response behaviours, particularly when complemented with the concepts of 'perceived risk' and of 'buyer involvement', discussed in the previous chapter.

The Foote, Cone and Belding (FCB) involvement grid

The various paths of the response process may be viewed from a more general framework, which includes the degree of involvement and the perception of reality mode. Brain specialisation theory proposes that anatomical separation of the cerebral hemispheres of the brain leads to specialised perception of reality: the left side of the brain (or the intellectual mode) and the right side (or the affective or sensory mode):

⬤ The left side, or *intellectual mode*, is relatively more capable of handling logic, factual information, language and analysis, that is the cognitive *'thinking'* function.

⬤ The right side, or *affective mode*, which engages in synthesis, is more intuitive, visual and responsive to the non-verbal, that is the *'feeling'* function.

In order to provide a conceptual framework which integrates the 'learn–feel–do' hierarchy with the consumer involvement and the brain specialisation theory, Vaughn (1986) presented a grid in which purchase decision processes can be classified along two basic dimensions: 'high–low' involvement and 'think–feel' perception of reality. Crossing the degree of involvement with the mode of reality perception leads to the matrix in Figure 5.1 in which we can see four different paths of the response process:

⬤ Quadrant (1) corresponds to a buying situation where product involvement is high and the way we perceive reality is essentially intellectual. This situation implies a large need for information due to the importance of the product and mental issues related to it. Quadrant 1 illustrates the *learning process* described earlier, where the sequence followed was: *'learn–feel–do*.

　　Major purchases with high prices and significant objective and functional characteristics, such as cars, electrical household goods and houses follow this process. Industrial goods also fall in this category. These factors suggest a need for informative advertising.

⬤ Quadrant (2) describes buying situations where product involvement is also high. Specific information is, however, less important than an attitude or an *emotional arousal*, since the product or brand choice reveals the buyer's system of values and personality and relates to the buyer's self-esteem. The sequence here is 'feel–learn–do'.

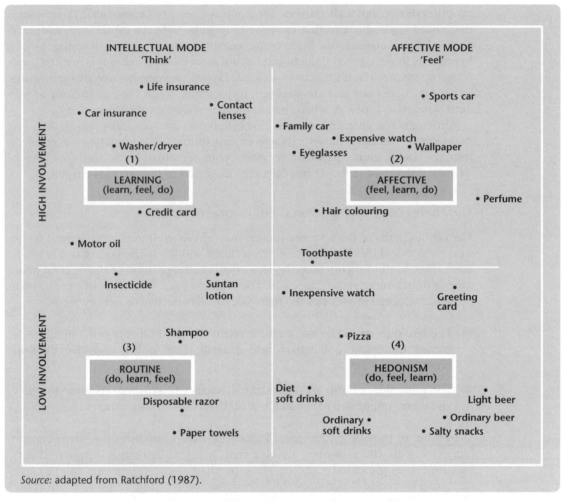

Source: adapted from Ratchford (1987).

Figure 5.1   The Foote, Cone and Belding involvement grid

In this category we find all products that have important social and/or emotional value, like perfumes, clothes, jewellery and motorcycles. These factors suggest a need for emotional advertising.

● Quadrant (3) describes product decisions, which involve minimal thought and a tendency to form buying habits for convenience. As long as the product fulfils the expected core service, we find *low product involvement* and routinised behaviour. Brand loyalty will be largely a function of habit. The hierarchy model is a *'do–learn–feel'* pattern.

Most food and staple package goods belong in this category, which is somewhat like a commodity limbo. As products reach maturity, they are likely to descend into this quadrant. These factors suggest a need for advertising, which creates and maintains habits and stimulates a reminder of the product.

● Quadrant (4) illustrates a situation where low product involvement coexists with the sensory mode. Products in this category cater to personal tastes involving imagery and *quick satisfaction*. The sequence is *'do–feel–learn'*.

In this category, we find products like beer, chocolates, cigarettes, jams and fast food restaurants. For these product categories, there is a need for advertising, which emphasises personal satisfaction.

Ratchford (1987) has measured the location of 254 consumer products on this grid from a sample of 1792 adults. Figure 5.1 presents a plot of products' average scores on the 'involvement and think/feel' scales for selected product categories.

> As can be seen, the results are generally intuitive. Insurance and household appliances tend to be high involvement/think; cars tend to have both think and feel elements; food items tend to be on the 'feel' side because of sensory nature; mundane household items such as bleach and paper towels tend to be on low involvement/think. (Ratchford 1987, p. 30)

An interesting observation emerging from consumer involvement analyses (see also Kapferer and Laurent, 1983) is the large number of 'low risk–low involvement' product decisions. This fact constitutes a challenge for the firm and suggests that marketing and communication strategies must be adapted to deal with this situation where consumers just do not care very much about a large number of purchase decisions they make. The rest of this chapter will examine various measures of these three levels of market response.

● ## Measuring the Cognitive Response

Cognitive response relates to knowledge, that is the totality of information and beliefs held by an individual or a group. Individuals store this information, which influences their interpretation of the stimuli to which they are exposed. The quantity and nature of the information retained varies according to cognitive styles (Pinson *et al.*, 1988) and perceptual capacities. *Perception* can be defined as:

> The process by which an individual selects, organises and interprets the information inputs to create a meaningful picture of the world. (Berelson and Steiner, 1964, p. 88)

Individuals will, in general, have different perceptions of the same situation, because of selective attention. Perception has a regulating function since it filters information. Some elements of information are retained either because they meet the needs of the moment, or because they come as a surprise: this is *selective perception and retention*. Other elements are perceived as altered when they contradict the specific framework of interest: this is *perceptual bias*. Finally, other elements are rejected because they are worrying or disturbing: this is *perceptual defence*.

> A study done in the USA reveals, for example, that only 32 per cent of smokers have read newspaper articles suggesting a link between cigarette smoking and the development of cancer of the larynx, as opposed to 60 per cent of non-smokers.

Clearly, the first objective of producers must be to overcome perceptual resistance and to propagate knowledge about their products and about their claimed distinctive features. This first stage conditions the development of any market demand.

Several measures of cognitive response have been developed. They can be grouped into three categories: brand awareness, advertising recall and perceived similarity.

Brand awareness

The simplest level of cognitive response is the knowledge of the existence of a product or a brand. Is the potential buyer aware of the brand existence within a given product category? Brand awareness can be defined as follows:

> The ability of a potential buyer to identify (recall or recognise) the brand with sufficient detail to propose, recommend, choose or use the brand to meet the need of a certain product category.

Thus, awareness establishes a link between the brand name and a product class. Information about brand awareness can be easily obtained by questioning potential buyers about the brands they know in the class of products under consideration. Three types of brand awareness can be distinguished:

- *Brand recognition* implies that the brand recognition precedes and leads to the need (I recognise brand A and I realise that I need such product category). Recognition is a minimal level of awareness, which will be particularly important at the point of purchase when choosing a brand.

- *Brand recall* implies that the need for a product category precedes and leads to the brand (I need that product category, I will buy brand A). Recall is a much more demanding test.

- *Top of the mind awareness* refers to the first-named brand in a recall test. The brand is ahead of all the other competing brands in a person's mind.

Brand recall is measured by unaided awareness; brand recognition is measured by aided or qualified awareness. *Unaided (or spontaneous) awareness* refers to the case where the respondent is questioned about a brand where the question makes no reference to any brand. *Aided (or prompted) awareness* refers to a set of brand names from a given product class which are presented to respondents, who are asked to note the ones they have heard of before. In the latter case, respondents may also be asked to specify their level of familiarity with the brand on a scale of three or five positions, as illustrated in Table 5.2. We then have a measure of *qualified awareness*.

Table 5.2   Measuring brand awareness

Unaided Awareness	Aided or Qualified Awareness	
Which brands of laptop computers do you know?	Among the following brands of laptop computers, indicate the brand(s) you know:	
....	Know very well:	....
....	Know by name only:	....
....	Don't know:	....

The responses to these simple questions provide useful information to allow the evaluation of the *capital of goodwill* (Nerlove and Arrow, 1962) or *brand equity* (Aaker, 1991) enjoyed by the brand or by the firm. The information provided by a brand awareness analysis is used as follows:

● To determine the *brand's share of mind*, that is the percentage of potential buyers who name the brand or the company as the first brand or company that comes to mind in the product category.

● To identify the *trio of the best known brands* which are in direct competition in the minds of potential customers, that is the number of times a brand is mentioned in an unaided recall test in first, second or third position.

● To compare the observed changes in the *recall versus recognition scores* in an unaided versus an aided recall test. Some brands or companies have a weak evocative power; a product may be easily recognised due to its obvious link with the product class, but in an unaided recall test the product scores low (see Krugman, 1972).

● To compare the correlation between the *awareness score and market share* of each brand with regard to the market average performance; some brands enhance their awareness better than others and are situated above the market average (see Assael and Day, 1968).

● To construct a *one-dimensional interval scale*, based on the law of comparative judgements (Thurstone, 1959). This method is used to obtain a ranking as well as measures of distance between brands in terms of awareness.

● To compare awareness scores (aided and unaided) between *different groups of buyers* and thereby identify zones of weakest awareness where remedial action should be taken.

It is worth remembering that a high awareness score is a key brand asset to the firm, which takes years to build and which requires significant and repetitive advertising investments. Brand awareness is a key component of brand equity, even if it alone cannot create sales. On the concept of brand equity, see Aaker (1991).

In addition, apart from the identification of the brand itself, measures of knowledge may also relate to the identification of some of its characteristics, such as usual places of sale, current advertising themes and price levels.

Advertising recall

Advertising recall scores are commonly used as intermediate measures of advertising effectiveness. They are also used with different variations to measure new product acceptance. Various impact scores are available which measure the percentage of readers or viewers who correctly identify the advertisement or the message after an advertising campaign. There are a large number of variants of impact scores (see, for example, Franzen *et al.*, 1999). The following three measures of print advertising effectiveness, obtained from interviews, recur regularly:

● *Noted score*: the percentage of readers who say they previously saw the advertisement in the magazine (ad recognition).
● *Saw–associated or proved name registration (PNR) score*: the percentage of individuals who correctly identify the product and advertiser with the advertisement.
● *Read most:* the percentage who say they read more than half of the written material in the advertisement.

These impact scores are collected after several exposures and are cumulative scores. Another useful impact score, called the *'beta (ß) score'* (Morgensztern, 1983) or day-after score, is a more revealing measure. It is defined as:

The percentage of individuals who, when exposed for the first time to a new message, memorise the brand and at least one of the visual or textual elements of the advertisement.

Comparisons of beta scores from different advertising campaigns show enormous fluctuations between campaigns with the same intensity within a medium as well as between advertising media (see Table 5.3). Companies specialising in this kind of analysis, such as Daniel Starch in the USA, also provide 'adnorms' showing the average scores for each product category for the year. This information enables advertisers to compare their advertisement's impact with those of competition.

Table 5.3 Comparing impact scores of media advertising (%)

Media	Beta Scores		
	Average scores	Minimum scores	Maximum scores
Television (30 seconds)	27	9	70
Dailies (1/4 page mono)	35	0	75
Dailies (1/2 page mono)	27	3	69
Magazines (colour page)	19	6	46
Magazines (dps colour)	27	6	46

Source: Carat, Belgium.

The comparison of impact scores, obtained from a large number of advertisements shows that:

● The prior level of brand awareness has a significant effect on scores of advertising recall; the greater the brand awareness, the higher the impact of the message.

● Some product categories benefit from a recall above average.

● Recall measured in terms of 'saw–associated' scores is better among the upper social classes.

● Creative factors, advertisement formats, use of colour and visualisation of the product in the advertisement are factors that explained the variance of observed scores.

These scores are only intermediate measures of advertising effectiveness and give no indication about advertising's ultimate effectiveness, which should ideally help to produce sales. These intermediate measures are nevertheless useful since they enable advertisers to verify whether the advertisement has actually succeeded in breaking the wall of indifference of the target audience. Observed differences in recall scores can be explained by the attractiveness of the message, by the element of surprise, incongruity and originality. The comparison of qualitative scores (agreement, credibility, originality) shows that consumers perceive differences between advertisements by product category. These differences also exist between brands within the same class of products.

The remembering and forgetting of advertising

Studying the dynamics of recall scores provides some knowledge about the evolution of recall over time and allows the determination of optimal advertising scheduling given the communication objective.

Experiments done in this domain (Morgensztern, 1983) have established that the proportion of individuals retaining an induced opinion change decrease geometrically over time. The rates of depreciation of recall, however, vary largely with the contents to be retained. Figure 5.2, based on an experiment conducted by Watts and McGuire (1964), illustrates this point.

One can see that recall of the message topic drops sharply after one week (from 95 to 60 per cent), but then keeps on at this level; on the other hand, recall of the arguments used in the message sees a much sharper drop in the first week (from 72 to 28

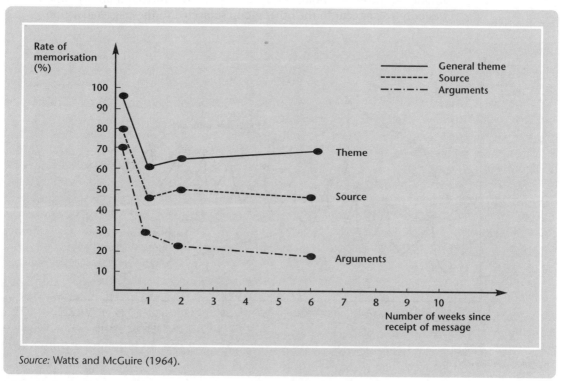

Source: Watts and McGuire (1964).

Figure 5.2   Induced opinion change as a function of time

per cent) and then continues to decay to reach more or less 20 per cent in the sixth week. One observes a similar but less abrupt pattern for recall of the message source. Thus, advertisers have very little time at their disposal to get the value of the investment on communication that they have made.

The repetition of the message clearly has an effect on people's ability to remember over time. Many experiments have been carried out, namely by Zielske (1958) and Zielske and Henry (1980), which have underlined the relation between the change in the recall rate and different advertising schedules. In his study of 1958, Zielske measured the impact on recall of two advertising campaigns of thirteen newspaper advertisements each.

The plan of this experiment was to expose one group of women to 13 different advertisements from the same newspaper advertising campaign at four week intervals (staggered action). Every four weeks for a year an advertisement was mailed to women in this group. A second group of women received a total of 13 advertisements, mailed one-week apart (intensive action). Recall of the advertising, aided only by mention of the product class, was obtained by telephone interviews throughout the study, with no single individual being interviewed more than once.

The recall of advertising by both groups, as reported by Zielske, is shown in Figure 5.3. These data emphasise the nature of response rather than the interim decay. The following observations emerge:

● After thirteen weekly exposures (intensive action), the rate of recall registered among exposed households was 63 per cent; after thirteen monthly exposures, it was only 48 per cent in the other group subjected to the staggered action.

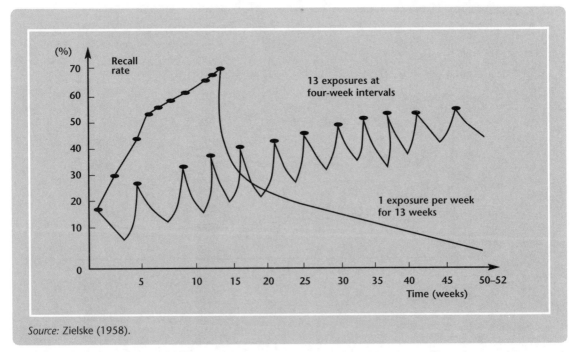

Source: Zielske (1958).

Figure 5.3   Dynamic evolution of recall as a function of time and number of exposures

⬤ During the period of 52 weeks, however, the average percentage of households who could recall the advertising was 29 per cent in the case of the staggered action and only 21 per cent in the other group.

⬤ In the case of weekly exposures, four weeks after the end of the campaign the rate of recall drops by 50 per cent and six weeks later by 66 per cent.

⬤ The rate of forgetting decreases as the number of repetitions increases; three weeks after one exposure to the message, the recall rate drops from 14 to 3 per cent, that is a depreciation rate of 79 per cent; after thirteen exposures, the recall rate drops from 48 to 37 per cent in three weeks, which is a depreciation rate of only 23 per cent.

Similar results were obtained with another experiment done in 1980 (Zielske and Henry) with television advertising, again involving actions with the same intensity but different schedules. The forgetting mechanisms are very powerful and memory loss is very rapid, implying the necessity for a sufficient number of repetitions of the message.

> A television campaign consisting of 6 repetitions in its first wave, and creating a 60 per cent rate of recall, should not be interrupted for more than three months if one doesn't want to see the rate drop below 20 per cent. (Morgensztern, 1983, p. 210)

Large fluctuations will exist between different campaigns, according to their relevance and to the creative value of their messages. The same phenomenon of rapid forgetting is also observed with other media, the daily press in particular.

How to overcome the buyers' wall of indifference or perceptual defence is not obvious. Yet, if this condition is not met, nothing will happen where attitude and behaviours are concerned. As long as advertising information is not perceived, understood and memorised, it does not exist for the potential buyer. Informing is not sufficient; one must also communicate. For a comprehensive review on how advertising affects consumers, see Vakratsas and Ambler (1999).

Perceived similarity analysis

Multidimensional scaling of perceived similarity is a method used for understanding how a brand is positioned in the minds of potential buyers *vis-à-vis* competing brands. This is done through the construction of perceptual maps which give a visual representation of perceived similarities among brands without formulating any prior hypotheses concerning the causes of the perceived similarities or dissimilarities. Thus, the method is a *non-attribute-based approach*, which does not ask respondents to rate the brands on designated attributes, but rather asks them to make some summary judgements about the brands' degree of similarity.

For this reason, non-attribute-based perceptual maps can be considered as a form of cognitive response, even though there exists an underlying evaluation in the comparative judgements provided by the respondent. Multidimensional scaling of perceived similarities is based on the following assumptions:

⬤ Any product or brand (any object) is perceived by the individual as a *bundle of characteristics or attributes*.

These characteristics are used as *criteria for comparing* brands, which are part of their evoked set.

If each of the *K* characteristics is geometrically represented along one *axis*, that is by one dimension of a *K*-dimensional space, each brand or object will represent one point in this space and the co-ordinates of this point will be the evaluations of the product according to each characteristic.

In practice, it is observed that potential buyers' perceptions of products or brands are based on a small number of dimensions, rarely more than two or three, called macro-characteristics.

These privileged dimensions, or macro-characteristics, are identified and are used to compare the positioning of the different brands. Multidimensional similarity analysis finally leads to perceptual maps where each point represents a brand and the distance between points measures the approximate degree of similarity perceived by respondents. Exhibit 5.1 succinctly describes the estimation procedure followed in such analyses.

Exhibit 5.1

Multidimensional Scaling Analysis: Description of the Estimation Procedure

■ The objective is to develop a non-attribute-based multidimensional map to characterise the perceived relationships among a set of brands competing within a given market segment.

■ A representative sample of respondents is asked to rank all possible pairs of the studied brands according to their perceived degree of similarity. We thus have a triangular matrix where the entries are simple ranks, or ordered relationships by increasing dissimilarity. For *N* compared brands, we will have $N(N - 1)/2$ different entries.

■ The objective of the method is to seek a configuration of points of minimum dimensionality that most nearly matches the original order of perceived distances among brands. That is a geometric configuration in which the physical distances between points are monotone (that is in the same order) with the original similarity judgements.

■ To find this configuration, generally the computer program operates iteratively. It starts with a given (arbitrary) configuration in $N - 1$ dimensions. It generates an initial solution and then assesses how well the ordering of the actual distances between the brands matches the original ranking of similarity and determines whether the fit can be improved. It then reduces the number of dimensions and repeats the process with the objective of finding the lowest dimensionality for which the monotonicity constraint is closely met.

■ Once the best configuration is identified, the last step is to interpret the retained dimensions and to discover the underlying macro-characteristics used by the respondents to compare the brands.

Source: Adapted from Churchill (1995).

Figure 5.4 is an example of a non-attribute-based perceptual map. It depicts the market for jams in Belgium. The analysis, based on a random sample of 400 respondents, brings to the fore the existence of two dimensions in respondents' perceived similarity.

- The first dimension (horizontal) contrasts industrial jams with home-made jams. Price differences are significant between these two types of product.

- The second dimension contrasts private brands (Sarma, GB and Delhaize) with manufacturers' brands. Note that these two groups of brands have more or less the same ranking on the first dimension, implying that respondents perceive them as similar as far as this characteristic is concerned.

We have a visual representation of perceived similarities between the brands according to two dimensions, which summarise the market perceptions. These results may appear trivial, in that they do not provide any new information to the manufacturer. Nevertheless, they are important because:

- The analysis made it possible to identify the two dimensions spontaneously used by consumers when they mentally compare brands, in this example, the perception of 'industrial versus home-made' and the contrast of 'private brands versus manufacturers' brands'.

- The analysis brings to the fore the structure of the market in each subgroup by identifying whether or not the brands are perceived as direct substitutes.

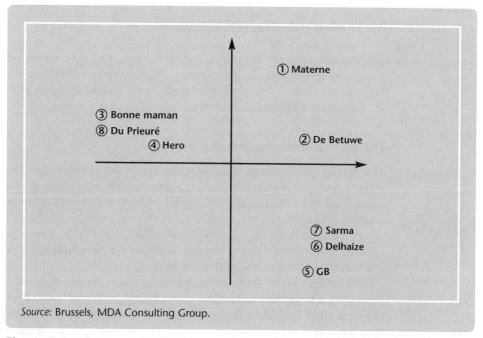

Source: Brussels, MDA Consulting Group.

Figure 5.4   An example of a non-attribute-based perceptual map: the market for jams in Belgium

● The analysis allows each firm to contrast the positioning perceived by the market with the positioning sought for the brand.

The method of multidimensional analysis does, however, have *problems*, which ought to be underlined:

● When the number of brands to be evaluated becomes large, the task facing respondents is very tedious. If there are 7 brands to compare, 21 pairs of brands need to be ranked, which might overwhelm the cognitive abilities of respondents.

● Interpretation of the axes is not always obvious and normally requires additional information.

Despite these difficulties, this method of structuring the market has the following *advantages:*

● The method preserves the multidimensional nature of market perceptions.
● The dimensions, or comparative criteria, are not *a priori* imposed.
● Inputs are simple non-metric ranking data, which are in principle easy to obtain from respondents when the number of objects to compare is not large.

In order to be fully operational, multidimensional scaling analysis needs to be complemented with an attribute-based approach, which relies on attribute-by-attribute assessments of the various brands. In general, this approach is the objective of affective response measurements (Green and Rao, 1972).

● Measuring the Affective Response

The affective response is evaluative. It is no longer based only on simple knowledge. It also includes feelings, preferences, intentions and favourable or unfavourable judgements about a brand or an organisation. Several operational measures are also available to market analysts, with attitude as a central concept.

The evoked and consideration sets

The brands that become alternatives to the buyer's choice decision are generally a small number, collectively called his *evoked set*. The size of the evoked set is at best a fraction of the brands that he is aware of and a still smaller fraction of the total number of brands that are actually available in the market. The *consideration set* is the subset of brands known and/or tried, which have a non-zero probability to be selected by the buyer. The composition of the consideration set varies over time and as a function of the consumption situation.

The consideration set is more restrictive than the evoked set. As illustrated in Figure 5.5, a buyer can be familiar with a brand and even have experienced it, and at the same time have no intention to buy or to repurchase. To identify the consideration set, one has to know the brands considered as valid alternatives for the next purchase occasion.

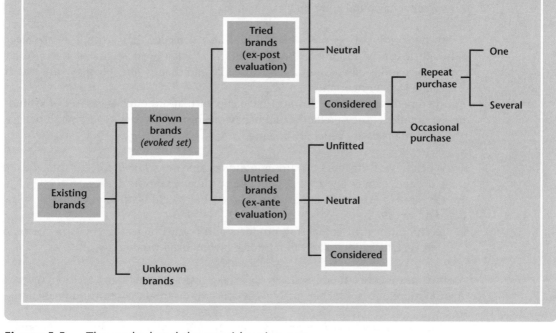

Figure 5.5   The evoked and the consideration sets

In the consumer goods sector, it is believed that the average number of known brands may vary between ten and twenty according to the class of products, whereas the average size of the consideration set is three to five brands (Jarvis and Wilcox, 1977). The notion of the consideration set is important; there is little chance that a brand will get adopted if it is not part of this set. It is in the producer's interest to know which brands or suppliers are on the shortlist of potential customers.

Definition of attitude

A central notion in affective response is the *concept of attitude*. A classical definition of attitude is the one given by Allport (1935):

> The mental process by which an individual – on the basis of past experience and stored infor-mation – organises his perceptions, beliefs and feelings about a particular object and orien-tates his future behaviour.

In this definition, we find the three levels or components of market response defined in the first section of this chapter:

● Attitude is based on a *series of information* about the object being evaluated, which is progressively stored by the individual (cognitive component).

● Attitude is oriented and reflects feelings, positive or negative, or *evaluation* regarding the object (affective component).
● Attitude is dynamic and is a *predisposition to respond*; as such, it has predictive value (behavioural component).

Psycho-sociologists (see Fishbein, 1967) also consider that attitude is *persistent*, although it can be modified; that it is *structured*, in the sense that it has internal consistency and is based on evaluative criteria; and that its *intensity* may vary widely or retain a state of neutrality.

Experimental studies in this area have shown that although measures of attitude are not infallible, they predict actual behaviour reasonably well. To be more precise, the following facts are generally accepted:

● When buyers' attitudes towards a brand become more favourable, its use tends to grow and, conversely, an unfavourable attitude heralds its decline.
● Consumers' attitudes help explain market shares held by different brands (Assael and Day, 1968).
● As the number of competing products and brands increases, the firm needs to intervene to maintain and to reinforce favourable attitudes.

Since measures of attitude are likely to be taken before a purchasing decision, they are of great importance for market analysis, as concerns diagnosis, control and prediction:

● *Diagnosis*: knowledge of a brand's strengths and weaknesses helps identify opportunities and/or threats facing a brand.
● *Control*: measures of attitudes taken 'before' and 'after' help evaluate the effectiveness of strategies aimed at changing the attitude towards the brand.
● *Prediction*: knowledge of attitudes helps predict the market response to a new or modified product, without having to rely on ex-post observations.

Given the importance of this notion, considerable attention has been given during the last twenty years to attitude measurement issues, not only in psycho-sociology research (Rosenberg, 1956; Fishbein, 1967), but also in marketing research (Wilkie and Pessemier, 1973).

The multi-attribute product concept defined in the previous chapter serves as the conceptual basis for modelling attitude. As mentioned earlier, two estimation procedures can be used for measuring a multi-attribute model: the 'compositional' approach or the 'decompositional' approach. These two approaches will be examined successively.

The compositional multi-attribute model

The multi-attribute product concept has been defined in the previous chapter. Let us briefly review the basic ideas of this notion, as they are summarised in Table 4.1:
● Individuals perceive a brand or a product as bundle of attributes.
● Each individual does not necessarily attach the same importance to attributes.
● Individuals hold certain beliefs about the degree of presence of attributes in each brand that is evaluated.

● Individuals have a utility function for each attribute, associating the degree of expected satisfaction or utility with the degree of presence of the attribute in the object.
● Individuals' attitude is structured, that is based on processing the stored information.

The most widely used multi-attribute model is the model developed by Fishbein (1967) and by Bass and Tarlarzyck (1969) which can be formalised as follows:

$$A_{ij} = \sum_{k=1}^{n} w_{jk} \cdot x_{ijk}$$

where

A_{ij} = attitude of individual j about brand i
w_{jk} = relative importance to individual j of attribute k
x_{ijk} = perceived degree of presence of attribute k in brand i by individual j (score)
n = number of determinant attributes (k = 1 to n)

This formula is a weighted average of evaluation scores. To estimate this model, the market analyst needs an importance score for each attribute and an evaluation (or performance) score of the brand with respect to each attribute. A numerical example is given in Table 5.4, where six brands of laptop computer are evaluated according to five determinant attributes.

Table 5.4   A compositional multi-attribute model

Brands of laptop computer	Attributes					Overall score[3]	
	Compact-ness	Autonomy	Power	Keyboard	Screen	Mean	Adjusted
Brand A	6	8	9	8	7	7.50	7.68
Brand B	7	8	7	8	9	7.60	7.58
Brand C	5	9	9	8	8	7.55	7.86
Brand D	7	8	9	7	9	7.85	7.95
Brand E	8	8	5	6	7	7.00	7.08
Brand F	9	2	5	6	7	5.80	5.07
Importance	0.30	0.25	0.20	0.15	0.10	1.00	1.00
Differentiation[1]	1.41	2.56	1.97	0.98	0.98	–	–
Determinance[2]	0.25	0.38	0.23	0.09	0.06	1.00	1.00

1. Differentiation of a particular attribute is measured by the standard deviation of the scores on that attribute.
2. Determinance is obtained by multiplying the importance score by the differentiation score and by standardising those products to have a sum equal to 1.
3. The mean score is calculated using the importance scores, while the adjusted mean score is determined using the determinance scores.

If the potential buyer evaluates brands in a linearly additive fashion, the selected laptop computer will not necessarily be the most compact nor the one with the most readable screen, the most powerful, the most convenient keyboard, and so on. The selected computer, however, will be that which is 'globally' best for this buyer, taking into account all of the relevant attributes and their relative importance. In this example, the model suggests that brand D will be preferred by the market.

Non-compensatory models of attitude

In the previous example, we can verify that Fishbein's model is compensatory, that is low points on an attribute are compensated by high points obtained for other attributes. In this model, the multiplicative relations between importance and performance, the summation over all attributes and the nature of the scores show that it is a linear compensatory attitude model. This fact allows high scores in some attributes to compensate for low ratings in others.

This way of evaluating brands is not necessarily the most effective and one can imagine that an individual may face an absolute constraint on a price level. In this kind of situation, evaluation is no longer compensatory because one criterion dominates.

In Exhibit 5.2 the major non-compensatory models of attitude are defined. The most common observation is a two-stage choice procedure. At the first stage, the potential buyer adopts a conjunctive model allowing him to eliminate products not satisfying his minimal requirements. At the second stage, the remaining products are subjected to compensatory evaluation or lexicographic ordering.

Exhibit 5.2

Non-compensatory Decision and Attitude Models

■ **DISJUNCTIVE MODEL**
Instead of setting minimum standards on different attributes and rejecting alternatives that do not meet all those minima, the buyer sets a high standard for *one or few attributes* and then considers buying only those brands meeting or exceeding the standards on these attributes only.

■ **CONJUNCTIVE MODEL**
The buyer has some *minimum cut-off level* in mind for each important attribute. He or she rejects alternatives that fall below the minimum on any one of those attributes. The buyer will favour the brand(s) that exceed the minimum requirements on all-important criteria. A high score on one attribute will not compensate for a below minimum level on another.

■ **LEXICOGRAPHIC MODEL**
In a lexicographic model, the buyer first *ranks criteria or attributes* in order of importance. Next, all brands or choice alternatives are compared on the most important attribute. If one brand scores higher on the most important criterion than any other brands, then it is chosen. If not (suppose it is tied with two others), then the inferior brands are eliminated and comparisons are made among the tied brands using the second most important attribute. The procedure is continued until a final superior brand remains to be chosen or until no further brands can be eliminated.

Measuring attribute determinance

To empirically measure attitude, the attributes used as choice criteria by the target group must be identified. A distinction must be made between attribute 'salience', 'importance' and 'determinance' as already discussed in Chapter 4. Briefly:

● *Salience* corresponds to the fact that the attribute is in the respondent's mind at a given moment.
● *Importance* reflects the value system of the individual.
● *Determinance* reflects the ability of a particular attribute to discriminate among alternative brands.

Thus, determinance refers to important attributes, which help differentiate among objects being evaluated. If an important attribute is equally represented in all competing brands, it clearly does not allow discrimination among them, and is not a determinant in the choice. Measuring determinance implies not only a measure of importance, but also a *differentiation score*, which is a measure of perceived difference between brands with respect to each attribute.

Determinance is then obtained by multiplying scores of importance and differentiation. Differentiation may be measured by a direct question about perceived differences between brands for each attribute using, for example, a scale of 1 (no difference) to 5 (great difference). A simpler method would be a measure of dispersion for a differentiation score (such as standard deviation of evaluation scores), as illustrated in Table 5.4. This method would prevent rendering the task of respondents too demanding.

Clearly, it is with respect to determinant attributes that it is interesting to situate different competing brands in the market. In the example of Table 5.4, global attitude scores are calculated first with the importance scores and then with the determinance scores. The model predicts that individual *j* will prefer computer D. But the ranking of computers B and C is modified, however, when the determinance scores are used.

The importance/performance matrix

An attribute can be considered as very important by a buyer and not be perceived as present in a particular brand. The problem then is whether to reinforce the attribute's presence in the product or to use better communication to increase awareness and/or conviction about the attribute's presence. To confront importance and performance scores, it is convenient to use a matrix similar to the one presented in Figure 5.6 where the attributes of a brand are situated along two dimensions (Martilla and James, 1977). The horizontal axis indicates the importance of the attributes from low to high and the vertical axis represents their perceived performance from low to high. The placements of attributes on this two-dimensional grid suggest the suitable strategy for each.

● In the upper-right quadrant are located the *'strengths'*, that is attributes evaluated high both in importance and performance. The brand has a strong image for these criteria, which must be highlighted in the communication.

● In the quadrant just below are the brand *'weaknesses'*: these attributes are high in importance but rated low in performance. In this case the firm has to act and make efforts to improve its performance.

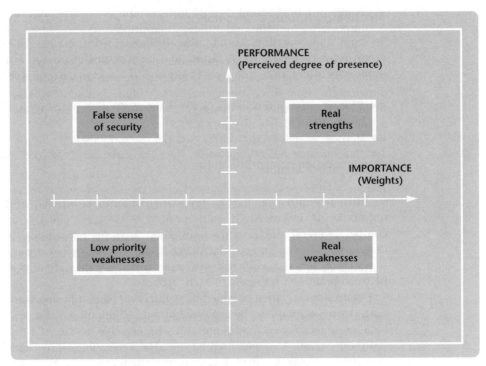

Figure 5.6 The importance/performance matrix

● In the upper-left quadrant are the *'false problems'*, the criteria rated high in performance, but low in importance. This implies that an overkill has occurred. Perhaps the resources committed to these attributes should be reallocated.

● Finally, in the quadrant below are the *'false strengths'*: these attributes are rated low both in importance and performance. They are considered low priority and hence require no additional action.

The determinance versus relative performance matrix

This analysis is useful to identify the components of a brand image and the communication programme to support this image. This matrix as outlined above has two weaknesses, however, which limits its usefulness for identifying the brand's sustainable competitive advantage:

● First, performance of the brand on a particular attribute is defined in absolute terms ignoring performance *vis-à-vis* competitors. In reality, buyers do not evaluate an object in a competitive vacuum but in comparative terms. Thus, *relative performance* scores should be determined for each attribute by reference to priority competitor(s).

● Second, as discussed above, importance scores do not recognise the *determinance* of an attribute. Determinant attributes are those that discriminate well among competing brands and directly influence buyer choice. Thus, focusing solely on importance may misguide strategy definition.

The extended 'importance–performance' analysis is designed to rectify these two weaknesses by incorporating a relative performance dimension and a determinance dimension. Three levels of determinance (high, medium low) are combined with three levels of relative performance, (competitive advantage, parity or disadvantage) as shown in the matrix of Figure 5.7.

Attribute-based perceptual maps

The problem of *redundancy* remains as a final question about the relevance of attributes. Two attributes are said to be redundant when there is no difference in their significance.

> For example, in a study of the heavy trucks market in Belgium, two criteria of 'loading capacity' and 'engine capacity' were spontaneously evoked as important attributes. The two criteria are being used interchangeably, neither existing without the other.

If two determinant attributes are retained, but they both indicate the same characteristic, this situation is equivalent to selecting only one attribute. The analyst should establish a list of determinant but non-redundant attributes.

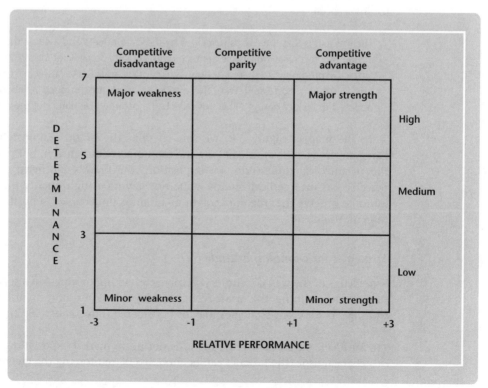

Figure 5.7   Determinance versus relative performance analysis

Exhibit 5.3

Principal Components Analysis

The method used for this purpose is factorial analysis, for example principal components analysis (PCA). This method is a statistical technique which organises and summarises a set of data (the *N* determinant attributes in this case) into a reduced set of factors called the principal components or 'macro-characteristics', which are independent of each other and which contrast best the objects under study (see Hair *et al.*, 1992). The output of a PCA is an attribute-based perceptual map. Each brand is positioned along the two or three retained components, which can be interpreted by the correlation observed between these principal components and each attribute. The interpretation of a perceptual map resulting from a PCA is as follows: two brands are close on the perceptual map if they are evaluated in the same way according to all retained attributes. Two attributes are close if they lead to the evaluation of brands in the same manner.

Brand image studies measure customers' perceptions and help discover market expectations. The perceptual map of Figure 5.8 illustrates this point. This map is based on the rating scores of 12 attributes obtained from a sample of regular users of skin-care and make-up brands. A principal components analysis (Exhibit 5.3) of these scores identified two macro-attributes, which summarise 83 per cent of the total variance.

The first axis is total quality as perceived by the respondents and include the following micro-attributes: 'technical quality, 'extent of product line', 'quality of packaging', 'information', 'attractive promotions'. These attributes are mentally opposed to 'attractive prices'. The second axis is strongly correlated with the attributes 'medicare products', 'laboratory tests' and opposed to 'luxury design'. This axis reflects the paramedical nature of these products.

In the map of Figure 5.8, we can see that the brands Rubinstein, Lauder and Lancôme are well positioned along the total quality dimension, but poorly placed on the paramedical dimension. By opposition, the brands Biotherm and Clarins are perceived as paramedical brands while not having a high quality image. It is interesting to observe that the upper-right quadrant is unoccupied, a positioning probably difficult to defend.

Strategies for changing attitude

Knowledge of the way consumers perceive competing products in a segment is important in determining the strategy to be adopted to modify an unfavourable positioning. Six different strategies may be considered (Boyd *et al.*, 1972):

● *Modifying the product.* If the brand is not up to market expectations of a particular characteristic, the product can be modified by reinforcing the given characteristic.

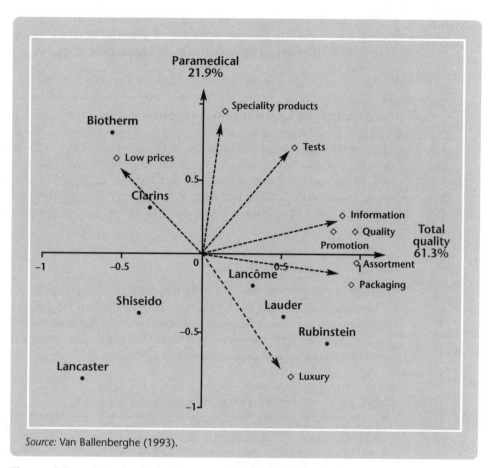

Source: Van Ballenberghe (1993).

Figure 5.8 Attribute-based perceptual map: the skin-care and make-up market

● *Modifying attribute weights.* Convince the market that more importance ought to be attached to a particular characteristic that the brand exhibits well.

● *Modifying beliefs about a brand.* The market may be badly informed and underestimate some real distinctive qualities of the brand. This entails perceptual repositioning.

● *Modifying beliefs about competing brands.* This strategy is to be used if the market overestimates some characteristics of competitors. It implies the possibility of using comparative advertising.

● *Attracting attention to neglected attributes.* This strategy usually involves the creation of a new benefit not yet considered by the target segment.

● *Modifying the required attribute level.* It is possible that the market expects a quality level that is not always necessary, at least as far as some applications are concerned. The firm can try to convince the segment that the quality offered for that particular dimension is adequate.

The major advantage of multi-attribute models over simple overall attitude measure is in gaining an understanding of the attitudinal structure of the segment under study, in order to identify the most appropriate strategies of positioning and communication.

⬤ Measuring the Behavioural Response

The simplest and most direct measure of behavioural response is given by sales data for the product or brand, complemented by an analysis of the market share held within each segment covered. Other types of information are useful for interpreting sales data and formulating a valid diagnostic of the positioning of the product, that is information about purchasing habits and also information about after-purchase behaviour.

Analysis of purchasing habits

The aim of this analysis is to establish the profile of the buying behaviour by segment of consumers within the product category being studied. Information is required on three types of behaviour: *acquisition, utilisation and possession*. Table 5.5 presents the main elements of information being sought. These elements vary by product category and must be adapted to each particular situation.

Table 5.5 Information on purchasing behaviour

Questions	Acquisition	Use	Possession
What?	Regular brand Last brand bought	Type of use Substitute products	Brand now on hand
How much?	Quantity per purchase	Consumption per week Most important use	Quantity owned
How?	Purchasing situation	Mode of use	Mode of storage
Where?	Usual place of purchase	Usual place of use	Usual place of storage
When?	Date of last purchase Interpurchase timing	Usual period of use	Length of storage
Who?	Person who buys	Person who uses	Person who holds

The description of buying behaviour is facilitated by using the following basic questions: *what, how much, how, where, when* and *who*.

- ⬤ *What* allows the definition of the evoked set of brands and identification of possible substitutes.
- ⬤ *How much* provides quantitative information on the volume of purchases and consumption and on storage habits.
- ⬤ *How* highlights different ways of purchasing (hire purchase, instalment plan) and different uses to which the product is put.

- *Where* is important for identifying the main distribution networks used, places of consumption and storing of the product.
- *When* helps get knowledge about situation factors and consumption opportunities, as well as the rhythm of purchase and repurchase.
- *Who* aims to identify the composition of the buying centre and the role of its members (buyer, user, payer).

These questions are useful to guide the collection of market primary data and to build a market information system.

The family viewed as a buying decision centre

As mentioned before, the question of the *buying centre* and its structure is fundamental in industrial marketing. It is also important regarding consumer goods, since buying decisions are hardly ever made by isolated individuals and mostly made within the family, which, in fact, constitutes a buying centre comparable to the one observed in an organisation.

Knowledge of purchasing habits implies identification of the respective roles (buyer, user, payer) of the mother, the father and the children, and this by product category and at different stages of the buying process. These questions are important to marketers, who must adapt their product, price and communication policies to their real client (Davis and Rigaux, 1974), especially since the distribution of the roles and influence of spouses tends to change, due in particular to the rapidly changing role of women in society. One of the first proposed typologies suggests four allocations of roles (Herbst, 1952):

- autonomous decision by the husband or the wife,
- dominant influence of husband,
- dominant influence of wife,
- synchretic decision, that is, taken together.

The role of children is still to be taken into account. Comparison of the results of studies on the allocation of roles for various product categories shows that the influence of spouses varies greatly according to the type of product (Davis and Rigaux, 1974).

Pras and Tarondeau (1981, p. 214) emphasise that the aim of this kind of research is to define the strategies to be adopted due to a better understanding of the behaviour of the target group. Their relevance can be summarised as follows:

- properly choose the persons to be questioned,
- determine the content of advertising messages,
- choose the best adapted support material,
- adapt product conception to the needs of the person with greatest influence, choose the most appropriate distribution network.

Mastering this set of information about buying habits will contribute to a significant improvement in the firm's marketing practice and thus increase the impact of behavioural response.

Market share analysis

Company or brand sales, measured in volume or in value, are the most direct measures of the market behavioural response. Sales analysis can be misleading, however, since it does not reveal how the brand is doing relative to competing brands operating in the same reference market. An increase in sales may be due to a general improvement in market conditions and have nothing to do with the brand's performance, or the increase may be hiding a deterioration of the brand's position, for instance when it has grown but less than its rivals. To be useful, sales analysis must therefore be complemented by a market share analysis, ideally in volume within each segment covered.

Calculating market shares assumes that the firm has clearly defined its *reference market*, that is the set of products or brands that compete with it. The method of defining a reference market is described in Chapter 7.

Once the reference market has been determined, market share is simply calculated as follows:

$$\text{Market share} = \frac{\text{Brand A unit sales}}{\text{Total unit sales}}$$

The reason for measuring market share is to eliminate the impact of environmental factors, which exert the same influence on all competing brands and thus allow a proper comparison of the competitive power of each. Nevertheless, as suggested by Oxenfeldt (1969), the notion of market share needs to be used with caution, keeping the following considerations in mind:

- The level of market share depends directly on the choice of the basis of comparison, that is on the *reference market*. It is important to check that this basis is the same for all the brands.

- The hypothesis that *environmental factors* have the same influence on all brands is not necessarily verified. Some brands may be better or less well placed with respect to some environmental factors.

- When *new brands* are introduced into a market, the share of each participant must necessarily drop, without there being any bad performance, even if some brands resist the entry of a new competitor better than others.

- Market shares can sometimes fluctuate because *of accidental or exceptional factors*, such as a large order.

- Sometimes the firm may deliberately provoke a drop in market share because, for example, a distribution network or a market segment is being abandoned.

Irrespective of the definition adopted for the reference market, various measures of market share can be calculated:

- *Unit market share*, that is company or brand sales in volume expressed as percentage of total sales of the reference market.

● *Value market share* is calculated on the basis of turnover rather than sales in units. A market share in value is often difficult to interpret because changes in market share reflect a combination of volume and price changes.

● *Served-market share* is calculated, not relative to the total reference market, but relative to sales in the market segment(s) addressed by the firm. Note that the served-market share is always larger than overall market share.

● *Relative market share* compares the firm's sales with that of its competitors, thus excluding the firm's own sales. If a firm holds 30 per cent of the market, and its top three competitors hold respectively 20, 15 and 10 per cent, and the 'others' 25 per cent, relative market share will be 43 per cent (30/70). If relative market share is calculated by reference to the top three competitors, then the firm's relative market share is 67 per cent (30/45). Relative market shares above 33 per cent are considered to be strong.

● *Relative market share to leading competitor* is calculated by reference to the leading competitor's sales. In the previous example, the dominant firm has a relative market share of 1.5 (30/20). The relative market share of the other firms is obtained by dividing their market share by that of the leading competitor, that is 0.67, 0.50 and 0.33, respectively, in this example.

Measuring market shares can raise problems depending on the availability of the necessary information. To measure served-market share implies that the firm is in a position to evaluate total sales in each segment. Similarly, relative market share assumes knowledge of sales achieved by direct competition. Obtaining this information varies in levels of difficulty from sector to sector.

In the field of consumer goods, market shares are available through syndicated consumer or dealer panels or through scanning diary panels. In the other fields, in cases where government organisations and trade associations do not provide this information, it is up to the *marketing information system* to arrange how to purchase or to create this information, which is vital for tracking sales performance.

Quality of market share analysis

Quality market share analysis helps predict future performance. The critical question addressed is: *What makes up our market share?* Traditional market share measures in units or in value should be complemented by an analysis of the customer base, as shown in the following examples (see Table 5.6), where two competitors having the same market share are compared.

Table 5.6   Quality market share analysis (%)

	Brand A	Brand B
EXAMPLE 1		
Market share	30	30
Composition of customer base:		
High profit	15	5
Switchable	15	50
Unprofitable	5	15
Loyal	65	30
EXAMPLE 2		
Market share	30	30
Composition of customer base:		
Growers	40	20
Maintainers	25	30
Decliners	35	50

Source: CDI Point of View (1992).

The question is: *Which 30 per cent market share is preferable?* Clearly, Competitor A has:

● Less risk with fewer 'switchables' customers.
● A stronger financial position fuelled by more 'high profit' customers.
● Fewer 'unprofitable' customers draining its resources.

Competitor B's outlook is not so bright. With few 'high profit' customers and 50 per cent of its customer base at risk in 'switchables', we can anticipate flat or declining sales and unattractive profitability. Similar analyses of the customer base can be made, for instance, on how many customers are growing, maintaining or declining in their spending.

Market share movement analysis

Consumer and dealer panels provide detailed information on market shares by region, segment, distribution network, and so on. Such data allow the implementation of more refined types of analysis, used to interpret gains or losses in market shares.

Parfitt and Collins (1968) have shown how to decompose market share into a number of components, which help to interpret and to predict its development:

● *Penetration rate* is the share of buyers, that is the percentage of buyers of brand x compared to the total number of buyers in the reference product category.

● *Exclusivity rate* is defined as the share of total purchases in a product category reserved for brand x. This rate is a measure of the loyalty attached to brand x, given that buyers have the possibility of diversifying their purchases and acquiring different brands in the same product category.

● *Intensity rate* compares average quantities purchased per buyer of brand x with average quantities purchased per buyer of the product category.

A brand's market share can then be calculated from these three components. Thus,

$$\text{Market share} = \text{Penetration rate} \times \text{Exclusivity rate} \times \text{Intensity rate}$$

Let x denote the brand and c the reference product category to which x belongs. Let us also adopt the following notation:

N_x = Number of buyers of x;
N_c = Number of buyers of c;
Q_{xx} = Quantity of x purchased by buyers of x;
Q_{cx} = Quantity of c purchased by buyers of x;
Q_{cc} = Quantity of c purchased by buyers of c.

It can be verified that

$$\text{Market share} = \frac{Q_{xx}}{Q_{cc}} = \frac{N_x}{N_c} \cdot \frac{Q_{xx}/N_x}{Q_{cx}/N_x} \cdot \frac{Qc_x/N_x}{Q_{cc}/N_c}$$

To express market share in value, a relative price index must be added: the ratio of the brand's average price to the average price charged by all competing brands. This definition of market share can be generally applied. It permits the identification of the possible causes of observed movements in market share. The following are possible explanations of a fall in market share:

● the brand is losing customers (lower penetration rate),
● buyers are devoting a smaller share of their purchases of the product to this particular brand (lower exclusivity rate),
● buyers of the brand are purchasing smaller quantities compared to the quantities bought on average by buyers of the product (lower intensity rate).

By tracking these market indicators over time, the market analyst can identify the underlying causes of market share changes and suggest corrective measures accordingly.

Measures of market share can be used from two different perspectives, as an *indicator of competitive performance* or as an *indicator of competitive advantage.* In the first case, market shares should, as much as possible, be calculated over finer divisions, that is by segment, by distribution network or by region. In the second case, a more aggregate basis would be more suitable because it would better reveal the strength of the market power held by the firm and the possible existence of economies of scale or of learning curve effects.

Estimating marketing response functions

A marketing response function is a relationship that links buyers' response expressed in terms of volume or market share, to one or more marketing variables. Response functions are generally obtained from historical data through econometric analysis. Quantitative estimation of response functions leads to *elasticity coefficients* measuring demand or market share sensitivity to a variation in one of the explanatory variables, such as price, advertising or household income. The notion of elasticity is defined in more detail in Appendix 5.1.

Response functions are useful because their estimations, based on observations on different markets, different segments or different product categories, improve one's understanding of buyers' response mechanisms. Thus one progressively builds a more rigorous basis for future marketing programmes (see Assmus *et al.*, 1984).

Table 5.7   Selected estimates of marketing variables elasticities

Product Categories	Number of Brands	Advertising Elasticities[1]	Price Elasticities	Distribution[2] Elasticities
Soft drinks	5	0.070	−1.419	1.181
Yoghurt	2	0.031	−1.100	−
Confectionery	2	0.034	−1.982	2.319
TV sets	4	0.122	−	−
Cigarettes	1	0.154	−1.224	−
Bank services	5	0.003	−	0.251
Cars transported by rail	1	0.184	−1.533	−
Coffee	1	0.036	−2.933	1.868
Fruits	1	0.095	−1.229	−
Electric shavers	18	0.219	−2.460	0.909
Gasoline	19	0.024	−0.600	0.923
Shampoos	11	0.036	−1.762	−
Insecticides	9	0.058	−	−
Deodorants	11	0.054	−	−
Detergents	6	0.084	−	−
Suntan lotion	11	0.300	−	−
Average: study 1976[3]	**N = 107**	**0.094**	**−1.624**	**1.243**
Female hygiene	6	0.010	−1.405	0.958
Dishwashers	2	0.029	−1.692	−
Detergent	1	0.049	−2.009	−
Jam	3	0.022	−2.672	2.757
Automobiles	8	0.093	−2.004	−
Average: study 1988[4]	**N = 20**	**0.041**	**−1.956**	**−**
Average: 1976 and 1988	N = 127	0.081	−1.735	1.395

Source: J.J. Lambin (1976, 1988).
1. These elasticities are average elasticities.
2. Based on Nielsen indices of distribution coverage.
3. The observation basis is the brand per country: the countries are: Belgium, France, the Netherlands, FRG, Denmark, Italy, Norway, Sweden.
4. The observation basis is Belgium.

By way of illustration, Table 5.7 presents estimates of the marketing variables elasticities for a sample of 127 brands operating on the European market and coming from 21 different product categories. These elasticity coefficients observed for the distribution, price and advertising variables are directly useful for forecasting and control. They constitute good starting points for simulation exercises designed for analysing the implications of alternative marketing programmes (Lambin, 1972).

In consumer markets, the use of response functions is now largely facilitated by constant improvement in databases. This development has come about as a result of technological innovation; the progressive but irreversible introduction of *scanning systems* in retail stores and increasing computerisation of marketing information systems in the firm (Nielsen Researcher, 1981). Market analysts now have at their disposal more reliable information on market shares, selling prices, advertising, promotions, out-of-stocks, and so on. The most important change in this area is in the frequency of data, which is now available weekly rather than on a bimonthly or monthly basis. This weekly frequency gives more timely and sensitive information to assist the market analyst in assessing competitive response and brand performance. Direct causal relationships between market shares and the marketing variables can also be established. Figure 5.9 presents the penetration curve of a new brand described successively in terms of bimonthly, monthly and weekly observations. Causal data, that is the marketing variables active during the launching period, are shown in the lower part of the graph, below the time scale. It is clear that bimonthly and monthly data completely mask the market response. The weekly observations, on the other hand, show the causal relationship very clearly.

Post-purchase behaviour

Having bought and used the product, the consumer or buyer develops a new attitude, based mainly on the degree *of satisfaction or dissatisfaction* that is felt after using the product. This positive or negative attitude will lead to a post-purchase behaviour which determines the product's acceptance and also the repeat purchase rate if it is the case of a product bought repeatedly.

The buyers' satisfaction will be a function of the degree of concordance existing between their expectations of the product on the one hand, and their perception of its performance on the other. If the result conforms to their expectations, there is satisfaction; if it is higher, satisfaction is greater; if it is lower, there is dissatisfaction. The notion of expected result goes back to Lewin's (1935) *aspiration level theory.* Lewin's analysis is based on the following propositions:

> Every time someone feels the need or desire for something, he or she identifies (a) a level of satisfaction, called the realisation level, perceived as already obtained; (b) a level of satisfaction expected by the purchase, the aspiration level and (c) the highest possible level of satisfaction, the ideal level.

Individuals' aspiration levels are formed on the basis of their experiences, as well as the promises made in the firm's advertising about its products' performances. Individuals' aspirations develop differently according to their personality. Some set their aspiration level at a *minimum*, which they intend to surpass. This attitude describes risk aversion. Others set their level at a *maximum*, representing an objective they endeavour to approach, but do not expect to attain. Here, aspiration level acts as a stimulus. Finally, others set their level roughly to the *average* of the results already obtained, reflecting an equality between aspiration level and realisation level.

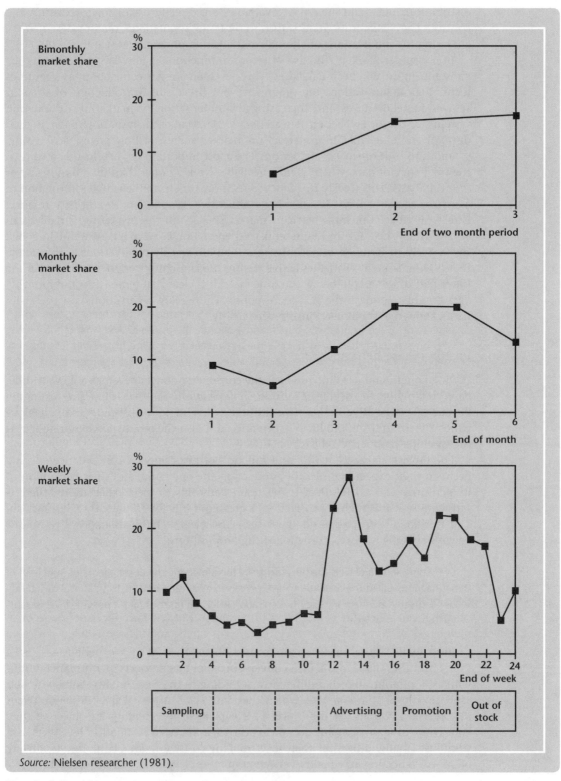

Source: Nielsen researcher (1981).

Figure 5.9　Penetration curves of a new product

Aspirations are not static, but develop continuously. As emphasised in Chapter 3, individuals constantly seek stimulation and novelty. If successful, aspirations tend to amplify. They are also influenced by performances of other members of the group to which the individual belongs. Expectation theory therefore suggests adopting a communication policy based on the product's likely performances, and avoiding inconsiderate promises which can only create dissatisfaction, by contradicting or invalidating buyers' expectations.

The brand loyalty concept

There are several approaches for operationally defining brand loyalty and for long the most popular one was based on the observation of purchase sequence. For example, a 12-trial purchase sequence of: AABAACAADAAE would qualify a consumer as being loyal to Brand A according to a per cent-of-purchase definition, but not according to most sequence definitions which require three or four consecutive purchases of the same brand as the criterion of loyalty. This purely behavioural view of loyalty has clear limitations, because attention is focused entirely on the *outcome of*, rather than the *reasons for*, behaviour.

> For example, is the woman who always buy Brand A because it is the cheapest, 'loyal' in the same sense as the woman who buys brand A because she prefers it? And what of the woman who buys brand A because it has the most favourable shelf space or because it is the only nationally advertised and distributed brand carried by the store in which she shops? (Day, 1969)

It is clear that, underlying the loyalty behaviour, there is an *evaluative process or an attitudinal component* linked to the purchaser's degree of satisfaction that must be identified. The repeat purchase behaviour is a necessary but not sufficient condition for defining brand loyalty. Jakoby and Kyner (1973) have presented six criteria considered necessary and collectively sufficient for defining brand loyalty.

> Brand loyalty is (1) the biased (that is non random), (2) behavioural response (that is purchase), (3) expressed over time, (4) by some decision-making unit, (5) with respect to one or more alternative brands out of a set of such brands, and (6) is a function of psychological (decision-making, evaluative) processes. (Jakoby and Kyner, 1973)

The term '*decision-making unit*' implies that the decision-maker need not be (a) the user or even the purchaser of the product, but can also be the prescriber. Similarly, the decision-making unit can be an individual or a collection of individuals (family or organisation). The fifth condition is important because it introduces the concept of *multibrand loyalty or brand repertoire*: individuals can be and frequently are multibrand loyal. A brand switch can occur within a set of brands to which the buyer remains loyal. This behaviour is revealing of a loyal behaviour to a reduced set of brands, a construct close to the consideration set concept described above (see Figure 5.5).

The brand (or company) loyalty concept is important in several respects and in particular in view of the relationship existing between loyalty and satisfaction – as discussed in the next section – and also because of the impact of customer loyalty on corporate profitability, as illustrated in Figure 5.10 and Exhibit 5.4.

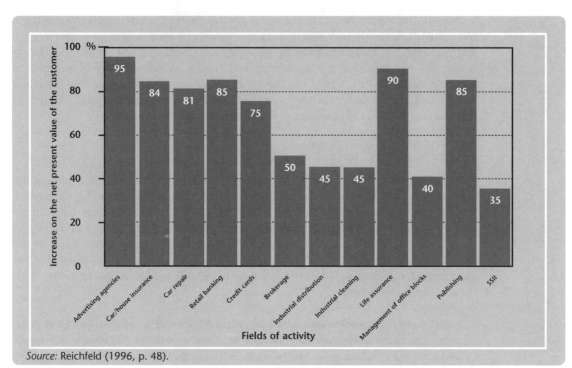

Source: Reichfeld (1996, p. 48).

Figure 5.10　Impact of a five per cent increase of the loyalty rate on the net present value of a customer

Brand switching analysis

A simple indicator of consumer satisfaction in a competitive market is the buyers' repeat purchase rate over time. Brand switching analysis is also useful to forecast the brand dynamic evolution. Note that this approach is based on the analysis of *purchase sequences*. Consider the market share development of brands A, B and C shown in Figure 5.11.

Exhibit 5.4

Customer Longevity is Profitable

The more a customer is loyal, the more he contributes to the profitability, since the costs of finding a new customer are borne only once. If every year, 5 per cent of the customer base quit and must be replaced, it means that a customer has an average life of twenty years. If the loyalty rate can be increased from 95 per cent to 96 per cent thanks to a higher customer satisfaction level, only 4 per cent of customers have to be replaced and the average customer life jumps to 25 per cent, with a resulting strong improvement of the firm's profitability.

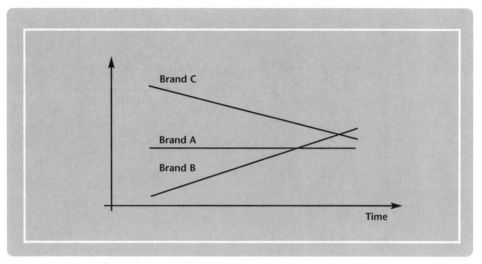

Figure 5.11   The dynamics of market share movements

The stability of brand A's market share can be interpreted in two very different ways:

- a fixed number of consumers buys the same quantity of brand A at regular intervals,
- the number of consumers dropping brand A is equal to the number of consumers adopting brand A; entry rate then compensates exit rate exactly.

On the basis of aggregate market data, it is not possible to decide which is the true state. Similarly, one could give the following explanations for brand B's growth:

- brand B has a fixed number of loyal buyers to whom new buyers are added at a regular pace,
- entry rate is higher than exit rate,
- the number of brand B's buyers remains unchanged, but some of them are purchasing an increased quantity per buying occasion.

Here again, the available information does not permit us to discriminate between these possible explanations.

To keep the analysis simple, let us limit ourselves to a market composed of two competing brands. As shown in Figure 5.12 each particular purchasing act, viewed in a dynamic perspective, can be described in terms of three origins and three destinations. For each brand, we can thus define a loyalty rate and an attraction rate. These switching rates can be defined as follows:

- The *loyalty rate* is the percentage of buyers who, having purchased brand A in the previous period $(t - 1)$, continue to buy brand A in the current period (t).
- The *attraction rate* is the percentage of buyers who, having purchased a competing brand in period $t - 1$, purchase brand A in period t.

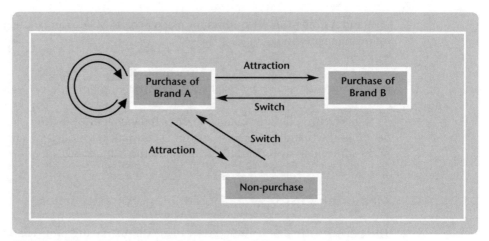

Figure 5.12 The brand switching dynamic

These proportions, called *transition probabilities*, can be estimated through survey or on the basis of panel data. To illustrate, the transition probabilities observed in the Belgian market among six makes of heavy trucks are presented in Table 5.8.

Table 5.8 Example of brand switching analysis: the heavy duty truck market

Replaced Brands in Period (t)	Brands Purchased in Period ($t + 1$)						
	Daf	Mercedes	Renault	Scania	Volvo	Others	Market share in t
Daf	55.2	15.3	1.3	2.3	11.4	13.5	7.6%
Mercedes	8.2	59.5	2.4	2.3	11.1	15.5	15.3%
Renault	9.0	9.2	53.0	5.0	1.2	22.6	3.2%
Scania	8.1	13.3	0.0	65.6	5.1	5.9	3.3%
Volvo	15.5	12.9	1.2	1.7	60.0	7.7	5.2%
Others	11.7	17.1	4.8	2.9	10.3	53.2	63.4%
Market share in $t + 1$	14.6%	23.2%	5.3%	4.8%	13.2%	38.9%	100.0%

Source: MDA Consulting Group, Brussels.

These transition probabilities allow the market analyst to explain market share movements over time, to describe the underlying competitive dynamics and to formulate predictions on market developments assuming that the observed transition probabilities will remain unchanged within a reasonable planning horizon.

If α denotes loyalty rate and β attraction rate, brand A's market share in future period $t + 1$ will be

$$MS\ (t + 1) = \alpha\ MS\ (t) + \beta[1 - MS(t)]$$

Brand A's long-run or equilibrium market share, MS(e), can be calculated from the following expression:

$$MS(e) = \frac{\text{Attraction rate}}{(1 - \text{loyalty rate}) + (\text{attraction rate})} = \frac{\beta}{(1 - \alpha) + \beta}$$

Note that equilibrium market share is independent of the initial market share. It describes the brand's trajectory, assuming constant transition probabilities. This type of dynamic analysis is particularly useful at the launch stage of a new product.

Measuring Customer Satisfaction and Dissatisfaction

The buyer's satisfaction is at the heart of the marketing process and yet it is only recently that companies have begun to systematically measure the degree of satisfaction felt by consumers. Previously, analysis was restricted to internal measures of quality such as ISO-9000. The most obvious level of satisfaction would seem to be the level of sales or market share, just as the number of complaints would be the sign of dissatisfaction.

In fact, things are much more complicated. There can be a big difference between what the company thinks customers want and what the customer is really looking for. In other words, the gap between the designed and the expected quality may be very large, even if the customer never formally expresses his or her dissatisfaction. This is why it is necessary to directly interview customers to assess scientifically their level of satisfaction/dissatisfaction. The value of this type of study is also to permit international comparisons for the same brand from country to country and to allow longitudinal analyses to keep track of the changes in satisfaction over a certain period.

The behaviour of dissatisfied customers

In a meta-analysis of customer satisfaction studies based on 500 surveys conducted in Europe in all business sectors, with an average of 300 interviews per survey, Goderis (1998, p. 285) obtained the following data:

● only 2.9 per cent of sales transactions result in complaints *made directly* to the company,
● on average, 28.6 per cent of transactions result in *indirect complaints* to the sales representatives, neighbours, friends, and so on,
● in addition, 9.2 per cent of the complaints are never communicated.

There are two different explanations for this last group. Buyers have either minimised the problem or they were pessimistic about the outcome of a complaint, given the dominant position of the supplier or because, in previous instances, a complaint has remained unanswered.

Thus, in total, 40.7 per cent of the transactions of an average firm may cause problems to customers, a level of dissatisfaction that is not well reflected by the tip of the iceberg, that is the 3 per cent of formal complaints.

In so far as a complaint is efficiently handled by after-sales service, the negative consequences for the firm can be limited. On the other hand, a real problem remains with the 30 per cent group of dissatisfied customers who do not communicate with the supplier but who could really affect market share in the long run. This is why the adoption of a proactive attitude here is important by measuring regularly the level of satisfaction/dissatisfaction of different customer groups and identifying their causes. Remember that, in sectors where primary demand is non-expandable, 80 to 90 per cent of the turnover is due to existing customers. It is easy to understand why it is important to maintain satisfaction for this portfolio of existing customers.

An additional argument is provided by analysis of the behaviour of dissatisfied customers whose complaints were well handled by the firm. The findings reported in the Goderis study (1998, p. 286) have shown the following results:

● For satisfied customers, the average repeat purchase rate is 91 per cent.

● Among customers who had made a complaint but had received a poor response from the firm, the repeat purchase rate drops to 54 per cent.

● Of dissatisfied customers who had complained and had received an appropriate response from the firm, the repeat purchase rate was 96 per cent, a rate higher than that observed for satisfied customers.

Problem customers are (a) those dissatisfied but who do not complain and (b) those who complain but are not happy with the way their complaint has been treated by the company. The loss of customers comes from these two groups which constitute a form of negative advertising by word of mouth, costly for the firm and very difficult to control. Research findings (Rhoades, 1988) show that *dissatisfied customers will tell ten other people about their bad experience with a company or a brand'.*

● Three important conclusions can be drawn from these various studies on dissatisfied customers' behaviour:

● The level of satisfaction/dissatisfaction is key input data in the market information system of any company.

● A complaint is not necessarily negative because the customer will accept a problem to the extent the company finds a good solution to the problem.

● Complaints are important sources of information, allowing a company to better understand customer needs and their perception of the product quality.

Current complaint management is only one aspect, necessary but insufficient, of a total quality programme aiming at complete customer satisfaction.

The satisfaction–loyalty relationship

As already underlined, a high level of satisfaction leads to increased customer loyalty and increased customer loyalty is the single most important driver of long-term financial performance. The relationship between satisfaction and loyalty has been empirically established, namely by Jones and Sasser (1995), as shown in Figure 5.13.

According to conventional wisdom, the relationship between satisfaction and loyalty should be a simple linear relationship: as satisfaction increases, so does loyalty. A research conducted at Rank Xerox and replicated by Jones and Sasser (1995)

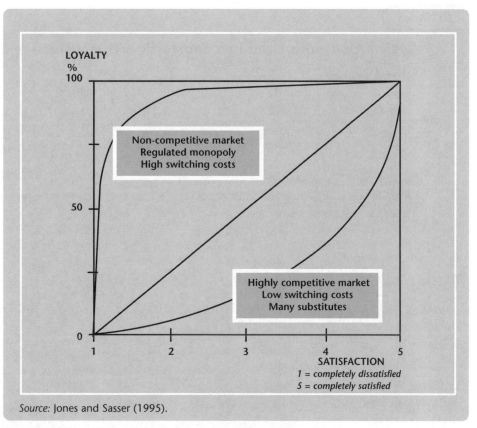

Source: Jones and Sasser (1995).

Figure 5.13   The satisfaction–loyalty relationship

showed a much more complex relationship. The two extreme curves of Figure 5.13 are representative of two different competitive situations:

● *In non-competitive markets* – the upper-left zone – satisfaction has little impact on loyalty. These markets are typically regulated monopolies like telecommunication, electrical or transportation utilities; or market situations where switching costs are very high. Customers in fact have no choice; they are captive customers. This situation can change rapidly, however, if the source of monopoly disappears, because of deregulation or the emergence of alternative technology.

● *In competitive markets* – the lower-right zone – where competition is intense with many substitutes and low switching costs, a very large difference is observed between the loyalty of *'satisfied'* (score of 4) and *'completely satisfied'* (score between 4 and 5) customers. This was namely the discovery made at the Xerox Corporation:

its totally satisfied customers were six times more likely to repurchase Xerox products over the next 18 months than its satisfied customers. (Jones and Sasser, 1995, p. 91)

Exhibit 5.5

Typical Questions Used in a Satisfaction/Dissatisfaction Study

1. Overall evaluation
Generally speaking, how do you evaluate your overall degree of satisfaction concerning your supplier:

Overall satisfaction: 1 2 3 4 5 6 7 8 9 10

2. Evaluation for each attribute
How do you evaluate the importance and your level of satisfaction regarding each of the following attributes:

Importance: 1 2 3 4 5 6 7 8 9 10

Performance: 1 2 3 4 5 6 7 8 9 10

3. Repeat purchase intention
Would you buy your next product ABC from the same supplier?

Yes: .... No: .... Don't know yet: ....

Why: .... Why: .... Why: ....

The implications are profound. Merely satisfying customers who have the freedom to make choices is not enough to keep them loyal. The only truly loyal customers are totally satisfied customers.

Methods of measuring satisfaction/dissatisfaction

The conceptual model underlying satisfaction/dissatisfaction research is simply the attitude multi-attribute model discussed earlier in this chapter. The questions concern the importance of each attribute and the degree of perceived presence of the attribute (performance) in the evaluated product or service.

The interviewing procedure is in three steps. First, the overall level of satisfaction is obtained from the respondent; then importance and performance scores are requested for each attribute on a 10-point rating scale. Finally, repeat purchase intentions are measured. The typical questions used are presented in Exhibit 5.5. This type of questionnaire is preferably administered by telephone, experience having shown that dissatisfied customers are the most likely to respond to a mail questionnaire, thereby undermining the sample representativeness.

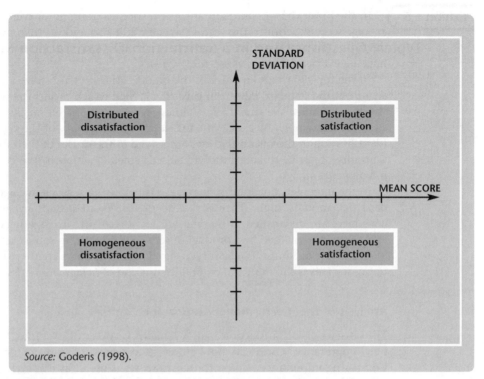

Figure 5.14   The satisfaction–dissatisfaction matrix

This type of questionnaire can be given regularly to representative samples of customers of the same company in different markets, or to customers of different companies in the same market. In this latter case, we have syndicated studies, which offer the advantage of allowing comparisons of competitors.

Analysis of customer satisfaction

The first step is to calculate the average performance score for each attribute as well as its standard deviation. These scores are then compared with the average scores observed in the sector or the scores obtained by priority competitors. This comparison will result in a good picture of how the market perceives the quality of the product, viewed as a package of benefits.

The performance scores obtained on the attributes are situated along two axes: on the horizontal axis are placed the average performance scores and on the vertical axis the standard deviations for these scores. A high standard deviation means that few respondents have the same opinion and a low standard deviation will, in contrast, show that most customers share the same opinion.

The choice of a cut-off point for these two axes is always a sensitive problem. It is common practice to use the average score observed in the sector or the score of the priority competitor. We then have a two-by-two matrix defining four quadrants as shown in Figure 5.14.

In the lower right-hand quadrant, the attributes of brand or company X have an average score superior to the sector's average and also a lower than average standard deviation. This means that customers are generally satisfied and agree to say so. We have here a case of *homogeneous satisfaction*.

In the top right-hand quadrant, the brand's attributes also have an above average score, but the standard deviation this time is high which means that customers have varying opinions. We thus have a situation of *distributed satisfaction*, which can be caused, for example, by a lack of consistency in the quality of the services provided. Identification of the dissatisfied customers and of the causes of their dissatisfaction is a priority objective to adopt individualised remedial action before customers switch to competition.

In the upper-left quadrant, the average is below the sectoral average and the standard deviation is high. This is a case of *distributed dissatisfaction*; most of the customers are dissatisfied, but some are less dissatisfied than others. This state of affairs can be explained by a product or service ill adapted to some customer group(s).

In the last quadrant, the lower left-hand one, customers are dissatisfied and agree to say so. This is the most unfavourable situation of *homogeneous dissatisfaction*.

Analysis of the 'performance/importance' ratios

The satisfaction/dissatisfaction matrix remains very descriptive. Integrating the attributes' importance scores can now allow us to develop a tool for decision making. Comparing importance and performance scores is useful as it is a check on whether or not the package of benefits provided by the product or the service is adapted to customer expectations.

The degree of importance is normally higher than the degree of performance. If the performance score is very inferior, the customer will judge the product as not adequate. In the opposite case, the company offers a product or service of much higher quality than expected and we have an overkill. There is no sense in being very good for an attribute which is of no or little importance. On the other hand, having a poor level of quality for an important attribute can have a very negative impact on the company's image. This is why it is essential to establish a ranking of attributes by order of decreasing importance so as to identify the priority attributes to concentrate upon.

To measure the product's degree of adaptation, the ratio 'performance/importance' will be used as shown in Figure 5.15. On the horizontal axis is the ratio 'performance/importance'; on the vertical axis are the standard deviations of the satisfaction scores. The cut-off point is fixed at a standard deviation of 1 and at a value of 0.9 for the 'performance/importance' ratios. The horizontal axis is subdivided into four distinct zones:

- ⬤ *Zone 1*: the 'performance/importance' (P/I) ratio is above 100 per cent: performance is higher than the importance given to the attribute. This is the case of overkill where too many resources are allocated to a particular attribute.

- ⬤ *Zone 2*: the P/I ratio is between 90 and 100 per cent; the level of satisfaction on important attributes is good.

- ⬤ *Zone 3*: the P/I ratio is included between 80 and 90 per cent; the level of performance is insufficient as compared to the attributes' importance.

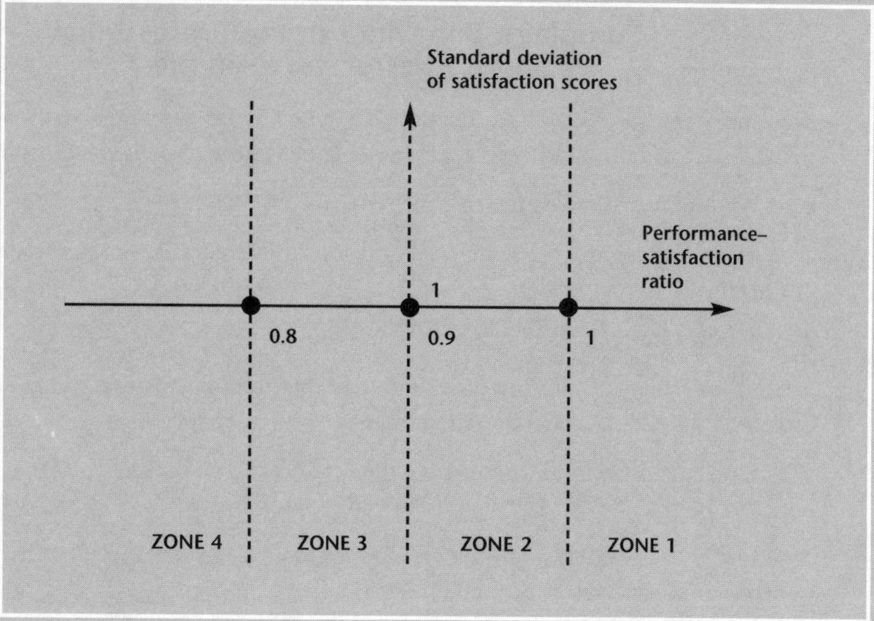

Figure 5.15   Analysis of the performance–importance ratios

⬤ *Zone 4*: the P/I ratio is below 80 per cent; performance is much lower than the importance of the attributes.

This information is useful in identifying the weak points of a product and in identifying the action to be taken by priority.

Satisfaction–dissatisfaction response styles

Customers can and do engage in multiple responses to satisfaction or dissatisfaction. The typology proposed by Jones and Sasser (1995) is particularly useful. Six types of loyalty behaviour are proposed:

⬤ The *apostle*: a delighted customer who tells other prospective customers.
⬤ The *loyalist*: a satisfied customer but who does not tell other people.
⬤ The *defector*: a dissatisfied customer who keeps quiet.
⬤ The *terrorist*: a very dissatisfied customer who talks too much.
⬤ The *mercenary*: a customer who is mostly satisfied but who would do anything to obtain a better deal.
⬤ The *hostage*: a customer, satisfied or not, who has no option or no other choice.

Each company should analyse its customer base using this typology in order to adapt its response behaviour. An example of such an analysis is presented in Exhibit 5.6.

Exhibit 5.6

Complaint Behaviour in the Professional Service Sector: an Example

Dart and Freeman (1994) have developed a typology of response styles among professional service clients; three factors or types of complaint behaviour were identified:

■ *Voice*: responses directed towards the firm.

■ *Private*: word-of-mouth communication and/or discontinuance of the relationship with the firm.

■ *Third party*: complaining to external agencies.

In a cluster analysis conducted on a sample of 224 respondents among business users of professional services (accounting), four segments were identified:

■ *Passives (42%)*: customers whose intentions to complain are below average on the three factors, especially for voicing complaints directly to the firm.

■ *Voicers (34%)*: dissatisfied customers who are more likely to complain to the firm and to engage in negative word-of-mouth behaviour.

■ *Irates (5%)*: customer who demonstrate above average private response such as negative word-of-mouth or switching firms.

■ *Activists (19%)*: customers who are likely to engage in above average behaviour in all three types of complaint behaviour.

Source: Dart and Freeman (1994).

From loyalty to delight

More and more firms are today addressing the importance of *delighting the customer* as an extension of providing basic satisfaction (Schlossberg, 1990). In this perspective, satisfying customers is viewed as a minimum, corresponding to an objective standardised quality (zero defects), while customers are looking for customisation quality, that is attention to their individual needs. Levels of quality beyond merely adequate quality or mere satisfaction could have important behavioural consequences, such as a greater loyalty, as shown in Table 5.9.

Table 5.9   Levels of customer response to quality

Customer Response	Customer loyalty	Need stated by the customer	Service received
Dissatisfaction	None	Yes	Below customer expectations
Satisfaction	Low–high	Yes	Within customer expectations
Delight (surprise and joy)	Very high	No	Beyond customer expectations

Source: adapted from Domingo (1997, p. 279).

Customer delight is the reaction of customers when they receive a product or a service that not only satisfies, but also provides unexpected value or unanticipated satisfaction. As stated by Chandler (1989, p. 30)

> Customer satisfaction is largely a static process that focuses on today and deals with known circumstances and known variables. Providing customer delight is a dynamic, forward-looking process that takes place primarily in the unknown environment... Going beyond satisfaction to customer delight will provide a distinct advantage to the company that does it first and does it well consistently.

Delight and surprise require the imagination, resourcefulness and common sense of the service provider. To delight their customers, many companies have to modify their business mission definition and adopt the *solution-to-a-problem* approach described in Chapter 6. In the airline business, this would mean the following changes:

- from being in the transport business to being in the service business;
- from flying planes to serving passengers;
- from managing in-flight service to managing the total service, from pre-flight to post-flight;
- from treating passengers like baggage to treating passengers like kings.

In a survey made by Quantas Airways of passenger needs (see Exhibit 5.7), out of 22 items, 'no lost baggage' and 'no damaged baggage' were Nos 1 and 2 respectively ahead of 'good quality meals' and 'on-time arrival'. Passengers treat their baggage as extensions of themselves and therefore expect airlines to treat their baggage with the same respect and care.

The Brand Equity Concept

The last few years have seen brand equity become one of the hottest topics in business among professionals and academic researchers as well (Aaker, 1991, 1996;

Exhibit 5.7

Airline Delight: an Example

If you dropped your cash-filled wallet in an airline seat, your natural expectation is that it is gone forever. You would be *satisfied* if the ground staff handled your report promptly with a promise, even without guarantees, that they would try their best to recover your wallet. You would be *annoyed* if you encountered red tape and indifference when you filed the report. You would be *delighted* if the airline found your wallet in no time and notified you that you could get your wallet with all the cash intact at the airline counter in your next destination. You would be *surprised* if an airline staff member carried your wallet to your home. As a delighted and surprised customer, you would write an unsolicited letter of compliment to the airline management; you would also become a loyal frequent flyer and tell the whole world about your wonderful experience with the airline. (Domingo, 1997, p. 282)

Kapferer, 1995b), although economists adopted the concept many years previously (Nerlove and Arrow, 1962). Two definitions are currently used:

> Broadly stated, brand equity refers to the 'capital of goodwill' accumulated by a brand and resulting from past marketing activities. (Nerlove and Arrow, 1962)

Alternatively,

> A consumer perceives a brand's equity as the 'value added' to the functional product or service by associating it with the brand name. (Aaker, 1991)

In both definitions the concept refers to the brand's strength which can vary largely among brands and which is determined by its awareness, personality perceived quality, leadership or stock value. When confronted with the measurement problem, difficulties arise, and Feldwick (1996) suggests referring to three possible distinct senses:

1. The total value of a brand as a *separable asset*, when it is sold or included in a balance sheet.
2. The strength of customers' *attachment to a brand* revealed namely by the price premium customers are ready to pay.
3. The set of perceptions, associations or beliefs, both cognitive and affective, the customer has about a brand, which is traditionally called the *brand image*.

These three different meanings are linked and the causal chain would be (1) brand image, (2) brand strength, (3) brand value. Let us first review the roles played by the brand in a market economy.

The functions of a brand

The brand plays an important role in a market economy, not only for the customer but for the producer as well. Following Kapferer and Thoenig (1989) and Lambin (1989), five distinct functions of direct use to the buyer can be identified with four functions of strategic importance for the firm:

- A *landmarking function*. A brand name is perceived by the potential buyer as a message proposing a specific package of attributes both tangible and intangible, and the buyer uses this information to guide his (or her) choice given the needs or the consumption situation confronted. In this sense, the brand is a *signal* to potential buyers who can identify, at a low personal cost, the set of existing solutions to their problems. By structuring supply, this brand's landmarking function contributes to the market transparency, a service particularly useful in industrialised economies where brands proliferate.

- A *decision simplification function*. The brand is a simple and practical way to memorise the brand characteristics and to put a name to a specific assortment of benefits. Easy to memorise and to recognise, the brand makes possible a *routine purchase behaviour*, thereby reducing the time spent shopping, a task more and more perceived as a bore by buyers attracted by more stimulating activities. Similarly, the advertiser having promoted a promise on the market, can simply re-advertise the brand name or simply its logo. Thus, from a semiotics perspective, the brand's logo, colour and sign are very important. On this topic see the excellent work of Paulo de Lencastre (1997).

● *A guarantee function.* A brand is a signature, which identifies the producer and creates a long-term responsibility, since the brand owner commits himself to give a specific and constant level of quality. A brand represents a pact between brand owner and consumer. The more a brand is known, the more this pact is binding, since the producer cannot afford to deceive his customer base and to undermine the brand's accumulated capital of goodwill. The fiction of 'generic products' without brand names, popular a few years ago, has triggered strong negative reactions from the consumerists who rightly want the product's origin to be clearly identified.

● *A personalisation function.* The diversity of taste and preferences is central in a market economy. To meet this diversity, firms market differentiated products, not only on tangible attributes, but on the intangibles as well, such as emotion, aesthetics, social image, and so on. Brands give consumers the opportunity to claim their difference, to demonstrate their originality, to express their personality through their brand choices. Viewed in this perspective, the brand is a social communication mean which give to consumers the possibility to privilege certain attributes in their choices, thereby communicating their value system.

● *A pleasure-giving function.* In affluent societies, consumers' primary or basic needs are largely met, and the needs for novelty, change, surprise, stimulation become vital necessities. As seen in Chapter 3, the need to try varied experiences, to live different lifestyles, the chance to try new products and to have new sources of satisfaction form an important subject matter in this type of society. Brands like Swatch, Club Med, Marlboro, McDonald's, Cartier, Coca-Cola and so on contribute to the fulfilment of those needs through their branding policies.

To these five functions mainly useful to the buyer, four other roles of a brand must be added which are critical for the firm's long-term and competitive strategy:

● *A communication function.* The brand is of strategic importance to manufacturers because it enables the firm to communicate directly with end-consumers regardless of the actions of the middlemen. This communication link is vital to the survival of many of the world's leading grocery companies. Without brands, such manufacturers would be at the mercy of large retail chains whose influence and power over the last ten years have grown dramatically.

● *A protection function.* Property rights (trade marks, patent, copyrights) protect the brand name against imitations or counterfeiting. The firm can take action for infringement of patent or trade marks in order to establish its intellectual property rights. A brand owner can register the brand in several product categories according to an international classification. He thereby has a clear legal title, which enables him to oppose any fraudulent imitation, forgery or counterfeit. A centralisation procedure (Convention of Madrid) facilitates registration at the international level, but it was only in 1993 that the concept of a European Community brand was established along with common rules of property rights

The History of Selected Brands

The need to associate a new product with a brand name implies the use of the company name or its founder's name. Cinzano is one of the oldest names in business. As long ago as 1757, Carlo Stefano Cinzano and Giovanni Giacomo Cinzano were distilling the beverage that bears their name in a factory near Turin. Among the brands born during the last century, some of them are still alive and well: Nestlé (the milky flour from Henri Nestlé, 1867), Maggi (soups from Jules Maggi, 1883), Levi's (from Levi Strauss & Co, 1856), the biscuits of Mr Lefèvre and Miss Utile (1856) became the brand Lu, similarly the aperitif anise from Pernod (1850). Today, the brand is a part of our daily environment.

(de Maricourt, 1997, p. 693). This protection function for manufacturers' brands is particularly important today in view of the 'copycat' own-label strategy adopted by some large retail chains in France and in the UK (see Kapferer, 1995b), and also by manufacturers based in Latin America or in Asia.

- *A positioning tool*. It is the same landmarking function described above but viewed from the brand owner's side. A brand gives the firm the opportunity to position its offering *vis-à-vis* competition, to express its difference and to claim its distinctive characteristics. This positioning function is very important for advertising communication, particularly in markets where comparative advertising is authorised. Viewed in this perspective, the brand is a competitive weapon, which contributes to increase the market transparency. Is it necessary to repeat that this process of competitive emulation remains the best protection for consumers against abuse of power?

- *A capitalisation function*. The brand, and in particular the brand image, serves to capture not only the past advertising investments put into it, but also the capital of satisfaction generated by the brand. Many brands are more than one hundred years old (see Exhibit 5.8). To the firm, they constitute a valuable asset, an intangible capital, resulting from several years of past advertising investments. Brands therefore introduce stability into businesses; they allow planning and investment in a long-term perspective.

To conclude this section, the brand is a valuable asset for the firm, a capital to be managed, maintained and developed, which is the outgrowth from the buyers' perceptions and from the signals produced by the brand owner.

Measuring brand image

The brand or corporate image can be defined in the following terms:

The set of mental representations, both cognitive and affective, a person or a group of persons, holds vis-à-vis a brand or a company.

A good understanding of the brand image and of its perceived strengths and weaknesses is an indispensable prerequisite to any strategy and communication platform definition. In this respect, it is useful to make a distinction between three levels of brand image analysis:

1. The *perceived image* or how the others see and perceive the brand: an outside-in perspective, based on field interviews within the reference market or segment.
2. The *actual image* or the reality of the brand, with its strengths and weaknesses identified by the firm through an internal audit.
3. The *desired image* or the way the brand wishes to be perceived by the target segment as a result of a positioning decision.

Clearly important differences can exist between these three levels of image measurement and reconciliation may be necessary:

- A gap may exist between the actual image and the perceived image, in a positive or negative sense.

- If the gap is in favour of the brand, communication has an important role to play in the reconciliation process; in the opposite case, the brand concept must be revised.

- A gap may also occur between the desired image and the reality of the brand, that is its know-how, its quality or its communication; it is the credibility of the positioning strategy which is at stake here.

This last problem is particularly acute in service firms where the contact personnel directly contribute to the perceived image of the firm. Internal marketing has an important role to play here.

To measure the perceived image, the analysis will be based on the three levels of market response examined in this chapter, using successively indicators of the cognitive, affective and behavioural response. The attitudinal measures described above – namely the evaluation of the package of benefits provided by the brand – are particularly useful, since they lead to an *image profile*, illustrated by the 'importance–performance' matrix or by an attribute-based perceptual map.

Exhibit 5.9

Price Advantages of the Strongest Brands

To gauge how important brands are to customers during the purchase process, Court *et al.* (1996) from McKinsey examined 27 case studies, based on over 5000 customer interviews in the USA, Europe and Asia. On average, prices of the strongest brands (in terms of the brand's importance behind the decision to buy) were 19 per cent higher than those of the weakest brands. Relative to second-tier brands, the leading brands commanded an average price premium of 5 per cent.

Source: Court *et al.* (1996, p. 178).

Measuring a brand's strength

A brand's strength is directly related to the degree of attachment or loyalty of customers to a brand. The best test of brand loyalty is probably to know what a consumer will do if his (or her) preferred brand is not on the shelves in the store: will she switch to another brand or will she visit another store?

One can identify at least five indicators of a brand's strength:

1. *A lower price sensitivity.* A strong brand displays a stronger resistance to a price increase than its competitors. In Europe, for instance, one has observed that the market share of Japanese cars was more sensitive to price increases than that of European cars.

2. *Acceptable price premiums.* A brand is strong if people are prepared to pay more for it (see Exhibit 5.9). Conversely, a weak brand has to propose a price lower than the price charged by its competitors, as typically observed for distributors' brands.

3. *Exclusivity rate.* The more loyal customer is the one for whom the brand represents a higher share of category requirement. For instance, someone who buys seven jars of Nestlé coffee in ten coffee purchasing occasions is more loyal than someone who buys only three.

4. *Dynamic loyalty rate.* An alternative to share of category requirement is to look at patterns of purchasing over time, and use this to estimate the probability of a consumer buying the brand on the next purchase occasion.

5. *Positive attitudinal measures.* Indicators such as familiarity, esteem, perceived quality, purchase intentions (brand loyalty) and so on, are also good indicators of a brand's strength.

The brand's strength and its translation into maximum acceptable price, or value price, will be analysed in more detail in Chapter 13.

Valuation methods of brand equity

The problem of brand valuation as separable assets raises financial and accounting issues, which are beyond the scope of this book. The greatest difficulty is separability, since the brand value can be intertwined both with the tangible product and related physical resources and with other intangible assets, such as human resources, managerial know-how, company image and so forth. Aaker (1991) has proposed five general approaches to assessing the value of brand equity:

1. The measurement of the price premium attached to a particular brand compared to the price levels in the product category.

2. The impact of the brand name upon the customer evaluation of the brand as measured by preference, attitude or intent to purchase.

3. The cost of establishing a comparable name and business, that is the replacement value of the brand in the reference market.

4. To use the stock price as a basis to evaluate the value of the brand equities of a firm. The argument is that the stock market will adjust the price of a firm to reflect future prospects of its brands.

5. The discounted present value of future earnings attributable to brand equity assets. The problem here is to provide such an estimate.

Other valuation methods exist. To go further on this topic, see Stobart (1995) from the Interbrand group and in particular Sheppard (1994, pp. 85–101). See also Macrae (1996).

Chapter summary

A buyer's response means all mental or physical activity caused by a marketing stimulus. The various response forms of the buyer can be classified in three categories: cognitive response, which relates to retained information and knowledge, affective response which concerns attitude and evaluation, and behavioural response which describes the actions taken, not only at the moment of purchase but also after the purchase. A learning process supposes that the individual, like the organisation, reaches these three stages successively and in this order: learn–feel–do. Other sequences of response are observed depending on the degree of the buyer's involvement and his (or her) mode of reality perception. The main measures of the cognitive response are awareness, recall or recognition and perceived similarity. Regarding the affective response, the concept of attitude is central. The multi-attribute product concept defined in Chapter 4 serves as a conceptual basis for modelling attitudes. Two estimation procedures can be used for measuring a Fishbein multi-attribute model: the 'compositional' approach and the 'decompositional' approach through conjoint analysis. Attitude measurements are summarised in the 'importance–performance' matrix and also in attribute-based perceptual maps. Non-compensatory models of attitude can be used in more complex cases. Measures of the behavioural response are purchasing habits analysis, market share movements analysis and econometric marketing response functions. Post-purchase behaviour is based mainly on the degree of satisfaction–dissatisfaction of customers. A good indicator of customer satisfaction is its loyalty rate. For fast moving consumer goods (FMCG), brand switching analysis is also very useful. In advanced economies, satisfying the customer is a minimum; the real objective is to delight customers. The brand equity concept can be used in three distinct senses: the total value of a brand as a separable asset; the brand strength or the consumer attachment to a brand; and the brand image.

QUESTIONS AND PROBLEMS

1. Look at Figure 5.1. How would you rank electric razors, mustard, microcomputers, chocolates pralines, painkillers, garden hoses, costume jewellery? What kind of information would you use to justify your ranking?

2. Select a consumer product category you know well and prepare a questionnaire to measure unaided, aided and qualified awareness of the main competing brands within the category. How would you proceed to analyse the results?

3. Brand A has a 30 per cent occupation rate and a 60 per cent exclusivity rate. Buyers of this brand usually consume the same quantity of the product, as do the buyers of competing brands. What is brand's A market share? If the exclusivity rate drops to 50 per cent what will be its market share?

4. Two brands are competing in the same reference market. Brand A has a loyalty rate of 80 per cent and an attraction rate of 30 per cent. The market shares are respectively 30 per cent for brand A and 70 per cent for brand B. What are the expected equilibrium market shares of these two brands if the loyalty and attraction rates remain unchanged? What would you do if you were the brand manager of brand B?

5. Compare four makes of microcomputers using four attributes (A, B, C and D) having the following determinance rates: 0.40/0.30/0.20/0.10. The score obtained (on a 10-point rating scale) by the brands on the four attributes are: A = 10/8/6/4; B = 8/9/8/3; C = 6/8/10/5; D = 4/3/7/8. Compute a total utility score for each brand using these data. Compare and interpret the results.

6. In a brand image study, measures of perception of four brands (A, B, C and D) from the same product category were obtained from a sample of respondents. The importance scores of the four determining attributes are: 0.40/0.30/0.20/0.10. The performance scores for each brand are the following: A = 8/4/4/1; B = 8/3/5/3; C = 6/6/5/3; D = 5/9/6/5. Which brand will be preferred by the market if the buyers use (a) the compensatory model as decision rule, (b) the disjunctive model, (c)the conjunctive model with a minimum of 5 required for each attribute, (d) the lexicographic model?

Appendix 5.1

Defining the Notion of Elasticity

The elasticity of demand, with respect to a marketing variable, measures the responsiveness of the quantity demanded for a product or a brand to a change in the level of the marketing variable.

Specifically, if we consider price (p) as the marketing variable under study, price elasticity is defined as the rate of percentage change in quantity (q) demanded relative to the percentage change in price, or

$$\varepsilon_{q,p} = \frac{\% \text{ change of } q}{\% \text{ change of } p} = \frac{dq/q}{dp/p} = \frac{dq}{dp} * \frac{p}{q}$$

For the generally assumed case, demand increases as price decreases.

Demand is said to be 'elastic' with respect to price, if the ratio is greater than one in absolute terms; it is 'inelastic' if price elasticity is less than one.

Elasticity is normally not the same at each level of the marketing variable. When the response function is as follows:

$$q = a \cdot p^{\beta}$$

the exponent ß is the elasticity assumed constant between two levels ($q1$, $p1$) and ($q2$, $p2$). It can be determined as follows:

$$\varepsilon_{q,p} = \frac{\log(q_1/q_2)}{\log(p_1/p_2)}$$

If the response function is

$$q = a + \beta \ln s$$

where s is the advertising expenditure, the elasticity coefficient is variable and is given by

$$\varepsilon_{q,s} = \frac{\beta}{q}$$

A distinction must be made between short- and long-term elasticity. If the dynamic advertising response function is as follows:

$$Q = \alpha + \beta \sum_{i=0}^{\infty} \lambda^i s_{t-i}$$

the cumulative advertising elasticity is equal to

$$\varepsilon_{q,s} = \frac{\beta}{1-\lambda} \cdot \frac{S}{Q}$$

where λ denotes the rate of the implied geometric progression. Other forms of the response functions are of course possible.

Bibliography

Aaker, D.A. (1991) *Managing Brand Equity*, New York, The Free Press.

Aaker, D.A. (1996) *Building Strong Brands*, New York, The Free Press.

Allport, G.W. (1935) Attitudes, in: Murchison, C.A. (ed.), *A Handbook of Social Psychology*, Worcester MA, Clark University Press, pp. 798–844.

Assael, H. and Day, G.S. (1968) Attitudes and Awareness, Predictors of Market Shares, *Journal of Advertising Research*, **8**, December, pp. 10–17.

Bass, F.M. and Tarlarzyck, W.W. (1969) A Study of Attitude Theory and Brand Preferences, *Journal of Marketing Research*, **9**, pp. 93–5.

Bauer, R.A. (1960) Consumer Behavior as Risk Taking, in: Hancock, A.S. (ed.), *Proceedings Fall Conference of the American Marketing Association*, pp. 389–98.

Berelson, B. and Steiner, G.A. (1964) *Human Behavior: An Inventory of Scientific Findings*, New York, Harcourt Brace Jovanovich.

Boyd, H.W., Ray, M.L. and Strong, E.C. (1972) An Attitudinal Framework for Advertising Strategy, *Journal of Marketing*, **35**, April, pp. 27–33.

CDI Point of View (1992) *Quality of Market Share*, Boston MA, Corporate Decisions.

Chandler, C.H. (1989), Quality: Beyond Customer Satisfaction, *Quality Progress*, **22**, February, pp. 30–2.

Churchill, G.A. (1995), *Marketing Research, Methodological Foundations*, 6th edn, Chicago IL, Dryden Press.

Court, D., Freeling, A., Leiter, M. and Parsons, A.J. (1996) Uncovering the Value of Brands, *The McKinsey Quarterly*, No. 4, pp. 176–8.

Dart, J. and Freeman, K. (1994) Dissatisfaction Response Styles Among Clients of Professional Accounting Firms, *Journal of Business Research*, **29**: 75–81.

Davis, H.L. and Rigaux, B.P. (1974) Perceptions of Marital Roles in Decision Processes, *Journal of Consumer Research*, **1**: 51–62.

De Lencastre, P. (1997) *L'identification de la marque, un outil de stratégie marketing*, CIACO, Louvain-la-Neuve.

De Maricourt, R. (ed.) (1997) *Marketing Européen: Stratégies et Actions*, Paris, Publi Union.

Domingo, R.T. (1997) *Quality Means Survival*, Singapore, Prentice Hall.

Feldwick, P. (1996) What Is Brand Equity Anyway, and How Do You Measure It? *Journal of Market Research Society*, **38**(2): 85–104.

Festinger, L. (1957) *A Theory of Cognitive Dissonance*, New York, Harper & Row.

Fishbein, M. (1967) Attitudes and Prediction of Behavior, in: Fishbein, M. (ed.), *Readings in Attitude Theory and Measurement*, New York, John Wiley & Sons, pp. 477–92.

Franzen, G. *et al.* (1999) *Brands and Advertising*, London, Admap Publications.

Goderis, J.P. (1998) Barrier Marketing: From Customer Satisfaction to Customer Loyalty, *CEMS Business Review*, **2**(4).

Green, P.E. and Rao, V.R. (1972) *Applied Multidimensional Scaling*, New York, Holt, Rinehart & Winston.

Green, P.E. and Srinivasan, V. (1978) Conjoint Analysis in Consumer Research: Issues and Outlook, *Journal of Consumer Research*, **5**, September, pp. 103–23.

Hair, J.F., Anderson, R.E., Tatham, R.L. and Black, W.C. (1992) *Multivariate Data Analysis*, New York, Maxwell Macmillan.

Herbst, P.G. (1952) The Measurement of Family Relationships, *Human and Relations*, No. 5, pp. 3–35.

Howard, J. A. and Sheth, J.N. (1969) *The Theory of Buyer Behavior*, New York, John Wiley & Sons.

Jakoby, J. and Kyner, D.B. (1973), Brand Loyalty versus Repeat Purchasing Behavior, *Journal of Marketing Research*, **10**: 1–19.

Jarvis, L.P. and Wilcox, J.B. (1977) Evoked Set, Some Theoretical Foundations and Empirical Evidence, in: Howard, J.A. (ed.) *Consumer Behavior Applications of Theory*, New York, McGraw-Hill.

Jones, T.O. and Sasser, W.E. (1995) Why Satisfied Customers Defect?, *Harvard Business Review*, **73**, November–December, pp. 88–99.

Kapferer, J.N. (1995) Brand Confusion: Empirical Study of a Legal Concept, *Psychology and Marketing*, **12**(6): 551–68.

Kapferer, J.N. (1995) Stealing Brand Equity: Measuring Perceptual Confusion Between National Brands and Copycat Own Label Products, *Marketing and Research Today*, May, pp. 96–102.

Kapferer, J.N. and Laurent, G. (1983) *La sensibilité aux marques*, Paris, Fondation Jours de France.

Kapferer, J.N. and Thoenig, J.C. (1989) *La marque*, Paris, Ediscience international.

Kotler, P. (1991) *Marketing Management*, 7th edn, Englewood Cliffs NJ, Prentice-Hall.

Krugman, H.E. (1965) The Impact of Television Advertising: Learning without Involvement, *Public Opinion Quarterly*, Autumn, pp. 349–55.

Krugman, H.E., (1972) Low Recall and High Recognition of Advertising, *Journal of Advertising Research*, **86**, February–March, pp. 79–85.

Lambin, J.J. (1972) A Computer On-line Marketing Mix Model, *Journal of Marketing Research*, **9**, May, pp. 119–25.

Lambin, J.J. (1976) *Advertising, Competition and Market Conduct in Oligopoly over Time*, Amsterdam, North-Holland.

Lambin, J.J. (1988) *Synthèse des études récentes sur l'efficacité économique de la publicité*, CESAM unpublished working paper, Belgium, Louvain-la-Neuve.

Lambin, J.J. (1989) La marque et le comportement de choix de l'acheteur, in: Kapferer, J. and Thoenig, J.C. (eds), *La marque*, Paris, Ediscience international.

Lavidge, R.J. and Steiner, G.A. (1961) A Model for Predictions Measurement of Advertising Effectiveness, *Journal of Marketing*, **25**, October, pp. 59–62.

Leventhal, R.C. (1996) Branding Strategy, *Business Horizons*, September–October, pp. 17–23.

Lewin, K. (1935) *A Dynamic Theory of Personality*, New York, McGraw-Hill.

Macrae, C. (1996) *The Brand Chartering Handbook*, Harlow, Addison-Wesley.

Martilla, J.A. and James, J.C. (1977) Importance–performance Analysis, *Journal of Marketing*, **41**(1): 77–9.

Morgensztern, A. (1983) Une synthèse des travaux sur la mémorisation des messages publicitaires, in: Piquet, S.(ed.) *La publicité, nerf de la communication*, Paris, Les Editions d'Organisation.

Nielsen Researcher (1981) *Utilizing UPC Scanning Data for New Products Decisions*, No. 1.

Nerlove, M. and Arrow, K. (1962) Optimal Advertising Policy under Dynamic Conditions, *Economica*, **29**: 131–45.

Oxenfeldt, A.R. (1969) How to Use Market Share Measurement, *Harvard Business Review*, January–February, pp. 59–68.

Parfitt, J.H. and Collins, B.J.K. (1968) The Use of Consumer Panels for Brand Share Prediction, *Journal of Marketing Research*, **5**, May, pp. 131–45.

Palda, K.S. (1966) The Hypothesis of a Hierarchy of Effects, *Journal of Marketing Research*, **3**: 13–24.

Pinson, C., Malhotra, N.K. and Jain, A.K. (1988) Les styles cognitifs des consommateurs, *Recherche et Applications en Marketing*, **3**(1): 53–73.

Pras, B. and Tarondeau, J-C. (1981) *Comportement de l'acheteur*, Paris, Editions Sirey.

Ratchford, B.T. (1987) New Insights about the FCB Grid, *Journal of Advertising Research*, **27**: 30–1.

Reichfeld, F.F., (1996) *L'effet loyauté*, Paris, Dunod.

Rhoades, K. (1988) The Importance of Consumer Complaints, *Protect Yourself*, January, pp. 115–18.

Rogers, E.M. (1962) *Diffusion of Innovations*, New York, The Free Press.

Rosenberg, M.J. (1956) Cognitive Structure and Attitudinal Affect, *Journal of Abnormal and Social Psychology*, **53**: 367–72.

Schlossberg, H. (1990) Satisfying Customers Is a Minimum: You Really Have to Delight Them, *Marketing News*, **24**, May 28, pp. 10–11.

Sheppard, A. (1994) Adding Brand Value, in: Stobart, P. (ed.) *Brand Power*, London, Macmillan, pp. 85–110.

Stobart, P. (ed.) (1995) *Brand Power*, London, Macmillan.

TARP (1979, 1986), *Consumer Complaint Handling in America*, Washington DC, US Office of Consumer Affairs.

Thurstone, L.L. (1959) *The Measurement of Values*, Chicago IL, University of Chicago Press.

Vakratsas, D. and Ambler, T. (1999) How Advertising Works: What Do we Really Know?, *Journal of Marketing*, **63**, January, pp. 26–43.

Van Ballenberghe, A. (1993) Le comportement des consommateurs en période de promotion: analyse des perceptions des marques, unpublished working paper, IAG, Louvain-la-Neuve, Belgium.

Vaughn, R. (1986) How Advertising Works: A Planning Model Revisited, *Journal of Advertising Research*, **20**, February–March, pp. 57–65.

Watts, W.A. and McGuire, J.W. (1964) Persistence of Induced Opinion Change and Retention of Inducing Message Content, *Journal of Abnormal and Social Psychology*, **68**: 233–41.

Wilkie, W.L. and Pessemier, E.A. (1973) Issues in Marketing's Use of Multi-Attribute Attitude Models, *Journal of Marketing Research*, **10**, November, pp. 428–41.

Zielske, H.A. (1958) The Remembering and the Forgetting of Advertising, *Journal of Marketing*, **24**, January, pp. 239–43.

Zielske, H.A. and Henry, W.A. (1980) Remembering and Forgetting Television Ads, *Journal of Advertising Research*, **20**, April, pp. 7–13.

Market-driven Strategy Development

STRUCTURE OF THE BOOK

PART ONE The Changing Role of Marketing

The role of marketing in the firm and in a marketing economy
CHAPTER ONE

From marketing to market-driven management
CHAPTER TWO

PART TWO Understanding Customer Behaviour

The customer choice behaviour
CHAPTER THREE

The marketing information system
CHAPTER FOUR

The customer's response behaviour
CHAPTER FIVE

PART THREE Market-driven Strategy Development

Needs analysis through market segmentation
CHAPTER SIX

Market attractiveness analysis
CHAPTER SEVEN

Competitiveness analysis
CHAPTER EIGHT

Formulating a market strategy
CHAPTER NINE

The strategic marketing plan
CHAPTER TEN

PART FOUR Market-driven Management Decisions

Market-driven new product decisions
CHAPTER ELEVEN

Market-driven distribution decisions
CHAPTER TWELVE

Market-driven pricing decisions
CHAPTER THIRTEEN

Market-driven communication decisions
CHAPTER FOURTEEN

Market-driven advertising decisions
CHAPTER FIFTEEN

PART FIVE Ten Case Studies in Market-driven Management

1. **The Lander Company** *W.J. Stanton*
2. **The WILO Corporation** *R. Köhler*
3. **TV: Cold Bath for French Cinema** *A. Riding*
4. **Ecover** *D. Develter*
5. **Volvo Truck Belgium** *J.J. Lambin*
6. **The Petro-equipment Company** *J.J. Lambin*
7. **Sierra Plastics Company** *W.J. Stanton*
8. **Tissex** *G. Marion*
9. **Newfood** *G.S. Day et al.*
10. **SAS: Meeting Customer Expectations** *D.L. Kurtz and K.E. Clow*

chapter six

Needs analysis through market segmentation

One of the first strategic decisions a firm has to make is to define its reference market and to choose the customer segment(s) to target. This choice implies the splitting of the total market into groups of customers with similar needs and behavioural or motivational characteristics, and which constitute distinct market opportunities. A firm can elect to serve all possible customers or to focus on one or several specific segments within the reference market. This segmentation of the reference market is generally done in two steps, corresponding to different levels of total market desegregation. The first step, called *macro-segmentation*, has the objective of identifying 'product markets', while in the second, called *micro-segmentation*, the goal is to uncover customers' 'segments' within each product market previously identified. Using this mapping of the reference market, the firm will then evaluate the attractiveness of each product market and/or segment (see Chapter 8) and assess its own competitiveness (see Chapter 9). This chapter describes a general methodology for segmenting a market and also presents alternative ways of international segmentation.

Chapter learning objectives

When you have read this chapter, you should be able to:

1. identify a target market and the objectives of market segmentation;
2. describe the advantages and disadvantages of the different segmentation methods;
3. explain the requirements for effective segmentation;
4. define the objectives of strategic positioning;
5. discuss the different approaches of international market segmentation.

Macro-segmentation Analysis

In the majority of markets, it is almost impossible to satisfy all customers with a single product or service. Different consumers have varying desires and interests. This variety stems from diverse buying practices and basic variations of customers' needs and the benefits they seek from products. Increasingly, therefore, companies have found it essential to move away from mass marketing towards target marketing strategy, where the focus is on a particular group of customers. This identification of target customer groups is market segmentation, where the total market is desegregated into subgroups, with similar requirements and buying characteristics. Knowing how to segment a market is one of the most important skills a firm must possess. Segmentation defines what business the firm is in, guides strategy development and determines the capabilities needed in the business unit.

Defining the reference market in terms of solution

Implementing a market segment strategy should begin with a business definition statement that reveals the true function or purpose of the firm in a customer-oriented perspective. Three fundamental questions should be addressed:

- What business(es) are we in?
- What business(es) should we be in?
- What business(es) should we not be in?

To answer these questions in a customer-oriented perspective, the business definition should be made in generic terms, that is in terms of the 'solution' sought by the customer and not in technical terms, to avoid the risk of myopia. The rationale behind the *solution approach* has been explained in Chapter 4. It can be summarised as follows:

- To the buyer, the product is what it does.
- No one buys a product *per se*. What is sought is a solution to a problem.
- Different technologies can produce the same function.
- Technologies are fast changing, while generic needs are stable.

It is therefore important for the market-oriented firm to define its reference market in terms of a generic need, rather than in terms of a product. Here are some examples of market reference definitions:

- *Derbit Belgium* is operating in the European roofing market and manufactures membranes of APP-modified bitumen. The company defines its market as follows: 'We are selling guaranteed waterproof solutions to flat roofing problems in partnership with exclusive distributors and highly qualified roofing applicators.'

- *Sedal*, a small French company manufacturing metallic ventilation grids, defined its business as the 'air and temperature control' business and expanded its offerings to air ventilation and air conditioning systems (see Figure 6.1).

- *Automatic Systems* manufactures gates and doors, but defines its business as the sales of 'access control solutions' and offers its customers the hardware and the software (security systems) as well.

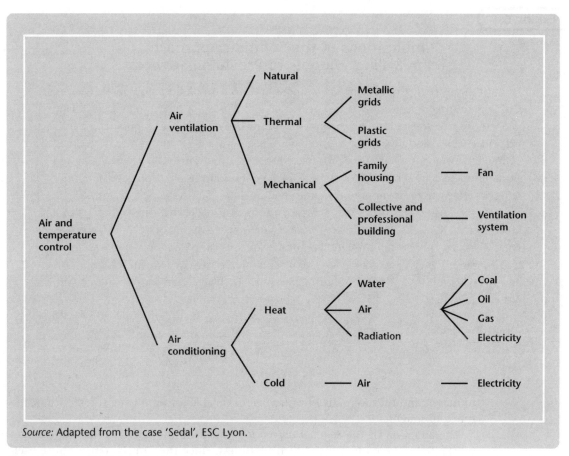

Source: Adapted from the case 'Sedal', ESC Lyon.

Figure 6.1   Defining the business: an example

⬤ *IBM* defines its mission in the following terms: 'we are in the business of helping customers solve problems through the use of advanced information technology. We are creating value by offering the solutions, products and services that help customers succeed.'

Ideally, the business definition should be stated in terms narrow enough to provide practical guidance, yet broad enough to stimulate imaginative thinking, such as openings for product line extensions or for diversification into adjacent product areas. At the Grumman Corporation, the guidelines for the mission statement advise:

We should be careful not to confine the market boundaries by our existing or traditional product participation. The market definition analysis is purposely meant to create an outward awareness of the total surrounding market, and of its needs and trends that may offer opportunity for, or on the other hand challenges to, our current or contemplated position. (Hopkins, 1982, p. 119)

The business definition is the starting point for strategy development. It helps identify the customers to be served, the competitors to surpass the key success factors

Exhibit 6.1

Implications of the Solution Approach:
From Selling Widgets to Providing Services

From General Electric Co. to Wang Laboratories Inc., from Xerox Corp. to Hewlett-Packard Co., American companies that a few years ago got almost all their profits from selling widgets are rapidly transforming themselves into service providers. Computer companies like Unisys Corp. and IBM Corp. are designing, installing and running other companies' computer operations. Document processors like Xerox and Pitney Bowes Inc. now run mailrooms and copy centres and distribute documents electronically. Honeywell redesigns refineries. Hewlett-Packard not only designs and operates data systems, but also pays for the whole package and then leases it out. 'Customers want to finance a solution, not a little piece of it', says Ann Livermore, vice-president of Hewlett-Packard's service operations. The move to services is one of the hottest strategies in US business, and it is driven by changes at the very foundations of manufacturing. 'Services generate huge cash flows and today's businesses are run for cash flow', said Nicholas Heymann an analyst with NatWest securities.

Source: Deutsch (1997).

to master and the alternative technologies available for producing the service or the function sought.

The adoption of the *solution approach* in defining the reference market changes substantially the nature of the firm's business, since the firm is transforming itself into a *service provider*. As evidenced in Exhibit 6.1, a growing number of firms, particularly in hi-tech sectors, are moving in that direction.

Conceptualisation of the reference market

The objective is to define the reference market in the buyer perspective and not from the producer's point of view, as is too often the case. As suggested by Abell (1980), a reference market can be defined in three dimensions:

● Customer group or *who* is being satisfied; customer functions or needs.
● *What* is being satisfied; and the technologies used to meet the needs.
● *How* customer needs are being satisfied.

We thus have a three-dimensional framework, as shown in Figure 6.2. To segment the market, the first step is to identify the relevant criteria for describing each of these three dimensions.

Functions

We refer here to the need to be fulfilled by the product or the service. Examples of functions would be:

Home interior decoration; international transportation of goods; waterproof roof protection; rust prevention; teeth cleaning; deep versus shallow drilling; diagnostic imaging; and so on.

Functions have to be conceptually separated from the way the function is performed (that is the technology). The dividing line between 'functions' and 'benefits' is not always clear, as functions are narrowly subdivided or as assortments of functions are considered, for example, teeth cleaning plus decay prevention, shampoo with anti-dandruff treatment. Thus, functions can also be defined as a package of benefits sought by different customer groups.

Customers

We describe the different customer groups that might buy the product. The most common criteria used are:

households versus industrial buyers, socio-economic class, geographic location, type of activity, company size, original equipment manufacturer versus user, decision-making unit, and so on.

At this level of macro-segmentation, only broad customer characteristics are retained. For consumer goods, more detailed criteria are often necessary, such as age group, benefits sought, lifestyle, purchase behaviour, and so on. This is the object of micro-segmentation.

Technologies

These describe the alternative ways in which a particular function can be performed for a customer.

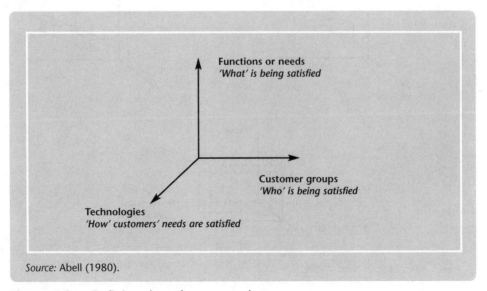

Source: Abell (1980).

Figure 6.2 Defining the reference market

For example, paint or wallpaper for the function of home interior decoration; road, air, rail or sea for international transportation of goods; bitumen or plastic for roof protection; toothpaste or mouthwash for teeth cleaning; X-ray, ultrasound or computerised tomography for diagnostic imaging, and so on.

As underlined above, the technology dimension is dynamic, in the sense that one technology can displace another over time. For example, ultrasound, nuclear medicine and CT scanning as alternative imaging diagnostic techniques are displacing X-rays. Similarly, electronic mail is tending to displace printed materials in the field of written communication.

Market boundary definitions

Using this framework, we may distinguish between a 'product market', a 'solution market' and an 'industry' (Figure 6.3):

● A specific customer group, seeking a specific function or assortment of functions based on a single technology defines a *product market*.

● A *solution market* is defined by the performance of given functions in given customer groups, but including all the substitute technologies to perform those functions. It corresponds to the concept of 'category'.

● An *industry* is based on a single technology, but covers several businesses, that is several functions or assortments of functions and several customer groups.

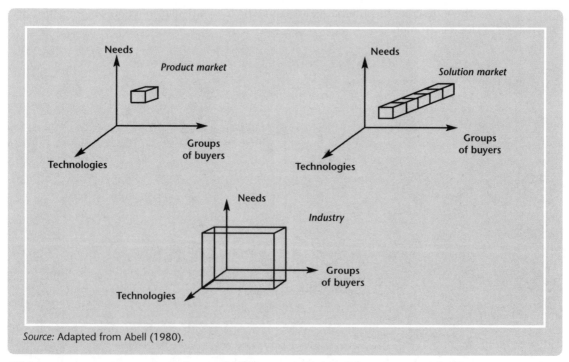

Source: Adapted from Abell (1980).

Figure 6.3 Market boundaries definition

These alternative boundary definitions correspond to different market coverage strategies, each having their own merits and weaknesses. The *industry* definition is the most traditional one, but also the least satisfactory because it is supply-oriented and not market-oriented. From a marketing point of view, this definition of the reference market is much too general, since it includes a large variety of functions and customer groups.

> In the household appliances industry, for example, this would include microwave ovens and laundry irons, two very different products in terms of growth potential and of customers' behaviour characteristics.

However, most industrial and foreign trade statistics are industry-based and it is therefore difficult to avoid industry definitions completely.

The *solution market* definition is very close to the generic need concept and has the merit of emphasising the existence of substitute products or technologies for performing the same function. A technological innovation can dramatically change existing market boundaries. The monitoring of substitute technologies is enhanced by this reference market definition. The major difficulty stems from the fact that the technology domains involved may be very different.

> Customers with a need for a 6 mm hole will normally use a metal twist drill, but some segments are finding lasers or high-pressure water jets to be a better solution. Also, Companies that refine cane sugar wrestle with this question often. Their product is a sweetener, but the needs of soft drink and candy manufacturers for sweetening can be satisfied with sugar made from corn (fructose) or sugar beets. Depending on market conditions, these alternatives may be cheaper. Should they offer all sweetening materials? (Day, 1990, p. 27)

The *solution market* definition is very useful for giving directions to R&D and for suggesting diversification strategies and also for organising markets. *Category management* is based on this concept, which also modifies substantially the marketing mix concept (see Exhibit 6.2).

The *product market* definition is the most market-oriented definition. It corresponds to the notion of 'strategic business unit' (SBU) and is very close to the real world market. This market definition automatically dictates four key elements of the firm's strategic thrust:

● The customers to be served.
● The package of benefits to be provided.
● The competitors to surpass.
● The capabilities to acquire.

This partitioning of the total reference market into product markets will guide market coverage decisions and will determine the type of organisational structure to adopt. One shortcoming of this market definition is the difficulty of finding appropriate market measurements, most government statistics being industry-based and not market-based.

Exhibit 6.2

The Marketing Mix and the *Solution-to-a-Problem* Approach

- *Product*: a solution to a problem and the package of benefits that the product represents.
- *Category*: the set of products giving a solution to the buyers' problem.
- *Place*: a convenient access to the solution sought by the buyer.
- *Price*: all the costs, including price, supported by the buyer to acquire the solution sought.
- *Advertising*: the messages and signals communicated about the solutions available and about their distinctive qualities.
- *Selling*: the negotiation process or the dialogue organised with the potential buyer in his search for the appropriate solution to his (or her) problem.

Development of a macro-segmentation grid

Once the relevant segmentation variables are identified, the next task is to combine them to develop a segmentation grid. To illustrate this process, let us consider the market of heavy-duty trucks. The identified segmentation variables are the following:

- *Functions*: regional, national and international transport of goods.
- *Technologies*: air, rail, water and road.
- *Customers*: types of activity: own account, professional transporters and renting companies; size of fleet: small (1–4 trucks), medium (4–10 trucks) and large (>10 trucks).

If we consider all possible combinations, we have here a total of 108 ($3 \times 4 \times 3 \times 3$) possible segments. To refine the analysis, let us adopt the following rules:

- Ignore transportation modes other than road transportation but establish a distinction between trucks below and above 16 tonnes.
- Forget about truck renting companies.
- Subdivide regional transport into three categories: distribution, construction and others.

We now obtain 60 ($5 \times 2 \times 2 \times 3$) segments as shown in Table 6.1, which is still much too high. The size of these segments varies widely, however, as the figures of Table 6.1 show. Those numbers represent the percentage of registered licence plates for trucks within each segment. Each segment does not necessarily have to be considered, as the pertinence analysis should demonstrate.

Table 6.1 Macro-segmentation of the truck market (% total truck population)

Activity/functions	Fleet size and weight						Total
	Small (1–4)		Medium (4–10)		Large (>10)		
	<16t	>16t	<16t	>16t	<16t	>16t	
Own account transporters	Segment 1: 19.3%				Segment 2: 11.1%		
Distribution	7.3	4.5	1.1	1.8	0.4	2.1	16.2
Construction	0.1	1.1	0.9	1.4	1.7	1.6	6.8
National	4.7	1.6	1.4	3.8	1.7	3.6	16.8
International	1.3	0.9	0.2	1.3	–	1.4	5.1
Others	–	0.6	0.3	–	2.5	–	3.4
Professional transporters	Segment 3: 13.9%				Segment 4: 26.1%		
Distribution	1.1	0.8	0.9	1.6	–	1.6	6.0
Construction	0.2	1.6	–	0.4	–	1.2	3.4
National	1.4	1.5	1.4	3.0	2.5	8.5	18.3
International	0.2	0.7	0.5	6.1	0.4	14.7	22.6
Others	–	0.4	–	–	–	–	0.4
Total	16.3	13.7	6.7	19.4	9.2	34.7	100.0

Source: Lambin and Hiller (1990).

Pertinence analysis

In developing an operational segmentation grid, the following rules should be adopted:

● The analyst should start with the longest list of segmentation variables to avoid overlooking meaningful criteria.
● Only those variables with a truly significant strategic impact should be isolated.
● Collapsing together variables that are correlated can reduce the number of variables.
● Some cells are generally unfeasible combinations of segmentation variables and therefore can be eliminated.
● Some segments can be regrouped if the differences among them are not really significant or their size is too small.
● The segmentation grid should include potential segments as well and not only segments that are currently occupied.

In the case of Volvo Trucks company, re-examination of the segmentation grid suggested the regrouping of the most similar segments that must be served together, to retain eventually *four major segments* which altogether represent 70.4 per cent of the total truck population in the Belgian market.

This phase is the most difficult one. The task is to conciliate realism and operationality, two often contradictory objectives. When eliminating segments, one must eliminate only the unfeasible combinations of segmentation variables but keep the empty cells, which, while currently unoccupied, could become potential segments in the future.

Testing the macro-segmentation grid

To verify the usefulness of the grid, the company's customers and direct competitors should be located in the different segments. The objective is to evaluate the potential of each segment in terms of size and growth, and to measure the market share held by the firm within each segment. The questions to examine are the following:

● Which segment(s) display the highest growth rate?
● What is our present market coverage?
● Where are our key customers located?
● Where are our direct competitors located?
● What are the requirements of each segment in terms of service, product quality, and so on?

The following questions can also help decide whether or not two products belong to the same strategic segment:

● Are the main competitors the same?
● Are their customers or groups of customers the same?
● Are the key success factors the same?
● Does divesting in one affect the other?

Positive answers to these four questions would tend to show that both products belong to the same product market. The answers to these questions will also help the firm to define its market coverage strategy and to regroup segments having the same requirements and/or the same competitors.

Finding new segments

Some segmentation variables are readily apparent as a result of industry convention or established norms for dividing buyers. Macro-segmentation analysis goes beyond conventional wisdom and accepted classification schemes and gives the opportunity for discovering new ways of segmenting the market. In searching for potential new segments, the following questions should be considered:

● Are there other technologies to perform the required functions?
● Could an enhanced product perform additional functions?
● Could the needs of some buyers be better served by reducing the number of functions and possibly lowering the price?
● Are there other groups of buyers requiring the same service or function?
● Are there new channels of distribution that could be used?
● Are there different bundles of products and services that could possibly be sold as a package?

Finding new ways to segment the market can give the firm a major competitive advantage over rivals (Porter 1985, p. 247).

Reference market coverage strategies

Reference market coverage decisions will be made on the basis of the 'attractiveness/competitiveness' analysis of the different product markets (see Chapter 10). The firm can consider different market coverage strategies:

● *Focused strategy*. The market boundaries are defined narrowly in terms of functions, technology and customer groups. This is the strategy of the specialist seeking a high market share in a narrow niche.

● *Functional specialist*. The firm serves a single or narrow set of functions but covers a broad range of customers. The market boundaries are defined narrowly by function, but broadly by customer group. Firms manufacturing intermediate components fall into this category.

● *Customer specialist*. The market boundaries are defined broadly by function but narrowly by customer group. The focus is on the needs of a particular group of customers. Companies specialising in hospital equipment belong to this category (see Figure 6.4 as an example).

● *Mixed strategy*. The firm is diversifying its activities in terms of functions and/or customer groups.

● *Full coverage*. The market boundaries are defined broadly by function and customer group. The firm covers the whole market. A steel company is a good example of this kind of market.

In most cases, market coverage strategies can be defined in only two dimensions, functions and customer groups, because in general the firm masters only one technology, even if substitute technologies exist.

For example, jam is in direct competition with melted cheese and chocolate paste. Because manufacturing requirements are so different, none of the firms operating in the sector of fruit transformation also has industrial operations in these adjacent sectors.

In some cases, however, firms define their businesses in terms of several substitute technologies, such as General Electric in the diagnostic imaging market (see Abell, 1980).

In a given sector of activity, business definitions may differ from one competitor to another. A firm specialising in a particular function can be confronted by a rival specialising in a particular customer group interested in the same function. The first competitor will probably have a cost advantage over the second, who will be probably more efficient in terms of distribution or customer service. The competitor analysis system should help identify the distinctive qualities of direct competitors.

Changes in market boundaries

Under the pressure of technological progress and changing consumption habits, definitions of market boundaries keep on changing along any one of three dimensions: functions, technologies or customers:

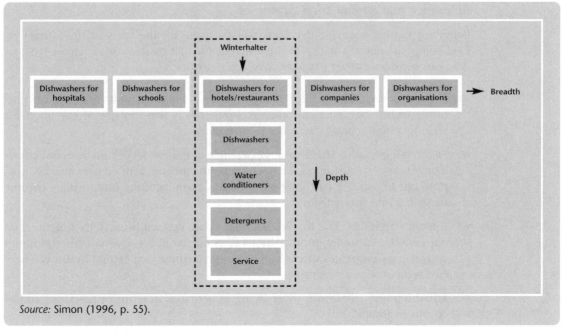

Source: Simon (1996, p. 55).

Figure 6.4　Market coverage strategy: depth rather than breadth – Winterhalter's strategy

● *Extension to new customer groups* through a process of adoption and diffusion, for example, adoption of microcomputers in the classroom.

● *Extension to new functions* through a process of systematisation and through the creation of products to serve a combination of functions, for example, telephone sets combined with a fax and with an automatic answering device.

● *Extension to new technologies* through a process of technological substitution, for example, electronic mail replacing printed mail.

These changing forces explain the changing profiles of product life cycles, a key criterion for assessing the attractiveness of product markets. The product life cycle (PLC) model will be analysed in the next chapter.

● Micro-segmentation Analysis

The objective of micro-segmentation is to analyse the diversity of customers' require-ments in a more detailed way within each of the product markets (or macro-segments) identified at the stage of macro-segmentation analysis. Within a particular product market, customers seek the same core service, for instance, time measure-ment in the watch market. However, keeping in mind the multi-attribute product concept, the way the core service is provided and the secondary services that go with the core service can be very different. The goal of micro-segmentation analysis is to identify customer groups searching for the same package of benefits in the product.

This can lead to a differentiation strategy to obtain a competitive advantage over rivals by doing a better job of satisfying customer requirements.

Market segmentation versus product differentiation

A distinction should be clearly made between segmentation and differentiation, two key marketing concepts.

Product *differentiation* provides a basis upon which a supplier can appeal to selective buying motives. Chamberlin (1950, p. 56) has defined this concept in the following way:

> A general class of product is differentiated if any significant basis exists for distinguishing the goods (or services) of one seller from those of another. Such a basis may be real or fancied, so long as it is of any importance whatever to buyers, and leads to a preference for one variety of a product over another.

The products are differentiated if the consumer believes that they are different.

While product differentiation is based on distinctions among products, market *segmentation* is based on distinctions among prospects that constitute the market (Smith, 1956). Recognition of the heterogeneity of customers has led firms to appeal to segments of what once might have been considered a homogeneous market. Generally, segmentation is viewed as a process of market desegregation. It may be useful to view it as a process of consumer aggregation.

> The firm could consider each buying unit as a segment. However, at least some economies of scale should be possible if these buying units were clustered into fewer groups. Buying units are aggregated in segments in such a way that there is a maximum homogeneity of demand within segments and maximum heterogeneity of demand between segments. Continuation of the aggregation process eventually leads to the formation of a single segment: the market as a whole. The firm must determine the level of aggregation that will generate the optimal profits. (Dalrymple and Parsons, 1976, p. 143)

Thus, product differentiation is a supply concept, while market segmentation is a demand concept.

Steps in market segmentation

The implementation of a micro-segmentation analysis consists of four basic steps:

● *Segmentation analysis*, or subdividing product markets into distinct groups of potential buyers having the same expectations or requirements (homogeneity condition), and being different from customers who are in other segments (heterogeneity condition).

● *Market targeting*, or selecting particular segment(s) to target, given the firm's strategic ambition and distinctive capabilities.

● *Market positioning*, or deciding how the firm wants to be perceived in the minds of potential customers, given the distinctive quality of the product and the positions already occupied by competitors.

● *Marketing programming* aimed at target segments. This last step involves the development and deployment of specific marketing programme(s) specially designed to achieve the desired positioning in the target segment(s).

The first step, segmentation analysis, can be implemented in four different ways:

● *Descriptive segmentation*, which is based on socio-demographic characteristics of the customer irrespective of the product category.

● *Benefit segmentation*, which considers explicitly the product category and the person's system of values.

● *Lifestyle segmentation*, which is based on socio-cultural characteristics of the customer, irrespective of the product category.

● *Behavioural segmentation*, which classifies customers on the basis of their actual purchasing behaviour in the marketplace.

Each of these segmentation methods has its own merits and weaknesses, which will be discussed in the following sections.

Descriptive or socio-demographic segmentation

Socio-demographic segmentation is an indirect segmentation method. The basic assumption embedded in this buyer's classification is the following:

> People having different socio-demographic profiles also have different needs and expectations regarding products and services.

This is obvious in many fields. Women and men have different needs for products like clothes, hats, cosmetics, jewellery, and so on, and similarly for teenagers or senior citizens, for low- and high-income households, for rural versus urban households, and so on. Thus, socio-demographic variables are used as proxies for direct need analysis.

The most commonly used variables are: sex, age, income, geographic location, education, occupation, family size and social class, all variables which reflect the easily measurable vital statistics of a society.

Frequently, a socio-demographic segmentation combines several variables, as shown in Figure 6.5. The case analysed here is that of a recently launched new brand in the food sector. The market response is described by reference to two dependent variables: the proportion of households having purchased the brand (market occupation rate) and the average quantity purchased per household (market penetration rate). The national average is at the intersection of the two dotted lines, the other points describing the behaviour of different socio-economic subgroups.

> For instance, one observes that the highest occupation rates are within the subgroups denoted respectively 4/13/7/18: (region 3), (age group 50–64), (large cities), (classes A+B). Similarly, the market penetration rate is higher within the following subgroups: 3/14/8/17: (region 2), (age group 65 and higher), (middle size cities), (household composition: 5 persons and higher).

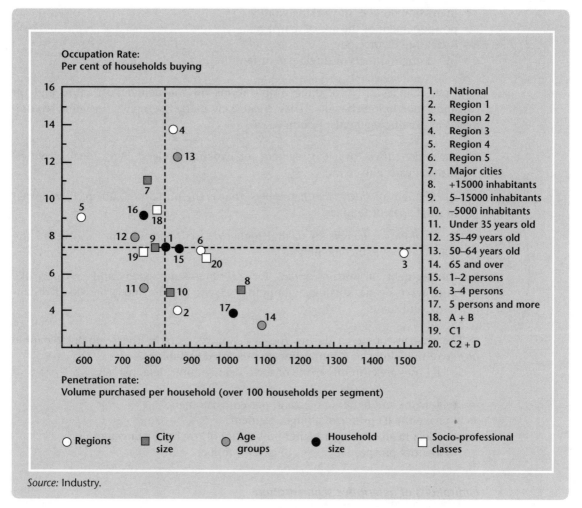

Figure 6.5 Socio-demographic segmentation: the case of a food product

This information is essential to verify whether the target group has been reached and, if not, to adjust the marketing programme accordingly.

Usefulness of socio-demographic data

The *merits* of socio-demographic segmentation are its low cost and ease of application. In most markets, information on socio-demographic variables is readily available in published sources. In addition, consumer panels use these criteria in their monthly or bimonthly reports on a similar base across the main European countries.

Also, in recent years significant socio-demographic changes have been observed in industrialised countries. Among these changes are:

● declining birth rate,
● increase in life expectancy,

● increasing number of working women,
● postponement of the age of marriage,
● increasing divorce rate,
● increasing numbers of single-parent families.

These changes all have direct implications on the demand structure and on consumer purchase behaviour. They create new market segments and new requirements in existing segments. Examples are:

● the *senior citizen* (over 65) segment for banking services, recreational activities, medical care, and so on;

● the segment of *single-adult households,* that is the unmarried, divorced, widowed or single-parent families;

● the *dual-income households* having higher discretionary income, also called the 'DINKS' (double income no kids);

● the segment of *working women* for all time-saving goods and services, like microwave ovens, catalogue shopping, easy-to-prepare foods, fast-food restaurants, and so on.

The changes observed during the last twenty years in the socio-demographic profile of the European Community are presented in Table 6.2.

Several uses are currently made of socio-demographic data, namely:

● to describe and better understand present customers,
● to have the ID profile of a target segment,
● to select media having a higher probability of reaching a target group,
● to identify prospective buyers of a new product.

Limitations of descriptive segmentation

Socio-demographic segmentation (as well as behavioural segmentation) is *ex-post analysis* of the kind of people who make up specific segments. The emphasis is on describing the characteristics of segments rather than on learning what causes these segments to develop. This is why it is called 'descriptive segmentation'.

Another major weakness is the *declining predictive value* of socio-demographic segmentation in industrialised countries as, increasingly, different persons adopt the same consumer behaviour with the growing standardisation of consumption modes across social classes. In other words, the fact of belonging to the upper class no longer necessarily implies the existence of a purchase behaviour different from that of a middle-class person. Today, two consumers of the same age, same family structure and same income may have extremely different behaviours and attitudes, reflected in different buying habits, product preferences and sometimes completely opposite reactions to advertising. Socio-demographic segmentation must be complemented by other methods to understand and predict a buyer's behaviour.

Table 6.2   Changes in the socio-demographic profile of the European Community

	YESTERDAY (The 1960s)	TODAY (Year 2000)
Total population	296,082	347,316
Age groups		
less than 20 years old	94,075	84,768
over 60 years old	45,594	70,321
Births		
Fertility rate	2.61	1.48
Births outside marriage (per 1000 births)	48.6	199.9
Infant mortality (per 1000 births	34.8	8.2
Life expectancy		
Men	67.3	72.9
Women	72.7	79.5
Private households		
Number	111,485	130,878
Persons per household	2.8	2.6
% single household	22.3	26.1
Number of marriages	2362.7	1884.9
Divorce rate (over total population	0.5	1.6
Active population		
Men	70.1	67.8
Women	40.9	44.0

Source: Eurostat (1991, 1996).

Benefit segmentation

In benefit segmentation, the emphasis is placed on differences in peoples' values and not on differences in socio-demographic profiles. Two persons identical in terms of socio-demographic profiles may have very *different value systems*. Moreover, the same person having different experiences with products can hold different values towards each product that is purchased.

> For example, a person who buys a refrigerator because it is the cheapest available may want to buy the most expensive TV set simply because of its superior design. Or, the individual who pays a high price for a bottle of wine may own a very cheap watch.

Thus, as discussed in Chapter 3, the value or the benefit sought in purchasing a particular product is the critical motivational factor to identify. The objective of benefit segmentation is to explain differences in preferences and not simply to give ex-post descriptions of purchase behaviour.

A classic example of benefit segmentation analysis is due to Yankelovich (1964) in the watch market. His approach reveals three distinct segments, each representing different values attributed to watches by each of three different groups of consumers:

● *Economy segment*. This group wants to pay the lowest possible price for any watch that works reasonably well. If it fails within a year, they will replace it (23 per cent of buyers).

● *Durability and quality segment*. This group wants a watch with a long life, good workmanship, good material and good styling. They are willing to pay for these product qualities (46 per cent of buyers).

● *Symbolic segment*. This group wants useful product features and meaningful emotional qualities. The watch should suitably symbolise an important occasion. Here, a well-known brand name, fine styling, a gold or diamond case and a jeweller's recommendation are important (31 per cent of buyers).

Without such an understanding, the demographic characteristics of the buyers were most confusing. It turns out, for example, that people with both the highest and the lowest incomes buy the most expensive watches. On the other hand, some upper-income consumers are no longer buying costly watches, but are buying cheap, well-styled watches to throw away when they require servicing. Other upper-income consumers, however, continue to buy fine, expensive watches for suitable occasions (Yankelovich, 1964).

At one time, most watch companies were oriented almost exclusively towards the third segment, thus leaving the major portion of the market open to attack and exploitation. The US Time Company, with the Timex brand, took advantage of this opening and established a very strong position among buyers in the first two segments.

Required market data

Benefit segmentation (Haley, 1968) requires obtaining detailed information on consumer value systems. Each segment is identified by the benefits it is seeking. It is the total package of benefits sought, which differentiates one segment from another, rather than the fact that one segment is seeking one particular benefit and another a quite different benefit. Individual benefits are likely to have appeal for several segments. In fact, most people would like as many benefits as possible. However, the relative importance they attach to individual benefits when forced to make trade-offs can differ a great deal and, accordingly, can be used as an effective criterion in segmenting markets. Thus, opportunities for segmentation arise from *trade-offs* consumers are willing to make among the benefits possible and the prices paid to obtain them.

Thus, the *multi-attribute product concept* (see Chapter 5) is the implied behavioural model in benefit segmentation. Its implementation requires the following information from a representative sample of target consumers:

● The list of attributes or benefits associated with a product category.
● An evaluation of the relative importance attached to each benefit.
● A regrouping procedure of consumers with similar rating patterns.
● An evaluation of the size and profile of each identified segment.

Thus, in the dental and mouth hygiene market for instance, the attributes identified through consumer research were the following: whiteness, freshness, good taste, product appearance, decay prevention, gum protection and economy. The next question was to ask respondents to divide 100 points among each of the toothpaste attributes according to how important each characteristic was for them when selecting a brand of toothpaste. Four segments were identified as shown in Table 6.3 (Haley, 1968). Supplementary information has also been collected about the people in each of these segments:

Table 6.3   Benefit segmentation of the toothpaste market

Benefits sought	Benefit segments			
	Sensory	Sociable	Worriers	Independents
Flavour, appearance	***	*	*	*
Brightness of teeth	*	***	*	*
Decay prevention	*	*	***	*
Low price	*	*	*	***

*** most important.
Source: adapted from Haley (1968).

- The *decay prevention segment* contains a large number of families with children. They are seriously concerned about the possibilities of cavities and show a definite preference for fluoride toothpaste.

- The *sociable segment*, which comprises people who show concern for the brightness of their teeth, is quite different. It includes a relatively large group of young married couples. They smoke more than average and their lifestyle is very active.

- The *sensory segment* is particularly concerned with the flavour and the appearance of the product. In this segment, a large portion of the brand users are children. Their use of spearmint toothpaste is well above average.

- The *independent segment* is price-oriented and shows a dominance of men. It tends to be above average in terms of toothpaste usage. People in this segment see very few meaningful differences between brands.

Benefit segmentation has important implications for the product policy of the firm. Once marketing understands the expectations of a particular consumer group, new or modified products can be developed and aimed at people seeking a specific combination of benefits.

Limitations of benefit segmentation

The greatest difficulty in applying this approach lies in the selection of the benefits to emphasise, mainly in the consumer goods markets. When market analysts ask consumers what benefit they want in a product, they are not likely to provide very new information about product benefits, since they are not highly introspective. If direct market analysis is supplemented with information about consumers' problems, however, new insights can be obtained.

> For example, in the toothpaste market, protection of gums is a new benefit promoted by brands having adopted a paramedical positioning. This is the outcome of dental hygiene analysis conducted with the dental profession.

Another difficulty of benefit segmentation stems from this fact: if we are gaining in understanding of consumer preferences, we are losing in terms of knowledge of the socio-demographic profiles of different customer groups. How do we reach, selectively, the 'worriers'? Thus, additional information must be collected to be able to describe these segments in socio-demographic terms.

Benefit segmentation analysis requires the collection of primary data, always a costly exercise. In addition, sophisticated multivariate measurement techniques (cluster analysis) must be used to identify the different customer groups. In some cases, however, interesting insights on benefits sought can be obtained through qualitative research, as illustrated in Table 6.4 with an example from the hi-fi chains market.

Table 6.4   Hi-fi chains market: benefit segments and principal benefits sought

■ **THE TECHNICIANS**
  – Mean to enjoy high-fidelity sound in its technical aspects.
  – Look for the quality and purity of the sound.
  – Mostly interested in the technical features without being necessarily qualified.

■ **THE MUSICIANS**
  – Mean to enjoy music.
  – Look for the spirit of the music, its musical space and colour.
  – Mostly interested in the musical interpretation without necessarily having a great musical culture.

■ **THE SNOBS**
  – Mean to show their resources, taste and aesthetic sense.
  – Look for prestige, demonstration effects and social integration.
  – Often poorly informed, tend to buy what is known and safe.

■ **THE OTHERS**

Segmenting markets with conjoint analysis

The method of conjoint analysis has been described and illustrated in Chapter 4. As explained, the focus of conjoint analysis is on the measurement of buyer preferences for product attribute levels and of the buyer benefits generated by the product attributes. Since measurements are made at the individual level, if preference heterogeneity exists, the market analyst can detect it and regroup individuals displaying the same utilities.

An empirical example will clarify the methodology. The application involves a bimonthly book magazine which publishes new book reviews, book guidance and advice, book digests and short articles. The editor is considering three alternative modifications of the editorial content:

● Concentrating on book reviews and analyses and dropping all the other editorial sections *(book review)*.
● Concentrating on guidance and advice on a larger number of books using standardised evaluation grids *(reader's guide)*.
● Limiting the number of book reviews, but adding a section on literary news with interviews of authors and special topical sections *(literary news)*.

A *do nothing* alternative is also considered, that is to keep the present editorial content unchanged. As to the selling price, three levels are considered: the present price of 142BF, an increased price of 200BF and a decreased price of 100BF, the number of pages remaining unchanged (30 pages). A questionnaire was mailed to 400 respondents selected among a group of readers and 171 valid questionnaires were used to estimate the utility functions. A cluster analysis programme was then used to regroup the respondents having the same utilities. As shown in Table 6.5, four different segments were identified:

Table 6.5   Benefit segmentation through conjoint analysis:
book review example

Attributes	Segment 1 (35.5%)	Segment 2 (21.0%)	Segment 3 (11.3%)	Segment (32.2%)
Content				
Book review	−6.1	1.2	−6.2	−1.8
Book guide	−6.4	−6.9	2.9	−3.1
Present content	0	0	0	0
Literary news	0.3	−2.1	−6.8	−3.3
Range:	6.7	9.1	9.7	3.3
Price				
100BF	0.5	0.6	0.3	1.1
142BF	0	0	0	0
200BF	−0.7	−0.6	−0.4	−1.0
Range:	1.2	1.2	0.7	2.1

Source: adapted from Roisin (1988).

● In *segment 1*, the respondents seem to be happy with the present editorial content. They react very negatively to the first two alternatives, and positively, but without enthusiasm, to the 'literary news' concept.

● In *segment 2*, there is a clear preference for the 'book reviews' concept and a negative attitude towards the other two editorial concepts.

● In *segment 3*, it is the 'reader's guide' concept which is preferred, the other two being clearly rejected.

● In *segment 4*, the present editorial content is the best alternative, but the range of utilities is also the smallest.

Thus in terms of benefits sought, the four segments are very different. As to the prices, the largest price sensitivity is observed in segment 4, as evidenced by the range, while segments 1 and 2 react in a very similar way, segment 3 being the least price sensitive. Analysis of the composition of these four segments showed that segment 4 was largely composed of librarians, while high-school teachers were an important group in segment 3.

For a comprehensive review of the contributions of conjoint analysis in market segmentation, see Green and Krieger (1991).

Behavioural segmentation

Usage segmentation attempts to classify consumers on the basis of their actual purchase behaviour in the marketplace. As such, it is also a descriptive and ex-post segmentation method. The criteria most commonly used are product usage, volume purchased, and loyalty status:

- *Product-user segmentation.* A distinction can be made between users, non-users, first users, ex-users, potential users and occasional versus regular users. A different selling and communication approach must be adopted for each of these user categories.

- *Volume segmentation.* In many markets, a small proportion of customers represents a high percentage of total sales. Often, about 20 per cent of the users account for 80 per cent of total consumption. A distinction between heavy, light and non-users is often very useful. Heavy users, or key accounts, deserve special treatment.

- *Loyalty segmentation.* Among existing customers a distinction can be made between hard-core loyal, soft-core loyal and switchers. Markets like cigarettes, beers and toothpaste are generally brand-loyal markets. Keeping loyal customers is the objective of relationship marketing. Appropriate marketing strategies can be developed to attract competitors' customers or to increase the loyalty of switchers.

Socio-cultural or lifestyle segmentation

As mentioned above, socio-demographic criteria are losing predictive value in affluent societies as consumption patterns become more and more personalised. Individuals from the same socio-demographic groups can have very different preferences and buying behaviour, and vice versa.

Socio-cultural segmentation, also called *lifestyle* or *psychographic segmentation*, seeks to supplement demographics by adding such elements as activities, attitudes, interests, opinions, perceptions and preferences to obtain a more complete consumer profile. It attempts to draw human portraits of consumers adding detail at the less obvious levels of motivation and personality. Wells and Tigert make the following point:

> Demographics have been and continue to be extremely useful, but they are unsatisfying. They lack colour. They lack texture. They lack dimensionality. They need to be supplemented by something that puts flesh on bare statistical backbone' (Wells and Tigert, 1971, published in Wells, 1974, p. 37).

The basic objective is to relate personality-type variables to consumer behaviour. Lifestyle descriptors are used as proxies for personality traits. 'Lifestyle' refers to the overall manner in which people live and spend time and money. A person's lifestyle (or psychographic profile) can be measured and described in a number of ways:

- At the most stable and persistent level is the person's *valuing system and personality traits*, which are, of course, more difficult to measure.

- At an intermediate level, a person's *activities, interests and opinions* reveal her or his value system.

- At a superficial level, but directly observable, consumers' lifestyles are reflected by the *products and services purchased* and by the way in which buyers are using or consuming them.

Valette-Florence (1986) suggests defining a person's lifestyle as the interaction of these three levels: the group of persons having a similar behaviour at each of these levels is homogeneous in terms of lifestyle. Thus a *lifestyle is the outgrowth of a person's value system, attitudes, interests and opinions (AIO) and of the individual's consumption mode*. It describes the sort of person she (or he) is and at the same time it differentiates her (or him) from other persons.

Lifestyle studies can be conducted at one of these three levels. The closer we are to actual purchase decisions, the easier the measurements, but also the more volatile the conclusions. The largest majority of empirical lifestyle studies have been conducted at the AIO level, where research measures:

- People's *activities* in terms of how they spend their time.
- Their *interests*, what they place importance on in their immediate surroundings.
- Their *opinions* in terms of views of themselves and the world around them.

Some basic *demographic* characteristics such as their stage in the life cycle, income, education and where they live. Table 6.6 lists the elements included in each major dimension of lifestyle.

Table 6.6   Lifestyle dimensions

Activities	Interests	Opinions	Demographics
Work	Family	Themselves	Age
Hobbies	Home	Social issue	Education
Social events	Job	Politics	Income
Vacation	Community	Business	Occupation
Entertainment	Recreation	Economics	Family size
Club membership	Fashion	Education	Dwelling
Community	Food	Products	Geography
Shopping	Media	Future	City size
Sports	Achievements	Culture	Life cycle

Source: Plummer (1974).

Lifestyle studies provide a broad everyday view of consumers, a living portrait that goes beyond flat socio-demographic descriptions and helps understand actual consumer behaviour.

Examples of General Lifestyle Statements

■ I find myself checking the prices in the grocery stores even for small items (price conscious).
■ An important part of my life and activities is dressing smartly (fashion conscious).
■ I would rather spend a quiet evening at home than go out to a party (homebody).
■ I like to work on community projects (community minded).
■ I try to arrange my home for my children's convenience (child oriented).

Source: Wells and Tigert (1971).

Lifestyle research methodology

In a typical lifestyle study, a questionnaire is developed containing a set of statements measuring the lifestyle dimensions relevant to the product category under study. Each dimension is measured by several statements or propositions to which respondents indicate the extent of their agreement or disagreement on a five-point Likert scale ranging from 'definitely disagree' to 'definitely agree'. Examples of lifestyle statements are presented in Exhibit 6.3. If the relevant dimension is 'price conscious', then it will be measured by consumers agreeing or disagreeing with 5 or 6 statements similar to those given in Exhibit 6.3 under the dimension 'price conscious'.

Typically, several different statements are introduced into the questionnaire to measure the same concept. Approximately 200 to 300 AIO statements may be included. In addition to the AIO statements, information is also collected on product usage and on demographic characteristics.

Armed with these three sets of data (AIO statements, product usage and demographics), the market analyst constructs user profiles. The analysis involves relating levels of agreement on all AIO items with the levels of usage on a product and with demographic characteristics. The procedure is the following:

● Factor analysis is used to reduce the set of statements to a summary set of factors.
● Each respondent's scores on the factors are computed.
● Respondents are then clustered into segments that are relatively homogeneous using a cluster analysis program.
● The clusters are then labelled by the factors that most typify each cluster.
● Finally, the segments are cross-tabulated with demographic and usage variables to help characterise the identified segments.

An example of general lifestyle segmentation of the European market is presented in Figure 6.6.

Usefulness of lifestyle segmentation

The results of lifestyle studies are stocked and regularly updated. Factorial analyses are used to uncover principal components or macro-characteristics and meaningful clus-

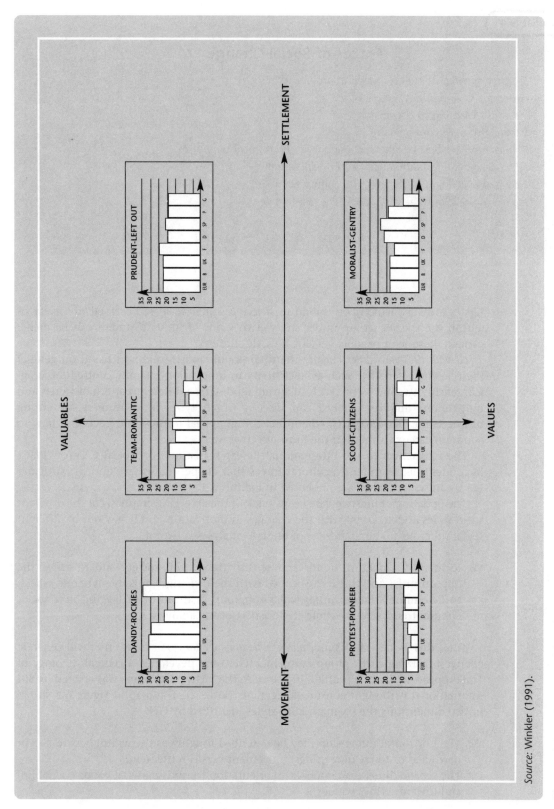

Figure 6.6 European lifestyle segmentation

Source: Winkler (1991).

Exhibit 6.4

Forces of Social Change

Self-development. Affirming oneself as an individual.

Hedonism. Giving priority to pleasure.

Plasticity. Adapting to circumstances.

Vitality. Exploiting one's energy.

Connectivity. Relating to others: clicking in and out, mixing cultures.

Ethics. Searching for authenticity and meaning in life.

Belongings. Defining social links and cultural identities.

Inertia. Actively, or more often passively, resisting change.

Source: Hasson (1995).

ters of answers, which correspond to *stereotypes* or *socio-styles* observed in society or within the specific group under study. Two kinds of lifestyle studies can be made: general lifestyle or product-specific lifestyle studies.

General lifestyle studies classify the total population into groups based on general lifestyle characteristics, such as 'receptivity to innovation', 'family centred', 'ecological sensitivity', and so on. Each subgroup represents a different pattern of values and motivations and the analyst can discern which types of consumers are strong prospects for their products, what other things appeal to these prospects and how to communicate with them in the most effective way.

The researchers of the International Research Institute on Social Change (RISC) have identified eight socio-cultural forces that shape our society and in particular European society. They are presented in Exhibit 6.4.

The updating of lifestyle data keeps track of the changing emphasis of the different socio-styles and keeps up with the changes in motivation and behaviour of different social subgroups. The usefulness of lifestyle analyses is twofold:

- to identify emerging trends and sensitivities within society and to assess the opportunities and threats associated with these changes; it is the dynamic aspect;
- to determine whether a particular subgroup is ahead of or lagging in a socio-cultural trend; it is the more static aspect of the analysis.

Thus, this process shows up *leading indicators of changes* or trends that will generate changes. In Europe, the group Europanel (GFK) has developed a general typology of 16 European socio-style profiles. In the USA, the VALS programme was created by SRI International with eight consumer segments (VALS-2). The map in Figure 6.6 shows in two dimensions the six main Euro-styles identified by GFK.

- The horizontal dimension may be described roughly as the willingness to accept new ideas or to try new things: movement versus settlement;
- The second dimension opposes an orientation towards material goods (valuables) and towards ethics (values).

A third dimension opposing rational and emotional behaviour has been observed but is not represented here. Having this map, it is possible to overlay the pattern of product (or brand) usage or attitude and to compare the kinds of people who are heavy users of the product category and/or of the brand.

In *product-specific lifestyle* studies, the objective is to understand consumer behaviour related to a particular product or service. The AIO statements are then more product-specific. To illustrate, here are examples of AIO statements adapted to the credit cards market:

- I like to pay cash for everything I buy.
- I buy many things with a credit card or a charge card.
- In the past year, we have borrowed money from a bank or finance company.
- To buy anything other than a house or a car on credit is unwise.

Lifestyle research methodology also has some important advantages over motivation research and depth interviews: (a) samples are large; (b) conclusions do not rely heavily on interviewer interpretation of relatively unstructured responses; (c) data are easily analysed by a variety of well-understood statistical methods; and (d) less highly trained interviewers can be employed.

Problems in lifestyle research

Lifestyle research was at a time very popular in marketing research, particularly among advertising people, although several researchers have initially expressed considerable reservations as to its validity and predictive value. A certain number of methodological issues are still unresolved:

- To date, there is *no explicit theoretical model*, that specifies the key concepts of lifestyle to be explored and their hypothesised relations to purchase behaviour. In most cases, it is a trial-and-error procedure that is adopted.

- As a consequence, *the selection of lifestyle dimensions* and indicators is largely based on intuition, hunches and the researcher's imagination. Lifestyle researchers do not agree on what variables should be included. The end result is a very large number (up to 300) statements included in the questionnaire; a way out facilitated by increasing computer capacities.

- Lifestyle analyses belong to the class of causal studies, since the objective is to explain why people behave as they do. To demonstrate the existence of a causal relationship requires a *well-conceived experimental design* and careful testing of the observed relationship. Evidence of a relationship does not necessarily imply causality. Spurious correlations as well as spurious non-correlations exist and the lack of prior research design can cause faulty interpretation of data.

- Traditionally, the association between lifestyle data with variables like product usage, brand loyalty, and so on. are examined by direct cross-tabulations, while the *multivariate nature of data* suggests the use of multivariate statistical techniques.

- Questions are also raised regarding the *reliability of the measuring instrument*. Can we expect reliable and valid responses from a questionnaire which takes several hours to complete and may lead to boredom or fatigue?

Several of the methodological issues raised here are critical and question the *internal and external validity* of general lifestyle studies. This means that its users must make special efforts to be careful in measurements, statistical analyses and interpretations of results if they are to uncover valid information on consumer behaviour. It is up to the market analyst to verify whether the basic validity conditions are indeed fulfilled.

These are basic questions to which every professional user has the right to receive precise answers, since they will determine the validity of lifestyle analyses. As underlined in Chapter 5, marketing research has to deal with *accredited knowledge*, since management is primarily interested in making decisions on accurate and unbiased data. The absence of satisfactory answers to these methodological issues, combined with the data inaccessibility and with the secrecy of the questionnaire, explains the low degree of interest in these studies in the scientific community.

In spite of the methodological issues in lifestyle research, the socio-cultural approach is both interesting and promising. It is an undeniable improvement over segmentation methods based on just economic and socio-demographic criteria. For a systematic analysis of the methodological issues raised by lifestyle research and for the remedies suggested, see Green and Wind (1974) and Valette-Florence (1986, 1988).

Business-to-Business Market Segmentation

Conceptually, there is no difference between business-to-business (or industrial) and consumer market segmentation, but the criteria used to segment the market vary greatly. The same distinction between macro- and micro-segmentation can be made. The method of macro-segmentation described earlier in this chapter is of direct application. The micro-segmentation criteria tend to be different, however.

Benefit segmentation

As for consumer goods, *benefit segmentation* is the most natural method. It is based on the specific needs, in general well defined, of the business-to-business customer. In industrial markets, this means classifying the customers by type of industry or by end-use. End-users are generally looking for different benefits, performance or functions in a product. Industrial products often have a wide range of possible uses, for instance in electric motors, ball bearings, steel sheets, and so on. The classification by industry type points out the priority needs and their relative importance.

By way of illustration, let us consider the case of a company specialising in the manufacture of small electric motors, a product that has a very large number of possible uses. For each end-use, beyond the core function, one or several product characteristics may be particularly important. This is the case for the following three industrial applications:

● Motors incorporated in petrol pumps: security norms (spark-free) are essential.
● Motors incorporated into computers or in medical instruments used in hospitals: the response time must be instantaneous.
● Motors incorporated in industrial sewing machines; resistance to frequent stopping and starting is important and fast reaction is secondary.

The functions of an industrial good and their importance in the customer's industrial process vary according to whether it is a major equipment good (turnkey factory, steel mill, alternator) or secondary equipment good (radiator, light trucks, typewriter); semi-finished intermediate products (coated steel sheets); parts to be incorporated (electric motors, gear shifts); finished goods (tools, oil); raw materials (coal, grease, polyurethane foam); services (engineering, industrial cleaning, maintenance) (see Figure 3.8). In each case, the perceived economic value of the product by the customer will be very different.

It is important to recall that in many business-to-business sectors, sales are based on orders with detailed specifications. In this type of market situation, the product is naturally adjusted to the particular needs of the customer.

Descriptive segmentation

Demographic or descriptive segmentation is based on criteria describing the profile of the industrial customer. These criteria generally concern activity, geographic location, size, shareholder composition, and so on (for an example see Figure 6.7). Many companies choose to have separate sales service for large and small customers. Large customers are directly serviced by the company while small customers will be dealt with by distributors.

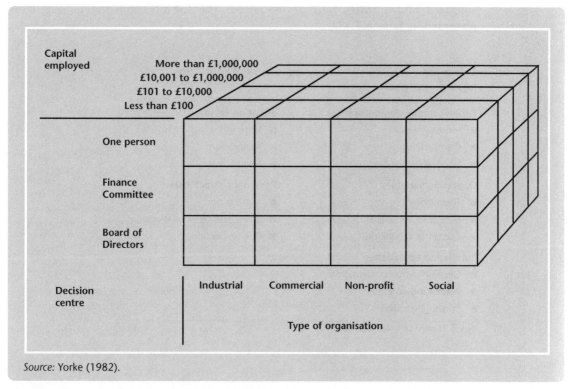

Source: Yorke (1982).

Figure 6.7 Example of descriptive segmentation in the business-to-business service sector: the corporate banking market

Behavioural segmentation

Behavioural *segmentation* is important for industrial markets. Its purpose is to develop a strategy for approaching business-to-business customers according to their structures and the way their buying decision centre operates. The way a buying decision centre works was discussed in Chapter 3 of this book, where we also saw that the buying process can be more or less formalised according to the complexity of decisions and organisational structures.

In some companies, buying is centralised and precise rules govern the purchase decisions. Other companies, in contrast, decentralise buying and the approach to such a company will be similar to that used for a smaller firm. Other characteristics of the buying centre are also important: motivations of different members of the buying team, the different forces at play between the representatives of different functions, the degree of formalism and the length of time necessary for a decision. These behavioural characteristics are not usually directly observable and thus are often hard to identify. However, as seen above, these are important things for sales people to be aware of.

Because of the complexity and variety of possible bases for segmentation industrial markets, Shapiro and Bonona (1983) have expanded the use of macro- and micro-segmentation into what is called a *nested approach*. This method assumes a hierarchical structure of segmentation bases that move from very broad or general bases to very organisation-specific bases. Rather than a two-step process, the nested approach allows three, four or five steps. The list of segmentation criteria is presented in Table 6.7.

Table 6.7 Business-to-business segmentation: the nested approach

Organisational demographics	Situation factors
■ Industry sectors	■ Urgency
■ Company size	■ Application
■ Geographic location	■ Size of order
Operating variables	**Personal characteristics**
■ Technology	■ Motivation
■ User–non-user status	■ Buyer and seller relationship
■ Customer capabilities	■ Risk perception
Purchasing approaches	
■ Decision centre organisation	
■ Purchasing policies	
■ Purchasing criteria	

Source: Shapiro and Bonona (1983).

The simplest way to segment industrial markets is to use broad descriptive characteristics, such as industrial sectors (NACE or SIC category), company size, geographic location or end-market served. This information is easily accessible since this type of data is readily available through government agencies, which publish detailed industrial classifications. Benefit segmentation is also easier in industrial markets than in consumer markets, because users are professional people who have less difficulty in expressing their needs and in qualifying the relative importance of different product attributes.

Implementation of a Segmentation Strategy

Having completed the market segmentation analysis phase we have a segmentation grid which describes the different existing segments. The next step for management is to make decisions regarding the segments to target and the positioning to adopt within the targeted segments. The final stage is to define the type of marketing programme to adopt within each chosen segment. A preliminary question must be raised, however: to verify to what extent the requirements for effective segmentation are met.

Requirements for effective segmentation

To be effective and useful a segmentation strategy should identify segments that meet four criteria: differential response, adequate size, measurability and accessibility.

Differential response

This is the most important criterion to consider when choosing a segmentation strategy. The segments must be different in terms of their sensitivity to one or several marketing variables under the control of the firm. The segmentation variable should maximise the behavioural difference between segments (heterogeneity condition) while minimising the differences among customers within a segment (homogeneity condition).

A key requirement is to avoid segment overlapping, the risk being the possibility of cannibalism among products of the same company but targeted to different segments. The more a product has distinctive and observable characteristics, the more homogeneous the segment will be.

We must, however, remember that segment homogeneity does not necessarily imply that all categories of buyers are mutually exclusive. An individual may of course belong to more than one segment. Products from different segments may be bought by the same person for different people within the household, for different types of use or just for the sake of variety. Observation of shopping trolleys outside a supermarket often shows that brands from both the high and the low end of the range have been purchased at the same time. One segment does not necessarily cover the buyers, but rather the products purchased by the buyers.

Adequate size

Segments should be defined so that they represent enough potential customers to provide sufficient sales revenue to justify the development of different products and marketing programmes.

Identified segments must represent a market potential large enough to justify developing a specific marketing strategy. This condition affects not only the size of the segment in volume and frequency of buying but also its life cycle. All markets are affected by fashion. It is essential to verify that the targeted niche is not temporary and that the product's lifespan be economically long. Finally, the size requirement also implies that the added value of the product, because of its specificity, will be financially worthwhile, in the sense that the market price acceptable by the target segment is sufficiently rewarding for the firm.

Meeting this requirement often implies a trade-off between two logics: the logic of marketing management, which tries to meet the needs of the market through a narrow definition of segments in order to adapt the firm's offering to the diversity of market needs as best as possible, and the logic of operations management, which emphasises the benefits of economies of scale through standardisation and long production runs.

Measurability

Before target segments can be selected, the size, purchasing power and major behaviour characteristics of the identified segments must be measured. If the segmentation criteria used are very abstract, such information is hard to find. For example, if the prospects were companies of a certain size, it would be easy to find information about their number, location, turnover, and so on. But a segmentation criterion like 'innovativeness of companies' does not lend itself to easy measurement and the firm would probably have to conduct its own market survey. Abstract criteria are often used in benefit and lifestyle segmentations, while descriptive segmentation is based on more concrete and observable criteria.

Accessibility

Accessibility refers to the degree to which a market segment can be reached through a unique marketing programme. There are two ways to reach prospects:

- *Customer self-selection* involves reaching a more general target while relying on the product and appeal of advertising to the intended target group. These consumers select themselves by their attention to the advertisements.

- *Controlled coverage* is very efficient because the firm reaches target customers with little wasted coverage of individuals or firms who are not potential buyers.

Controlled coverage is more efficient from the firm's point of view. This communication strategy implies a good knowledge of the socio-demographic profile of the target group, which is not always the case when using benefit or lifestyle segmentation. The main characteristics of each segment can be summarised in a segmentation grid, as shown in Figure 6.8.

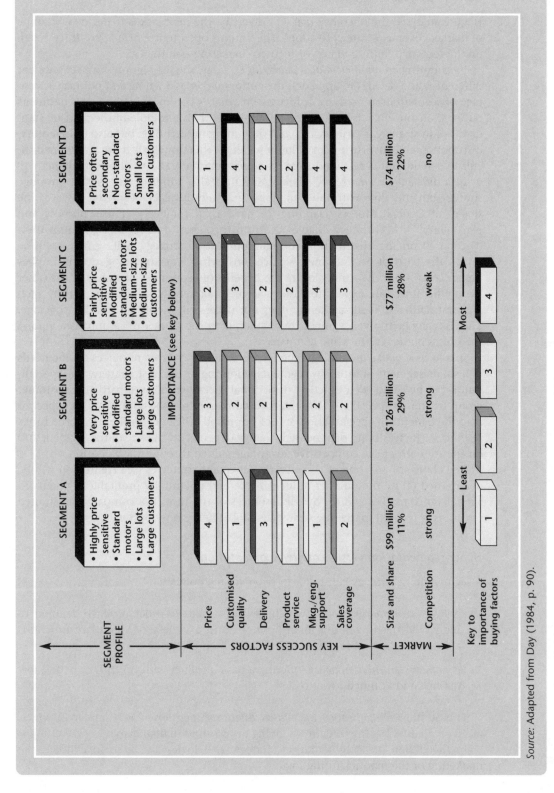

SEGMENT PROFILE		SEGMENT A	SEGMENT B	SEGMENT C	SEGMENT D
		• Highly price sensitive • Standard motors • Large lots • Large customers	• Very price sensitive • Modified standard motors • Large lots • Large customers	• Fairly price sensitive • Modified standard motors • Medium-size lots • Medium-size customers	• Price often secondary • Non-standard motors • Small lots • Small customers

IMPORTANCE (see key below)

KEY SUCCESS FACTORS					
Price	4	3	2	1
Customised quality	1	2	3	4
Delivery	3	2	2	2
Product service	1	1	2	2
Mkg./eng. support	1	2	4	4
Sales coverage	2	2	3	4

MARKET					
Size and share	$99 million 11%	$126 million 29%	$77 million 28%	$74 million 22%
Competition	strong	strong	weak	no

Key to importance of buying factors

Least ← → Most

1   2   3   4

Source: Adapted from Day (1984, p. 90).

Figure 6.8 Typical segmentation grid: comparative analysis of segment profiles

Market targeting strategies

Having analysed the reference market's diversity, the next task is to decide what type of market coverage strategy to adopt. The options open to the firm are of three types: undifferentiated, differentiated or focused marketing (Smith, 1956).

By adopting an *undifferentiated marketing* strategy, the firm ignores market segment differences and decides to approach the entire market as a whole and not take advantage of segmentation analysis. It focuses on what is common in the needs of buyers rather than on what is different. The rationale of this middle-of-the-road or standardisation strategy is cost savings, not only in manufacturing, but also in inventory, distribution and advertising. In affluent societies, this strategy is more and more difficult to defend as it is rarely possible for a product or a brand to please everyone.

In a *differentiated marketing* strategy, the firm also adopts a full market coverage strategy but this time with tailor-made programmes for each segment. This was the slogan of General Motors, claiming 'to have a car for every "purse, purpose and personality"'. This strategy enables the firm to operate in several segments with a customised pricing, distribution and communication strategy. Selling prices will be set on the basis of each segment's price sensitivity. This strategy generally implies higher costs, since the firm is losing the benefits of economies of scale. On the other hand, the firm can expect to hold a strong market share position within each segment. Differentiated marketing does not necessarily imply full market coverage. The risk may be to over-segment the market, with the danger of cannibalism among the excess brands of the same company.

In a *focused marketing* strategy, the firm is concentrating its resources on the needs of a single segment or on a few segments, adopting a specialist strategy. The specialisation can be based on a function (functional specialist) or on a particular customer group (customer specialist). Through focused marketing, the company can expect to reap the benefits of specialisation and of improved efficiency in the use of the firm's resources. The feasibility of a focused strategy depends on the size of the segment and on the strength of the competitive advantage gained through specialisation.

The choice of any one of these market coverage strategies (see Figure 6.9) will be determined (a) by the number of identifiable and potentially profitable segments in the reference market and (b) by the resources of the firm. If a company has limited resources, a focused marketing strategy is probably the only option.

Hyper-segmentation versus counter-segmentation

A segmentation strategy can result in two extreme policies:

- A *hyper-segmentation policy*, which develops made-to-order products tailored to individual needs, offering many options and a variety of secondary functions along with the core function and this at a high cost.

- A *counter-segmentation policy*, offering a basic product with no frills or extras, few options and at much lower cost.

This is the *standardisation–adaptation* dilemma mentioned in Chapter 2, which faced companies having to define a global or transnational strategy.

In the design of a segmentation strategy, two logics are often in conflict: the marketing or the manufacturing logic:

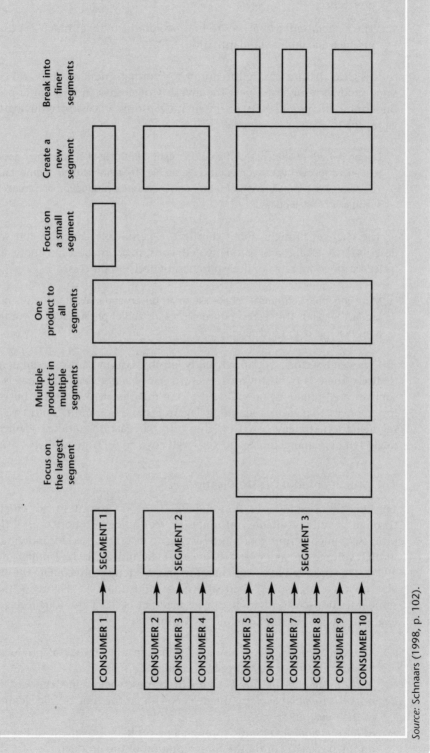

Figure 6.9 Examples of market coverage strategies

Source: Schnaars (1998, p. 102).

● The *marketing logic* calls for maximum adaptation to the diversity of needs and leads to the development of products customised by reference to client individual preferences.

● The *manufacturing logic* tries to improve productivity as much as possible through product maximum standardisation.

It is clear that increasing the number of formats, designs, sizes and colours of the same product in order to meet the diversity of needs can be counter-productive and undermine the productivity of the manufacturing process by reducing the potential gains due to economies of scale.

> During periods of affluence of the golden sixties, in the field of consumer goods, companies tended to follow hyper-segmentation strategies by refining their segmentation strategies. The result was a proliferation of brands, an increase of production and marketing costs and eventually of retail prices.

The changes brought about during the period of economic and social turmoil described in Chapter 2 gradually led consumers to become more aware of the 'price/satisfaction' ratio in their purchasing decision process.

> More and more consumers behave like smart buyers and make trade-offs between price and product benefits. The success of generic brands and of private labels in Western economies is an example of this evolution.

In several sectors, and particularly in the fast moving consumer goods sector (FMCG), there is trend towards a return to *voluntary simplicity*, that is towards less sophisticated products, providing the core function without frills, but sold at much lower prices thanks to their high level of standardisation. Thus, we have here a segmentation strategy based on the 'price/satisfaction' ratio, a segment too often neglected by manufacturers and very well covered by large retailers.

The process of mass customisation

The adaptation–standardisation dilemma can be solved in an efficient manner through readily available information technology, robotics and flexible work processes which permit goods and services to be customised for individual customers in high volume and at a relatively low cost (Tarondeau, 1982; Lampel and Mintzberg, 1997). This so-called *mass customisation* process tends to reconcile the two traditionally opposed logics described above. As illustrated in Figure 6.10, the choice standardisation–customisation can be made at each of the four levels of the value chain: design, fabrication, assembly, distribution:

● *At the fabrication level*, through the design of a universal product or through modular design or customisable products.

● *At the use level by the user himself* who can use the product the way he wants.

● *At the distribution level*, by the dealers who, at the time of sale, adapt the product to their customers' needs.

● *At the communication stage*, through a perceptual or cosmetic differentiation based on the packaging or on the representation of the product.

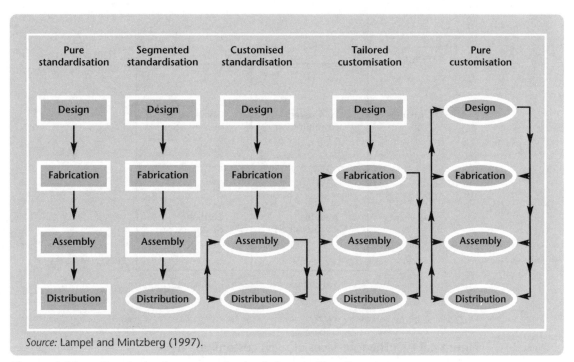

Source: Lampel and Mintzberg (1997).

Figure 6.10   Customisation strategies in the manufacturing process

As illustrated by Figure 6.11, the problem of mass customisation can be addressed by reference to two dimensions: first the presence or absence of *product modification*; second by the presence or absence of its *presentation*. Four distinct approaches to customisation can be identified (Gilmore and Pine, 1997):

⬤ *Collaborative customisation*: collaborative customisers conduct a dialogue with individual customers to help them articulate their needs, to identify the precise offering that fulfils those needs and to make customised products for them.

⬤ *Adaptive customisation*: adaptive customisers offer one standard, but customisable, product that is designed so that users can alter it themselves, thanks to a modular design.

⬤ *Cosmetic customisation*: cosmetic customisers present a standard product differently for different customers.

⬤ *Transparent customisation*: transparent customisers provide individual customers with unique goods or services without letting them know explicitly that those products and services have been customised for them.

Each of these strategies enables the firm to avoid the pitfalls of mass manufacturing and to adapt their offering in order to best serve their customers while keeping the benefits of economies of scale.

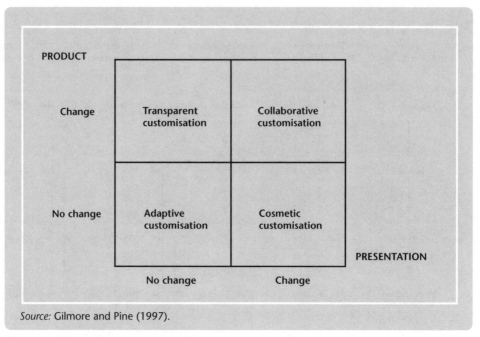

Source: Gilmore and Pine (1997).

Figure 6.11　The four faces of mass customisation

Product positioning strategies

Once the market coverage decisions are made, the next step is to decide on the positioning strategy to adopt within each target segment. Selection of the positioning strategy provides the unifying concept for the development of the marketing programme. Positioning indicates how the firm would like to be perceived in the minds of target customers. Positioning can be defined as follows:

> Positioning is the act of designing and communicating the firm's offer so that it occupies a distinct and valued place in the target customers' mind. (Ries and Trout, 1981)

Positioning is mostly relevant when coupled with a segmentation analysis, which requires a positioning by segments instead of a single positioning for the total market. Positioning strategy is the operational way to implement a differentiation strategy. The typical questions to address here are the following:

● What are the distinctive features and/or benefits, real or perceived, considered as the most important from the buyer's point of view?
● What are the perceived positions of the main competing brands according to these features and/or benefits?
● Given the strengths and weaknesses of our brand and the positions already occupied by competing brands, what is the best positioning to adopt?
● What is the most appropriate marketing programme for achieving the chosen positioning?

Thus, not all brand or product differences are meaningful to buyers. As will be discussed in Chapter 9, the source of differentiation should be 'unique', 'important' to the buyer, 'sustainable', 'communicable' and 'affordable'.

Alternative bases for positioning

Wind (1982, pp. 79–80) has identified six alternative bases for positioning. These are:

● Positioning on product features.
● Positioning on benefits, on problem solution or needs.
● Positioning for specific usage occasion.
● Positioning for user category.
● Positioning against another product.
● Product class dissociation.

Other positioning bases exist, such as, for example, lifestyle positioning.

Selecting a positioning basis

When selecting a positioning basis, a certain number of conditions must be carefully met:

● To have a good understanding of the *present positioning* of the brand or firm in the customers' minds. This knowledge can be acquired through brand image studies, as described in Chapter 5.

● To know the present positioning of *competing brands*, in particular those brands in direct competition.

● To select one positioning and to identify the most relevant and credible *arguments* which justify the chosen positioning.

● To evaluate the potential *profitability* of the contemplated positioning, while being suspicious of false market niches invented by advertising people or discovered through an invalidated qualitative study.

● To verify whether the brand has the required *personality potential* to achieve the positioning in the minds of consumers.

● To assess the *vulnerability* of the positioning. Do we have the resources required to occupy and defend this position?

● To ensure *consistency* in the positioning with the different marketing mix instruments: pricing, distribution, packaging, services, and so on.

Once the positioning strategy is adopted and clearly defined, it is much simpler for marketing people to translate this positioning in terms of an effective and consistent marketing programme.

In the positioning decision, the price/quality ratio is a key factor. Figure 6.12 illustrates the structure of a typical market made up of four positioning alternatives. In this example, brand A is inadequately positioned because it is too costly for the mass market and has insufficient perceived quality to appeal to the premium or to the luxury segments.

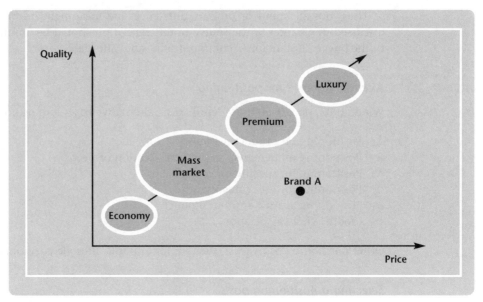

Figure 6.12 Positioning alternatives in a typical market

Attribute-based perceptual maps

When the number of benefits to consider is large, attribute-based perceptual maps are useful to identify the different packages of benefits and to describe the perceived positioning of the major competing brands. As shown in Exhibit 6.5, to illustrate we refer to a study of the toothpaste market aiming to verify the way consumers perceive a paramedical brand extension of the brand Signal, called Signal-plus. In this analysis, 24 product benefits were identified through unstructured group discussions.

Exhibit 6.5

The Package of Benefits of a Paramedical Brand of Toothpaste

Good for children	Traditional
Protects gums	Prevents tartar
Prevents decay	Fresh breath
Expensive	Pleasant texture
Sold in pharmacy	Economical
Much advertised	Unpleasant taste
Whitens teeth	For the whole family
Cavity protection	Strong taste
Young	Pleasant advertising
Medical	Friendly
Funny colours	Less effective than claimed
With fluoride	Attractive packaging

A representative sample of 130 respondents in the 12–30 age group were exposed to the 12 leading brands of toothpaste and asked to rate them by simply noting their perceptions as to the absence or presence (0, 1) of each particular benefit in each brand. These data were fed into a computer program called Factorial Correspondence Analysis (ANAFACO) to determine the association of the benefits with the brands. Three dimensions have been identified:

● The first axis sets the paramedical aspect (medical, sold in pharmacy, expensive, unpleasant taste) against the pleasurable aspect of the product (young, pleasant texture, attractive packaging). This axis shows an inertia rate of 41 per cent and compares two distribution channels, the food and drug networks.

● The second axis compares the attribute of the specific dental anti-cavities treatment (fluoride, anti-cavities, children like it) with the more general attributes of dental hygiene (whitens teeth, strong taste, pleasant advertising). The inertia rate here is 21 per cent.

● A third axis also emerges, which isolates a relatively new benefit sought: gum care opposed to the traditional cosmetic toothpaste. The inertia rate here is 13 per cent. In total, we thus have an explained variance of 75 per cent.

The two-dimensional map identified is presented in Figure 6.13, which provides management with a picture of the market for all competing brands and for the benefits associated with the brands:

● *Segment 1* groups the medical brands perceived as giving 'gum protection', being 'sold in pharmacies', 'expensive' and with 'unpleasant taste'.

● *Segment 2* groups the cosmetic brands, emphasising 'fresh breath', being 'friendly', with a 'pleasant taste', 'attractive packaging' and 'pleasant texture'.

● *Segment 3* groups the anti-cavity brands and emphasises 'white teeth', 'good for children', 'pleasant colours', 'with fluoride', and 'pleasant advertising'.

The promise in segment 3 is friendlier than in segment 1, but is coupled with a more serious promise: cavity prevention. Thus, this type of perceptual map permits management to evaluate the way segments perceive the different brands and whether the intended positioning has been reasonably well achieved.

● ## International Segmentation

With the globalisation of the world economy, opportunities are growing to create demand for universal products. International segmentation is a way in which a global approach can be adopted to sell a physically similar product worldwide. The objective is to discover in different countries and/or regions groups of buyers having the same expectations and requirements *vis-à-vis* products, despite cultural and national differences. Those segments, even if they are small in size within each country, may represent in total a very attractive opportunity for the international firm. To adjust to local differences, the physical product can be customised through services, accessories or inexpensive product modifications. The potential for globalisation is not the same for

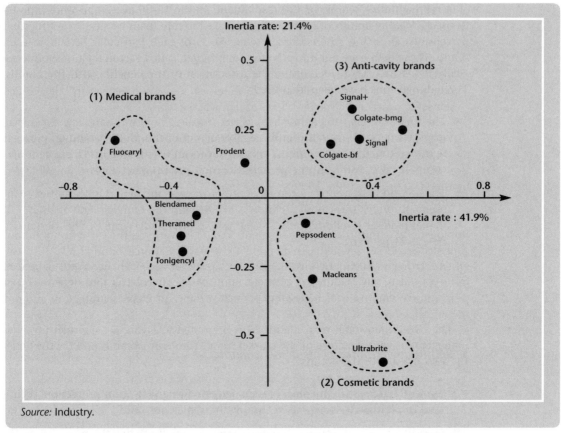

Figure 6.13 Product positioning analysis: the toothpaste market in Belgium, 1985

each product category and different approaches can be adopted. For a review of the literature on this topic, see Hassan and Katsanis (1991).

Identification of global market segments

Global market segmentation can be defined as the process of identifying specific segments, whether they be country groups or individual buyer groups, of potential customers with homogeneous attributes who are likely to exhibit similar buying behaviour. There are three different approaches for global segmentation: (a) identifying clusters of countries that demand similar products; (b) identifying segments present in many or most countries; and (c) targeting different segments in different countries with the same product (Takeuchi and Porter, 1986, pp. 138–40).

Targeting country clusters

Traditionally, the world market has been segmented on geographic variables, that is by *grouping countries* that are similar in terms of climate, language, religion, economic development, distribution channel, and so on. Products rarely require modification or tailoring for every single country, except for such things as labelling and the language used in the manuals and catalogues.

> On the European scene, natural clusters of countries would be, for example, the Nordic countries (Denmark, Norway, Sweden and maybe Finland); the Germanic countries (Germany, Austria, part of Switzerland), the Iberian countries, and so on. With this country segmentation strategy, products and communication would be adapted for each group of countries.

Within the European Community, an argument in favour of this country approach lies in the very high diversity of the different countries, as evidenced by the comparison of their socio-demographic profiles. See the social portrait of Europe published by the EC (Eurostat, 1996, 1999).

However, this approach presents three potential limitations: (a) it is based on country variables and not on consumer behavioural patterns, (b) it assumes total homogeneity within the country segment, and (c) it overlooks the existence of homogeneous consumer segments that might exist across national boundaries. With the growth of regionalism within Europe, the second assumption becomes more and more a limiting factor. In fact, with the elimination of country borders more European firms are defining their geographic market zones by reference to regions and not to countries.

Selling to universal segments across countries

As discussed in Chapter 2, several trends are influencing consumption behaviour on a global scale and many consumer products are becoming more widely accepted globally, such as consumer electronics, automobiles, fashion, home appliances, food products, beverages and services. Many of these products respond to needs and wants that cut across national boundaries.

Thus, even if product needs overall vary among countries, there may be a segment of the market with identical needs in every country. The challenge facing international firms is to identify these *'universal' segments* and reach them with marketing programmes that meet the common needs of these potential buyers. These universal segments are most likely to be high-end consumers, sport professionals, executives of multinational companies or, in general, sophisticated users, because these groups tend to be the most mobile and therefore the most likely to be exposed to extensive international contacts and experiences.

> A growing market segment on a global scale is composed of consumers aspiring to an 'élite lifestyle'. This élite, in Tokyo, New York, Paris, London, Hong Kong, Rio de Janeiro, and so on, is the target of brands that fit the image of exclusivity like Mercedes, Gucci, Hermès, American Express, Gold Card, Chivas, Godiva, and so on.

Such high-end brands can be targeted internationally to this universal segment in exactly the same way they are currently positioned in their respective home market. This international segmentation strategy is illustrated in Figure 6.14. The size of universal segments can be small in each country. What is attractive is the cumulative volume. For example, Godiva pralines are present in more than 20 different countries all over the world, sometimes with modest market shares. It is nevertheless the world's leading chocolate maker.

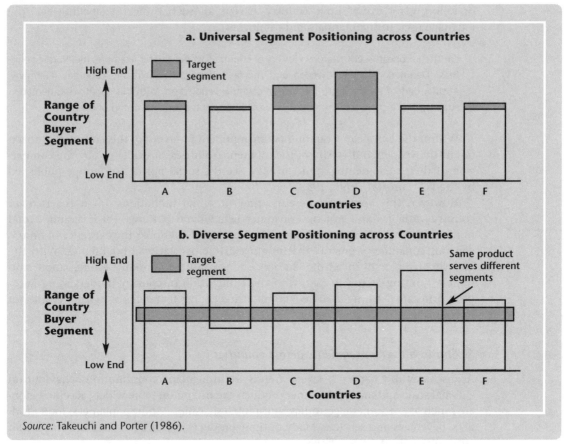

Source: Takeuchi and Porter (1986).

Figure 6.14   International segmentation: two different market positioning strategies

Targeting diverse segments across countries

Even if product needs vary among countries, the same product can sometimes be sold in each country but in different segments, by adopting different market positioning based on non-product variables such as distributive networks, advertising and pricing. This approach is illustrated in Figure 6.14 (see also Exhibit 6.6).

> The positioning adopted for the Canon AE-1 provides a good example of this international segmentation approach. The AE-1 was targeted towards young replacement buyers in Japan, upscale first-time buyers of 35-mm single-lens reflex cameras in the USA, and older and more technologically sophisticated replacement buyers in Germany. Three different marketing programmes were developed for Japan, the USA and Europe (Takeuchi and Porter, 1986, p. 139).

This approach requires important adaptations of communication and selling strategies which contribute to increasing costs or at least to preventing cost decreases as a consequence of standardisation.

Of the three segmentation approaches, universal segmentation is the most innovative and also most likely to give the firm a significant competitive advantage, because product and communication can be standardised and transferred among countries (see Figure 6.15 as an example). This gives the brand a reputation and a coherence in image and positioning which is internationally reinforced. The diverse segmentation approach has the merit of taking into consideration differences in consumer behaviour among countries and of introducing adaptations to accommodate these differences. On the other hand, because of these country-to-country adaptations, the brand image in each country will probably be different.

The case of universal segments

The global approach in segmenting world markets looks for similarities between markets. The traditional international approach is multidomestic, that is it tends to ignore similarities. The global approach actively seeks homogeneity in product, image, marketing and advertising message, while the multidomestic approach maintains unnecessary differences from market to market. The goal, however, is not to have a uniform product line worldwide. Rather the goal is to have a product line that is as standardised as possible, while recognising that allowances for some local conditions are both necessary and desirable.

Exhibit 6.6

The Case of Black & Decker

The case of Black & Decker provides a good illustration. Black & Decker is established in 50 countries and manufactures in 25 plants, 16 of which are outside the USA. It has a very high level of brand awareness worldwide, sometimes in the 80–90 per cent range. For Black & Decker the potential economies of scale and cost savings of globalisation were considerable. The challenges to be overcome were the following:

■ Different countries have different safety and industry standards that make complete standardisation impossible.
■ European and American consumers have very different responses to product design and even to colours.
■ Consumers use the products in different ways in different countries. For example, Europeans are more power-oriented in their electric tools than Americans.

As a consequence of this diversity, the multidomestic organisation approach produced staggering product proliferation. The company had hundreds of products worldwide and relatively few interchangeable among countries. As a result of the globalisation approach implemented between 1980 and 1990, Black & Decker has developed global products. The rule now is that any new product must be designed for a world market. People within the organisation are expected to think 'world product' first; anything else has to be justified.

Source: Farley (1986, p. 69).

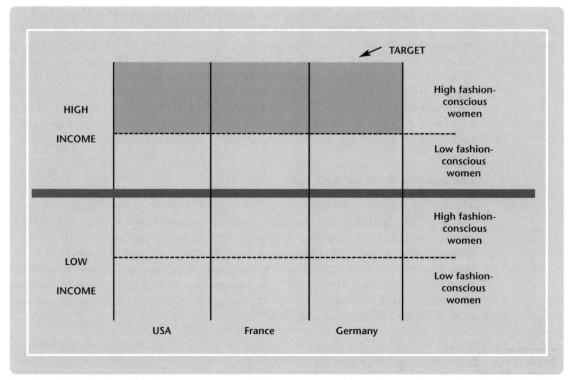

Figure 6.15   Example of a transnational segment: the high fashion market

Trade-off between standardisation and customisation

In the great majority of market situations, some degree of adaptation will be necessary. The essence of international segmentation can be summarised as follows: *think of global similarities and adapt to local differences*. This perspective should help management to determine similarities across national boundaries while assessing within-country differences. The different strategies susceptible to adoption, depending on the diversity of expectations and cultural background, are presented in Table 6.8 Three types of product policy can be considered:

- *Universal Product*: the physical product sold in each country is identical except for labelling and for the language used in the manuals.

- *Modified Product*: the core product is the same, but some modifications are adopted, such as voltage, colour, size or accessories, to accommodate government regulations or to reflect local differences in taste, buying habits, climate, and so on.

- *Country-tailored Product*: the physical product is substantially tailored to each country or group of countries.

The financial and cost implications of these alternative product policies are, of course, particularly important.

Table 6.8   Strategies of international segmentation

| | Expectations of segments | | | | |
| Global marketing strategies | Homogeneous | | Similar | | Different |
	Same Culture	Different Culture	Same Culture	Different Culture	
1. Unchanged product and operational marketing	1	–	–	–	–
2. Unchanged product and adapted operational marketing	–	2	2	2	–
3. Adapted product and operational marketing	–	–	–	3	3
4. New product and specific operational marketing	–	–	–	–	4

Source: Blanche (1987).

Establishing a world brand

Every product does not have the same global potential, and some products may be easier than others to develop as world brands. Several brands are on the market that are recognised as world brands: Coca-Cola, Marlboro, Kodak, Honda, Mercedes, Heineken, Swatch, Canon, Gucci, British Airways, Perrier, Black & Decker, Hertz, Benetton, McDonald's, Godiva and many others. It is worth noting that the popularity of these brands is independent of the attitude towards their country of origin.

In reality, the global potential of a product is closely linked to the universality of the benefit sought. To the extent that a product is a proven success in meeting the needs of a particular group of buyers in a given country, it is logical to expect a similar success with the same group of people in another country, provided of course the product is adapted to local consuming habits or regulations. In other words, as suggested by Quelch and Hoff (1986), the driving factor in moving towards global marketing should be 'the efficient worldwide use of good marketing ideas rather than scale economies from standardisation'.

The closer the product to the *high-tech/high-touch poles*, the more universal it is. These two product categories have in common the fact of (a) being high-involvement products and of (b) sharing a common language (Domzal and Unger, 1987, p. 28):

● *High-tech products* appeal to highly specialised buyers who share a common technical language and symbols. This is the case among computer users, tennis players and musicians, who all understand the technical aspects of the products. This is true for heavy machinery, computer hardware and financial services, but also for personal computers, video equipment, skiing equipment, and so on. The mere existence of a common 'shop talk' facilitates communication and increases the chance of success as global brands.

● *High-touch products* are more image-oriented than features-oriented products, but they respond to universal themes or needs, such as romance, wealth, heroism, play, and so on. Many products like perfume, fashion, jewellery and watches are sold on these themes.

For these two product categories, buyers all over the world are using and understanding the same language and the same symbols. Worldwide brand standardisation appears most feasible when products approach either end of the high-tech/high-touch spectrum (Domzal and Unger, 1987, p. 27).

Chapter summary

In a market-oriented company, the target market is identified in the buyer's perspective, that is by reference to the 'solution' sought by the customer and not in technical terms. Given the diversity of buyers' expectations, the choice of a target market implies the partitioning of the total market into subgroups of potential customers with similar needs and behavioural characteristics. A first level of market segmentation, called macro-segmentation, splits the market by reference to three criteria: (a) solutions or functions performed, (b) groups of buyers and (c) technologies. A key output of this exercise is a segmentation grid, which can help to decide on the market coverage strategy, and which can also be used as an instrument to discover new potential segments. The objective of micro-segmentation is to analyse the diversity of potential customer profiles in a more detailed way within each previously identified macro-segment. Four micro-segmentation methods exist which each have their own merits and weaknesses: socio-demographic, benefit, lifestyle and behavioural segmentation. Different market coverage strategies can be considered: undifferentiated or standardised marketing, differentiated or focused marketing. To be effective, a segmentation strategy must meet four criteria: differential response, adequate size, measurability and accessibility. Having selected one or several target segment(s), the next step is to decide upon a positioning strategy for each segment, which will be communicated to the target group. International segmentation is a key issue in global marketing. The objective is to identify supranational or universal segments that can be reached with a standardised marketing programme.

QUESTIONS AND PROBLEMS

1. Use the macro-segmentation method based on the three criteria 'function/buyers/technologies' in one of the following industrial sectors: paint, fax, banking services, medical imaging. In each case, define the product-markets, the market and the industry.

2. A European importer of a Japanese camera wishes to have a benefit segmentation analysis of the European market. Construct a segmentation grid that seems appropriate and propose a procedure to collect the required market data to verify the value of the proposed segmentation scheme.

3. In a survey conducted in the photo developing market, the following data have been collected from a representative sample of amateur photographers:

Segment	Quality	Price	Convenience	Speed	Return	Diverse
1	6.80	5.83	5.83	5.50	5.66	3.96
2	6.71	4.76	3.38	4.00	4.66	3.80
3	4.60	6.60	6.20	5.80	3.40	2.60
4	6.47	6.28	5.42	3.66	2.80	2.57
5	6.90	3.45	5.63	4.45	3.54	3.36

Scores are mean values on a 7-point scale where 1 meant 'not important' and 7 meant 'extremely important'.
Source: Sheth *et al.*, (1999, p. 452).

Analyse these data and describe the type of benefit package sought by different groups of buyers.

4. Pick two magazines targeting a specific socio-demographic group (for example, teenagers, seniors, housewives or an ethnic group). Select three or four advertisements and try to identify the positioning sought by the advertisers.

5. In affluent societies, consumers are increasingly seeking solutions adapted to their specific problems. For the firm the question is to know how far to go in segmenting a market. Analyse the factors in favour of a fine market segmentation strategy (hyper-segmentation) and the arguments which, in contrast, suggest a standardised strategy (counter-segmentation).

6. In affluent societies, one observes a growing fragmentation of markets, buyers requesting more and more products adapted to their specific needs. How can we reconcile this fact with the objectives of global marketing which emphasise a strategy of standardisation of products and brands across the entire world?

Bibliography

Abell, D.F. (1980) *Defining the Business: The Starting Point of Strategic Planning*, Englewood Cliffs NJ, Prentice Hall.

Blanche, B. (1987) Le marketing global: paradoxe, fantasme ou objectif pour demain?, *Revue Française du Marketing*, No. 114.

Chamberlin, E.H. (1950) *The Theory of Monopolistic Competition*, Cambridge MA, Harvard University Press.

Day, G.S. (1984) *Strategic Market Planning*, St Paul, West Publishing.

Day, G.S. (1990) *Market-driven Strategy*, New York, The Free Press.

Dalrymple, D.J. and Parsons, L.J. (1976) *Marketing Management: Text and Cases*, New York, John Wiley & Sons.

Deutsch, C.H. (1997) A New High-Tech Code: From Widgets to Service, *International Herald Tribune*.

Domzal, T. and Unger, L.S. (1987) Emerging Positioning Strategies in Global Marketing, *The Journal of Consumer Marketing*, **4**(4): 23–40.

Eurostat (1991, 1996) *A Social Portrait of Europe*, Brussels, European Commission.

Farley, L.J. (1986) Going Global: Choices and Challenges, *The Journal of Consumer Marketing*, **3**(1): 67–70.

Gilmore, J.H. and Pine, B.J. (1997) The Four Faces of Mass Customization, *Harvard Business Review*, **75**(1): 91–101.

Green, P.E. and Wind, Y. (1974) Some Conceptual, Measurement and Analytical Problems in Lifestyle Research, in: Wells, W.D. (ed.) *Life Style and Psychographics*, Chicago IL, American Marketing Association.

Green, P.E. and Krieger, A.M. (1991) Segmenting Markets with Conjoint Analysis, *Journal of Marketing*, **55**, October, pp. 20–31.

Haley, R.I. (1968) Benefit Segmentation: A Decision Oriented Tool, *Journal of Marketing Research*, **32**, July, pp. 30–5.

Hassan, S.S. and Katsanis, L.P. (1991) Identification of Global Customer Segments, *Journal of International Consumer Marketing*, **3**(2): 11–29.

Hasson, L. (1995) Monitoring Social Change, *Journal of the Market Research Society*, No. 37, pp. 69–80.

Hopkins, D.S. (1982) *The Marketing Plan*, New York, The Conference Board.

Lambin, J.J. and Hiller, T.B. (1990) Volvo Trucks Europe, in: Kerin, R.A. and Peterson, R.A. (eds) (1993) *Strategic Marketing Problems*, Boston MA, Allyn & Bacon.

Lampel, J. and Mintzberg, H. (1997) *Customizing Customization*, Sloan Management Review, **36**(4): 21–30.

Plummer, J.T. (1974) The Concept and Application of Life Style Segmentation, *Journal of Marketing*, **38**, January, pp. 33–6.

Porter, M. (1985) *Competitive Advantage*, New York, The Free Press.

Quelch, J. and Hoff, E.G. (1986) Customizing Global Marketing, *Harvard Business Review*, **64**, May–June, pp. 59–68.

Ries, A and Trout, J. (1981) *Positioning: The Battle for your Mind*, New York, McGraw-Hill.

Roisin, J. (1988) *Etude du concept d'une revue littéraire: une application de l'analyse conjointe*, Louvain-la-Neuve, IAG.

Schnaars, S.P. (1998) *Marketing Strategy: Customers and Competition*, 2nd edn, New York, The Free Press.

Shapiro, B.P. and Bonona, T.V. (1983) *Segmenting Industrial Markets*, Lexington MA, Lexington Books.

Sheth, J., Mittal, B. and Newman, B.I. (1999) *Customer Behavior, Consumer Behavior and Beyond*, Fort Worth, Dryden Press.

Simon, H. (1996) *Hidden Champions*, Boston MA, Harvard Business School Press.

Smith, W.R. (1956) Product Differentiation and Market Segmentation as Alternative Strategies, *Journal of Marketing*, **21**, July, pp. 3–8.

Takeuchi, H. and Porter, M.E. (1986) Three Roles of International Marketing in Global Industries, in: Porter, M.E. (ed.), (1987) *Competition in Global Industries*, Boston MA, Harvard Business School Press.

Tarondeau, J.C. (1982) Sortir du dilemme flexibilité-productivité, *Harvard-l'Expansion*, Spring, pp. 25–35.

Valette-Florence, P. (1986) Les démarches de styles de vie: concepts, champs d'investigation et problèmes actuels, *Recherche et Applications en Marketing*, **1**(1–2).

Valette-Florence, P. (1988) Analyse structurelle comparative des composantes des systèmes de valeurs selon Kahle et Rokeach, *Recherche et Applications en Marketing*, **3**(1): 15–34.

Wells, W. (1974) *Life Style and Psychographics*, Chicago, American Marketing Association.

Wells, W.D. and Tigert, D.J. (1971) Activities, Interests and Opinions, *Journal of Advertising Research*, **35**: pp. 27–34.

Wind, J.Y. (1982) *Product Policy: Concepts, Methods and Strategy*, Reading MA, Addison-Wesley.

Winkler, A.R. (1991) Euro-styles in Panel Analyses, in: *Europanel Marketing Bulletin*, Europanel Coordination Center, Nyon Switzerland.

Yankelovich, D. (1964) New Criteria for Market Segmentation, *Harvard Business Review*, March–April, pp. 83–90.

Yorke, D.A. (1982) The Definition of Market Segments for Banking Services, *European Journal of Marketing*, **16**(3): 14–22.

chapter seven

Market attractiveness analysis

The output of a segmentation analysis takes the form of a segmentation grid displaying the different segments or product markets, which belong to the reference market. The next task is to assess the business opportunity of each of these segments in order to decide which segment(s) to target. *Attractiveness analysis* has the objective of measuring and forecasting the size, life cycle and profit potential of each segment or product market. Measuring the sales potential of a market is the responsibility of strategic marketing. These market projections will then be used by general management to calibrate investments and production capacity. Market potential forecasting and measurement is a key input for these decisions. The objective of this chapter is to review the major concepts of demand analysis and to describe briefly the main sales forecasting methods.

Chapter learning objectives

When you have read this chapter, you should be able to:

1. describe the major concepts of demand analysis and their structure;

2. explain the structure of demand for consumer and industrial goods, for durable and non-durable goods and for services;

3. explain how to detect growth opportunities in a given market through gap analysis;

4. describe the product life cycle (PLC) model and its strategic implications at each phase of the PLC;

5. discuss the main demand forecasting methods, their respective merits and conditions for application.

● Basic Concepts in Demand Analysis

At its simplest level, the demand for a product or service is the quantity sold. At the outset it is important to distinguish clearly between two levels of demand: primary demand or total market demand, and company demand (also called selective demand).

> The primary demand for a particular product is the total sales volume bought by a defined customer group, in a defined geographic area, in a defined time period, and in a defined economic and competitive environment.

The term *product category need*, or *category need* is also commonly used. Thus, primary demand measurement implies prior definition of the segment or product market. Also, it is a function of both environmental and of total industry marketing efforts.

> Company demand is the company or brand's share of primary demand.

It, too, is a *response function*. Its determinants are environmental factors and company (or brand) marketing factors. These demand determinants fall into two categories: environmental factors which are outside the control of the firm and the factors under control, that is the marketing mix or the total marketing pressure exerted by the firm to support its brand.

The notion of market potential

Market potential represents the upper limit of demand in a defined period of time. The relationship between primary demand and total industry marketing efforts is depicted in Figure 7.1(a) The response function is S-shaped with total demand on the vertical axis and total marketing efforts on the horizontal axis. The curve of Figure 7.1(a) is defined for a constant macro-environment.

Typically, the relationship is not linear. Some minimum level of demand (Q_0) will occur at zero marketing effort; as the total marketing pressure on the market increases, sales also increase, but at a decreasing rate. Beyond a certain level of marketing intensity, primary demand reaches an upper limit (Q_m) called the saturation level or the *current market potential*.

The level of primary demand is influenced not only by the total marketing efforts made the firms operating in the segment, but also by environmental factors. A change in the socio-economic environment will move the response curve vertically, as illustrated in Figure 7.1(b). A distinction must be made, therefore, between a movement along the response curve and a shift of the response curve itself.

> Two scenarios (or market demand functions) are represented in Figure 7.1(b): a scenario of prosperity and a scenario of recession. Under the prosperity scenario, the forecast or expected level of total sales is $E(Q)$, assuming the level M for total industry marketing effort. Now, if the recession scenario prevails, to achieve the same sales volume, total marketing effort should be at the level M' and not M.

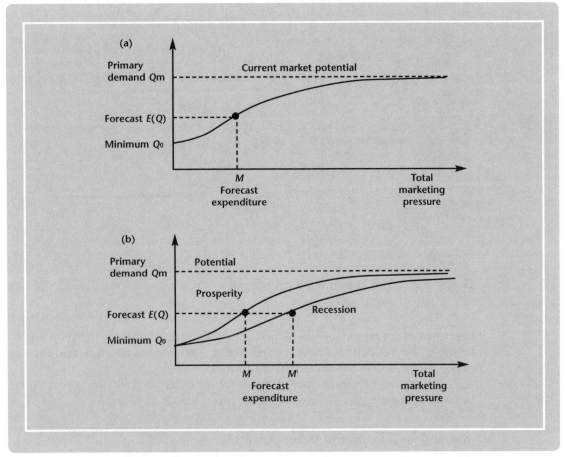

Figure 7.1   The relationship between primary demand and total marketing intensity

Firms cannot do much about the prevailing market scenario, except to try to anticipate future environmental conditions as best as possible. In the turbulent environment of the 1990s this is a particularly difficult task and many firms are systematically developing alternative scenarios to increase their capacity to react quickly to a sudden crisis in the environment.

In Figure 7.1(b), the current market potential corresponds to the saturation level Q_m. This level is not static, however. It evolves over time under the influence of diffusion and contagion effects, and tends towards its upper limit, which is the absolute market potential.

Expansible versus non-expansible primary demand

The gap between the minimum (or present) level of primary demand and its maximum level reflects the size of the market opportunity. In the first part of the curve, demand is said to be *expansible*, that is the level of primary demand is easily affected by the size and intensity of total marketing efforts. Primary demand elasticity is high and each firm contributes to the development of the total market. In the

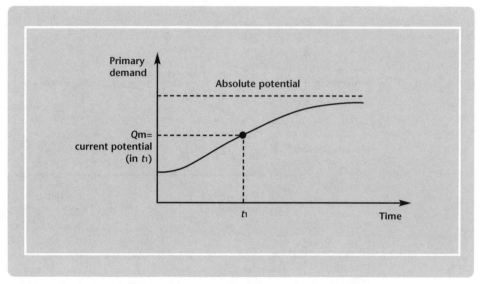

Figure 7.2   The absolute market potential

upper part of the response curve, demand becomes inelastic and the market is said to be *non-expansible*. Further increase in marketing intensity has no impact on the size of the market, which has reached its maturity stage.

Thus, in a non-expansible market the size of the market is fixed. Any sales increase in favour of a particular firm necessarily implies a market share gain.

Absolute versus current market potential

A potential market may develop over a certain period, not only because of economic factors but also through the influence of cultural and social factors, which tend to stimulate consumer habits. For instance, environmental concern is growing and this may encourage the demand for anti-pollution equipment. Similarly, the use of computers in small and medium-sized companies has grown under the influence of diffusion, learning and contagion phenomena, independently of the total marketing efforts made by the companies operating in the sector. Thus, there is a difference between the *current market potential* and the *absolute market potential*:

Current market potential is the limit approached by primary demand as total industry marketing efforts tend towards infinity, in a given environment and in a given time period.

Absolute market potential corresponds to the total sales level (in volume or value) that would be observed if every potential user consumed the product at the optimum frequency rate and at the full rate per use occasion.

Thus, the absolute market potential (AMP) defines the upper limit of the market size under the somewhat artificial assumption of optimum market coverage. The concept is useful, however, for assessing the size of a business opportunity and for estimating the growth opportunity in a particular market given the present level of demand. Three assumptions are made concerning usage of the product in order to derive the absolute market potential:

- Everyone who could reasonably be expected to use the product is using it.
- Everyone who is using it is using it on every use occasion.
- Every time the product is used, it is used to the fullest extent possible (that is full dosage, full serving, and so on).

An example of estimation of absolute market potential is presented in Exhibit 7.1.

The current market potential is time-dependent, as illustrated in Figure 7.2. Its evolution over time is caused by external factors such as change in consumption habits, cultural values, disposable income, technological changes, level of prices, government regulations, and so on. The firm has no direct control over these factors, yet they have a decisive influence on the development of the market. Occasionally, firms are indirectly able to influence these external causes (through lobbying, for instance), but their power is limited. Most of the firm's efforts, therefore, are directed towards the anticipation of changes in the environment.

The determinants of demand

As already underlined, market demand is not a fixed number but a function which relates the level of sales to its causes, termed *demand determinants*. The causes of sales are twofold: external or uncontrollable causes and internal or controllable causes.

Exhibit 7.1

Estimating Industry Absolute Market Potential for Mouthwash

- **Number of Potential Users:**
    - Assume that everyone 5 years and older is a potential user.
    - Approximately 90 per cent of the US population.
    - US population: 222 million.
    - Number of potential users: 90 per cent (222 m) = 200 million.
- **Number of Use Occasions per Year:**
    - Assume that each potential user can use mouthwash twice a day.
    - Number of use occasion per year:
        200 million people x 2/day x 365 days
        = 146 billion use occasions per year.
- **Full Use on Each Occasion:**
    - Assume that full use (or full dosage) is 1 oz per use.
    - The absolute market potential is therefore: 146 billion oz per year.
    - An average of 16 oz per bottle.
    - Result: 9125 billion bottles per year.

Source: Weber (1976, p. 66).

As indicated in Chapter 1, the *controllable factors* fall into four basic categories, popularly known as the 'four Ps' (McCarthy, 1960) or the marketing mix: product, place, price and promotion. This set of marketing factors constitutes the total offering of the firm to the buyers in hopes of meeting their needs at a profit. They are the main determinants of company demand.

Let us note that this traditional manner to define the marketing action variables is not really customer-oriented but rather company-oriented. As already discussed in Chapter 6 (see Exhibit 6.2), viewed from the customer's perspective, the four Ps can be redefined in the following way:

● *Product*: a solution to a problem and the package of benefits that the product represents.

● *Place*: a convenient access to the solution sought by the buyer.

● *Price*: all the costs, including price, borne by the buyer to acquire the solution sought.

● *Advertising*: the messages and signals communicated about the solutions available and about their distinctive qualities.

● *Selling*: the negotiation process or the dialogue organised with the potential buyer in his search for the appropriate solution to his (or her) problem.

As for the *uncontrollable factors*, they are the other participants or actors to be dealt with in the marketplace, which the firm does not control. As shown in Chapter 2, in the general case, there are four types of market participants active in the market.

● The firm's *end-customers* (buyer, user or payer) with their changing needs and expectations, that have to be met with an appropriate and attractive marketing programme.

● The *distributors*, or intermediate customers (wholesalers, retailers, industrial distributors), with their own constraints and objectives in the distribution channel, but who cannot be bypassed by the firm.

● The *competitors* targeting the same customers in the reference market who cannot be ignored and who have to be outperformed by the firm.

● The *macro-marketing environment*, that is the economic, social political and ecological factors, which influence the level of primary demand in the reference market and which have to be anticipated.

To these traditional market participants, in some markets one must add the *prescribers*, that is those market actors who recommend the use of some products.

In the home building market, for instance, architects are important prescribers for many products like heating systems, kitchen equipment, windows, and so on. Similarly, in the pharmaceutical market doctors have a strong influence in the adoption of a new drug. Their roles cannot be ignored and specific communication actions must be undertaken to inform them and to gain their support.

It is up to the market analyst to identify and to understand as best as possible the role and the influence of these external factors, in order to adapt the marketing mix to account for them.

● Structure of Primary Demand

Demand analysis, measurement and forecast are the primary responsibility of market research. The goal is to estimate in quantitative terms the size of the market potential and the current level of demand, and to formulate forecasts of its future development over a number of years. Aggregate estimates of total demand are rarely available and the role of the market analyst is to identify and estimate the key components of market potential. The structure of demand is different for consumer products (durable or non-durable goods), for industrial goods and for services.

Demand for consumer goods

Demand estimates are usually based on two factors: the number of potential users (n) and the rate of purchase (q). Thus, we have

$$Q = n \cdot q$$

where Q designates total demand in units. Similarly, total sales revenue will be given by

$$R = n \cdot Q \cdot P$$

where R denotes total sales revenue and P the average price per unit. The empirical measurement of these basic concepts raises different issues depending on the type of product category. We will examine the demand structure for the main product categories.

Demand for non-durable consumer products

If the consumer good is *not linked to the use of a durable good*, total demand can be estimated in the following way:

- Number of potential consuming units.
- Proportion of customers using the product (market occupation rate).
- Size or frequency of purchases (market penetration rate).

The distinction between *occupation rate* and *penetration rate* is important to identify the priority objectives in a market development strategy: increase the number of users or increase the average quantity used per user.

The absolute market potential is determined by assuming a 100 per cent occupation rate and the optimum penetration per use occasion. The current level of primary demand implies data on current purchasing behaviour. These data can sometimes be obtained from trade associations, from government publications or through primary market research. A major problem in measuring current demand is the degree to which purchase rates vary among different buyer groups. Only primary sources of market research, such as consumer panels, can provide this type of data.

If the consumer good is *linked to the use of a durable good* (soap and washing machines, for instance), the equipment rate of households must also be considered, in addition to the utilisation rate of the equipment. We thus have:

- Number of potential consuming units.
- Household rate of equipment.
- Equipment utilisation rate.
- Consumption rate per use occasion.

Here also, the absolute market potential can be determined assuming a 100 per cent equipment rate, an average utilisation rate and an average consumption rate which is technically defined in most cases. As for the estimation of the level of current market demand, primary market research data are necessary.

Demand for durable consumer goods

In this case, a distinction must be made between first equipment demand and replacement demand. The components of *first equipment demand* are:

- The number of effective users and rate of increase of their equipment rate.
- The number of new users and equipment rate of these new using units.

The diffusion rate is an important factor in the growth of first equipment demand within the target population. The analysis of penetration curves for similar products is very useful this respect.

Replacement demand is more complex to estimate. The following components of replacement demand must be identified and estimated:

- Size of the current population.
- Age distribution of the current population.
- Service life of the equipment (technical, economic or fashion obsolescence).
- Scrappage rate.
- Substitution effect (new technologies).
- Mortality rate of users.

Replacement demand is directly dependent on the rate at which owners scrap a product because of wearing out or obsolescence. Market analysts can estimate *scrappage rates* either by examining the technical service life of a product or the historical long-term rate of voluntary scrappage.

If historical data on scrappage rates can be calculated from a sample of users, market analysts can use actuarial methods to estimate the replacement potential for products of different ages.

Replacement demand depends directly on the size of the current population and on the service life of the durable good. The replacement rate is not necessarily identical to the scrappage rate. Scrappage rate designates the fraction of the stock of existing durable goods, which is sent to breakage, or in other words which disappears. A durable good can be obsolete because its economic performance has become inferior or simply because it is out of fashion in the eyes of the users.

> ### Exhibit 7.2
>
> ## Estimating Replacement Demand: an Example
>
> By way of an example let us look at the car market. Let us assume that the average technical service life is around 10 to 11 years. If the expectation is to have a service life of 12.5 years, the yearly scrappage rate will be around 8 per cent, which represents a level of replacement demand of 1.7 million cars, given the current size of the car population. If, in contrast, the expected service life were only 9 years, the scrappage rate would be 11.1 per cent with a level of replacement demand of 2.1 million.

In general, one tends to consider that scrappage rates are proportional to the length of the physical life cycle of the products of a given product category. In other words, if the average duration is 12 years, the annual scrappage rate should in theory be equal to its reciprocal, that is, 8.3 per cent.

The predictions made about the technical service life of a durable good will have a direct impact on the expected level of primary demand in the years to come.

Some of the data required to estimate the size of primary demand can be derived from times series sales data, namely the size of the population and its age distribution. The age distribution can also be estimated through sampling of car owners, for instance, when they decide to replace their old equipment. The estimated replacement rates do not permit us to identify, however, the type of obsolescence responsible for the replacement decision. A technically well-functioning product can be replaced for economic reasons, for instance, if the operating costs of newly developed products are sharply reduced. It can also be replaced for psychological reasons when the user is sensitive to the design of the new models. Finally, at the time of the replacement decision, the buyer can also decide to switch to another product category performing the same core function.

> Significant technical progress has been made in the market of central heating systems, with low temperature boilers, which are much more economical in terms of fuel consumption. This innovation has accelerated the replacement rate of existing boilers. In parallel, other technologies have also improved their technical performance, like heat pumps which, for many applications, were substituted for traditional fuel heating systems.

In most Western economies' markets, household equipment rates are very high and close to the maximum and therefore the largest share of sales of durable goods corresponds to a replacement decision.

The demand for consumer services

The demand for services can be estimated as described above for consumer goods. It depends on the number of potential consumers and on the frequency rate of use of the service. Services have, however, a certain number of characteristics that greatly impact the marketing management of them. These characteristics are due to their intangible and perishable nature and to the fact that their production implies direct contact with the service person or organisation. The managerial implications of these characteristics are significant (Shostack, 1977; Berry, 1980).

Classification of services

There are a large variety of services and several attempts have been made to classify them in a meaningful way. One classification system is based on the evolution of services in five categories:

1. *Unskilled personal services.* This category includes housekeeping, janitorial work, street cleaning, and so on as observed in a traditional society.

2. *Skilled personal services.* These emerged as society became more industrialised ñ as it passed out of the subsistence stage, as needs arose for government services, repair businesses, and retail/wholesale specialists.

3. *Professional services.* As products became more plentiful, highly skilled specialists appeared, such as lawyers, accountants, consultants and marketing researchers.

4. *Mass consumer services.* Discretionary income gave rise to any number of consumer service industries that flourished because of scale effects. These include national and international transport, lodging, fast food, car rental and entertainment companies.

5. *High-tech business services.* The growth in the use of sophisticated technologies has created a need for new services as well as more efficient older ones. Thus, in recent years, we have seen a rapid growth in repair services relating to information processing, telecommunications and other electronic products.

Services can also be classified by whether they are *equipment or people-based*, by the *extent of customer contact*, by a *public or private* organisation.

Intangibility of services

Services are *immaterial*. They exist only once produced and consumed. They cannot be inspected before purchase and the selling activity must necessarily precede the production activity. As the consumer goods firm, the service firm is selling a *promise of satisfaction*. But contrary to a consumer good, the service sold has no physical support, except the organisational system of the service firm when visible to the customer. The service cannot be seen, touched, smelled, heard or tasted prior to the purchase, except when service firms have tangible assets or physical structures (buildings, aircraft, hotel facilities, and so on) that are used to perform the service.

Thus, from the buyer's point of view the uncertainty is much larger and the communication role of the firm is to reduce that uncertainty by providing physical evidence, signs, symbols or indicators of quality. On this topic, see Levitt (1965) and Zeithmal *et al.* (1990).

Perishability of services

Since services are intangible, they cannot be stored. The service firm has a service production capacity, which can be used only when demand is expressed. Demand peaks cannot be accommodated and the potential business is lost.

> For example, if an airliner takes off with 20 empty seats, the revenue that these 20 seats could have produced is lost forever. In contrast, if a pair of jeans does not sell today, a retailer can store it and sell it at a later time.

Perishability can cause the reverse to occur. Demand can be greater than supply. In this situation, for example, the airline does not have enough seats for everyone. Customers are left at the gate and the sale is lost.

Thus, a key challenge for service firms is to better synchronise supply and demand, by adjusting production capacity, that is by reshaping supply, but also by reshaping demand through pricing incentives and promotions.

Inseparability of services

Services are produced and consumed at the same time, and the customer participates in the process of service production. The implication is twofold here. First, the service provider necessarily has a direct contact with the customer and is part of the service. There is a large human component involved in performing services. Thus, standardisation is difficult because of the personalised nature of services. Second, the client participates in the production process and the service provider–customer interaction can also affect the quality of the service.

An implication of these characteristics is the difficulty of maintaining a constant level of quality of the services. Total quality control of services is a major issue for the service firm. The components of service quality are described in Chapter 10.

Variability of service quality

A distinction is usually made between *search quality* goods or services that can be evaluated prior to purchase, *experience quality* goods that can be evaluated only after purchase and *credence quality* goods and services difficult to evaluate even after the purchase. Services tend to be high in experience and credence qualities. It is particularly the case for the services provided by consultant, lawyers, doctors, accountants, advertising agencies, and so on.

In discussing service quality, four characteristics of services should be kept in mind:

● Service quality is more difficult for the consumer to evaluate than the quality of goods, because services tend to be high in *experience* and *credence* qualities.

● Service quality is based on consumers' perception, not only of the outcome of the service, but also on their evaluation of the process by which the service is performed.

● Service quality perception results from a comparison of what the consumer expected prior to the service and the perceived level of the service received. Different individuals can have different perceptions and different prior expectations.

⬤ A *human factor* is heavily involved in the process of service delivery and therefore a stable and fully standardised level of quality is more difficult to achieve. Different individuals will perform differently in delivering the same service and the same service provider can have a different performance level from one time to another.

To go further on the issue of service quality measurement see Zeithmal *et al.* (1990) and Berry (1999). For a good text on services marketing, see Kurtz and Clow (1998).

Implications for services management

These characteristics of the demand for services have direct implications on the management of services and firms must try to reconcile, (a) productivity constraints leading to standardisation and to the maximum use of information technology, (b) quality control objectives, leading to the development of personal interaction with customers, and finally (c) differentiation objectives. As illustrated in Figure 7.3, service delivery activities can be classified by reference to two main dimensions at two levels each: *labour intensity* of the service delivery activity and *degree of interaction and customisation*.

As shown in Figure 7.3, using these two dimensions, four types of service activities can be identified:

⬤ *Service factories.* Service businesses that have a relatively low labour intensity and a low degree of customer interaction, like airlines, trucking, hotels and resorts.

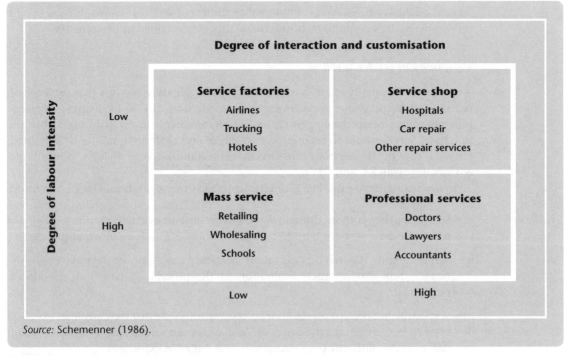

Source: Schemenner (1986).

Figure 7.3   The service process matrix

⬤ *Service shops*, where the degree of customer interaction or customisation increases. These service businesses still have a high degree of plant and equipment relative to labour, but they offer more interactions and customisation; hospitals, car repair garages and restaurants are examples of service shops.

⬤ *Mass service.* These businesses have a high degree of labour intensity but a rather low degree of interaction and customisation, such as retailing, schools, laundry, cleaning, and so on.

⬤ *Professional services.* When the degree of interaction with the customer increases and/or customisation of this service becomes the watchword, mass services give way to professional services: doctors, lawyers, accountants, architects are classic examples.

This classification of services is not necessarily fixed as service firms innovate or modify their service operations.

For example, with the advent of fast food, interaction and customisation for the consumer have been lowered dramatically, as has labour intensity. Fast food restaurants are moving to the service factory quadrant.

Similarly, in the retailing sectors, the expansion of catalogue stores, electronic commerce and warehouse stores has shifted the emphasis of traditional retailing operations towards a lower degree of labour intensity. The opposite evolution is also observed in retailing with the proliferation of boutiques within stores, where interaction and customisation are stressed. In this last example, the evolution is from the lower left quadrant to the lower right quadrant.

The demand for industrial goods

We have seen in Chapter 3 that industrial demand is actually *derived* from the consumer marketplace. Thus, industrial marketers must be cognisant of conditions in their own markets, but must also be aware of developments in the markets served by their customers and by their customers' customers. Of course, many industrial products are far removed from the consumer and the linkage is difficult to see. This separation becomes more apparent as the number of intermediate customers increases between a given manufacturer and the end-user. In other cases, the linkage is quite clear, such as the impact of car sales on the steel industry.

Thus, if consumers are not buying homes, autos, clothing, stereos, educational or medical services, there will be less need for lumber, steel, cotton, plastics, computer components and hospital forms. Consequently, industry will require less energy, fewer trucking services and not as many tools or machines. (Morris, 1988, p. 390)

The planning task can become quite complex when a manufacturer's output is used in a wide variety of applications.

The demand for industrial goods is structured differently according to whether they are consumable goods, industrial components or industrial equipment. The data needed for the evaluation of demand are practically identical to the data for consumer goods, with only few exceptions.

Exhibit 7.3

Estimating the Demand for a Consumable Industrial Product

The Cleanchem Company has developed a water treatment chemical for paper manufacturers. Total paper shipments in the Northeast region represent a value of $700 million. Data found in trade reports and information received from the local water utility show that paper mills use 0.01 gallons of water per dollar of shipment value. Cleanchem engineers recommend a minimum of 0.25 ounces of the water treatment chemical per gallon of water and 0.30 ounces per gallon of water to be optimal. The absolute market potential is estimated to range between 1,750,000 ounces ($700 million x 0.01 x 0.25) and 2,100,000 ounces. These estimates must be adjusted for the activity level of paper mills. (Morris 1988, p. 183)

The demand for industrial consumable goods

We have here products that are used by the industrial firm but not incorporated in the fabricated product. The components of demand are the following:

- Number of potential industrial users (by size).
- Proportion of effective users (by size).
- Level of activity per effective user.
- Usage rate per use occasion.

The usage rate is a technical norm easy to identify. The number of companies classified by number of employees, payroll, value of shipments, and so on can be obtained in the Census of Manufacturers. An example is presented in Exhibit 7.3.

The current proportion of effective users in this example is the major source of uncertainty.

The demand for industrial components

Industrial components are used in the product fabricated by the customer. Thus, their demand is directly related to the volume of production of the client company. The components of their demand are the following:

- Number of potential industrial users (by size).
- Proportion of effective users (by size).
- Quantity produced per effective user.
- Rate of usage per product.

Producers of car parts are a good example of a sector that responds to this type of demand. As illustrated in Figure 7.4, fluctuation in consumer demand for cars will eventually result in a variation of the demand for their components. Thus a careful observation of the evolution of demand for the end product is imperative for the producer of industrial components who wishes to predict his own demand.

The demand for industrial equipment

Here we have products such as industrial machines or computers that are necessary to the production activity. They are durable goods and thus the distinction between primary and replacement demand is important. *Primary equipment demand* is determined by the following factors:

● Number of companies equipped (by size).
● Increase of the production capacity.
● Number of new-user companies (by size).
● Production capacity.

Replacement demand is determined by the following factors:

● Size of the existing population.
● Age distribution and technology level of the population.
● Distribution of the product life spans.
● Rate of replacement.
● Effect of product substitution.
● Effect of reduction of production capacity.

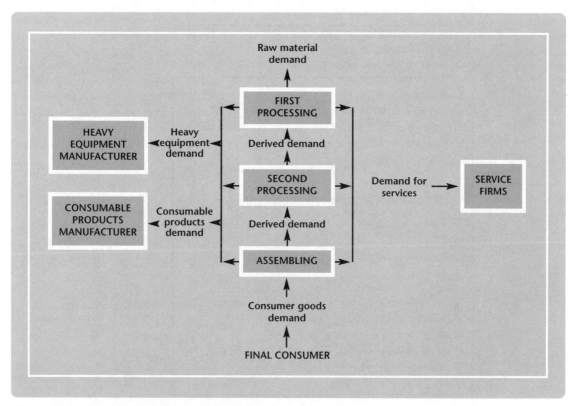

Figure 7.4   The derived demand for industrial equipment

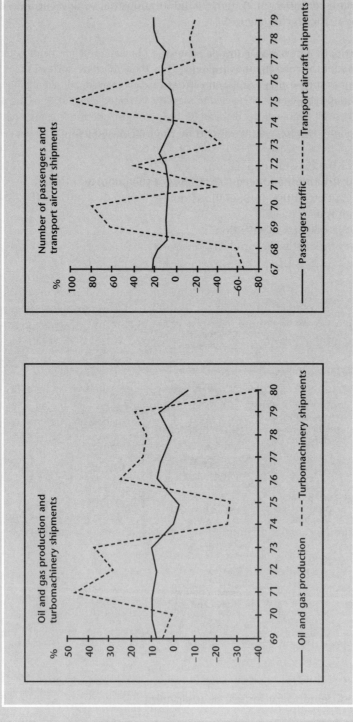

Source: Bishop *et al.* (1984).

Figure 7.5 Examples of volatile equipment demands

The acceleration effect

The demand for industrial equipment is directly related to the production capacity of the client companies, and thus even a small fluctuation in final demand can translate into a very large variation in the demand for industrial equipment. This phenomenon is known as the *acceleration effect*.

> For example, suppose that the life span of a population of machines is ten years. If the demand for the consumer goods produced by these machines increases by 10 per cent, 10 per cent of the existing population will need to be replaced, and an additional 10 per cent production capacity will be needed to meet the increased demand. Thus the demand for the machines will double. If the demand for the consumer goods decreases by 10 per cent, the required production capacity will only be 90 per cent, and thus the 10 per cent that fail will not need to be replaced. Thus the demand for the machines falls to 0.

The *volatility of the demand for industrial equipment* means that for accurate demand forecasting, companies must analyse both their own demand and the final demand of the companies they supply. The data in Figure 7.5 show evidence of an 'acceleration effect' in two different markets.

Marketing implications of industrial derived demand

In addition to the difficulty of forecasting sales, derived demand also has implications for operational marketing. The dynamic industrial firm may decide to target its selling efforts not only on the immediate customer but also towards *indirect customers* further down the production chain, as shown in Figure 7.6.

> Thus Recticel has advertised the benefits of its polyurethane foam to armchair and sofa distributors and to the general public as well. Its goals are twofold here: first to encourage end-users and distributors to place demands upon various furniture manufacturers to begin using the Recticel foam as a component in their production process; and second, to provide promotional efforts for furniture manufacturers currently using Recticel's product.

By focusing efforts further down the industrial chain, the industrial firm is adopting a *pull strategy* which complements more traditional selling efforts targeted at direct customers (*push strategy*). To limit their dependence on direct customers, dynamic industrial firms have to adopt a proactive marketing behaviour and to play an active role in demand stimulation at each level of the industrial chain.

Growth opportunity analysis

The gap between the current and the absolute level of primary demand is indicative of the rate of development or underdevelopment of a product market. The larger the gap, the greater the growth opportunity; conversely, the smaller the gap, the closer the market is to the saturation level.

Weber (1976) has developed a framework, called gap analysis, to analyse the gaps between absolute market potential and current company sales. Four growth opportunities are identified as shown in Figure 7.7: the usage gap, the distribution gap, the product line gap and the competitive gap. The *competitive gap* is due to sales of directly

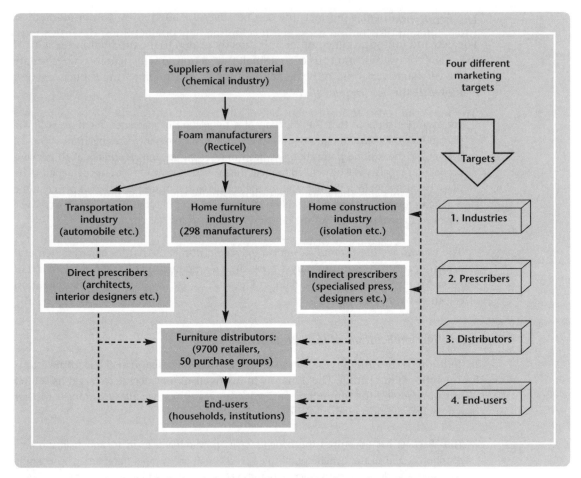

Figure 7.6   Example of derived demand: the market for polyurethane foam

competitive brands within the product market and also to substitute products. The other gaps present growth opportunities that will be briefly reviewed below.

Distribution gaps

The *distribution gap* is due to absence or inadequate distribution within the product market. Three types of distribution gap can be observed:

- The *coverage gap* exists when a firm does not distribute the relevant product line in all geographic regions desired.

- The *intensity gap* exists when a firm's product line is distributed in an inadequate number of outlets within a geographic region where the firm has distribution coverage.

- The *exposure gap* exists when a firm's product lines have poor or inadequate shelf space, location, displays, and so on within outlets where the firm does have distribution for the product.

Sales of a particular product line can be adversely affected by any or all of these three different distribution gaps. Before adopting new product lines, the firm should try to close these distribution gaps.

Usage gaps

The *usage gap* is due to insufficient use of the product. Three types of usage gap can be identified:

● The *non-user gap*, that is the customers who could potentially use the product but are not using it.
● The *light user gap*, that is the customers who use the product but do not use it on every use occasion.
● The *light usage gap*, that is the customers who use the product but by less than a full use on each use occasion.

A strategy aiming at closing these gaps will contribute to the development of primary demand and will therefore benefit all competing firms as well.

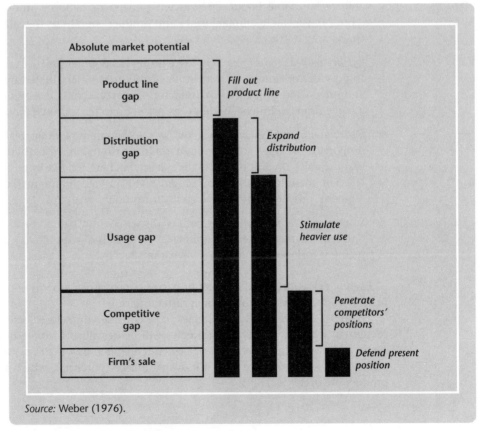

Source: Weber (1976).

Figure 7.7 Growth opportunity analysis

Product line gaps

The product line gap is caused by the lack of a full product line. Seven types of product line gaps could exist:

- *Size-related product line gaps*. Product 'size' can be defined along three dimensions: 'container size' for consumables like soft drinks or detergents, 'capacity' for durables like refrigerators or computers and 'power' for car engines or industrial machinery.

- *Options-related product line gaps*. Optional features can be offered by a firm desiring to cater to specific demands of individual customers. Cars serve as one good example. By offering a large number of options, car manufacturers can produce a large number of cars, each one in some way different from every other one.

- *Style, colour, flavour and fragrance-related product line gaps*. Style and colour can be important for clothing, shoes, appliances, cars, and so on; flavours and fragrances can become important means of expanding product lines in food and drink products, tobaccos, toiletries, and so on.

- *Form-related product line gaps*. One form of a product may be more attractive for customers than another. Possible dimensions of form include method or principle of operation (petrol versus electric mowers), product format (antacids: chewable, swallowable liquid, effervescent powder or tablets); product composition (corn oil, vegetable oil margarine) and product containers (resealable, returnable, throwaway bottles, easy-open cans).

- *Quality-related product line gaps*. Price lining is a popular practice used by marketers to provide consumers with a choice of products differentiated by overall quality and prices. Sporting goods manufacturers market tennis rackets and golf clubs in a range from beginners' models (low price) up to professional models (high price).

- *Distributor brand-related product line gaps*. Many manufacturers realise a significant proportion of their sales through selling to retailers who then put their own brand names on the products, like Saint Michael for Marks and Spencer in the UK. For manufacturers who recognise the private brand market as a separate segment, private brands can account for product line gaps.

- *Segment-related product line gaps*. As discussed in Chapter 6, a firm can adopt different market coverage strategies. A firm has a product line gap for any segment for which it does not have a product.

Each of these identified product line gaps constitutes a growth opportunity for the firm through innovation or product differentiation.

The types of development strategies to be considered to close these gaps are briefly presented in Figure 7.7. Those strategies will be described in more detail in Chapter 10. In addition to these *development strategies* operated by the firms, one must add the *natural changes* in the size of the industry market potential, which is linked to the product life cycle.

The Product Life Cycle Model

In attractiveness analysis, market potential analysis is a first, and essentially quantitative, step. The analysis must be completed by a study of the product life cycle, or the evolution of the potential demand for a product or service over time. An essentially dynamic concept borrowed from biology, the product life cycle (PLC) model takes the form of an S-shaped graph comprising five phases. The first phase is a take-off, or introductory phase, followed by an exponential growth phase, a shake-out phase, a maturity phase and a decline phase. Figure 7.8(a) presents an idealised representation of the PLC, while Figure 7.8(b) portrays the life cycle of audio products in France, and in particular long-playing records and the compact disc.

The determinants of the product life cycle model

Before moving to an explanation of the PLC, its stages and its marketing implications, it is important to explain what type of products should be dealt with in a life cycle analysis.

> Should it be a category of products (computers), a particular type of product within the category (microcomputers), a specific model (laptop computers or note books) or a specific brand (Compaq)?

While a life cycle analysis at any level can have value if properly conducted, the most useful level of analysis is that of a *product market*, in the sense given in Chapter 6. A product market lends itself best to a life cycle analysis because it best describes buying behaviours within a particular product category and it most clearly defines the frame of reference: *a product seen as a specific package of benefits, targeted to a specific group of buyers*. The same product can very well have different life cycle profiles in different geographic markets or different segments within the same market. Every product market has its own life cycle which reflects not only the evolution of the product, largely determined by technology, but also the evolution of primary demand and of its determinants. Thus, a clear distinction should be made between the product life cycle (PLC) and the brand life cycle (BLC).

The product-market life cycle (PLC) model

For a product market, primary demand is the principal driving force and its determining factors are both non-controllable environmental factors and industry's totally controllable marketing variables. One of the most important non-controllable factors is the *evolution of technology*, which pushes towards newer, higher performance products, and makes older products obsolete. A second factor is the *evolution of production and consumption norms*, which makes certain products no longer suitable for the market and calls for others. Thus, the PLC model portrays the sales history of a particular product technology, which constitutes one specific solution (among many others) for a specific group of buyers to a market need.

These factors exist in all business sectors, which does not however exclude the possibility that certain better protected product markets have a much longer life cycle than others. The life cycle also remains largely influenced by industry marketing efforts, particularly when the market is expanding. Dynamic companies are the driving force in a market, guiding its evolution, development and eventual

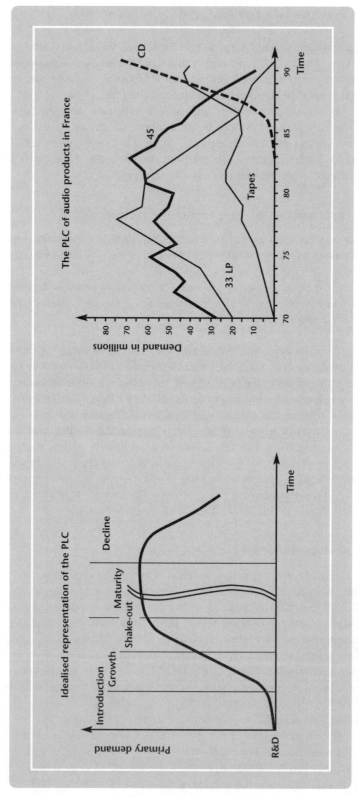

Figure 7.8 The product life cycle concept

relaunch sparked by modifications to the product. The PLC is thus not fixed, and research in the field has identified a great variety of life cycle patterns (Cox, 1967; Swan and Rink, 1982).

The brand life cycle (BLC) model

For a particular brand, *selective demand* is the driving element. It is determined by the evolution of the reference market, but with an added competitive factor: the share of total marketing efforts for the particular brand compared with other competing brands. Thus it is perfectly possible to find a brand in decline in an expanding market, or vice versa.

> The CEO of Procter and Gamble does not believe in the product life cycle model, and cites as an example the brand Tide, launched in 1947 and still in a growth phase in 1976. In reality, the product was modified 55 times in its 29 year existence to adapt to market changes including consumption habits, characteristics of washing machines, new fabrics, and so on. (Day, 1981, p. 61)

It is clear that the life cycle of a brand is essentially determined by factors under the control of the company: the marketing strategy adopted and the amount of effort dedicated to it. Caron (1996) studied the historical evolution of more than one thousand brands and identified five phases in the typical brand life cycle (BLC), as shown in Figure 7.9, a profile very similar in fact to the one observed by Hinkle (1966) in the USA in the food and cosmetic markets. The phases of the BLC are briefly described in Exhibit 7.4. In this chapter, we will refer to the life cycle of a product market (PLC) and no longer to that of a specific brand (BLC).

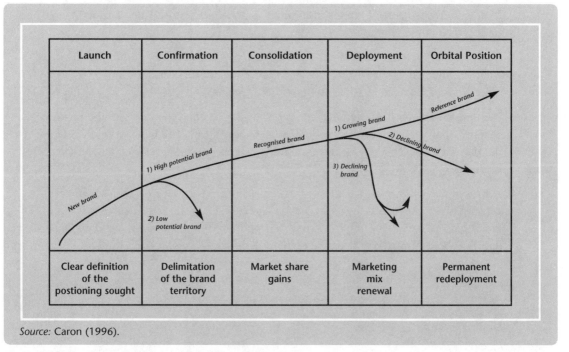

Source: Caron (1996).

Figure 7.9   The five phases of the brand life cycle

Strategic implications of the product life cycle

As product markets grow, mature and decline over time, marketing strategy must evolve with the changing buyers' behaviour and competitive environment. To say that a product has a life cycle implies four things:

● The economic and competitive environment is different at each phase.
● The priority strategic objective must be redefined at each phase.
● Products' cost and profit structures are different at each phase.
● The marketing programme must be adapted in each stage of the PLC.

The shortening of the PLC is a major challenge for the innovative firm which has less and less time to achieve its objectives.

Exhibit 7.4

The Brand Life Cycle

Caron (1996) reports that Carré Noir has studied the strategy of a sample of one thousand brands and has observed that the typical brand life cycle comprises in total five phases. In about 85 per cent of the studied cases the BLC was limited to two or four.

1. *Launch*. More than one million of brands are registered every year in the world, of which 61,583 in France in 1995. During this phase, the new brand concentrates its marketing efforts to claim its identity.

2. *Confirmation*. Once the fashion effect has gone, sales of the low potential brands fall and these brands are delisted from the distributors' purchasing centres. The surviving brands delimit their brand territory.

3. *Consolidation*. The recognised brands have to reaffirm their national and/or international strategic ambition, claim their difference, improve their distribution rate, and so on. The objective is to 'hold' and to increase their market share.

4. *Deployment*. Thanks to a constant renewal of their marketing mix to meet the market changes, the expanding brands redeploy and conquer a new breed of consumers. Some do not find rejuvenating ideas to reinvent themselves and decline. Others have accidents.

5. *Orbital position*. The brand is fully in charge. Rich from its accumulated experience, consolidated by its success, by its reputation and its status among its customer base, the brand has reached a high orbit. To keep that position, the brand will have to continuously create its own style and language that will be assimilated by its customers.

Even in this final phase, the brand remains threatened. The five difficult phases of development (see Figure 7.8) look like a real combat track.

Source: Adapted from Caron (1996).

The introductory phase

In the introductory phase, the market is often (not always) characterised by a slow growth of sales because of various environmental factors:

● The first of these is the *technology uncertainty*, which is often not yet entirely mastered by the innovating company that has to exploit its first-mover advantage (see Exhibit 7.5). In addition, the technology may still be developing or evolving in reaction to the first applications, and thus the producer cannot yet hope to produce at maximum efficiency.

● *Distributors* are a second environmental force, and can be very reluctant at this stage to distribute a product which has not yet proven itself on the larger market. In addition, an industrial distributor will need to familiarise himself with the product, its technical characteristics and its principal functions, which will additionally slow the process.

● *The potential buyers* make up a third environmental factor. They can often be slow to change their consumption or production habits because of switching costs and caution towards the innovation. Only the most innovative of consumers will be the first to adopt the new product. This group constitutes a rather small initial segment for a product in the introduction phase, and is thus another contributing factor to slow sales.

● A final environmental force is the *competition*. Typically, the innovating company is without direct competition for a period of time, depending of the strength of the patent protection if any. Substitute product competition can still be very strong, however, except in the case of breakthrough innovation.

This phase is characterised by a high degree of uncertainty because, as technology is still developing, competitors are not yet identified, the reference market is blurred and there is little market information available. The more revolutionary the innovation, the larger the uncertainty.

Exhibit 7.5

First-mover Advantage: Myth or Reality?

FIRST-MOVER ADVANTAGES	FREE-RIDER ADVANTAGES
Image and reputation	Risk reduction in time and money
Brand loyalty	Lower R&D costs
Opportunity for the best market position	Lower education costs
Technological leadership	Entry through heavy promotion
Opportunity to set product standards	Technological leapfrog
Access to distribution	Imposing a new standard
Experience effects	Learning from a changing market
Patents as barrier to entry	Shared experience
Switching costs as barrier to entry	

Source: Adapted from Schnaars (1998, pp. 160–5).

Internal company factors which also characterise the introduction phase include highly negative cash flows, large marketing expenses, high production costs, and often large R&D costs to be amortised. All of these factors put the new product in a very risky financial position. For this reason, the shorter the introduction phase of the product, the better for the company's profitability.

The *length of the introductory phase* of the PLC is a function of the speed of adoption of the less innovative potential buyers, which is influenced by various factors:

- Importance to the buyer of the new product's benefits.
- Presence or absence of adoption costs to be borne by the buyer.
- Compatibility of the product with current modes of consumption or production.
- Observable nature of the new product's benefits.
- Possibility of trying the new product.
- Competitive pressures inducing buyers to adopt the innovation.

Given these factors, the company's highest priority strategic objective is *to create primary demand* as rapidly as possible and thus to keep the introduction phase as short as possible.

This priority objective includes:

- Creating awareness of the product's existence.
- Informing the market of the new product benefits.
- Inducing potential customers to try the product.
- Securing channels for current and future distribution.

Thus the marketing strategy in the early phase of the PLC typically stresses market education objectives. To respond to these priorities, the *marketing programme* in the introduction phase will tend to have the following characteristics:

- A basic, core version of the product.
- An exclusive or selective distribution system.
- A low price sensitivity situation.
- An informative communication programme.

Several alternatives exist as to the types of launching strategies, particularly in terms pricing: the dilemma of 'skimming versus penetration' pricing will be discussed in more detail in Chapter 12.

The growth phase

If the product successfully passes the test of its introduction to the market, it enters into the *growth phase*. This phase is characterised by growth of sales at an accelerating rate. The causes of this growth are the following:

- The first satisfied users become repeat customers and influence other potential users by word of mouth; thus the rate of occupation of the market increases.
- The availability of the product due to wider distribution gives the product more visibility, which then further increases the product's diffusion in the market.

⬤ The entrance of new competitors increases the total marketing pressure on demand at a moment when it is expansible and strongly elastic.

An important characteristic of this phase is the regular decrease of production costs due to the increase in the volume produced. The effect of experience also begins to be felt. Prices have a tendency to decrease, which allows progressive coverage of the entire potential market. Marketing expenses are thus spread over a strongly expanding sales base, and cash flows become positive.

The characteristics of the *economic and competitive environment* change markedly:

⬤ Sales are growing at an accelerating rate.
⬤ The target group is now the segment of early adopters.
⬤ New competitors enter the market.
⬤ The technology is well diffused in the market.

To meet these new market conditions, the *strategic marketing objectives* are changed as well. They now include:

⬤ Expanding the size of the total market.
⬤ Maximising the occupation rate in the market.
⬤ Building a strong brand image.
⬤ Creating brand loyalty.

To achieve these new objectives, the *marketing programme* will also be modified, as follows:

⬤ Product improvements and features addition strategy.
⬤ Intensive distribution and multiple channels strategy.
⬤ Price reductions to penetrate the market.
⬤ Image building communication strategy.

This primary demand development strategy requires large financial resources, and, if the cash flows are positive and profits rising, the equilibrium break-even point is not necessarily reached yet.

At this time, there is no intensive competitive rivalry in the product market, since the marketing efforts of any firm contribute to the expansion of the total market and are therefore beneficial for other firms.

The shake-out phase

This is a transitory phase where the rate of sales growth is decelerating, even though it remains above that of the general economy. The target group is now the majority of the market. The weakest competitors start dropping out, as the result of successive decreases in the market price, and the market is becoming more concentrated. The competitive and economic environments once again have changed:

⬤ Demand is increasing at a slower rate.
⬤ The target is the majority group in the market.

● The weakest competitors are dropping out of the race because of the reduced market prices.
● The industrial sector is more concentrated.

The key message of the shake-out phase is that things will be more difficult in the market because of the slowing down of total demand. Competing firms are led to redefine their priority objectives in two new directions:

● First, the strategic emphasis must shift from developing primary demand to building up or maximising *market share*.
● Second, *market segmentation* must guide the product policy to differentiate the firm from the proliferation of 'me too' products and to move away from the core market. The majority rule has become the majority fallacy.

The new *priority objectives* are:

● To segment the market and to identify priority target segments.
● To maximise market share in the target segments.
● To position the brand clearly in consumers' minds.
● To create and maintain brand loyalty.

To achieve these objectives, the *marketing programme* will stress the following strategic orientations:

● Product differentiation guided by market segmentation.
● Expansion of distribution to obtain maximum market exposure.
● Pricing based on the distinctive characteristics of the brands.
● Advertising to communicate the claimed positioning to the market.

The shake-out period can be very short. The competitive climate becomes more aggressive and the key indicator of performance is market share.

The maturity phase

Eventually, the increase of primary demand slows down and stabilises at the growth rate of the real GNP or the rhythm of demographic expansion. The product is in the *phase of maturity*. The majority of products can be found in this phase, which usually has the longest duration. The causes of this stabilisation of global demand are the following:

● The rates of occupation and penetration of the product in the market are very high and very unlikely to increase further.
● The coverage of the market by distribution is intensive and cannot be increased further.
● The technology is stabilised and only minor modifications to the product can be expected.

At this stage, the market is very segmented as companies try to cover all the diversity of needs by offering a wide range of product variations. Over the course of this phase the probability of a technological innovation to relaunch the PLC is high, as everyone in the industry tries to extend the life of the product.

The emerging trends observed in the shake-out period have materialised and the characteristics of the *economic and competitive environment* are the following:

- Non-expansible primary demand growing at the rate of the economy.
- Durable goods demand is determined by replacement demand.
- Markets are highly segmented.
- The market is dominated by a few powerful competitors and the market structure is oligopolistic.
- The technology is standardised.

The firm's *priority objective* is to defend, and if possible to expand, market share and to gain a sustainable competitive advantage over direct competitors. The tools to be used for achieving this objective are basically of three types:

- To differentiate the products through quality, feature or style improvements.
- To enter new market segments or niches.
- To gain a competitive advantage through the non-product variables of the marketing mix.

The slowing of market growth certainly has an impact on the competitive climate. Production capacity surpluses appear and contribute to the intensification of the competitive situation. Price competition is more frequent, but has little or no impact on primary demand, which has become inelastic to price. It will only affect the market share of the existing competitors. Inasmuch as the industry succeeds in avoiding price wars, this is the phase where profitability is highest, as shown in Figure 8.8. In theory, this profitability will be as strong as the market share retained is high.

The decline phase

The *decline phase* is characterised by a structural decrease in demand for one of the following reasons:

- *New, more technologically advanced products* make their appearance and replace existing products with the same function.

- Preferences, tastes or *consumption habits* change with time and render products outdated.

- Changes in the social, economic and political *environment*, such as modifications in environmental protection laws, make products obsolete or simply prohibited.

As sales and potential profits decrease, certain companies disinvest and leave the market, while others try to specialise in the residual market. This represents a valid option if the decline is progressive (see Exhibit 7.6). Except in a turnaround of the market, which is sometimes observed, the abandonment of the technologically outdated product is inevitable. In Table 7.1 a summary of the marketing strategies over the PLC is presented and in Table 7.2 the reader will find a PLC evaluation grid.

Table 7.1 Marketing programme over the product life cycle

Phase of the Product Life Cycle	Macro-marketing Environment	Priority Strategic Objectives	Marketing Programme
Introduction	■ Slow growth of primary demand ■ Target: segment of innovators ■ Monopoly, or few rivals ■ Fast technological evolution	■ To create primary demand ■ To educate potential users ■ To induce trial purchase ■ To secure large distribution	■ Core product – basic model ■ Selective or exclusive distribution ■ Skimming or penetration pricing ■ Generic and informative communication
Growth	■ Growth at an accelerating pace ■ Target: segment of early adopters ■ Entry of new competitors ■ Diffused technology	■ To expand primary demand ■ To increase market occupation rate ■ To build brand or corporate image ■ To create brand or corporate loyalty	■ Improved product with new features ■ Intensive distribution and market coverage ■ Price reductions to enlarge the market ■ Image building communication
Shake-out	■ Growth at a declining pace ■ Target: majority of the market ■ Weakest rivals start dropping out ■ Second-generation technology emerges	■ To target specific segments ■ To maximise market share ■ To position the brand clearly ■ To create and maintain brand loyalty	■ Differentiation based on segmentation ■ Intensive distribution ■ High price and value pricing strategy ■ Brand positioning communication
Maturity	■ Non-expandable primary demand ■ Highly fragmented market ■ Few powerful rivals dominate ■ Standardised technology	■ To differentiate products ■ To enter new segments or niches ■ To refine the positioning strategy ■ To add new product features	■ Differentiation based on segmentation ■ Return to selective distribution ■ Forms of non-price competition ■ Brand positioning communication
Decline	■ Zero growth or declining market ■ Target: segment of laggards ■ Competitors leave the market ■ Outdated technology	■ To divest quickly or selectively ■ To become the industry specialist ■ To slow down the decline of the market	■ Limited product line and range ■ Highly selective distribution ■ High prices due to low price sensitivity ■ Communication to loyal customers

The PLC model as a conceptual framework

More than a planning tool, the life cycle model is a *conceptual framework* for analysing the forces which determine the attractiveness of a product market and which provoke its evolution. Markets evolve because certain forces change, provoking pressures or inciting changes. These changing forces are important to identify, and for that purpose the PLC model is useful (Levitt, 1965).

Exhibit 7.6

Is the Minicassette Eternal?

Philips was the first to introduce in the market the minicassette for tape recorders. After more than 30 years, and despite the competition from CDs (also invented by Philips), about three billion cassettes are sold every year worldwide. Philips has made the product universal by offering the licence at no cost to other manufacturers, thereby imposing its standard. The minicassette is compatible not only with recorders but also with car radios and with Walkmans. In fact it is compatible with any form of recording or listening. From the beginning, the cassette was launched with a massive marketing support at a low price. Since then several technical improvements have been made which have opened more selective markets with higher added value. The life of this product seems eternal.

Source: Le Figaro-Economie, 6 January 1992.

Diversity of actual PLC profiles

A difficulty in interpretating the PLC model comes from the fact that available experimental observations show that the PLC profile does not always follow an S-curve as suggested by the model. Rink and Swan (1979) identified as many as twelve different profiles. Sometimes products escape the introduction phase and enter directly into growth; others skip the maturity phase and pass directly from growth to decline; still others skip decline and find a new vigour after a brief slowdown, and so on (see Figure 7.10). Thus there is not only one type of evolution that will invari-ably intervene, and it is often difficult to determine in which phase a product is currently situated. This difficulty reduces the utility of the concept as a planning tool, and even more so as the duration of the phases varies from one product to another, not to mention from one country to another for the same product.

> In 1960, most of the European producers of TV sets had planned their production capacity for colour TV (at that time in the introductory phase) by reference to the PLC of colour TV in the USA, which had a very long introductory phase. In Europe, however, the market penetration was very rapid, the European market and environment being very different.

The different profiles observed can be explained by the evolution of the following explanatory factors: technology, consumption habits and company dynamism. The PLC model does not exempt the market analyst from a systematic analysis of the driving forces at the origin of these changes. The obvious difficulty is to determine, before the facts, the type of evolution that will prevail.

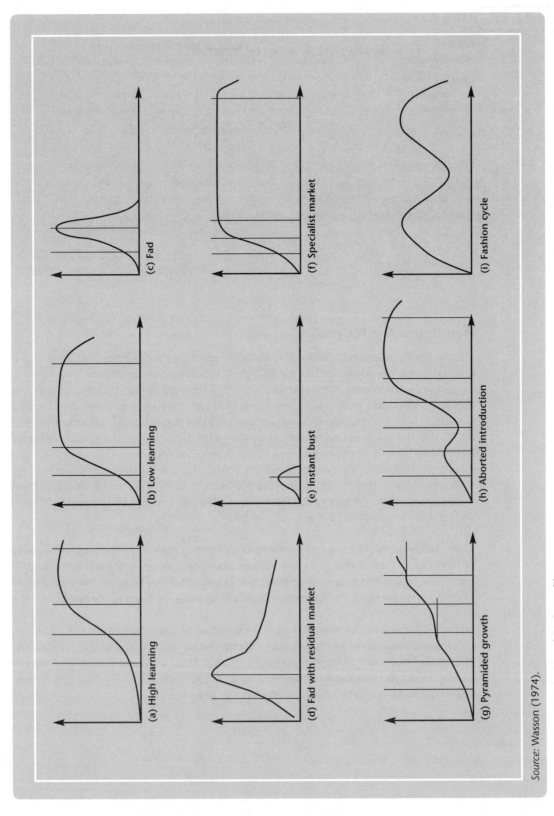

Source: Wasson (1974).

Figure 7.10 Diversity of PLC profiles

Table 7.2 Product life cycle evaluation grid

Market characteristics	Phases of the Product Life Cycle				
	Introduction	Growth	Shake-out	Maturity	Decline
PRIMARY DEMAND					
Slow growth	———	———	———	———	———
Fast growth	———	———	———	———	———
Slowing down	———	———	———	———	———
Decreasing	———	———	———	———	———
NEW COMPETITORS					
Some	———	———	———	———	———
Many	———	———	———	———	———
Few	———	———	———	———	———
Even fewer	———	———	———	———	———
REAL PRICES					
Stable	———	———	———	———	———
Decreasing	———	———	———	———	———
Erratic	———	———	———	———	———
RANGE OF PRODUCTS					
Increasing	———	———	———	———	———
Few changes	———	———	———	———	———
Decreasing	———	———	———	———	———
DISTRIBUTION					
Low growth	———	———	———	———	———
Fast growth	———	———	———	———	———
Few changes	———	———	———	———	———
Decreasing	———	———	———	———	———
PRODUCT MODIFICATIONS					
Few	———	———	———	———	———
Many	———	———	———	———	———
Very few	———	———	———	———	———
COMMUNICATION CONTENT					
Core service	———	———	———	———	———
Main attributes	———	———	———	———	———
New uses	———	———	———	———	———
Secondary attributes	———	———	———	———	———

Source: Taylor (1986, p. 27).

Product rejuvenation strategies

Another explanation of the observed differences in the profiles comes from the fact that companies can act upon the pattern of the PLC profile by innovating, repositioning the product, promoting its diffusion to other groups of consumers, or modifying it in various manners. Throughout the life cycle, the dynamic firm will try to pursue the following objectives:

⬤ Shortening the introduction phase.
⬤ Accelerating the growth process.

● Prolonging the maturity phase.
● Slowing the decline phase.

The ideal profile of a PLC is one where the development phase is short, the introduction brief, the growth phase rapid, the maturity phase long and the decline long and progressive. The initiatives taken by an innovating firm can thus modify the life cycle profile of a product market.

A classic example of a life cycle with successive product relaunches is the nylon industry, where the growth phase was prolonged several times due to successive technological innovations. (Yale, 1964)

It is clear that if all the competitors in a product market consider maturity or decline inevitable, the phases risk being realised sooner than expected.

Some industrial sectors, once considered as declining or stagnant, have suddenly experienced a new lease of life resulting from a rejuvenating supply-led innovation adopted by a manufacturer or by a distributor.

Ikea, in the home furniture distribution, Swatch in the watches market, Benetton in the garment market and Kinepolis in the movie distribution market are good examples of placid or stagnant markets rejuvenated.

The relevant question to examine is to know whether the product market is really in decline or whether it is the strategy adopted by the competing firms within the product market which is obsolete or delivers only limited value to customers?

How to reconcile growth and profit objectives?

The structure of the financial flows which accompany the (idealised) evolution of primary demand over time is described in Figure 7.11. One observes that, in the general case considered here, the financial flows are very unevenly allocated among the different phases of the PLC. In phases 1 and 2, past investments and marketing expenditures heavily undermine the profitability which can remain negative for a significant period of time, particularly in markets where the introductory phase is long. It is only in the shake-out or even in the maturity phase that the innovating firm reaches the profitability zone, having recouped previous losses and achieving higher gross profit margins and lower costs due to experience of economies of scale effects.

A golden managerial rule resulting from this cost and revenue allocation along the PLC is to maintain permanently a balanced structure of the firm's product portfolio in terms of profitability and growth. It is clear, for example, that a firm having 85 per cent of its turnover achieved by products or activities situated in phases 1 or 2 of the PLC, would have a high growth potential, but would certainly be confronted with severe liquidity or cash flow problems being unable to generate enough cash to finance the firm's expansion. It is often the case for promising hi-tech companies having plenty of new product ideas, but not enough cash to finance them. Conversely, a firm achieving 85 per cent of its turnover through products or activities situated in phases 4 or 5, would have substantial financial means, but would be highly vulnerable in terms of growth potential, being

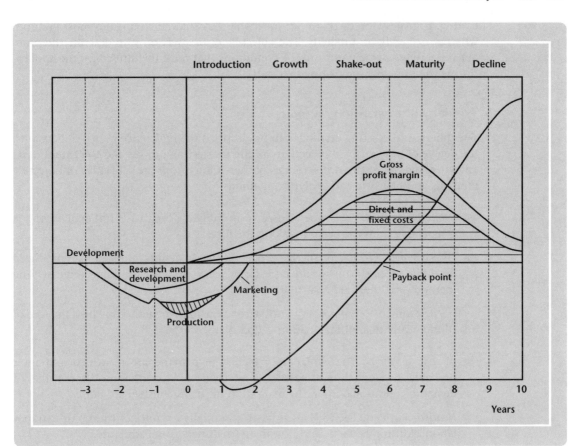

Introduction Growth Shake-out Maturity Decline

Figure 7.11 Financial flows and the PLC

completely dependent on a market turnaround or on a sudden decline of primary demand in its main reference markets.

A balanced product portfolio implies the presence of so-called *cash cow products* generating more cash than required for their development, and so-called *problem children products* or new products having a high growth potential but requiring substantial financial support to ensure their development. These objectives of balanced portfolio structure are at the basis of the portfolio analysis methods developed in Chapter 9 of this book.

● Methods of Demand Measurement

The application of the PLC model implies the ability to formulate forecasts of the evolution of primary demand in a given product market, be they qualitative or quantitative. This problem has become particularly complex in Western economies because of the turbulence of the environment and the radical nature of the changes observed over the course of the last decade. In light of these difficulties and the importance of forecasting errors, certain analysts came to speak of the futility of forecasting. In reality, forecasting is an inevitable task that all companies must perform, whether explicitly or implicitly. The objective of this section is to describe the problems of forecasting demand and the conditions that must be fulfilled for the application of the principal forecasting methods.

Typology of forecasting methods

The different forecasting methods can be classified with reference to two dimensions: the degree of interpersonal objectivity of the forecasting process and the extent of its analytical nature. At the two extremes of these dimensions are subjective or objective methods and heuristic and analytical methods:

- *Subjective methods.* The process used to formulate a forecast is not explicit and is inseparable from the person making the forecast.

- *Objective methods.* The predictive process is clearly defined and can be reproduced by other people, who would necessarily come up with the same forecast. The methods used here are quantitative.

This first dimension opposes quantitative to qualitative methods, where the role of intuition, creativity and imagination is dominant.

- *Analytic methods.* The explanatory factors of demand are identified and their probable future values predicted; one then deduces the probable value of demand, conditional upon the realisation of the established scenario.

- *Heuristic methods.* The forecast is based essentially on rules of thumb or extrapolation of historical facts, and not on an identified causal structure.

This second dimension deals with the analytical character of the forecasting approach, which opposes extrapolation methods to explanatory methods, be they qualitative or quantitative.

As shown in Figure 7.12, the intersection of these two dimensions allows one to classify the different demand forecasting methods in four categories. In what follows, we shall briefly review the main methods used, neglecting the case of naïve methods.

Forecasting methods based on expert judgements

When the forecast formulated does not rest on objective data but rather on the judgements of managers or consumers, the forecasting methods used are said to be expert judgement-based. The 'expert' is assumed to base his or her judgement on a group of explanatory factors, to estimate their chances of occurrence and their likely impact on the level of demand.

Thus, underlying this approach there is a *causal structure*, a set of judgements upon the explanatory factors of demand and their probability of occurrence, in the framework of one or several scenarios. This causal structure is unique to the expert, and another expert confronted with the same problem could come up with different conclusions using the same information. The expert approach presents the advantage of allowing exchange and confrontation of ideas, because of the existence of an explicit causal structure. The three judgement-based methods most often used are:

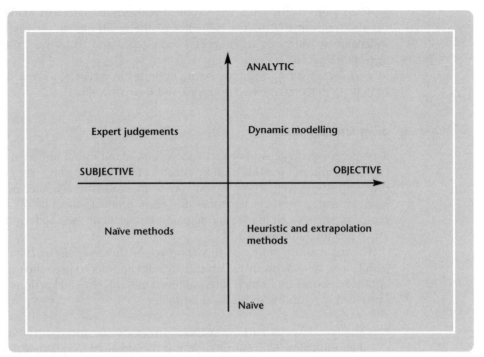

Figure 7.12 Typology of demand forecasting methods

management judgements, sales force estimates and buyers' intentions.

Management judgements

The forecast is determined by the *vision, intuition or imagination* of the individual who formulates it. Managers are asked to give their best guesses or estimates, with their degree of uncertainty, taking, for example, the form of probabilities.

This approach is, to a certain degree, always present in a company. It is frequently observed in organisations dominated by managers who orient their actions only on the basis of their own views. The value of this approach will obviously depend on the values of the experience and the intuition of the managers. The major disadvantage of this approach is its difficulty of communication and the absence of any possibility of verification or disapproval. One way to reduce the subjectivity of individual judgement is to have a *panel of managers* who discuss possible forecasts and try to reach a consensus. A somewhat better way to arrive at subjective estimates is to use the *Delphi method*.

Under this procedure, the judgements of individuals in a group of experts are solicited anonymously (usually by questionnaire). Then the median judgement is computed and communicated to the individuals in the group, who are again asked to make a new judgement. In practice, it has been found that such a procedure quickly leads to a consensus, typically within two rounds. (Phillips, 1987)

The Delphi method has been applied with some success in marketing. Its major drawback lies in the biasing influence of the feedback. An alternative is to obtain independent estimates from several individuals and to average them to yield an aggregate forecast.

Decision support systems have been developed in recent years to assist management in making judgement-based decisions and forecasts.

Sales force estimates

Sales people are in general very knowledgeable about future potential sales to existing customers and can provide useful estimates of the untapped market potential in their own territory as well. The simplest way to proceed is to ask sales people for overall sales estimates in their territories for each product under a set of assumptions regarding the level of marketing support. Management then adds up the estimates to arrive at a total for the firm.

The main shortcoming of this approach is the *vested interest problem* since sales people may systematically underestimate sales in order to keep their quota low and to appear subsequently as high sales achievers. Several remedial actions can be taken to improve the reliability of the sales estimates:

- Asking sales people to assess their own degree of uncertainty (or confidence) in their estimates. This information can then be used to qualify the forecast.
- Combining each sales person's estimate with an estimate provided by the regional sales manager.
- Applying a correction factor to each person's estimate based on his or her history of over- or under-reporting.

Involving the sales force in the sales forecasting process is important for motivating the sales force and for gaining acceptance of the sales quotas. It is also interesting to have sales forecasts available at very desegregated levels, such as region, territory, customer, and so on.

Buyers' intentions surveys

A last judgemental method is to estimate demand directly on the basis of stated intentions to purchase provided by buyers. Buyers' intentions can be analysed at two different levels: (a) the general level of buyers' expectations and confidence about their present and future personal finance and/or about the economy or (b) the level of a specific product class or a brand. In the European Union two general surveys of buyers' intentions are periodically carried out.

The first is the EU quarterly survey on consumers' sentiments or confidence about the economy and about their personal economic situation. Consumers are also asked to express their intentions to purchase major durable goods within the next three months. These data are then used to construct an *index of consumer confidence* which can be used as an early indicator of shifts in retail sales.

In the field of industrial goods, central banks within the EU conduct monthly surveys among industrial firms regarding their expectations and/or intentions about investments, employment, production capacity utilisation and current state of orders and shipments for both domestic and international markets. These data, available for each major industrial sector, are used to construct an *index of industry confidence*, which has proved to be a reliable early indicator of economic recession or recovery. Firms are using this information to anticipate shifts in the level of demand.

Various firms carry out their own surveys of consumer intentions, especially when testing a new product concept. A typical question on buyers' intentions looks like that presented in Table 7.3.

Table 7.3   Typical question on buyers' intentions

Do you intend to buy a new car within the next six months?					
No chance	Slight possibility	Fair possibility	Good possibility	High probability	Certain
(0)	(0.20)	(0.40)	(0.60)	(0.80)	(1.00)

The frequencies observed for the two upper classes of this purchase probability scale can be used to generate potential market estimates and/or brand shares.

When one comes to intentions about the purchase of a specific good or brand, specific intentions surveys have been found to be of more limited value than general surveys. Intentions are not always related strongly to behaviour, except when *advanced planning* is required, as is the case for major product or service purchases, such as cars, housing, holiday trips, and so on.

Subjective methods have obvious limitations, but they nevertheless provide a useful starting point in demand estimation. However, they should be used conjointly with more objective methods.

Heuristic and extrapolation forecasting

When the analytic structure of the forecasting process is weak, but when the forecast rests on objective market data, the methods used are said to be heuristic methods. They are either rules of thumb, loosely based on empirical data, or extrapolations of current sales.

The chain ratio method

This method is an extension of the absolute market potential given earlier in this chapter, which calls for identifying all potential buyers (n) in the product market or segment and for assuming optimum use of (q) the product by each potential user. Two examples of application have been provided, one for a consumer good (see Exhibit 7.1) and one for a consumable industrial good (see Exhibit 7.3). The determination of the current level of primary demand in these two examples would require estimates of the current occupation rates.

The chain ratio method involves the use of successive adjusting percentages to break down the absolute potential to come to the demand for a particular product or brand. To illustrate, let us consider the case of a company selling a compound to be used in conjunction with the usual water-softening chemicals used for treating water in boiler systems. The market is dominated by a monopolist, but many factories are

Exhibit 7.7

Example of Application of the Chain Ratio Method

- Water consumption by factories equipped with boiler systems = 7,500,000 hl.
- Softener use ratio per litre of water = 1 per cent.
- Percentage of factories using water-softening products = 72 per cent.
- Compound use ratio per litre of softener = 9 per cent.
- The *current market potential* is
  7,500,000 hl × 0.01 × 0.72 × 0.09 = 486,000 litres.
- Percentage of factories using the chemical compound = 54 per cent.
- The current level of primary demand is
  750,000,000 hl × 0.01 × 0.72 × 0.09 × 0.54 = 262,440 litres.
- If the target market share for Company A is 40 per cent, the expected sales volume in this particular area will be 104,976 litres.

still non-users of the compound. To determine the expected sales volume of this new compound in a particular geographic area, an estimate can be made as shown in Exhibit 7.7.

The difficulty of this method is the choice of the different multipliers if no primary research data are available. Moreover, error in any one multiplier will carry throughout the analysis, given the dependency of each level on preceding levels. The way out is to adopt different multipliers to generate, not a single estimate, but a range of estimates. In any case, this method should be used along with other procedures or complementary analyses.

Buying power index

In the field of consumer goods a popular technique is the buying power index (BPI) method. The objective is to measure the attractiveness of a market by a weighted average of the three key components of any market potential:

- The number of potential consuming units.
- The purchasing power of these consuming units.
- The willingness to spend of these consuming units.

Indicators of these components are identified by region, province, district, community or city and a weighted average index is computed for each area.

Two approaches are possible here: to use a standard BPI developed by marketing research companies or to develop an index tailored to the specific products and market of a particular firm.

Standard BPIs are in general based on the three following indicators: total population, per capita income and retail sales. The relative buying power of any area i is given by

$$\text{BPI}_i = 0.5(C_i) + 0.3(Y_i) + 0.2(W_i)$$

where

C = percentage of total population in area i
Y = percentage of income originating from area i
W = percentage of retail sales in area i

The weights adopted in the BPI equation are those used by the *Sales and Marketing Management* magazine which, in the USA, publishes BPIs in July of each year. They are derived empirically through regression analyses and they apply mainly to mass products moderately priced. Other weights can be adopted if necessary, as well as additional indicators. Similar BPIs are published by Chase Econometrics for the main regions of the EU, and by *Business International* for 117 countries throughout the world.

Tailor-made BPIs would typically keep the same three basic components of buying power, but would include indicators more directly related to the business plus possibly other indicators to reflect competitive conditions or local characteristics. An example of a tailor-made BPI is presented in Table 7.4.

The market studied is the soft drink market. The indicators used to compute the buying power index are number of households with children, private disposable income, and number of hotels, restaurants and cafés within each area. These data, expressed in percentages of the total, are available for 14 sales territories. The buying power index is a simple average of the three percentages of each territory. Its predictive value has been verified by correlating the BPI with product category sales in each area.

In Table 7.4, the BPI is used to assess the market penetration of brand A within each area. To estimate potential sales of each territory, the BPI is multiplied by the expected national sales for the brand. Other strategic goals or local conditions must, of course, be considered. Some firms also use the BPI as a guide to allocate their total advertising budget among the different sales territories.

Table 7.4 Sales performance evaluation per territory

Territory	Brand A sales	Percentage of total sales	Buying Power Index (%)	Performance index
1	2,533	3.53	4.31	0.82
2	8,458	11.80	7.84	1.51
3	3,954	5.52	5.89	0.94
4	19,619	27.37	20.28	1.35
5	3,780	5.27	4.75	1.11
6	3,757	5.24	13.24	0.40
7	5,432	7.58	7.74	0.87
8	3,701	5.16	3.97	1.30
9	3,028	4.22	3.19	1.32
10	3,820	5.33	9.16	0.58
11	2,433	3.39	3.70	0.92
12	5,736	7.00	7.32	0.96
13	2,569	3.58	2.96	1.21
14	2,861	3.99	3.65	1.09
Total	71,681	100.0	100.0	–

Trend decomposition and extrapolation

The purpose of trend analysis is to decompose the original sales series into its principal components, to measure the past evolution of each component and to project this evolution into a near future. It is evident that this projection has no meaning beyond the short term, that is the period of time for which one can consider that the characteristics of the phenomenon being studied do not change measurably. However, these conditions exist rather often in practice, because inertia also exists in the environment. Five different components can be identified in a typical sales time series:

● A *structural component*, that is the long-term trend, generally linked to the life cycle of the product market.
● A *cyclical component*, represented by fluctuations around the long-term trend, provoked by medium-term changes in economic activity.
● A *seasonal component*, or recurrent short-term fluctuations due to diverse causes (weather, holidays, calendar structure, and so on).
● A *marketing component* reflecting short-term promotional actions, temporary price cuts or out-of-stock situations.
● An *erratic component*, which reflects the impact of complex phenomena, poorly understood, unpredictable and non-quantifiable.

For each component, a parameter is estimated on the basis of the regularities observed in the past: long-term average growth rate, short-term fluctuations, seasonal coefficients and special events. These parameters are then used to generate a sales forecast, assuming that their past values will remain unchanged during the next period.

Exponential smoothing

This approach forecasts sales as a weighted average of sales observed in a number of past periods, with the largest weights being placed on sales observed in the most recent periods. The sales forecast for the next period is given by

$$\bar{Q}_t = \alpha \, Q_t + (1 - \alpha) \, Q_t - 1$$

where

$$\begin{aligned}
\bar{Q}_t &= \text{smoothed sales for the current period} \\
\alpha &= \text{smoothing constant, where } 0 < \alpha < 1 \\
Q_t &= \text{current sales in period } t \\
\bar{Q}_t - 1 &= \text{smoothed sales as computed in period } t - 1
\end{aligned}$$

The smoothing constant is a number between 0 and 1 and must be selected by the market analyst. Low values of α are appropriate when sales change slowly, whereas high values are relevant for rapid changes in sales. Computer programs are available to select the best value of α by trial and error on historical data.

To illustrate, let us examine the data presented in Table 7.5. Quarterly sales in volume have been seasonally adjusted. The objective is to find the optimal value for α, the smoothing constant. The data of 1992 are used to test the predictive value of the model.

Table 7.5   Seasonally adjusted quarterly sales: an example

Quarter	1987	1988	1989	1990	1991	1992	Seasonal index
1	105	106	112	121	124	130	0.908
2	101	111	115	117	125	127	0.996
3	100	110	110	117	129	132	1.153
4	108	110	117	118	122	124	0.943

To forecast sales for the first quarter of 1992, we need the smoothed sales as estimated for the preceding periods. For example, the smoothed sales for the first quarter of 1988 are then,

$$\overline{Q}_{88} = (0.10)\ (106) + (0.90)\ (105) = 105.1$$

where seasonally adjusted sales for 1987 have been used for the smoothed sales because the latter are not available when one begins exponential smoothing. Similarly, for the other quarters we have successively,

$$\overline{Q}_{89} = (0.10)\ (112) + (0.90)\ (105.1) = 105.9$$
$$\overline{Q}_{90} = (0.10)\ (121) + (0.90)\ (105.9) = 107.3$$
$$\overline{Q}_{91} = (0.10)\ (124) + (0.90)\ (107.3) = 109.0$$

Thus, the forecast for the first quarter of 1992 is based on past sales and is equal to

$$E(Q_{92}) = Q_{91} = 109.0$$

Note that the sales forecast is always included between current sales and smoothed sales for the current period. The error of forecasting can be computed as

$$\text{Forecasting error} = \frac{109.0 - 130}{130} = 16.2 \text{ per cent}$$

This a very large prediction error, which can be caused by the small value of the smoothing constant α since, in this example, sales are rapidly increasing. A value of 0.80 for α gives smoothed sales for 1991 equal to 127.60, reducing the forecasting error to 1.1, a much better performance.

A large number of different techniques exist, incorporating more than one smoothing constant. For an overview of these methods, see Makridakis and Wheelwright (1973). The main shortcoming of exponential smoothing methods is their inability to really 'forecast' the evolution of demand, in the sense that they cannot anticipate a turning point. At most, they can rapidly integrate a modification in sales. This is why these methods are termed 'adaptive forecasting models'. For numerous management problems, this 'after the fact' forecast is none the less useful since the causes of sales tend to operate in a regular manner. Thus, the use of previous sales levels as predictors of future levels often works satisfactorily.

The explanatory model building approach

'Objective' and 'analytical' forecasting methods are the most advanced methods, scientifically speaking. They are based upon the construction of *explicative mathemat-*

ical models, which allow the simulation of market situations in alternative scenarios. In its basic philosophy, mathematical modelling is very similar to the expert approach described above: identifying a causal structure, constructing one or several scenarios and deducting the probable level of demand in each of them. The difference comes from the fact that *the causal structure was established and validated experimentally in objectively observable and measurable conditions.*

Identification of the causal structure

The identification of the causal structure of the phenomenon under study is the starting point for any model building exercise. Let us take as an example the case of a distributor who wishes to increase the loyalty rate of his customers and who is trying to identify the best means of reaching this result. The questions to be asked are the following:

⬤ What are the determining factors behind the *image* of a distributor?
⬤ How does this image influence the *visit frequency* of stores?
⬤ What other factors explain customer *satisfaction*?
⬤ To what extent does the level of satisfaction generate long-term customer store *loyalty*?

Rather typically, we are faced here with successive causal relationships where the first dependent variable (*image*) becomes the explanatory variable of a second dependent variable (*visit frequency and satisfaction*), which then explains *loyalty*. This is obviously a set of hypotheses based on the observation of buyer behaviour and on assumptions or reasoning suggested by behavioural theory. These hypotheses should be verified (or disproved) on the basis of empirical data gathered by the market analyst. If confirmed, the model could then be used to guide the distributor's decisions.

Dynamic modelling

Peeters (1992) has developed a dynamic model for estimating the demand for lorries on different European markets. The demand function adopted is the following:

Demand = F(Production, Interest rates, Prices, Error term)

where

       Demand   = monthly registrations of lorries weighing 15 tonnes and more
       Production = monthly index of industrial production
       Interest   = monthly interest rate of state guaranteed bonds
       Price   = index of fuel prices.

Data are deseasonalised and expressed as logarithms. The mathematical model used is a dynamic model which describes the structure of the market response as follows:

⬤ the *production* variable is introduced under a distributed lag model taking the shape of a decreasing geometric progression from t to $t - k$ with a rate of 0.4557 (Koyck model);

- the *interest rate variable* comes into the model with an 8-month lag, which means that the time lag of a change in the interest rate on demand is 8 months; this lag was identified through an iteration procedure;

- the *price* variable is also introduced with an 8-month lag;

- the *error term* also has a dynamic structure as it is composed of a weighted sum of the preceding error terms (*U*) and of a random term (*e*).

The demand equation, estimated through a numerical method of maximum likelihood, is the following:

$$Q_t = 5.503 + 1.7479 \cdot \text{Prod}_t + 0.7960 \cdot \text{Prod}_{t-1} + 0.3630 \cdot \text{Prod}_{t-2} + ...$$
$$- 0.1899 \cdot \text{Interest}_{t-8} - 0.4767 \cdot \text{Price}_{t-8}$$
$$+ 0.2463 \cdot U_{t-1} + 0.1389 \cdot U_{t-2} + 0.2602 \cdot U_t{-}3 + e_t$$
$$N = 86 \qquad DW = 1.989 \qquad R^2 = 0.865$$

The quality of the statistical fit is measured by the usual statistical indicators. The determination coefficient here is 0.865. The *t tests* measuring the precision of the individual coefficients are also statistically significant at the 5 per cent level or higher. The interpretation of the coefficients is straightforward since they are elasticities. Thus, as an example:

- the cumulative total effect (sum of effects for all lags) of the industrial production variable is 2.907, which means that a 1 per cent increase of the industrial production index generates an increase of 2.9 per cent of truck registrations;

- a decrease in the interest rate of 10 per cent causes, eight months later, an increase of 1.9 per cent of the demand for trucks;

- a 10 per cent increase in the price of fuel causes, eight months later, a decrease of 4.8 per cent in the demand for trucks.

The comparison of the observed and calculated sales via the model for the last ten months confirmed the goodness of fit.

Limitations of mathematical model building

The strength of this approach is that the model becomes an instrument of discovery and exploration of numerous and varied situations that the human mind could not exhaustively explore.

It is important to note that this approach is only valid as long as the causal structure identified remains stable. Forecasting with an explicative model thus also implies an extrapolation, but of the second degree. In a rapidly and profoundly changing environment, a mathematical model is incapable of anticipating the effect of a change the cause of which has not been taken into account in the model. A mathematical model thus lacks the ability to improvise, and cannot adapt to a profoundly modified environment, whereas an expert can.

The majority of forecasting errors are due to the fact that, at the moment of formulation of the forecast, it has been implicitly considered that the current tendencies will more or less maintain themselves in the future. This is rarely the case in the reality of social and economic life.

History can be an unreliable guide as domestic economies become more international, new technologies emerge and industries evolve. These abilities of anticipation must be developed and this assumes a good comprehension of the key driving factors and of the vulnerability of the company to environmental threats.

The scenario planning approach

The examination of the different possible forecasting approaches has shown the advantages and limitations of each. In reality, the approaches are very complementary and a good forecasting system should be able to make use of all of them.

In a turbulent environment, it is clear that intuition and imagination can be precious instruments of perception of reality and complementary to quantitative approaches, which, by definition, rely solely on observed facts. In addition, a purely qualitative approach runs certain risks, and as much as possible intuitions and visions should be analysed in the light of the facts available. What is important is thus the confrontation of these two approaches. The integration of the different methods evoked by the scenarios method is a good manner in which to approach a forecasting problem.

Description of scenario planning

A *scenario* can be defined as follows:

> A presentation of the key explanatory factors to be taken into consideration, and a description of the manner(s) in which these factors could affect demand.

A scenario is thus different from a forecast. A forecast is more a judgement which tends to predict a specific situation and which is to be taken or left on its own value. A scenario, on the other hand, is an instrument which is conceived for analysis and reflection, and namely:

- To give a better understanding of a market's situation and its past evolution.
- To sensitise the company to its interactions with the environment.
- To evaluate its vulnerability to threats.
- To identify possible lines of action.

Scenario planning avoids the danger of a single-point forecasts by allowing users to explore the implications of several alternative futures. By surfacing, challenging and altering beliefs, managers are able to test their assumptions in a non-threatening environment. Having examined the full range of possible futures, the company is well-positioned to modify its strategic direction as actual events unfold. Thanks to this sensitisation, the method allows the company to improve its anticipation capability and to develop its flexibility and adaptability. A scenario should be regarded together with others: one basic scenario and other alternatives based on key factors, as illustrated in Figure 7.13.

Methodology of scenario planning

The key steps in the scenario planning process are the following:

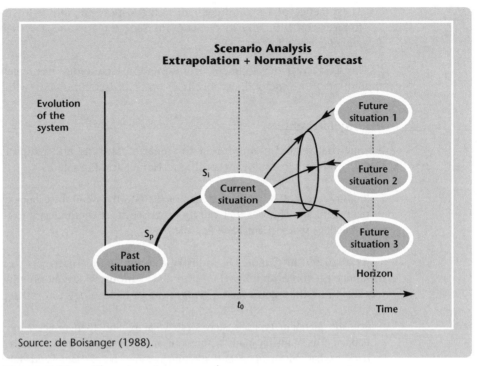

Figure 7.13   The scenario approach

⬤ Determine the model's scope and time frame.

⬤ Identify the current assumptions and mental models of the individuals who influence these decisions.

⬤ Create divergent, yet plausible, scenarios of how the future might evolve along with underlying assumptions.

⬤ Test the impact of key variables in each scenario.

⬤ Develop action plans based on either the most robust solutions that play well across scenarios, or the most desirable outcome towards which a company can direct its efforts.

⬤ Monitor events as they unfold to test the corporate direction and be prepared to modify it as required (Shoemaker, 1995).

This approach, which is based upon the conviction that the future can never be completely measured and controlled, presents several advantages for management:

⬤ First, it sensitises the company to the uncertainties which characterise any market situation; in a turbulent environment, sound management implies the *ability to anticipate* the evolution of the environment.

⬤ The scenario method facilitates *integration of the different forecasting approaches*, qualitative or quantitative.

The practice of this approach introduces more flexibility in management and induces the company to develop alternative plans and a system of *contingency planning* (see Chapter 11).

The spectacular development of information technology has largely facilitated the application of this method, notably in allowing its decentralisation within the company.

Industry foresight

A somewhat related methodology to scenario planning and which is gaining popularity is industry foresight. According to Hamel and Prahalad,

> Industry foresight is based on deep insights into the trend in technology, demographics, regulation, and lifestyles that can be harnessed to rewrite industry rules and create new competitive space. (Hamel and Prahalad, 1994, p. 76)

As discussed in Chapter 9, industry foresight helps managers to understand and influence the forces shaping the future of the industry. Developing industry foresight requires more than good scenario planning or technology forecasting.

> Scenario planning typically starts with what is, and then projects forward what might happen. The quest for industry foresight often starts with what could be, and then works back to what must happen for that future to come about. (Hamel and Prahalad, 1994, p. 82)

Also, industry foresight is the product of many people's visions.

Chapter summary

The key demand concepts are 'primary' versus 'company' demand, 'absolute' versus 'present' market potential, 'end' versus 'derived' demand, 'first equipment' versus 'replacement' demand for durable goods. The objective of demand analysis is to give an empirical content to these concepts through market research in order to objectively assess the attractiveness of each potential target segment and to identify the determinants of demand. These concepts are useful for detecting growth opportunities in the reference market through gap analysis. The product life cycle model is a conceptual framework which describes the evolution of primary demand in a dynamic perspective. A large variety of profiles exist for the PLC which can be explained by the evolution of technology and consumption habits and by the size of industry marketing efforts. The competitive situation and the financial structure (turnover and profits) are different at each stage of the PLC and the priority strategic objective and the marketing programme must be adapted accordingly. Demand forecasting methods can be classified by reference to two dimensions: the degree of interpersonal objectivity and the extent of the analytical approach. A distinction is made between 'subjective' and 'objective' methods and 'heuristic' or 'analytic' methods. Each of these methods has advantages and limitations but they are complementary. A good forecasting system should be able to make use of all of them. In a turbulent environment, emphasis is placed on flexibility and speed of adaptation. Thus, a foresight rather than a forecasting system, is preferable.

QUESTIONS AND PROBLEMS

1. What is the relationship between current market potential and absolute market potential? Describe the factors which determine the level and the evolution of these market potential concepts.

2. You must estimate the size of the absolute market potential as well as the current level of equipment of households for microwaves in a given country. Describe the information as well as the methods needed to gather this information.

3. How does the price elasticity of primary demand develop during the various phases of its product life cycle? What are the factors explaining this evolution and what are the managerial implications for the firm?

4. How would you proceed to develop a buying power index which would allow you to evaluate the market potential for life insurance on a regional base within a given country?

5. You are asked to measure young people's attitude towards advertising in general. Describe the causal structure that should guide the search for information.

Bibliography

Berry, F.W. (1980) Services Marketing is Different, *Business Magazine*, May–June.

Berry, L. (1999) *Discovering the Soul of Service*, New York, The Free Press.

Bishop,W.S., Graham, J.L. and Jones, M.H. (1984) Volatility of Derived Demand in Industrial Markets and its Management Implications, *Journal of Marketing*, **48**, pp. 95–103.

Business International (1991) Indicators of Market Size for 117 Countries, *Weekly Report*, July 7.

Caron, G. (1996) Le devenir des marques, Quel devenir...?, *Futuribles*, February, pp. 27–42.

Cox, W.E. (1967) Product Life Cycle: Marketing Models, *Journal of Business*, **40**, October, pp. 375–84.

Day, G.S. (1981) The Product Life Cycle: Analysis and Application Issues, *Journal of Marketing*, **45**, pp. 60–7.

de Boisanger, P. (1988) Réduire l'imprévu à l'imprévisible, *Futuribles*, March, pp. 59–67.

Eiglier, P. and Langeard, E. (1987) *Servuction*, Paris, Ediscience International.

Hamel, G. and Prahalad, C.K. (1994) *Competing for the Future*, Boston, Harvard Business School Press.

Hinkle, J. (1966) *Life Cycles*, New York, Nielsen.

Kurtz, D.L. and Clow, K.E. (1998) *Services Marketing*, New York, John Wiley & Sons.

Levitt, T. (1965) *L'imagination au service du marketing*, Paris, Economica.

McCarthy, J. (1960) *Basic Marketing: A Managerial Approach*, 1st edn, Homewood IL, R.D. Irwin.

Makridakis, S. and Wheelwright, S.C. (1973) *Forecasting Methods for Management*, New York, John Wiley & Sons.

Morris, M.H. (1988) *Industrial and Organizational Marketing*, Columbus OH, Merrill.

Peeters, R. (1992) *Total Truck Demand in Europe: A Case Study*, IAG, Université Catholique de Louvain, Louvain-la-Neuve.

Phillips, L. D. (1987) On Adequacy of Judgemental Forecasts, in: Wright, G. and Aytol, P. (eds) *Judgemental Forecasting*, New York, John Wiley & Sons.

Rink, D.R. and Swan, J.E. (1979) Product Life Cycle Research: A Literature Review, *Journal of Business Research*, September, pp. 219–42.

Schemenner, R.W. (1986) How Can Service Business Survive and Prosper?, *Sloan Management Review*, Spring.

Schnaars, S.P. (1998) *Marketing Strategy*, New York, The Free Press.

Shoemaker, P.J.H. (1995) Scenario Planning: A Tool for Strategic Thinking, *Sloan Management Review*, Winter, pp. 25–40.

Shostack, G.L. (1977) Breaking Free from Product-marketing, *Journal of Marketing*, **41**, April, pp. 73–80.

Swan, J.E. and Rink, D.R. (1982) Fitting Market Strategy to Varying Product Life Cycles, *Business Horizons*, January–February, pp. 72–6.

Taylor, J.W. (1986) *Competitive Marketing Strategies*, Radnor PA, Chilton Book Company.

Wasson, C.R. (1974) *Dynamic Competitive Strategy and the Product Life Cycle*, St Charles, Challenge Books.

Weber, J.A. (1976) *Growth Opportunity Analysis*, Reston VA, Reston Publishing.

Wilkie, W.L. (1990) *Consumer Behavior*, 2nd edn, New York, John Wiley & Sons.

Yale, J.P. (1964) The Strategy of Nylon's Growth: Create New Market, *Modern Textiles Magazine*, February.

Zeithmal, V.A., Parasuraman, A. and Berry, L.L. (1990) *Delivering Quality Service*, New York, The Free Press.

chapter eight

Competitiveness analysis

Having evaluated the intrinsic appeal of the product markets and segments in the reference market, the next stage of strategic marketing is to analyse the climate or the *competitive structure* of each of the product markets, and then evaluate the nature and intensity of the *competitive advantage* held by the various competitors in each market. A product market may be very attractive in itself, but not so for a particular firm, given its strengths and weaknesses and compared to its most dangerous competitors. Therefore, the aim of measuring business competitiveness is to identify the kind of competitive advantage that a firm or a brand can enjoy and to evaluate to what extent this advantage is sustainable, given the competitive structure, the balance of existing forces and the positions held by the competitors.

Chapter learning objectives

When you have read this chapter, you should be able to:

1. define a competitive advantage which is sustainable in a target market;

2. describe the nature and strengths of the competitive forces at play in an industry;

3. assess the impact of the competitive situation on the strategic and operational marketing objectives;

4. predict the type of competitive behaviour to expect given the competitive environment;

5. explain the importance of differentiation as a source of competitive advantage;

6. use the experience curve to measure the extent of a cost advantage or disadvantage over direct competitors;

7. understand the concept of international competitive advantage.

The Notion of Competitive Advantage

Competitive advantage refers to those characteristics or attributes of a product or a brand that give the firm some *superiority over its direct competitors*. These characteristics or attributes may be of different types and may relate to the product itself (the core service), to the necessary or added services accompanying the core service, or to the modes of production, distribution or selling specific to the product or to the firm. When it exists, this superiority is relative and is defined with respect to the best-placed competitor in the product market or segment. We then speak of the most dangerous competitor, or the *priority competitor*. A competitor's relative superiority may result from various factors, and the value chain model is particularly useful to identify them. Generally speaking, these can be classified into three main categories, according to the nature of competitive advantage they provide.

The quality competitive advantage

A quality competitive advantage is based on some distinctive qualities of the product which give *superior value to the buyer*, either by reducing its costs or by improving its performance and which therefore give the firm the capacity to charge a price higher than competition.

An external competitive advantage gives the firm increased *market power*. It can force the market to accept a price above that of its priority competitor which may not have the same distinctive quality. A strategy based on an external competitive advantage is a *differentiation strategy*, which calls into question the firm's marketing know-how, and its ability to better detect and meet those expectations of buyers which are not yet satisfied by existing products.

To succeed with an external advantage strategy, the price premium the customer is willing to pay must exceed the cost of providing that extra value.

The cost competitive advantage

A cost competitive advantage is based on the firm's superiority in matters of cost control, administration and product management, which bring *value to the producer* by enabling it to have a lower unit cost than its priority competitor.

Internal competitive advantage results from better *productivity*, thus making the firm more profitable and more resistant to price cuts imposed by the market or by the competition. A strategy based on internal competitive advantage is a *cost domination strategy*, which mainly calls into question the firm's organisational and technological know-how. To succeed, a cost strategy must offer acceptable value to customers, so that prices are close to the average of competitors. If too much quality is sacrificed to achieve a low-cost position, the price discount demanded by customers will more than offset the cost advantage.

The search for a sustainable competitive positioning

These two types of competitive advantage have distinct origins and natures, which are often incompatible because they imply different abilities and traditions. Figure 8.1 shows the two aspects of competitive advantage, which can be expressed as questions:

● *Market power*: to what extent are buyers willing to pay a price higher than the price charged by our direct competitor?

● *Productivity*: is our unit cost higher or lower than the unit cost of our direct competitor?

The horizontal axis in Figure 8.1 refers to maximum acceptable price and the vertical axis to unit cost. Both are expressed in terms of percentages compared to the priority competitor:

● The *productivity* dimension enables a brand or firm to position itself in terms of cost advantage or disadvantage compared to its priority competitor. A positioning in the upper part of the axis reveals a cost disadvantage and a cost advantage on the lower part.

● The *market power* dimension describes the position of the brand by reference to its buyers' maximum acceptable price compared to that of its priority competitor. A positioning to the right indicates a high brand strength and the capacity to charge a premium price. A positioning to the left suggests, on the other hand,

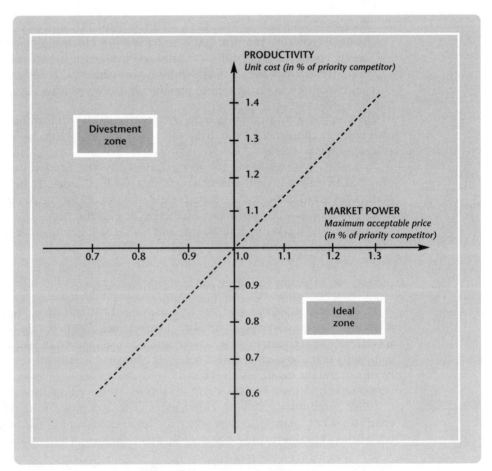

Figure 8.1   Competitive advantage analysis

that the brand has a weak market power and that it has to adopt a price lower than its priority competitors to be accepted by the market.

In Figure 8.1, the bisecting line separates the favourable and unfavourable positions. Four different competitive positionings can be identified:

1. The positioning in the *upper-left quadrant* is disastrous since the brand accumulates handicaps. The brand has a cost disadvantage over its priority competitor and has no market power to offset this cost handicap through a price premium. Sooner or later, a divestment or retreat strategy will have to be adopted.

2. The *lower-right quadrant* is the ideal situation where the brand would have the best of both worlds: low cost due to high productivity and high market-acceptable price due to high market power. A situation rarely observed in the real world, these two positionings imply two different corporate cultures.

3. The *lower-left quadrant* depicts the positioning of a brand having a cost advantage but a weak market power compared to its direct competitor. The strategy to adopt here is to target price sensitive market segments with a modest operational marketing budget or to subcontract operational marketing, for instance, to a large retail chain.

4. The *upper-right quadrant* describes a situation frequently observed in highly industrialised countries: the firm has a cost handicap but has a market power sufficiently strong to offset the cost handicap through a higher market-acceptable price. The strategy here is to search for higher added value and/or higher quality activities that will justify a price premium in the eyes of the buyer.

The purpose of measuring business competitiveness is to allow the firm to find its own position on these axes and deduce its strategic priority objectives for each of the products of its portfolio.

To find its position along the *market power axis*, the firm will use information provided by brand image studies which, as seen in Chapter 5, help measure the brand's perceived value and estimate price elasticities. As for the *productivity axis*, the experience law can be used when applicable or else the firm can use information provided by the marketing intelligence unit which has, among other things, the task of monitoring competition.

Competitive advantage based on core competencies

A more general way to look at the type of competitive advantage refers to the *core competency concept* developed by Prahalad and Hamel (1990). A core competence is a special skill or technology that creates unique customer value (see Exhibit 8.1). A company's specialised capabilities are largely embodied in the collective knowledge of its people and the organised procedures that shape the way employees interact. These core competencies can be viewed as the roots of a firm's competitive advantage.

When appropriately applied, core competencies can create sustainable sources of competitive advantage over time which are implementable in other seemingly unrelated fields of business. To be sustainable, a core competency should:

● provide significant and appreciable *value to customers* relative to competitor offerings;

⬤ be *difficult for competitors to imitate* or procure in the market, thereby creating competitive barriers to entry;

⬤ enable a company to access a *wide variety of seemingly unrelated markets* by combining skills and technologies across traditional business units.

Identifying and developing core competencies involves isolating key abilities within the organisation and then honing them into a definition of the organisation's key strengths (Rigby,1997). As reviewed in the following chapter, successful diversification strategies are often based on core competencies.

Operational versus strategic competitive advantage

The search for a sustainable competitive advantage is at the core of the strategy formulation process and is one of the main responsibilities of strategic marketing. A company can outperform rivals only if it can establish a difference that it can preserve. In this perspective a distinction can be made here between operational and strategic competitive advantages (Porter, 1996).

Gaining an operational competitive advantage in a given reference market means performing *similar activities better than rivals perform them*. It might mean:

⬤ being better by offering a higher quality or a same quality at a lower price;
⬤ being better by offering a product reducing customers' costs;
⬤ being better by offering lower cost and better quality at the same time;
⬤ being faster in meeting customers' products or services;
⬤ being closer to the customer and providing assistance in use.

Constant improvements in operational effectiveness are necessary to achieve superior profitability, but it is not usually sufficient. Staying ahead of rivals on the basis of

---

Exhibit 8.1

Three Examples of Core Competencies

■ 3M's competency was founded originally on sticky tape. Over time it has built from this unique bundle of skills in substrates, coatings, adhesives and various ways of combining them. These core competencies have allowed it to enter and excel in businesses as diverse as 'Post-it' notes, magnetic tape, photographic film, pressure-sensitive tapes and coated abrasives.

■ Casio's core competencies are in miniaturisation, micro-processor design, material science and ultra-thin precision casings, the same skills it applies in its miniature card calculators, pocket TVs, musical instruments and digital watches.

■ Canon, the number one in photography, thanks to its ability to combine and integrate optical and micro-electronic technologies and high precision mechanics was able to move from photography to video, low price photocopiers, colour photocopiers, ink jet printers, laser printers and fax.

operational effectiveness becomes harder every day because of the rapid diffusion of best practices. Competitors can quickly imitate management techniques, new technologies, input improvements and superior ways to meet customers' needs.

In contrast, gaining a strategic competitive advantage is about being different. It means (a) deliberately choosing a *different set of activities from rivals'* or (b) performing *similar activities but in a different way*, to deliver a unique mix of values. As illustrated in Exhibit 8.2, Ikea, the global furniture retailer based in Sweden, has chosen to perform activities differently from rivals.

In the search for a competitive advantage, it is important to make a clear distinction between these two types of competitive advantage, because a strategic positioning is likely to be more sustainable in the long term than an operational competitive advantage.

Forces Driving Industry Competition

The notion of extended rivalry, due to Porter (1982), is based on the idea that a firm's ability to exploit a competitive advantage in its reference market depends not only on the direct competition it faces, but also on the role played by rival forces, such as potential entrants, substitute products, customers and suppliers. The first two forces constitute a direct threat; the other two an indirect threat, because of their bargaining power. It is the combined interplay of these five competitive forces, described in Figure 8.2, which determines the profit potential of a product market. Clearly, the dominant forces determining the competitive climate vary from one market to another. Using Porter's analysis, we will examine the role of these four external competitive forces successively. The analysis of rivalry between direct competitors will be left for later in this chapter.

Exhibit 8.2

The Strategic Positioning of Ikea

Ikea, the global furniture retailer based in Sweden, has clear strategic positioning. Ikea targets young furniture buyers who want style at low cost. In contrast with the typical furniture store, Ikea serves customers who are happy to trade off service for cost. Instead of having a sales associate trail customers around the store, Ikea uses a self-service model based on clear, in-store displays. Rather than rely solely on third-party manufacturers, Ikea designs its own low-cost, modular, ready-to-assemble furniture to fit its positioning. Although much of its low-cost position comes from having customers 'do-it-yourselves', Ikea offers a number of extra services that its competitors do not. In store child-care is one. Extended hours are another. Those services are uniquely aligned with the needs of its customers, who are young, not wealthy, likely to have children (but no nanny), and, because they work for a living, have a need to shop at odd hours.

Source: Adapted from Porter (1996, p. 65).

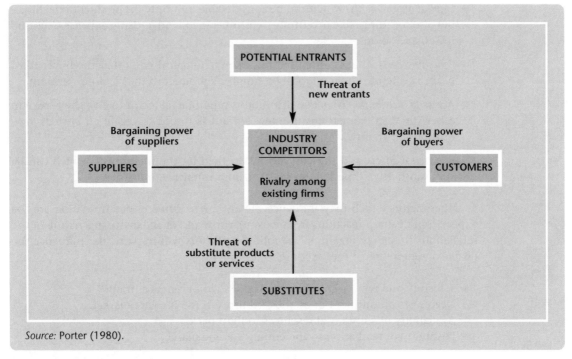

Figure 8.2   The forces driving industry competition

Threat of new entrants

Potential competitors, likely to enter a market, constitute a threat that the firm must limit and protect itself against, by creating barriers to entry. Potential entrants can be identified as follows:

- Firms outside the product market which could easily surmount the barriers to entry.
- Firms for which entry would represent a clear synergy.
- Firms for which entry is the logical conclusion of their strategy.
- Clients or suppliers who can proceed to backward or forward integration (Porter, 1980, p. 55).

The importance of the threat depends on the *barriers to entry* and on the strength of reaction that the potential entrant can expect. Possible barriers to entry are as follows:

- *Economies of scale*. These force the entrant to come in at large scale or else risk having to bear cost disadvantage.

- *Legal protection* obtained through patents, as we have seen in the case of the conflict between Kodak and Polaroid.

- *Product differentiation* and brand image, leading to a high degree of loyalty among existing customers who show little sensitivity to newcomers.

● *Capital requirements*, which can be considerable, not only for production facilities, but also for things like inventories, customer credit, advertising expenses, start-up losses, and so on.

● *Switching costs*, that is, one-time real or psychological costs that the buyer must bear to switch from an established supplier's product to that of a new entrant.

● *Access to distribution channels*: distributors might be reluctant to give shelf space to a new product; sometimes the new entrant is forced to create an entirely new distribution channel.

● *Experience effects* and the cost advantage held by the incumbent, which can be very substantial, especially in highly labour-intensive industries.

Other factors which may influence the entrant's degree of determination are the expectation of sharp reactions from existing firms and of the dissuasive nature of the retaliations they may organise. The following factors will in particular influence the degree of deterrence in the response:

● A history and reputation of aggressiveness *vis-à-vis* new entrants.
● Degree of commitment of established firms in the product market.
● Availability of substantial resources to fight back.
● Possibility of retaliation in the entrant's home market.

Put together, sustainable entry barriers and the ability to respond are the elements that determine the entry deterring price.

Threat of substitute products

Substitute products are products that can perform the same function for the same customer groups, but are based on different technologies. Referring back to the distinctions made in Chapter 6, substitute products go hand in hand with the definition of a market which is the 'set of all technologies for a given function and a given customer group'. Such products are a permanent threat because a substitution is always possible. The threat can be intensified, for instance, as a result of a technological change which modifies the substitute's quality/price as compared to the reference product market.

> The price decline in the microcomputer market has contributed to stimulate the development of electronic communication at the expense of traditional typographic equipment. Desktop publishing is taking over and many documents are now printed in house and not subcontracted to outside printing companies.

Prices of substitute products impose a ceiling on the price firms in the product market can charge. The more attractive the price–performance alternative offered by substitutes, the stronger the limit on the industry's ability to raise prices (Porter, 1982, p. 25).

> This phenomenon is observable, for instance, in the market of primary energy sources. The successive increases of oil prices has stimulated the development of alternative energy resources like solar and nuclear energy.

Clearly, substitute products that deserve particular attention are those that are subject to trends improving their price–performance trade-off with the industry's product. Moreover, in such a comparison, special attention needs to be given to switching costs (real or psychological) which can be very high and, as far as the buyer is concerned, offset the impact of the price differential.

Identifying substitute products is not always straightforward. The aim is to search systematically for products that meet the same generic need or perform the same function. This can sometimes lead to industries far removed from the main industry.

> For example, in the home-interior decoration market, the alternative technologies are: paint, wallpaper, textile, panels of wood, and so on. In the goods transportation market, the alternative technologies are: air, road, rail and water.

It would be insufficient simply to look at the common practices in the major customer groups, because the information risks appearing too late. Therefore it is necessary to have a permanent monitoring system of major technological developments in order to be able to adopt a proactive rather than a reactive behaviour. In this perspective, the concept of *solution market* presented in Chapter 6 is useful because it induces the firm to define upfront its reference market in terms of the alternative technologies susceptible to perform the same core service to the buyer.

Bargaining power of buyers

Buyers have a bargaining power *vis-à-vis* their suppliers. They can influence an activity's potential profitability by forcing the firm to cut prices, demanding more extensive services, better credit facilities or even by playing one competitor against another. The degree of influence depends on a number of conditions (Porter, 1980, pp. 24–7):

- The buyer group is concentrated and purchases *large volumes* relative to seller sales; this is so for large distributors, and, in France, for large shopping centres.
- The products that buyers purchase from the industry represent a significant fraction of their *own costs*, which drives them to bargain hard.
- The products purchased are standard or *undifferentiated*. Buyers are sure that they can always find alternative suppliers.
- The buyers' *switching costs*, or costs of changing suppliers, are few.
- Buyers pose a *credible threat of backward integration*, and are therefore dangerous potential entrants.
- The buyers have *full information* about demand, actual market prices and even supplier costs.

These conditions apply equally to consumer goods as well as industrial goods; they also apply to retailers as against wholesalers, and to wholesalers as against manufacturers. Such a situation, where buyers' bargaining power is very high, is seen in Belgium and France in the food sector, where large-scale distribution is highly concentrated and can even dictate its terms to manufacturers.

These considerations underline the fact that the choice of buyer groups to target is a crucial strategic decision. A firm can improve its competitive position by a *customer selection policy*, whereby it has a well-balanced portfolio of customers and thus avoids any kind of dependence on the buyer group.

Bargaining power of suppliers

Suppliers can exert bargaining power because they can raise the prices of their deliveries, reduce product quality or limit quantities sold to a particular buyer. Powerful suppliers can thereby squeeze profitability out of an industry unable to recover cost increases in its own prices.

> For instance, the increase in the price of basic steel products, imposed in Europe between 1980 and 1982 by the Davignon plan, contributed to profit erosion in the downstream steel transformation sector. Intense competition prevented firms in this sector from raising their prices.

The conditions making suppliers powerful are similar to those making buyers powerful (Porter, 1980, pp. 27–9):

● The supplier group is dominated by a few companies and is more concentrated than the industry it sells to.
● It is not facing other substitute products for sale to the industry.
● The firm is not an important customer of the supplier.
● The supplier's product is an important input to the buyer's business.
● The supplier group has differentiated its products or has built up switching costs to lock the buyers in.
● The supplier group poses a credible threat of forward integration.

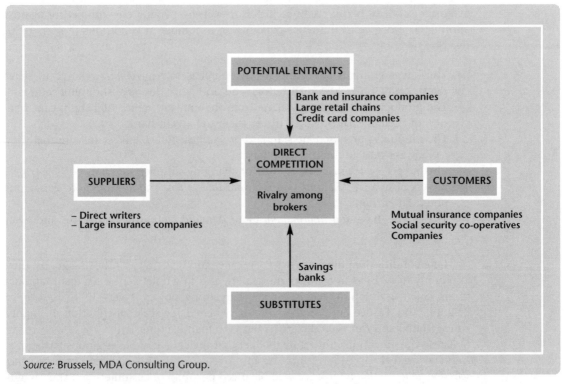

Source: Brussels, MDA Consulting Group.

Figure 8.3   Competition analysis: the private insurance brokers market

Note that the labour force used in a firm must also be recognised as a supplier. As such, and according to its degree of organisation and unionisation, labour exercises significant bargaining power which can greatly affect potential profits in an industry.

These four factors of external competition, together with rivalry among existing firms within the same product market, determine a firm's potential profitability and market power.

By way of illustration, the results of a competitive structure analysis in the private insurance brokerage market are presented in Figure 8.3.

Competitive Advantage Based on Market Power

The intensity and form of the competitive struggle between direct rivals in a product market vary according to the nature of the actual competitive structure. This defines the degree of interdependence between rivals and the extent of *market power* held by each competitor. To analyse a particular market situation, it is convenient to refer to the various competitive structures proposed by economists, for which numerous theoretical and empirical studies exist. Four competitive structures are generally distinguished: pure (or perfect) competition, oligopoly, monopolistic (or imperfect) competition and monopoly. We will examine each of these alternatives successively and describe the expected competitive behaviour in each case.

Pure or perfect competition

Perfect competition is characterised by the existence in the market of a large number of sellers facing a large number of buyers. Neither of the two groups is powerful enough to influence prices. Products have clearly defined technical characteristics, are perfect substitutes and sell at the market price, which is strictly determined by the *interplay between supply and demand*. In this kind of market, sellers have no market power whatsoever, and their behaviour is not affected by their respective actions. Key features are therefore the following:

- Large number of sellers and buyers.
- Undifferentiated and perfectly substitutable products.
- Complete absence of market power for each player.

This kind of situation can be seen in industrial markets for unbranded products, and in the *commodity markets*, such as soft commodities and the minerals and metals market. These are normally organised markets (terminal markets) such as the London Metal Exchange (LME) or the various commodity futures exchanges. In a perfectly competitive market, the interplay between supply and demand is the determining factor. As far as the firm is concerned, price is given (the dependent variable) and the quantity supplied is the action variable of interest.

To improve performance, the firm's only possible courses of action are either to modify its deliveries to the market, or to change its production capacity upward or downward, depending on the market price level. In the short term, it is essential for the firm to keep an eye on competitors' production levels and on new entrants in order to anticipate price movements.

In the long term, it is clearly in the firm's interest *to release itself from the anonymity of perfect competition* by differentiating its products to reduce substitutability, or by creating switching costs to the buyers in order to create some form of loyalty. One way of achieving this, for example, is to exercise strict quality control accompanied by a branding policy.

A number of countries exporting food products follow this kind of strategy to maintain their product's price and demand levels: Colombian coffee, Spanish oranges, Cape fruits and Swedish steel are attempts at this type of differentiation.

Another way is to develop, downstream in the industrial chain, higher added value activities incorporating the commodity, with the objectives of stabilising the level of demand and gaining protection from wild price fluctuations.

It is for instance, the strategy followed by the steel industry which diversifies its activity by entering downstream in sectors of transformation of primary steel products such as steel shingles of steel storage equipment.

How to escape from the anonymity of price competition?

This question is relevant for all the basic products labelled *commodities*, that is standard products sought by buyers for their core function at the lowest possible price. This the case for most agricultural products (wheat, corn, coffee, cocoa, sugar and so on), non-ferrous products (copper, tin, aluminium, cobalt and so on), chemical and petrochemical products, but also for products like fruit, concentrated fruit juice, textiles, and so on. For the majority of theses commodities organised markets, or bourses, exist like the London Metal Exchange (LME) or the London Commodity Market, where it is the interplay of supply and demand that determines *the market price*, which is then used as a reference price by the buyers and imposed on the seller.

From the commodity firm's point of view, two steps are required to escape from this competitive stalemate: (a) a systematic search for differentiation opportunities and (b) a fine market segmentation to undercover segments of buyers having more demanding purchase criteria.

A commodity is also a bundle of attributes

In approaching the commodity buyer, it is essential to keep in mind a global view of his problem and to analyse buyers' needs in terms of a *solution to his problem* and not only in terms of quantity to be sold. As explained above, to the buyer a product is a package of benefits or a bundle of attributes (see Figure 3.6) which of course comprises the core service or function, but also peripheral services, necessary or added, which accompany the core service provided by the commodity. In a pure competition market, only the core service is identical from one rival to the other and cannot therefore justify a price premium. But the seller can still differentiate himself from competition through the other services or attributes of the bundle, such as services, guarantee, assistance in use, technical support, and so on, and that, not only at the purchase phase, but also at each phase of the cycle *acquisition–use–maintenance–destruction–recycling* of the commodity.

Table 8.1 The search for differentiation opportunities

Value Creation	Value Delivery Mode	
	Through Product	Through Service
Consistency	Quality control	Reliability
Customisation	Adaptation	Assistance
Convenience	Packaging	Just-in-time

Source: Hill *et al.* (1998).

The problem is to discover what are the sensitive services to which the buyer is likely to respond and at what phase of the cycle. Hence the importance of a fine market segmentation. As shown in Table 8.1, differentiation opportunities always exist, even in commodity markets, either through value creation or through delivery mode.

Segmentation of commodity markets

In commodity markets, it is common practice to segment their customers by product and consuming industry and not by reference to their purchasing behaviour. In reality, no market is completely homogeneous in terms of customers' needs or expectations and, as explained in Chapter 6, the objective of market behavioural segmentation is to uncover customer(s) group(s) having different purchase criteria, more specific or more demanding, and who would be ready to pay a price higher than the reference market price to obtain exactly what they need.

According to Booz Allen and Hamilton (Hill *et al.*, 1998) three types of customers always exist, even in commodity markets: the incorrigibles, the potentials and the gold standard customers:

● The *incorrigibles*, also called the price sensitive buyers, are the pure price buyers who treat suppliers as the enemy and focus exclusively on current delivered price. They are primarily concerned with the cost, as the product usually represents a major portion of their total product cost or because their needs are fairly standard. They will switch suppliers for even the slightest price differential. Unfortunately they constitute half of the market or more. They are not attractive customers but so prevalent, that no supplier can seriously think about refusing them.

● The *potentials*, or the service customers, also place a high emphasis on pure price, but are occasionally willing to entertain the notion of selective relationships involving certain products or services. Customers in this segment, representing 30–45 per cent of the market, have some degree of interest in partnering in certain circumstances for reducing delivery costs, to avoid supply interruptions or for specific industrial applications. Once it is possible to move the dialogue beyond delivery price, the potential for differentiation exists.

● The *gold standard customers*, also called the commitment-focused customers, value long-standing relationships through which superior product applications can be developed and employed in their own products and processes. They will pay a premium price for offerings that deliver true value in terms of process enhancement, cost reduction or benefits to end-user. They typically represent a small portion of the total market, anywhere from 5 to 25 per cent.

Booz, Allen and Hamilton (BAH) reports that one study in steel strapping found that 8 per cent of the customers fit into this last category, while another piece of research carried out by BAH found that segment ranging as high as 22 per cent in some chemical markets.

While most wheat buyers require wheat to meet only two or three specifications, demanding buyers such as the Japanese may have a list of 20 requirements. Using its computerised capacity to monitor the precise content of the wheat in all 1500 of Australia's silos, the Australian Wheat Board track down the hard-to-find wheat the Japanese demand. Across all their customers, the Board earn a high price realisation of $2 a ton, a significant advantage in a low margin business. (Hill *et al.*, 1998, p. 29)

Table 8.2   How steel end-users choose suppliers

Purchase criteria used by buyers	Segments: buyers choose suppliers by:		
	Price (*n*=113)	Service (*n*=91)	Commitment (*n*=96)
Lowest price	3.4	2.3	2.5
Emergency response	3.4	3.7	3.2
On-time delivery	3.6	3.8	3.2
Responsive inside sales	2.9	3.5	2.8
Responsive after sales	2.3	2.3	2.3
Short lead time	3.1	3.3	2.5
Technical support	2.2	2.3	2.8
Industry commitment	2.9	2.2	2.7
Investment in mill	2.0	1.8	2.4
EDI links	1.4	1.4	1.9
Investment in R&D	1.4	1.9	2.4

Criteria rated on a scale of 1 (not important) to 4 (very important).
Source: Schorsch (1994).

As shown in Table 8.2, an in-depth appreciation of the needs of customers (in this example, the steel industry) reveals differentiation opportunities for the seller who can propose offerings having superior value to the buyer. An interesting observation made in this steel survey reported by McKinsey (Schorsch, 1994) is that each industry segment contains price, service and commitment buyers. Performance requirements simply do not correlate with industry segments (car customers, pipe and tube makers, construction, and so on.)

Oligopoly

Oligopoly is a situation where the number of competitors is low or a few firms are dominant. As a result rival firms are highly interdependent. In markets concentrated in this way, each firm knows well the forces at work and the actions of one firm are felt by the others, who are inclined to react. Therefore, the outcome of a strategic action depends largely on whether or not competing firms react.

The more undifferentiated the products of existing firms, the greater the dependence between them will be; in this case we talk about *undifferentiated oligopoly*, as opposed to *differentiated oligopoly*, where goods have significant distinctive qualities of value to the buyers. Oligopolistic situations tend to prevail in product markets having reached the maturity phase of their life cycle, where primary demand is stagnant and non-expansible.

The mechanisms of a price war

In undifferentiated oligopoly, products are perceived as 'commodities' and buyers' choices are mainly based on price and the service rendered. These conditions are therefore ripe for intense price competition, unless a dominant firm can impose a discipline and force a leading price. This situation is one of *price leadership*, in which the dominant firm's price is the reference price used by all competitors. On the other hand, if price competition does develop, it generally leads to reduced profitability for everyone, especially if primary demand is non-expansible. A *price war* then gets under way, as follows:

● A price cut initiated by one firm creates an important market share movement due to buyers attracted by the reduced price.

● The firm's market share increases. Other firms feel this immediately, given that their own shares drop. They begin to adopt the same price cut to overturn the movement.

● Price equality between rivals is restored, but at a lower level, which is less profitable for all.

● Since primary demand is non-expansible, the price cut has not contributed to increasing the market size.

Lack of co-operation or discipline causes everyone's situation to deteriorate. In a non-expansible market, competition becomes a *zero-sum game*. Firms seeking to increase sales can only achieve it at the expense of direct competitors. As a result, competition is more aggressive than when there is growth, where each firm has the possibility of increasing its sales by simply growing at the same pace as primary demand, that is with constant market share.

Alternative competitive behaviour

In a stagnant oligopolistic market, explicit consideration of competitors' behaviour is an essential aspect of strategy development. *Competitive behaviour* refers to the attitude adopted by a firm in its decision-making process, with regard to its competitors' actions and reactions. The attitudes observed in practice can be classified into five typical categories:

● *Independent behaviour* is observed when competitors' actions and/or reactions are not taken into account, either implicitly or explicitly, in the firm's decisions. This attitude is observed in particular with regard to operational decisions, and is sometimes seen even in the case of strategic choices, in firms with a dominant market position.

● *Co-operative behaviour* corresponds to a confident or complacent attitude which seeks, tacitly or explicitly, understanding or collusion rather than systematic confrontation. Tacit agreement is frequently seen between medium-sized firms; explicit or cartel agreement, on the other hand, takes place more between large firms in oligopolistic markets which are not subject to competition regulations or which are controlled very little in this respect. Anti-trust officials in the USA and the Competition Commission in the EU are actively pursuing cartel agreements and can impose severe fines and prison sentences (see Exhibit 8.3).

● *Follower behaviour* is based on an explicit consideration of competitors' actions; it consists of adapting one's own decisions to the observed decisions of competitors, without, however, anticipating their subsequent reactions. If all existing competitors adopt this kind of behaviour, a succession of mutual adaptations is observed, until stability is achieved.

● *Leader behaviour* is a more sophisticated behaviour. It consists of anticipating competitors' reactions to the firm's own decisions, assuming they have the previous type of behaviour; here, the firm is assumed to know its rivals' reaction function and to incorporate it when elaborating its strategy. As strategic marketing develops, it is seen ever more frequently in oligopolistic markets, where competition laws are strictly enforced.

● *Aggressive or warfare behaviour* also consists in anticipating competitors' reactions to the firm's decisions. But in this case, rivals' behaviour is assumed to be such that they always adopt the strategy most harmful to their adversaries. This type of behaviour is mainly observed in oligopolistic markets where primary demand is stagnant and any one firm's gains must be at the expense of the others. This kind of situation is analysed in game theory as a 'zero sum' game, with optimal strategy being the one with the lowest risk of loss.

Exhibit 8.3

Anti-trust Laws in Action

Two top European companies have been fined a record $725 million in the US for their part in a nine-year conspiracy to control the market of vitamins. A former executive was jailed for four months and fined $100,000 for his role in the cartel. The cartel lasted almost a decade and involved a highly sophisticated and elaborate conspiracy to control everything about the sale of these products. The companies acted as if they were working for the same business, referred to by executives as Vitamins Inc. Executives met once a year for a summit to fix their annual budget, setting prices, carving geographic markets and setting volumes of sales. The summit was followed by monitoring meetings, quarterly reviews and frequent correspondence. The European Commission was also investigating whether pharmaceutical companies had been involved in a vitamin price fixing cartel.

Source: The Financial Times, 21 May 1999.

The most frequent behaviour in undifferentiated oligopoly is of the follower or leader kind. It is, however, not rare to observe aggressive behaviour of the kind described in game theory, especially as regards price decisions, with the risk of leading to price wars which are generally harmful to all.

Marketing warfare

In industrialised economies, oligopolistic situations are frequent. In many industrial sectors, firms face each other with weakly differentiated products, in stagnant and saturated markets, where one firm's gains are necessarily another's losses. A key factor in success is thwarting competitors' actions. This kind of competitive climate obviously breeds the adoption of *marketing warfare*, which puts the destruction of the adversary at the centre of preoccupations. Kotler and Singh (1981), Ries and Trout (1986), Durö and Sandström (1988) have taken the analogy with *military strategy* even further and proposed various typologies of competitive strategies directly inspired from von Clausewitz (1908). As put by Ries and Trout (1986, p. 7):

> The true nature of marketing is not serving the customer, it is outwitting, outflanking and outfighting your competitors.

This point of view is in conflict with the market-driven orientation presented in Chapter 2, which suggests that a balance should be maintained between customer and competitor orientations. What is the advantage, indeed, of beating competitors in products that the customer does not want?

Competitive reaction matrix

Firms compete with one another by emphasising different elements of the marketing mix and by insisting differently on each component of the mix. The competitive reaction matrix presented in Table 8.3 is a useful instrument for analysing alternative action–reaction patterns among two competing companies (Lambin, 1976, pp. 22–7). The matrix might include two brands, the studied brand and its priority competitor, and three or four components of the marketing mix, such as price, media advertising, promotion or product quality.

> In Table 8.3, the horizontal rows designate the actions initiated by our brand A. The alternative actions might be to cut price, increase advertising or improve quality. The responses of brand B, the direct competitor, are represented by the vertical columns. The coefficients in the matrix are the reaction probabilities of brand B reacting to brand A's move.

On the diagonal we have the *direct reaction probabilities*, or the likelihood of brand B responding to a move of brand A with the same marketing instrument, that is meeting a price cut with a price cut. Off diagonal, we have the *indirect reaction elasticities*, or the probabilities of brand B responding to brand A with another marketing instrument, for example, meeting a price cut with increased advertising. These reaction elasticities can be estimated by reference to past behaviour or by seeking management's judgement concerning the strengths and weaknesses of competition. Once the matrix is developed, management can review each potential marketing action in the light of probable competitor reactions.

The entries of the matrix are probabilities, as in Table 8.3, their horizontal sum must be equal to one.

For example, if management considers that there is a 70 per cent chance that competition will meet our price cut, but only a 20 per cent chance that it will meet a quality increase, it might consider that a quality increase programme will help more to develop a unique marketing approach than the price cut, since it is less likely to be imitated.

Table 8.3   Competitive reaction matrix

Brand A Actions	Competing Brand B's Reactions		
	Price (p)	Advertising (a)	Quality (x)
Price	$P_{p,p}$[1]	$P_{p,a}$	$P_{p,x}$
Advertising	$P_{a,p}$	$P_{a,a}$	$P_{a,x}$
Quality	$P_{x,p}$	$P_{x,a}$	$P_{x,x}$

1. The first subscript is for the brand initiating the move; the second for is for the rival's response.
Source: Lambin (1976, p. 24).

The competitive matrix is useful in helping to develop a distinctive marketing approach to the market and to anticipate competitors' reactions. More columns can be added, representing other marketing instruments. Delayed responses can also be analysed. For an example of an application in the electric razor market, see Lambin *et al.* (1975).

Competitor analysis system

The attitude to be adopted towards competitors is central to any strategy. This attitude must be based on a refined analysis of competitors. Porter (1980, p. 47) describes the purpose of analysing competitors as follows:

The objective of a competitor analysis is to develop a profile of the nature and success of the likely strategy changes each competitor might make, each competitor's probable response to the range of feasible strategic moves other firms could initiate, and each competitor's probable reaction to the array of industry changes and broader environmental shifts that might occur.

There are four areas of interest which constitute the structure to guide the collection and analysis of information about competitors. The relevant questions are the following:

● What are the competitors' major objectives?
● What is the current strategy being employed to achieve the objectives?
● What are the capabilities of rivals to implement their strategies?
● What are their likely future strategies?

The first three parts of the analysis are the background data needed to predict the future strategies. Together, these four areas of information collection and analysis compose a fairly complete picture of the competitors' activities. Some companies have discovered the importance of competitor analysis. Some examples are:

- IBM has a commercial analysis department with thousands of branch office representatives responsible for reporting information about the competition.
- Texas Instruments has employees analyse government contracts won by competitors to discern their technological strengths.
- Citicorp has an executive with the title 'manager of competitive intelligence'.
- McDonald's distributes a Burger King and Wendy's Competitive Action Package to its store managers.

Strong competitive interdependence in a product market is not very attractive, because it limits the firm's freedom of action. To escape it, the firm can either try to differentiate itself from rivals, or seek new product markets through creative market segmentation.

Imperfect or monopolistic competition

Monopolistic competition is halfway between competition and monopoly (Chamberlin, 1950). There are many competitors whose market powers are evenly distributed. But their products are differentiated in the sense that, from the buyer's point of view, they possess significantly distinct characteristics and are perceived as such by the whole product market. Differentiation may take different forms: for example the taste of a drink, a particular technical characteristic, an innovative combination of features which provides the possibility of a variety of different uses, quality and extent of customer services, the distribution channel, power of brand image, and so on. Monopolistic competition is therefore founded on a *differentiation strategy* based on external competitive advantage.

Conditions for successful differentiation

For a *differentiation strategy* to be successful, a number of conditions need to be present:

- The differentiation should provide something which is *unique*, beyond simply offering a low price (see Exhibit 8.4).
- The element of uniqueness must represent some *value* to buyers.
- This value can either represent a better *performance* (higher satisfaction), or reduced cost.
- The value to buyers must be high enough for them to be prepared to pay a *price premium* to benefit from it.
- The element of differentiation must be *sustainable*; in other words, other rivals should not be able to imitate it immediately.
- The price premium paid by buyers must exceed the *cost supplement* borne by the firm to produce and maintain the element of differentiation.
- Finally, in so far as the element of differentiation is not very apparent and is unknown by the market, the firm must produce *signals* to make it known.

The effect of differentiation is to give the firm some degree of *market power*, because it generates preferences, customer loyalty and lower price sensitivity. The buyer's

Exhibit 8.4

The Search for Differentiation Ideas

A differentiation strategy gives the firm the opportunity to claim its difference with its direct competitors. This strategy makes it possible at the same or at a higher price, to increase market share or to keep it unchanged. This strategy is feasible only if some distance exists on one or several important product attributes compared to the competition. Chetochine (1997, p. 141) suggests four differentiation dimensions susceptible to create that distance *vis-à-vis* direct rivals.

A product or service can be different because it has one or several of the following innovative features: reformulating, simplifying, accelerating or improving:

- **Reformulating**: a product or service based on another technology or on another way to proceed, even if it produces similar results at the same price (phone banking).
- **Simplifying**: a product which saves effort, steps or energy (the Windows software).
- **Accelerating**: a product which generates time savings compared to traditional products (the self-scanning system in supermarkets).
- **Improving**: a product providing the user with better service or better performance (Pentium in microcomputers).

A product can distance itself from rivals on several dimensions. Phone banking, for example, is at the same time a new procedure, simplifying and accelerating, but not necessarily better in terms of service quality.

Source: Adapted from Chetochine (1997).

bargaining power is thus partially neutralised. Differentiation also protects the firm from rival attacks, given that as a result of the element of differentiation, substitution between products is reduced. The monopolistic firm is relatively independent in its actions *vis-à-vis* its rivals. Finally, it also helps the firm to defend itself better against suppliers and substitute products. *This is the typical competitive situation that strategic marketing seeks to create* (for an example see Figure 8.4).

In monopolistic competition, the firm offers a differentiated product and thus holds an external competitive advantage. This 'market power' places it in a protected position, and allows the firm to earn profits above the market average. Its strategic aim is therefore to exploit this preferential demand, while keeping an eye on the value and duration of the element of differentiation.

Measuring market power

The degree of *market power* is measured by the firm's ability to dictate a price above that of its priority competitors. One measure of this sensitivity is the price elasticity of the firm's or differentiated product's selective demand. The lower this demand elasticity, the less volatile or sensitive will market share be to a price increase.

If brand A has price elasticity equal to –1.5 and brand B an elasticity of –3.0; the same price increase of 5 per cent will lower demand for A by 7.5 per cent and demand for B by 15 per cent.

Therefore, a firm or brand with market power has a less elastic demand than a poorly differentiated product. As a result, it is in a position to make the group of buyers or consumers who are sensitive to the element of differentiation accept a higher price.

The brand strength refers to the buyers' degree of attachment or loyalty to a brand or company. Probably the best test of brand loyalty would be to know what a customer would do if she (or he) does not find her preferred brand in the visited store. Will she switch to another brand or will she visit another store?

As already presented in Chapter 5, one can identify at least five indicators of a brand's strength:

1. *A lower price sensitivity.* A strong brand displays a stronger resistance to a price increase than its competitors.

2. *Acceptable price premiums.* A brand is strong if people are prepared to pay more for it (see Table 8.4). Conversely, a weak brand has to propose a price lower than the price charged by its competitors.

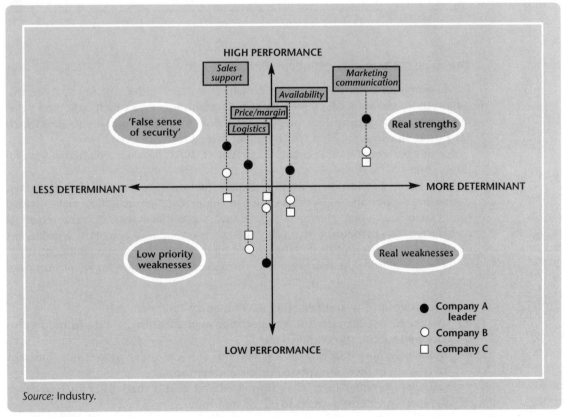

Source: Industry.

Figure 8.4 Impact of a successful differentiation strategy: an example from the office equipment market

3. *Exclusivity rate*. The more loyal customer is the one for whom the brand represents a higher share of category requirement.

4. *Dynamic loyalty rate*. An alternative to share of category requirement is to look at patterns of purchasing over time, and use this to estimate the probability of a consumer buying the brand on the next purchase occasion.

5. *Positive attitudinal measures*. Indicators like familiarity, esteem, perceived quality, purchase intentions (brand loyalty) and so on, are also good indicators of a brand's strength.

Example of price premiums charged by powerful brands are presented in Table 8.4.

Table 8.4 Examples of price premium available to strong brands

Price premium available to Hertz and Avis compared with		Price premium available to IBM compared with		Price premium available to British Airways compared with	
Budget	20.4%	Apple	10.0%	Virgin	11.0%
EuroDollar	22.5%	Compaq	17.0%	Delta	41.0%
Europcar	24.0%	Amstrad	40.0%	Air-India	45.0%
		Dell	46.0%		

Source: Thomas (1993).

The value chain in differentiation analysis

In the search for a source uniqueness on which to base a differentiation strategy, two pitfalls should be avoided: (a) identify elements of uniqueness which customers value but that the firm is incapable of supplying; (b) identify elements of uniqueness which the firm is able to supply but which are not valued by customers.

For this purpose the value chain model (Porter, 1982) provides a particularly useful framework.

Every firm is a collection of activities that are performed to design, produce, market, deliver and support its products. As shown in Figure 8.5, these activities can be divided into two broad types, *primary* activities and *support* activities. A value chain is constructed for a particular firm on the basis of the importance and of the separateness of different activities and also on the basis of their capacity for creating differentiation.

By way of illustration, representative sources of differentiation for *primary activities* could be:

● *Purchasing*: quality and reliability of components and materials.
● *Operations*: fast manufacturing, defect-free manufacturing, ability to produce to customer specifications and so on.
● *Warehousing and distribution*: fast delivery, efficient order processing, sufficient inventories to meet unexpected orders and so on.
● *Sales and marketing*: high advertising level and quality, high sales force coverage and quality, extensive credit to buyers and so on.
● *Customer service*: in-use assistance, training for customers, fast and reliable repairs and so on.

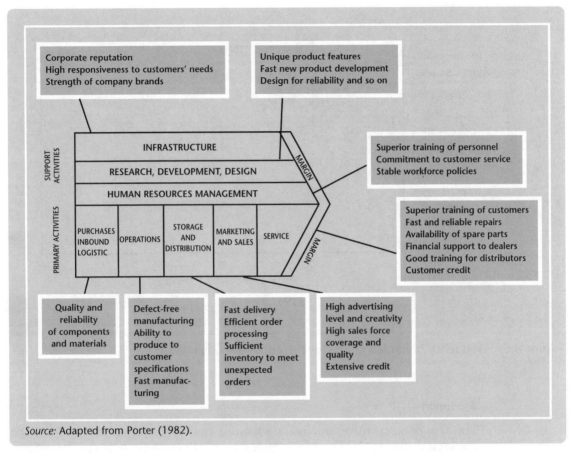

Source: Adapted from Porter (1982).

Figure 8.5   The generic value chain model

Similarly, for *support activities*, potential sources of differentiation are:

● *Human resources*: superior training of personnel, commitment to customer service, stable workforce policies and so on.
● *R&D:* unique product features, fast new product development, design for reliability and so on.
● *Infrastructure*: corporate reputation, responsiveness to customers needs and so on.

The objective is to identify the drivers of uniqueness in each activity, that is the variables and the actions through which the firm can achieve uniqueness in relation to competitors' offerings and provide value to the buyer. The merit of the value chain model is to suggest that the search for a sustainable competitive advantage is the role of every function within the organisation and not only of the marketing function.

It is interesting in this respect to make reference to the work of Simon (1996), already quoted in this book, who has analysed the strategies adopted by a sample of 122 firms (a majority of German firms) which are (a) world or European leaders in their reference market, (b) of small or medium size and (c) unfamiliar to the general public. Inspection of Figure 8.6 shows that the type of competitive advantage held by those *Hidden Champions* is largely based on product superiority.

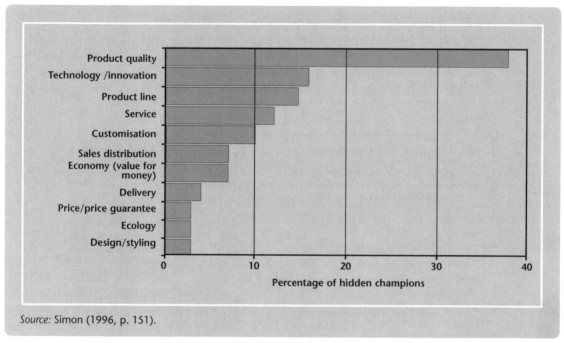

Source: Simon (1996, p. 151).

Figure 8.6 Frequency of hidden champions' competitive advantage

Monopoly

This type of competitive structure is a limiting case, as for perfect competition. The market is dominated by a single producer facing a large number of buyers. Its product is therefore, for a limited period of time, without any direct competitor in its category. This kind of situation is observed in the introductory stage of a product's life cycle, namely in emerging industries characterised by high technology innovations.

If monopoly exists, the firm has a market power which in principle is substantial. In reality, this power is rapidly threatened by new entrants who are attracted by the possibility of growth and profits. The foreseeable duration of monopoly then becomes an essential factor. It will depend on the innovation's power and the existence of sustainable barriers to entry. A monopoly situation is always temporary, due to the rapid diffusion of technological innovations. We saw in the previous chapter the strategic options and the risks that characterise innovation monopoly. A monopolist is also subject to competition from substitute products.

The logic of state or government monopolies is different from that of private firms. It is no longer the logic of profit, but that of public good and public service. Fulfilling these objectives in public services is hard because there is no incentive to adopt a market orientation. On the contrary, the public or state organisation favours the adoption of a self-centred or bureaucratic orientation. This is one of the reasons in favour of the policy of deregulation adopted in many European countries.

This problem is dealt with in the field of social marketing, or marketing of non-profit organisations, which has developed quite substantially over the last few years.

The dynamics of competition

Concluding the analysis of competitive forces, it is clear that market power and profit potential can vary widely from one market situation to another. We can thus put two limiting cases aside: one is the case where profit potential is almost zero; in the other case, it is very high. In the first case, the following situation will be observed:

● Entry into the product market is free.
● Existing firms have no bargaining power as against their clients and suppliers.
● Competition is unrestrained because of the large number of rival firms.
● Products are all similar and there are many substitutes.

This is the model of *perfect competition* dear to economists. The other limiting case is where profit potential is extremely high:

● There are powerful barriers that block entry to new competitors.
● The firm has either no competitors or a few weak competitors.
● Buyers cannot turn to substitute products.
● Buyers do not have enough bargaining power to make prices go down.
● Suppliers do not have enough bargaining power to make increased costs acceptable.

This is the ideal situation for the firm which will have a very strong *market power*. Market reality is obviously somewhere in-between these two limits. It is the interplay of competitive forces that favours one or other of these situations.

● Competitive Advantage Based on Cost Domination

Gaining market power through successful product differentiation is one way to gain a competitive advantage. Another way is to achieve cost domination *vis-à-vis* competition through better productivity and cost controls. Cost reductions can be achieved in many ways. In many industries, where the value added to the product accounts for a large percentage of the total cost, it has been observed that there is an opportunity to lower costs as a firm gains experience in producing a product.

The observation that there exist *experience effects* was made by Wright (1936) and the Boston Consulting Group (1968) who, towards the end of the 1960s, verified the existence of such an effect for more than 2000 different products, and deduced a law known as the *experience law* (see Exhibit 8.5). This law, which has had great influence on the strategies adopted by some firms, translates and formalises at the firm level what economists study at the aggregate level: improvements in productivity. We will first present the theoretical foundations of the experience law, and then discuss its strategic implications.

The experience law defined

The strategic importance of the experience law stems from the fact that it makes it possible not only to forecast one's own costs, but also to forecast competitors' costs. The law of experience stipulates that:

> The unit cost of value added to a standard product, measured in constant currency, declines by a constant percentage each time the accumulated production doubles.

Exhibit 8.5

The Mathematics of Experience Curves

The mathematical expression for the experience curve is as follows:

$$C_p = C_b \cdot (C_p/Q_b)^{-\varepsilon}$$

where

C_p = projected unit cost
C_b = base unit cost
Q = experience: cumulated volume of production
ε = constant: unit cost elasticity

Thus we have

$$\text{Projected cost} = \text{Base cost} \times \left(\frac{\text{Projected experience}}{\text{Base experience}} \right)^{-\varepsilon}$$

The cost elasticity (ε) can be estimated as follows:

$$\frac{C_p}{C_b} = \left(\frac{Q_p}{Q_b} \right)^{-\varepsilon}$$

and hence

$$\varepsilon = -\left(\frac{\log C_p - \log C_b}{\log Q_b - \log Q_b} \right)$$

In practice, it is convenient to refer to a doubling of experience. When the ratio of projected experience to base experience is equal to 2 (that is, $Q_p/Q_b = 2$) we obtain

$$\frac{C_p}{C_b} = 2^{-\varepsilon}$$

where $2^{-\varepsilon}$ is defined as Lambda (λ), the slope of the experience curve.

A certain number of points in this definition deserve further comments:

● The word 'experience' has a very precise meaning: it designates the *cumulative number of units produced* and not the number of years since the firm began making the product.

● Thus the growth of production per period must not be confused with the growth of experience. Experience grows even if production stagnates or declines.

● The experience law is a *statistical law* and not a natural one; it is an observation which is statistically verified in some situations, but not always. Costs do not spontaneously go down; they go down if someone pushes them down through productivity improvements.

● Costs must be measured in *constant monetary units*, that is, they must be adjusted for inflation. Inflation can hide the experience effect.

● The experience effect is always stronger during the *launch and growth stages* of a new product's development cycle; later improvements are proportionally weaker and weaker as the product market reaches maturity.

● The experience law applies only to *value added costs*, that is costs over which the firm has some control, such as costs of transformation, assembly, distribution and service. Recall that value added is equal to selling price minus input costs: the cost of value added is given by unit cost minus input costs.

In practice, total unit cost is often used as the basis of observation of experience effects, especially because it is more easily accessible than value added cost. The error introduced in this way is not too high when the cost of value added represents a large proportion of the total unit cost.

Causes of experience effects

Several factors contribute to drive unit costs down the experience curve (Figure 8.7). They are the improvements adopted by management in the production process as a result of learning from accumulated output. Abell and Hammond (1979) have identified seven sources of experience effects:

● *Labour Efficiency*. As workers repeat a particular task, they become more dextrous and learn improvements and short-cuts which increase their efficiency.

● *Work Specialisation and Methods Improvements*. Specialisation increases worker proficiency at a given task.

● *New Production Processes*. Process innovations and improvements can be an important source of cost reductions, such as the introduction of robotics or of computer-assisted systems.

● *Better Performance from Production Equipment*. When first designed, a piece of production equipment may have a conservatively rated output. Experience may reveal innovative ways of increasing its output.

● *Changes in the Resource Mix*. As experience accumulates, a producer can often incorporate different or less expensive resources in the operation. For instance, less skilled workers can replace skilled workers, or automation can replace labour.

● *Product Redesign*. Once the firm has a clear understanding of the performance requirements, a product can be redesigned to incorporate less costly materials and resources.

These factors are all under the control of the firm. They are part of the general policy of the firm of productivity improvements aiming at making an equivalent product for

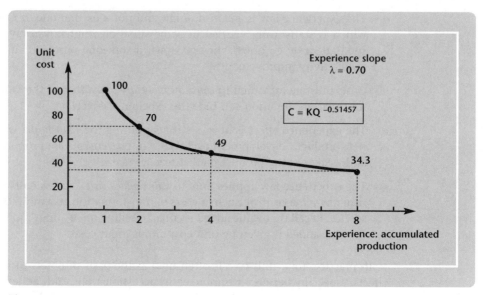

Figure 8.7   Example of an experience curve

less cost or at making a better product for the same cost or a combination of the two. Thus experience *per se* does not generate cost reductions, but rather provides *opportunities for cost reductions*. It is up to management to exploit these opportunities.

To what extent are experience effects different from *scale effects*? Scale effects are different from experience effects, even if in practice it is difficult to separate the two. Two major differences exist:

- Scale effects arise from the size of the operation, while experience effects accrue over time. The time dimension is what makes them different. Confusion between the two effects arises because size increases as experience accumulates.

- Another important difference exists. Cost advantages due to size always exist: fixed costs are divided by a larger number of units, thereby diminishing the unit cost. Cost advantages due to experience do not occur naturally: they are the result of concerted efforts to diminish costs.

Thus, scale effects can exist as a consequence of experience effects. For instance, the cost of capital (relative to that of its competitors) should decline as the firm becomes bigger and gains access to more and cheaper sources of capital. But scale effects can also exist independently of experience effects and vice versa.

Formulation of the experience law

The general expression of the experience curve is the following:

$$\text{Expected cost} = \text{Reference cost} \left(\frac{\text{Expected cumulative production}}{\text{Reference cumulative production}} \right)^{-\varepsilon}$$

It is common practice to refer to a doubling of the accumulated production. The ratio between the expected experience (Q_p) and the reference experience (Q_b) is then equal to 2 and one has

$$\text{Expected cost} = \text{Reference cost} \cdot (2)^{-\varepsilon}$$

where $2^{-\varepsilon}$ is denoted by the Greek letter λ, and called the experience slope.

In the above equation, if ($\varepsilon = 0.515$, λ the experience slope is equal to 0.70 and C_p will be equal to $0.70(C_b)$. This means that the unit expected cost of production C_p, when the cumulative volume doubles, will be equal to 70 per cent of the reference cost (C_b).

$$\text{Expected cost} = (\text{Reference cost}) \cdot (\text{Experience slope})$$

The experience slope, λ, measures therefore the percentage of cost reduction to its reference value. In Table 8.5., the values of λ, the experience slope for different values of the cost elasticity (ε), for lambda values from λ 70 to 100 per cent.

Table 8.5 Relationship between the cost elasticity and the experience slope

Experience slope (λ)	1.00	0.95	0.90	0.85	0.80	0.75	0.70
Cost elasticity (ε)	0	0.074	0.152	0.234	0.322	0.450	0.515

In Figure 8.7 we can see that the cost of the first unit is 100F and that of the second is 70F. When the cumulative quantity has doubled from 1 to 2, unit cost has decreased by 30 per cent; the cost of the fourth unit will therefore be 49F, the cost of the eighth unit 34.3F, of the sixteenth 24F, and so on. In this example, the rate of cost decline is 30 per cent per doubling, and the experience slope is 70 per cent. This corresponds to a cost elasticity of –0.515.

Often, the co-ordinates of an experience curve are expressed on a logarithmic scale, so as to represent it as a straight line. The larger the slope of the curve, the steeper the straight line. Experience slopes observed in practice lie between 0.70 (high degree of experience effect) and 1.00 (zero experience effect). The Boston Consulting Group observes that most experience curves have slopes between 70 and 80 per cent.

Table 8.6 Annual percentage of cost reduction due to experience effects

Experience curve slope	Annual market growth rate				
	2%	5%	10%	20%	30%
90%	0.3	0.7	1.4	2.7	3.9
80%	0.6	1.6	3.0	5.7	8.1
70%	1.0	2.5	4.8	8.0	12.6
60%	1.4	3.5	6.8	12.6	17.6

Source: Hax and Majluf (1984).

For a given firm, the impact of experience effects depends not only on its experience slope, but also on the speed at which experience accumulates. The possibility of reducing costs will be higher in sectors which have rapidly growing markets; similarly, for a given firm, the potential for cost reduction is high if its market share increases sharply, irrespective of whether or not the reference market is expanding. The figures in Table 8.6 give expected percentage reductions in annual costs for different experience slopes and different rates of sales growth.

Statistical estimation of experience curves

The statistical estimation of experience curves is made with historical data on unit costs (sometimes on the basis of unit prices) and on cumulative quantities, which should ideally cover several doublings of cumulated volume. Analysis of different cost components should in principle be carried out separately in order to pinpoint those that are behaving differently. For each group, unit costs are considered against cumulative volume, and after logarithmic transformations a line is fitted by the method of least squares. The estimated function is then used to forecast future costs for each of the components.

Two measurement problems occur regularly in estimating experience curves: the non-availability of competitors' cost data and the choice of the experience measurement units. To overcome the first problem, average prices for the industry as a whole are used. An alternative is to accept the assumption that all players in a particular product market are driving the same experience curve, an acceptable assumption if the same technology is prevalent. As to the experience measurement unit, the total number of units produced may not always be the most appropriate basis for measuring cumulative experience.

> For instance, the experience curve phenomenon may not be readily discernible if a firm manufacturing refrigerators in various sizes ranging from 2 cubic feet to 26 cubic feet of storage space were to employ the number of units produced as a measure of cumulative experience. Cubic feet of refrigeration space may be a more appropriate measure when the experience phenomenon is examined at the aggregate product level (Kerin *et al.*, 1990, p. 117).

The estimated experience curves are only valid if the conditions that gave rise to past observations remain stable: the firm manufactures the same product according to the same process and technology. These conditions are in reality never fully satisfied. Like many management tools, the experience law is more a tool of analysis than an accurate forecasting instrument. Nevertheless, it is of great value in analysing disparities in competitive capacity and evaluating the significance of competitive cost advantage.

Strategic implications of the experience law

The experience law helps us understand how a competitive advantage can exist based on a disparity in unit costs between rival firms operating in the same market, and using the same means of production. The strategic implications of the experience law can be summarised as follows:

● The firm with the largest cumulated production will have the *lowest* costs, *if the experience effect is properly exploited.*

● The aggressive firm will try to drive down as *rapidly as possible* its experience curve, so as to build a cost advantage over its direct competitors.

● The goal is to grow faster than priority competitors, which implies *increased relative market share*.

● This growth objective is best achieved *right at the start*, when gains in experience are most significant.

● The most effective way of gaining market share is to adopt a *price penetration* strategy, whereby the firm fixes price at a level which anticipates future cost reductions.

● This strategy will give the firm *above normal profit* performance.

Thus, in an experience-based strategy, building market share and penetration pricing are the key success factors for achieving a competitive advantage based on cost domination. Figure 8.8 illustrates the mechanism of a price penetration policy.

> The firm anticipates the movement of its unit cost in terms of cumulative production. It sets itself a target to reach which implies a faster sales growth than in the reference market and hence an increase in its relative market share. The selling price, when launching the product, is determined with respect to this anticipated volume. Once the level of experience has been reached, future cost decreases will be reflected in the price to maintain the advantage over priority competitors.

The pricing strategy illustrated by Figure 8.8(b) is more frequently observed because it is less risky: the price is reduced in parallel with the cost decline.

Assessing competitive costs disparities

If cumulative production does lead to the expected cost reduction, and if the dominant firm manages to protect the benefit of the experience it acquires, the experience effect creates an entry barrier to new entrants and a cost advantage for the leader. Firms with low market shares will inevitably have higher costs, and if they fix their prices at the same level as the dominant competitor they have to suffer heavy losses.

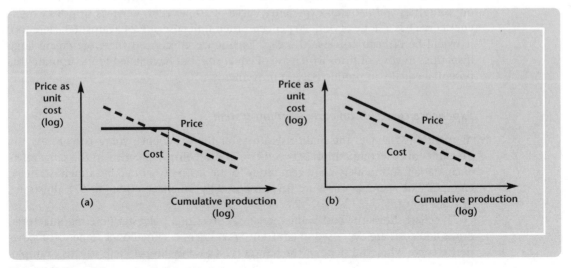

Figure 8.8   Price penetation strategy

Furthermore, the firm with the highest market share also enjoys larger cash flows. It can reinvest in new equipment or new processes and thus reinforce its leadership.

To illustrate, let us examine the data in Table 8.7. A comparison is made of movements in unit costs as a function of experience, for experience slopes equal to 70 per cent, 80 per cent and 90 per cent respectively.

Let us consider the case of two firms, A and B, using the same technology and having the same initial conditions; they both have an experience slope of 70 per cent. Firm A is at its first doubling of cumulative production, while firm B is at its fourth. Their costs are 70 and 24, respectively. One can imagine that it might be quite hard for firm A to close this gap, given that it needs to increase its market share quite considerably to achieve cost parity.

Table 8.7 Evolution of unit cost as a function of experience effects

Cumulative production (x 1000)	Number of doublings	Slope of the experience curve		
		70%	80%	90%
1	–	100	100	100
2	1	70	80	90
4	2	49	64	81
8	3	34	51	73
16	4	24	41	66
32	5	17	33	59
64	6	12	26	48

Now let us assume that the two firms A and B have the same experience; they are both at their fourth doubling. However, firm A has better exploited cost reduction opportunities and is on an experience curve of 70 per cent, whereas firm B's experience curve has a slope of only 90 per cent; their unit costs are 24 against 66. Here too, it would be difficult to close the gap. Experience effects can therefore create large disparities in costs of firms which are of equal size, but have failed to incorporate this potential equally in productivity improvements.

Experience curves as an early warning system

As mentioned above, the main usefulness of the experience curve is to assess the dynamics of cost competition between two or more firms operating in the same reference market and to alert management as to the necessity of making timely strategic changes. The example of Figure 8.9, proposed by Sallenave (1985, p. 67), illustrates this last point.

The chart shows the cost and experience curves of a polyester fibre manufacturer. Prices and costs are expressed in constant $/kg. Prices declined on a 75 per cent experience curve while the slope of the cost curve was only 86 per cent. In this example,

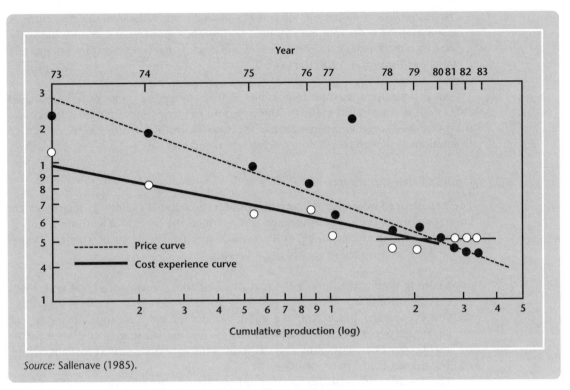

Source: Sallenave (1985).

Figure 8.9 The experience curve as an early warning system

management of the plant could have predicted years before it was too late that the cost and price curves were converging rapidly.

In 1980, the plant made no profit. Its management immediately embarked on a cost reduction programme, but at the same time demand slowed down. The plant was unable to operate at capacity level, which would have made the cost reduction programme effective. Unit costs remained unchanged. The plant closed down in 1983.

Had management read the early warning given by the experience curve analysis, it would have reacted early enough to decide between several possible remedial actions:

● Increase the capacity of the plant to accumulate faster and drive the unit cost down.
● Retool and/or improve the production process to operate on a 75 per cent cost slope, that is a slope compatible with the price slope.
● Specialise in special purpose fibres and sell them at a higher price than the normal price for regular polyester fibre.
● Sell the plant while it was profitable or convert it to another production line.

Thus, the experience curves can be used to anticipate future developments and *to simulate contemplated strategies*. The simulation exercise can be very instructive, as the following example shows.

Consider a firm with 6 per cent of a market that is growing at an 8 per cent real growth rate and whose leader has 24 per cent share. To catch up with the leader's share, our firm would have to grow at a 26 per cent growth rate in nine years, if the leader held its share by growing at the 8 per cent industry rate. That means expanding at over three times the industry rate for nine years, and that sales and capacity have to expand by 640 per cent (Abell and Hammond, 1979, p. 118).

This is typically a 'mission impossible'. Before embarking on an experience-based strategy, it is essential to calculate the time and the investment required to achieve the objective. Some companies, such as Texas Instruments, use experience curve simulations systematically before pricing a new product.

Limits of the experience law

The experience law is not universally applicable; it holds mainly in sectors where large scale brings economic advantage and in which the process of learning is important (Abernathy and Wayne, 1974). To be more specific, situations in which the experience law is of little relevance are the following:

● Learning potential is low or the part of value added cost in the total cost is not very significant.
● One competitor has access to a special source of supplies, thus having a cost advantage which bears no relation to its relative market share.
● Technology changes rapidly and neutralises the experience-based cost advantage.
● The market is not price sensitive.
● There is large potential for product differentiation.

Thus, if a firm is dominated by a competitor having a major cost advantage, two basic strategies can be adopted to circumvent the experience advantage:

● A *differentiation strategy* offering distinctive features valued by the buyer, who is ready to pay a premium price that would offset the cost handicap.

● A *technological innovation strategy* that would place the firm on a new and steeper experience curve, thereby neutralising the cost advantage of the current market leader.

The experience law is not of general application. To avoid misuse of the experience curve theory, it is important to verify the validity of the assumptions on which the theory is based.

The experience curve gives the firm an *operational competitive advantage*. As already mentioned, this type of advantage is not always sustainable in the long term because of the rapid diffusion of best practices in a given sector, which enables competitors to easily imitate and neutralise the cost advantage.

The competitive advantage matrix

A competitive advantage can be obtained in different ways, depending on the competitive structure and on the market characteristics. The Boston Consulting Group (Lochridge, 1981), which greatly contributed to spreading the law of experience, has proposed a classification of market situations which helps in identifying the type of competitive advantage to pursue. Two classification criteria are used:

● The size of the competitive advantage.
● The number of ways of achieving competitive advantage.

One then obtains a matrix, presented in Table 8.8. Horizontally, we have the size of the advantage, which can be small or large. Vertically, we have the number of ways to achieve advantage, which can be few or many. To each of the quadrants corresponds a particular market situation requiring a specific strategic approach. The four types of industry are: volume, specialisation, fragmented and stalemate industries:

Table 8.8   The competitive advantage matrix

Number of ways to achieve competitive advantage	Size of the competitive advantage	
	Small	**Large**
Many	Fragmented	Specialisation
Few	Stalemate	Volume

Source: Lochridge (1981).

● *Volume industries* are those where sources of competitive advantage are few and where cost advantage is the major opportunity. It is typically in this market situation that experience and/or scale effects manifest themselves, and where a large relative market share is a precious asset. Profitability is closely related to the size of market share as postulated by the experience curve theory.

● *Specialisation industries* are those with many ways of obtaining a sizeable competitive advantage. In these markets, the potential for differentiation is high, as is the case in situations of monopolistic competition, described earlier. Products have significant distinctive qualities from buyers' points of view, and they in turn are prepared to pay prices above those of direct competitors. In this kind of situation, the scale/experience effect brings no particular advantage. It is the value of differentiation or specialisation that counts and determines profitability. Total market share has little value; it is market share in a specific segment or niche which is critical, even if the size of the niche is small.

● In *fragmented industries*, sources of differentiation are many, but no firm can create a sustainable and decisive advantage over its rivals. Scale brings no significant economies and a dominant market share does not lead to lower costs. On the contrary, increased costs, linked to the complexity of the situation, limit the optimal size of the firm. Many service firms are good examples of a fragmented sector. Large and small firms can coexist with very different profitability. Market share has no effect, irrespective of the way it has been calculated. In this category, one can classify women's clothing, restaurants and car repair and maintenance services. In many cases, the best strategy is to transform a fragmented activity into a volume or specialised activity.

● In *stalemate industries*, the ways of obtaining a competitive advantage are few, as in the case of volume industries. But unlike these, accumulated experience does not constitute a competitive advantage. On the contrary, it is sometimes the newcomers who have the most efficient tools of production, because they have the most recent investment. In situations where technology is easily available, as in the steel industry or basic chemicals, competitiveness is more dependent on the age of the investment rather than the size of the firm: the last firm to invest benefits from lowest operating costs.

We can therefore see that an experience-based strategy can in fact only be applied in commodity-based, volume-sensitive industries, in which low cost is one of the few potential sources of achieving competitive advantage.

The International Competitive Advantage

International trade theory has traditionally placed the emphasis on country comparative advantages. The focus was on a country's natural endowments, its labour force and its currency's values as main sources of competitiveness. Recently, economists have turned their attention to the question how countries, governments and even private industry can alter the conditions within a country to create or reinforce the competitiveness of its firms. The leader in this area of research is Michael Porter (1990).

Industries globalise because shifts in technology, buyer needs, government policy or country infrastructure create major differences in competitive position among firms from different nations or make the advantage of global strategy more significant (Porter, 1990, p. 63).

According to Porter four broad attributes contribute to shape the environment in which local firms compete. These attributes promote or impede the creation of competitive advantage:

1. *Factor Conditions*. The nation's position in factors of production such as skilled labour or infrastructure, necessary to compete in a given industry. Porter notes that although factor conditions are very important, more so is the ability of a nation to continually create, upgrade and deploy its factors and not only the initial endowment.

2. *Demand Conditions*. The nature of home demand for the industry's product or service. The quality of home demand is more important than the quantity of home demand in determining competitive advantage. By quality, Porter means a highly competitive and demanding local market.

3. *Related and Supporting Industries*. The presence or absence in the nation of supplier industries and related industries that are internationally competitive. A firm that is operating within a mass of related firms and industries gains and maintains advantages through close working relationships, proximity to suppliers, and timeliness of product and information flows.

4. *Firm Strategy, Structure and Rivalry*. The conditions in the nation governing how companies are created, organised and managed and the nature of domestic rivalry. Porter notes that no one operational strategy is universally appropriate. It depends on the fit and flexibility of what works for that industry in that country at that time.

In the analysis of home demand composition, Porter identifies three home demand characteristics particularly significant in achieving a national competitive advantage:

● *Large Share of Home Demand.* A nation's firms are likely to gain competitive advantage in global segments that represent a large share of home demand but account for a less significant share in other nations. These relatively large segments receive the greatest and the earliest attention by the nation's firms, but tend to be perceived as less attractive by foreign competitors. The nation's firms may gain advantages in reaping economies of scale.

A good example is Airbus Industries' entry into commercial airliners. Airbus identified a segment of the European market that had been ignored by Boeing: a relatively large capacity plane for short hauls. Such a need was quite significant in Europe with its numerous capital cities within short flying distances and served by few airlines, in sharp contrast with the US situation.

● *Sophisticated and Demanding Buyers.* A nation's firms gain competitive advantage if domestic buyers are, or are among, the world's most sophisticated and demanding buyers for the product or service. Such buyers provide a window into the most advanced buyer needs. Demanding buyers pressure local firms to meet high standards in terms of product quality and services.

Japanese pay great attention to writing instruments, because nearly all documents have until recently been hand-written in Japan due to the impracticality of typewriters in reproducing Japanese characters. Penmanship is an important indication of education and culture. Japanese firms have been the innovators and have become world leaders in pens. (Porter, 1990, p. 91)

● *Anticipatory Buyer Needs.* A nation's firms gain advantages if the needs of home buyers anticipate those of other nations. This means that home demand provides an early warning indicator of buyer needs that will become widespread.

Scandinavian concern for social welfare and for the environment tends today to be ahead of that in the United States. Swedish and Danish firms have achieved success in a variety of industries where the heightened environmental concern anticipates foreign needs, such as in water pollution control equipment. (Porter, 1990, p. 92)

The composition of domestic demand is at the root of national advantage. The effect of demand conditions on competitive advantage also depends on other factors presented above. Without strong domestic rivalry, for example, rapid home market growth or a large home market may induce complacency rather than stimulate investment. Without the presence of appropriate supporting industries, firms may lack the ability to respond to demanding home buyers.

Chapter summary

Competitive advantage refers to a product superiority held by the firm over its direct competitor. Competitive advantages can be classified in two main categories: external advantages based on market power due to superior value to the buyer and internal advantages based on productivity generating a cost advantage. A firm's ability to exploit a competitive advantage depends on the strength, not only of direct competition, but also of other rival forces, such as potential entrants, substitute products, customers and suppliers. The intensity of direct competition varies according to the extent of market power held by each competitor. In an oligopoly, the degree of interdependence among rivals is high and explicit consideration of competitors' behaviour is an essential aspect of strategy development. In a monopolistic situation, products are differentiated in a way which represents a value to the buyer, either by reducing their cost or by improving their performance. The effect of product differentiation is to give the firm some degree of market power, customer loyalty and weaker price sensitivity. This is the typical competitive situation that strategic marketing seeks to create for the firm. Another way to gain a competitive advantage is cost domination through better productivity and cost controls. In many industries, there is an opportunity to lower costs as experience increases in producing a product. The strategic importance of the experience law stems from the fact that it is possible not only to forecast one's own costs, but also to forecast competitors' costs. Porter has identified four determinants of international competitive advantage which can be used by governments or management to create a favourable context in which a nation's firms compete.

QUESTIONS AND PROBLEMS

1. What differences do you see between a differentiated oligopoly and a situation of monopolistic competition? More specifically, what will be the expected competitive behaviour in each case?

2. What are the reaction strategies to be contemplated by a firm leader in its market which is confronted with a price cutting strategy initiated by a competitor having a very low market share?

3. Give an example of a sustainable external competitive advantage for each of the following sectors: mineral waters, fire insurance, highly specialised machine tools.

4. What type of development strategy can be adopted by a small firm dominated in its reference market by an aggressive and powerful competitor having a strong cost advantage?

5. The Springer Manufacturing Corporation is considering producing and delivering 40 units of an industrial plating machine to a new customer. The customer has indicated that the maximum feasible price for each plating machine is $5000. The average cost of building the first unit is estimated by research and development to be $8000. In the past, the company has usually operated along an experience curve of 85 per cent.

Several executives believe the potential price of $5000 is too low. Prepare an analysis that answers their concern. In your analysis show the average and the total costs and the total revenue received for the following units: 1, 2, 3, 4, 8, 16, 32, 40.

6. Try to identify the threats of the competitive environment for one of the following industrial sectors: private insurance brokerage, typographic industry, television.

Bibliography

Abell, D.E. and Hammond, J.S. (1979) *Strategic Market Planning*, Englewood Cliffs NJ, Prentice Hall.

Abernathy, W. and Wayne, K. (1974) The Limits of the Experience Curve, *Harvard Business Review*, **52**, September–October, pp. 109–18.

Boston Consulting Group (1968) *Perspectives on Experience*, Boston.

Chamberlin, E.H. (1950) *The Theory of Monopolistic Competition*, Cambridge MA, Harvard University Press.

Chetochine, G. (1997) *Stratégies d'entreprise face à la tourmente des prix*, Rueil Malmaison, Editions Liaisons.

Durö, R. and Sandström, B. (1988) *Le marketing de combat*, Paris, Les Editions d'Organisation.

Hax, A.C. and Majluf, N.S. (1984) *Strategic Management: An Integrative Perspective*, Englewood Cliffs NJ, Prentice Hall.

Hill, S.I., McGrath, J. and Dayal, S. (1998) How to Brand Sand?, *Strategy and Business/Booz, Allen & Hamilton*, Second Quarter, pp. 22–34.

Kerin, R.A., Mahajan, V. and Varadjan, P.R. (1990) *Contemporary Perspectives on Strategic Market Planning*, Boston, MA, Allyn and Bacon.

Kotler, P. and Singh, R. (1981) Marketing Warfare in the 1980s, *Journal of Business Strategy*, Winter, pp. 30–41.

Lambin, J.J. (1976) *Advertising, Competition and Market Conduct in Oligopoly over Time*, Amsterdam, North-Holland and Elsevier.

Lambin, J.J., Naert, P.A. and Bultez, A. (1975) Optimal Marketing Behavior in Oligopoly, *European Economic Review*, **6**, pp. 105–28.

Lochridge, R.K. (1981) *Strategies in the Eighties*, The Boston Consulting Group Annual Perspective.

Porter, M.E. (1980) *Competitive Strategy*, New York, The Free Press.

Porter, M.E. (1982) *Competitive Advantage*, New York, The Free Press.

Porter, M. (1990) *The Competitive Advantage of Nations*, London, Macmillan.

Porter, M. (1996) What is Strategy?, *Harvard Business Review*, November–December, pp. 61–78.

Prahalad, C.K. and Hamel, G. (1990) The Core Competence of the Corporation, *Harvard Business Review*, May–June, pp. 79–91.

Ries, A. and Trout, J. (1986) *Marketing Warfare*, New York, McGraw-Hill.

Rigby, D.K. (1997) *Management Tools and Techniques: An Executive Guide*, Boston MA, Bain.

Sallenave, J.P. (1985) The Use and Abuse of Experience Curves, *Long Range Planning*, **18**, January–February, pp. 64–72.

Schorsch, L.L. (1994) You Can Market Steel, *The McKinsey Quarterly*, No. 1, pp. 111–20.

Simon, H. (1996) *The Hidden Champions*, Boston MA, Harvard Business School Press.

Thomas, R. (1993) The Valuation of Brands, *Marketing and Research Today*, May, pp. 79–90.

Von Clausewitz, C. (1908) *On Wars*, London, Routledge & Kegan.

Wright, T.P. (1936) Factors Affecting the Cost of Airplanes, *Journal of Aeronautical Sciences*, **3**, pp. 16–24.

chapter nine

Formulating a market strategy

The objective of this chapter is to examine how a market-driven firm can select the appropriate competitive strategy to achieve an above-average profit performance in the different business units included in its product portfolio. Two sets of factors determine the performance of a particular business unit: first, the overall attractiveness of the reference market where it operates, and second, the strength of its competitive position relative to direct competition. The reference market's attractiveness is largely determined by forces outside the firm's control (see Chapter 7), while the business unit's competitiveness can be shaped by the firm's strategic choices (see Chapter 8). Product portfolio analysis relates attractiveness and competitiveness indicators to help guide strategic thinking by suggesting specific marketing strategies to achieve a balanced mix of products that will ensure growth and profit performance in the long run. In this chapter, we shall first define the conceptual bases of portfolio analysis and then describe the types of mission or objectives the firm should assign to each of its business units given their differentiated positions along the attractiveness–competitiveness dimensions. Finally, we shall discuss the strategic alternatives open to the firm in the field of international development.

Chapter learning objectives

When you have read this chapter, you should be able to:

1. conduct a product portfolio analysis, using either the BCG growth-share matrix or the multi-factor portfolio matrix;
2. discuss the merits and limitations of these two product portfolio analysis methods;
3. understand the different views of strategy;
4. describe the objectives and risks associated with the choice of a specific generic strategy;
5. define the different strategic options a firm can contemplate in designing a development or growth strategy;
6. describe the different competitive strategies a firm can consider *vis-à-vis* its rivals and their conditions of application;
7. discuss the objectives and the various forms of international development.

● Product Portfolio Analyses

The purpose of a product portfolio analysis is to help a multi-business firm decide how to allocate scarce resources among the product markets they compete in. In the general case, the procedure consists in cross-classifying each activity with respect to two independent dimensions: the attractiveness of the reference market where the firm operates, and the firm's capacity to take advantage of opportunities within the market. Various portfolio models have been developed, using matrix representations where different indicators are used to measure attractiveness and competitiveness. Here we shall concentrate on the two most representative methods: the Boston Consulting Group's (BCG) method called the 'growth-share' matrix (Boston Consulting Group, 1972; Henderson, 1970) and the 'multi-factor portfolio' matrix attributed to General Electric and McKinsey (Hussey, 1978; Abell and Hammond, 1979). Although the two methods have the same objectives, their implicit assumptions are different and the two approaches will likely yield different insights (Wind *et al.*, 1983).

The BCG growth-share matrix

The BCG matrix is built around two criteria: the reference market's growth rate (corrected for inflation), acting as an indicator of attractiveness, and market share relative to the firm's largest competitor, measuring competitiveness. As shown in Figure 9.1., we have a double entry table where a cut-off level on each axis creates a grid with four quadrants:

● Along the *market growth* axis, the cut-off point distinguishing high-growth from low-growth markets corresponds to the growth rate of the GNP in real terms, or to the (weighted) average of the predicted growth rates of the different markets in which the products compete. In practice, high-growth markets are often defined as those growing by more than 10 per cent per year. Markets growing by less than 10 per cent are deemed low-growth.

● Similarly, on the *relative market share* axis the dividing line is usually put at 1 or 1.5. Beyond this level, relative market share is high; below, it is low.

Thus the matrix relies on the concept of relative market share to leading competitor (see Chapter 6), which calculates the ratio of unit sales for one firm to unit sales for the largest share firm.

If company A, for example, has a 10 per cent share of the market and the largest share belongs to company B, with 20 per cent, then company A has a relative market share of 0.5 (10 per cent/20 per cent). It has a low market share since the ratio is less than one. Similarly, company B has a relative market share of 2 (20 per cent/10 per cent). It has a high share of the market.

The use of relative market share is based on the assumption that market share is positively correlated with experience and therefore with profitability (see Chapter 8). Therefore the competitive implications of holding a 20 per cent market share are quite different if the largest competitor is holding 40 per cent or only 5 per cent.

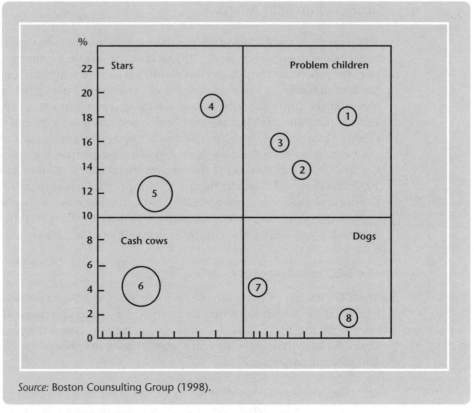

Figure 9.1 The BCG growth-share matrix

We thus obtain four different quadrants, each of which defines four fundamentally different competitive situations in terms of cash flow requirements and which need to be dealt with by specific objectives and marketing strategies.

Basic assumptions of the growth-share matrix

There are two basic assumptions underlying the BCG analysis: one concerns the existence of experience effects, and the other the product life cycle (PLC) model. These two assumptions can be summarised as follows:

● Higher relative market share implies cost advantage over direct competitors because of experience effects; where the *experience curve concept* applies, the largest competitor will be the most profitable at the prevailing price level. Conversely, lower relative market share implies cost disadvantages. The implication of this first assumption is that the expected cash flow from products with high relative market share will be higher than those with smaller market shares.

● Being in a fast *growing market* implies greater need for cash to finance growth, added production capacity, advertising expenditures, and so on. Conversely, cash can be generated by a product operating in a mature market. Thus, the *product life cycle model* is employed because it highlights the desirability of a balanced mix of products situated in the different phases of the PLC.

The implication of this second assumption is that the cash needs for products in rapidly growing markets are expected to be greater than they are for those in slower growing ones. As discussed above, these assumptions are not always true. On this topic, see Abell and Hammond (1979, pp. 192–3).

Defining the type of business

Keeping in mind these two key assumptions, we can identify four groups of product markets having different characteristics in terms of their cash flow needs and/or contributions:

● *Low Growth/High Share* or *Cash Cow* Products. These products usually generate more cash than is required to sustain their market position. As such, they are a source of funds for the firm to support diversification efforts and growth in other markets. The priority strategy is to 'harvest'.

● *Low Growth/Low Share*, *Dogs* or *Lame Ducks* Products. Dogs have a low market share in a low-growth market, the least desirable market position. They generally have a cost disadvantage and few opportunities to grow, since the war is over in the market. Maintaining these products generally turns into a financial drain without any hope of improvement. The priority strategy here is to 'divest' or in any case to adopt a low profile and to live modestly.

● *High Growth/Low Share* or *Problem Children* Products. In this category we find products with low relative market shares in a fast growing market. Despite their handicap vis-à-vis the leader, these products still have a chance of gaining market share, since the market has not yet settled down. However, supporting these products implies large financial means to finance share building strategies and to offset low profit margins. If the support is not given, these products will become dogs as market growth slows down. Thus, the alternatives here are to build market share or to divest.

● *High Growth/High Share* or *Stars* Products. Here we have the market leaders in a rapidly growing market. These activities also require a lot of cash to finance growth; but because of their leading position they generate significant amounts of profits to reinvest in order to maintain their market position. As the market matures, they will progressively take over as cash cows.

Every activity can be placed in a matrix similar to Figure 9.1. The significance of an activity can be represented by a circle of size proportional to sales volume, sales revenue or profit contribution. This analysis should be made in a dynamic way, that is by tracking the progression or movements of each business unit over a period of time, as illustrated in Figure 9.2.

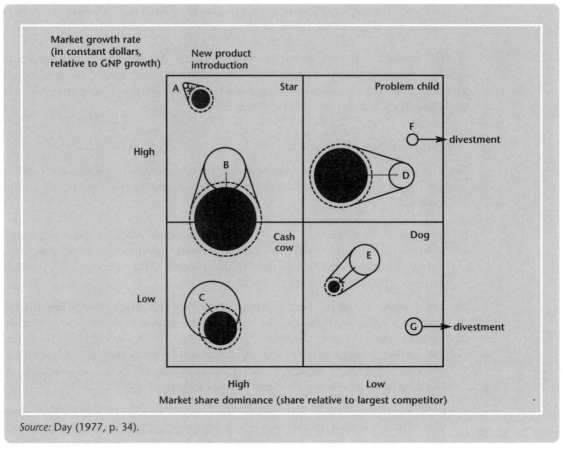

Source: Day (1977, p. 34).

Figure 9.2 Dynamic analysis of a product portfolio

Diagnosing the product portfolio

In this approach, it is important to properly define the reference market in which the activity is competing. Relative market share compares the strength of a firm relative to its competitors. If the market is defined too narrowly the firm appears as the segment leader; if it is too wide, the firm appears too weak. The following points arise from the analysis:

● The position in the matrix indicates the *credible strategy* for each product: maintain leadership for stars; abandon or low profile for dogs; selective investment and growth for problem children; maximum profitability for cash cows.

● The position in the matrix helps evaluate *cash requirements and profitability potential*. Profits are usually a function of competitiveness; cash requirements generally depend on the phase of the product's life cycle, that is, on the reference market's degree of development.

● Allocation of the firm's total sales revenue or profit contribution according to each quadrant allows *balancing of the product portfolio*. The ideal situation is to have products that generate cash and products in their introductory or growing stage that will ensure the firm's long-term viability. The needs of the second category will be financed by the first.

Based on this type of diagnostic, the firm can envisage various strategies either to maintain or to restore the balance of its product portfolio. To be more specific, it allows the firm:

● To develop *portfolio scenarios* for future years on the basis of projected growth rates and tentative decisions regarding the market share strategies for the various activities, assuming different competitive reaction strategies.

● To analyse the potential of the existing product portfolio, and to put a figure on the *total cash flow* it can expect from each activity, every year, until the end of its planning horizon.

● To analyse the *strategic gap*, that is the observed difference between expected performance and desired performance.

● To identify the *means to be employed* to fill this gap, either by improving existing products' performance, or by abandoning products that absorb too much cash without any realistic hope of improvement, or finally by introducing new products that will rebalance the portfolio structure.

Too many ageing products indicate a danger of decline, even if current results appear very positive. Too many new products can lead to financial problems, even if activities are quite healthy, and this type of situation inevitably risks loss of independence.

Figure 9.3 describes two successful and two unsuccessful trajectories that can be observed for new or existing business units:

● The *'innovator' trajectory*, which uses the cash generated by the cash cows to invest in R&D and to enter the market with a product new to the world that will take over from existing stars.

● The *'follower' trajectory*, which uses the cash generated by the cash cows to enter as a problem child in a new market, dominated by a leader, with an aggressive market share build-up strategy.

● The *'disaster' trajectory*, whereby a star product evolves to the problem children quadrant as a consequence of insufficient investment in market share maintenance.

● The *'permanent mediocrity' trajectory* involves a problem child product evolving to the dogs quadrant as a consequence of the failure to build market share for the product.

Let us remember that this type of diagnostic is only valid if the underlying assumptions mentioned earlier hold true. But, as already mentioned, the links between market share and profitability on the one hand and growth rate and financial requirements on the other are not always observed (see Abell and Hammond, 1979, pp. 192–3).

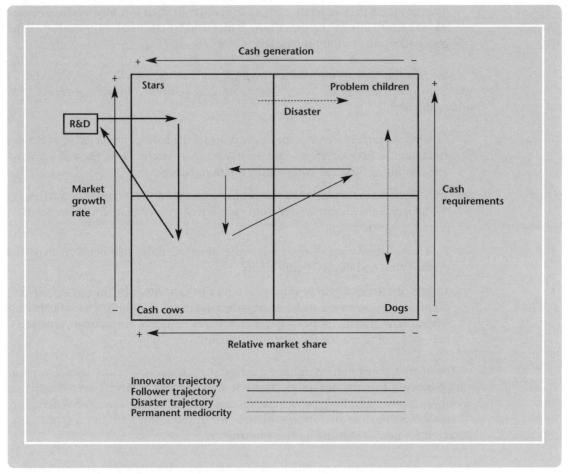

Figure 9.3 Portfolio scenarios alternative

Limitations of the growth-share matrix

The most important merit of the BCG method is undoubtedly that it provides an appealing and elegant theoretical development which establishes a clear link between strategic positioning and financial performance. It is true that the initial assumptions are restrictive. But if they are true, they allow accurate analysis and valuable recommendations. General managers can thus concentrate on the major strategic problems and analyse the implications of alternative business strategies. Furthermore, the method is based on *objective indicators* of attractiveness and competitiveness, thus reducing the risk of subjectivity. Finally, it should also be added that the matrix provides a *visual, vivid and easy to comprehend synthesis* of the firm's activities, thus facilitating communication.

There are, however, a number of *limitations and difficulties* which need to be emphasised because they reduce the generality of the approach:

⬤ The implicit hypothesis about the relation between relative market share and cash flows means that this technique can only be used when there is an experience effect, that is in *volume industries*, as we saw in the previous chapter (see Table 8.8). Thus the experience effect might be observed in only some product markets and not in all the product markets which are in the firm's portfolio.

● The method is based on the notion of 'internal' competitive advantage only and does not take into account any *'external' competitive advantage* enjoyed by the firm or the brand as a result of a successful differentiation strategy. Thus, a so-called 'dog' could very well generate cash despite its cost disadvantage if the market accepts the paying of a premium price for the product, given its distinctive qualities.

● Despite its simple appearance, some *measurement problems* can arise. Should the definitions of the product market be broad or narrow? What share of what market? How do we determine market growth rate? Wind *et al.* (1983) have shown that the analysis is very sensitive to the measures used. For a discussion of these questions, see Day (1977, pp. 35–7).

● The recommendations of a portfolio analysis remain very vague and at most constitute *orientations* to be clarified. To say that in a given product market a strategy of 'harvest' or 'low profile' should be adopted is not very explicit. In any case, it is insufficient for an effective determination of policies regarding prices, distribution, communication, and so on. The main purpose of a portfolio analysis is to help guide, but not substitute for, strategic thinking.

These limitations are serious and restrict the scope of the growth-share matrix significantly, which is not equally useful in all corporate situations. Other methods based on less restrictive assumptions have been developed.

The multi-factor portfolio matrix

The BCG matrix is based on two single indicators. But there are many situations where factors other than market growth and share determine the attractiveness of a market and the strength of a competitive position.

Clearly, a market's attractiveness can also depend on factors such as market accessibility, size, existing distribution network, structure of competition, favourable legislation, and so on.

The market for portable computers is in principle highly attractive if we judge it by its high growth rate. There are, however, many other factors, such as rapid change in demand, expected price changes, products' fast rate of obsolescence, intensity of competition and so on, which make this a risky and therefore relatively less attractive market.

Similarly, a firm's competitive advantage may be the result of strong brand image or commercial organisation, technological leadership, distinctive product qualities, and so on, even if its market share is low relative to the major competitor.

When, in 1982, IBM introduced its personal computer, its competitiveness was very low according to the BCG matrix, since its market share was zero. Yet many analysts perceived IBM's competitive potential as very high because of its reputation in the computer market, its important technological know-how, its available resources and its will to succeed.

It is clear that several factors need to be taken into account to measure correctly the market's attractiveness and the firm's competitiveness potential. Instead of using a single indicator per dimension, multiple indicators can be used to assess attractiveness and competitiveness and to construct a composite index for each dimension. For an extensive list of possible factors, see Abell and Hammond (1979, p. 214). Thus, the BCG matrix described in the preceding section may be viewed as a special case of a more general theory relating market attractiveness and business competitiveness.

Development of a multi-factor portfolio grid

To illustrate, Table 9.1 presents a battery of indicators selected to measure the *attractiveness* of five product markets from the textile industry, as well as a series of indicators evaluating the competitiveness of the company Tissex, which operates in these five product markets.

Since each situation is different, the relevant list of factors has to be identified and a multi-factor portfolio grid is necessarily company-specific. The selection of the relevant factors is a delicate task and should involve several people from the strategic marketing group and from other departments as well. Precise definition of each indicator must be given and the nature of the relationship should be clearly determined. Once the grid is developed, each product market is evaluated against each indicator:

● A scale of 5 points is used, with 'low', 'average' and 'high' as reference points for scores equal to 1, 3 and 5, respectively.

● As far as indicators of competitiveness are concerned, ratings are not attributed 'in abstract', but relative to the most dangerous competitor in each product market or segment.

● If some indicators appear to be more important than others, weighting can be introduced, but the weights must remain the same for every activity considered.

● The ratings should reflect, as much as possible, future or expected values of the indicators and not so much their present values.

● A summary score can then be calculated for each product market's global attractiveness and the firm's potential competitiveness.

Contrary to the BCG approach, subjective evaluations enter into these measures of attractiveness and competitiveness. But the process may nevertheless gain in interpersonal objectivity, to the extent that many judges operate independently. Their evaluations are then compared in order to reconcile or to explain observed differences and disagreements. This process of reconciliation is always useful in itself.

Interpretation of the multi-factor grid

We then obtain a two-dimensional classification grid similar to the BCG matrix. It is current practice to subdivide each dimension into three levels (low, average, high), thus obtaining nine squares, each corresponding to a specific strategic position.

Table 9.1 An example of multi-factor portfolio grid

Indicators of attractiveness	Weight (100)	Weak 1 2	Moderate 3 4	Strong 5
		Evaluation scale		
Market accessibility	——	Outside Europe and USA	Europe and USA	Europe
Market growth rate	——	≤5%	5%–10%	≥10%
Length of the life cycle	——	≤2 years	2–5 years	≥5 years
Gross profit potential	——	≤15%	15%– 25%	≥25%
Strength of competition	——	Structured oligopoly	Unstructured competition	Weak competition
Potential for differentiation	——	Very weak	Moderate	Strong
Concentration of customers	——	Very dispersed	Moderately dispersed	Concentrated

Indicators of competitiveness	Weight (100)	Weak 1 2	Moderate 3 4	Strong 5
		Evaluation scale		
Relative market share	——	≤1/3 leader	≥1/3 leader	Leader
Unit cost	——	> direct competitors	= direct competitors	< direct competitors
Distinctive qualities	——	'Me too' product	Moderately differentiated	'Unique selling proposition'
Technological know-how	——	Weak control	Moderate control	Strong control
Sales organisation	——	Independent distributors	Selective distribution	Direct sales
Image	——	Very weak	Fuzzy	Strong

Interpretation of the multi-factor grid

We then obtain a two-dimensional classification grid similar to the BCG matrix. It is current practice to subdivide each dimension into three levels (low, average, high), thus obtaining nine squares, each corresponding to a specific strategic position.

Each zone corresponds to a specific positioning. The firm's different activities can be represented by circles with an area proportional to their share in the total sales revenue or profit contribution. The four most clearly defined positionings are those corresponding to the four corners of the matrix in Figure 9.4:

● In quadrant C, both the product market's attractiveness and the firm's competitive potential are high; the strategic orientation to follow is *offensive growth*. The characteristics are similar to those of 'stars' in the BCG matrix.

● In quadrant A, both attractiveness and competitiveness are low; strategic orientation is *maintenance without investment* or *divestment*. We have the case of 'dogs' as in Figure 9.1.

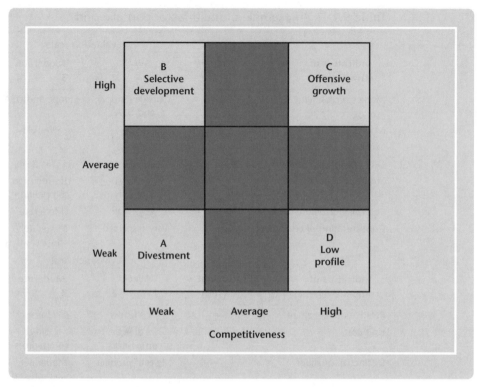

Figure 9.4 Multi-factor portfolio grid

● Quadrant B depicts an intermediate situation: competitive advantage is low, but the reference market's attraction is high. This is typically the case of 'problem children'. The strategy to follow is *selective growth*.

● In quadrant D, we have the opposite situation. Competitive advantage is high but market attractiveness is low. A skimming and maintenance strategy without major new investment is called for. This is the equivalent of the 'cash cows' positioning in the BCG matrix.

The other intermediate zones correspond to strategic positions which are less clearly defined and often hard to interpret. The fuzzy value of the summary scores can reflect either very high marks on some indicators and very low marks on others, or simply an average evaluation on all the criteria. The latter case is often observed in practice and reflects imprecise information or simply lack of it.

Choice of future strategy

We thus have a visual representation of the firm's growth potential. By extrapolating each activity's expected growth under the assumption of 'no change' strategy, the firm is in a position to assess its future position. Alternative strategic options can also be explored, such as:

● *Investing to hold* aims at maintaining the current position and keeping up with expected changes in the market.

● *Investing to penetrate* aims at improving the business position by moving the business unit to the right of the grid.

● *Investing to rebuild* aims at restoring a position which has been lost. This revitalisation strategy will be more difficult to implement if the market attractiveness is already medium or low.

● *Low investment* aims at harvesting the business, that is the business position is exchanged for cash, for example, by selling the activity at the highest possible price.

● *Divestment* aims at leaving markets or segments of low attractiveness or segments where the firm has not the capacity to acquire or to sustain a competitive advantage.

Figure 9.5 shows an example of multi-factor portfolio analysis. It represents the portfolio of a firm from the food industry. Note that product markets' attractiveness is very average and the firm's competitiveness is evaluated as low for almost all the products considered. The future of this firm is clearly very bleak.

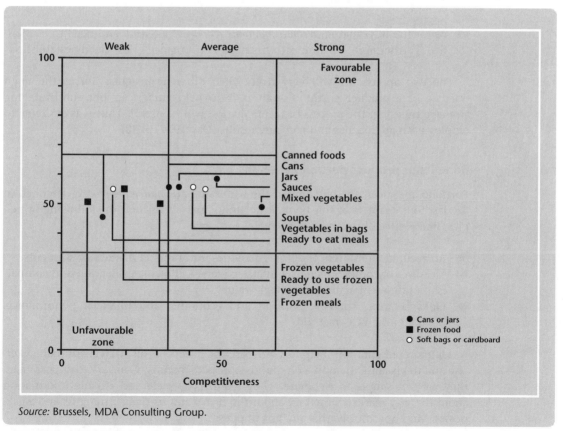

Source: Brussels, MDA Consulting Group.

Figure 9.5   Example of a multi-factor portfolio

Evaluation of the multi-factor portfolio grid

The *multi-factor portfolio model* leads to the same kind of analyses as the BCG matrix, with one major difference: the link between competitive and financial performance (that is cash flow) is lost. However, since this model is not based on any particular assumption, it does overcome many of the shortcomings of the BCG method and it is more widely applicable. Furthermore, it is much more flexible because the indicators used are company-specific.

The use of these types of matrix suffers nevertheless from certain *limitations*:

● Measurement problems are more delicate and *risk of subjectivity* is much higher here. This shows up not only in the choice of indicators and their possible weighting, but especially when it comes to marking the criteria. The risk of subjectivity is greater for indicators of competitiveness, where there is necessarily self-evaluation.

● When the number of indicators and the number of activities to evaluate are high, the *procedure becomes heavy* and demanding, especially when information is scarce or imprecise.

● The *results are sensitive* to the ratings and to the weighting systems adopted. Manipulation of weights can produce a desired position in the matrix. It is therefore important to test the sensitivity of results to the use of alternative weighting systems.

● As for the BCG matrix, *recommendations remain very general* and need to be clarified. Furthermore, the link with financial performance is less clearly established.

The two approaches will very likely yield different insights. But as the main purpose of a product portfolio analysis is to help guide, but not substitute for, strategic thinking, the process of reconciliation will be useful. Thus it is desirable to employ both approaches and compare results (Day 1977, p. 38).

Benefits of product portfolio analyses

Portfolio analysis is the outcome of the whole *strategic marketing process* described in the last four chapters of this book. A portfolio analysis rests on the following principles, irrespective of the method used:

● An accurate division of the firm's activities into product markets or segments.
● Measures of competitiveness and attractiveness allowing evaluation and comparison of different activities' strategic values.
● Links between strategic position and economic and financial performance, mainly in the BCG method.

Matrix representations help to synthesise the results of this strategic thinking exercise and to visualise them in a clear and expressive manner. Contrary to appearances, they are not simple to elaborate. They require complete and reliable information about the way markets function, about the firm's and its rivals' strengths and weaknesses. More specifically, this analysis implies:

⬤ Considerable effort to *segment the reference market*. This is particularly important, because the validity of the recommendations is conditioned by the initial choice of segmentation.

⬤ Systematic and careful collection of *detailed information*, which does not normally exist as such and needs to be reconstituted by cross-checking and probing; quality of results also depends on the reliability of this information.

This kind of analysis cannot be improved and it relies particularly on top management's complete support. Such a tool is obviously not a panacea, but it has the merit of emphasising some important aspects of management:

⬤ It moderates *excessively short-term* vision by insisting on keeping a balance between immediately profitable activities and those that prepare the future.
⬤ It encourages the firm to keep both market *attractiveness and competitive potential* in mind.
⬤ It establishes *priorities* in allocation of human as well as financial resources.
⬤ It suggests differentiated development strategies per type of activity on a more data-oriented basis.
⬤ It creates a *common language* throughout the organisation and fixes clear objectives to reinforce motivation and facilitate control.

The main weakness of methods of portfolio analysis is that they can give an image of the present, or indeed of the recent past, and devote too little time to assessing future changes and strategic options for dealing with these changes. There is also a risk of too mechanistic an application of these methods. As already underlined, different methods could lead to very different classifications. The tools described here must be viewed more as guides to informed reasoning than as prescriptive tools.

These matrices can also be used in a dynamic perspective, for instance in comparing the present market positions held within each product market with the targeted positions for the next period. The matrix presented in Figure 9.6 is useful with this respect because it permits us to analyse the changing competitive positions of each business unit over time (Hussey, 1978).

Portfolio models in practice

In a survey of the Fortune 1000 industrial firms, Haspeslagh (1982) studies the usefulness of portfolio analysis. Some of his findings follow:

⬤ As of 1979, 36 per cent of the Fortune 1000 firms and 45 per cent of the Fortune 500 firms had introduced the portfolio model approach to some extent. About 14 per cent of the Fortune 1000 were engaged in the process of portfolio planning in which the portfolio became a central part of the management process.

⬤ The decision as to which portfolio model to use was not regarded as critical. Considered fundamental to portfolio planning were (a) defining the business units; (b) classifying those business units according to their attractiveness and competitiveness; and (c) using this framework to assign financial objectives.

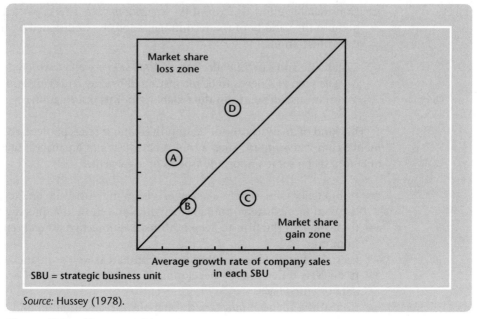

Source: Hussey (1978).

Figure 9.6 The growth matrix

⬤ As to the benefits of portfolio analysis, one-third of the respondents felt that the most important benefit was achieving a better understanding of their businesses, which in turn led to better strategic decision making. Another one-third felt that the key benefits were improved resource allocation, strategic reorientation and exit and entry decisions.

The survey also showed that firms using product portfolio models clearly had a longer time horizon than those not using portfolio planning. A more recent survey done by Hamermesch (1986) comes to the same conclusions.

More recently, in a multi-year international research project survey sponsored by the consultancy firm Bain & Company about management tools and techniques (Rigby, 1998), it appears that portfolio analyses have 43 per cent utilisation rate among the survey's respondents (4137 responses from senior managers in 15 countries around the world) and strategic planning a 90 per cent utilisation rate (Figure 9.7).

A portfolio analysis leads to different strategic recommendations according to the positioning of activities in the portfolio. As we saw, such recommendations are mainly general guidelines, such as invest, maintain, harvest, abandon, and so on, which require clarification and need to be put in a more explicit operational perspective.

⬤ **The Choice of a Generic Strategy**

The first step in elaborating a development strategy is to clarify the nature of the *sustainable competitive advantage* which will serve as the basis for later strategic actions and tactics. We saw in the previous chapter that competitive advantage can

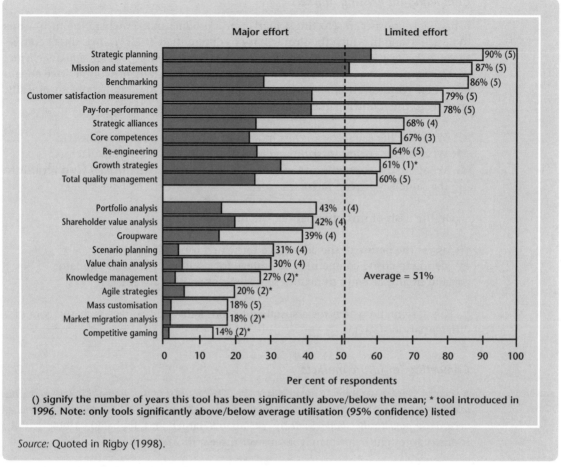

Figure 9.7 Utilisation rates of management tools

be described by reference to two aspects (see Figure 9.1): *productivity* (cost advantage) and *market power* (advantage in terms of maximum acceptable price). The question is to know which of these two aspects should be given priority, given the firm's characteristics, its strengths and weaknesses and those of its rivals. In other words, which advantage is 'sustainable' in a given product market? This question can be examined in two perspectives: within the framework of existing markets and of future markets.

Two ways to approach strategy

What is strategy? Two different views of strategy can be adopted, which are more complementary than opposed. The first view of strategy, promoted by M. Porter (1985, 1996), is mostly relevant when the objective is to target existing or articulated needs in existing markets, while the second, promoted by G. Hamel and C.K. Prahalad (1994), is more oriented towards latent needs and future markets.

Competing for existing markets

A first view consists in selecting a market or a product market where the firm wants to be active and in which the firm will try to differentiate itself *vis-à-vis* direct competition, *either by performing different activities from rivals or by performing similar activities in different ways* (Porter, 1996). Identifying a strategic sustainable competitive advantage then requires an analysis of the competitive structure, and more specifically, answers to the following questions:

- What are the *key success factors* in a given product market or segment?
- What are the firms' *strengths and weaknesses* with regard to these factors?
- What are the strengths and weaknesses of the firms' *direct rival(s)* with regards to the same key success factors?

On the basis of this information, the firm can:

- assess the nature of the advantage for which it is best placed;
- decide to create competitive advantage for itself in a particular domain;
- and finally, attempt to neutralise rivals' competitive advantage.

This systematic search for a sustainable competitive advantage is at the core of a differentiation strategy.

Competing for future markets

A second view of strategy is more proactive. The goal here is… *to build the best possible assumption base about the future (through foresight) and thereby develop the prescience needed to proactively shape industry evolution* (Hamel and Prahalad, 1994, p. 73). Industry foresight helps managers answer three critical questions:

- First, what new types of customer benefit should we seek to provide in five, ten or fifteen years?

Exhibit 9.1

The Value Strategy of Motorola

Motorola dreams of a world in which telephone numbers will be assigned to people, rather than places; where small hand-held devices will allow people to stay in touch no matter where they are; and where the new communicators can deliver video images and data as well as voice signals. For this world to become reality, Motorola knows that it will have to strengthen its competencies in digital compression, flat screen displays, and battery technology. Motorola also knows that to capture a significant share of a burgeoning consumer market, it will have to substantially increase the familiarity of its brand with customers around the world.

Source: Hamel and Prahalad (1994, p. 74).

● Second, what new competencies will we need to build or acquire to offer these benefits to customers?
● Third, how will we need to reconfigure the customer interface over the next few years?

This view of strategy is more proactive, since the objective here is to identify, understand and influence forces shaping the future of industry. As illustrated by Hamel and Prahalad, the US firm Motorola has such a point of view (Exhibit 9.1). More than a differentiation strategy of being better, faster, simpler, cheaper, and so on, the objective here is more fundamental and is to regenerate the core strategy of the firm and to reinvent the industry.

Kim and Mauborgne (1997) have proposed five recommendations in what they call a *value strategy* development:

● Challenge the inevitableness of industry conditions.
● Competition is not the benchmark.
● Focus on what most customers value.
● Ask what would we do if we were starting anew.
● Think in terms of the total solution buyers seek.

To adopt *value or discontinuous innovation strategy*, it is necessary to create solutions to problems customers do not even know they have. Discovering new solutions means going beyond the old ones by challenging the fundamental rules of business and redrawing the boundaries to create new markets and industries.

Generic strategies in existing markets

Generic strategies will be different according to the type of competitive advantage sought, that is whether they are based on productivity and therefore cost advantage, or whether they rest on an element of differentiation and are therefore based on a price premium. Porter (1980, p. 35) suggests there exist four generic competitive strategies to outperforming other firms in an industry: overall cost leadership, differentiation, focused differentiation or cost focus (Figure 9.8).

Overall cost leadership

This first generic strategy is based on *productivity* and is generally related to the existence of an experience effect. This strategy implies close scrutiny of overhead costs, of productivity investments intended to enhance the value of experience effects and of product design costs, and on cost minimisation in service, selling, advertising and so on. Low cost relative to competitors is the major preoccupation of the entire strategy.

Having a cost advantage constitutes an effective protection against the five competitive forces (see Figure 9.2):

● Relative to its *direct competitors*, the firm is in a better position to resist a possible price war and still make a profit at its rivals' minimum price level.
● Powerful *buyers* can only drive down prices to the level of the most efficient competitor.

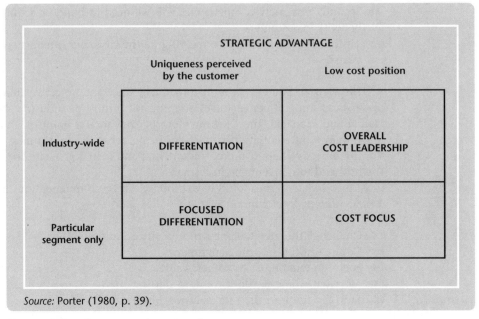

Source: Porter (1980, p. 39).

Figure 9.8   Four generic strategies

- Low cost provides a defence against powerful *suppliers* by providing more flexibility to cope with input cost increases.
- A low cost position provides substantial *entry barriers* in terms of scale economies or cost advantage.
- A low cost position usually places the firm in a favourable position *vis-à-vis substitutes* relative to competitors in the industry (Porter, 1980, p. 36).

Thus, cost leadership protects the firm against all five competitive forces, because the least efficient firms are the first to feel the effects of the competitive struggle.

Differentiation

The objective here is to give distinctive qualities to the product which are significant to the buyer and which create something that is perceived as being unique. What the firm tends to do is to create a situation of monopolistic competition in which it holds some *market power* because of the distinctive element (Chamberlin, 1950).

We saw before that differentiation can take many forms: design or brand image, technology, features, customer service, dealer network, and so on (see Levitt, 1980). Differentiation, like cost domination, protects the firm from the five competitive forces, but in a very different way:

- Relative to its *direct rivals*, differentiation provides the firm with insulation against competitive rivalry because of brand loyalty and resulting lower price sensitivity. It also increases margins, which avoids the need for a low cost position.

- The resulting customer loyalty, and the need for a competitor to overcome uniqueness, provide *entry barriers*.

● Higher profitability increases the firm's ability to resist cost increases imposed by powerful *suppliers*.

● Finally, the firm that has differentiated itself to achieve customer loyalty should be better positioned *vis-à-vis substitutes* than its competitors (Porter, 1980, p. 37).

Successful differentiation enables the firm to realise higher profits than its rivals because of the higher price the market is willing to accept and despite the fact that costs are generally higher. This type of strategy is not always compatible with high market share, since most buyers are not necessarily prepared to pay a higher price, even though they recognise product superiority.

Differentiation strategies generally imply large investments in operational marketing, particularly in advertising expenditures to inform the market about the product's distinctive qualities.

Focus

A third generic strategy is focusing on the needs of a particular segment, group of buyers or geographic market, without claiming to address the whole market. The objective is to take a restricted target and to serve its narrow strategic target more effectively than competitors who are serving the whole market. It implies either differentiation or cost domination, or both, but only *vis-à-vis* the particular target.

For example, a paint manufacturer can decide to address professional painters only, excluding the public at large, car manufacturers and the naval industry.

In the car industry, Mercedes only addresses the high end of the market, but it covers that segment more effectively than other car manufacturers having a full line of models.

The focus strategy always implies some limitations on the overall market share achievable. A focus strategy can give the firm a large share of the market in the targeted segment, but it may be low relative to the whole market.

Risks associated with generic strategies

The choice of one strategy against another is not a neutral decision, in the sense they involve differing types of risks and also different priority preoccupations in the organisation. Exhibit 9.2 summarises the risks inherent in each generic strategy.

The implementation of these strategies implies different resources and different know-how:

● A cost domination strategy assumes sustained investment, a high degree of technological competence, close control of manufacturing and distribution costs and standardised products to facilitate production.

● A differentiation strategy assumes significant marketing know-how as well as technological advance. The ability to analyse and anticipate trends in market needs plays a fundamental role here. Interfunctional co-ordination between R&D, production and marketing is vital.

Exhibit 9.2

Risks Associated with Generic Strategies

Risks of Overall Cost Leadership

■ Technological changes that nullify past investments or learning.

■ Low cost learning by industry newcomers or followers, through imitation or through their ability to invest in state-of-the-art facilities.

■ Inability to see required product or marketing change because of the attention placed on costs.

■ Inflation in costs that narrows the firm's ability to maintain enough of a price differential to offset competitors' brand images or other approaches to differentiation.

Risks of Differentiation

■ The cost differential between low cost competitors and the differentiated firm becomes too great for differentiation to hold brand loyalty. Buyers sacrifice some of the features, services or image possessed by the differentiated firm for large cost savings.

■ Buyers' needs for the differentiating factor fall. This can occur as buyers become more sophisticated.

■ Imitations narrows perceived differentiation, a common occurrence as industries mature.

Risks of Focus

■ The cost differential between broad range competitors and the focused firm widens to eliminate the cost advantages of serving a narrow target or to offset the differentiation achieved by focus.

■ The differences in desired products or services between the strategic target and the market as a whole narrows.

■ Competitors find sub-markets within the strategic target and out-focus the focused.

Source: Porter (1980, pp. 45–6).

Finally, a *concentration* strategy also assumes the previous characteristics *vis-à-vis* the targeted segment.

● Assessing Growth Opportunities

There are growth objectives in most strategies considered by firms, whether they are of sales growth, market share, profits or size. Growth is a factor that influences firm vitality, stimulates initiatives and increases motivation of personnel and management. Independent of this element of dynamism, growth is necessary in order to survive assaults from competitors, thanks to the economies of scale and experience effects it generates.

A firm can envisage growth objectives at three different levels:

Exhibit 9.3

Nestlé's Development Strategy

The question facing Nestlé now is how can the world's biggest food company which is either No. 1 or a strong No. 2 in its core categories in major markets, continue to grow? Major acquisitions, like the ones Nestlé made in the 1980s are no longer possible, because of regulatory problems. Instead, Nestlé says it will focus on organic growth, extending brands and moving others to global status and exploring new ways of reaching the consumer, including loyalty clubs and online selling. It will look at smaller acquisitions to round up its portfolio.

Source: Wall Street Journal Europe, 24 June 1999.

- A growth objective within the reference market it operates; we shall refer to this as *intensive growth*.
- A growth objective within the industrial chain, lateral expansion of its generic activity, backwards or forwards; this is *integrative growth*.
- A growth objective based on opportunities outside its normal field of activity; this is *growth by diversification*.

To each of these growth objectives correspond a number of possible strategies. It is interesting to examine them briefly.

Intensive growth

A strategy of *intensive growth* is called for when a firm has not yet fully exploited the opportunities offered by its products within its 'natural' reference market (see Exhibit 9.3). Various strategies may be envisaged: market penetration, market and product development strategies.

Market penetration strategies

A market penetration strategy, also called *organic growth*, consists of trying to increase or maintain sales of current products in existing markets. Several options are open:

Primary demand development: to increase size of total market by expanding primary demand, for example:

- Broadening the customer base by converting non-users into users (see Exhibit 9.4).
- Increasing the frequency of purchase among present users.
- Increasing the average quantity purchased per use occasion.
- Identifying and promoting new uses.

Note that this strategy can benefit all competitors since it influences primary demand more than selective demand.

Exhibit 9.4

Campbell Soup Co. Stimulates Soup Consumption

Campbell Soup noted that US soup consumption is growing again, up 3 per cent so far this fiscal year (1999). That's good news for Campbell, which has a US market share of about 80 per cent despite some inroads by generic supermarket brands in recent years. Soup accounts for nearly half of the Campbell's revenue. In a remarkable about-face for Campbell, it has been investing heavily to develop new products that will make it easier for consumers to eat soup. Among the new products that the company expects to roll out nationally in the fall: tomato soup in resealable plastic bottle and single serving, microwaveable soups. Other products are also in the pipeline, including refrigerated gourmet soup in a pouch. The company is also trying to sell more soup through restaurants, convenience stores, cafeterias and college dining halls. Campbell is testing a soup-dispensing machine that works like a soda fountain in 7–11 stores, and is trying out other soup products with McDonald's and Subway. Some at the company even talk about one day selling soup from Campbell kiosks.

Source: Adapted from *Wall Street Journal Europe*, 20 May 1999.

Market share increase strategy: to increase sales by attracting buyers from rival brands, through significant spending on marketing mix variables. For example:

- Improved product or service offering.
- Repositioning the brands.
- Aggressive pricing.
- Significant reinforcement of the distribution and service network.
- Major promotional efforts.

This more aggressive strategy will be mainly observed in market situations where primary demand is non-expansible, having reached the maturity phase of the product life cycle.

Market acquisition: to increase market share substantially by acquisition or joint venture. For example:

- Acquisition of competitor to obtain its market share.
- Joint venture to achieve control of a significant market share.

Market position defence: to defend current market position (that is customer relationships, network, share, image, and so on) by adjusting the marketing mix. For example:

- Product or service minor modifications or repositioning.
- Defensive pricing.
- Sales and distribution network reinforcement.
- Stepped-up or redirected promotional activities.

Market rationalisation: to modify significantly the markets served to reduce costs and/or increase marketing effectiveness. For example:

● Concentration on most profitable segments.
● Use of the most effective distributors.
● Limiting individual customers served via minimum volume requirements.
● Selective abandonment of market segments.

Market organisation: to influence, using legally accepted practices, the level of competition within one's industry to enhance economic viability. For example:

● Establishment of industry-wide competitive rules or guidelines, usually under government supervision.
● Creation of joint marketing research organisations to improve information systems.
● Agreement on capacity stabilisation or reduction.

These last three strategies are more defensive, aiming at maintaining the level of market penetration.

Market development strategies

A *market development strategy* refers to a firm's attempt to increase the sales of its present products by tapping new or future markets. This objective can be achieved using four alternative approaches.

Unarticulated needs among served customers: to propose solutions to customers' needs not yet perceived or expressed. The objective here is to lead customers with new products (like instant photography), to educate them and to create a new market through a supply marketing strategy.

New market segments: to reach new (unserved) groups of customers within the same geographic market. For example:

● Introducing an industrial product to the consumer market or vice versa.
● Selling the product to another customer age group (sweets to adults).
● Selling the product to another industrial sector.

New distribution channels: to distribute the product through another channel of distribution, complementary to the current ones (see Exhibit 9.5). For example:

● Adopting a direct marketing system for specific groups of customers.
● Distributing the products through vending machines.
● Developing a franchise system parallel to the existing network.

Geographic expansion towards other parts of the country or to other countries. For example:

● Shipping existing products to foreign markets relying on local agents or on an independent worldwide trading company.

Exhibit 9.5

Sony's New Strategy: From a Box Company to Becoming an Information Technology Company

Sony Corp. announced a sweeping corporate overhaul Tuesday aimed at decisively changing the company's identity from a manufacturer of consumer electronics to a provider of digital network services. Sony's President, Mr Idei, says Sony's new focus would be the network business: essentially the business of linking consumers to a variety of services either through their computers or their televisions. 'We have to make it possible for Sony's customers to directly link themselves with our products and services and for Sony to distribute its movies, music, games and personal finance tools and services directly to its customers.' In other words, the company intends to supply not only the computers and television sets through which people will gain access to its movies and music but also the pipeline. 'In the past three years, we have made a lot of efforts to move from being a "box" company to becoming an information technology company', Mr Idei said in an interview.

Source: Strom (1999).

- Creating an exclusive network of distributors to handle foreign business.
- Acquiring a foreign company in the same sector (see Exhibit 9.6).

Market development strategies rely mainly on the distribution and marketing know-how of the firm.

Product development strategies

A *product development* strategy consists of increasing sales by developing improved or new products aimed at current markets. Several different possibilities exist.

Discontinuous innovations: to launch a new product or service that represents a major change in the benefits offered to customers and in the behaviour necessary for them to use the product. Customers must in some way discontinue their past patterns to fit the new product into their lives (mobile telephone and self-banking are good examples).

Features addition strategy: to add functions or features to existing products in order to expand the market. For example:
- Increasing the versatility of a product by adding functions.
- Adding an emotional or social value to a utilitarian product.
- Improving the safety or convenience of the product.

Product line extensions strategy: to increase the breadth of the product line by introducing new varieties to increase or maintain market share. For example:

- Launching different packages of different sizes.
- Launching different product categories under the same umbrella brand name (see Exhibit 9.7).

Exhibit 9.6

The Internationalisation Strategy of Wal-Mart Stores, Inc.

After months of speculation, Wal-Mart Stores Inc. of the US made landfall in Britain in June 1999, with a deal that will more than double the size of the company's overseas operations. In a surprise move, the world's biggest retailer pounced on Asda Group PLC, the UK's third-largest food retailer, offering to buy the company for £6.72 billion, or 220 pence for each Asda share. If approved, the purchase would substantially expand Wal-Mart operations in Europe, which are now only in Germany. More importantly Wal-Mart's jump across the pond is likely to accelerate the already fierce retail competition in the UK and the rest of Europe – and spark further consolidation in the Continent's highly fragmented retail sector. European retailers, in Britain and elsewhere have good reasons to fear what is being dubbed the *Wal-Mart-ing* of the Continent. Worldwide more than 100 million people shop at Wal-Mart stores each week, and compared with Europe, the retail tactics can only be described as aggressive. Wal-Mart features sprawling, cavernous stores with, on average, over 1,000,000 items (food and non-food) on sale, and touts its low prices, long hours and smiling staff. Further, the arrival of the euro and its promise of a borderless, unified market in enticing. The common currency is expected to simplify purchasing and distribution, and homogenize consumer tastes, retail observers say. In turn, these changes will ease the way foreign retail invaders to stake a claim on a continent that had previously seemed remote and structurally old-fashioned, compared with the fast-moving, more technologically advanced US market.

Source: Adapted from *The Wall Street Journal Europe*, 15 June 1999.

● Increasing the number of flavours, scents, colours or composition.
● Offering the same product in different forms or shapes.

The strategy of line extension can lead to product proliferation and the question of cannibalisation and synergistic effects should be addressed explicitly.

Product line rejuvenation strategy: to restore the overall competitiveness of obsolete or inadequate products by replacing them with technologically or functionally superior products. For example:

● Developing a new generation of more powerful products.
● Launching environmentally friendly new models of existing products.
● Improving the aesthetic aspects of the product.

Product quality improvement strategy: to improve the way a product performs its functions as a package of benefits. For example:

● Determining the package of benefits sought by each customer group.

- Establishing quality standards on each dimension of the package of benefits.
- Establishing a programme of total quality control.

Product line acquisition: to complete, improve or broaden the range of products through external means. For example:

- Acquisition of a company with a complementary product line.
- Contracting for the supply of a complementary product line to be sold under the company's name.
- Joint venture for the development and production of a new product.

Product line rationalisation: to modify the product line to reduce production or distribution costs. For example:

- Product line and packaging standardisation.
- Selective abandonment of unprofitable or marginal products.
- Minor product redesign.

The lever used in product development strategies is essentially R&D. These strategies are generally more costly and risky than market development strategies.

Integrative growth

An integrative growth strategy is justified when a firm can improve profitability by controlling different activities of strategic importance within the industrial chain. It describes a variety of make-or-buy arrangements firms use to obtain a ready supply of strategic raw materials and a ready market for their outputs. Examples include ensuring stability of supplies, controlling a distribution network, or having access to information in a downstream activity to secure captive markets. There is a distinction between backward integration, forward integration and horizontal integration.

Exhibit 9.7

The Nivea Story of Brand Extension

The Nivea story begins with the ground-breaking discovery of the first water-in-oil emulsifier (Eucerit). In 1911, Carl Beiersdorf initiated the development of a skin creme based on such an emulsion. In December of that year the world's first long-lasting skin creme came into the market, named Nivea from the Latin word 'nivius' meaning 'snow-white'. Today, the blue tin of Nivea creme is the first skin care brand sold all over the world. Always using the blue box logo as positioning reference, the Nivea brand encompasses facial care, hair care, shaving, bathing/shower, baby care and sun care products, sold in 140 countries. Throughout the vicissitudes of almost a century of change, one thing has remained the same: Nivea means gentle care. Beiersdorf's dermatological expertise enables it to offer consistent high quality at a reasonable price, to take good care of you.

Backward integration

A *backward integration* strategy is driven by the concern to maintain or to protect a strategically important source of supplies, be it raw or semi-processed materials, components or services. In some cases, backward integration is necessary because suppliers do not have the resources or technological know-how to make components or materials which are indispensable to the firm.

Another objective may be to have access to a key technology which might be essential to the success of the activity. For example, many computer manufacturers have integrated backwards in the design and production of semiconductors in order to control this fundamental activity.

Forward integration

The basic motivation for a *forward integration* strategy is to control outlets without which the firm will choke. For a firm producing consumer goods, this involves controlling distribution through franchises or exclusive contracts, or even by creating its own chain stores, such as Yves Rocher or Bata. In industrial markets, the aim is mainly to ensure the development of downstream industries of transformation and incorporation that constitute natural outlets. This is how some basic industries actively participate in creating intermediary transformation activity.

> In the steel industry for example, Cockerill in Belgium has created Phoenix Works, specialising in coating and galvanising sheet steel, Polypal developing and manufacturing industrial storage systems and Polytuile, manufacturing roof coverings with steel sheet.

In some cases, forward integration is done simply to have a better understanding of the needs of buyers of manufactured products. The firm creates in this case a subsidiary playing the role of a pilot unit: to understand problems of users in order to meet their needs more effectively. The adoption of *solution-to-a-problem* strategy generally implies some form of forward integration. The new development strategy adopted by Xerox provides a good example of a forward integration strategy (see Exhibit 9.8).

Horizontal integration

A *horizontal integration* strategy has a totally different perspective. The objective is to reinforce competitive position by absorbing or controlling some competitors. There can be various arguments for this: neutralising a dangerous rival, reaching the critical volume so as to benefit from scale effects, benefiting from complementarity of product lines and having access to distribution networks or to restricted market segments (see Exhibit 9.9).

Growth by diversification

A strategy of *growth by diversification* is justified if the firm's industrial chain presents little or no prospect of growth or profitability. This may happen either because competitors occupy a powerful position, or because the reference market is in decline. Diversification implies entry into new product markets. This kind of

Exhibit 9.8

The Xerox Forward Integration Strategy: Becoming a Key Player in the Digitalised Office

Picture a revolution led by the ink-stained guys who come to fix the office copier. Instead of yanking out jammed paper, they've become systems experts who build a digital highway that lets you scan documents in Brazil, weave them into customised booklets in New York, and print on demand in London – with software to alter American spelling. Where they once hauled toner, the white shirts now sell industry-specific 'solutions' that change the way you shuttle information. This the game plan of G. Richard Thoman, president of Xerox Corp. Instead of just pushing products, Thoman wants Xerox to be a partner. He aims to build digital networks linking Xerox wonders to PCs and servers, putting to work a recently acquired army of systems specialists. Thoman is intent on pushing Xerox products into new markets at the far edge of the info age. One of the hottest is customised printing, where companies are using Xerox products to individualise their communications with customers as never before. For a book wholesaler in Germany, Xerox systems are already being used to print paperback reorders on demand. When book titles can be digitalised and ordered up by stores on demand, the savings in inventory alone could shift the economics of the business. 'We are positioning ourselves around knowledge', says Thoman, '...and the document is the DNA of knowledge.' Therefore, Thoman must push Xerox further into a world where customers turn to it for more than a 'box'. In the office that Thoman has in mind, clients don't just buy the next copier or printer from Xerox. They also let Xerox hook its copier into an office network and use its software to reshape the way the network channels information. And if Thoman is really lucky, Xerox will be asked to manage the whole printing process – turning an equipment sale into a much more juicy service contract. Such outsourcing grew 35 per cent for Xerox last year, to $2.7 billion or 14 per cent of revenues.

Source: Adapted from *Business Week*, 12 April 1999, pp. 63–8.

growth strategy is as such more risky, since the jump into the unknown is more significant. It is usual to establish a distinction between concentric diversification and pure diversification.

Concentric diversification

In a *concentric diversification* strategy, the firm goes out of its industrial and commercial network and tries to add new activities, which are related to its current activities technologically and/or commercially. The objective is therefore to benefit from synergy effects due to complementarity of activities, and thus to expand the firm's reference market.

For example, the Sports Division of Fabrique Nationale (FN) in Belgium, the leading European manufacturer of hunting weapons, has gradually diversified and added to its product line other sporting goods, such as golf clubs, fishing rods, tennis rackets and windsurfing boards. The aim was on the one hand to compensate for the decline in the hunting market, and on the other to take full advantage of a specialised distribution network of sporting goods controlled by FN, the Browning network in the USA in particular.

A concentric diversification strategy usually has the objectives of attracting new groups of buyers and expanding the reference market of the firm.

Pure diversification

In a pure diversification strategy, the firm enters into new activities which are unrelated to its traditional activities, either technologically or commercially. The aim is to turn towards entirely new fields so as to rejuvenate the product portfolio. At the end of 1978, for example, Volkswagen bought Triumph-Adler, which specialises in informatics and office equipment, for this very reason.

Diversification strategies are undoubtedly the most risky and complex strategies, because they lead the firm into unknown territory. To be successful, diversification requires important human as well as financial resources. Drucker (1981, p. 16) considers that a successful diversification requires a common core or unity represented by common markets, technology or production processes. He states that without such a unity core, diversification never works; financial ties alone are insufficient. Other organisational management specialists believe in the importance of a *corporate culture* or a *management style* which characterises every organisation and which may be effective in some fields and not others.

The rationale of diversification

Calori and Harvatopoulos (1988) study the rationales of diversification in French industry. They identify two dimensions. The first relates to the *nature of the strategic*

Exhibit 9.9

Fujitsu and Siemens to Link Europe Operations

Fujitsu Ltd., the Japanese computer giant, and Siemens AG, the German electronic conglomerate, announced plans to create the world's fifth-biggest computer maker by merging their European operations. On the strength of ultralight notebooks, Internet server and mainframes, the Japanese–German venture ambitiously aims to break into a global industry dominated by US technology manufacturers such as Compaq Computer Corp. 'We want to end the domination of US PC vendors,' said Judith Grindal, spokeswoman for Fujitsu Computers (Europe) Ltd. With users now treating many personal computers as 'commodity boxes', keeping prices under perpetual pressure, Siemens and Fujitsu need a critical mass of purchasing power, sales volume and marketing channels to compete. 'The main goal is really economies of scale, although Siemens won some market share in recent years, on a worldwide basis, their PC business is clearly too small.'

Source: International Herald Tribune, 18 June 1999.

Exhibit 9.10

The Diversification Strategy of Bic

For an outside observer, the entry of Bic in the disposable lighter and razor markets could be viewed as a double diversification strategy. In reality, it is not true for Bic which defines its core business as the distribution of moulded plastic disposable mass consumer products. For disposable pens, lighters or razors, the required core competencies are the same. The key success factors for those products rely essentially on technology (plastic injection), advertising, point of sales promotion and penetration in a large diversity of distribution channels. From a strategy point of view, all those products belong to the same domain of activity... and Bic means: 'cheap, relaxed life, a simple and convenient product'.

Source: Strategor (1997, p. 154).

---

objective: diversification may be defensive (replacing a loss-making activity) or offensive (conquering new positions). The second dimension involves the *expected outcomes* of diversification: management may expect great economic value (growth, profitability) or first and foremost great coherence and complementarity with their current activities (exploitation of know-how).

Cross-classifying these two dimensions gives rise to four logics of diversification, as shown in Table 9.2:

Table 9.2   The rationales of diversification

Type of objective	Expected outcome	
	Coherence	Economic value
Offensive	Expansion	Deployment
	(Salomon)	(Taittinger)
Defensive	Relay	Redeployment
	(Framatome)	(Lafarge)

Source: Calori and Harvatopoulos (1988).

- *Expansion*, whereby the firm tries to reinforce its activity (offensive aim) while taking full advantage of its know-how (coherence). This kind of diversification strategy has been followed by Salomon, for example, world leader in ski bindings, which has gone into the market for ski boots, then the market for cross-country skiing and more recently into manufacturing golf clubs and ski poles.

- *Relay*, which seeks to replace a declining activity (defensive objective), while using high quality staff (coherence). Framatome followed this strategy at the end of the 1970s, when the market for nuclear plants started to shrink.

● *Deployment* is an offensive strategy seeking high economic value. This was the case for Taittinger diversifying into the deluxe hotel business.

● *Redeployment* which is defensive in nature but seeks a new channel for growth. This strategy was followed by Lafarge which merged with Coppée and entered into biotechnology when faced with decline in the building industry.

Two more particular logics must be added to these basic ones: diversification driven by image improvement (the logic of image), and diversification driven by the will to watch the growth of a new promising technology (the logic of window).

Diversification strategy based on core competencies

A particular form of diversification is based on the resources or the competencies that a firm considers as fundamental and intrinsically part of its core business (see Chapter 8). These core *competencies* can be used in different domains of activities as long as the objective of coherence is met.

As a general rule, any successful diversification strategy is more or less based on synergies coming from the main activity of the firm. The provisional assessment of core competencies, talents or knowledge synergies between the present and the contemplated domain of activity constitutes a critical challenge in the design of a diversification strategy. The main risk is the over-evaluation of competencies' synergy between the two fields of activity, as in the FN case described above and as in the Bic case, with the failed launching of cheap perfume bottles targeted to the youth market.

It is important that management define the logic of diversification from the outset and as clearly as possible. Upon this logic will depend the criteria for assessing and selecting potential activities. The alternative growth strategies reviewed in this chapter are summarised in Exhibit 9.11.

● Choosing a Competitive Strategy

An important element of a growth strategy is taking explicit account of competitors' positions and behaviour. Measuring business competitiveness (Chapter 8) helps to evaluate the importance of the firm's competitive advantage compared with its most dangerous rivals, and to identify their competitive behaviour. The next task is to set out a strategy based on a realistic assessment of the forces at work, and to determine the means to achieve defined objectives.

Kotler establishes a distinction between four types of competitive strategy; his typology is based on the level of market share held and comprises four different strategies: market leader, market challenger, market follower and market nicher (Kotler, 1997, p. 319).

Market leader strategies

In a product market, the market leader is the firm that holds a dominant position and is acknowledged as such by its rivals. The leader is often an orientation point for competitors, a reference that rival firms try to attack, to imitate or to avoid. The best-

Exhibit 9.11

Alternative Growth Strategies

1. INTENSIVE GROWTH: TO GROW WITHIN THE REFERENCE MARKET

1.1   Penetration Strategy: Increase sales of existing products in existing markets:
- Primary demand development.
- Market share increase.
- Market acquisition.
- Market position defence.
- Market rationalisation.
- Market organisation.

1.2   Market Development Strategy: Increase sales of existing products in new markets:
- Target new market segments.
- Adopt new distribution channels.
- Penetrate new geographic markets.

1.3   Product Development Strategy: Increase sales in existing markets with new or modified products:
- Features addition strategy.
- Product line extensions strategy.
- Product line rejuvenation strategy.
- Product quality improvement strategy.
- Product line acquisition.
- Product line rationalisation.
- New product development strategy.

2. INTEGRATIVE GROWTH: TO GROW WITHIN THE INDUSTRIAL CHAIN

2.1   Backward integration.

2.2   Forward integration.

2.3   Horizontal integration.

3. GROWTH BY DIVERSIFICATION: TO GROW OUTSIDE THE INDUSTRIAL CHAIN

3.1   Concentric diversification.

3.2   Pure diversification.

known market leaders are IBM, Procter & Gamble, Kodak, Benetton, Nestlé, L'Oréal, and so on. A market leader can envisage different strategies.

Primary demand development

The market leader is usually the firm that contributes most to the growth of the reference market. The most natural strategy that flows from the leader's responsibility is to *expand total demand* by looking for new users, new uses and more usage of its products. Acting in this way, the market leader contributes to expanding the total market size which, in the end, is beneficial to all competitors. This type of strategy is normally observed in the first stages of the product's life cycle, when total demand is expansible and tension between rivals is low due to high potential for growth of total demand.

Defensive strategies

A second strategy open to a firm with large market share is a *defensive strategy*: protecting market share by countering the actions of the most dangerous rivals. This kind of strategy is often adopted by the innovating firm which finds itself attacked by imitating firms once the market has been opened. This was the case for IBM in the mainframe computer market, for Danone in the fresh products market, for Coca-Cola in the soft drink market, and so on. Many defensive strategies can be adopted:

- Innovation and technological advance which discourages competitors.
- Market consolidation through intensive distribution and a full line policy to cover all market segments.
- Direct confrontation, that is direct showdown through price wars or advertising campaigns.

We have seen this type of strategy between firms such as Hertz and Avis, Coca-Cola and Pepsi Cola, and Kodak and Polaroid.

Aggressive strategies

A third possibility available to a dominant firm is an *offensive strategy*. The objective here is to reap the benefits of experience effects to the maximum and thus improve profitability. This strategy is based on the assumption that market share and profitability are related. In the previous chapter, we saw that this relationship was mainly observed in volume industries, where competitive advantage is cost-based. Its existence has also been empirically established by works of PIMS (Buzzell *et al.*, 1975) and confirmed by Galbraith and Schendel (1983). Although increasing market share is beneficial to a firm, there exists a limit beyond which the cost of any further increase becomes prohibitive. Furthermore, an excessively dominant position also has the inconvenience that it attracts the attention of public authorities who are in charge of maintaining balanced competitive market conditions. This, for instance, is the task of the Competition Commission within the EU, and of anti-trust laws in the USA. Dominant firms are also more vulnerable to attacks by consumer organisations, who tend to choose the most visible targets, such as Nestlé in Switzerland and Fiat and Montedison in Italy.

Demarketing strategy

A strategy open to a dominant firm: *reduce its market share* to avoid accusations of monopoly or quasi-monopoly. Various possibilities exist. First, it can use *demarketing* to reduce the demand level in some segments by price increases, or reduce services as well as advertising and promotion campaigns. Another strategy is *diversification* towards product markets different from those where the firm has a dominant position. Finally, and in a very different perspective, a last strategy could be a *communication or public relations strategy* with the objective to promote the social role of the firm *vis-à-vis* its different publics.

> For example, mass food distributors having a dominant position in some markets, like to enhance their role in the fight against inflation through their pricing policy and namely through the launching on a large scale of 'no frills-low price' private labels which are 30 to 40 per cent less expensive than national brands.

In some cases, anti-trust laws may force companies to downsize.

Market challenger strategies

A firm that does not dominate a product market can choose either to attack the market leader and be its challenger, or to become a follower by falling into line with the leader's decisions. Market challenger strategies are therefore aggressive strategies with a declared objective of taking the leader's position.

The challenger faces two key questions: (a) the choice of the battleground from which to attack the market leader and (b) evaluation of the latter's reactive and defensive abilities.

In the *choice of the battleground*, the challenger has two possibilities: frontal attack or lateral attack. A *frontal attack* consists of opposing the competitor directly by using its own weapons, and without trying to use its weak points. To be successful, a frontal attack demands a balance of power heavily in favour of the attacker. In military strategy, this balance is normally put at 3 to 1.

> For example, when in 1981 IBM attacked the microcomputer market with its PC, its marketing tools, advertising in particular, were very clearly superior to those of Apple, Commodore and Tandy, which dominated the market (*Business Week*, 25 March 1985). Two years later IBM had become the leader.

Lateral attacks aim to confront the leader over one or another strategic dimension for which it is weak or ill prepared. A lateral attack may, for example, address a region or a distribution network where the leader is not well represented, or a market segment where his or her product is not well adapted. A classic market challenger strategy is to launch a price attack on the leader: offer the same product at a much lower price. Many Japanese firms adopt this strategy in electronics or cars (Kotler *et al.*, 1985, p. 91).

This strategy becomes even more effective when the leader holds a large market share. If the latter were to take up the lower price, it would have to bear large costs, whereas the challenger, especially if it is small, only loses over a low volume.

> The major European steel producers severely suffered from price cuts offered by the Italian Bresciani mini-steelworks. The same phenomenon is observed in the oil market with 'cut-price firms' such as Seca in Belgium, Uno-X in Denmark and Conoco in Great Britain; dominant firms (BP, Exxon, Shell, and so on) had more to lose in a price war.

Lateral or indirect attacks can take various forms. There is direct analogy with military strategy and one can define strategies of outflanking, encircling, guerrilla tactics, mobile defence, and so on. See on this topic Kotler and Singh (1981) and Ries and Trout (1986).

Before starting an offensive move, it is essential to assess correctly a dominant firm's *ability to react and defend*. Porter (1980, p. 68) suggests using the three following criteria:

- *Vulnerability*: to what strategic moves and governmental, macro-economic or industry events would the competitor be most vulnerable?

- *Provocation*: what moves or events are such that they will provoke a retaliation from competitors, even though retaliation may be costly and lead to marginal financial performance?

● *Effectiveness of retaliation*: what moves or events is the competitor impeded from reacting to quickly and/or effectively given its goals, strategy, existing capabilities and assumptions?

The ideal is to adopt a strategy against which the competitor cannot react because of its current situation or priority objectives.

As was underlined earlier, in saturated or stagnant markets the aggressiveness of the competitive struggle tends to intensify as the main objective becomes how to counter rivals' actions. The risk of a strategy based only on *marketing warfare* is that too much energy is devoted to driving rivals away at the risk of losing sight of the objective of satisfying buyers' needs. A firm which is focusing entirely on its rivals tends to adopt a reactive behaviour which is more dependent on rivals' actions than the developments in market needs. A proper balance between the two orientations is therefore essential (Oxenfeld and Moore, 1978).

Market follower strategies

As we saw before, a follower is a competitor with modest market share who adopts an adaptive behaviour by falling into line with competitors' decisions. Instead of attacking the leader, these firms pursue a policy of 'peaceful coexistence' by adopting the same attitude as the market leader. This type of behaviour is mainly observed in oligopolistic markets where differentiation possibilities are minimal and cross-price elasticities are very high, so that it is in no one's interest to start a competitive war that risks being harmful to all.

Adoption of a follower's behaviour does not permit the firm to have no competitive strategy, quite the contrary. The fact that the firm holds a modest market share reinforces the importance of having clearly defined strategic objectives which are adapted to its size and its strategic ambition. Hamermesch *et al.* (1978) analyse strategies of small firms and show that these firms can overcome the size handicap and achieve performance sometimes superior to dominant rivals. In other words, not all firms with low market share in low-growth markets are necessarily 'dogs' or 'lame ducks'.

Hamermesch *et al.* (1978, pp. 98–100) have uncovered four main features in the strategies implemented by companies with high performance and low market share:

● *Creative Market Segmentation*. To be successful, a low market share company must compete in a limited number of segments where its own strengths will be most highly valued and where large competitors will be most unlikely to compete.

● *Efficient Use of R&D*. Small firms cannot compete with large companies in fundamental research; R&D should be concentrated mainly on process improvements aimed at lowering costs.

● *Think Small*. Successful low market share companies are content to remain small. Most of them emphasise profits rather than sales growth or market share, and specialisation rather than diversification.

● *Ubiquitous Chief Executive*. The final characteristic of these companies is the pervasive influence of the chief executive.

A market follower strategy therefore does not imply passivity on the part of the chief executive of the firm, rather the concern to have a growth strategy which will not entail reprisals from the market leader.

Market nicher strategies

A nicher is interested in one or few market segments, but not in the whole market. The objective is to be a large fish in a small pond rather than being a small fish in a large pond. This competitive strategy is one of the generic strategies we discussed earlier, namely focus. The key to a focus strategy is specialisation in a niche. For a niche to be profitable and sustainable, five characteristics are necessary (Kotler, 1997, p. 395):

- sufficient profit potential.
- growth potential.
- unattractive to rivals.
- market corresponding to the firm's distinctive competence.
- sustainable entry barrier.

A firm seeking a niche must face the problem of finding the feature or criterion upon which to build its specialisation. This criterion may relate to a technical aspect of the product, to a particular distinctive quality or to any element of the marketing mix.

From that point of view, it is interesting to refer once more to Simon (1996a, 1996b) – already quoted in the preceding chapter – who has analysed the strategies adopted by a sample of 122 firms (a majority of German firms) which are (a) world or European leaders in their reference market, (b) of small or medium size and (c) unfamiliar to the general public. The nine main lessons are summarised in Exhibit 9.12.

International Development Strategies

We emphasised in the first chapter that internationalisation of the economy means that a growing number of firms operate in markets where competition is global. As a result, international development strategies concern all firms, irrespective of whether they actively participate in foreign markets or not. We will examine here the stages of international development as well as the strategic reasoning of a firm that pursues an international marketing development strategy.

Objectives of international development

International development is no longer limited to large enterprises. Many small firms are forced to become international in order to grow, or simply to survive. Objectives in an international development strategy may be varied:

- To enlarge the *potential market*, thus being able to produce more and achieve better results thanks to economies of scale. For many activities, the critical volume is at such a level that it demands a large potential market.

- To extend the product's *life cycle* by entering markets which are not at the same development stage and still have expandable total demand, whereas in the domestic market of the exporting firm demand has reached the maturity phase.

Exhibit 9.12

The Nine Lessons from the Hidden Champions

1. **Set clear and ambitious goals**. Ideally a company should strive to be the best and to become the leader in its market.
2. **Define the market narrowly** and in so doing include both customer needs and technology. Do not accept given market definition but consider the market definition itself part of strategy. Stay focused and concentrated. Avoid distractions.
3. **Combine a narrow market focus with a global orientation**, involving worldwide sales and marketing. Deal as directly as possible with customers around the globe.
4. **Be close to customers in both performance and interaction**. Make sure that all functions have direct customer contacts. Adopt a value-driven strategy. Pay close attention to the most demanding customers.
5. **Strive for continuous innovation in both product and process**. Innovation should be both technology- and customer-driven. Pay equal attention to internal resources and competencies and external opportunities.
6. **Create clear-cut competitive advantage in both product and service**. Defend the company's competitive position ferociously.
7. **Rely on your own strengths**. Keep core competencies in the company, but outsource non-core activities. Consider cooperation as last resort rather than a first choice.
8. **Try always to have more work than heads**. elect employees rigorously in the first phase, then retain them for the long term. Communicate directly to motivate people and use employee creativity to its full potential.
9. **Practise leadership that is both authoritarian in the fundamentals and participative in the details**. Pay utmost attention to the selection of leaders, observing their unity of person and purpose, energy and perseverance, and the ability to inspire others.

Source: Simon (1996b).

- To diversify *commercial risk* by addressing buyers in different economic environments and enjoying more favourable competitive conditions.

- To control *competition* through diversification of positions on the one hand and surveillance of competitors' activities in other markets on the other.

- To reduce *costs of supplies and production* by exploiting different countries' comparative advantages.

- To exploit *excess production capacity* by exporting goods at low (marginal cost) prices.

- To achieve *geographic diversification* by entering new markets with existing products.

- To *follow key customers* abroad to supply or to service them in their foreign locations.

The phenomenon of globalisation of markets, already mentioned in Chapter 2, must also be added to these basic objectives: take advantage of the progressive liberalisation of world trade.

Forms of international development

A firm's internationalisation does not happen overnight, but results from a process that can be subdivided into six levels of growing internationalisation (Leroy *et al.*, 1978).

Exporting is the most frequent form. Often, the first attempts to export result from a necessity to clear surplus production. Later, exports can become a regular activity, but one which is reconstituted every year without there being any kind of medium- or long-term commitment to foreign countries. Relations are purely commercial.

The second stage is the *contractual stage*. Here the firm seeks more long-term agreements so as to stabilise its outlets, especially if its production capacity has been adjusted in terms of the potential to export. It will then sign long-term contracts, either with an importer or with a franchised distributor, or with a licensed manufacturer if it is an industrial firm.

In order to control the foreign partner or to finance its expansion, the firm may directly invest its own capital; this is the *participatory stage* which leads to commercial companies or co-ownership production.

After a few years, involvement can become absolute, with the firm owning 100 per cent of the capital of the foreign subsidiary; this stage is *direct investment* in a subsidiary with controlled management.

Gradually, the foreign subsidiary looks for ways of autonomous development, using local finance, national managers and its own programme of R&D which is distinct from the parent company. This is the *autonomous subsidiary stage*. If the parent company has many subsidiaries of this kind, this subsidiary becomes a multinational company. It would probably be more appropriate to use the term 'multidomestic', because it emphasises the point that each of these companies is more concerned about its own internal market, and the group's various companies coexist independently of each other.

The final stage of development is the one which is taking shape at the moment. It is the stage of the *global enterprise* that addresses the international market as if it were a single market. This kind of firm bases itself on interdependence of markets, and the latter are therefore no longer administered autonomously.

Stages of international organisation

To the various stages of international development there often correspond specific forms of organisation at the international level which reflect different views of international marketing. As already discussed in Chapter 1, Keegan (1989) suggests the following typology:

● *Domestic organisation.* The firm is focused on its domestic market, and exporting is viewed as an opportunistic activity. This type of organisation is frequent in the 'passive marketing' stage described in Chapter 1.

● *International organisation.* Internationalisation takes place more actively, but at this stage the firm's orientation is still focused on the home market, which is considered as the primary area of opportunity. The *ethnocentric* company, unconsciously, if not explicitly and consciously, operates on the assumption that home country methods, approaches, people, practices and values are superior to those found elsewhere in the world. Attention is mostly centred on similarities with the home country market. The product strategy at this stage is 'extension', that is products that have been designed for the home country market are 'extended' into markets around the world.

● *Multidomestic organisation.* After a certain period of time, the company discovers that the difference in markets demands adaptation of its marketing in order to succeed. The focus of the firm is now multinational (as opposed to home country) and its orientation is *polycentric*. The polycentric orientation is based on the assumption that markets around the world are so different and unique that the only way to succeed is to adapt to the unique and different aspect of each national market. The product strategy is adaptation, that is to change or adapt products to meet local differences and practices. Each country is managed as if it were an independent entity.

● *Global organisation.* A global market is one that can be reached with the same basic appeal and message and with the same basic product. Both the product and the advertising and promotion may require adaptation to local customs and practices, as illustrated in Table 6.8. The *geocentric* orientation of the global corporation is based on the assumption that markets around the world are both similar and different, and that it is possible to develop a global strategy that recognises similarities which transcend national differences while adapting to local differences as well. The basic notion of a world strategy can therefore be summarised as follows: 'think globally and act locally'.

This last stage is at the moment taking shape in the world and in particular in the European economy. It implies important changes in the logic of strategic marketing. On this topic, see Hamel and Prahalad (1994).

The dynamics of international strategy

The view of strategy, as presented in this chapter, is largely based on the five competitive forces model developed by Porter (see Figure 8.2) and also on the value chain model as a tool to uncover sources of competitive advantage (see Figure 8.5). Porter's five forces model has the merit of analysing at the same time the static or structural form of competition (the direct competitors) and its dynamic dimension, through the potential entrants and through the technological changes which stimulate the emergence of substitute products.

With the changes observed in the international macro-marketing environment, and in particular with the globalisation of the world economy and the acceleration of technological change, the dynamic component of competition has today a growing importance and has given place to a concept of strategy, proposed by Hamel and Prahalad (1994) based on a broader view of competitive advantage, which places more emphasis on the core competencies of the firm, that is on its capabilities and talents. As observed by Stalk *et al.* (1992, p. 62):

> When the economy was relatively stable, strategy could afford to be static. In a world characterised by durable products, stable consumer needs, well-defined national and regional markets

and clearly identified competitors, competition was a war of position in which companies occupied competitive space like squares on a chess board. ...Today, competition is a war of movement in which success depends on anticipation of market trends and quick response to changing customer needs. Successful competitors move quickly in and out of products, markets and sometimes even entire businesses, a process more akin to an interactive video game than to chess. In such an environment, the essence of strategy is not the structure of company's products and markets but the dynamics of its behaviour. And the goal is to identify and develop the hard-to-imitate organisational capabilities that distinguish a company from its competitors in the eyes of customers. (Stalk *et al.*, 1992 in: Stern *et al.*, 1998).

This view of strategy based on competencies places the emphasis on the behavioural aspect of strategy development and implementation – more on the '*how to?*' than on the '*what?*' – that is to say on the skills, talents, competencies and knowledge held by the firm all over the value chain.

These capabilities will enable the firm to design and develop efficient strategies of redeployment and diversification. These core competencies can be of very different nature:

- *Technology*. The mastership of a generic technology or of a set of convergent technologies leading to diversification towards new field of activity.

- *Savoir faire*. A know-how transferable to other domains of activity, such as the mastership of luxury goods' management like Cartier, Hermès, Taittinger, a mastership transferable to five-star hotel management. Or the mastership of consumer goods branding strategies for Danone.

- *Speed*. The ability to respond quickly to customer or market demands and to incorporate new ideas and technologies quickly into products.

- *Acuity*. The ability to see the competitive environment clearly and thus to anticipate and respond to customers' evolving needs and wants.

- *Innovativeness*: the ability to generate new ideas and to combine existing elements to create new sources of value.

The management of core competencies is taking on an ever growing importance in view of the fact that, in highly industrialised economies, many firms are transforming themselves into *service providers* (see Exhibits 9.5 and 9.8) and are moving towards what is called today a *knowledge society*. In most business today, knowledge seems to be the central resource and product at the same time. As underlined by Drucker (1993),

We are in a knowledge society where knowledge has taken precedence over traditional organisational resources, such as labour, capital and land. Knowledge in one form or another, is of central importance to the development of the sustainable competitive advantage of companies.

On the eve of the third millennium, the firm's most valuable asset lies more in its ability to identify, measure and exploit knowledge than in its financial assets. This *intellectual capital of knowledge*, tacit or explicit, can be its sharpest competitive weapon and will probably be the key success factor in the international competition of the years to come. To go further on this topic see Nonaka and Takeuchi (1995).

Chapter summary

Product portfolio analyses are designed to help guide a multi-product firm's strategic thinking by evaluating each activity with reference to indicators of attractiveness and of competitiveness. The growth-share matrix has the merit of simplicity and objectivity, but its underlying assumptions are restrictive and limit its scope of application. The multi-factor matrix is more widely applicable and more flexible because the indicators used are company-specific, but the risk of subjectivity is higher and the procedure is more demanding in terms of available information. In elaborating a development strategy, the firm should clarify the nature of the sustainable competitive advantage which will serve as the basis for later strategic actions and tactics. Two views of strategy exist, one which is more relevant in existing markets, the other being better adapted for strategy development in future markets. Three generic options can be adopted in existing markets: overall cost leadership, differentiation or focus. The choice of one generic strategy is not neutral, but implies different resources, know-how and risks. In assessing growth opportunities, growth objectives can be considered at different levels: within the reference market (intensive growth), within the supply chain (integrative growth) or outside the current field of activity (diversification). For each of these three development strategies, several options are open which should be systematically explored in a strategic thinking exercise. A development strategy should explicitly take into account competitors' positions and behaviour on the basis of a realistic assessment of the forces at work. One can distinguish four types of competitive strategies: market leader, market challenger, market follower or market nicher. As a consequence of the globalisation of the world economy, international development is no longer limited to large enterprises and is motivated by a variety of strategic objectives. A firm's internationalisation does not happen overnight but results from a process which can be subdivided into different stages of international involvement and also in various organisational forms.

QUESTIONS AND PROBLEMS

1. A manufacturer of electronic components for industrial applications has five business units shown in the table below.

Strategic Business Units (SBU)	Sales in units (million)	Number of competitors	Sales of top 3 competitors	Market growth rate
A	1.0	7	1.4/1.4/1.0	15%
B	3.2	18	3.2/3.2/2.0	20%
C	3.8	12	3.8/3.0/2.5	7%
D	6.5	5	6.5/1.6/1.4	4%
E	0.7	9	3.0/2.5/2.0	4%

Using the BCG growth-share matrix evaluate the strength of the company's current and future position. What development strategies should it consider to improve the position of each business unit? Define clearly the conditions of application of this portfolio analysis method.

2. Design a multi-factor portfolio grid for one of the following companies: Godiva International (chocolate pralines), Haagen-Dazs (ice-cream), Perrier (mineral water).

3. Which development strategy would you recommend for a small business firm having a very specialised and recognised know-how in a worldwide market, but which has very limited financial means?

4. In France and Belgium, the level of ice-cream consumption is much lower than in other European markets as well as in North America. You are responsible for a worldwide known brand of ice-cream; which development strategy(ies) would you consider in these two markets?

5. You are responsible for preparing a diversification programme for a company having a very strong know-how in the field of fruit purchase and transformation and which owns a well-known brand of jam and fruit preserves. Propose different avenues for diversification and assess their risks and opportunities.

6. Referring to Exhibit 9.5, how would you characterise the new development strategy adopted by Sony?

Bibliography

Abell, D.E. and Hammond, J.S. (1979) *Strategic Market Planning*, Englewood Cliffs NJ, Prentice Hall.

Boston Consulting Group (1972) *Perspectives on Experience*, Boston MA, The Boston Consulting Group.

Boston Consulting Group (1998) *Perspectives on Strategy*, New York, John Wiley & Sons.

Buzzell, R.D., Gale, B.T. and Sultan, G.M. (1975) Market Share, a Key to Profitability, *Harvard Business Review*, **53**, January–February, pp. 97–106.

Calori, R. and Harvatopoulos, Y. (1988) Diversification: les règles de conduite, *Harvard-L'Expansion*, **48**, Spring, pp. 48–59.

Chamberlin, E.H. (1950) *The Theory of Monopolistic Competition*, Cambridge MA, Harvard University Press.

Day, G.S. (1977) Diagnosing the Product Portfolio, *Journal of Marketing*, **41**, April.

Drucker, P.F. (1981) The Five Rules of Successful Acquisition, *The Wall Street Journal*, 15 October, p. 16.

Drucker, P.F. (1993) *Post Capitalist Society*, Oxford, Butterworth Heinemann.

Galbraith, C. and Schendel, D. (1983) An Empirical Analysis of Strategy Types, *Strategic Management Journal*, **4**, pp. 153–73.

Hamel, G. and Prahalad, C.K. (1994) *Competing For the Future*, Boston MA, Harvard Business School Press.

Hamermesch, R.G. (1986) Making Planning Strategic, *Harvard Business Review*, **64**, July–August, pp. 115–20.

Hamermesch, R.G., Anderson, M.J. and Harris, J.E. (1978) Strategies for Low Market Share Businesses, *Harvard Business Review*, **56**, May–June, pp. 95–102.

Haspeslagh, P. (1982) Portfolio Planning: Uses and Limits, *Harvard-L'Expansion*, Summer, pp. 58–72.

Henderson, B.B. (1970) *The Product Portfolio*, Boston, MA. The Boston Consulting Group.

Hussey, D.E., (1978) Portfolio Analysis: Practical Experience with the Directional Policy Matrix, *Long Range Planning*, **11**, August, pp. 2–8.

Keegan, W.J. (1989) *Global Marketing Management*, 4th edn, Englewood Cliffs NJ, Prentice Hall.

Kim, W.C. and Mauborgne, R. (1997) Value Innovation: The Strategic Logic of High Growth, *Harvard Business Review*, **75**(1): 102–12.

Kotler, P. (1997) *Marketing Management*, 7th edn, Englewood Cliffs NJ, Prentice Hall.

Kotler, P. and Singh, R. (1981) Marketing Warfare in the 1980s, *Journal of Business Strategy*, **2**, Winter, pp. 30–41.

Leroy, G., Richard, G. and Sallenave, J.P. (1978) *La conquête des marchés extérieurs*, Paris, Les Editions d'Organisation.

Levitt, T. (1980) Marketing Success through Differentiation – of Everything, *Harvard Business Review*, **58**, pp. 83–91.

McNamee, P. (1984) Competitive Analysis Using Matrix Displays, *Long Range Planning*, **17**, June, pp. 98–114.

Nonaka, I. and Takeuchi, H. (1995) *The Knowledge Creating Company – How Japanese Companies Create the Dynamics of Innovation*, New York, Oxford University Press.

Oxenfeld, A.R. and Moore, W.L. (1978) Customer or Competitor: Which Guide Lines for Marketing? *Management Review*, August, pp. 43–8.

Porter, M. (1980) *Competitive Strategy*, New York, The Free Press.

Porter, M.E. (1985) *Competitive Advantage*, New York, The Free Press.

Porter, M.E. (1996) What is Strategy? *Harvard Business Review*, November–December, pp. 61–78.

Ries, A. and Trout, J. (1986) *Warfare Marketing*, New York, McGraw-Hill.

Rigby, D. (1998) Management Tool Mania, *The Newsletter of Bain & Company, Benelux*, October.

Simon, H. (1996) *Hidden Champions*, Boston MA, Harvard Business School Press.

Simon, H., (1996) You don't Have to be German to be a 'Hidden Champion', *Business Strategy Review*, **7**(2): 1–13.

Stalk, G., Evans, P. and Schulman, L.E., (1992) Competing on Capabilities: The New Rules of Corporate Strategy, *Harvard Business Review*, March–April, pp. 57–69.

Stern, C.W. and Stalk, G. (eds) (1998) *Perspectives on Strategy*, New York, John Wiley & Sons.

Strategor (1997) *Stratégie, structure, décision, identité*, 3rd edn, Paris, InterEditions.

Strom, S. (1999) Sony, in a Giant Overhaul, Sets Sights on Networking, *International Herald Tribune*, 9 March.

Wind, Y., Mahajan, V. and Swire, D.S. (1983) An Empirical Comparison of Standardized Portfolio Models, *Journal of Marketing*, **47**, pp. 89–99.

chapter ten

The strategic marketing plan

Sound strategic thinking about the future must be spelled out in a written document which describes the ends and means required to implement the chosen development strategy. In the short term, the firm's success is directly dependent on the financial performance of its ongoing activities. In the longer run, however, its survival and growth imply the ability to anticipate market changes and to adapt the structure of its product portfolio accordingly. To be effective, this strategic and proactive thinking must be organised in a systematic and formal way. The role of strategic marketing planning is the design of a desired future and of effective ways of making things happen. Its role is also to communicate these choices to those responsible for their implementation. This planning task is of course particularly hard when great uncertainties prevail in the firm's environment. Anticipating the unexpected is also part of the strategic planning process. In this chapter, we shall build on the concepts and procedures described in previous chapters and examine the steps needed to make strategic marketing happen in the firm.

Chapter learning objectives

When you have read this chapter, you should be able to:

1. understand the usefulness of formal strategic planning;
2. define the structure and content of a strategic plan;
3. conduct an external and internal audit (SWOT analysis);
4. define operational objectives and action programmes;
5. prepare a projected profit and loss statement;
6. test the robustness of a strategic plan.

● Overview of Marketing Planning

The *raison d'être* of a strategic plan is to formulate the main strategic options taken by the firm, in a clear and concise way, in order to ensure its long-term development. These strategic options must be translated into decisions and action programmes. We shall briefly examine the overall structure of a plan and the benefits expected from strategic planning.

Overall structure of the strategic marketing plan

As shown in this book, the strategic marketing process can be summarised around *six key questions*. The answers provided to these questions constitute the backbone of the plan and also the objectives for the firm.

1. What business are we in and what is the *firm's mission* in the chosen reference market?

2. Within the defined reference market, what are the targeted product markets or segments and what is the *positioning strategy* likely to be adopted within each segment?

3. What are the key business *attractiveness factors* in each segment and what are the opportunities and threats presented by the environment?

4. Within each segment, what are the firm's distinctive qualities, strengths and weaknesses and *competitive advantages?*

5. Which *development strategy* and strategic ambition should be adopted for each activity in the firm's product portfolio?

6. How do these strategic options translate into *operational marketing programmes* defined in terms of product, distribution, pricing and communications decisions?

Once the answers to these questions are obtained as the result of a strategic marketing audit, the task remains to summarise the options taken, to define the means required to achieve the stated objectives, to design the specific action programmes and, last but not least, to prepare projected profit and loss statements for each activity and for the company as a whole.

In fact, a strategic marketing plan is nothing more than a financial plan, but with much more information on the origins and destinations of the financial flows. As illustrated by Figure 10.1, the strategic marketing plan has direct implications on all the other functions of the firm and vice versa:

● *Research and Development*: market needs must be met through new, improved or adapted products and services.
● *Finance*: the marketing *programme* is subject to financial constraints and to availability of resources.
● *Operations*: sales objectives are subject to production capacity and to physical delivery constraints.
● *Human Resources*: the implementation of the plan implies the availability of qualified and well-trained personnel.

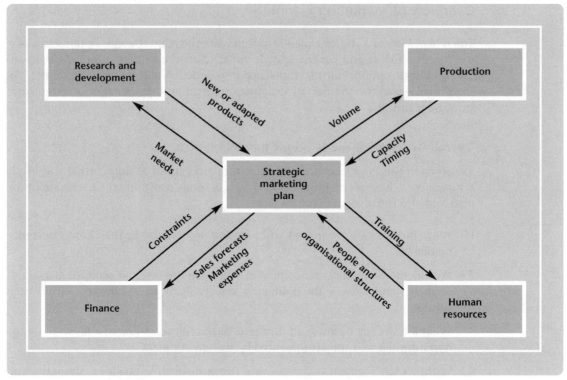

Figure 10.1   The strategic marketing plan: a cross-functional responsibility

Thus strategic planning will result in a better integration of all the company's functions and contribute to maximisation of efforts in reaching corporate goals. In a market-driven organisation, the mission of strategic marketing is to identify prospects for growth and profit given the company resources and *savoir faire*. As already emphasised in this book, this role is much broader than the traditional domain of marketing management, and implies interfunctional co-ordination.

Importance of strategic planning

Every company, even those reluctant to engage in the idea of formal planning, has to formulate forecasts in a minimum of three areas:

● The calibration of the *investment programme* required to meet the level of market demand or to penetrate a new product market.
● The *production programme* organisation needed, given the seasonality of sales and the periodicity of orders.
● The *financial liquidity*, based on income and expense forecasts, which is required to meet the financial liabilities.

These managerial problems are common to all companies and they imply that reliable sales forecasts should be handled properly.

In addition to this argument of necessity, other arguments in favour of formal strategic planning exist:

- The plan expresses the value system, philosophies and v
  This information gives people a *sense of direction* and a sens

- The plan presents the facts on 'where the business has come f
  stands'. The situation analysis helps to understand the *reasons* fo
  options taken by top management.

- The plan *facilitates co-ordination* among the different functions, maintains c
  tency in the objectives, and facilitates trade-offs among conflicting goals.

- The plan is a *monitoring instrument* which provides the opportunity to review the
  progress made in implementing the plan and to redirect parts of the action
  programme that are off target.

- The plan minimises the degree to which the company is taken by surprise to the
  extent that 'best case–worst case' scenarios have been explored.

- The plan encourages a more *rigorous management* of scarce resources by using standards, budgets, schedules, and so on, thereby reducing the risk of improvisation.

Most strategic plans are complemented by some form of *contingency plan* to be activated if certain events occur. Contingency plans are developed for factors which are
key to the survival of the company.

Objections to formal planning

Although strategic planning is a widely adopted practice, a certain number of firms
avoid using formal written strategic plans. Three types of objections to formal planning are usually given: the lack of relevant information, the futility of forecasting in
a fast-changing environment and the rigidity of planning.

Lack of needed information

Ideally the planner would have at hand all the pertinent information required on
industry and market trends, competitive intentions, market share, technological
innovations and so forth. The most common complaint concerns lack of adequate
information for the purpose of planning. On deeper investigation, however, it nearly
always turns out to be a case of too much information rather than too little. The real
problem is much more the lack of in-depth analysis.

The existence of a market information system, similar to the one described in
Chapter 4 (see Figure 4.1), is today a vital necessity to maintain the firm's competitiveness. Thus, market information and business intelligence systems must exist in
any case, and this is a costly operation with or without formal planning.

Futility of forecasting

In a turbulent environment, what good are strategic plans which will be contradicted
by future events? This attitude results from a misunderstanding as to the nature of
forecasting, which is erroneously likened to a crystal ball. As emphasised in Chapter
7, a forecast is a quantitative or qualitative estimate of what one expects, given a set
of assumptions on the environment. A forecast is not an end in itself, but a *forward
thinking exercise*, a tool used to increase the company's responsiveness and adapt-

tegic marketing plan 427

ews of top management.
of how to behave.
om and where it
the strategic
onsis-

d. This objective can be achieved even if the predicted

d commit the firm to a given direction, whereas adaptability
are required in a fast-changing environment. This objection
thoritarian planning style than planning itself. A plan should
ce creativity and quick reaction to changes. The mere fact of
sible changes in the market in advance will help to revise
ectives faster, whenever it is desirable to do so.
gic planning is widely used, as evidenced by various surveys
and in the USA (Haspeslagh 1982; Hamermesch, 1986; Greenley,
1987; Caeldries and Van Dierdonck, 1988). For an analysis of the main barriers to the
development of marketing plans, see McDonald (1991).

Content of a Strategic Marketing Plan

A strategic marketing plan typically sets out to answer the six key questions presented
at the beginning of this chapter. In this section, we shall describe the basic elements
of a strategic marketing plan and the type of information required on which to base
recommendations.

The mission statement

Sometimes called a *creed statement* or a statement of business principles, a *mission
statement* reveals the company's long-term vision in terms of what it wants to be and
who it wants to serve. It defines the organisation's value system and its economic and
non-economic objectives. The mission statement is important from both an internal
and external point of view:

- *Inside the company*, it serves as a focal point for individuals to identify with the
  organisation's direction and to ensure unanimity of purpose within the firm,
  thereby facilitating the emergence of a *corporate culture*.

- *From an external point of view*, the mission statement contributes to the creation of
  corporate identity, that is, how the company wants to be perceived in the marketplace by its customers, competitors, employees, owners and shareholders, and by
  the general public.

A mission statement should include at least the four following components.

History of the company

Knowledge of the past history of the company, its origin and successive transformations is always useful to understand its present situation and the weight given to
some economic or non-economic goals and objectives.

Materne-Confilux celebrated its 100th anniversary in 1987. This company has accumulated a broad experience in the field of purchase and transformation of fruits and has succeeded in maintaining a family managerial structure. This strong foothold in the fruit sector is a key factor to consider when exploring alternative diversification strategies.

In searching for a new purpose, a company must remain consistent with its past achievements and fields of competence.

Business definition

This is a key component in the mission statement. As emphasised in Chapter 3, what customers buy and consider valuable is never the product, but rather its utility, that is, *what a product or a service does for them* (Drucker, 1973, p. 61). Thus, the market definition should be written in terms of the benefit provided to the buyer. As discussed in Chapter 6, the three relevant questions to examine here are:

- What business(es) are we in?
- What business(es) should we be in?
- What business(es) should we not be in?

These are not easy questions to answer, particularly when the environment is changing very quickly. Ideally, the mission statement should be stated in terms narrow enough to provide practical guidance, yet broad enough to stimulate imaginative thinking, such as openings for product line extensions, or for diversification into adjacent product areas. At the Grumman Corporation, the guidelines for the mission statement advise:

'We should be careful not to confine the market boundaries by our existing or traditional product participation. The market definition analysis is purposely meant to create an outward awareness of the total surrounding market, and of its needs and trends that may offer opportunity for, or on the other hand challenges to, our current or contemplated position' (Hopkins, 1981, p. 119).

Every organisation has a unique purpose and reason for being. This uniqueness should be reflected in the market definition. In a market-driven organisation, the market definition will reflect the degree of customer orientation of the firm. By adopting a business definition formulated in terms of generic need or in terms of *'solution to a problem'*, the firm emphasises its market orientation and limits the risk of market myopia.

Corporate goals and restraints

Goals set the direction for both long- and short-term development and therefore determine limitations and priorities to comply with. These general goals, usually defined at the corporate level, are constraints within which the strategic plan must be developed. They should be clearly defined in advance to avoid proposals that contradict objectives of general management or corporate shareholders.

These goals may be economic but also non-economic. Examples are: a minimum rate of return on investment, a growth objective, the conservation of the family ownership of the company, the refusal to enter particular fields of activity, or a minimum level of employment, and so on.

The description of *available company resources* (capacity, equipment, human resources, capital, and so on), also forms part of the restraints and should be made explicit in order to avoid the adoption of a 'mission impossible' given the resources needed. *Codes of conduct and corporate ethics* for dealing with others (customers, distributors, competitors, suppliers, and so on) should also be formulated.

Basic strategic choices

Independent of the general goals imposed at the corporate level by general management, basic strategic options can be defined for each strategic business unit. For example, the extent of the *strategic ambition* and the role played by the firm in the target segment, that is leader, follower, challenger or nicher, may be defined. The strategic ambition must of course be compatible with the available resources of the firm.

Reference could be made here also to the three *basic positioning strategies* suggested by Porter (1980) and discussed in Chapter 8: cost advantage, differentiation and focus. The type of competitive advantage sought should also be defined. At this stage of the strategic plan, only broad orientations are given. They will be redefined in quantitative terms in the action programmes developed for each business unit.

In a survey conducted in the USA, out of a total of 181 responses received, 75 organisations provided a formal description of their mission statements. The main components included are summarised in Table 10.1.

Table 10.1 What components are included in a mission statement
(A survey: $N = 75$)

■ Customer	Who are the company's customers?
■ Products and services	What are the firm's products or services?
■ Location	Where does the firm compete?
■ Technology	What is the firm's core technology?
■ Concern for survival	What are the commitments to economic objectives?
■ Philosophy	What are the basic beliefs, values, aspirations and philosophical priorities?
■ Self-concept	What are the firm's major strengths and competitive advantages?
■ Public image	What are the firm's public responsibilities and what image is desired?
■ Concern for employees	What is the firm's attitude towards its employees?

Source: David (1989).

External audit – market attractiveness analysis

This external audit – also called *opportunities and threats* analysis – is the first part of the situation analysis. As explained in Chapter 7, an attractiveness analysis examines the major external factors, that is the factors which are out of the control of the firm, but that may have an impact on the marketing plan. The following areas should be reviewed:

● Market trends
● Buyer behaviour
● Distribution structure
● Competitive environment
● Macro-environmental trends
● International environment.

These external factors may constitute *opportunities or threats* that the firm must try to anticipate and monitor through its marketing information system and through business intelligence. In what follows, we shall simply list the critical questions to raise in each of these areas. The precise type of information required will of course differ by product category: consumer durable or non-durable goods, services or industrial goods.

Market trends analysis

The objective is to describe, segment by segment, the total demand's general trends within a three- to five-year horizon. The task is to position each product market in its life cycle and to quantify the market size. Both unit volume and monetary values should be identified. The key demand concepts to examine were reviewed in Chapter 7.

Questionnaire 1: Reference market trends

● What is the size of the total market, in volume and in value?
● What are the trends: growth, stagnation, decline?
● What is the average per capita consumption?
● How far are we from the saturation level?
● What is the rate of equipment per household or per company?
● What is the average lifetime of the product?
● What is the share of replacement demand of total demand?
● What is the seasonal pattern of total sales?
● What are the main substitute products performing the same service?
● What are the major innovations in the sector?
● What are the costs per distribution channel?
● What is the structure of the distributive system?
● How will supply–demand relationships affect price levels?
● What is the level of total advertising intensity?
● What are the most popular advertising media?

This list is certainly incomplete. It simply illustrates the type of information required. If the product studied is an industrial good, several information items should pertain not only to the direct customers' demand, but also to the demand expressed further down the line in the industrial chain by the customers of the direct customers.

Customer behaviour analysis

The task here is to analyse customer behaviour in terms of purchasing, use and possession. In addition to a description of buyers' purchasing habits, it is also useful to know the buying process and to identify the influencing factors.

Questionnaire 2: Customer behaviour analysis

● Per segment, what is the customer's socio-demographic profile?
● What is the composition of the buying centre?
● Who is the buyer, the user, the payer?
● What is the decision process adopted by the customer?
● What is the level of involvement of the buyer, the user, the payer?
● What are the main motivations of the buying decision?
● What is the package of benefits sought by the buyer, the user, the payer?
● What are the different uses of the product?
● What changing customer demands and needs do we anticipate?
● What are the purchasing frequency and periodicity?
● To which marketing factors are customers most responsive?
● What is the rate of customer satisfaction or dissatisfaction?

These descriptive data must be complemented with measures of the cognitive and affective response (recall, attitudes, preferences, intentions, and so on), as well as with brand or company image analyses.

Distribution structure analysis

This part of the external audit is probably more relevant in the field of consumer goods than in the sector of industrial goods, where direct distribution is common practice. The objective is to assess the future development of distribution channels and to understand the motivations and expectations of the company's trading partners.

Questionnaire 3: Structure and motivation of distribution

● What are industry sales by type of outlet?
● What are product type sales by type of outlet?
● What are product type sales by method of distribution?
● What is the concentration ratio of distribution?
● Is distribution intensive, selective or exclusive?
● What is the share of advertising assumed by distributors?
● What change does one observe in the assortments?
● What is the market share held by private brands?
● Which market segments are covered by the different channels?
● What are the total distribution costs?
● What is the distribution margin for each channel of distribution?
● What kind of distributor support is currently provided?
● What is the potential of direct distribution?

The distributor, as a business partner, has strong negotiation powers *vis-à-vis* the firm. One of the roles of a distribution analysis is to assess the degree of autonomy or dependence of the firm in the distributive system.

Competitive environment

The competitive structure of a market sets the framework within which the firm will operate. As Porter (1980) has said: 'The essence of strategy formulation is coping with

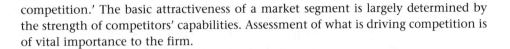

competition.' The basic attractiveness of a market segment is largely determined by the strength of competitors' capabilities. Assessment of what is driving competition is of vital importance to the firm.

Questionnaire 4: Competition Analysis

- What is the market's competitive structure?
- What is the market share held by the top three to five rivals?
- What type of competitive behaviour is dominant?
- What is the strength of competing brands' images?
- What is the nature of the competitive advantage of direct competitors?
- To what extent are these competitive advantages well protected?
- What are the competitors' major objectives?
- What is the current strategy being used to achieve the objectives?
- What are the strengths and weaknesses of competitors?
- What are their likely future strategies?
- Are there entry barriers in this market?
- Which are the main substitute products?
- What is the bargaining power of customers and suppliers?

The gathering of this type of information implies the development of a *competitor intelligence system*. For a more detailed framework of competitor analysis, see Porter (1980, Chapter 3).

Macro-environmental trends

This section describes the macro-environmental trends – demographic, economic, political/legal and socio-cultural – that bear on the studied market's future development. These external factors can provide productive opportunities or severe limitations for the company's products.

Questionnaire 5a: Economic macro-environment

- What is the expected GNP rate of growth?
- What major economic changes could affect our business?
- What is the expected level of employment?
- What is the expected rate of inflation?
- Do these trends affect our business and how?

Questionnaire 5b: Technological environment

- What major changes are occurring in product technology?
- How can we adjust our activities to cope with these changes?
- What major generic substitutes might replace our product?
- Do we have the required R&D capabilities?
- Do we need to update our equipment and at what cost?

Questionnaire 5c: Socio-demographic and cultural macro-environment

● What are the major demographic trends that affect our business?
● What is the cultural climate within which our business operates?
● Are present and future lifestyles favourable to our business?
● Is society's attitude towards our business changing?
● Are there changes in society's values that could affect our business?

Questionnaire 5d: Political and legal macro-environment

● Are there any specific changes in the law that affect our company?
● Are there legal or political areas that affect our customers?
● Which regulations could affect our advertising or selling strategy?
● Is our industry subject to criticisms from consumer organisations?
● Are there political or legal trends that could be used to our advantage?

Questionnaire 5e: International environment

● To what extent are we dependent on imports for key components?
● What is the economic and political stability of the supplier country?
● What alternatives do we have should our imports be interrupted?
● What is the economic and political stability of the customer countries?
● What opportunities does the European single market represent?
● Are there emerging global segments in our business?
● Is our business affected by changing world trade patterns?

Questionnaire 5f: Ecological environment

● Are our products environmentally friendly?
● Do we use processes or raw materials which threaten the environment?
● Is green marketing a potential strategy for our company?
● Is our industry a potential target for environmentalists?
● How can we improve the ecological quality of our products?

Questionnaire 5g: Industry and corporate ethics

● Does our company or industry have a stated code of ethics?
● What is the ethical level of our industry?
● Are industry values in alignment with those expected by society?
● How could our industry improve its ethical practice?

This information, dealing with the macro-environment of the firm, is indispensable for exploring alternative scenarios of market development. Generally, at least two scenarios will be explored: a base scenario, but also one or several alternative scenarios based on vulnerability factors.

The sources of information are numerous and varied, but often very scattered. Professional organisations and local chambers of commerce have economic data available for their members to use in planning. In addition to national statistics and foreign trade institutes, international financial institutions like the Bank for International Settlements (BIS), the International Monetary Fund (IMF), the World Bank (WB), the Office for Economic Co-operation and Development (OECD), the United Nations (UN), and so on, are the major public sources, with periodic publications readily available. University research centres and large international consulting firms, like Business International, McKinsey, the Economist Intelligence Unit, and so on, also publish newsletters, articles and monographs which are very useful for planning purposes.

Internal audit – company competitiveness analysis

The objective of the internal audit, also called the company strengths and weaknesses analysis, is to assess company resources and to identify the type of sustainable competitive advantage on which to base the development strategy. *Strengths and weaknesses* are internal factors, in contrast with opportunities and threats, which are external factors. Company strengths (or distinctive qualities), point to certain strategies the company might be successful in adopting, while company weaknesses point to certain things the company needs to correct. A competitiveness analysis should not be abstract. Reference to competition in general is too vague. Therefore, competition should be referred to in terms of the most dangerous competitors, called priority competitors.

To illustrate, *distinctive qualities* for a brand of laptop computer, as compared to those of the priority competitor, might be:

- An excellent brand awareness and an image of high quality.
- Dealers who are knowledgeable and well trained in selling.
- An excellent service network and customers who know they will get quick repair service.

The *weaknesses* of the same brand could be:

- The screen quality of the brand is not demonstrably better than the quality of competing machines, yet screen quality can make a big difference in brand choice.
- The brand is budgeting only 5 per cent of its sales revenue for advertising and promotion while major competitors are spending twice that level.
- The brand is priced higher relative to other brands without being supported by a real perceived difference in quality.

The strengths of the company or of the brand constitute potential *competitive advantages* on which to base the positioning and the communication strategy. The weaknesses determine the *vulnerability* of the brand and require remedial action. Some weaknesses may be structural, that is linked to the size of the firm and therefore difficult to correct. Examples of structural weaknesses are:

- National market share leadership, if not accompanied by international distribution, creates a home country vulnerability to the extent that the local company has little freedom for retaliation in the country of foreign competitors.

- If total sales volume is generated by a single powerful distributor, the company has weak bargaining power.

- A small or medium-sized company does not have the financial capability to use the most powerful media, like television advertising.

So a distinction must be made between the weaknesses that the company can correct and therefore which become priority issues that must be addressed in the plan, and the high risk structural weaknesses which are beyond the control of the firm and which require a high degree of surveillance.

Competitiveness analysis is organised much like attractiveness analysis. The major difference comes from the fact that the company, and not the market, is the central subject of the analysis.

Company current marketing situation

Data on the served markets for each of the products of the company's portfolio, in volume and market shares for several years and by geographical areas, are presented, as well as data on the current marketing mix.

Questionnaire 6: Product portfolio analysis

● What is the rate of current sales per product, segment, distributive channel, region and country, and so on, in volume and value?
● What is the current market share per product category, segment, distributive channel, region, country, and so on?
● How does the quality of our products compare with that of competition?
● How strong is the company's product brand image?
● Does the firm have a complete product line?
● What is the structure of our portfolio of customers?
● How concentrated is our total turnover?
● What is the age profile of our product portfolio?
● What is the contribution margin per product, segment, channel, and so on?
● What is the current level of nominal and relative prices?

This analysis is to be repeated for each product of the company's portfolio. Profit and loss statements for the last three years should be presented along with the current budget. A typical profit and loss statement is shown below in Table 10.6.

Priority competitor analysis

Priority competitor(s) should be identified for each product market. For each of these competitors, the same data collected for the company products will be gathered and compared as shown in Table 10.2 (see also Appendix 10.1). Other information is required to assess the strength of priority competition.

Questionnaire 7: Priority competition analysis

● What is the relative market share?
● Does competition have a cost advantage?
● What is the relative price?
● What is the competitive behaviour of rivals?
● How strong is the image of competing products?
● On what basis are competing products differentiated?
● How large are their financial resources?

Table 10.2   Priority competitors' analysis form
(each factor must be evaluated on a 10-point scale)

Marketing variables	Our product	Competitor 1	Competitor 2	Competitor 3
Product				
Quality:	——	——	——	——
Company price:	——	——	——	——
Product line:	——	——	——	——
Packaging:	——	——	——	——
Evaluation on				
■ Attribute 1:	——	——	——	——
■ Attribute 2:	——	——	——	——
■ Attribute 3:	——	——	——	——
Distribution				
Dist. number:	——	——	——	——
Dist. value:	——	——	——	——
■ channel 1:	——	——	——	——
■ channel 2:	——	——	——	——
■ channel 3:	——	——	——	——
Facing:	——	——	——	——
Margin:	——	——	——	——
Discounts:	——	——	——	——
Promotion:	——	——	——	——
Sales force				
Size of sales force:	——	——	——	——
Quality:	——	——	——	——
Call frequency:	——	——	——	——
Training:	——	——	——	——
Advertising				
Size of budget:	——	——	——	——
Media mix:				
■ medium 1:	——	——	——	——
■ medium 2:	——	——	——	——
■ medium 3:	——	——	——	——
Advertising copy:	——	——	——	——
Advertisement quality:	——	——	——	——
Promotion				
Size of budget:	——	——	——	——
Type of promotion:				
■ Consumer price:	——	——	——	——
■ Distribution margin:	——	——	——	——
■ Other promotions:	——	——	——	——
Services				
Range of services:	——	——	——	——
Delivery terms:	——	——	——	——
After-sales service:	——	——	——	——
Research and development				
Size of budget:	——	——	——	——
Staff:	——	——	——	——
Performance in R&D:	——	——	——	——
Marketing research				
Quality of MIS:	——	——	——	——
Data banks:	——	——	——	——
Performance:	——	——	——	——

● What is their retaliation capacity in case of frontal attack?
● Which are their major sources of vulnerability?
● What type of aggressive actions could they take?
● What kind of retaliatory or protective actions could we adopt?
● What changes could modify the present balance of power?
● Is competition able to destroy our competitive advantage?

With the information provided by questionnaires 6 and 7, a product portfolio analysis can be conducted using one of the procedures described in Chapter 9.

Distribution penetration analysis

Distributors, a company's partners in the marketing process, control the access to the end-users' market and play an important role in ensuring the success of the contemplated marketing programme. In addition, if they are powerful buyers they have a strong bargaining power *vis-à-vis* their suppliers. In fact, distributors must be viewed as intermediate customers just like end-user customers. The role of *trade marketing* is to analyse the needs and requirements of these intermediate customers in order to develop a mutually satisfactory exchange relationship.

Questionnaire 8: Distribution analysis

● How many distributors do we have in each channel?
● What is our penetration rate in number and value in each channel?
● What is the sales volume by type of distributor?
● What are the growth potentials of the different channels?
● What are the efficiency levels of the different distributors?
● Are the present trade terms motivating for distributors?
● What changes could modify relationships with our dealer network?
● Should the firm consider changing its distribution channels?
● What is the potential of direct marketing in our business?
● Are there new forms of distribution emerging in the market?

The objectives pursued by the firm and by its distributors are not exactly the same and conflicts can arise in the channels. Distributors are no longer passive intermediaries in most markets. The role of 'trade marketing' is to ensure that distributors are viewed by the firm as partners and as intermediate customers.

Communication programme analysis

Mass media advertising, interactive advertising, personal selling, publicity, and so on are powerful competitive weapons if properly used, that is, when the target markets are well chosen and when the content of the communication programme is well in line with the product positioning, pricing and distribution strategies.

Questionnaire 9: Communication programme analysis

● What is the advertising intensity compared to direct competition?
● What is the advertising cost per thousand target buyers per medium?

● What is the communication effectiveness of media advertising?
● What are the consumers' opinions on the advertisement content?
● What is the number of reply coupons stimulated by direct advertising?
● How well are the advertising objectives defined?
● What is the sales or market share effectiveness of advertising?
● What is the impact of advertising on awareness, attitude, intentions?
● What is the average number of sales calls per sales representative per week?
● What is the number of new customers per period?
● What is the sales force cost as a percentage of total sales?

These questionnaires should be used as guidelines for periodically reviewing the company's marketing situation within the framework of a marketing audit.

Pricing policy analysis

Price is the only component of the marketing mix generating income, by contrast with the other marketing instruments. Price also has the highest visibility in the marketplace and can be easily compared with rivals.

Questionnaire 10: Pricing policy analysis

● What is the price elasticity of primary demand?
● What is the price elasticity of our own demand or market share?
● What are the market 'maximum acceptable' prices of our brands?
● At what level are the perceived value prices of our brands?
● How do our prices compare with direct competitors' prices?
● Is price sensitivity very different from one segment to another?
● What is our policy in terms of price discounting?
● Are our prices stated in euros competitive in the European market?
● What type of price adjustment do we have to consider in the European market?

It is important to keep in mind that price is a determining factor in the brand positioning strategy and that it must be compatible with the other elements of the marketing mix.

● Objectives and Programmes

At this point, management knows the major issues and has to make some basic decisions about the objectives. Using the information provided by the strategic marketing audit and by the positioning statement, the firm's identified priority objectives must then be translated into operational action programmes.

Definition of objectives

Every firm has several objectives which can be grouped into two broad categories: marketing and non-marketing objectives:

● *Non-marketing objectives* have been described in the firm's mission statement. They describe the overall value system of the company and as such they apply for all market targets.

● *Marketing objectives* are of three types: sales, profit and customers. They should be defined for each product market or segment.

Sales objectives

It is a quantitative measure of the impact the firm 'wants' to achieve in the future within a particular product market. It is not simply a forecast of what one 'expects' may occur in the future. It is an active, not a passive, statement about the future. Sales objectives can be stated in currency, in volume or in market share. Examples of sales-oriented objectives are presented in Table 10.3.

Table 10.3   Examples of sales-oriented objectives

■ Achieve total sales revenue of $2,150,000 by the end of 1999.
■ Attain a 20 per cent market share of the management distance learning market.
■ Reach a sales volume of 150,000 units per year.

● *Sales revenue* objectives are the most convenient way to express a sales objective because they are easily integrated in the accounting and financial system. Sales revenue may be misleading, however, if not adjusted for inflation and also for modifications in the sales mix if, for example, the share of high-priced products has changed from one period to another.

● *Unit sales* represent the best indicator provided there is no change in the volume definition. In the soft drink sector, for example, it is current practice to think in terms of case sales. What about cases of 12 or 18 bottles? Conversion to 'litre equivalent cases' must be made. In many markets a meaningful unit definition simply does not exist. For example, in life insurance the number of policies taken out is not a good indicator of sales performance.

● *Market share*, as discussed in Chapter 6, is the best indicator of competitive performance. Also, in volume industries where experience effects occur, high market share implies a cost competitive advantage over direct competition.

Sales data are a key element in the projected income statement. They must be translated into financial terms.

Profit objectives

Marketing, as for all other functions within the firm, must be accountable for profits. The inclusion of formal profit objectives forces marketing people to estimate the cost implications of the stated sales objectives. Examples of profit objectives are presented in Table 10.4.

Table 10.4   Examples of profit objectives

- Produce net profits of $150,000 before tax by December 1999.
- Earn an average 15 per cent return on investment during the next 5 years.
- Produce a dollar contribution of $350,000 at the end of the fiscal year.

The definition of profit objectives implies a close interfunctional co-ordination within the firm. A statement of profitability cannot be made without a close look at the cost–volume relationship and capacity constraints. For new products, the investment in fixed costs and working capital, in addition to manufacturing and marketing costs, should be analysed before launching. Similarly, the marketing expenses involved in implementing the proposed marketing strategy must be carefully evaluated and their expected contribution to sales and/or market share development assessed. Go back to Figure 1.2 for a description of the interrelationships between the key managerial functions.

Customer objectives

Customer objectives are deduced from the positioning statement. They describe the type of behaviour or attitude the firm would want customers to have towards its brands or services. Examples of customer objectives are presented in Table 10.5.

Table 10.5   Examples of customer objectives

- Create at least a 60 per cent awareness for brand A within the 15–25 age group by the end of 1999.
- To increase by 20 per cent the repeat purchase rate of brand A within the 15–25 age group by the end of 1999.
- To position brand A at the high end of the market in the mind of consumers belonging to the upper income bracket.

These customer objectives are important because they provide directions to advertising people for the development of communication strategies and for supporting the positioning theme adopted.

Integration of objectives

Kotler (1997, p. 99) suggests starting with the profit objectives and deducing the required sales and customer objectives:

> For example, if the company wants to earn $1,800,000 profit, and its target profit margin is 10 per cent on sales, then it must set a goal of $18 million in sales revenue. If the company set an average price of $260, it must sell 69 230 units. If it expects total industry sales to reach 2.3 million units, that is a 3 per cent market share. To maintain this market share, the company will have to set certain goals for consumer awareness, distribution coverage, and so on.

Thus, the line of reasoning is the following:

- to define the expected net profit;
- to identify the turnover required to achieve this result;
- given the current average company price, to determine the required sales volume (in units);
- given the expected level of primary demand in the reference segment, to calculate the corresponding required market share;
- given this target market share, to determine the target objectives in terms of distribution and communication.

The corresponding *marketing objectives* should therefore be:

- to achieve a given turnover, which represents an increase over previous year of x per cent;
- This would imply a sales volume of x units, corresponding to a y per cent market share;
- to determine the level of brand awareness required to achieve this market share objective and also the required proportion of purchase intentions within the target segment;
- to determine the increase of distribution rate;
- to maintain the average company price.

This logical and apparently simple procedure is difficult to implement in the real world because it implies complete knowledge of the functional relationships between market share and price, market share and distribution, market share and awareness, and so on. The merit of this approach is to identify clearly the required information for sound marketing planning.

Characteristics of good objectives

Sound marketing objectives should have the following characteristics. They must be (a) clear and concise, avoiding long statements and phrases; (b) presented in a written form to facilitate communication and to avoid altering objectives over time; (c) stated within a specific time period and (d) in measurable terms; (e) consistent with overall company objectives and purpose; (f) attainable but of sufficient challenge to stimulate effort; and (g) name specific results in key areas, such as sales, profits and consumer behaviour or attitudes (Stevens, 1982, pp. 80–2).

In addition, individual responsibilities should be clearly defined as well as the calendar and the deadlines to be met.

Selection of the strategic path

To define an objective is one thing. To know how to reach that objective is another story, since the very same objective can be achieved in different ways.

A 10 per cent revenue increase can be obtained, for instance, by increasing the average selling price, or by expanding total demand through a price decrease, or by increasing market share without price change but through intensive advertising or promotional actions.

Clearly these alternative actions are not substitutes and their efficiency will vary according to market and competitive situations. Thus, beyond the general directions given by the basic strategic options discussed in Chapter 9, it is necessary to specify the action programmes segment by segment.

If the strategic option is to defend current market position with existing products in an existing segment, the alternative actions to consider in a *market position defence strategy* could be:

- Product or service modifications, for example new features or packaging, or product repositioning through concept advertising.
- Sales, distribution and service network reinforcement.
- Stepped-up or redirected promotional activities.
- Defensive pricing through bundling or premium pricing.

If the objective is to complete, improve or broaden the range of products, the alternative of a *product line extension strategy* could be:

- Filling gaps in the existing product line.
- Introduction of new products to serve untapped segments in related business areas.
- Systematic brand proliferation to blanket the market.
- Acquisition of a company with a complementary product line.
- Contracting for the supply of a complementary product line to be sold under the company's name.
- Joint venture for the development and production of a new product line.

If the objective is *international development* by shipping existing products to foreign markets, the alternatives could be:

- Use of an independent, worldwide trading company.
- Use of a network of export agents to handle all foreign business.
- Setting up of a network of distributors or import agents in target markets.
- Acquisition of a foreign company in the same industrial sector.
- A joint venture to enter a restricted foreign market.

These alternative strategy paths may have very different implications in terms of resources, both financial and human, and their feasibility must be carefully assessed.

The strategy statement

The strategy statement requires making basic choices among the strategy alternatives. It is a summary overview designed to state 'how' the objectives for the business unit will be met. The strategy statement will govern not only marketing planning, but the manufacturing, financial and R&D functions. It is the mainstream guidance from which all subsequent planning functions flow. The strategy statement should address the following:

- Market segments selected and targeted.
- Positioning relative to direct competition.

● Product line requirements, mix, extensions, and so on.
● Channels of distribution, direct, indirect, and so on.
● Pricing and price structure.
● Personal selling.
● Advertising and promotion.
● After-sales, warranty, services, and so on.
● Marketing research.

The strategy statement should not exceed two or three pages of text. At this point, general management should review and approve the objectives.

Criteria for selecting a strategic option

A certain number of simple rules, inspired by military strategy, should be followed in selecting a strategy:

● *Feasibility:* assess skills and resources constraints.
● *Strength:* always try to have a strength advantage.
● *Concentration:* avoid scattering of efforts.
● *Synergy:* ensure co-ordination and consistency in efforts.
● *Adaptability:* be ready to respond to the unexpected.
● *Parsimony:* avoid waste of scarce resources.

In the 1990s environment, forward thinking is a dynamic exercise which requires adaptability and flexibility (Gilbreath, 1987).

Design of the marketing programme

The expected level of sales of a given brand is a function of the intensity and continuity of operational marketing efforts. The support given to each product of the firm's portfolio must be described with precision and summarised in financial terms in a projected profit and loss statement.

Alternative marketing programmes

In the design of the marketing programme, the product or brand manager has to decide on the level of each of the key marketing mix instruments, that is price, advertising, visit frequency of the sales force to distributors, promotional activities to organise to support the brand in the distributive network, and so on. Since these marketing instruments are partly substitutable, the brand manager can explore the sensitivity of the break-even volume to different combinations of the marketing mix variables.It is common practice to establish a base programme and then to analyse the implications of alternative scenarios. By way of illustration, let us consider the following (fictitious) case.

> The direct cost of a new product is £10 (C); the annual depreciation cost plus the share of general overhead (F) add up to £38,000. Executive opinion held that £16 is a price (P) on the low side while £24 is a price on the high side; and that £10,000 is a low budget for advertising (S) and personal selling (V) respectively, and £50,000 is a high budget. This yields eight strategy combinations.

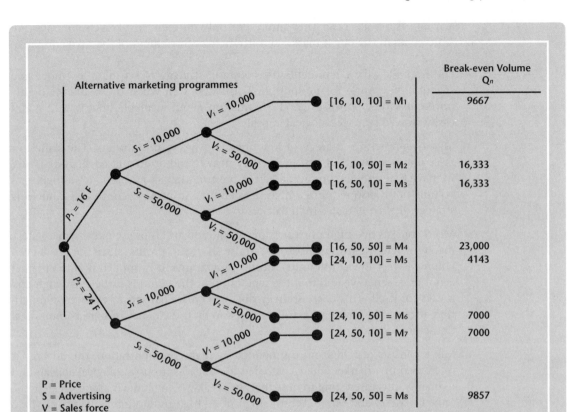

Source: Adapted from an example presented by Kotler (1964, p. 44).

Figure 10.2 Minimum volume requirements as a function of marketing mix

The break-even volume can be estimated as a function of the elements of the marketing mix as follows:

$$Q_n = \frac{F + S + V}{P - C}$$

The break-even volume will vary with the product price and the amount of marketing effort devoted to the new product,

$$Q_n = \frac{38\,000 + S + V}{P - 10}$$

In Figure 10.2, eight alternative marketing programmes are listed for this product along with the implied break-even volume. For example, in the case of Mix 1, one has,

$$Q_1 = \frac{38\,000 + 10\,000 + 100\,000}{16 - 10} = 9\,667 \text{ units}$$

Each mix is a polar case. They imply not only different break-even volumes, but also differences in the target market sensitivity to each element of the marketing mix:

● For example, Mix 1 represents the common strategy of setting a low price and spending very little for promotion. This works well when the market is highly price conscious, possesses good information about available brands, and is not easily swayed by psychological appeals.

● Mix 4 represents a strategy of low price and heavy promotions. The same low price policy as in Mix 1 is supported by heavy promotion and advertising. Thus, we have here the maximum marketing pressure that should produce a high sales volume but it also requires a high sales volume to break even. In this launching strategy, the firm creates high barriers to entry.

● Mix 5 consists of a high price and low promotion and is used typically in a seller's market where the firm wants to maximise short-run profits, since the break-even volume is very low (4143 units). In this programme, it is implied that the market is not price sensitive and that the reputation of the brand is sufficiently high and speaks for itself. This entry strategy does not create barriers of entry to competition attracted by the high market prices and by the absence of high communication costs.

● Mix 8 consists of a high price supported by high communication; this strategy is often used in a market where customers are sensitive to psychological appeals and to quality. It is interesting to note that the break-even volume is approximately the same for Mix 1 and Mix 8. Yet, the high price, high promotion character of Mix 8 promises greater losses or greater profits for deviations from the break-even volume.

The other mixes (Nos 2, 3, 6, 7) are variations on the same themes, with the additional feature that different assessments are made of the comparative effectiveness of advertising and personal selling. The alternatives presented here opposed a push versus a pull communication strategy. But it should be noted that while the division of a given budget between advertising and personal selling affects the actual sales volume, it does not affect the break-even volume.

The sales multiplier concept

In the field of fast moving consumer goods (FMCG), sales evolution beyond the first year is mainly determined by the repeat purchase rate. This rate is often difficult to estimate with precision. If the firm has information on the sales patterns of similar products, the product's penetration curve can be estimated on this basis. For example, the observation made by the firm could be the following:

Brand sales in this type of product category have a short life cycle; they reach their maximum level after twelve months, stay on this plateau during the second year and then decay during the third year at a rate which varies with the size of marketing efforts.

If the average decay rate observed for similar products is 20 per cent, third-year sales would then be 80 per cent of second-year sales. The sales multiplier of first-year sales over three years would then be 2.80 (1+1+0.80). This number (2.80) is called the sales multiplier or *'blow-up factor'*. With this information, it is possible to develop a *projected profit and loss statement* over three years.

Risk or sensitivity analysis

A projected profit and loss statement, such as presented in Table 10.7 below, is based on assumptions about the sales growth rate and the size of the marketing budget. Management knows that this information is imperfect and risk analysis consists in testing the sensitivity of these assumptions on expected sales and profit.

Given the absence of reliable information on the trial and repeat purchase rates of the product, first-year and subsequent years' sales cannot be determined with precision, and it is therefore useful to have a range of likely sales, and not only a point estimate, to assess the risk implications of the project. Suppose that the brand manager's opinion is summarised in the following terms:

> The product manager is satisfied with the sales estimate of 2 million cases for the first year, although admitting that it contains some uncertainty. When pressed, however, the product manager will admit that sales could be as low as 1 million cases in the first year, but points out that sales might also exceed the estimate by as much as 1 million cases. The operational definition of these extremes is that each has no more than 1 in 10 chance of occurring.

Using these estimates, one can derive a probability distribution for first-year sales and calculate the expected value of sales. The objective is to assess the risk of having a sales volume inferior to the break-even volume during the first year. The probability distribution is presented in Table 10.6.

Table 10.6 Expected value of sales and profit

Sales[1]		Probability	Expected sales	Conditional payoffs	Expected profit
Classes	Mid-point				
0.5–1.0	0,75	0.10	0,075	–6,455	–0,646
1.0–1.5	1,25	0.20	0,250	–2,759	–0,552
1.5–2.0	1,75	0.25	0,438	+0,938	+0,235
2.0–2.5	2,25	0.25	0,562	+4,635	+1,159
2.5–3.0	2,75	0.10	0,275	+8,331	+0,833
3.0–3.5	3,25	0.10	0,325	+11,028	+1,203
Total:	–	1.00	$E(q) = 1,925$	–	$E(\pi) = 2,232$

1. In million cases or dollars.

The expected value of sales is 1,925,000 cases, which is very close to the deterministic estimation. There is, however, a 3 in 10 ten chance that the sales volume in the first year will fall below the break-even volume. This is a significant risk.

Risk can also be measured in financial terms by computing the value of perfect information or the cost of uncertainty. The expected value of the choice given perfect information (VPI) is obtained by computing the expected value of the best conditional payoffs of Table 11.11.

$$E(VPI) = 0.10(0)+0.20(0)+0.25(0,938)+0.25(4,635)+0.10(8,331)+0.10(11,028)$$

That is,

$$E(VPI) = \$3,430 \text{ million}$$

Without perfect information, the optimal action is to go ahead, with an expected payoff of \$2,232 million. Thus the expected gain from perfect information (or the uncertainty cost) is:

$$\$3,430 \text{ million} – \$2,232 \text{ million} = \$1,198 \text{ million}$$

One observes that the uncertainty cost is high compared to the expected gain. Another way to assess the risk is simply to observe, referring to column 5 in Table 10.6, that there are 30 chances out of 100 to have a loss of at least \$2,759,000 on this project. The cost of uncertainty measures in a way the opportunity cost of a decision taken under imperfect information. This amount also measures the value of additional information.

The marketing budget

Once the course of action is identified, a detailed description of the means required will be made for each component of the marketing mix. The strategy statement allows the product manager to prepare a supporting budget, which is basically a projected profit and loss statement. A standard structure of a projected profit and loss statement is presented in Table 10.6.

The strategy statement gives a general direction which must then be translated into specific actions for each component of the marketing mix with a description of the resources available to implement those actions. These resources include human and financial resources; they are described in the action programme and in the budget.

The *action programme* includes a detailed description of the actions to be undertaken. In addition to financial considerations, the budget should also specify the timing of the action programmes and the responsibilities, that is who is in charge of what. An example of budget structure is presented in Table 10.7.

Negotiation of the marketing budget

Different budgeting modes can be adopted to design a strategic marketing plan. The ideal procedure should be as simple as possible and involve the whole organisation and in particular the functions responsible for the plan implementation. The most popular budgeting process observed in a survey of 141 companies (Piercy, 1987, p. 49), is the *bottom-up/top-down* process:

> Managers of the sub-units in marketing submit budget requests, which are co-ordinated by the chief marketing executive and presented to top management, who adjust the total budget size to conform with overall goals and strategies.

A good strategic marketing plan should be a written document: it takes the form of a contract. To be effective the plan should have the following characteristics:

Table 10.7 Projected profit and loss statements form

SEGMENT: _____ PRODUCT: _____ ZONE: _____							
	Year −3 (19)	Year −2 (19)	Year −1 (19)	Current Year (19) Budget	(19) Estimated	Year +1 (20)	Year +2 (20)
■ **TOTAL MARKET**							
– Volume (units)	——	——	——	——	——	——	——
– Dollar sales ($)	——	——	——	——	——	——	——
■ **COMPANY SALES**							
– Volume (units)	——	——	——	——	——	——	——
– Marker share	——	——	——	——	——	——	——
– Sales revenue($)	——	——	——	——	——	——	——
■ **DIRECT COST**							
■ **GROSS PROFIT MARGIN**							
– Value	——	——	——	——	——	——	——
– % of net turnover	——	——	——	——	——	——	——
■ **DIRECT MARKETING COSTS**							
– Promotions	——	——	——	——	——	——	——
– Discounts	——	——	——	——	——	——	——
– Folders and mailing	——	——	——	——	——	——	——
– Miscellaneous	——	——	——	——	——	——	——
– Total direct costs	——	——	——	——	——	——	——
■ **SEMI-FIXED MARKETING COSTS**							
– Media advertising	——	——	——	——	——	——	——
– POS	——	——	——	——	——	——	——
– Public relations	——	——	——	——	——	——	——
– Total semi-fixed costs	——	——	——	——	——	——	——
■ **FIXED MARKETING COSTS**							
– Marketing department	——	——	——	——	——	——	——
– Sales force	——	——	——	——	——	——	——
– Market research	——	——	——	——	——	——	——
– Sampling	——	——	——	——	——	——	——
– Miscellaneous	——	——	——	——	——	——	——
– Total fixed costs	——	——	——	——	——	——	——
■ **TOTAL COSTS**							
– in % of net turnover	——	——	——	——	——	——	——
■ **NET CONTRIBUTION**							
– Value	——	——	——	——	——	——	——
– in % of net turnover	——	——	——	——	——	——	——
■ **NET CUMULATIVE CONTRIBUTION**	——	——	——	——	——	——	——

⬤ To be sufficiently standardised as to permit fast discussion and approval.

⬤ To consider alternative solutions to be adopted if environmental conditions change or if corrective actions have to be taken.

⬤ To be regularly re-examined or updated.

● To be viewed as a managerial aid, which implies being (a) strict on the applications of corporate goal and on long-term strategic options, and (b) flexible on short-term forecasts.

● The planning horizon is in general a three-year moving horizon.

Usually, every month there is a comparison between current and expected results in order to monitor closely the implementation of the plan and to facilitate the adoption of fast remedial actions.

Gap analysis

In summarising the objectives of each business unit, it is instructive to project the current performance trends to verify whether the projected performance is satisfactory. If gaps appear between the current and the desired performance, then strategic changes will need to be considered. The graph presented in Figure 10.3 illustrates the contribution of growth opportunities under two growth scenarios:

● An 'all things being equal performance', where growth is achieved through a penetration strategy based on existing products and existing markets, assuming no change in the current strategy.

● A 'desired performance', where growth is the outcome of the proposed marketing programme and of different growth opportunities.

As shown in Figure 10.3, the gap between these two performance levels can be subdivided into two parts:

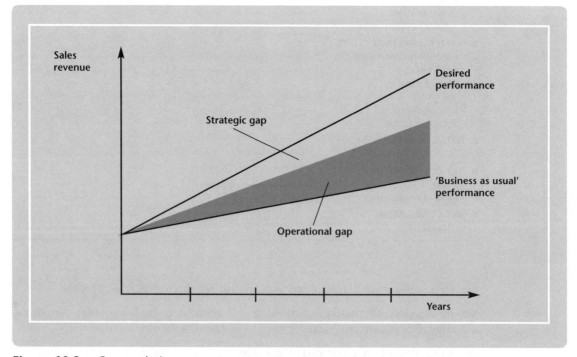

Figure 10.3 Gap analysis

An *'operational gap'*, which reveals the improvement potential of existing businesses that could be achieved through a market and product rationalisation strategy, that is reducing costs and/or improving marketing effectiveness, while keeping the structure of the product portfolio unchanged.

A *'strategic gap'*, which requires new growth opportunities, that is new products, new markets, international development, diversification or integration.

These growth opportunities should be listed in order of priority and their potential financial contribution to the desired performance evaluated.

Vulnerability Analysis and Contingency Planning

The value of strategic planning is a continuing topic for debate. Not long ago, planning departments enjoyed a high status within the corporate organisation. Today, most corporate planners downplay their formal planning roles. Experience with such largely unforeseen upheavals as the two oil crises of the 1970s, the stock market crash of 1987, the Gulf war, the East European revolutions, and so on has revealed the shortcomings and the limitations of rigid planning procedures. Under fairly static conditions, planning works well, but when faced with uncertainties, turbulence, unanticipated market and competitive changes, general management becomes suspicious of the forecasts of revenue and profit performance that come from the business units.

Testing the robustness of a strategic plan

Just because a strategy must be developed and implemented under turbulent and uncertain conditions is no reason to abandon the discipline of structured planning. Planning is necessary for the functioning of the firm. To improve strategic planning performance, it is therefore important to test the robustness of the proposed strategy. Gilbreath (1987) suggests applying a 'shake test' to the proposed strategy.

> When structural or mechanical engineers wish to determine the reaction of a proposed design to mechanical vibrations, they either model it mathematically and calculate its response to input vibrations or, if feasible, build a prototype, put it on a special 'shaking table' and actually witness the outcome. This is called a 'shake test'… It is proposed that a similar exercise be applied to strategic plans – giving them the shake test before the unforgiving test our markets and competitors will surely apply (Gilbreath, 1987, p. 47).

Day (1986) proposed testing the robustness of a proposed strategy through the following seven 'tough questions' to be examined by corporate management and operating managers:

Suitability: is there a sustainable advantage given the potential threats to and opportunities for the business and in light of the capabilities of the firm?

Validity: are the assumptions realistic? What is the quality of the information on which these assumptions rely?

Feasibility: do we have the skills, resources and commitment?

- *Consistency*: does the strategy hang together? Are all elements of the strategy pointing in the same direction?
- *Vulnerability*: what are the risks and contingencies?
- *Adaptability*: can we retain our flexibility? How could the strategy be reversed in the future?
- *Financial desirability*: how much economic value is created? What is the attractiveness of the forecast performance relative to the probable risk? (adapted from Day, 1986, pp. 63–8).

Examples of vulnerability factors are presented in Table 10.8. Given the rapidity of environmental change, the test should be applied periodically to facilitate adaptability and revision. A good way to proceed is to apply this shake test with the assistance of outside persons to avoid the risk of myopia and wishful thinking.

Table 10.8   Identifying vulnerability factors

Vulnerability Factors	Stability Factors
Reliance on fads	Projection of lasting symbols
Single use	Multiple use of products
Technology dependence	Technology transcendence
Single distribution network	Multiple distribution network
Heavy capital investment	Leasing, renting and joint ownership
Prescriptive identities	Non-restrictive identities
Building with products outside our control	Building with unchanging needs

Source: Adapted from Gilbreath (1987).

Vulnerability analysis

The vulnerability of a strategic plan is determined by two factors: the strategic importance of risk and the degree of control the firm has over the risk factor. The risk factor is a combination of (a) the impact of extreme but plausible values on overall performance, and (b) the likelihood that these extreme values could occur during the planning period.

The vulnerability grid presented in Figure 10.4 can be used to position the different risk factors and to isolate those few that could cause the most damage. To each quadrant there corresponds a specific risk situation which requires appropriate action:

- In the *strategy quadrant*, that is where both risk and degree of control are high, the risk factors are subject to company control, need to be understood very well, are the focus of major strategic actions and should be tightly monitored.

- In the *vulnerability quadrant*, the risks are high but the degree of control is weak. The factors positioned here are critical and must be continuously monitored. Contingency plans should be developed.

- In the *fine-tuning quadrant*, the risks are low but the degree of control high. These factors are controlled and managed by operational management.

- In the *non-strategy quadrant*, both risk and degree of control are low and the factors positioned here will be included in the base scenario.

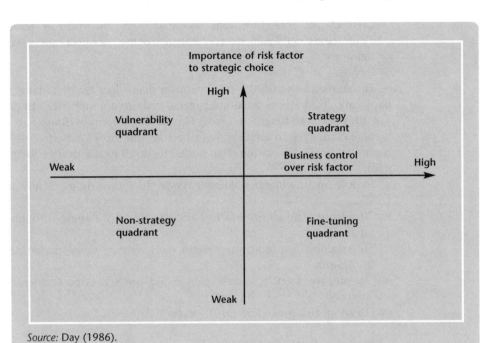

Source: Day (1986).

Figure 10.4   Vulnerability grid

The vulnerability quadrant deserves particular attention, since major and unanticipated crises could come from these risk factors. Alternative strategies should be developed for these risk factors.

Strategic surprise management

In spite of the best planning efforts, some issues or unexpected changes will slip by the environmental monitoring system and become 'crises' or *'strategic surprises'* in Ansoff's terminology (1984). A crisis is characterised by four elements:

● The issue arrives suddenly, unanticipated.
● It poses novel problems in which the firm has little prior experience.
● Failure to respond implies either a major financial reversal or loss of a major opportunity.
● The response is urgent and cannot be handled promptly enough by the normal systems and procedures (Ansoff, 1984, p. 24).

The combination of these four elements creates major problems for the firm. A crisis or disaster can be any emergency that happens suddenly, that disrupts the routine of the organisation and that demands immediate attention. Examples of crises are numerous.

The 'Nestlé kills babies' affair, the Tylenol incident, the Union Carbide disaster in Bhopal, the Société Générale of Belgium's take-over bid, the Pan Am Boeing 747 crash at Lockerbie, the

Chernobyl and Three Mile Island nuclear accidents, the mad cow disease in the UK, the dioxin scandal in Belgium, the contamination of the Coca-Cola cans in France and Belgium, and so on.

The suddenness and the prospect of a major loss create a danger of widespread panic, and 'business as usual' managerial systems are inefficient to deal with a crisis. The firm needs to invest in a *crisis recovery plan*, because disaster recovery planning is more conducive to a rational perspective and more cost-effective if the process is begun before a crisis, rather than pulled together in the heat of battle (Phelps, 1986, p. 6).

To develop a *contingency planning system* the following steps must be taken:

⬤ To identify the *sensitive factors* and the zones of danger through a vulnerability analysis.
⬤ To establish a monitoring system with *warning signals* based on early-warning indicators.
⬤ To prepare a *crisis recovery plan* based on a previously identified alternative strategy.
⬤ To adopt this procedure for the *major risks*.

According to Ansoff (1984) and Lagadec (1991), a *crisis recovery plan* should have the following characteristics:

⬤ A emergency communication network which crosses normal organisational boundaries, filters the information and rapidly communicates with the entire organisation.

⬤ A repartition of top management responsibilities between three groups: one in charge of the organisation's morale control and maintenance; one in charge of 'business as usual'; and one in charge of the response to the surprise.

⬤ A strategic task force to deal with the surprise whose members cross normal organisational lines.

⬤ The task force and communication networks are pre-designed and trained under non-crisis conditions before they are put to the actual test.

This procedure will not eliminate the occurrence of completely unexpected events but will contribute to reduce the consequences of major risks which can be identified. As put by Augustine (1995, p. 151), '*when preparing for crises, it is instructive to recall that Noah started building the ark before it began to rain*'. To go further on the topic of crisis management, see the excellent book by Lagadec (1991).

The new roles of global strategic planning

Business International (1991) has conducted a survey with 18 of the world's leading global companies on three continents to gain insights into their approaches to global planning. The 10 most frequently mentioned functions of corporate planners are the following:

- Compiling of information for top management.
- Competitor research.
- Forecasting.
- Consulting services.
- Creating a common language.
- Communicating corporate culture.
- Establishing and communicating corporate objectives.
- Group facilitation and team leadership.
- Guardianship of the planning system.
- Developing planning methods.

Most corporate planners downplay their formal planning roles and instead emphasise their functions as 'facilitators', 'communicators' or 'consultants'. They see their role less as representatives of corporate authority than as consultants charged with assisting the divisions in developing their own plan and strategies.

Chapter summary

This chapter has provided a scheme for developing a formal strategic marketing plan. The role of strategic planning is to design a desired future for the company and to define effective ways of making things happen. The plan summarises, in a formal way, the marketing strategy development phase. One of the key elements of the strategic plan is the mission statement which should reveal the company's long-term vision of what it wants to be and whom it wants to serve. The strategic plan is based on an external audit. The environment is ever-changing and complex and the firm must constantly scan and monitor the environment to identify the main threats and opportunities. The assessment of strengths and weaknesses is also an essential task in the strategic process. The objective is to evaluate company resources in order to identify a sustainable competitive advantage on which to base the development strategy. Using the information collected in the external and internal audits (swot analysis), the next task is to define priority objectives to be translated into operational action programmes and in a marketing budget. Testing the robustness of a strategic plan is useful to improve the strategic planning performance. Also, in the current turbulent environment, vulnerability and risk analysis is required to help the firm anticipate the unexpected through contingency planning and crisis management.

QUESTIONS AND PROBLEMS

1. What difference do you see between a marketing plan and a marketing strategy?
2. Pick a company whose activities and corporate goal you know well and prepare a mission statement.

3. How do you associate as closely as possible the different echelons within the firm with the preparation and the adoption of a strategic plan? Compare the merits and the weaknesses of the 'top-down' and the 'bottom-up' budgeting processes?

4. Referring to Table 10.7, give examples of three vulnerability factors and three stability factors to be used to test the robustness of a strategic plan.

5. What are the chances that strategic planning will succeed in a company whose chief executive is not interested in it and delegates the task to staff people?

6. List five variables on which success in the home construction industry depends.

7. Since it is natural for managers to want to justify their actions and decisions, is it possible for a company to make a truly objective appraisal of its strengths and weaknesses?

8. A financial executive questions the need for formal planning. Prepare a defence of strategic marketing planning.

Bibliography

Ansoff, H.I. (1984) *Implanting Strategic Management*, Englewood Cliffs NJ, Prentice Hall.

Augustine, N.R. (1995) Managing the Crisis you Tried to Prevent, *Harvard Business Review*, **73**(6): 147–58.

Business International (1991) *The Changing Face of Corporate Planning in the 1990's*, Bimonthly Report, August 19.

Caeldries, F. and Van Dierdonck, R. (1988) How Belgian Businesses Make Strategic Planning Work?, *Long Range Planning*, **21**(2): 41–51.

David, F.R. (1989) How Companies Define Their Mission?, *Long Range Planning*, **22**(1): 90–7.

Day, G.S. (1986) Tough Questions for Developing Strategies, *The Journal of Business Strategy*, **6**(3): 67–75.

Drucker, P. (1973) *Management, Tasks, Responsibilities, Practices*, New York, Harper & Row.

Gilbreath, R.D. (1987) Planning for the Unexpected, *The Journal of Business Strategy*, **8**(2): 44–9.

Greenley, G. (1987) An Exposition into Empirical Research into Marketing Planning, *Journal of Marketing Management*, **3**(1).

Hamermesch, R.G. (1986) Making Planning Strategies, *Harvard Business Review*,.**64**, pp. 115–20.

Haspeslagh, P. (1982) Portfolio Planning Uses and Limits, *Harvard Business Review*, **60**, pp. 58–72.

Hopkins, D.S. (1981) *The Marketing Plan*, New York, The Conference Board, Report No. 801.

Kotler, P. (1964) Marketing Mix for New Products, *Journal of Marketing Research*, **1**, pp. 43–9.

Kotler, P. (1997) *Marketing Management*, 7th edn, Englewood Cliffs NJ, Prentice Hall.

Lagadec, P. (1991) *La gestion des crises*, Paris, Ediscience International.

McDonald, M.H.B. (1991) Ten Barriers to Marketing Planning, *The Journal of Consumer Marketing*, **8**, pp. 45–58.

Piercy, N.F. (1987) The Marketing Budgeting Process: Marketing Management Implications, *Journal of Marketing*, **51**(4): 45–59.

Phelps, N.L. (1986) Setting Up a Crisis Recovery Plan, *The Journal of Business Strategy*, **6**(4): 5–10.

Porter, M.E. (1980) *Competitive Strategy*, New York, The Free Press.

Stevens, R.E. (1982) *Strategic Marketing Plan Master Guide*, Englewood Cliffs NJ, Prentice Hall.

Appendix 10.1

The Search for a Sustainable Competitive Advantage in the Value Chain

MANAGERIAL FUNCTIONS	EVALUATION[1]				
	1	2	3	4	5
MARKETING:					
High relative market share					
Brand reputation					
High distribution coverage					
Size of the sales force					
Effective sales force					
Level of sales training					
Quality sales support					
Low relative price					
Balanced customer portfolio					
Size of the advertising budget					
Advertising quality (creativity)					
Marketing data bank					
Fast delivery					
Training for dealers					
Fine-tuned segmentation					
Customers' level of satisfaction					
Extent of product line					
OPERATIONS:					
Large production capacity					
Convenient location of production units					
Extension potential					
Advanced technology					
Age of equipment					
Total quality control					
Equipment versatility					
Availability of quality labour force					
Fast manufacturing					
Quality, reliability of components					
Flexible manufacturing					
Production to customer specifications					
Defect-free manufacturing					
Fast, reliable repairs					
FINANCE:					
High cash flow					
Good profitability					
Availability of credit					
Availability of capital					
Low debt ratio					
High stock turnout					
No long-term debt					
Good return on equity					
Efficient invoicing					
Good customer credit					

1. 1= not at all important; 5 = very important.

(continued overleaf)

MANAGERIAL FUNCTIONS	EVALUATION[1]				
	1	2	3	4	5
ADMINISTRATION:					
Qualification of personnel					
Sufficient inventory					
Strategic, attractive location of office					
Low operating costs					
Good customer after-sales service					
Good training programmes					
Up-to-date office equipment					
Office automation					
Efficient order processing					
TECHNOLOGY:					
Fast new product development					
Up-to-date technology					
Engineering know-how					
Product patents					
Process patents					
High creativity in R&D					
Good management of R&D					
High R&D budget					
Performance of R&D					

1. 1= not at all important; 5 = very important.

part four

Market-driven Management Decisions

STRUCTURE OF THE BOOK

PART ONE The Changing Role of Marketing

The role of marketing in the firm and in a marketing economy

CHAPTER ONE

From marketing to market-driven management

CHAPTER TWO

PART TWO Understanding Customer Behaviour

The customer choice behaviour

CHAPTER THREE

The marketing information system

CHAPTER FOUR

The customer's response behaviour

CHAPTER FIVE

PART THREE Market-driven Strategy Development

Needs analysis through market segmentation

CHAPTER SIX

Market attractiveness analysis

CHAPTER SEVEN

Competitiveness analysis

CHAPTER EIGHT

Formulating a market strategy

CHAPTER NINE

The strategic marketing plan

CHAPTER TEN

PART FOUR Market-driven Management Decisions

Market-driven new product decisions	Market-driven distribution decisions	Market-driven pricing decisions	Market-driven communication decisions	Market-driven advertising decisions
CHAPTER ELEVEN	CHAPTER TWELVE	CHAPTER THIRTEEN	CHAPTER FOURTEEN	CHAPTER FIFTEEN

PART FIVE Ten Case Studies in Market-driven Management

1. **The Lander Company** *W.J. Stanton*
2. **The WILO Corporation** *R. Köhler*
3. **TV: Cold Bath for French Cinema** *A. Riding*
4. **Ecover** *D. Develter*
5. **Volvo Truck Belgium** *J.J. Lambin*
6. **The Petro-equipment Company** *J.J. Lambin*
7. **Sierra Plastics Company** *W.J. Stanton*
8. **Tissex** *G. Marion*
9. **Newfood** *G.S. Day et al.*
10. **SAS: Meeting Customer Expectations** *D.L. Kurtz and K.E. Clow*

Market-driven new product decisions

The objective of this chapter is to analyse the concepts and procedures which allow a firm to implement new product development strategies. Redeployment, diversification and innovation are at the heart of all development strategies. In a constantly changing environment, a company must continuously re-evaluate the structure of its portfolio of activities, meaning the decisions to abandon products, modify existing ones or launch new products. These decisions are of the utmost importance to the survival of the company and involve not only the marketing department, but all of the other functional areas as well. In this chapter, we shall examine the ways of establishing a *dialogue* between the various functional areas which play a role in the development of a new product. We do this in such a way as to minimise the risks in the strategy during the innovation process. A recent global survey on innovation published by A.D. Little (1997) reveals that the down-sizing era of the 1990s is over and that companies are placing high strategic priority on growth through innovations.

Chapter learning objectives

When you have read this chapter, you should be able to know and understand:

1. the nature, the risks and the success factors of innovations;

2. the organisational procedure of the new product development process;

3. the methods of idea generation;

4. the methods of idea screening;

5. the steps to follow in the design of a launching marketing plan;

6. the concept of portfolio of projects;

7. the dimensions of quality viewed from the buyer's perspective.

● Assessing the Risk of Innovations

The expression 'new product' is used loosely to describe a whole spectrum of innovations ranging from very minor, such as a change in an existing product, to very major, such as perfecting a new medicine resulting from years of research and development. Clearly, the risk varies greatly in these two examples and the nature of the risk in each one is completely different. Therefore it is important to evaluate accurately the diversity of innovations and their specific risks. After having defined the elements which constitute innovation, we will examine the different classifications of innovations as well as the principal factors which explain the success, or failure, of new products.

Strategic role of innovations

New product decisions are complex and risky decisions, but they are of vital importance for the development and the survival of the firm. The acceleration of technological change has reinforced this importance. In 1995, the share of sales derived from new or improved products commercialised within the previous five years was 45 per cent on average (Page, 1993). This percentage is even higher for high-tech products and tends to increase with time:

> 1976–1981: 33 per cent
> 1981–1986: 40 per cent
> 1986–1990: 42 per cent
> 1990–1995: 45 per cent

New products also have a decisive impact on corporate profits. A study made by the Product Development and Management Association (PDMA), indicated that:

> On average 23.2 per cent of 1990 profits came from internally developed new products introduced during the previous five years. Furthermore, this percentage is expected to increase to 45.6 per cent for new products introduced during the 1990–1994 period (Page, 1993, p. 285).

One American study (1999) found that the overall rate of return for some 17 successful innovations made in the 1970s averaged 56 per cent. Compare that with the 16 per cent average return on investment for all-American business over the past 30 years (*The Economist*, 1999).

This data observed in the United States cannot be transposed as such to European markets; they remain nevertheless very instructive. The data presented in Table 11.1 are interesting to assess the importance of R&D expenditures among the world champions.

Components of an Innovation

In Chapter 2 we saw that there was a distinction between an invention and an innovation. The latter is defined as the original implementation of a concept, discovery, or invention. According to Barreyre (1980, p. 10), an innovation may be subdivided into three elements (see Exhibit 11.1):

Table 11.1 The world champions in R&D

Companies	R&D expenditures in billions £	R&D in % of sales revenue	Companies	R&D expenditures in billions £	R&D in % of sales revenue
General Motors	4.98	4.9	NTT	1.54	3.7
Ford Motors	3.85	4.1	Volkswagen	1.49	3.9
Siemens	2.75	7.6	Intel	1.43	9.4
IBM	2.62	5.5	Hoechst	1.35	7.7
Hitachi	2.35	5.9	Bayer	1.34	7.2
Toyota	2.11	3.7	Sony	1.32	5.2
Matsushita-Electric	2.03	5.7	Northern Telecom	1.30	13.9
Daimler-Benz	1.91	4.6	Johnson & Johnson	1.30	9.5
Hewlett-Packard	1.87	7.2	Bell Canada	1.24	8.8
Ericsson Telefon	1.86	14.5	Philips	1.22	5.3
Lucent Technologies	1.84	11.5	Roche	1.21	15.5
Motorola	1.67	9.2	Honda Motor	1.17	4.7
Fujitsu	1.65	7.8	Pfizer	1.17	15.8
NEC	1.63	7.0	Microsoft	1.17	16.9
Asea Brown Boweri	1.61	8.5	Boeing	1.17	4.2
El du Pont de Nemours	1.58	5.8	Glaxo Wellcome	1.15	14.4
Toshiba	1.55	6.1	Alcatel Alsthom	1.11	6.8
Novartis	1.54	11.8	Robert Bosch	1.10	7.0

Source: The Department of Trade and Industry, *IHT*, 4–5 July (1998).

● A *need* to be satisfied, or a function(s) to be fulfilled.
● The *concept* of an object or entity to satisfy the need, in other words, the 'new idea'.
● The *inputs* comprising of a body of existing knowledge as well as materials and available technology, which allow the concept to become operational.

The degree of risk associated with an innovation will thus depend on two factors:

● The degree of originality and complexity of the concept, which will determine the reception by the market and transfer costs for the user (*market risk*).
● The degree of technological innovation pertaining to the concept, which will determine the technical feasibility of the innovation (*technology risk*).

Added to these two intrinsic risks is the degree of familiarity that the firm itself has with the market and technology (*strategy risk*).

Too often a product is said to be new, simply because it is new for the firm, while it is not necessarily new for the buyers. It is therefore important to establish a distinction between a *novelty* and an *innovation*. What is new is not necessarily an innovation.

New products – from foods to health and beauty aids – continue to inundate customers with choices, according to Marketing Intelligence Service LTD's annual new products report. With

Components of an Innovation: Two Examples

- **The disengageable T-bar and downhill skiing**
  - The *need*: to avoid the long and tiresome process of climbing back up snow-covered slopes.
  - The *concept*: traction by a disengageable cable with a seat.
  - The *technology*: mechanics
- **The problem of aeronautic vibrations**
  - The *need*: to eliminate the vibrations that affect electronic equipment in an aeroplane.
  - The *concept*: a sort of mesh covering.
  - The *technology*: a resilient steel weave.

25,181 new product launches in 1998, against 25,261 in 1997, the pace of new introductions still far surpasses the 14,254 new products that arrived in the market place in 1987. The percentage of these new products considered as truly innovative is minimal. Only 5.9 per cent of the products launched last year featured original characteristics, about the same percentage as in the previous year. (*Marketing News*, March 1999)

A true innovation is a product, a service, a concept which brings a new solution to the buyers' problems, either by providing a better solution than the existing ones proposed by competition, or by offering a new or an additional function.

Typology of innovations

Four possible criteria for classifying innovations emerge: (a) the degree of newness for the firm; (b) the intrinsic nature of the innovation concept; (c) the innovation's origin and (d) the behavioural change implied for the user of the innovation.

Degree of newness for the company

Assessing the degree of newness for the company is important because it is this newness which determines, at least in part, the company's competitiveness or competitive capacity. As Table 11.2 suggests, the more a company explores new territory, the greater the strategy risk. Four distinguishable levels of risk for a new product are as follows:

- *Known market and product*: the risk is doubly limited because the firm relies on its distinctive abilities.
- *New market, known product*: the risk is essentially a commercial one and success relies heavily on the marketing know-how of the firm.
- *Known market, new product*: the risk is technical in nature and success relies on the firm's technical know-how.

● *New market, new product*: the risks cumulate and we find the characteristics of a diversification strategy.

Table 11.2 Assessing the newness of an innovation for the firm

Newness of the product for the firm	Newness of the market for the firm	
	Low	**High**
High	New products for the firm	New products for the firm
	Present customers	New customer groups
	New product line	Diversification strategy
Low	Reformulated products	Extension of existing products
	Present customers	New customer groups
	Next generation – improved products	Addition to existing product lines

Source: Adapted from Booz, Allen and Hamilton (1982).

When considering product *newness*, it is important to distinguish between products 'new to the world' and 'new to the company'. Booz *et al.* (1982) established the following typology, based on a study of 700 companies and 13,000 new industrial and consumer products:

● New-to-the-world products	10 per cent
● New product lines	20 per cent
● Additions to existing product lines	26 per cent
● Improvements in/revisions to existing products	26 per cent
● Repositioning	7 per cent
● Cost reductions	11 per cent
	100 per cent

Note that a small percentage of innovations are new to the world (10 per cent), while the majority of innovations (70 per cent) essentially involve line extensions or modifications of existing products.

Nature of the innovation: technological versus organisational

A second classification of innovations deals with the intrinsic nature of the new idea. Based on this, we distinguish between commercial and technological innovations.

Technological innovation deals with the physical characteristics of the product, whether at the level of the manufacturing process (float glass), the use of a new ingredient (steel cord in radial tyres), the use of a new primary material (polyurethane foam), completely new products (composite materials), new finished products (compact disc), new physical conditioning of the product (instant coffee) or complex new systems (the high speed train).

The technological innovation results in the application of exact sciences for industrial practices. These innovations usually come from laboratories or R&D departments. Some of these innovations require a lot of technology and capital (nuclear industry, space industry), while others require a lot of technology and very little capital (consumer electronic industry). From the customer's point of view, a technological innovation is embodied in the product itself.

An *organisational or commercial innovation* deals mostly with the modes of organisation, distribution and communication inherent in the commercialisation process of a product or service. For example, the new presentation of a product (its design), a new means of distribution (Amazon on the Internet), a new advertising medium (advertising on-line), a new combination of aesthetics and function (Swatch watches), a new packaging (the Evian compactable bottle), a new system of payment (the Proton card) or a new way of selling (Caddy Home).

Thus, commercial innovation deals with all that is linked to getting the product from the manufacturer to the end-user. It also results in the application of the human sciences. In this sense, it is organisational in nature and does not concern itself specifically with scientific and technical progress. Commercial innovation examines matters of imagination, creativity and know-how more so than those of financial resources.

Often these innovations require very little capital outlay and technology. However, some commercial innovations may require considerable financial resources, like the installation of a computerised banking network.

Admittedly, the boundary between these two types of innovation is blurred in the sense that technological innovations sometimes lead to commercial innovations.

For example, the progress achieved in information technology has led to the development of credit cards, which have revolutionised systems of payment and sales.

The inverse is also true: certain organisational changes encourage technological innovations. For example, the generalisation of self-service in distribution contributed to the development of scanning and computerised banking systems.

Technological innovations are generally considered 'heavier' that is they require greater financial means and are therefore more risky. Commercial innovations are generally 'lighter' and less risky, but also more easily copied.

Origin of innovations: the firm or the market

As discussed in Chapter 1, a distinction can be made between a *market-pull innovation*, that is one that directly answers observed needs, or a *technology-push* innovation, that is one that results from R&D efforts. This distinction is equally valid for technological or commercial innovations.

As explained in Chapter 1, this distinction is important because these innovations imply different marketing strategies: *response marketing* for innovation coming from the market and *supply or creative marketing* for technology-led innovations. Technology-push innovations are often discontinuous innovations, fulfilling needs not explicitly articulated by potential adopters, and anticipating market demand to be created by operational marketing. For these reasons, these innovations are generally more risky.

A synthesis of American and European contributions in the area of innovations, notably in the industrial sectors, reveals that about 60 to 80 per cent of successful products in many industries have been developed in response to market demand and needs against 40 to 20 per cent for technology-push innovations. Consumer-based innovations often result in better sales growth (Urban *et al.*, 1987, p. 23).

These observations suggest that consumer needs and demand are prime sources of successful products.

> R&D isn't worth anything alone, it has to be coupled with the market. The innovative firms are not necessarily the ones that produce the best technological output, but the ones that know what is marketable. (E. Mansfield, published in *Business Week*, 8 June, 1976)

Thus, while a proactive strategy must include R&D, it must also have a strong market orientation that is critical to the successful development of new products.

Discontinuous innovations

A discontinuous innovation is new product or service that represents major changes in the benefits offered to customers *and* in the behaviour necessary for them to use the product. Customers must in some way *discontinue* their past patterns to fit the new product into their lives.

Table 11.3   Nature and origin of innovations

Nature of the innovation	Origin of the innovation	
	The market	The firm
Technological	Green products	Compact disc
Commercial	Cash and carry	Toys 'R' Us store

In Table 11.3, innovations are classified according to the intensity of (1) the technological change of the product itself and of (2) the behavioural change required from the user of the innovation. Four types of innovations can be identified:

- *Technological improvements* contribute to better functional performance of a product with no impact on user behaviour. In this category are innovations such as line extension, reformulated or improved products being cheaper, simpler, smaller, faster and easier to use.

- *Technological discontinuity* groups innovations which represent major technological changes but which do not really modify consuming or using habits, as has been the case for the facsimile and for compact discs.

- *Organisational discontinuity* designates innovations with a weak technological change, but which nevertheless imply a behavioural change among users (see Table 11.4), as is the case for selective waste disposal (brown and white glass, plastic bottles, paper, cardboard, used batteries, and so on).

● *Discontinuous or breakthrough innovations* designate new products or services resulting from major technological changes and which significantly modify the behaviour necessary to use them. This is typically the case with home computers and electronic shopping.

Table 11.4   Innovation and customer behaviour

Behavioural change	Technological change	
	Low	High
High	Organisational discontinuity (Kinépolis, Caddy Home)	Discontinuous innovation (GSM, Internet)
Low	Technological improvement (Fax with standard paper)	Technological discontinuity (electronic replaces electromechanical systems)

Receptivity to innovation can be very different according to the type of innovation. As a general rule, technological innovations directly compatible with existing beliefs and practices are more easily adopted than innovation requiring considerable effort to learn how to use these products.

For example, most users of microcomputers are little concerned by the fact that their PC uses Motorola or Intel chips. By contrast, they would probably be very reluctant to adopt a PC not compatible with their usual word processing software.

Importance of discontinuous innovations

In highly industrialised economies, where the majority of basic needs are well fulfilled, a company can redefine its business and catch its competitors off guard by developing strategic innovations, which break the rules of the game, and attack established industry practice. These *disruptive* or *discontinuous* innovations can be defined as follows,

An innovation resulting from a new combination of resources or being able in a new way to fill existing wants and creating a new product or service concept, which changes the rules of the game, destabilises the competitive position of rivals and gives the innovator a competitive advantage difficult to neutralise. (Adapted from Bijon, 1984, p. 101)

By definition, a discontinuous innovation is new to the firm and new to the market. Disruptive innovations are particularly effective for relaunching an activity having reached the maturity phase of its PLC.

A good example is the case of Toys 'R' Us, the American leader in the toy market, who created a completely different new store concept: the 'Kids' World'. In a space twice as large as a conventional store, are grouped all the goods related to the child's universe: toys, confectionery, garments, furniture, and so on in shelves adapted to the size of children. The paradox is that Toys 'R' Us has created a discontinuity simply by playing the role of any distributor: not simply selling toys but staging children's life. (Auckenthaler *et al.*, 1997, p. 87)

Once more we are confronted here with an argument already presented in Chapter 1 about the limits of response marketing. A product policy entirely focused on the objective of fulfilling existing needs and wants is certainly less disruptive and less risky, but also less attractive in terms of growth and profit potential for the firm.

In designing an innovation policy, it is therefore important to maintain a good balance between continuous and discontinuous innovations. To place too much weight on articulated needs and on applied research at the expense of supply pull product concepts based on fundamental research, can create a technological gap difficult to overcome. Whatever the innovation strategy, based on technological or organisational creativity, what matters is that the market orientation is present within the firm as a business philosophy shared by everyone and every function.

High-technology marketing

As emphasised in Chapter 2, the pace of technological change has considerably accelerated in recent years, and technology-push innovations have become the major source of competitive advantage in many fast-growing markets (see Table 11.5). A question often raised is whether the marketing of high-technology innovations – or high-technology marketing – is different from traditional marketing.

Table 11.5 European position in key technologies (share of the world in %)

Key Technologies	EU	United States	Japan
Electric and electronic components	29.7	34.3	31.3
Audio-visual-telecom	26.0	32.2	38.7
Informatics	26.1	50.9	19.9
Instrumentation	39.3	39.2	16.1
Pharmaceutical products	29.3	54.1	9.0
Biotechnology	39.5	29.4	25.2
New materials	53.8	26.5	12.9
Industrial environmental processes	63.2	14.4	19.4
Transports	51.7	29.2	6.6

Source: *Vigie info*, Jan–March 1996, No. 17.: in *Futuribles*, July–August 1996, p. 33.

High-technology industries have specific characteristics, which differentiate them from more classic industrial sectors. They are science-intensive activities in continuous change, leading to unexpected applications often ahead of expressed market needs, striding across the boundaries of economic activity and upsetting the established balance of existing industrial sectors. The main characteristics of high-tech activities are summarised as follows:

- *Shorter Product Life Cycles*. Most industrial products have 10- to 15-year life cycles, while high-technology products rarely last more than three to five years. Moreover, copying and 'reverse engineering' from competition is common practice. Thus, speed in market development is a strategic issue.

● *Creative Supply*. It is rarely clear where fundamental research will lead, and innovations are often impossible to predict. At the early stage of an emerging technology, it is not even apparent where the new technology will find applications. Once the technology is developed, the goal is to move quickly to the market and to apply the 'meta-technology' or 'technology platform' to as many products as possible. Thus the technology creates the market.

● *Blurred Competitive Environment*. The market boundaries are not well defined and competitive threats can come from very different technological horizons. Technological uncertainties remain high and entry and exit of competitors is constant. The boundaries of existing sectors or market segments are modified and one observes either regrouping of segments into a new reference market – for example the office automation market – or splitting of a traditional market into specialised segments.

These characteristics of high-technology industries have implications for the new product development process, namely speed and flexibility in product development (Stalk, 1988), close co-operation with customers and systematic monitoring of the technological environment. Thus, in high-technology markets, strategic marketing has a crucial role to play, particularly in the 'R&D–production–marketing' interface, and also creating market demand.

● The Dimensions of New Product Success or Failure

The available information on the success rate of new products is limited and sometimes contradictory:

● In 1971, the Nielsen Research Company observed a 47 per cent success rate of new brands in a study based on a sample of 204 new products from the health and beauty aids (106), household (24) and grocery (74) markets. In a similar study done in 1962, but based on a smaller sample of 103 new brands, the observed success rate was 54.4 per cent (*The Nielsen Researcher*, 1971, p. 6).

● In the study performed by Booz *et al.* (1982), the success rate observed over the 1977–81 period was 65 per cent, against 67 per cent in the same study done over the 1963–68 period (Booz *et al.*, 1982 p. 7).

● In a UK study conducted in 1990 on a sample of 86 British firms and of 116 Japanese firms operating in the United Kingdom, the success rate was 59.8 per cent for the Japanese firms and 54.3 per cent for the British firms (Edgett *et al.* 1992, p. 7).

● In the 1993 PDMA study (Page, 1993, p. 284), the success rate observed on a sample of 189 firms was 58 per cent.

● Also instructive is A.D. Little's global survey on innovations (1997) based on a sample of 169 companies from all over the world and the survey 'Innovation in industry' published by *The Economist* (1999).

Obviously, the estimations fluctuate widely. In the best cases, the probability of success is a little better than one in two. This implies that investing a large proportion of available funds in R&D and spending a great deal on commercialisation are unproductive. In other words, there is no correlation between large investments in R&D commercial spending and the success rate of a product.

Effective management of an innovation

Booz *et al.* also analysed the success rate of innovations at different stages of the new product development process. As seen in Figure 11.1, this process is composed of five stages. The observed success and failure rates from both the 1968 and 1981 studies are represented.

On examining the data, one can observe that the success rate increases continuously from 36 per cent in the first phase to 71 per cent in the fifth. This implies that the evaluation process was effective. It is also instructive to compare these data with the same observations found in the 1968 study. It reveals that the selection process has become more discriminating, as the probability for success in the last phase rose from 50 per cent in 1968 to 71 per cent in 1981. This improvement in new product selection is probably due to the change in spending distribution from 1968 to 1981. In other words, a different proportion of money was spent during each phase.

Indeed, one can observe that a large proportion of resources was spent during the first phases (21 per cent in phases 1 and 2 during 1981, as compared to 10 per cent in 1968). In contrast, 37 per cent of resources were spent in phase 3 in 1981, compared with 28 per cent in 1968. On the other hand, 25 per cent of resources was allocated to the commercial phase in 1981, as compared to 48 per cent in 1968.

These data suggest that the companies have increased upfront strategic marketing analysis while reducing the share of the total expended on commercialisation efforts.

Companies that have excellent records of successful new product introductions conduct more analyses early in the process and focus their idea and concept generation. And they conduct more rigorous screening and evaluation of the ideas generated. (Booz *et al.*, 1982, p. 12)

To reinforce the strategic marketing analysis at the beginning of the new product development process seems to be profitable. Using the data published by Booz *et al.* and computing the weighted average of the success rates observed at each phase, the estimated success rate in 1981 is 57 per cent against 37 per cent in 1968, a 54 per cent improvement. This gain in new product management effectiveness is dramatically illustrated in Figure 11.2 which compares the mortality rate of new product ideas in 1968 and 1981. The data were taken from the 1982 study carried out by Booz *et al.*

In 1968, on average, out of 58 *new product ideas*, 12 passed the initial filtering test. Of these 12.7 remained after an extensive study of their profitability potential. Only 3 of these went on to the product development stage, 2 to market testing and only one was a commercial success. It can therefore be concluded that 58 new product ideas were considered for every successful new product.

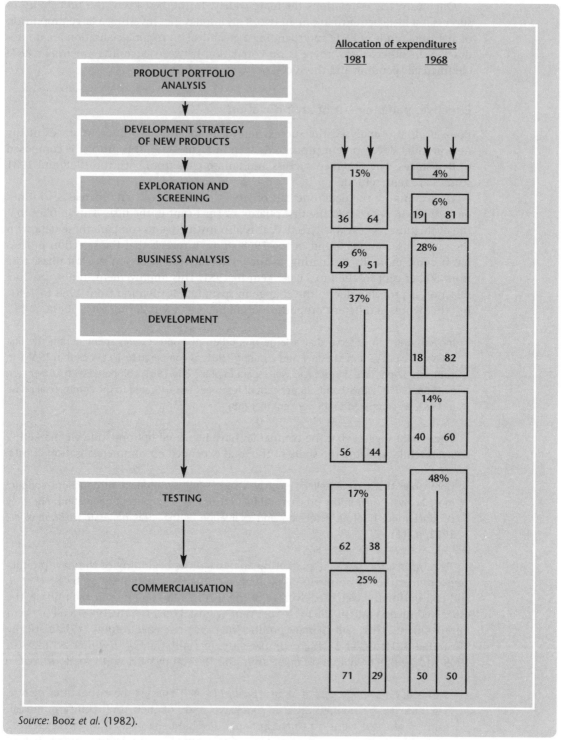

Source: Booz et al. (1982).

Figure 11.1   The new product development process

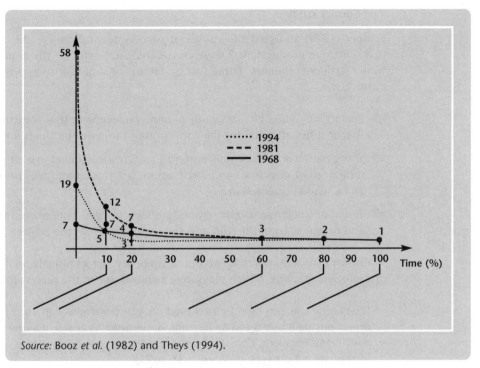

Source: Booz *et al.* (1982) and Theys (1994).

Figure 11.2 Mortality curve of new product ideas

● In 1981, as a result of increased attention to the market and of increased sophistication in segmenting the market, only 7 ideas were required to generate one successful new product.

The PDMA study (Page, 1993) is less optimistic and reports a 9 per cent rate.

Out of 100 new product ideas that enter their development process, 26.6 of them are typically tested in some formal manner, 12.4 of them are introduced into the market, and 9.4 are typically commercially successful. (Page, 1993, p. 284)

In a similar study conducted in the metallurgic sector in Belgium, Theys (1994) observed about the same mortality curve: out of 19 ideas, one product was introduced into the market.

Increased strategic marketing is therefore profitable for the company since it improves the productivity of its investments in the conception and development phases. This allows the company to reduce its spending in operational marketing in the launch and commercialisation.

Success factors of new products

Analysing the factors which explain the success or failure of innovations is particularly instructive and confirms the preceding conclusions. Several available studies, done in both the USA and Europe, have produced results which are remarkably similar.

The Cooper study

Cooper (1979) analysed the causes of success and failure of 195 industrial products. Of these products, 102 were considered successful by the company, while 93 were considered failures. Three success factors or dimensions appear to be the *keys to success*:

- ⬤ *Product uniqueness and superiority to competing products*: that is existence of distinctive qualities allowing for the conception of superior products for the user.

- ⬤ *Strong market orientation and marketing proficiency*: detailed market potential study, well-targeted sales force and distribution, test market and trial prior to launching and a market orientation.

- ⬤ *Technical and production synergy and proficiency*: a good fit between the engineering and design skills of the firm and the requirements of the project.

Cooper's study shows that two out of three key factors directly relate to the quality of strategic marketing, which plays here a crucial role in the success of an innovation.

> The observed success rates for new products that perform well in one of the above three dimensions are 82, 79.5 and 64 per cent, respectively. Moreover, if a new product is strong in all three dimensions, it has a success rate of 90 per cent; if it is weak in all three areas, the success rate is 7 per cent. (Cooper, 1981, p. 75)

It is also important to emphasise that these three key success factors are all under the firm's control. Thus, success is directly determined by the quality of management and not just by chance, nor by the situation or by the environment the firm is facing. The message is clearly: 'It matters not what situation you face; it matters more what you do about it'.

The *NewProd* methodology developed by Cooper in 1979 has since been applied to a large number of companies and the results available in 1993 in the NewProd III project are based on retrospective analysis of 203 actual new product projects in 125 industrial product firms (Cooper, 1993, p. 57). As in the initial study some of these projects were successes and others failures. The results broadly confirm the observations made in 1979 and also bring some additional information.

As in the initial study, the key success factor is clearly *the existence of a superior product that delivers unique benefits to the user*. When the high-advantage products (the top 20 per cent) are contrasted with those with the least degree of differentiation (the bottom 20 per cent), the superior products:

- ⬤ had an exceptional success rate of 98.0 per cent, versus only 18.4 per cent for undifferentiated ones;
- ⬤ had a market share of 53.5 per cent, versus only 11.6 per cent for 'me too' new products;
- ⬤ had a rate of profitability of 8.4 out of 10 (versus only 2.6 out of 10 for undifferentiated products);
- ⬤ met company sales and profit objectives to a greater degree than did undifferentiated products (Cooper, 1993, p. 58).

Fifteen key lessons for success in new product development were identified by Cooper. They are summarised in Table 11.6.

Table 11.6 Fifteen key lessons for new product success

1. The number one success factor is a unique superior product: a differentiated product that delivers unique benefits and superior value to the customer.

2. A strong market orientation – a market-driven and customer-focused new product process – is critical to success.

3. Look to the world product: an international orientation in product design, development and target marketing provides the edge in product innovation.

4. More pre-development work – the homework – must be done before product development gets under way.

5. Sharp and early product definition is one of the key differences between winning and losing at new products.

6. A well-conceived, properly executed launch is central to new product success. And a solid marketing plan is at the heart of the launch.

7. The right organisational structure, design and climate are key factors in success.

8. Top management support does not guarantee success, but it sure helps. But many senior managers get it wrong.

9. Synergy is vital to success – 'step-out' projects tend to fail.

10. Products aimed at attractive markets do better; market attractiveness is a key project-selection criterion.

11. New product success is predictable; and the profile of a winner can be used to make sharper project-selection decisions to yield better focus.

12. New product success is controllable: more emphasis is needed on completeness, consistency and quality of execution.

13. The resources must be in place.

14. Speed is everything! But not at the expense of quality of execution.

15. Companies that follow a multistage, disciplined new product game plan fare much better.

Source: Cooper (1993, p. 76).

The Booz, Allen and Hamilton study in the USA

In the previously mentioned Booz *et al.* study (1982), the following factors were identified as contributing to the success of new products:

Product fit with market needs	85 per cent
Product fit with internal functional strengths	62 per cent
Technological superiority of product	52 per cent
Top management support	45 per cent
Use of new product process	33 per cent
Favourable competitive environment	31 per cent
Structure of new product organisation	15 per cent

The two most important factors in successful new product introductions are the fit of the product with market needs and with internal functional strengths. Having a technologically superior product, receiving support from top management and using a multiple-step new product process are additional factors contributing to new product success. The relative importance of these factors, however, varies significantly by industry and by type of product being introduced.

The British study of Edgett, Shipley and Forbes

When respondents were asked in this study to identify factors that have contributed to a successful new product, the most frequently cited variable overall was that successful new products were well matched to customer needs. This reflects the need for a consumer-oriented approach to development programmes rather than a production-oriented approach. Only one in four respondents considered skilful marketing to be a factor in new product success. A comparison of the success factors is presented in Table 11.7.

Table 11.7   Factors contributing to new product success

Success factor of product	% of companies	
	Japanese (n = 116)	British (n = 86)
■ Well matched to customer needs	69.8	75.6
■ Superior to competition:		
– in quality	79.3	59.3
– in reliability	69.8	45.3
– in value for money	58.6	61.6
– in design	55.2	48.8
■ Highly price competitive	41.4	27.9
■ Well matched to company objective and image	39.7	34.9
■ Unique	36.2	29.1
■ Skilfully marketed	27.6	25.6
■ Based on good marketing research	27.6	18.6
■ Launched into large markets	20.7	16.3
■ Created synergy in production or marketing	16.4	18.6
■ Avoiding competitive markets with satisfied customers	7.8	10.5
■ Avoiding dynamic markets where product launches are common	2.6	4.7

Source: Edgett et al. (1992).

Compared with British companies, the Japanese rated the need to develop a superior product significantly higher in terms of product quality, reliability and offerability at highly competitive prices This suggests that Japanese firms believe that to be successful in an increasingly cluttered marketplace, the product must also have a competitive advantage (Edgett et al., 1992, p. 8).

The Belgian study in the chemical sector

A Belgian survey covering a sample of 163 chemical new products carried out by de Moerloose (1999) revealed that *new product success* was understood by the surveyed managers as financial success (profitability) rather than technological, commercial or strategic success. The four key success factors identified are the following:

1. The major success factor is *filling a need*, be it latent or explicit. This implied very early detection of the need in the product development process and emphasis on problem solution rather than on technological performance.

2. The second key success factor is *superior value* for the customer. Delivering a new service, benefit or function or delivering the same service with a better perform-ance. This product superiority may simply result from competitors' weaknesses.

3. The third success factor observed was the *strength of the new product delivery mode* to the market, that is the operational marketing intensity in terms of distribution, advertising and promotion. This observation is consistent with the view that operational marketing can be very efficient if the strategic option (filling a need with a superior product) is solid.

4. The fourth direct success factor is *technological synergy*. The financial success is higher when the firm takes advantage of learning and/or scale effects in R&D and in the production process.

It is important to note that these four key success factors are all under the control of the firm. Thus, new product success is the outcome of appropriate managerial actions and not due to chance or good luck. This observation confirms the previous findings of Cooper (1993).

In addition to these key success factors directly related to performance, *indirect or interacting factors* were also identified:

1. The attractiveness of the *reference market* in terms of growth potential and of strength or weakness of the competitive environment. Typically two factors beyond the firm's control.

2. A new product selection procedure based on a sound exploitation of existing commercial *synergies*, that is the pre-existence of required commercial competencies.

3. The setting of an appropriate *organisational structure* to support the new product development process: top management support, existence of a champion, good communication and interfunctional co-ordination. It was observed that these factors were particularly instrumental in the creation of superior value.

4. Finally, when we are in situations where the new products clearly fill a need, it has been observed that the required level of marketing pressure is lower.

The survey also showed that the success factors remain unchanged for whatever type of innovation (technological, commercial, or customer group). An important result of this study was to observe the moderating effect of some variables on the success factors (see de Moerloose, 1999).

⬤ Organisation of the New Product Development Process

The data presented in the previous section illustrate the *high risk* involved in launching a new activity. This risk may be reduced, however, by implementing a systematic evaluation and development procedure for new products. The key success factors are those which are controllable by the company. The purpose of this section is to examine the procedures and organisational methods which reduce the risk of failure throughout the innovation process. The objective is to organise a *systematic and continuous dialogue* between the relevant functions within an organisation, that is R&D, marketing, operations and finance. In a market-driven company, developing a new product is a *cross-functional effort*, which involves the entire organisation.

A workable organisational structure

If it is true that top management has the final say in decisions concerning new product launches, it remains the case that an organisational structure with specific responsibilities is essential in managing and co-ordinating the entire innovation process. Different organisational structures are possible. Large companies have created *new product management* functions or *new product departments*, as Nestlé, Colgate Palmolive, Johnson & Johnson and General Foods have done.

Cross-functional organisational structures

A more flexible solution, which is available to all companies regardless of their size, is the *new products committee* or *venture team* in charge of a specific project.

- ⬤ *New products committee* is a permanent group of persons which meets periodically, say, once a month. It is composed of individuals from different functions (that is R&D, operations, marketing, finance and human resources). Ideally, it is presided over by the managing director, whose responsibility is to organise and manage the development process of a new product from its conception to its launching.

- ⬤ *Self-organising project teams* or 'venture teams' are groups formed for the development of a specific project (task force). This group is composed of people from various departments, from which they are temporarily separated, either completely or partially. This allows better concentration on the creation of a new activity.

The PDMA study is instructive on the evolution observed on the organisational structures used for new product development. The respondents were asked to indicate which of six forms of new product organisation structure best described the ones used by their firm (see Table 11.8). The multi-disciplinary team was by far the most widely used organisation with a score of 76 per cent of the sample businesses while the new product department had a score of only 30 per cent (Page, 1993, p. 276).

Table 11.8   Organisational structures used for new product development

Organisational Structures	Per cent
Multi-disciplinary team	76.2
New product department	30.2
Product manager	30.2
New product manager	25.9
New product committee	16.9
Venture team	6.9

Source: Page (1993, p. 277).

No matter which organisational structure is adopted, the most important thing is a *structure open to the ideas of new activities*. The objective is to institutionalise preoccupation with new products within the company and to do so in a way which is flexible and favours an entrepreneurial approach to problems.

Two processes are currently adopted by innovative companies, the sequential or the parallel development process.

Sequential development process

The *sequential development process*, evidenced by the Booz *et al.* study (1982), is where the project moves step by step from one phase to the next: concept development and testing, feasibility analysis, prototype development, market test and production. The whole process is described in Figure 11.3.

The merits of the sequential approach have already been discussed. But although it contributes to reducing the new product failure rate, it also has some shortcomings:

- First, the sequential process in itself leaves little room for integration since each functional specialist passes the project to the next one.

- The move to the next phase is done only after all the requirements of the preceding phase are satisfied. A bottleneck in one phase can slow or even block the entire process.

- Moreover, this product planning process is slow and requires long lead times. It avoids errors, but at large cost in terms of time.

Changes in the market, entry of new competitors and risk of copying often result in a product arriving too late in the market. Thus long lead times can very well increase rather than reduce the risk of failure. This will be particularly important for high-technology products, where speed is a key success factor.

Parallel development process

The *parallel development process* advocated by Takeuchi and Nonaka (1986) speeds the process by relying on self-organising project teams whose members work together from start to finish. Under this organisational scheme, the process development

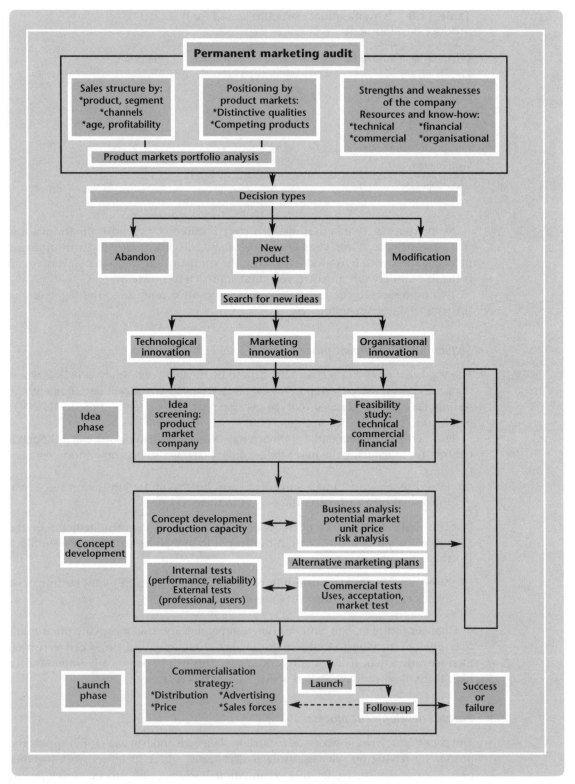

Figure 11.3 The sequential development process of new products

process emerges from the constant interaction of a multi-disciplinary team. Rather than moving in defined, highly structured stages, the process is born out of the team members' interplay. One of the potential benefits of the parallel development process is the *overlapping of the tasks* assumed by the different departments.

> While design engineers are still designing the product, production people can intervene to make sure that the design is compatible with production scale economies and marketing people can work on the positioning platform to communicate to the market.

The parallel development process is described in Figure 11.4. The merits of this organisational structure are important:

- The system facilitates better cross-functional co-ordination since each function is associated in the entire development process.

- Several activities can be organised simultaneously, which accelerates the process because the amount of recycle and rework – going back and doing it again – is greatly reduced.

- Each activity is better controlled since it directly determines the subsequent activities.

- Substantial time savings are made due to the more intensive work and to the improved spontaneous co-ordination.

This type of organisational structure, because it stresses multi-functional activities, promotes improved teamwork. To go further on this topic see Larson and Gobeli (1988).

Idea generation

Naturally, the development process for innovation begins with researching new product ideas, which are in line with the chosen development strategy. Some companies adopt an empirical approach to this problem, relying on a spontaneous stream of ideas originating from external and internal sources. However, the mortality rate of

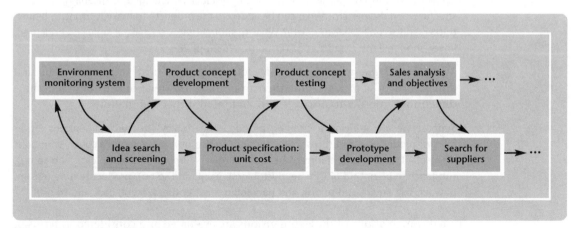

Figure 11.4   Parallel development of new products

these ideas is very high; therefore, it is essential to feed on new ideas regularly. Generally, ideas, especially good ones, do not happen by themselves; organisation and stimulation are needed to generate them. A company may use different methods for collecting ideas. These methods try to anticipate the change in needs and not simply respond to the demands expressed by the market. This is a 'proactive' versus a 'reactive' approach. A creative idea is nothing but an unexpected combination of two or more concepts. *Creativity* can therefore be defined as

> the intellectual exercise of linking information in an unpredictable way so as to produce a new arrangement.

Idea generation methods can be grouped into two broad categories: (a) functional analysis methods which analyse products in order to identify possible improvements, and (b) methods which interview directly or indirectly buyers or consumers to detect unsatisfied needs or ill resolved problems with the existing products.

Methods of functional analysis

The rationale behind functional analysis methods is that a product's users can provide useful information on how the product could be modified and improved:

● *Problem/opportunity analysis* starts with the consumer. It is linked to the study of user behaviour in order to identify the kinds of problems a user may encounter during use of the product. Every problem or difficulty brought up could give rise to a new idea for improvement or modification. This modification is frequently used in industrial market studies with a panel of user clients.

● The *attribute listing* method has the same objectives as problem analysis, but instead of examining how the consumer uses the product, it examines the characteristics of the product itself. The method consists of establishing a list of the principal characteristics and then recombining them in such a way as to create some improvement. Osborn defined a list of questions intended to stimulate ideas for new products.

> Can the product be used in any new way? What else is like the product and what can be learned from this comparison? How can the product be changed in meaning, function, structure, and use pattern? What can be added to the product? To make it stronger, longer, thicker, and so on? What to delete? What to subtract, how to make it smaller, condensed, lower, shorter, lighter, and so on? (Osborn, 1963, pp. 286–7).

● *Morphological analysis* consists of identifying the most important structural dimensions of a product and then examining the relationship between these dimensions in order to discover new and interesting combinations.

> Suppose we are studying a cleaning product. The six key structural dimensions are as follows: product support (brush, rag, sponge, and so on), ingredients (alcohol, ammonia, disinfectant, and so on), things to be cleaned (glass, carpet, sinks, walls, cars, and so on), substance to be got rid of (grease, dust, blood, paint, and so on), product texture (cream, powder, salt, liquid, and so on), and packaging (box, bottle, aerosol, bag, and so on).

Paired combinations of these dimensions are evaluated and considered in terms of their potential value as new products.

A last method for idea generation must be added, one that is old but very effective: the *suggestion box*. This can prove to be very helpful if certain rules are followed. Two rules are particularly important: follow up promptly on the proposed ideas and provide a complete recognition system to motivate employees.

There are other and varied methods for idea generation. Systematic analysis of competitive products through *reverse engineering* is also widely used. For a more exhaustive description of these methods, see Wind (1982, Chapter 9). The most important objective for a firm is to keep a permanent portfolio of new product ideas, which is sizeable enough to allow the firm to face the competition in an environment where innovation is omnipresent.

Creativity groups and brainstorming

Methods which are likely to stimulate creativity can be grouped into two categories: unstructured and structured methods. *Unstructured methods* are essentially based on imagination and intuition. These methods are usually implemented in the form of *creativity groups*, relying on the hypothesis that a group of individuals is usually more creative than a person working alone. This assumption is based on the synergy effect or the interaction between group members.

Brainstorming is probably the most popular method, mostly because it is easy to organise. The only goal of a brainstorming session is to produce as many ideas as possible. Six to ten participants with diverse backgrounds and experience, from both within and outside the company, are gathered together and are given the objective of generating the greatest possible number of ideas on a particular theme in a spontaneous manner. The major rules governing a brainstorming session, according to Osborn (1963, p. 156), are the following:

⬤ No evaluation of any kind is permitted, since criticism and judgement may cause people to defend their ideas rather than generate new and creative ones.

⬤ Participants should be encouraged to think of the wildest ideas possible.

⬤ Encourage a large number of ideas.

⬤ Encourage participants to build upon or modify the ideas of others, as combinations or modifications of previously suggested ideas often lead to new ideas that are superior to those that sparked them.

This type of exercise is usually very effective; it is not out of the ordinary for a group to generate more than 100 ideas during a brainstorming session. Another somewhat more structured method is synectics (Gordon, 1965).

Synectics is another creativity method developed by Gordon (1965), which tackles the problem indirectly. The assumption is that habits prevent the development of a really new vision of a too familiar problem (see Exhibit 11.2).

For a professional whose reflexes and perceptions of the environment have been moulded by a growing market and confirmed by success, it is very difficult to see the opportunity of doing the same thing differently. The acquired professionalism hides the perception of new way of operating. The adoption of a discontinuous strategy requires new reflexes and a distance from traditional activities. (Bijon, 1984, p. 104)

Exhibit 11.2

Selected Examples of Prediction Errors

1895: Lord Kelvin, President of the Royal Society (UK):
'It is impossible to design flying machines heavier than air'.

1899: Charles Duell, Director of the Patent Office (USA):
'Everything has already been invented'.

1905: Grover Cleveland, President of United States:
'Reasonable women will never ask for the right to vote'.

1920: Robert Millikan, Nobel prize for physics:
'Man will never be able to exploit atomic power'.

1947: Thomas J. Watson Sr., President of IBM Corp:
'I believe that there is a total market for approximately five computers'.

1977: Ken Olsen, CEO Digital Equipment Corp:
'Why would people like to have a computer at home?'

Source: Quoted by de Branbandère (1998, pp. 99–107).

To become creative, it is sometimes necessary to take some distant view and to make a 'creative detour', before coming back to the problem under study. Once the problem is formulated in different, but related contexts, one is led to discover analogies and to propose more relevant and creative ideas.

New product generation from customer ideas

The idea generation methods presented so far are usually *manufacturer-active*, that is the manufacturer plays the active role (see Table 11.3). In industrial markets, von Hippel (1978) has shown that often a customer request for a new product can generate a new product idea, at least in situations where the industrial customer is overtly aware of his new product need.

In the consumer goods sector, the role of the consumer is essentially that of a respondent, 'speaking only when spoken to'. It is the role of the manufacturer to obtain information on needs for new products and to develop a responsive product idea. In the industrial good sector, it is often the role of the *would-be customer* to develop the idea for a new product and to select a supplier capable of making the product. We have here a *customer-active paradigm*.

Table 11.9   Search for ideas for new industrial products

Nature of Customer Need	Accessibility of New Product Opportunity to Manufacturer-Managed Action	
	Low	**High**
Overt	Customer active only	Customer and/or manufacturer active
Latent	Neither	Manufacturer active 1 only

Source: von Hippel (1978).

Any statement of need made by a professional customer contains information about what a responsive solution should be. Consider the following statement of need of manufacturing firm X:

> (a)… we need higher profits in our semi-conductor plant; (b)… which we can get by raising output… (c)… which we can best do by getting rid of the bottleneck in process step D… (d)… which can best be done by designing and installing new equipment… (e)… which has the following functional specifications… (f)… and should be built according to these blueprints. (von Hippel 1978, p. 41)

This need statement already contains the key elements of the solution to a problem sought by the would-be customer. The firm needs only to instruct its R&D and manufacturing people to manufacture the product according to the customer specifications spontaneously provided. This example underlines the importance of a systematic dialogue with customers to generate new product ideas.

In the field of industrial goods, there are also several markets in which *everyone knows* what the customer wants, but progress in technology is required before the desired product can be realised.

> In the computer, plastics and semi-conductor industries, every one knows that the customer wants more calculation per second and per dollar in the computer business; every one knows that the customer wants plastics which degrade less quickly in sunlight; and everyone knows that the semi-conductor customer wants more memory capacity on a single chip of silicon.

In these sectors, a customer request is not required to trigger a new product, only an advance in technology.

Idea generation methods are numerous and varied. Cooper (1993, p. 133) proposes a list of 25 different methods. What is important for the firm is to have permanently a *portfolio of new product ideas* sufficiently diversified to enable the firm to meet the challenge of competition in an environment where innovation is permanent and a key success factor for survival and development.

Idea screening

The objective of the second stage in the development process is to screen the ideas generated in order to eliminate the ones that are incompatible with the company's resources or objectives or simply unattractive to the firm. The purpose is to spot and drop unfeasible ideas as soon as possible. This is therefore an *evaluation phase* which presupposes the existence of criteria for choice. The goal of this screening is not to do an in-depth analysis, but rather to make a quick, inexpensive, internal evaluation about which projects merit further study and which should be abandoned. Therefore this is not yet a feasibility study, but simply a preliminary evaluation.

Typically, the new product committee is in the best position to do the screening. A single and effective method is the *evaluation grid* which has the following basic principles:

● An exhaustive inventory of all the *key success factors* (KSF) in each functional area: marketing, finance, operations and R&D.
● Each factor or group of factors is weighted to reflect its *relative importance*.
● Each new product idea is scored against each KSF by the *judges* of the new product committee.
● A desirability or *performance index* is calculated.

This procedure ensures that all the important factors have been systematically and equally considered and that the objectives and constraints of the company have been attended to.

When computing the performance index, it is preferable to adopt a *conjunctive method* and not a simple weighted average procedure (compensatory approach). As seen in Chapter 5, the conjunctive method does not result in a global score, but aids in identifying ideas, which are or are not compatible with the company's objectives or resources. The conjunctive approach presupposes that a maximum and minimum level of performance for each project has been specified. Only those ideas which satisfy each specified threshold are retained.

Several standard evaluation grids exist in the marketing literature, the best known being that of O'Meara (1961) and of Steele (1988). Such checklists provide a useful guideline for ideas evaluation. Ideally, an evaluation grid should be tailor-made and be adapted to the company's own needs. It is up to the new product committee to establish an appropriate structure, which reflects the corporate objectives and the unique situational factors of the firm. Figure 11.5 shows an evaluation grid used in a consumer goods company to evaluate the marketing feasibility of new product ideas. Similar grids have been developed for the other functions: R&D, operations and finance.

Cooper (1993, see Appendix C, p. 335) has also developed a diagnostic and screening grid. The questionnaire comprises thirty questions to be answered by several judges who evaluate the project on each criterion on a 10-point scale and who express their degree of confidence on their own evaluation, also on a 10-point scale. The profile of the project is then evaluated and compared with the observed profiles of hundreds of projects, which belong to the NewProd data bank. The simulation model provides a probability of success and also analyses the strong and the weak points of the project.

Concept development

At this phase of the development process, we move from 'product ideas' to *product concepts*. The ideas having survived to the screening phase are now defined in more elaborated terms. A *product concept* can thus be defined as:

New product idea: —————————— Score: ——

INDICATORS OF ATTRACTIVENESS	SCORES				Not relevant
	Very good	Good	Weak	Very weak	
1. Market trend	Emerging	Growing	Stable	Declining	
2. Product life	10 years plus	5–10 years	3–5 years	2–3 years	
3. Spread of diffusion	Very fast	Fast	Slow	Very slow	
4. Market size (volume)	>10 000 tons	5000–10 000 tons	1000–5000 tons	1000 tons	
5. Market size (value)	1 billion	0.5–1 billion	100–500 million	>100 million	
6. Buyer's needs	Not met	Poorly met	Well met	Very well met	
7. Receptivity of distribution	Enthusiastic	Positive	Reserved	Reluctant	
8. Advertising support required	Weak support	Moderate support	Important support	Strong support	
9. Market accessibility	Very easy	Easy	Difficult	Very difficult	

INDICATORS OF COMPETITIVENESS	SCORES				Not relevant
	Very good	Good	Weak	Very weak	
1. Product's appeal	Very high	High	Moderate	Weak	
2. Distinctive qualities	Exclusivity	Major distinctive quality	Weak distinctive quality	'me too' product	
3. Strength of competition	Very weak	Weak	High	Very high	
4. Duration of exclusivity	> 3 years	1–3 years	< 1 year	< 6 months	
5. Compatability with current products	Very good	Good	Weak	Very weak	
6. Level of price	Lower price	Slightly lower	Equal price	Higher price	
7. Compatability with existing distribution network	Fully compatible	Easily compatible	Compatible but difficult	New network	
8. Capacity of the sales force	Very good	Good	Weak	Very weak	
9. Level of product quality	Clearly superior	Superior	Same	Inferior	

Source: Brussels, MDA Consulting Group.

Figure 11.5 Example of a new product screening grid

A written description of the physical and perceptual characteristics of the product and of the 'package of benefits' (the promise) it represents for the identified target group(s) of potential buyers'

This is more than a simple technological description of the product, since the product's benefits to the potential user are emphasised. The product concept definition highlights the notion of a product as a package of benefits. In defining the concept, a company is forced to be explicit in its strategic options and market objective. A clear and precise definition of the product concept is important in many respects:

● The concept definition describes the *positioning sought* for the product and therefore defines the means required to achieve the expected positioning.

● The product concept is a kind of *specification manual* for R&D, whose job it is to examine the technical feasibility of the concept.

● The description of the product's promise serves as a *briefing* for the advertising agency that is in charge of communicating the new product's claims to the marketplace.

Thus, the product concept defines the *reference product market* in which the future product should be positioned. Four questions come to mind:

● Which attributes or product characteristics do potential buyers react favourably to?
● How are competitive products perceived with regard to these attributes?
● What niche could the new product occupy, considering the target segment and the positions held by competition?
● What is the most effective marketing means that will achieve the desired positioning?

The answers to these questions presuppose the existence of a fine-tuned market segmentation analysis, which is able to quantify the size of the potential market.

Designing a green product concept

Sensitivity towards the environment is today a must for business success and the accountable firm should assess the environmental implication of a new product not only at the concept development phase, but also at each phase of the product life cycle from *cradle to grave* as discussed in Chapter 2 of this book. Numerous opportunities exist for refining existing products or developing new ones that meet environmental imperatives and satisfy consumers' expectations. These opportunities must considered in a proactive way very early in development process. Ideas for action are presented in Exhibit 11.3 (Ottman, 1993, see Chapter 5).

While adopting the green product concept, the firm has to be careful and must *prove its environmental credentials in scientific terms* and by reference to the entire life cycle of the product. This is not always easy, because *green is relative* and also because large uncertainties remain on the ecological impact of products and raw materials.

According to a study conducted in France (Peixoto, 1993), 33 per cent of consumers – the True-Blue Greens and the Greenback Greens – are active environmentalists. These consumers avoid buying products from a company with a questionable environmental reputation and are much more likely to buy greener types of products. According to an American study, active environmentalist consumers, on average, would pay a 4.6 per cent price premium for certain environmentally sound products (Ottman, 1993, p. 43). The size of this segment of green activists is growing regularly.

Concept testing

Concept testing represents the first investment (other than managerial time) a firm has to make in the development process. It consists of submitting a description of

Exhibit 11.3

The Green Product Concept: Ideas for Action

- Source and reduce packaging.
- Eliminate or lightweight packaging.
- Concentrate products.
- Use bulk packaging or large sizes.
- Develop multi-purpose products.
- Use recycled content.
- Conserve natural resources, habitats and endangered species.
- Make products more energy efficient.
- Maximise consumer and environmental safety.
- Make products more durable.
- Make products and packaging reusable or refillable.
- Design products for remanufacturing, recycling and repair.
- Take products back for recycling.
- Make products and packaging safe to landfill or incinerate.
- Make products compostable.

Source: Ottman (1993).

the new product concept to an appropriate group of target users to measure the degree of acceptance.

The product concept description may be done in one of two ways: neutral, that is with no 'sell', or by a mock advertisement, which presents the concept as if it were an existing product. The former is easier to do and avoids the pitfall of the inevitable and uncontrollable creative element inherent in an advertisement. The advantage of the advertisement, however, is that it more accurately reproduces the buying atmosphere of a future product and is therefore more realistic.

The following descriptions illustrate 'neutral' and 'advertising' forms of concept testing, respectively, for a new dessert topping.

Here is a new dessert topping made of fruit and packaged in a spray can. It comes in four flavours: strawberry, cherry, apricot and redcurrant. It can be used in cakes, puddings and frozen desserts.

Here is a new delicious fruit topping for desserts conveniently packaged in a spray can. These new toppings will enhance the desserts you serve your family. Your choice among four flavours: strawberry, cherry, apricot and redcurrant will certainly embellish all your desserts including cakes, puddings, frozen desserts and more.

Twenty to fifty people with varying socio-demographic profiles are gathered to assess the degree of concept acceptance. They are shown slides or videos on the new concept and asked to react to it with questions similar to those presented in Table 11.10.

Table 11.10　　Key questions in concept testing

1. Are the benefits clear to you and believable?
2. Do you see this product as solving a problem or filling a need for you?
3. Do other products currently meet this need and satisfy you?
4. Is the price reasonable in relation to the value?
5. Would you (definitely, probably, probably not, definitely not) buy the product?
6. Who would use this product, and how often would it be used?

Source: Kotler, (1997, p. 325).

Obviously, the key questions in Table 11.10 is the one dealing with intentions to buy (question 5). A score of positive intentions (that is 'would definitely buy' and 'would probably buy' responses grouped together) that adds up to less than 60 per cent is generally considered insufficient, at least in the field of consumer goods.

Predictive value of intentions

Results from concept testing should be interpreted with care, especially when the concept is very new. Consumers are asked to express their interest in a product, which they have never seen or used. They are therefore often unable to judge whether or not they would like the new product. Numerous products, which received mediocre scores during the concept-testing phase, actually turned out to be brilliant successes. Inversely, expensive failures were avoided using concept testing.

Measuring intentions to buy is not always the best indication of the respondents' degree of conviction regarding a new product's ability to solve problems or to satisfy unmet needs. Yet, this is clearly a key success factor. In a test situation, respondents may express a willingness to purchase a new product out of simple curiosity or concern for keeping up with the latest innovation, or a need for variety. In light of this, scores for intention tend to overestimate the true rate of acceptance.

In order to deal with this problem, Tauber (1973) suggests using concept-testing results based on measurements of perceived needs as well as of purchase interest. In an experiment on eight new product concepts, Tauber observed that virtually all the respondents who claimed that a product solved a problem or filled an unmet need had a positive intention to purchase the new product, while a considerable number of respondents who expressed purchase interest did not believe the product solved a problem or filled an unmet need. This observation suggests that overstatement of purchase intent may be simply those with curiosity to try but with little expectation of adopting. Thus, basing new product decisions on purchase intent data could be misleading in predicting the true rate of product adoption for regular use.

A more reliable way to estimate the adoption rate of a new product for regular use would be to base the decision on the percentage of people giving an affirmative answer to both questions, that is *they do intend to buy and they are convinced that the new product solves a problem or fills an unmet need.*

The adjusted purchase intent rates of Table 11.11 illustrate the argument. The ranking of the eight product concepts is significantly different from the ranking observed for the positive purchase intention.

Table 11.11   Interpretation of intention-to-buy scores

New product concepts	A	B	C	D	E	F	G	H
Gross intentions: Percentage of respondents with positive buying intention	—							
Adjusted intentions: Percentage of respondents with positive intentions and convinced of the novelty of the product	71	62	60	60	51	46	44	22
Rate of conviction: Percentage of respondents convinced within the group	45	37	18	19	27	37	10	19
with positive intentions	63	59	30	31	53	79	26	86

Source: Tauber (1973).

Conjoint analysis

More elaborate approaches to concept testing may be used, including the *conjoint analysis*, which has been successfully used over the last few years (Green and Srinivasan, 1978). The distinctive value of conjoint analysis is to allow the impact of the product concept's key characteristics on product preferences, information which is not revealed by an overall reaction to the concept. The basic principles of this method were described in Chapter 4 and an example was presented in Chapter 6.

In concept testing, conjoint analysis helps in answering the following questions:

● What is the partial utility or *value* that a target group attaches to different characteristics of the product concept?
● What is the *relative importance* of each product characteristic?
● What kind of *trade-offs* are potential buyers ready to make between two or more product characteristics?
● What will be the *share of preferences* with regard to different product concepts each representing a different bundle of characteristics?

The collected data are simple rankings of preference for the various concept combinations. Each concept constitutes a different assortment of characteristics. These preference data are submitted to one of the conjoint analysis algorithms and the output is partial utilities for each component of the product concept and for each individual respondent.

Conjoint analysis results provide the market analyst with four useful results:

● The identification of the *best concept*, that is the combination of concept components with the highest utilities, among all possible combinations.

● Information on what will be the *utility or disutility of any change* in the concept characteristics. This enables a selection of the most attractive trade-offs among concept components.

● Information on the *relative importance* of each component.

● Possibility of constructing *segments* based on the similarity of the respondents' reactions to the tested concepts.

On the basis of these results, alternative scenarios can be developed and the expected share of preferences estimated in each case.

The problems raised by concept testing are usually less subtle in *industrial markets*, since industrial clients' needs are generally more clearly specified. Moreover, the respondent is a professional, and trade-off analysis is a more natural way of thinking. Conjoint analysis has many applications within industrial markets. For an interesting application see the Clarke Equipment Case (Clarke, 1987).

Example of a concept test

To illustrate the contribution of conjoint analysis, let us examine the following example. The product studied is a hairspray, targeted at the Belgian market and defined in terms of the following five characteristics:

● *Design*: two designs are considered: the existing one and a new one.
● *Product's claim*: 'styling spray', 'extra strong hair spray' or 'fixing spray'.
● *Price*: three price levels are considered; 109, 129 and 149 Belgian francs.
● *Product Range*: the product may be offered singly or included in a range comprising a gel, a mousse and a styling cream.
● *Brand*: the brand may be A, B or C.

These variables give a total of 108 possible combinations for new product concept ($2 \times 3 \times 3 \times 2 \times 3$). Using a fractional factorial design we can reduce the number of concepts to be tested to 18. All pertinent information on each of the characteristics is retained, but information on interactions of orders greater than 2 are lost. In order to estimate partial utilities, regression analysis is conducted, using binary variables (0, 1) to describe the presence or absence of the product characteristics at each level. Figure 11.6 shows the average utility curves obtained from the sample examined.

The results show that consumers are very sensitive to the brand name and that they noticeably prefer brand B to the other brands. They also show the price elasticity to be –0.81. The new design is also clearly preferred over the old one. With regard to the product's claim, there appears to be very little sensitivity on the part of the respondents, who probably understand the claim poorly (Rochet, 1987).

These results are useful to develop alternative launching scenarios and to obtain estimates of the likely rate of adoption of the new product concept.

● Business Analysis and Marketing Programming

Once the product concept has been developed and accepted by top management, it is up to the marketing department to quantify the market opportunity and to develop alternative marketing programmes. This implies sales forecasting and market penetration objectives under different marketing budgets. The economic viability of the new product within the chosen time horizon must be assessed and the risk of the new venture evaluated.

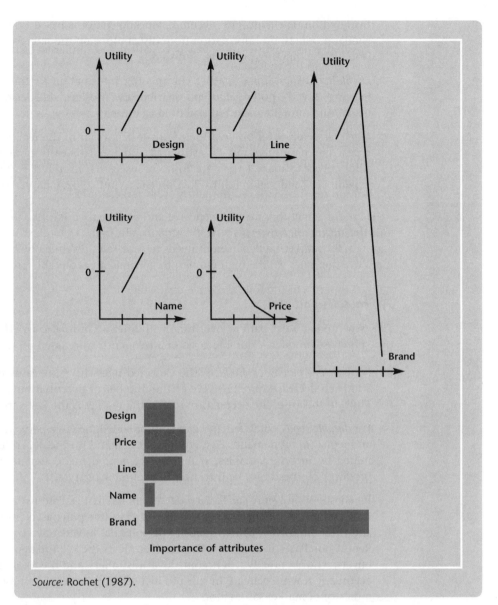

Figure 11.6 Example of conjoint analysis: hairspray products

Estimating sales volume

Estimating the sales projection for the first three years is the first problem to examine, which will condition the rest of the analysis. Given estimates of total potential sales in the target segment, what will be the expected sales volume or market share of the new product under different assumptions regarding the size of the marketing efforts? Different methods to approach this question can be used: subjective methods, feasibility studies and methods based on a test market:

● *Subjective methods* rely on the marketing information system of the firm, but also on experience, judgement and on information accumulated more or less informally within the firm. This accumulated knowledge is based on sales history of similar products, on information from distributors, on the sales force, on comparison with competing products, and so on.

⬤ *Feasibility studies* aim to gather the missing information in the field by interviewing directly potential users, distributors, retailers, and so on. Purchasing intention scores are collected and used to estimate sales volume.

⬤ *Market tests* allow for observation of buyer behaviour in the real world. Trial and repeat purchase rates can be estimated and used for early projection of sales. Alternatives to market tests are in-home use tests, mini-test panels, laboratory experiments and regional introduction (see Wind, 1982, Chapter 14).

These three methods are not exclusive and may be used jointly where uncertainty and the degree of newness for the company are high. Regardless of the approach adopted, the marketing department needs to set a sales revenue objective and to estimate whether sales will be high enough to generate an acceptable profit to the firm.

Typical sales patterns

The new product sales pattern over time will differ according to whether it is a one-time purchase product, a durable good or a frequently purchased product:

⬤ For *one-time purchased products*, the expected sales curve increases steadily, peaks and then decreases progressively as the number of potential buyers diminishes. Thus, in this case, the occupation rate of the market is the key variable.

⬤ For *durable goods*, total demand can be subdivided into two parts: first equipment and replacement demand. First equipment demand is time dependent and determined by income variables, while replacement demand is determined by the product's obsolescence, be it technical, economic or style.

⬤ Purchases of *frequently purchased products* can be divided into two categories: first-time and repeat purchases. The number of first-time purchasers initially increases and then diminishes as the majority of potential buyers have tried the product. Repeat purchases will occur if the product meets the requirements of a group of buyers, who eventually will become loyal customers, and the total sales curve will eventually reach a plateau. In this product category, repeat purchases are the best indicator of market satisfaction.

The typical sales patterns for trial, repeat and total sales of a frequently purchased product are presented in Figure 11.7.

Panel data projection methods

In the case of frequently purchased products, the Parfitt and Collins theorem (1968) can be used to decompose market share, as shown in Chapter 5, and to generate *market share projections*. These measures are normally obtained from a consumer panel. As seen before, market share can be divided into three distinct components:

⬤ The *penetration rate* of a brand is defined as the cumulative trial, that is the percentage of buyers having made a trial purchase at time t; this rate first

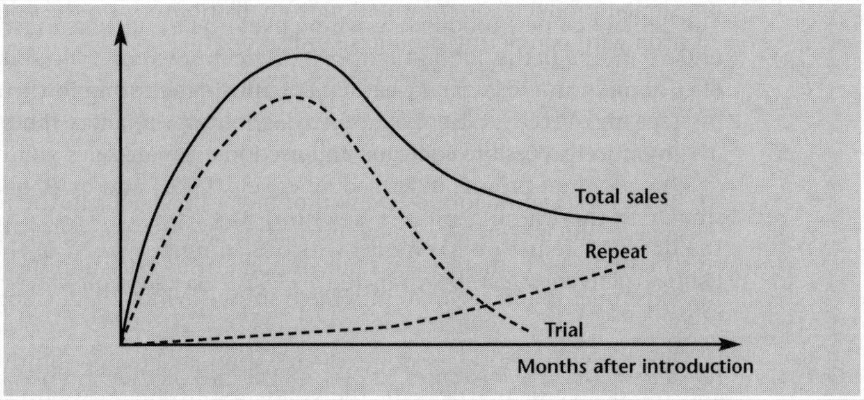

Figure 11.7   Typical sales pattern for trial and repeat sales

increases after launching and then tends to stabilise fairly rapidly as the stock of potential first-time buyers diminishes.

● The *repeat purchasing* rate is expressed as the proportion of total purchases in the product field by those buyers having tried the product. After a certain number of purchases, the repeat purchase rate will level off to some equilibrium state.

● The *intensity rate*, or buying level index, compares the rate of quantities purchased of the studied brand to the average quantities purchased within the product category. A distinction can be made here between heavy, light or average buyers (by volume) in the product field.

The *expected market share* is estimated by multiplying these three values.

Suppose that the estimated rate for trial purchase is 34 per cent and that the repeat purchase rate is around 25 per cent. If the average quantities purchased are the same for the brand and the product category, the expected market share will be:

$$34 \text{ per cent} \times 25 \text{ per cent} \times 1.00 = 8.5 \text{ per cent}$$

In cases of segmented markets, the expected market shares are calculated for each group. For example, the buying level index may vary according to the type of buyer. It may reach 1.20 for heavy buyers and 0.80 for light buyers. The expected market share in each of these cases will be around 10.2 and 6.8 per cent, respectively.

This kind of market share projection can be quickly formulated after the first few months of launching a new product. This method also allows for measurement of the impact that advertising and promotional activities have on market share. For more on this topic, see Parfitt and Collins' seminal article (1968).

No method can estimate future sales with certainty. Therefore, it is useful to give a range of estimations, with minimum and maximum sales, in order to assess the extent of risk implied by the new product launch.

The customer adoption process

The design of a new product-launching plan, to be effective, must be based on a good understanding of the adoption process of the innovation followed by the target group of customers. In the general case, the adoption process can be described as a sequence of steps (see Table 11.12) followed by the prospect, from the stage of innovation discovery to its possible adoption or rejection.

This adoption process described by Rogers (1962) and by Robertson (1971) is very similar to the learning process described in Chapter 5 (Table 5.1) and also to the Lavidge and Steiner (1961) model which is commonly used in the analysis of advertising effectiveness. As shown in Table 11.12, this adoption process can be subdivided into six phases.

1. *Knowledge*: the customer knows of the product's existence; informative advertising and word-of-mouth communication play an important role at this stage.

2. *Comprehension*: it is based on knowledge and represents the customer's conception of what the product is and what functions it can perform.

3. *Attitude*: as explained in Chapter 5, attitude is thought of as the predisposition of the individual to evaluate an object of his environment in a favourable or unfavourable manner. Concept advertising, distributors and prescribers are the main sources of influence.

4. *Conviction*: the individual realises a favourable attitude, is convinced of the product's superiority and that purchase is the appropriate course of action.

5. *Trial*: the individual uses the product on a limited scale, stimulated by a promotion or by sampling.

6. *Adoption*: the customer accepts the product and continues to purchase and/or use it. The adoption process is now complete and it is the intrinsic product quality that will determine the level of satisfaction.

Table 11.12   The adoption process of an innovation

Stages of the Process	Hierarchy of Effects (Lavidge and Steiner, 1961)	Adoption Process (Robertson, 1971)
Cognitive level	Awareness ↓ Knowledge ↓	Knowledge ↓ Comprehension
Affective level	Liking ↓ Preference ↓	Attitude ↓ Conviction ↓
Behavioural level	Conviction ↓ Purchase ↓ Loyalty/Forgetting	Trial ↓ Adoption

In the design of a launching plan, it is therefore important to select the types of marketing instrument better adapted to each stage and to monitor the progress made by the target group along the adoption process.

Duration of the diffusion process

The speed of diffusion will be a function of the type of innovation. As explained in Chapter 7, five characteristics have been found to affect diffusion speed (Rogers, 1962, 1995, p. 208):

● *Relative advantage*: the degree of improvement that the innovation represents over existing alternatives (fax machines' superiority over telex).

● *Complexity*: the inherent difficulty associated with the new idea or product. High levels of complexity can make it more expensive for a customer in terms of learning costs (personal computers).

● *Compatibility*: how well the innovation fits with the existing practices of potential adopters. If customers have to modify their prior use patterns, changeover or adoption costs exist and the speed of diffusion will be slower. Conversely, if the product is fully compatible with prior use, the adoption can be very rapid (fluoridated toothpaste versus the electric toothbrush).

● *Communicability*: the ease with which the essence of the innovation can be conveyed to potential adopters. Some benefits have a high degree of visibility and some products lend themselves well to usage demonstration like cars, telephones, VCRs, and so on. Conversely, innovations with long-term benefits (like health protection) are more difficult to promote and therefore are susceptible to diffuse more slowly.

● *Trialability*: the innovation's capability of being tried out in a smaller scale prior to purchase, thereby reducing the adoption costs.

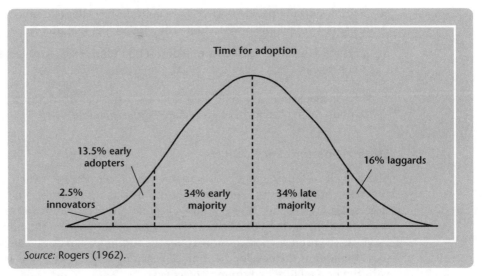

Source: Rogers (1962).

Figure 11.8   Adopter categorisation based on relative time of adoption

Other factors can also determine the speed of diffusion like the degree of uncertainty of the innovation itself, particularly in the case of discontinuous innovations (Frambach, 1995). Three sources of uncertainty may exist:

⬤ Uncertainty concerning the reality of the benefits claimed, particularly when those benefits are expected in the long term.
⬤ Uncertainty concerning the adoption costs (resistance to change) associated with the implementation of the innovation in the customer's life or organisation.
⬤ Uncertainty concerning the pace of innovation itself and the length of its product life cycle.

The analysis of these factors prior to the launching of the innovation is useful to evaluate correctly the duration of the introductory phase and also to design the most appropriate communication programme.

Categories of adopters

Rogers (1962, p. 5) defines the diffusion process as *the manner in which new ideas, products, or practices spread through a culture*, or (in marketing terms) through a target market. Rogers proposed classifying adopters by reference to the timing of adoption into five types, ranked from those who first adopt the innovation to those who come last to the adoption phase (see Figure 11.8). The basic assumption is that the numbers of people falling into each category will approximate a normal distribution.

1. *Innovators* (2.5 per cent): the very early purchasers of the innovation; they are independent, venturesome and willing to try new ideas at some risk. They represent a very small proportion of the market.

2. *Early adopters* (13.5 per cent): a larger group, composed of opinion leaders in their social group. They adopt new ideas early, but with prudence.

3. *Early majority* (34 per cent): they adopt new ideas before the average person but they need information and they are not leaders.

4. *Late majority* (34 per cent): they are sceptical; they adopt an innovation only after a majority of people have tried it. They follow the majority rule.

5. *Laggards* (16 per cent): they are tradition bound; they are suspicious and resistant to changes.

This categorisation approximately follows a normal distribution, its cumulative distribution taking the form of an *S-shaped diffusion* curve.

Dynamic performance analysis

The launch of a new product is a strategic decision process, which concerns every function within the firm and not only the marketing function. The success of this process largely depends on a sound co-ordination of each function involved. Moreover, the time factor is important and may modify the profitability of the new product. To ensure a good co-ordination, the firm must have at its disposal analytical tools to monitor the development process step by step and to assess its conformance with the profitability and timing objectives.

Assessing the financial risk

For each strategy, it is important to determine as precisely as possible when the elimination of risk is supposed to occur. There are three levels of risk, identified in Figure 11.9.

● The *simple break-even point*, the moment where the new activity leaves the zone of losses and enters into the zone of profits.

● The *equilibrium break-even point*, when the present value of total receipts covers the present value of total expenses. The company has recouped its capital layout.

● The *capital acquisition point*, the point where the new activity generates a financial surplus allowing for reinvestments to prolong the economic life of the activity or for supporting the development of other businesses within the firm.

Ideally, the capital acquisition point should be reached before the maturity phase of the product's life cycle in order to allow the company timely redeployment, that is before competitive pressure begins to erode profit margins. These three criteria will eventually determine the economic viability of the project. To be operational these criteria must be viewed in a dynamic perspective.

Dynamics of the development process

House and Price (1991) have developed a tracking system, called the Return Map which is used at Hewlett-Packard, which allow people working in cross-functional

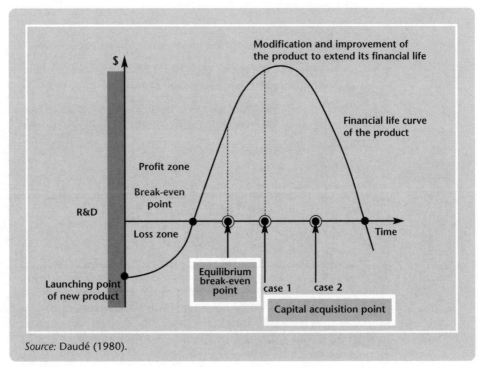

Source: Daudé (1980).

Figure 11.9 Assessing the financial risk of a new product

teams to assess the impact of their decisions and of their colleagues' decisions on the entire development process, both in terms of time and money.

The Return Map is simply a dynamic break-even chart. It is a two-dimensional graph displaying time and money on the *x*- and *y*-axes respectively. The *x*-axis is usually drawn on a linear scale, while the *y*-axis is drawn most effectively on a logarithmic scale, because for successful products the difference between sales and investments costs will be greater than 100:1. The *x*-axis is divided into three segments showing partitioned tasks and responsibilities: investigation, development and manufacturing. An example of application is presented in Figure 11.10.

Investigation took 4 months and costs about $400,000; development required 12 months and $4.5 million. Hence the total product development effort from beginning to manufacturing and sales release took 16 months and cost $4.9 million. See the 'investment' line in Figure 11.10. The manufacturing–sales phase started in period 16.

Sales for the first year were $56 million and for the second year $145 million. cumulative sales give a sense of how quickly the product was introduced and sold; In the first year, net profits of $2.2 million were less than expected. During the second year profits increased significantly, reached $13 million and passed through the investment line about 16 months after manufacturing. Thus, the chart tracks – in dollars and in months – R&D, manufacturing, sales and profit.

Several indicators of performance can be derived from the chart of Figure 11.10:

● Time to R&D (or TRD), the time and cost of the investigation phase until the start of the development phase.

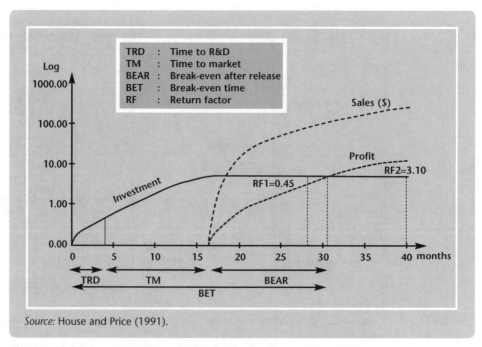

Source: House and Price (1991).

Figure 11.10　Dynamic analysis of the development process

● Time to market (or TM), the total development time from the start of the development phase to manufacturing release.

● Break-even after release (or BEAR) is the time from manufacturing release until the project investment costs are recovered in product profits.

● Break-even time (or BET). It is defined as the time from the start of the investigation until product profits equal the investment in development.

● Return factor (or RF) is a calculation of profit dollars divided by investment dollars at a specific point of time after the product has moved into manufacturing and sales.

In the example presented, the performance indicators are as follows:

TRD: 4 months and a cost of $0.4 million
TM: 12 months and a cost of $4.5 million
BEAR: 16 months
BET: 32 months
RF (year 1): 2.2/4.9 = 0.45
RF (year 2): 15.2/4.9 = 3.10

The effectiveness of the Return Map hinges on the involvement of all three major functional areas in the development and introduction of new products. The map captures the link between the development team and the rest of the company and the customer. It is a typical situation where a high level of market orientation of the entire firm is required.

Project evaluation procedure

How do we proceed to select priority projects when financial resources are limited, opportunities too many and the risks very different from one project to the other?

There is a vast literature in the field of capital budgeting on this topic, but the methods proposed are strictly financial, quantitatively oriented and do not consider qualitative criteria, which are often very important to assess the attractiveness of a particular project. Moreover, they required precise financial data, which often are not available at the evaluation phase of a project.

A crude but useful financial indicator is the *payback period index* (in years) which answers the question *when shall I get all my money back?* This index is calculated as follows:

$$\text{Payback} = \frac{\text{Development and commercial costs}}{(\text{Annual sales (\$/year)}) \cdot (\text{Profit margin as a \% of sales})}$$

This criterion is simple, easily understood and is based on data usually available at the evaluation phase. The reciprocal of this index gives a very crude estimate of the return as a percentage. Alternative and more rigorous methods are net present value (NPV) or discounted cash flow (DCF) as well as internal rate of return (IRR).

It is often useful to add explicitly a risk factor and qualitative indicators similar to those used in the screening grid (see Figure 11.5). We would then have a new project evaluation matrix similar to that presented in Figure 11.11. In this matrix the projects are evaluated along two dimensions:

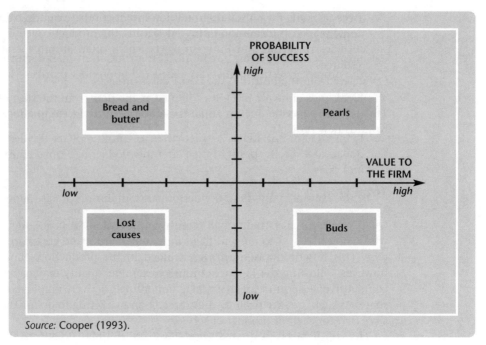

Source: Cooper (1993).

Figure 11.11   Portfolio analysis of new product concepts

The first horizontal dimension measures the *value to the firm* of each project, using a multi-attribute composite index based on quantitative and qualitative indicators reflecting the value of the project to the firm.

A second vertical dimension measuring the *probability of technological and/or commercial success of each project* as evaluated by management after the investigation or development phase.

We thus have a two-dimensional grid composed of four quadrants, where each project is represented by a bubble denoting the size of the resources to be devoted to each project:

In the upper right quadrant are the *Pearls*, that is projects having a high value to the firm and a high probability of success.

In the lower right quadrant, are the *Buds*, very desirable projects for the firm but still having a low probability of success.

In the upper left quadrant, are the *Bread and Butter* projects, with a good probability of success (and a low risk) but ordinary or low value to the firm.

In the lower right quadrant are the *Lost Causes*, the bad projects, a low commercial payoff and a low probability of success.

This project portfolio grid is used during the annual budgeting exercise to identify the priority projects. Decision rules might be:

allocate resources by priority to the development and the launching of Pearls projects;

- invest in some Buds projects to reinforce their competitiveness by gathering additional market information or by redesigning the product concept;
- cut back on Bread and Butter projects which often absorb too much time and resources;
- delete from the portfolio the Lost Causes projects.

This type of portfolio analysis is also useful to help the firm to allocate R&D efforts towards new projects.

Total Quality Strategy

Quality control has traditionally been considered as a purely defensive measure whose objective was to prevent flaws in manufacturing and eliminate defective products. This function was normally included in the production department. Today, however, following the Japanese industry example, quality management is seen as a competitive weapon of great strategic importance, actively employed to gain market share. As such, quality strategy calls directly on marketing to define the *expected excellence level* for each of product or service.

Quality from the buyer's point of view

For the buyer, a quality product does not necessarily mean a luxury good, but could simply mean a product that pleases, that is that fits the needs and expectations of a specific target group. Product quality can thus be defined as follows:

> The quality of a product is the degree of conformance of all of the relevant features and characteristics of the product to all of the aspects of a customer's need, limited by the price and delivery he or she will accept. (Groocock, 1986, p. 27)

Comparisons in quality only make sense between products designed to meet the same needs and sold at the same price level. Buyer satisfaction is a function of the degree of conformance between the buyer's expectations of the product and the perception of the product's overall performance.

It is buyers who dictate to the company the level of excellence to be attained, as a function of their own needs. Quality management implies, above all, a knowledge of the expectations and motivations to buy of the target group.

> The person who buys a Renault 5 does not expect the same kind of performance from the car as does the person who purchases a Mercedes 190E. Both products, however, may be quality products in the sense that they both meet the excellence level expected by the buyers given the price paid.

Considering the diversity of needs, the level of excellence for each product must be defined for each target segment. This implies a different package of benefits or 'set of values' corresponding to the expected quality level and to the accepted price range. Thus, designing a quality strategy presupposes a market segmentation analysis.

The key dimensions of quality

We have seen that buyers perceive a product as a bundle of attributes likely to supply the core service sought as well as other added services or benefits. Quality management implies breaking down total quality into components so as to establish norms or performance standards for each component.

The components of product quality

Garvin (1987) proposes eight dimensions or components of product quality:

● *Product or service performance*: the ability of a product to perform its basic function.
● *Proprietary features*: the range of other advantages a product offers in addition to its basic function.
● *Conformance*: adherence to norms or standards corresponding to a determined level of excellence (with a reduced tolerance margin).
● *Reliability*: the absence of failure or defective operation within a given time frame.
● *Durability*: the useful life span of a product or the frequency of product use before the product deteriorates.
● *Serviceability*: the extent, speed and efficiency of services offered before, during and after purchase.
● *Appearance or aesthetics*: the design, look, colour, taste, and so on of a product (that is a much more subjective component).
● *Perceived quality*: the reputation or perceived image of a product or brand.

A quality control programme will consist of establishing norms for each of these components and monitoring conformance to these norms. Each of these components represents an opportunity to differentiate the product with respect to competition.

The components of service quality

The same kind of process can be used in managing the *quality of services*, a much more complicated task because of its intangible nature (Lambin, 1987; Horovitz, 1987). This complexity is described in Figure 11.12.

The empirical studies conducted in France (Eiglier and Langeard, 1982) and in the United States (Parasuraman *et al.*, 1985) identified ten factors, which determine the perception of the quality of a service:

● *Competence* means the possession of the required skills and knowledge to perform the service.

● *Reliability* involves consistency of performance and dependability, and performing the service right the first time. It also means that the firm honours its promises.

● *Responsiveness* concerns the willingness or readiness of employees to provide service. It involves timeliness of service.

● *Accessibility* refers to both physical and psychological accessibility. Access involves approachability and ease of contact.

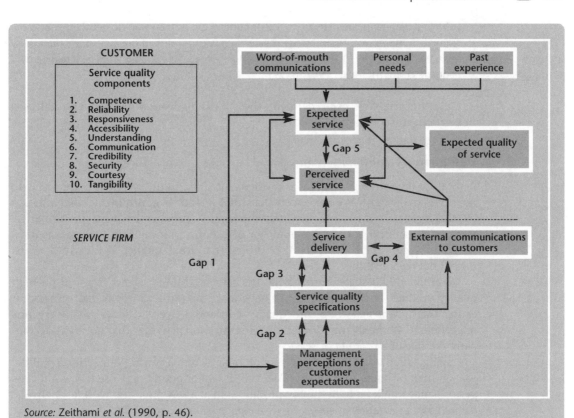

Source: Zeithami *et al.* (1990, p. 46).

Figure 11.12   The components of service quality

⬤ *Understanding* or knowing the customer involves making the effort to understand the customer's needs.

⬤ *Communication* means keeping customers informed in language they can understand and listening to them. It may mean that the company has to adjust its language for different customers.

⬤ *Credibility* involves trustworthiness, believability and honesty. It involves having the customer's best interest at heart.

⬤ *Security* is the freedom from danger, risk or doubt. It involves physical safety, financial and moral security.

⬤ *Courtesy* involves politeness, respect, consideration and friendliness of contact personnel.

⬤ *Tangibility* includes the physical evidence of the service: physical facilities, appearance of personnel, physical representation of the service, and so on.

These ten components of service quality are somewhat redundant (Parasuraman *et al.*, 1985, Table 1, p. 47). Each organisation must adapt them to its specific situation and establish quality norms, which constitute commitments to customers. These norms must be measurable.

Lufthansa has just included in its service promise: 'Businessmen want to get there, not wait.' Translated into norms, this message means: 'a passenger should not wait more than thirty minutes'. This statement also induces norms for baggage checks, flight times, schedules and baggage claim. (Horovitz, 1987, p. 99)

Once norms have been defined, they must be communicated and diffused throughout the company.

Designing a total quality strategy

A total quality strategy implies a unified, integrated and systematic approach to quality management. We have seen that total quality is multidimensional and can be disaggregated into two broad components: product quality (performance, features, reliability) and service quality (communication, responsiveness), as illustrated in Figure 11.13, which also shows that total quality is clearly a cross-functional responsibility.

Domingo (1997) suggests that what basically a customer wants is not just a high quality product, but one they could have at a low price and delivered on time or earlier. *Good, cheap and fast* or the 'quality, cost and delivery' trilogy. By delivery, one refers here to all the distribution and communication activities that normally accompany the sale of a product or service.

Having a high quality product does not make a company a TQM practitioner, if the price is high or uncompetitive or if delivery if late or poorly organised. A world class performance implies a high quality product sold at a low price and with fast delivery, *the universal expectation of any customer on any product or service anywhere.*

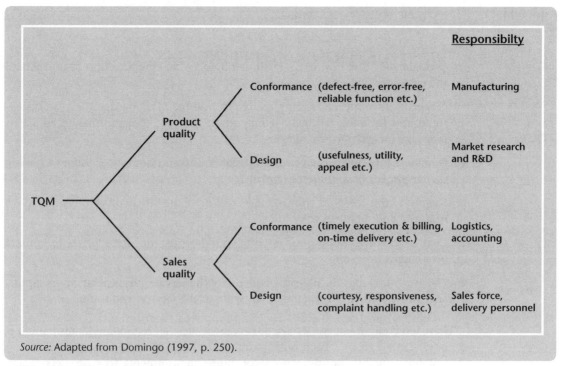

Source: Adapted from Domingo (1997, p. 250).

Figure 11.13　The components of total quality

Chapter summary

The term 'innovation' is used loosely to describe a whole range of cases ranging from minor to breakthrough innovations and it is important to evaluate accurately the diversity of innovations and their specific risks. The distinction between market-pull and technology-push innovations is particularly useful. Data available on new product success or failure show that the risk of failure is very high and that success is directly determined by the quality of management of the new product development process and not just by chance nor by the environment the firm is facing. The new product development process consists of three phases: (a) idea phase (idea generation and screening), (b) concept phase (concept development, concept testing, business analysis) and (c) launching phase. In market-driven companies this process tends to be more a parallel than a sequential development process in order to ensure better interfunctional co-ordination. The concept development phase is crucial for incorporating the market orientation upfront and also for adopting a thorough approach to product greening. In the business analysis, the economic viability of the new product must be assessed in a dynamic perspective under alternative marketing programmes and the risk of the new venture evaluated. The market-oriented firm tries to have a permanently balanced portfolio of projects, a useful tool for identifying priority projects. Total quality from the buyer's point of view refers to the degree of conformance between the product's perceived performance and the buyer's expectations. Quality is a multi-dimensional concept and a quality control programme will consist in establishing norms for each component of quality.

QUESTIONS AND PROBLEMS

1. Proceed to the morphological analysis of one of the following three products: office chair, an electric fryer, and a document binding system.

2. You are responsible for the launching of a new electronic device for automatic video recording of TV programmes through a system of code numbers (type Show-View). Prepare a written description of the product concept (a) to be communicated as a brief to the advertising agency and (b) to be used in a product concept test within a sample of housewives owning a video and belonging to the 40 years and over age group.

3. The Agrifood Company specialises in the manufacturing and selling of snacks and every year introduces into the market several products under its brand name. The PLC of this type of product is typically the one of a fad with a stable residual market after three years. Typically, first-year sales are on average 10,000 cases (35 packages per case); sales decline at a 30 per cent yearly decay rate over two years to stabilise at the level reached. According to product types, first-year sales can be 20 per cent higher or lower in 20 cases out of 100. The first-year advertising support is 10 million and 3 million during the two subsequent years. Retail price is 90F per package and the unit direct cost 33F. Each new product generates a fixed cost of about 3 million per year. Compute the break-even and the general equilibrium points over a period of three years given a

target profit rate of 10 per cent on an investment of 50 million. How would you proceed to assess the risk of this new product launching?

4. Give three examples of products new to the world, show the key components of these innovations and the type of risk the innovating firm will be confronted with.

5. In your opinion, what are the merits and demerits of the parallel and sequential approaches in the organisation of the new product development process?

6. The travel agency *Frontiers* has developed different tourist concepts using three characteristics – activity, site and price – each at three levels. These service concepts have been tested within three segments of potential customers: juniors, families and seniors. Through conjoint analysis, the following utilities were identified:

Characteristics		Segment: juniors	Segment: families	Segment: seniors
Activity:	culture	+0.10	-0.20	+0.20
	sport	+0.30	-0.10	-0.20
	leisure	-0.40	+0.30	0
Prices:	20,000 F/S	+0.50	+0.40	+0.30
	40,000 F/S	-0.10	-0.10	-0.10
	50,000 F/S	-0.40	-0.30	-0.20
Sites:	sea	+0.10	+0.50	-0.30
	mountain	+0.10	+0.10	-0.10
	cities	-0.20	-0.60	+0.40

Analyse the sensitivity of each segment to the different service characteristics. Which tourist service would you propose by priority to each segment? Would it be possible to develop a service concept that would suit the three segments?

Bibliography

Auckenthaler, B., Ducatte, J.-C. and Huz, T. (1997) *Réinventer l'innovation*, Rueil Malmaison, Editions Liaisons.

Barreyre, P.Y. (1980) Typologie des innovations, *Revue Française de Gestion*, January–February, pp. 9–15.

Bijon, C. (1984) La stratégie de rupture, *Harvard-L'expansion*, Autumn, pp. 98–104.

Booz, Allen and Hamilton (1982) *New Product Management for the 1980s*.

Clarke, D.G. (1987) *Marketing Analysis and Decision Making*, Redwood City, CA, The Scientific Press.

Cooper, R.C. (1979) The Dimensions of Industrial New Products Success and Failure, *Journal of Marketing*, **43**, Summer, pp. 93–103.

Cooper, D.G. (1981) The Myth of the Better Mousetrap: What Makes a New Product a Success, *Business Quarterly*, Spring, pp. 69–81.

Cooper, R.G. (1993) *Winning at New Products*, 2nd edn, Reading MA: Addison-Wesley.

Daudé, B. (1980) Analyse de la maîtrise des risques, *Revue Française de Gestion*, January–February, pp. 38–48.

de Brabandère, L. (1998) *Le management des idées*, Paris, Dunod.

de Moerloose, C. (1999) *Contingence du type de nouveauté sur le succès des produits nouveaux*, Louvain-la-Neuve, Institut d'administration et de gestion.

Domingo, R.T. (1997) *Quality Means Survival*, Singapore, Simon & Schuster Asia.

Economist, The (1999) *Innovation Industry Survey*, 20 February.

Edgett, S., Shipley, D. and Forbes, G. (1992) Japanese and British Companies Compared: Contributing Factors to Success and Failure in NPD, *Journal of Product Innovation Management*, **9**, pp. 3–10.

Eiglier, P. and Langeard, E. (1987) *Servuction: le marketing des services*, Paris, Ediscience international.

Frambach, R.T. (1995) Diffusion of Innovations in Business-to-Business Markets, in: Bruce, M. and Biemans, W.G. (eds), *Product Development*, New York, John Wiley & Sons.

Garvin, D.A. (1987) Competing on the Eight Dimensions of Quality, *Harvard Business Review*, **65**, November–December, pp. 101–9.

Gordon, J.J. (1965) *Stimulation des facultés créatrices dans les groupes de recherche synectique*, Paris, Hommes et Techniques.

Green, P.E. and Srinivasan, V. (1978) Conjoint Analysis in Consumer Research: Issues and Outlook, *Journal of Consumer Research*, September, pp. 103–23.

Groocock, J.M. (1986) The Chain of Quality, New York, John Wiley & Sons.

House, C.H. and Price, R.L. (1991) The Return Map: Tracking Product Teams, *Harvard Business Review*, **69**, January–February, pp. 92–100.

Horovitz, J. (1987) *La qualité des services*, Paris, InterEditions.

Kotler, P. (1997) *Marketing Management*, 9th edn, Englewood Cliffs, NJ: Prentice-Hall International.

Lambin, J.-J. (1987) Le contrôle de la qualité dans le domaine des services, *Gestion 2000*, **1**: 63–75.

Lavidge, R.J. and Steiner, G.A. (1961) A Model of Predictive Measurement of Advertising Effectiveness, *Journal of Marketing*, **25**, October, pp. 59–62.

Little, A.D. (1997) A Global Survey on Innovation, Boston, Arthur D. Little.

Nielsen Researcher, The (1971) New Product Success Ratio, **5**, pp. 4–9, Chicago, The Nielsen Company.

O'Meara, J.T. (1961) Selecting Profitable Products, *Harvard Business Review*, **39**, January–February, pp. 110–18.

Osborn, A.F. (1963) *Applied Imagination*, 3rd edn, New York, Charles Scribner's Sons.

Ottman, J.A. (1993) *Green Marketing*, Lincolnwood IL, NTC Business Books.

Parasumaran, A., Zeithaml, V.A. and Berry, L.L. (1985) A Conceptual Model of Service Quality and Its Implications for Future Research, *Journal of Marketing*, **49**, Autumn, pp. 41–50.

Parfitt, J.M. and Collins, J.K. (1968) Use of Consumer Panels for Brand Share Prediction, *Journal of Marketing Research*, **5**, May, pp. 131–45.

Page, A.L. (1993) Assessing New Product Development Practices and Performance: Establishing Crucial Norms, *Journal of Product Innovation Management*, **10**(4): 273–90.

Peixoto, O. (1993) Conscience verte des Français et Eco-marketing, *Revue Française du Marketing*, (142–3), pp. 198–202.

Rochet, L. (1987) *Diagnostic stratégique du potentiel d'extension d'une marque de laque*, Louvain-la-Neuve, Institut d'Administration et de Gestion.

Rogers, E.M. (1962, 1995) *Diffusion of Innovations*, 4th edn, New York, The Free Press.

Robertson, T.S. (1971) *Innovative Behavior and Communication*, New York, Holt, Rinehart and Winston.

Stalk, G. (1988) Time – The Next Source of Competitive Advantage, *Harvard Business Review*, July–August, pp. 41–51.

Takeuchi, H. and Nonaka, I. (1986) The New Product Development Game, *Harvard Business Review*, January–February, pp. 137–46.

Tauber, E.M. (1973) Reduce New Product Failures: Measure Needs as well as Purchase Interest, *Journal of Marketing*, **37**, July, pp. 61–70.

Theys, F. (1994) *Succês et échecs de l'innovation dans l'IFME*, IAG, Louvain-la-Neuve, Belgium.

Urban, G.L., Hauser, J.R. and Dholakia, N. (1987) *Essentials of New Product Management*, Englewood Cliffs NJ, Prentice Hall.

von Hippel, E. (1978) Successful Industrial Products from Customer Ideas, *Journal of Marketing*, **42**, January, pp. 39–49.

Wind, Y.S. (1982) *Product Policy: Concepts, Methods and Strategy*, Reading MA, Addison Wesley.

Zeithaml, V., Parasuraman, A. and Berry, L.L. (1990) *Delivering Quality Service*, New York, The Free Press.

chapter twelve

Market-driven distribution decisions

In most markets, the physical and psychological distance between producers and end-users is such that intermediaries are necessary to ensure an efficient matching between segments of demand and supply. Distributors and facilitating agencies are required because manufacturers are unable to assume by themselves, at a reasonable cost, all the tasks and activities implied by a free and competitive exchange process. The use of intermediaries means a loss of manufacturer control of certain distributive functions, since the firm subcontracts activities that could, in principle, be assumed by marketing management. Thus, from the firm's point of view, channel decisions are critical ones which involve developing a channel structure that fits the firm's strategy and the needs of the target segment. The design of a channel structure is a major strategic decision, neither frequently made nor easily changed. In this chapter, we shall first examine the channel design decisions from the manufacturer's point of view (see Figure 12.1) and then analyse the type of positioning strategies available to retailers in consumer markets.

Chapter learning objectives

When you have read this chapter, you should be able to:

1. explain the role and the functions performed by distribution channels in a market economy;

2. describe why companies use distribution channels and the tasks performed by these channels;

3. identify the main configurations of a distribution channel and analyse the distribution cost structure of each possible channel;

4. explain the different market coverage and communication strategies open to the manufacturer;

5. explain the strategic marketing issues facing the retailer;

6. understand the potential of e-commerce and direct marketing;

7. describe the alternative entry strategies in foreign markets open to the international firm.

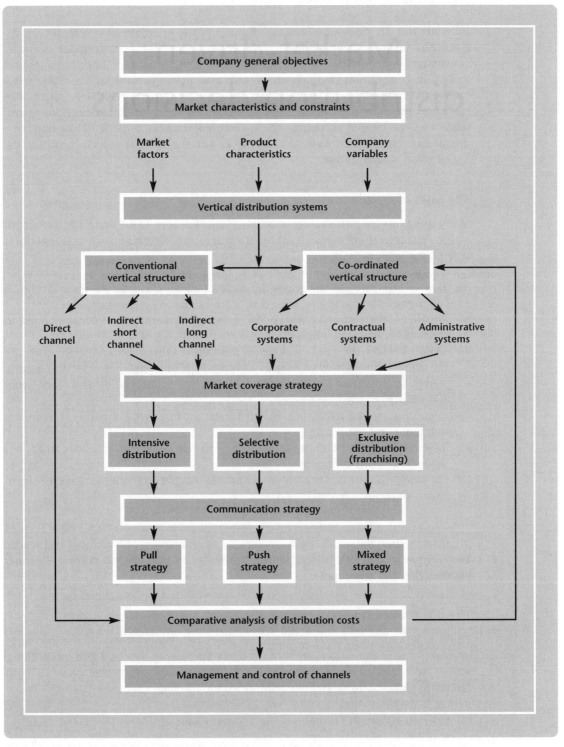

Figure 12.1 Overview of distribution channel decisions

● The Economic Role of Distribution Channels

A distribution channel is the structure formed by the interdependent partners participating in the process of making goods or services available for consumption or use by consumers or industrial users. These partners are the producers, intermediaries and end-users. Distribution channels are *organised* structures performing the tasks necessary to facilitate exchange transactions. Their role in a market economy is to bridge the gap between manufacturers and end-users by making goods available where and when they are needed and under the appropriate terms of trade. The functions of a distribution channels are to create time, space and state utilities which constitute the added value of distribution.

The tasks of distribution

Many functions are provided by channels of distribution. These occur for the benefit of the producer or consumer or both. For producers, distribution channels perform seven different functions:

- *Transporting*: to make the goods available in places close to consumers or industrial users.
- *Breaking of bulk*: to make the goods available in quantity or volume adapted to consumers' purchasing habits.
- *Storing*: to make the goods available at the time of consumption, thereby reducing the manufacturer's need to store its own products in company-owned warehouses.
- *Sorting*: to constitute a selection of goods for use in association with each other and adapted to the buyer's use.
- *Contacting*: to establish personalised relationships with customers who are numerous and remote.
- *Informing*: to collect and disseminate information about market needs and about products and terms of trade.
- *Promoting*: to promote the products through advertising and promotions organised at the point of sales.

In addition to these basic functions, intermediaries also provide services such as financial credit, guarantees, delivery, repairs, maintenance, atmosphere, and so on. The main economic role of distribution channels is *to overcome the existing disparities* between demand and supply.

The distribution flows

These functions give rise to distribution flows between partners in the exchange process. Some of these flows are forward flows (ownership, physical and promotion), others are backward flows (ordering and payment), and still others move in both directions (information). The five main flows are the following:

- *Ownership flow*: the actual transfer of legal ownership from one organisation to another.
- *Physical flow*: the successive movements of the physical product from the producer to the end-user.

- *Ordering flow*: the orders placed by intermediaries in the channel and forwarded to the manufacturer.
- *Payment flow*: successive buyers paying their bills through financial institutions to sellers.
- *Information flow*: the dissemination of information to the market and/or to the producer at the initiative of the producer and/or the intermediaries.

The key question in designing a channel of distribution is not whether these functions and flows need to be performed, but rather who is to perform them. These functions and the management of these distribution flows can be shifted between channel's partners. The problem is to decide who could perform these economic functions most efficiently: the producer, the intermediary or the consumer.

The rationale for marketing channels

The distribution functions cannot be eliminated, but rather simply assumed by other more efficient channel members. Innovations in distribution channels largely reflect the discovery of more efficient ways to manage these economic functions or flows. Various sources of efficiency enable intermediaries to perform distribution functions at a lower cost than either the customer or the manufacturer could by themselves. This is particularly true for consumer goods, which are distributed to a large number of geographically dispersed customers.

Contactual efficiency

The complexity of the exchange process increases as the number of partners increases. As shown in Figure 12.2, the number of contacts required to maintain mutual interactions between all partners in the exchange process is much higher in a decentralised exchange system than in a centralised one. Figure 12.2 shows that, given three manufacturers and five retailers who buy goods from each manufacturer, the number of contacts required amounts to 15. If the manufacturer sells to these retailers through one wholesaler, the number of necessary contacts is reduced to 8. Thus, a centralised system employing intermediaries is more efficient than a decentralised system of exchange, by reducing the number of transactions required for matching segments of demand and supply.

Economies of scale

By grouping the products of several manufacturers, intermediaries can perform one or more distribution tasks more efficiently than manufacturers. For example, a wholesaler's sales representative can spread costs over several manufacturers and perform the selling function at a lower cost per manufacturer than if each firm paid its own company sales representative.

Reduction of functional discrepancies

By purchasing large volumes of goods from manufacturers, storing them and breaking them down into the volume customers prefer to purchase, wholesalers and retailers enable manufacturers and their customers to operate at their more efficient scale.

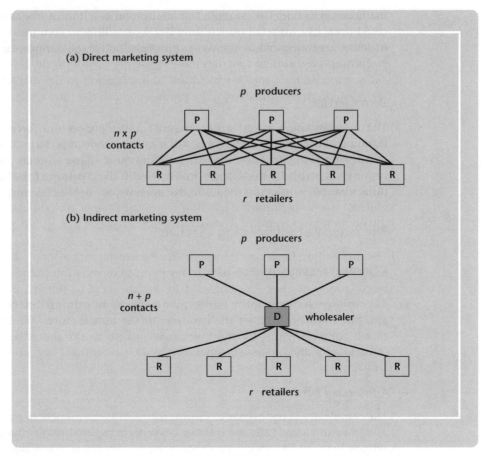

Figure 12.2   Contact efficiency of distributors

Rather than having to make small production runs to fill the orders of individual customers, manufacturers can achieve economies of scale. Similarly, their customers can buy small quantities without having their capital tied up in large inventories.

If a particular organisation is responsible for two separate functions (for instance manufacturing and distribution) that have different optimum levels of operations, there is a risk for one of the two functions, or even for each of them, to operate at a sub-optimum level. Costs go up and prices have to be higher. When some functions are subcontracted to middlemen the producer's costs and prices are lower.

Better assortment

At the manufacturer's level, the assortment of goods produced is largely dictated by technological considerations, whereas the assortment of goods consumers usually desire is dictated by the use situation. Typically, consumers desire a *limited quantity of a wide variety of goods*. The role of intermediaries is to create wide assortments and to make it possible for consumers to acquire a large variety of products from a single source with one transaction. This reduces the time and effort that consumers must expend in finding the goods they need. The same economy of effort also exists on the manufacturer's side. For example, a manufacturer of a limited line of hardware items could open its own retail outlets only if it were willing to accumulate a large variety of items generally sold at this type of outlet. In general, hardware wholesalers can perform this assortment function more efficiently than individual manufacturers.

Better services

The intermediary is close to the end-users and therefore can have a better understanding of their needs and desires and adapt the assortment to local situations.

The superior efficiency of intermediaries in a market system is not absolute however. A particular middleman will survive in the channel structure as long as the other channel partners in the exchange process consider that there is no other more efficient way to perform the function. Thus, the issue of who should perform various distribution tasks is one of relative efficiency.

● Channel Design Alternatives

The design of a channel structure implies decisions regarding the responsibilities to be assumed by the different participants in the exchange process. From the manufacturer's point of view, the first decision is whether or not to subcontract certain distribution tasks and, if so, to what extent to subcontract and under which trade conditions.

Types of intermediary

There are four broad categories of intermediary that a firm might include in the distributive network of its product: wholesalers, retailers, agents and facilitating agencies.

Wholesalers

These intermediaries sell primarily to other resellers, such as retailers or institutional or industrial customers, rather than to individual consumers. They take title of the goods they store and can provide quick delivery when the goods are ordered because they are usually located closer to customers than manufacturers. The case of wholesalers in the pharmaceutical industry described in Exhibit 12.1 is illustrative in this respect.

They purchase in large lots from manufacturers and resell in smaller lots to retailers. Wholesalers generally bring together an assortment of goods, usually of related items, by dealing with several sources of supply. In the food industry, full-service wholesalers have been confronted with the competition of mass retail distributors who have assumed by themselves the wholesaling function. Wholesalers have reacted by creating *voluntary chains* which consist of a wholesaler-sponsored group of independent retailers engaged in bulk buying and in common merchandising.

Retailers

Retailers sell goods and services directly to consumers for their personal, non-business use. Retailers take the ownership of the goods they carry, and their compensation is

Exhibit 12.1

Wholesalers in the Pharmaceutical Industry

■ How can 350 pharmaceutical laboratories and 250 suppliers of para-pharmaceutical products respond as rapidly as possible to the needs of 22,000 French pharmacies, knowing that 12 million health products are sold every day?

■ To do the job specialty wholesalers have covered French territory with warehouses to meet this demand. As a result, today 81 per cent of health products are distributed by these wholesalers. The remaining 19 per cent are delivered directly to hospitals (12 per cent) or to pharmacies (7 per cent).

■ Twice a day, pharmacists place their orders through teletransmission, to be served early afternoon before the end of schools' closing, or the following morning before the store is open. The staff have less than two hours to handle the orders.

Source: Le Monde, (16 March, 1993).

the margin between what they pay for the goods and the price they charge their customers. There are several schemes for classifying retailers. A traditional classification makes a distinction between three types of independent retailers: food retailers, specialty retailers and artisan retailers (bakers and butchers).

They can also be classified according to the level of service they provide (self-service versus full-service retailing) or according to their method of operation (low margin/high turnover or high margin/low turnover). Low margin/high turnover retailers compete primarily on a price basis, while high margin/low turnover retailers focus on unique assortment, specialty goods, services and prestigious store image. The number of independent retailers has drastically decreased in most European countries, mainly due to the competition of mass merchandisers.

Integrated distribution

Since the beginning of the century, profound changes have taken place in the distribution sector and it is useful to briefly summarise this evolution:

● The first revolution goes back to 1852 with the establishment in Paris of the first *department store*. The innovating principles were broad assortment, low mark-ups and rapid turnover, marking and displaying the prices, free entry without pressure or obligation to purchase. The best-known department stores today are, Harrods in London, Galeries Lafayettes in Paris, Macy's in New York, La Renascente in Milan, and so on.

● The next generation of stores was the *specialty-stores chain* located in suburban shopping centres closer to consumers. A store concept based on a limited assortment and economies of scale due to large purchased quantities.

● The next generation was the *popular store* which sells goods at low prices by accepting lower margins, working on higher volume and providing minimum service (typically Prisunic in France and Belgium).

● The fourth revolution is the *supermarket* revolution, a store concept based on self-service operations and designed to serve the consumer's total needs for food, laundry and household maintenance products. The one-stop shopping concept. Supermarkets have moved towards larger stores, the superstore or the *hypermarché* as Carrefour in France.

The supermarket concept has been extremely successful in Europe, in particular in the fast moving consumer goods sector. Six managerial rules characterised this selling formula:

● A broad assortment and wide variety of popular merchandise to facilitate multiple-item purchases and fast stock rotation.
● A low purchase price thanks to the high volume purchased and a strong bargaining power *vis-à-vis* suppliers.
● Low margins and low sales prices.
● Dynamic promotional activities in order to stimulate store traffic.
● Economies of scale on physical distribution (in transportation, handling and packaging).
● Long credit terms (typically 90 days) for products usually sold within 15 days in order to generate substantial financial by-products.

This selling formula has given a substantial competitive advantage to integrated distributors over independent retailers. The situation is changing today as new expectations emerge among consumers and as independent distributors propose new store concepts.

The new food discounters

The fifth revolution in mass merchandising is currently taking place with a new breed of retailers called the *hard discounters*, led mainly in Western Europe by the German distributors Aldi and Lidl (see Table 12.1). It is a retailing system characterised by the permanent and generalised adoption of low prices, thanks to a systematic cost control and limited service policies.

The main features of discount retailing, sometimes called *minimum marketing*, as observed in a typical Aldi store, are the following:

● a limited store size included between 3000 and 7000 square feet in the UK, the average size in France being 662 square metres (*LSA*, 1998);
● a small product range, approximately 600 lines, with a single offer per product category, mainly set out in full boxes on pallets;
● approximately 70 per cent of the range is own brand or at least a brand name with a 'packed exclusively for Aldi' qualification;
● prices aim to be 20–25 per cent lower than average major multiples;
● limited number (4 or 5) of multi-functional sales attendants;
● prices are memorised by checkout operators and there is no EpoS;

● only cash payments, credit cards are not accepted;
● plastic bags are charged for and the stores are often renovated warehouses or cinemas.

Table 12.1   The food discounters' share in Europe

Country	Discounter Share (%)
Germany	23
Belgium	20
Denmark	14
The Netherlands	9
Spain	9
United Kingdom	7.8
France	7.5
Italy	3

Source: Hogarth-Scott and Rice (1994) and *LSA* (1997).

According to a survey published by the *LSA* (1998), hard discounting is in good shape in France with more than 2000 units in 1998 and a growing market share of 6 to 7 per cent, with the German retail giants Lidl and Aldi leading, followed by Leader Price and ED Le Marché Discount. The growth of hard discounters is also significant in the UK with Aldi and Rewe (Penny) from Germany and Netto from Denmark. The two UK discount chains, Kwik Save and Lo Cost, dominate the discounting market.

Agents

These are functional intermediaries who do not take title of the goods with which they deal but who negotiate sales or purchases for clients or principals. They are compensated in the form of a commission on sales or purchases. They are independent business persons or freelance sales people who represent client organisations. Common types of agent include import or export agents, traders, brokers and manufacturers' representatives. Manufacturers' representatives usually work for several firms and carry non-competitive, complementary goods in an exclusive territory or foreign country.

Facilitating agencies

Facilitating agencies are business firms that assist in the performance of distribution tasks other than buying, selling and transferring title. From the firm's standpoint, they are subcontractors carrying out certain distribution tasks because of their specialisation or special expertise. Common types of facilitating agencies are: transportation agencies, storage agencies, advertising agencies, market research firms, financial agencies, insurance companies, and so on. These agencies are involved in a marketing channel on an as-needed basis and they are compensated by commissions or fees paid for their services.

Many different types of institutions participate in a distribution channel. The channel structure will be determined by the manner in which the different distribution tasks have been allocated among the channel participants.

Configurations of a distribution channel

Distribution channels can be characterised by the number of intermediary levels that separate the manufacturer from the end-user. Figure 12.3 shows the different channel designs commonly used to distribute industrial or consumer goods. A distinction can be made between direct and indirect distribution systems:

● In a *direct distribution system*, the manufacturer sells directly to the end-user and there is no intermediary in the channel. This structure is also called a direct marketing system.

● In an *indirect distribution system*, one or several intermediaries participate and bring the product closer to the final buyer. An indirect system is said to be 'short' or 'long' depending on the number of intermediary levels.

In the field of consumer goods, distribution channels tend to be long and involve several intermediaries, typically wholesalers and retailers. In industrial markets, chan-

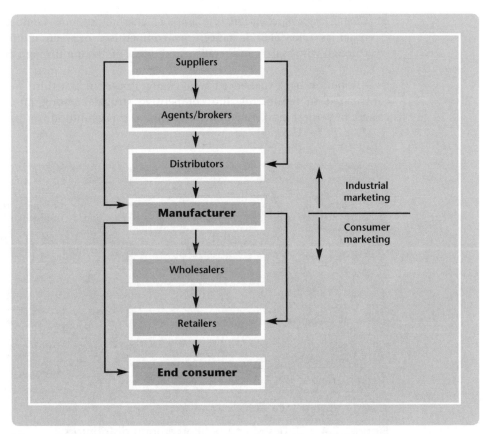

Figure 12.3 Structure of a conventional vertical marketing system

nels are generally shorter, particularly when buyers are large and well identified. From the producer's point of view, the longer the channel, the more difficult the problem of control.

In most market situations, companies use *multiple channels* to reach their target segments, either to create emulation among distributors or to reach separate target segments having different purchasing habits. For example, many industrial companies use distributors to sell and service small accounts and their own sales force to handle large accounts.

Types of competition among distributors

In a distributive network several types of competition may exist among distributors as shown in Figure 12.4:

● *Horizontal competition*. The same type of intermediaries at the same channel level competing with each other.

● *Intertype competition*. Different types of intermediaries at the same channel level competing with each other (self-service versus full service).

● *Vertical competition*. Channel members at different levels in the channel competing with each other, such as retailers integrating the wholesaling function or vice versa.

● *Channel system competition*. Complete channel systems competing with each other as units. For instance, the competition between indirect distribution through wholesalers and retailers and direct marketing through direct mail.

Distribution has experienced large changes over the last thirty years which have contributed to reinforcing the competitive struggle among intermediaries. The growth of vertical marketing systems illustrates this evolution.

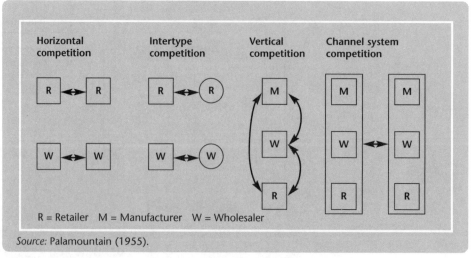

Source: Palamountain (1955).

Figure 12.4　Types of competition among distributors

Factors affecting the channel structure

The selection of a particular channel design is largely determined by a set of constraints related to market and buyer behaviour factors and to product and company characteristics. These factors and their implications for the channel configuration are described in Table 12.2.

Table 12.2   Factors affecting channel structure

Influencing factors	Channel structure		
	Direct	**Indirect short**	**Indirect long**
Market factors			
Large number of buyers		**	***
High geographical dispersion		**	***
Purchases in large quantity	***		
Buying highly seasonal		**	***
Product characteristics			
Perishable products	***		
Complex products	***		
Newness of the product	***	**	
Heavy and bulky products	***		
Standardised products		**	***
Low unit value		**	***
Company variables			
Large financial capacity	***	**	
Complete assortment	***	**	
High control sought	***	**	

Market factors

The number of potential buyers determines the *size of the market*. A very general heuristic rule about market size relative to channel structure is: if the market is large, the use of intermediaries is more likely to be needed. Conversely, if the market is small, a firm is more likely to avoid the use of intermediaries and to assume most of the distribution tasks. Also, the more *geographically dispersed* the market, the more difficult and expensive distribution is. The more geographically dispersed the market, the more likely it is that intermediaries will be used because of the high costs involved in providing adequate services to many dispersed customers.

Patterns of buying behaviour also influence the channel structure. If customers typically buy in very *small quantities* and if demand is highly *seasonal* a long distribution channel involving several intermediaries will be more appropriate.

Product variables

Characteristics of the product also determine the channel structure. Channels should be as short as possible for highly *perishable products*. Heavy and *bulky products* have very high handling and shipping costs and the firm should try to minimise these by shipping the goods only in truck-load quantities to a limited number of places; the channel structure should also be short.

Short structures are also desirable for *complex and technical products* requiring extensive after-sales service and assistance in use. Similarly, for *innovative products* requiring aggressive promotion in the introductory stage of the PLC, a shorter channel will facilitate the development and control of promotion activities aiming at creating product acceptance by the market. Long channel structures will be more adequate, on the other hand, when products are highly standardised and when they have *low unit value*. In this latter case, the costs of distribution can be shared by many other products handled by the intermediaries.

> For example, it would be difficult to imagine the sales of packages of crisps by the Smiths Company to the consumer. Only by spreading the costs of distribution over the wide variety of products handled by wholesale and retail intermediaries is it possible to buy a packet of crisps at retail for BF50.

A manufacturer's channel choice is also influenced by the *extent of its product line*. The manufacturer with only one item may have to use wholesaling intermediaries, whereas it could go directly to retailers if it made several products which could be combined on a large scale. A retailer ordinarily cannot buy a truckload of washing machines alone, but it might buy a truckload of mixed appliances.

Company variables

The key variables here are the size and the financial capability of the producer. Large firms in general have large financial resources and therefore the capacity to assume several distribution tasks directly, thereby reducing their dependence on intermediaries. Several distribution activities, such as transportation and storage, imply fixed costs. Large companies are better able to bear these costs. On the other hand, the use of intermediaries implies a cost which is proportional to the volume of activity, since their compensation takes the form of commissions on actual sales revenue. Therefore, small firms will be inclined to have extensive recourse to intermediaries. In some cases, the entire output is sold under the retailer's brand. The disadvantage of this arrangement is that the producer is completely at the mercy of its one large retailer.

Other considerations are also important. For example, the lack of marketing expertise necessary to perform the distribution tasks may force the firm to use the services of intermediaries. This happens frequently when the firm is penetrating new or foreign markets. Also, high-technology companies built upon the engineering abilities of management often rely heavily on distributors to do the marketing job. A manufacturer may establish as short a channel as possible simply because it wants to *control the distribution* of its product, even though the cost of a more direct channel is higher.

Vertical marketing systems

If the adopted channel structure is indirect, some degree of *co-operation* and co-ordination must be achieved among the participants in the channel (see Exhibit 12.2). Two forms of vertical organisation can exist: conventional vertical structures and co-ordinated vertical structures, called vertical marketing systems:

Exhibit 12.2

Forms of Co-operation between Resellers

Retailer Co-operatives

Groups of independent retailers form their own co-operative chain organisation. Typically, they agree to concentrate their purchases by forming their own wholesale operations. In many cases, they also engage in joint advertising, promotion and merchandising programmes.

Wholesale-sponsored Voluntary Chains

Wholesalers organise voluntary chains by getting independent retailers to sign contracts in which they agree to standardise their selling practices and to purchase a certain proportion of their inventories from the wholesaler. This gives the wholesaler greater buying power in its dealings with manufacturers. Some voluntary chains also have a common brand store.

Franchise Systems

Franchising is a form of co-operation between two distinct enterprises in which a supplier (franchiser) grants a dealer (franchisee) the right to sell products in exchange for some type of consideration, such as some percentage of total sales. The franchiser helps to furnish equipment, buildings, management know-how and marketing assistance. The franchisee must agree to operate according to the rules of the franchiser.

Rack Jobbing

Rack jobbers perform purchasing and stocking function for retailers. Impulse products that have short life cycles (such as toys, books, records) may be supplied by rack jobbers to avoid the inconvenience to retailers of having to deal with unfamiliar products. They physically maintain the goods by refilling shelves, fixing displays and maintaining inventory records. Retailers have only to furnish space. Thus limited-service wholesaler usually operates on a consignment basis. The retailer is remunerated by some percentage of sales.

Cash-and-Carry Wholesalers

Cash-and-carry wholesalers are limited-service wholesalers that sell to customers who will pay cash and furnish transportation or pay extra to have products delivered. The middlemen usually handle a limited line of products such as groceries, construction materials, electrical supplies or office supplies.

- In a *conventional vertical structure* each level of the channel behaves independently as a separate business entity seeking to maximise its own profit, even if it is at the expense of the overall performance of the distribution channel. This is the traditional way in which a distribution network works, where no channel member has control over the others.

- In a *co-ordinated vertical structure*, the participants in the exchange process behave like partners and co-ordinate their activities in order to increase their bargaining power and to achieve operating economies and maximum market impact. In this type of vertical organisation, a channel member takes the initiative of co-ordination, be it the manufacturer, the wholesaler or the retailer.

Several forms of vertical marketing system have emerged. A distinction is usually made between corporate, contractual and administered vertical marketing systems.

Corporate vertical marketing systems

In corporate vertically integrated marketing systems a particular firm achieves co-ordination and control through corporate ownership. The firm owning and operating the other units of the channel may be a manufacturer, wholesaler or retailer. Firms such as Bata in shoes and Rodier in clothing own their own retail outlets. However, it is not always the manufacturer that controls the channel system through forward integration. Backward integration occurs when a retailer or a wholesaler assumes ownership of institutions that normally precede them in the channel. Sears in the USA, for example, and Marks & Spencer in the UK have ownership interest in several manufacturing firms that are important suppliers of their private brands.

Contractual vertical marketing systems

In a contractual vertical marketing system, independent firms operating at different levels of the channel co-ordinate their activities through legal contracts that spell out the rights and duties of each partner. The three basic types of contractual system are: retail co-operatives, wholesale-sponsored voluntary chains and franchise systems. Franchise systems have expanded the most in recent years. Their organisation is discussed in more detail in the next section.

Administered vertical marketing systems

In this third system, firms participating in the channel co-ordinate their activities through the informal guidance or influence of one of the channel members (and not through ownership or contractual agreements). The leading firm, usually the manufacturer, bases its influence on the brand or company reputation or managerial expertise. Companies like L'Oréal in cosmetics and Procter & Gamble in detergents are examples of firms having successfully achieved this form of co-operation.

Vertical marketing systems have become the dominant mode of distribution in the field of consumer marketing over the last twenty years. They can be viewed as a new form of competition, *channel system competition*, setting complete channels against other complete channels, as opposed to traditional vertical competition, opposing channel members at different levels of the same channel, that is retailers versus wholesalers, manufacturer versus wholesaler, and so on. Vertical marketing systems help eliminate the sources of conflict that exist in conventional vertical structures, and increase of the market impact of their activities.

● Market Coverage Strategies

If the decision made by the producer is to use intermediaries to organise the distribution of its products, the firm must then decide on the number of intermediaries to use at each channel level to achieve the market penetration objective. Three basic market coverage strategies are possible:

- Hollywood distributes its chewing gums wherever possible: in food stores, tobacconists, drug stores, through vending machines, and so on.

- Pierre Cardin distributes his dresses and women's suits in carefully selected clothing stores and tries to be present in the most elegant shops.

- VAG (Volkswagen Audi Group) distributes its cars through exclusive dealerships; each dealer has an exclusive territory and no other dealer is authorised to carry the VAG makes.

Hollywood is adopting an *intensive* distribution strategy, Cardin a *selective* strategy and VAG an *exclusive* strategy. The best strategy for a given product depends on the nature of the product itself, on the objective being pursued and on the competitive situation.

Consumer goods classifications

In the field of consumer goods, the choice of a particular market coverage strategy is largely determined by the shopping habits associated with the consumers of the distributed product. Consumer goods fall into four subgroups: convenience goods, shopping goods, specialty goods and unsought goods. The purchasing behaviour associated with these products varies primarily in the amount and type of effort consumers exert in buying these products.

Convenience goods

Convenience products are purchased with as little effort as possible, frequently and in small quantities. We have here a routine buying behaviour. Convenience goods can be further subdivided into staple goods, impulse goods and emergency goods:

- *Staple goods* are purchased on a regular basis and include most food items. Brand loyalty facilitates routine purchase and the goods must be pre-sold, namely through repetitive advertising.

- *Impulse goods* are purchased without any planning (crisps, magazines, sweets, and so on). These goods must be available in many places; the packaging and the in-store displays in supermarkets are important in the sale of these products.

- *Emergency goods* are those needed to fill an unexpected and urgent need. These goods are purchased immediately as the need emerges and therefore they must be available in many outlets.

For these product categories, the firm has practically no alternative. These products require an intensive market coverage. If the brand is not found at the point of sale, consumers will buy another brand and the sales occasion will be lost.

Shopping goods

Shopping goods are high perceived-risk products. For these products, consumers are willing to spend time and effort to shop around and to compare product alternatives on criteria such as quality, price, style, features, and so on. Examples include major appliances, furniture and clothing, that is expensive and infrequently bought products. Prospective buyers visit several stores before making a decision and sales personnel have an important role to play by providing information and advice. For shopping goods maximal market coverage is not required and a selective distribution system will be more appropriate, more especially as the co-operation of the retailer is necessary.

Specialty goods

Specialty goods are products with unique characteristics and sufficiently important to consumers that they make a special effort to discover them. Examples would include specific brands, fancy goods, exotic foods, deluxe clothing, sophisticated photographic equipment, and so on. For these products, prospective buyers do not proceed to comparisons; they search for the outlet carrying the wanted product. Brand loyalty or the distinctive features of the product are the determining factors. For specialty goods, retailers are especially important; thus the firms of such goods will tend to limit their distribution to obtain strong support from the retailers. A selective or exclusive distribution system is the best option for the producer.

Unsought goods

Unsought goods are products that consumers do not know about or know about but do not consider buying. Examples are heat pumps, smoke detectors, encyclopaedias and life insurance. Substantial selling efforts are required for those products. The co-operation of the intermediaries is indispensable, or the firm must adopt a direct marketing system.

Other factors must be taken into consideration in the choice of a market coverage strategy. As a general rule, selective and exclusive distribution systems imply a higher level of co-operation among distributors, a reduction of distribution costs for the supplier and a better control over sales operations. On the other hand in both cases, there is a voluntary limitation of the product retail availability. Thus potential buyers will have to actively search for the product. The firm must therefore maintain a good balance between the benefits and the demerits of each distribution system.

Intensive distribution

In an intensive distribution system, the firm seeks the maximum possible number of retailers to distribute its product, the largest number of storage points to ensure a maximum market coverage and the highest brand exposure. This strategy is appropriate for convenience goods, common raw materials and low-involvement services. The advantages of intensive distribution are to maximise product availability and to generate a large market share due to the brand's broad exposure to potential buyers. There are, however, significant disadvantages or risks associated with this strategy:

● The sales revenue generated by the different retailers varies greatly, while the contact cost is the same for each intermediary. If the firm receives many small orders from an intensive network of small retailers, *distribution* costs (order processing and shipping) can become extremely high and undermine the overall profitability.

⬤ When the product has an intensive distribution in multiple and very diversified sales points, it becomes difficult for the firm to control its marketing strategy: discount pricing, poor customer service and lack of co-operation from retailers are practices difficult to prevent.

⬤ Intensive distribution is hard to reconcile with a *brand image* building strategy and with a specific product positioning strategy due to the lack of control of the distributive network.

For these reasons, market-driven companies are induced to adopt a more selective distributive system once the brand awareness objectives have been achieved.

Selective distribution

In a selective distribution system, the producer uses fewer distributors than the total number of available distributors in a specific geographic area. It is an appropriate strategy for shopping goods that customers buy infrequently and compare for differences in price and product features.

A selective distribution may also be the result of the refusal from distributors to carry the product in their assortment. To have a selective distribution, the firm must decide the criteria upon which to select its intermediaries. Several criteria are commonly used:

⬤ The *size of the distributor*, measured by its sales revenue, is the most popular criterion. In the majority of markets, a small number of distributors achieve a significant share of total sales revenue. In the food sector, for instance, the concentration ratio is very high in Switzerland, the UK and Belgium, where the first 5 distributors in the food sectors account for 82, 53 and 52 per cent respectively of the total turnover (Nielsen, 1997). In these conditions, it is obviously unprofitable to contact all distributors.

⬤ The *quality of the service* provided is also an important criterion. Intermediaries are paid to perform a certain number of well-defined functions and some dealers or retailers are more efficient than others.

⬤ The *technical competence* of the dealer and the availability of up-to-date facilities, mainly for complex products where after-sales service is important, is a third important criterion.

In adopting a selective distribution system, the firm voluntarily agrees to limit the availability of its product in order to reduce its distribution costs and to gain better co-operation from the intermediaries. This co-operation can take various forms:

⬤ Participating in the advertising and promotion budget.
⬤ Accepting new products or unsought products requiring more selling effort.
⬤ Maintaining a minimum level of inventory.
⬤ Transferring information to the producer.
⬤ Providing better services to customers.

The *main risk* of a selective distribution system is to have insufficient market coverage. The producer must verify whether the market knows the distributors handling the brand or the product. If not, the reduced availability of the product could generate significant losses of sales opportunities. It may happen that the firm has in fact no alternative and is forced to maintain a certain degree of selectivity in its distributive network. For example:

● A new product which is not yet a proven success will be accepted by a retailer only if it receives an exclusive right to carry the product in its territory.

● If the assortment is large because the consumer must be able to choose among several product forms (design, colour, size), selectivity will be necessary, otherwise the expected sales revenue will be too low to motivate the retailer.

● If the after-sales service implies long and costly training of the dealers, selectivity will be necessary to reduce the costs.

● If the firm decides to adopt a selective distribution system, it is important to realise that this decision implies the adoption of a 'short' indirect distribution channel. It is very unlikely indeed that wholesalers will agree to voluntarily limit their field of operation simply to meet the strategic objectives of the producer.

Exclusive distribution and franchise systems

In an exclusive distribution system, the manufacturer relies on only one retailer or dealer to distribute its product in a given geographic territory. In turn, the exclusive dealer agrees not to sell any competing brand within the same product category. Exclusive distribution is useful when a company wants to differentiate its product on the basis of high quality, prestige or excellent customer service. The close co-operation with exclusive dealers facilitates the implementation of the producer's customer service programmes. The advantages and disadvantages of exclusive distribution are the same as in selective distribution, but amplified. A particular form of exclusive distribution is franchising.

Franchising is a contractual, vertically integrated marketing system which refers to a comprehensive method of distributing goods and services. It involves a continuous and contractual relationship in which a *franchiser* provides a licensed privilege to do business and assistance in organising, training, merchandising, management and other areas in return for a specific consideration from the *franchisee*. Thus, the franchisee agrees to pay an initial fee, plus royalties calculated on the sales revenue, for the right to use a well-known trademarked product or service and to receive continual assistance and services from the franchiser. In fact, the franchisee is buying a proven success from the franchiser.

Types of franchise systems

The franchiser may occupy any position within the channel; therefore there are four basic types of franchise system:

● The *manufacturer–retailer* franchise is exemplified by franchised automobile dealers and franchised service stations. Singer in the USA, Pingouin and Yves Rocher in France are good examples.

- The *manufacturer–wholesaler* franchise is exemplified by the soft drink companies like Coca Cola and 7-Up who sell the soft drink syrups they manufacture to franchised wholesalers who, in turn, carbonate, bottle, sell and distribute to retailers.

- The *wholesaler–retailer* franchise is exemplified by Rexall Drug Stores, by Christianssens in toys and Unic and Disco in food.

- The *service sponsor–retailer* franchise is exemplified by Avis, Hertz, McDonald's, Midas and Holiday Inn.

The faster growing franchises include business and professional services, fast food, restaurants, car and truck rentals, and home and cleaning maintenance.

Characteristics of a good franchise

A good franchise must be above all a *transferable proven success*, which can be replicated in another territory or environment. According to Sallenave (1979, p. 11), a good franchise must:

1. Be related to the distribution of a *high quality* product or service.
2. Meet a *universal need* or want which is not country or region-specific.
3. Be a *proven success* in franchiser-owned and -operated pilot units which serve as models for the other franchisees.
4. Ensure the full transfer of *know-how* and to provide the training of the franchisee in the methods of doing business and modes of operation.
5. Offer to the franchisees *initial and continuing service* to gain immediate market acceptance and to improve modes of operation.
6. Have a regular *reporting and information system* which permits effective monitoring of the performance and collection of market information.
7. Specify initial franchise *fees* and the royalty fees based on the gross value of a franchisee's sales volume (generally 5 per cent).
8. Involve the franchisee in the *management* and development of the franchise system.
9. Specify *legal provisions* for termination, cancellation and renewal of the franchise agreement, as well as for the repurchase of the franchise.

Franchise systems constitute a viable alternative to completely integrated corporate vertical marketing systems. In a franchise system, *funds are provided by the franchisees*, who invest in the stores and in the facilities. From the franchiser's point of view, the establishment of franchised dealers is an ideal means to achieve rapid national or international distribution for its products or services without committing large funds and while keeping the control of the system through contractual agreements.

John Y. Brown, President of Kentucky Fried Chicken Corporation, has stated that it would have required $450 million for his firm to have established its first 2700 stores if they would have been company-owned. This sum was simply not available to his firm during the initial stages of its proposed expansion. The use of capital made available from franchisees, however, made the proposed expansion possible. (McGuire, 1971, p. 7)

Thus a franchise system is *an integrated marketing system controlled by the franchiser but financed by the franchisees*. A successful franchise is a partnership in which the mutual interests of both franchiser and franchisees are closely interdependent.

Benefits to the franchiser

The motivations of the franchiser for creating and developing a franchise system are the following:

1. To acquire funds without diluting control of the marketing system.
2. To keep high flexibility in the use of the capital collected for developing the system.
3. To avoid the fixed overhead expenses associated with distribution through company-owned branch units or stores.
4. To co-operate with independent business people, the franchisees, who are more likely to work hard at developing their markets than salaried employees.
5. To co-operate with local business people well accepted and integrated in the local community or in the foreign country.
6. To develop new sources of income based on existing know-how and marketing expertise.
7. To achieve faster sales development thanks to the snowball effect generated by the franchising of a successful idea.
8. To benefit from economies of scale with the development of the franchise system.

Franchisers provide both initial and continuous services to their franchisees (McGuire, 1971). *Initial services* include: market survey and site selection; facility

Table 12.3   Franchising in Europe

Countries	Number of franchisers	Number of franchisees	Turnover in billion Ecu	Number of jobs
Germany	530	22,000	14.6	230,000
Austria	210	3,000	1.6	40,000
Belgium	170	3,500	2.4	28,500
Denmark	98	2,000	1.0	40,000
Spain	288	13,161	6.8	69,000
Finland	76	1,464	1.2	14,000
France	470	23,750	9.2	355,000
UK	474	25,700	8.9	222,700
Hungary	220	5,000	2.6	45,000
Norway	125	3,500	3.0	
Holland	345	11,910	9.2	100,000
Portugal	220	2,000	1.0	35,000
Sweden	230	9,150	5.7	71,000
Czech Republic	40	80	0.83	760
Yugoslavia	18	620	0.56	2,810
TOTAL	3,950	150,225	80.59	1,303,928

Source: Fédération européenne de la franchise (1997).

design and layout; lease negotiation advice; financing advice; operating manuals; management training programmes and franchisee employee training. *Continuous services* include field supervision; merchandising and promotional materials; management and employee retraining; quality inspection; national advertising; centralised purchasing; market data and guidance; auditing and record keeping; management reports; and group insurance plans.

The franchise system is present in almost all business fields, and total franchise system sales have grown dramatically during the last decade. The number of franchise companies and franchisees active in each of the major markets of the EU is summarised in Table 12.3.

Benefits to franchisees

From the perspective of the potential franchisee, the most important appeal is to benefit from the franchiser's reputation of quality and corporate image. Franchising has several other strong appeals which explain the success of this distribution arrangement:

1. Franchising enables an individual to enter a business which would be prohibitively expensive if the individual tried to go it alone.
2. The amount of uncertainty is reduced, since the business idea has been successfully tested.
3. The extensive services provided by the franchiser, both initial and continuous, reduce the risks of the operation.
4. Franchising offers better purchasing power, access to better sites and the support of national advertising.
5. The introduction of new products and the constant rejuvenation of the product portfolio are made possible.
6. Managerial assistance in marketing and finance is provided.
7. The opportunity is provided for individuals to operate as independent business people within a large organisation.

Franchising is a very flexible organisation and many variants exist. *Three basic rules* must be met to have a successful arrangement:

- The will to work as partners.
- The right to mutual control.
- The value of the business idea.

This last condition is crucial. Franchising will work only if the business idea is a proven success. It is not a solution for a firm to declare itself a franchiser if there is no proven success.

Communication Strategies in the Channel

Gaining support and co-operation from independent intermediaries is a key success factor for the implementation of the firm's marketing objectives. To obtain this co-operation, two very distinct communication strategies can be adopted by the firm: a push strategy or a pull strategy. A third alternative is a combination of the two.

Push strategies

In a push communication strategy, the bulk of the marketing effort is devoted to incentives directed to wholesalers and retailers to induce them to co-operate with the firm, to carry the brands in their range, to keep a minimum level of inventory, to display the products and to give them enough visibility on their shelf spaces. The objective is to win *voluntary co-operation* by offering attractive terms of trade, that is larger margins, quantity discounts, local or in-store advertising, promotional allowances, in-store sampling, and so on. Personal selling and personal communication are the key marketing instruments here. The role of the sales representatives and of the merchandisers will be particularly important. Table 12.4 lists a variety of incentives the firm can use to increase the number of channel members.

Table 12.4 Incentives for motivating channel members

Functional performance	Examples of channel incentives
■ *Increased purchases or carry large inventories*	Large margins, exclusive territories, buy-in promotions, quantity discounts, buy-back allowances, free goods, shelf-stocking programmes
■ *Increased personal selling effort*	Sales training, instructional materials, incentive programmes for channel members' sales people
■ *Increased local promotional effort* – Local advertising	Co-operative advertising, advertising allowance; print, radio, TV ads for use by local retailers
– Increased display space	Promotion allowances tied to shelf space
– In-store promotions	Display racks and signs, in-store demonstrations, in-store sampling
■ *Improved customer service*	Service training programmes, instructional materials, high margins on replacement parts, liberal labour cost allowances for warranty service

Source: Boyd and Walker (1990).

A programme of incentives is indispensable to get the support of intermediaries. The larger their negotiation power, the more difficult it will be for the firm to obtain the support of distributors. In markets where distribution is highly concentrated, it is the intermediary who specifies the conditions for carrying the brand. The risk of an exclusive push strategy is the absence of countervailing power and the dependence of the firm on the intermediary who controls the access to the market.

The only alternative for the firm is the adoption of a direct marketing system which completely bypasses intermediaries. This is a costly operation, however, since all distribution tasks must then be assumed by the firm. Recent developments in communication technologies present new opportunities, however. The potential of direct or interactive marketing will be discussed in the final section of this chapter.

Pull strategies

When adopting a pull strategy, the manufacturer focuses its communication efforts on the end-user, bypassing intermediaries and trying to build company demand directly among potential customers in the target segment. The communication objective is to create strong customer demand and brand loyalty among consumers in order to pull the brand through the distribution channel, forcing the intermediaries to carry the brand to meet consumers' demand.

To achieve these objectives, the manufacturer will spend the largest proportion of its communication budget on media advertising, consumer promotions and direct marketing efforts aimed at winning end-customer preferences. If this branding policy is successful, the manufacturer has the power to influence channel participants and to induce them to carry the brand, since a substantial sales volume will be achieved. The strategic objective is to neutralise the bargaining power of the intermediary who could block access to the market.

> Procter & Gamble generally adopts a pull strategy in its new product launching strategies. However, the consumer advertising campaign starts only when the new brand has achieved almost 100 per cent distribution at retail. It goes without saying that such a result can be achieved only because P&G's sales reps are in position to demonstrate to retailers the advertising that will be organised to support the new product market introduction. Thus, retailers are willing to co-operate with the company.

Pull strategies imply in general large financial resources to cover the costs of brand image advertising campaigns. These costs are fixed overhead expenses, while the costs of a push strategy are proportional to volume and therefore easier to bear, particularly for a small firm.

In fact, a pull strategy must be viewed as a long-term investment. The goal of the firm is to create a capital of goodwill, a *brand equity*, around the company name or around the brand. A strong brand image is an asset for the firm and is the best argument for obtaining support and co-operation from intermediaries.

In practice, these two communication strategies are used in combination, and it is hard to imagine a market situation where no incentives would be used to motivate intermediaries. With the development of marketing expertise and the increased cost of personal selling, the trend among market-driven companies is to reinforce branding policies and pull communication strategies. As the average cost of a call to a customer made by a sales person keeps on increasing, the selectivity of mass media tends to improve and therefore to lower the unit cost of a contact through advertising.

● Distribution Cost Analysis

The distribution cost is measured by the difference between the unit sales price paid by the end-user and the unit cost paid to the producer by the first buyer. Thus, the distribution margin measures the *added value* brought by the distribution channel. If several intermediaries participate in the distribution process, the distribution margin is equal to the sum of the different distributors' margins. The margin of a particular distributor is equal to the difference between its selling price and its purchase cost. The two definitions coincide when there is only one intermediary in the channel.

Trade margins

A trade margin is often expressed as a percentage. This is sometimes confusing, since the margin percentage can be computed on the basis of purchase cost (C) or on the

Table 12.5 Definitions of trade margins

■ Trade margins:

Trade margin = Selling price – Purchase cost

$$D = P - C$$

■ Trade margin as percentage:

'of selling price' (discount)

$$D^* = \frac{P - C}{P}$$

'of purchase cost' (mark-up)

$$D^0 = \frac{P - C}{C}$$

■ Conversion rules:

$$D^* = \frac{D^0}{1 + D^0}$$

$$D^0 = \frac{D^0}{1 - D^0}$$

basis of selling price (P). The trade margin (D) is then referred to as a 'mark-up' or as a 'discount'. The conversion rules are presented in Table 12.5.

Suppose a retailer purchases an item for £10 and sells it at a price of £20, that is, at a £10 margin. What is the retailer's margin percentage? As a percentage of the selling price, it is

£10/£20 × 100 = 50 per cent

As a percentage of cost, it is

£10/£10 × 100 = 100 per cent

Trade margins are usually determined on the basis of selling price, but practices do vary between firms and industries.

Trade margins are based on a distributor's place in the channel and represent payment for performing certain distribution tasks. In some cases, several margins are quoted to distributors, as illustrated in Table 12.6. The manufacturer's problem of suggesting a list price, that is the final suggested price of the product, is more complex, as the number of intermediaries between the producer and the final consumer increases.

Comparison of distribution costs

The distribution margin compensates the distribution functions and tasks assumed by the intermediaries in the channel. If some of these distribution tasks are assumed directly by the producer, it will have to support the organisation and the costs implied. By way of illustration, Table 12.7 shows a cost comparison of two indirect distribution channels: a 'long' indirect channel involving two intermediaries, whole-salers and retailers, and a 'short' indirect channel involving only retailers, the whole-saling function being assumed by the manufacturer.

In the *indirect long channel*, most of the physical distribution tasks (storage and transportation) are taken on by wholesalers and the distribution costs are largely proportional to the rate of activity and covered by the wholesalers' distributors' margin. The manufacturer has to maintain a minimum sales administration unit and the overhead costs are minimised. In this type of conventional vertical marketing

Table 12.6   Developing a price structure

- Trade margins are based on a distributor's place in the channel and represent payment for performing certain distribution tasks.
- Prices are usually quoted to distributors as a series of numbers depending on the number of functions performed.
- In the case of large retail chains, we would have the following quotation:

'30, 10, 5, and 2/10, net 30'

The first three numbers represent successive discounts from the list price:

- 30 per cent: as functional discount for the position the retailer occupies in the channel;
- 10 per cent: as compensation for performing the storage function, usually performed by the wholesaler;
- 5 per cent: as an allowance for the retailer's efforts to promote the product through local advertising;
- 2/10: as cash discount, 2 per cent, as reward for payment of an invoice within 10 days;
- Net 30: the length of the credit period; if the payment is not made within 10 days, the entire invoice must be paid in full within 30 days.

Source: Adapted from Monroe (1979, p. 169).

organisation, however, the producer is dependent on the goodwill of the distributors and has only limited control on the sales organisation. To offset this handicap, the producer can create its own sales force (merchandisers) to stimulate sales at the retailers' level and also to use mass media advertising to create brand awareness and brand preference among end-users through a 'pull communication' strategy.

Examining now the cost structure of the *indirect short channel*, one observes that overheads or fixed costs represent the largest share of total distribution costs. It means that the manufacturer has to support the costs of the physical distribution functions and organise a network of warehouses plus a much more extensive sales administration unit. The financial costs involved in inventory management and the customers' accounts receivable are also completely assumed by the producer, as well as the selling function.

> By adopting a selective distribution strategy, the firm has to contact at least once a month 2500 retailers. One sales representative can perform on average 4.8 calls per day during 250 working days per year. The required sales force is therefore 25 sales representatives to achieve the market coverage objective.

Thus, adopting an indirect short distribution channel implies a major financial risk for the producer. The benefits of this strategy, however, are better control of the commercial organisation and a closer contact with the end-users.

The two cost equations are compared in Figure 12.5. One sees that the costs of distribution are the same at a certain level – the break-even level – of the total sales revenue. If the expected sales revenues are the same in both cases, the 'longer' channel will be preferred for any turnover inferior to the break-even level and conversely for any higher turnover. This observation is in line with the common observation that small companies tend to favour long distribution channels, their financial capacities being in general too weak to support the costs of a short distribution channel.

Table 12.7 Distribution cost analysis of two distribution channels

Distribution tasks	Indirect long channel		Indirect short channel	
	Cost	Comments	Cost	Comments
Transport		■ M→W: in charge of M – more expensive ■ W→R: in charge of R – cheaper	–	■ M→warehouses: in charge of M – cheaper ■ warehouses→R: in charge of R – more expensive
Assortment	Covered by the wholesaler margin: 16% of the manufacturer's sales revenue	■ in charge of W and R: complete assortment	–	■ in charge of R: risk of incomplete assortment
Storage		■ warehouses: in charge of W ■ stocks: in charge of W	$750 000 2.5% of sales revenue	■ 7 warehouses (fewer) ■ 4 rotations (rate 10%)
		■ customer in charge of W	1.25% of sales revenue	■ payment at 45 days (rate 10%)
Contact		■ in charge of W – risk of inertia	$500 000	■ 25 sales people at $20 000 more dynamic (push strategy)
Information	2.5% of sales revenue	■ push strategy on W and R	1.5% of sales revenue	■ pull strategy
Sales administration	$30 000	■ principally in charge of W; small team	$200 000	■ principally in charge of M; large team
Total cost	$30 000 + 0.185 (sales revenue)	■ cost proportional to the activity rate	$1 450 000 +0.0525 (sales revenue)	■ largest part of cost is fixed

M = Manufacturer   R = Retailer   W = Wholesaler

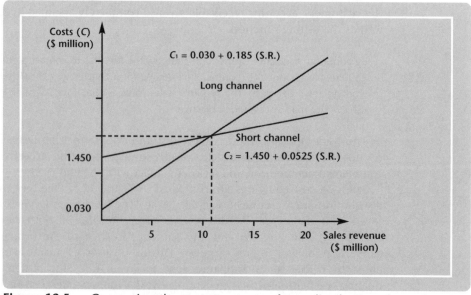

Figure 12.5 Comparing the cost structures of two distribution channels

In general, the sales revenue expectations are not the same for each distribution channel. The profitability rate of each channel will be determined as follows:

$$R = \frac{\text{Sales revenue} - \text{Distribution costs}}{\text{Distribution costs}}$$

where R is an estimate of the expected rate of return when all the costs are taken into account for each channel. This quantitative indicator must of course be interpreted with care and with due consideration of the more 'qualitative' factors discussed above.

The Retailer's Strategic Marketing

Significant changes have occurred during the 1990s in the way retailers, and in particular large retailers, perceive their roles in the exchange process. Traditionally, retailers have limited their role to intermediaries, acting rather passively between the producer and the consumer by simply performing the physical tasks of distribution and by making the goods available to consumers in the condition, place and time required by them. From this rather passive role, intermediaries are increasingly adopting an innovative and active role, thereby modifying the balance of power between manufacturers and retailers.

This evolution has coincided with significant socio-cultural changes in affluent economies which have induced retailers to redefine their roles as economic agents and to adopt a more market-driven perspective. From a traditional 'shop' or 'in-house' orientation, retailers are now discovering strategic marketing and are moving away from a business philosophy where the marketing function is confined to the physical distribution tasks and to the purchasing function.

Major changes in the retailing sector

The major changes of the macro-environment have been described in Chapter 2. In many West European countries, retailing has become a mature industry, and several indicators confirm this observation:

- Keeping pace with the growth of the economy, the retailing industry has experienced *zero or minimal growth* for several years, particularly in the food sector. The share of large retail chains has reached a plateau and is even declining in some markets.

- The *proliferation of retailers* has created over-capacity, and today a retailer must compete against a crowd of competitors, not only in the food sector, but also in sectors like clothing, household appliances and even in the newest product categories like home computers.

- *Competition* is intensive and based almost exclusively on price for all the branded products. In most product categories, consumers can buy exactly the same product or brand at a discount store at bargain prices as they could at a department store at its full price.

- In several European countries, a *high level of concentration* is observed among large distributors. Table 12.8 displays the concentration ratios of the top three distributors in the food sector. These distributors have substantial purchasing power (and bargaining power), reinforced recently by the creation of joint purchasing units at the European level.

Table 12.8 Market share in the food sector of the first three distributors in Europe, 1995

Countries	Groups	Market share (%)
Sweden	Ica, KF, D Group	95
Denmark	FDB, Dansk Supermarket, Dagrofa	63
Belgium	Gib, Delhaize, Aldi	58
Austria	BML, Spar, Adeg	56
Germany	Rai, Aidera, Aldin	47
Netherlands	A.Hein, Super Unie, Vendes	47
United Kingdom	Tesco, Sainsbury, Asda	45
Ireland	Dunnes, Power Super, Super Quinn	43
France	Intermarché, Leclerc, Carrefour	43
Spain	Pryca, Continente, Alcampo	20
Greece	Marinopoulos, Sklavenitis, Veropoulos	17
Italy	Coop, Végé, GS	11

Source: Nielsen/*LSA*, No. 1495, 6 June 1996.

All these characteristics – maturity, over-capacity, concentration and price competition – are typical of commodity markets, suggest that the retailing industry has become *commoditised*. This conclusion must be qualified, however, by country and by product category. Several factors explain this evolution:

● During the 1960s, *manufacturers' brand names* became prominent in a broadening range of product categories, and more and more retailers began featuring these brands. Thus, the presence of the brand in the retailer's assortment became the determining choice criterion in choosing a particular store. In the process, retailers abdicated much of their stores' marketing and positioning responsibilities to the manufacturers.

● This situation has stimulated the development of *discount stores*, who sell well-known brands exclusively on bargain pricing with minimum services.

● The proliferation of slightly differentiated brands and the adoption of *intensive distribution strategies* by manufacturers have also contributed to reducing store differentiation, most stores carrying the same assortments of brands.

● Retailers once had the major responsibility for *after-sales service*, and choosing a retailer was important when one bought products like appliances and consumer electronics. Now consumers can get after-sales service for most products independently of the retailer, and this type of store differentiation is also waning.

● The lack of customer services at retail to improve productivity has generated an important *self-production of services* by consumers which contribute to increase the 'total price' of mass distribution (de Maricourt, 1988).

● Finally, the tremendous growth in *bank credit cards* also contributes to undermine store loyalty. Consumers no longer choose a store because they have established credit there: bank cards entitle customers to buy items almost anywhere they please.

These factors have all contributed to reducing store differentiation and loyalty, to killing the concept of *shopping for enjoyment* and to modifying consumer's buying behaviour, particularly for working housewives attracted by other more rewarding and stimulating activities.

Changes in consumers' retail buying behaviour

Retail consumers today behave differently, not only because of the social and demographic changes described above, but also because they are more educated and professional in their purchase decisions. As already discussed in Chapter 2, one of the biggest changes is the rise of the *smart shopper*. Being a smart shopper implies several capabilities:

● Being informed about the products one wants to buy and being able to compare and choose independently of brand, advertising, store and sales person's recommendations. It means finding the best value for money.

● Being able to separate the product features and the benefits and services provided by a store to augment the product value. Smart shoppers distinguish between what is inherent in the product and can therefore be obtained anywhere they buy it, and what a specific store adds to the purchase. They routinely compare stores as well as brands on this basis.

● Being able to recognise that brands have become increasingly similar. They will not necessarily choose a well-known brand over a less-well-known one simply because it is familiar or because of its image. The product must also be viewed as offering superior value.

In addition, for many consumers, and for a broadening range of goods, shopping is no longer viewed as fun or recreational, but rather as a tedious task to be performed as economically and efficiently as possible. In their search for value, an expanding group of consumers seek not only good merchandise but savings of time and effort as well.

Differentiation strategies of the retailer

Confronted with these changes, the retailer has to review his traditional strategic positioning by redefining his *store concept* and by adopting a positioning which provides unique value to consumers. The adoption of a store differentiation strategy becomes a necessity in a market place where retailing has become commoditised. Thus the concepts of strategic marketing developed for product marketing can be directly applied to retail marketing.

The multi-attribute concept of a store

From the consumer standpoint, the store concept can be viewed as a package of benefits and the *multi-attribute product concept* described in Chapter 4 is useful here to help design the store concept. Six different characteristics or attributes can be identified in a store, which constitute as many action variables for the retailer:

- *Location*. This defines the territorial coverage or trading area within which to develop business relations. The alternatives are downtown location, community, suburban or regional shopping centres.

- *Assortment*. The number of product lines that will be sold, which implies decisions on the product assortment breadth (narrow or wide) and product assortment depth (shallow or deep) for each product line.

- *Pricing*. The general level of prices (high or low gross margins) and the use of loss-leaders, discount pricing and price promotions.

- *Services*. The extent of the service mix. A distinction can be made between pre-purchase services (telephone orders, shopping hours, fitting rooms, and so on), post-purchase services (delivery, alterations, wrapping, and so on) and ancillary services (credit, restaurants, baby sitting, travel agencies, and so on); see de Maricourt (1988).

- *Time*. The time required for a shopping trip. Proximity is the key factor, but also opening and closing hours, accessibility, ease of selection, fast completion of transaction and queuing time at checkout counters.

Exhibit 12.3

Two Examples of New Stores Concepts

Renting with purchase option

The store brand of the British Group Thorn, Crazy George's, offers consumers immediate possession of household durable goods through a system of renting combined with a purchase option. The clients hold the goods from the time of a first, very modest, down-payment, but have the ownership title only after several years of weekly instalments corresponding to a total cost increase of 50, 60 or 70 per cent compared to a full cash payment. Crazy George's promotes only well known brands and offers a full after-sales service. The buyer is served and serviced as in any other store. If the modest payments that have to be paid every week become too heavy a load, the buyer can discontinue the agreement at no cost, temporarily or definitely.

Second-hand trade

Based in France for two or three years, Cash Converters, the giant Australian distributor specialising in barters, already has 63 stores operating as sales-deposits outlets, targeted to people experiencing a difficult economic time and wishing to be paid cash when they want to get rid of some of their goods. A miserable price but cash paid. Cash Converters re-purchase goods at about 25 per cent of the initial price and resell them as second-hand goods at 50 per cent. In 1997, the total turnover of the chain reached FF200 million. The stores are full during weekends and the objective is to have 200 operating stores by the year 2000.

Source: Le Monde, 23 January 23 p. 118.

● *Atmosphere*. The layout of the store, but also the light, the space the musical ambience, the look and the interior decoration, and so on.

These store attributes are used by consumers when they compare retail stores. It is up to the retailer to define a store concept based on some innovative combination of these attributes and which constitutes a package of benefits differentiated from the competition (For example, see Exhibit 12.3).

Store positioning strategies

The positioning strategies to be adopted by the retailer vary with sectors. Retail outlets can be classified according two dimensions: the level of the gross margin (high or low) and the type of benefit sought by the consumer: symbolic or functional. We thus have a two-dimensional map as shown in Figure 12.6, which describes four distinct positioning strategies:

● Among the functional products sold with a high gross margin (upper left quadrant), we will have the *specialty stores* having selected or specialised assortments in food or in audio-visuals, computers, tools, and so on.

● Among the functional products with low margins are the 'everyday' food products sold in *supermarkets and superstores*, low price furniture (Ikea), do-it-yourself centres, cheap audio-visual goods, and so on.

● The symbolic products with high margins are sold through *prestige specialty stores*, like fashion stores (Benetton, Rodier), jewellery, watches, and so on.

● Symbolic products sold at low prices, these are distributed through *discount stores* selling national brands at prices lower than those prevailing in conventional stores.

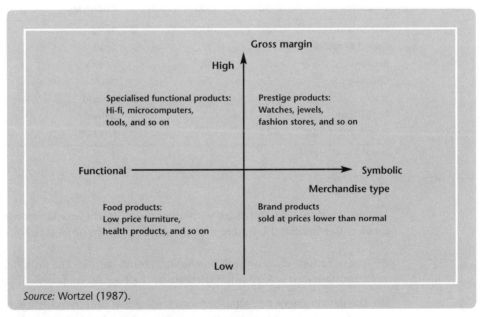

Source: Wortzel (1987).

Figure 12.6　Retail positioning strategies

Three basic store positioning strategies can be adopted by the retailer: product differentiation, service and personality augmentation, and price leadership:

● A *product differentiation* strategy is based on offering products that are intrinsically different, for example different brands or different styles from those in the same product category offered by other stores.

● In a *service and personality augmentation* strategy, a retailer offers products that are intrinsically similar to those offered by competitors, but adds specific services and personality to differentiate the store.

● A *price leadership* strategy means offering the same products as the competition at lower prices.

Several alternative positioning strategies can be contemplated by the retailer who has under his control several action variables. Thus, a strategic marketing plan can be elaborated and implemented through an action programme consistent with the chosen objectives to gain a sustainable competitive advantage over competition.

Private label development

Differentiation strategies based on private brand development have been successfully implemented by large retailers during the last decade. In Belgium, for instance, private labels' market shares increased from 11.4 per cent in 1983 to 19.8 per cent in 1992 (Nielsen, 1997). Private labels' market shares in the other European countries are presented in Table 12.9. See also the McKinsey study (Glémet and Mira, 1993a, b).

Table 12.9 Market share of private labels in Europe (%)

Countries	1992	1995	Countries	1992	1995
Switzerland	42	41	Sweden	10.7	11
United Kingdom	33	37	Spain	8	10
Belgium	16	22	Austria	7	9
Germany	17	22	Italy	4	7
France	15	18	Finland	5.4	n.d.
Netherlands	16	16	Ireland	3.6	n.d.
European average	12.6	–	Greece	3	3

Source: Nielsen (1997).

This development coincides with the growth of the market power held by large retailers (see Exhibit 12.4), due namely to three groups of factors:

● the creation of powerful *purchasing centres at the European level*, which has contributed to a substantial increase in the bargaining power of large retailers;

● the development of *centralised warehousing and delivery systems* which has created a physical barrier between the supplier and the local supermarket;

Exhibit 12.4

Major Retailers Ranked by Net Sales

Rank	Company	Core market	Core retail sector	Net sales ($ millions)
1.	Wal-Mart	US	Mixed retailer	117,958
2.	Sears	US	Variety/dept store	41,296
3.	Metro	Germany	Mixed retailer	32,855
4.	Rewe	Germany	Grocery	31,648
5.	J C Penney	US	Mail order variety store	30,546
6.	Aldi	Germany	Grocery discounter	30,287
7.	Tengelman	Germany	Mixed retailer	30,266
8.	Carrefour[1]	France	Grocery	29,387
9.	Tesco	UK	Grocery	26,970
10.	Ito-Yokado	Japan	Department store	26,080
11.	Ahold[1]	Netherlands	Grocery	25,932
12.	Intermarché	France	Grocery	24,601
13.	Daiei	Japan	Mixed retailer	24,349
14.	Auchan	France	Grocery	24,132
15.	J Sainsbury	UK	Grocery	23,770
16.	Safeway	US	Grocery	22,484
17.	Costco	US	Mixed retailer	21,874
18.	Promodes[1]	France	Grocery	19,213
19.	Jusco	Japan	Mixed retailer	18,533
20.	Pinault-Printemps-Redoute	France	Mail-order	15,482

Source: Euromonitor International: quoted in *Marketing News* (1999), 25 October, p. 3.
1. On 30 August, 1999, Carrefour merged with the Promodes Group.

- the generalisation of *electronic point of sales* (EPOS), a computerised system for recording sales at retail checkouts which give the retailer instant information on each product sold at the retail outlet.

As the result of these technological changes, one observes a shift in the balance of power between suppliers and retailers.

This increased market power has induced retailers to develop their own branding policies in order to improve their profitability. This private label strategy goes back more than twenty years in Western Europe, but it has been gaining a new dimension recently. Several types of private labels exist in the European market:

- *Store brand names*. The proposition here is to provide the same performance as national brands, but at more moderate prices. Typical examples are Delhaize, St Michael from Marks & Spencer, and Casino. The brand name is that of the chain and is used as a way of furthering the store's image.

● *Generic brands*. The products are unsophisticated, presented in simple package at lowest prices and without brand name. Typically the white products from GB in Belgium.

● *Invented brand names*. They are presented as regular brands by the retailer but they are distributed exclusively in the stores of the chain. Many retail chains sell invented brands such as Beaumont at Monoprix, O'Lacy at Asko and Saint Goustain and Chabrior at Intermarché.

● *First price*. Their role is to stave off the invasion of the hard discounters, namely Aldi. The name of the store is not mentioned.

It is worth noting that the development of private labels (see Table 12.10) has been stimulated by the growth of the 'first price' brands and by the dynamism of hard discounters like Aldi and Lidl (Germany and Denmark) and Kwik-Save (UK) which operate through warehouse retail stores.

Table 12.10 Compared perceptions of distributors' and manufacturers' brands in Europe

In %	Average	Germany	Spain	France	Italy	UK
PRICE						
Higher	3	3	2	2	3	1
Same	19	12	16	26	29	13
Lower	78	85	83	72	68	86
QUALITY						
Better	5	2	6	3	7	4
Same	78	90	73	78	71	77
Lower	17	8	21	19	22	18
TRUST						
More	6	3	7	4	10	5
Same	74	84	71	73	66	74
Less	21	12	22	23	24	21

Source: Secodip, IGD Europanel (1994).
See also *LSA* (1997).

This offensive of private labels has been fruitful and, as a consequence, national brands' loyalty is decreasing and suppliers are forced to reduce their price differentials.

In the USA, the Roper Organisation regularly measures brand loyalty. In 1988, 56 per cent of respondents claimed to know which brands to buy in entering the store; this figure dropped to 53 per cent in 1990 and to 46 per cent in 1991.

Marlboro's market share in the US dropped from 30 to 22 per cent, largely in favour of generic brands whose market share reached more than 30 per cent. To stop this erosion, Philip Morris reduced its price by 22 per cent. (The Economist, 1993)

It seems however that, in France and in the UK, private labels are stagnating at the current level reached. In a survey carried out in France by *LSA* (May, 1997), only 24 per cent of the consumers interviewed were in favour of an extension of the range of private brands in their usual store and 70 per cent were opposed, a result similar to that observed in 1995.

Exhibit 12.5

Who Produces Distributors' Brands?

Suppliers of private labels are generally small or medium size companies who do not have a strong national brand but who have a competitive and flexible production capacity. They are not the only ones to produce private labels. Large international groups also participate more or less recently, like McCain, BSN, Cadbury Schweppes, Kraft Jacobs Suchard, Yoplait, and so on (*Le Monde*, February, 1995). Some companies, like Northern Foods or Hillsdown in the UK, produce exclusively for distributors' brands, a targeted market segment in which they have expanded. Finally, small companies also specialise in the production of low price products for distributors.

Source: Santi (1997, p. 67).

Strategic objectives of distributors

Retailers' marketing strategies tend to become more sophisticated. They do not simply imitate existing products but develop new product concepts targeted to well defined market segments and which are then produced by international manufacturers specialising in private labels (see Exhibit 12.5). For retailers, three objectives can be pursued with private labels:

- To reduce power of manufacturers by reducing their volume and their brand franchise and to eliminate small competitors.
- To enhance category margins since private labels can deliver 5–10 margin points more than national brands.
- To provide a differentiated product to build the retailer's image.

This last objective is now gaining in importance among the most sophisticated and dynamic retailers.

As illustrated by Figure 12.7, different price/quality positioning strategies can be adopted by the distributor:

- *Same quality, cheaper*. It is the most frequent strategy adopted for store brands: to propose a level of quality similar to that offered by the leading national brand but at a price 15 to 20 per cent lower.

- *Lower quality, cheaper*. This strategy is based on the invented brand names and on the generic brands: to propose a lower level of quality in simplified packages at a price 30 to 40 per cent lower than the prices charged by national brands.

- *Better quality, same price*. To propose a level of quality higher than national brands at the same price. This positioning strategy is adopted by Sainsbury in the UK for a certain number of product categories, using invented brand names exclusively found in Sainsbury stores.

- *Better quality, higher price*. A less frequent strategy, adopted by distributors targeting the high end of the market with home-made or handicraft products (see Exhibit 12.6).

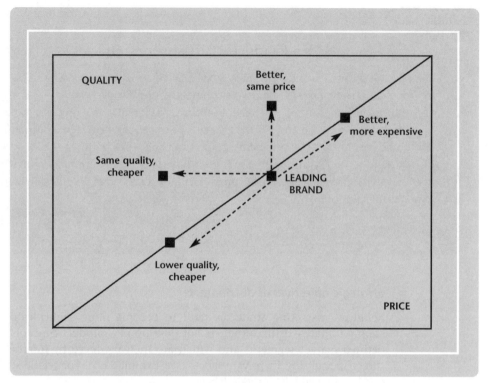

Figure 12.7　　Price quality ratios for private labels

As a result of these aggressive price label strategies, there is general pressure on prices. Within large supermarket chains, three types of brand are observed within a same product category:

Exhibit 12.6

Private Labels and the Euro

In, Portugal, Spain and particularly Italy, where one euro will be worth more than one unit of today's currency, the price difference between products will appear to be compressed. Were Britain to join the euro, the opposite would occur with £1 worth nearly 1.5 euros, and differentials would seem to expand. With prices in euros, supermarkets in the Mediterranean countries may find their own label products no longer look cheap beside branded products. A bar of branded chocolate or soap may currently retail for FF10 ($1.63) with an own-label version selling for FF8, a visible 20 per cent less. However the same products priced in euros would sell for around 1.5 euros and 1.2 euros. This penalises own brands in two ways. One is that people pay little attention to what comes after a decimal point. The second is that shoppers unfamiliar with the euro will not bother to work out the saving for themselves. Roughly 60 per cent of decisions to buy basic groceries take less than 20 seconds.

Source: *The Economist*, 14 March, 1998.

● *national brands* and preferably the brand leader in the product category (the A brands) and which are supported by heavy advertising and promotional activities;
● *own labels, store or umbrella brands* (the B brands) created by the retailer to improve profitability and to build the store image;
● *first prices* (the C brands) which are used as price-fighters to stop the *hard-discounters* by offering an alternative to customers.

In this competitive struggle, the weakest manufacturers' brands are the first to be eliminated from the supermarkets.

Strategic options for national brands

Confronted with the growing power of large supermarket retailers, what are the defence strategies for consumer brand manufacturers? Four basic strategic options exist:

● *Pull strategy*. To promote an innovative (unique) product or well-differentiated brand through creative segmentation and media advertising targeted to the end-consumer, in order to induce the distributor to list the brand in his assortment.

● *Direct marketing*. To bypass the retailers by adopting a *non-store marketing* strategy where purchases are made from the home and delivered to the home.

● *Subcontracting marketing*. To concentrate on R&D and manufacturing and to leave the marketing function to a well-diversified group of retailers.

● *Trade marketing*. To view distributors as intermediate customers and to design a retailer-driven marketing programme.

Before examining the potential of direct marketing, we shall first review the strategic options available to a national brand through a pull strategy and through trade marketing.

Alternative options in a pull strategy

From the manufacturer's point of view, the ideal situation is to have a well-differentiated brand, strongly supported by advertising and demanded by consumers. In this situation of manufacturer's domination, the distributor is captive and is forced to list the brand in his assortment. Such a situation is not likely to prevail indefinitely, however, and even big-name manufacturers can be threatened by private labels as illustrated by the success story of Classic Cola of Sainsbury against the mighty Coca-Cola.

> Classic Cola, a private label made by the Cott Corporation for J. Sainsbury in the United Kingdom, was launched at a price 28 per cent lower than Coca-Cola. Today the private label accounts for 65 per cent of total cola sales through Sainsbury and for 15 per cent of the UK cola market.

Once confronted with the private label challenge, how should national brands react (see Figure 12.8)? Hoch (1996) suggests four basic strategic moves that a national

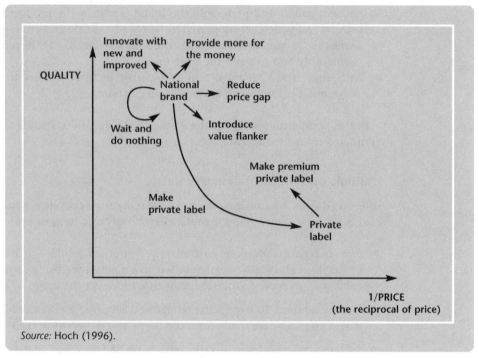

Source: Hoch (1996).

Figure 12.8　Strategic options for national brands

brand can make to improve its competitive position. These options are meant to be neither mutually exclusive nor exhaustive.

1. *Wait and do nothing*. In markets characterised by high volatility and fluctuation, it may be imprudent for a national manufacturer to react quickly and aggressively.

2. *Increase distance from private labels*. Distancing moves could be to 'provide more for money' or 'new and improved' products. It does necessarily imply line extensions which too often tend to dilute rather than enhance the core brand.

3. *Reduce the price gap*. Empirical evidence shows that small price gaps increased unit sales of national brands relative to the private label. Because consumers appear more willing to trade up quality rather down, price changes by national brands affect private labels more than corresponding changes by private labels affect national brand sales.

4. *Formulate a 'me too' strategy*. Two options are possible here. To introduce a 'value flanker' by offering a lower-priced, possibly lower-quality item to crowd out the private label. The risk here is to cannibalise sales currently accruing to the premium national brand. In another strategy, the national brand can elect to manufacture private labels directly for the retailer.

Regarding this last strategy, Quelch and Harding (1996, p. 103) suggest that private label manufacturing opportunities often appear profitable to manufacturers, because they are evaluated on an incremental marginal cost basis. If private label manufacturing were evaluated on a full cost rather than on an incremental basis, it would in many cases appear much less profitable. Every company considering producing private label goods should answer three questions: (a) what is the true contribution from private label products? (b) what fixed costs are attributable to private label production? (c) how much will the private label goods cannibalise the company's national brands?

Trade marketing

Trade marketing is simply the application of the marketing concept to distributors who are no longer viewed as 'intermediaries' in the channel but as partners or customers in their own right. The marketing process targeted to resellers or distributors can be subdivided into four phases:

- Segmentation of the reseller population, or the identification of groups of distributors having the same expectations from suppliers.
- Selection of one or several segment(s) to target by priority.
- Analysis of their needs, that is understand factors that shape resellers decisions, their functioning mode, their objectives and expectations (see Exhibit 12.7).
- Design of an adapted marketing programme.

Efficient order fulfilment is one domain of application of trade marketing where the benefits for the two parties are directly observable (see Exhibit 12.8). In this partnership approach, the goal is to maximise the profits for the entire supply chain. This requires (a) that the supplier is linked with store-shelf inventory data, which is

---

Exhibit 12.7

Generic Needs of Resellers

1. **Freedom to price and promote the merchandise**: freedom to price their merchandise in line with their own goals and interests; freedom from pressure to implement supplier-designed promotions.

2. **Adequate trade margins**: when selling at the manufacturer's suggested price, discount from the list price adequate to cover costs operation and to generate a profit.

3. **Protection from undue competition**: selling the merchandise to too many other resellers; selling the merchandise to off-price resellers; engaging itself in direct selling to end-users.

4. **Support from manufacturers**: training, advertising and promotion, merchandising, information on new developments on the market.

5. **Efficient order fulfilment**: minimise their inventory carrying costs; to avoid stockouts through joint management of inventory flows (see EDI and EWR, Exhibit 2.8).

Source: Sheth *et al.* (1999, pp. 663–8).

Exhibit 12.8

EDI and EWR: Two Important Tools of Trade Marketing

■ **EDI: Electronic Data Interchange**

This system of data interchange between suppliers and resellers is becoming more and more popular in the US and in Europe. Its principle is simple: to establish a direct connection which hooks together computers of the commercial partners via telephone lines to swap information. Once established, this connection facilitates and accelerates communication within the chain and generates substantial cost savings. One of the benefits of EDI is the time reduction for order taking. If order taking for 500 stores generally requires 12 hours, 10 minutes are sufficient with EDI. This operation is followed up by a control which takes two hours to validate the orders. EDI also contributes to the reduction of the execution costs of an order, from its initiation to its transmission: it is 3FF with EDI against 17FF with a magnetic support, and 54FF for a paper document. EDI creates a new management mode: the one of real time commerce.

■ **EWR: Efficient Warehouse Response**

EWR can be defined as a logistic partnership proposing an exchange of information through EDI. This communication between manufacturers and resellers is mainly concerned with inventory flows with the objective to achieve productivity gains at each level of the logistic chain. These cost savings are then shared between the channel partners. The main benefits expected are:
- Produce and sell as much as possible in real time;
- Reduce the number of stockouts;
- Gain a better understanding of stock movements and of demand to reduce real inventory;
- Rationalise the flow of merchandise to make economies of scale.

The most important field of application of EWR is the optimisation of the flow of goods; the other domains are organisation of sales promotions and new products development..

Source: Adapted from Vandaele (1998, Chapter 2).

updated immediately customers buy products from the store, (b) production based on real-time store sales forecast, (c) relocation by the supplier of warehouse facilities closer to the stores. These actions together minimise the inventory costs throughout the system, and the supplier is able to pass on the savings to resellers, and through them, to consumers. Both consumers and resellers get better value in terms of lower prices and merchandise availability due to reduced stockouts.

In order to manage this business-to-business relationship with resellers, suppliers will have to develop an in-depth understanding of their logistic problems, their desired store image and the perceived importance of a particular product category for the chain store's positioning. The most fundamental change is the shift from an adversarial practice to one of partnership. A good understanding of the objectives and constraints of the intermediate customer is a prerequisite for the development of a successful relationship marketing strategy. To go further on the subject of trade marketing see Vandaele (1998), Corstjens and Corstjens (1996) and Buzzell and Ortmeyer (1995).

Interactive or Direct Marketing

Direct marketing (that is a zero intermediary level channel) is current practice in industrial markets when potential buyers are few and products are sophisticated or custom made and of high unit value. The surprising fact in recent years is the development of this selling system in the field of consumer goods, largely as a result of the development of new communication media, such as telemarketing, direct response radio and television, electronic shopping (Minitel), and so on.

Direct marketing is defined by the Direct Marketing Association as:

> An interactive system which uses one or more advertising media to effect a measurable response and/or transaction at any location.

Thus, according to this definition, direct marketing does not necessarily imply non-store marketing, that is a marketing system without using intermediaries. To clarify the field, a distinction must be made between 'direct-order' marketing and 'direct-relationship' marketing:

- *In direct-order marketing*, purchases are made from the home and delivered to the home, and the firm distributes directly without using intermediaries. This is non-store marketing, and the techniques used are mail order catalogues, direct mail, telemarketing, electronic shopping, and so on.

- In *direct-relationship marketing*, the objective is to stimulate sales by establishing direct contacts with prospects and customers to create or maintain a continuing relationship.

Thus, direct-relationship marketing can very well coexist with a conventional vertical indirect marketing system. For this reason, the expression *interactive marketing* seems more appropriate than 'direct marketing', which refers essentially to non-store marketing practices.

The development of interactive marketing is indicative of a significant change in the exchange and communication process between producers and consumers in affluent economies. It suggests that the marketing monologue which prevails in most market situations tends to be replaced by a marketing dialogue, *customised marketing* being substituted for mass or segment marketing.

Rationale of direct-order marketing

Several factors explain the development of more direct marketing and communication systems:

- First, the considerable *cost increase of personal communication*. According to a study by Forsyth (1988), the average cost of a business sales call rose to $251.63 in 1987, that is 160 per cent of the 1977 cost of $96.79.

● Simultaneously, one observes a *weakening of mass media advertising's effectiveness*, caused by the proliferation of advertising messages and changing viewing habits in TV (zapping, VCR) combined with the rising cost of brand image advertising campaigns.

● Shopping is no longer associated with fun and excitement, and is perceived as a bore and as time-consuming by educated consumers who tend to give their time higher value. For consumers, catalogue shopping is a convenient shopping alternative.

● For the manufacturers, direct marketing presents several potential advantages. It allows *greater selectivity* in communicating with the market, personalisation of messages and the maintenance of a continuous relationship. From a strategic point of view, direct marketing gives the producer a way to bypass intermediaries and to reduce the firm's dependence on the goodwill of too powerful retailers.

● Finally, the formidable development of *low-cost computers*, with their immense storage and processing capabilities, has greatly facilitated the use of databases to record and keep track of commercial contacts with customers. This information is then used to reach them individually with highly personalised messages.

The economic incentive of increasing the productivity of marketing expenditure is very appealing.

The tools of direct marketing

Direct marketers can use a large variety of tools to reach potential customers, from traditional face to face to Internet on-line selling (see Table 12.11). The most important tools are: direct mailing, catalogue selling, telemarketing, television direct response marketing and on-line marketing:

● *Face-to-face selling* remains the preferred tool in business-to-business markets, where firms, having a limited and well-identified number of prospects, use their sales force to locate them and to develop them into customers.

● *Direct mail* has grown spectacularly during recent years thanks to the development of personalised data banks which permit high target-market selectivity. One European, in average, receives 46 mailings per year against 200 in the United States.

● *Catalogue selling* accounts for 2.5 per cent of retail sales in France. In Europe, several companies hold strong positions in this market: Les Trois Suisses, La Redoute, Manufrance, Otto Versand and Schikedanz, two German companies. In the United States, the leaders are Montgomery Ward and Sears and Roebuck. Distance selling accounts for more than 5 per cent in the United Kingdom and 7 per cent in the United States.

● *Telemarketing, or telephone marketing*, is experiencing a spectacular development with the generalised adoption of green (freephone) telephone numbers. In Europe, the most spectacular success in telemarketing has been achieved by Direct Line, a telephone sales service set up in Britain by the Royal Bank of Scotland. The great advantage of telemarketing is the rate at which calls can be made. It is quite realistic for even untrained sales personnel to make more than 50 telephone calls in a day, compared to 300 face-to-face calls in year. With specialist telesales personnel, the call rate can rise to hundreds per day.

● *Television marketing* consists of television spots, which persuasively describe a product and provide listeners with a green telephone number for ordering; this form of distance selling is still modest in Europe. It lends itself particularly well to products where the demonstration effect is important.

Table 12.11 Direct marketing expenditures in Europe in 1997

Countries	Direct mail (Ecu m)	Telemarketing (Ecu m)	On-line Advertising (Ecu m)	Total Direct Marketing (Ecu m)	Per capita DM Spend (Ecu)	Share of DM in traditional ad spend (in %)
Austria	989	–	–	989	122.5	70.3
Belgium	913	–	–	913	89.6	63.6
Denmark	725	22	–	747	141.1	59.1
Finland	428	–	–	428	83.2	45.8
France	5,348	521	–	5,869	91.1	71.8
Germany	6,567	2,240	1,273	10,080	107.4	59.6
Ireland	112	18	–	131	35.7	21.3
Italy	1,161	287	215	1,663	25.2	32.1
Netherlands	1,797	681	158	2,637	159.2	90.1
Portugal	35	–	–	35	3.6	4.6
Spain	1,886	104	13	2,003	50.6	51.4
Sweden	640	–	–	640	72.4	39.7
UK	2,861	2,506	131	5,449	91.0	39.7
EU total	23,464	6,380	1,789	31,634	88.9	–

Source: FEDMA (1999), 1998 Survey on Direct Marketing Activities in the EU.

The most promising distance selling method today is probably *on-line selling* on the Internet. On-line channels will be described in more detail in the next section and also in the next chapter.

Organisation of a direct-order marketing system

Direct-order marketing supposes the development of a marketing database system. The essence of the system is to communicate directly with customers and ask them to respond in a tangible way. A database system can be defined as follows:

> The development of a direct marketing campaign implies the creation of personalised messages containing an offer and an invitation to respond. The database is then used to record the response of customers and to adapt the next message.

The components of a direct marketing system are the following:

● *The Message Content.* The end objective is of course to achieve a sale, but the immediate objective is to create a dialogue and to maintain a relationship. The intermediate objective may be to obtain prospective leads, to reactivate former customers, to acknowledge receipt of an order, to welcome new customers, to inform customers and to prepare them for later purchase, to generate requests for catalogues or leaflets, to propose a visit to a showroom, and so on.

- *Personalised Messages.* This is the main superiority of direct marketing over mass media advertising. Instead of using standardised advertising messages and a 'shotgun' approach, a marketing database makes possible a 'rifle' approach and, at the extreme, a truly personalised message by including details relevant to the target customer and not to others.

- *The Offer.* To obtain a positive behavioural response from the prospect, the message must include an offer or a proposition sufficiently attractive to induce prospects to respond. In the simplest case, it is an offer to purchase the product. It could also be the proposal to inspect the product, a free sample or a free credit, participation in a contest or in a club, and so on. The attractiveness of the offer is a key success factor.

- *Measurable Response.* In an interactive marketing system, the key objective is to engage in a dialogue with individual customers, and it is therefore essential to obtain some kind of response. The ideal response is placing an order, but other forms of response are sought, such as agreeing to a sales appointment, returning a reply coupon, confirming receipt of information, agreeing to attend an exhibition, providing more information about needs and wants, and so on. In an interactive marketing system, potential customers are self-selected since only potentially interested customers will respond.

- *Database Marketing.* Any interactive marketing system implies the existence of a computerised database, A marketing database is

   an organised collection of data about individual customers, prospects or suspects that is accessible and actionable for such marketing purposes as lead generation, lead qualification, sale of a product or of a service, or maintenance of customer relationships. (Kotler, 1997, p. 721)

   The database must include, in addition to the personal identification elements, information on past purchase behaviour, preferred brands, size of orders, and so on. Thus, within the firm the capacity to handle prospects' reactions and personal orders must exist. This implies a considerable reinforcement of the sales administration and logistics departments.

- *Communication Mix.* The communication media used are mainly the personalised media like direct mail, catalogue marketing and telemarketing. Then come radio, magazine and television direct-response marketing and electronic shopping. Direct mail remains the most important medium.

One of the greatest advantages of direct marketing is that responses to campaigns are measured, enabling marketing management to identify the effectiveness of different approaches. It is testable and it permits privacy in that the marketing offer is not visible to the competition.

On-line selling through the Internet

On-line sales are still in their early stage of development in Europe, even if most experts agree that they will have a spectacular development until year 2000 (see Table 12.12). In France, out of over 1 million cyber spacers, only 5 per cent purchase from the Web for a total of FF50 million, a very small score compared to Minitel: 8 billion in 1997, of which 1.5 billion were just for the sole ticketing sales (*Le Figaro-Economie*, 7 April, 1998). In the USA, on-line sales accounted for FF16 billion in 1997 and should reach FF230 billion in 2002 (*Business Week*, 1998, p. 14).

In several sectors, electronic commerce is in direct competition with traditional retailers, particularly for goods like computer equipment (Dell computers), records and CDs (Music Boulevard), books (Amazon and Barnes and Noble Inc.) and travelling (Otto Versand).

Table 12.12 Online selling on the Web (%)

Retailers selling on the Web	1997	1998	Manufacturers selling on the Web	1997	1998
Yes	12	39	Yes	9	15
Plan to	22	37	Plan to	12	28
No Plans	54	24	Don't Plan to	71	57
Unsure	12	0	Unsure	8	0

Source: The Second Annual Ernst & Young Internet Shopping Study, 1999.

From the accumulated experience so far, several lessons can be learned (see Exhibit 12.9).

● Customers will be the first to benefit from electronic commerce because they can find on the Net a lot of comparative information about products, competitors and prices without leaving their home or office. Consumers, and particularly young-sters well familiarised with the computer technology, will be able to focus on objective criteria such as prices, performance, quality, and so on. They will become more demanding buyers. The traditional 'one-way' mass communication methods will become more and more incompatible with the *Net generation*.

● Electronic commerce will *stimulate price competition* as a result of the greater facility of price comparisons provided by the Web. For example, Music Boulevard is aggressively expanding in Europe and in Japan where CD prices are on average 30 per cent higher than in the US. In addition, by creating a site in Europe in a joint venture with the French Company Hachette, buyers do not have to pay custom duties. The same situation prevails for books whose wholesale prices are higher in the UK than in the US. Until recently, it was more interesting to buy on-line with Amazon (based in Seattle) than with Internet Bookshop (IBS) based at Cambridge. Price comparisons are further facilitated since January 1999, with retail prices quoted in euros.

● Electronic commerce will also facilitate and accelerate price changes and price adjustments since, on the Net, there is a quasi-permanent confrontation of demand and supply, as is the case with companies (airlines and hotels among

Exhibit 12.9

Business and the Internet in Europe

The precise impact of the Internet is still hard to quantify. One reason is its sheer rate of growth: every second, another seven people around the globe tap in for the first time. But enough data have emerged – and several companies have established enough of a track record – that the glimmerings of a new business era are becoming visible, one that should endure through eventual recessions. Business-to-consumer electronic commerce remains modest in scale – perhaps $8billion last year in America, according to Forrester, an American consultancy, compared with $43 billion-odd of business-to-business e-commerce. In the near future, retail commerce may hit obstacles. It has grown faster inside the United States than outside it, even though the biggest impact of the new technology may well be felt when consumers learn to use the border-hopping properties of the Internet to shop all round the world. In Europe, the Internet will help to turn the single currency into the foundation of a genuine single market for consumers. Yet Europeans are less prepared than Americans to buy electronically; they are less likely to have credit cards, have less experience of mail-ordering shopping, and are generally more conservative in their shopping habits; Even in America, reckons Forrester, business-to-consumer in 2003 will be worth no more than $108 billion, less than Wal-Mart's 1998 sales. Business-to-business e-commerce, in contrast, might well top $1.3 trillion in 2003.

The days when Europe could be considered a backwater in electronic commerce, lagging years behind development in the United States, are rapidly drawing to a close. Major European companies are adopting innovative strategies for e-commerce, consumers are shedding their inhibitions to purchasing on-line and the growth of free Internet service providers and low-cost approaches are making the Web more accessible. These factors have produced a virtuous circle of Internet growth that has enabled Europe to close the gap with the United States. Forrester Research Inc. expects Britain and Germany to go into the same hyper-growth stage of e-business about two years after America, with Japan, France and Italy a further two years behind.

Source: International Herald Tribune, 28 June, 1999 and The Economist, 26 June, 1999.

others) having adopted yield management for establishing their pricing policy (see Chapter 13).

Given the relatively low cost of opening an electronic store, small specialised retailers can easily enter the world market through the Web and compete directly with the most powerful rivals (see Exhibit 12.10).

● The most important domain of applications of electronic commerce seems to business-to-business markets, where distance selling has been common practice for a long time.

A certain number of factors which could inhibit the development of electronic commerce exist however and which maintain a certain degree of uncertainty about this new distribution system:

Exhibit 12.10

Two Pioneers of Electronic Commerce

Internet Shopping Network (*http://www.isn.com*) sells software and computer equipment. Founded in 1994, this company already has 10,000 customers, for a turnover $1.5 million of monthly sales. The Web site proposes 35,000 products, and received 30,000 visitors every day, of which 200 will place an order. The average basket is $200.

The company Amazon Books (*http://www.amazon.com.*) which sells more than 1 million books annually exclusively on the Internet, is the company having the largest number of customers in the Web. Every day, 40 per cent of sales are made to existing customers. Amazon offers at reduced prices the largest assortment of existing books. As each author or title selected by the buyers is automatically recorded on a data base, Amazon corresponds by Email with its customers to promote other books of interest to them. To build traffic on the site, Amazon does not hesitate to use international press advertising, namely the *Wall Street Journal* or the *International Herald Tribune*.

⬤ The high cost of access to the Web in Europe remains an issue. Bertelsman has calculated that, in Germany, 20 hours on-line on the Web represent in telephone bills only, a cost of $54 to $74 dollars against $29 in average in the US.

⬤ According to a survey by PricewaterhouseCoopers (1999), in both the US and the UK, comparison shopping for products was the main reason cited for logging on-line. In the US, only 36 per cent of all consumers who comparison shop on-line actually make a purchase, considerably lower than UK consumers, 50 per cent of whom end up buying what they research on the Internet.

⬤ For many Web users, the lack of confidentiality about transactions remains a preoccupation, as shown by the data presented in Exhibit 12.11.

How to create an electronic store?

The development of electronic commerce requires some standardisation of the internal procedures within the firm. We are here in the world of the virtual enterprise, which deals from a distance with its suppliers and customers, subcontracts logistics and reduces the staff to a minimum (see Exhibit 12.12). As described by Strauss and Frost (1999), the steps of an electronic transaction are the following:

⬤ In an *electronic catalogue*, the products are described in a pictorial form; the browser simply clicks on any text or icon to bring up more details about a particular product. The text presents and promotes the product's features and benefits.

⬤ The visitor who selects a product can directly place an order on a order form, where he identifies himself and gives the reference and number of his credit card.

⬤ Software installed on the server of the electronic store by a company specialising in electronic payments, immediately calls via the Internet the credit card network to verify that the card has not been stolen or blocked and that the customer is solvent. If the information comes back with a positive reply, it means that the payment has been made by the payment company. This message triggers the commercial process of the transaction.

● The details of the order made are transmitted from the Web server to the internal server of the firm. This information is recorded in the marketing data base which identifies a new customer in the accounting system and records the transaction. A message is also sent to the computer terminal of the delivery service which prepares the package to be collected by the shipping company.

● Simultaneously, information is sent back through the Internet to the logistic partner who will collect the merchandise and ship it to the customer.

Specialised software companies offer *merchant servers* to companies wishing to go on-line. These software organise the different functions of distance selling, like the design of the electronic catalogue, the payment system, the logistics, and so on. To go further on this topic, see Strauss and Frost (1999).

Exhibit 12.11

Internet: The Confidentiality of Information

If you do not go on-line, would you be more likely to start using the Internet, or not, if...? (answers in %)	YES	NO	Don't know
The privacy of your personal information and communication was protected	61	36	2
The cost was reduced	51	44	5
The use became less complicated	53	43	4
You had more control over businesses sending marketing messages that you did not want	39	56	5

If you were to use the Internet, how concerned would you be about each of the following possibilities?	5	4	3	2	1
The company you buy from uses personal information you provide to send you unwanted information	52	34	11	3	0
The company or one of its employees uses your credit card information to make purchases without your consent	80	12	6	2	0
In the course of the transaction, your credit-card information is made accessible to others who might use it without your consent	86	10	2	1	0

(5: very; 4: somewhat; 3: not very; 2: not at all; 1: don't know)

Source: Business Week, 16 March, 1998, p. 57.

Exhibit 12.12

Tesco Expands Home Shopping

Tesco is planning to roll out its home shopping service in stores across the country in the next few months, as the supermarket group attempts to cash in on the success of its free Internet service. The Tesco service allows customers to order their shopping on-line and have it delivered to their homes for £5. It will offer the service from 100 of its stores, enabling it to reach most of the country. The move comes after a two-year trial of the service involving 11 stores during which Tesco experimented with allowing customers to order by phone and fax. However, it has concluded that costs will be kept down if customers only order via the Internet. Tesco expects the service to expand its customer base by tempting shoppers who cannot travel or who live too far away from a super-market. The offer is also likely to appeal to Tesco's free Internet service, which was launched earlier this year. More than 200,000 people use Tesco as their Internet provider, with a further 10,000 joining each month.

Source: The *Independent*, 14 April, 1999.

Exhibit 12.13

Success Factors in On-line Selling to Consumers

Retailers		Manufacturers	
Success factors	Importance rates	Success factors	Importance rates
Having a well-designed, easy-to-use site	2.97	Having a well-designed, easy-to-use site	2.94
Having a strong company brand	2.81	Being allied with the right search engine	2.61
Selling well-known branded products	2.50	Having strong company brand	2.52
Being allied with the right search engines	2.48	Aggressively advertising and promoting the site	2.42
Aggressively advertising and promoting the site	2.45	Selling well-known branded products	2.39
Being a fast-follower	2.35	Being a first-mover	2.26
Having strong executive leadership	2.29	Being a fast-follower	2.10
Offering competitive prices on-line	2.10	Having strong executive leadership	2.03
Being a first-mover	1.87	Offering competitive prices on-line	1.77

Most important success factors ranked on a scale of 1–3: 1: not important; 2: somewhat important; 3: very important.

Source: The Second Annual Ernst & Young Internet Shopping Study (1999).

Is electronic commerce profitable?

Is the Net market too perfect for profits? The question is relevant in view of the low profitability displayed by 'Netrapreneurs' who often failed to turn a profit (see *Business Week*, 22 June, 1998, p. 83). The Net market has indeed most of the characteristics of a perfect or 'frictionless' market, that is fierce price competition, dwindling product differentiation and vanishing brand loyalty (Kuttner, 1998, p. 12):

● Full price information
● Worldwide comparison of sellers' offerings
● Strong bargaining power of more adroit customers
● Low entry barriers
● Weak potential for differentiation
● Lack of protection for innovations
● Message selection controlled by customers
● Volatile behaviour of buyers
● Equal access opportunities for all sellers.

In this type of competitive environment, close to pure competition as discussed in Chapter 8, the seller has no market power and therefore his potential for profit is non-existent in the long term. The challenge for on-line merchants is to find ways to differentiate themselves in this new competitive space, to maintain visibility, to create defensible market positions and to forge an institutional identity or brand.

Different methods can be used to attract and interact with a relatively large number of a visitors in target group. On this topic, see Watson *et al.* (1998). Despite these difficulties, most experts predict soaring sales by the year 2003 in the US and in Europe (see Table 12.13).

Table 12.13   On-line sales are soaring in the US (billion $)

Years	1998	1999	2000	2001	2002	2003
Computing electronics	19.7	50.4	121.4	229.1	319.1	395.3
Motor vehicles	3.7	9.3	22.7	53.2	114.3	212.9
Petrochemicals	4.7	10.3	22.6	48.0	96.8	178.3
Utilities	7.1	15.4	32.2	62.9	110.6	169.5
Paper office products	1.3	2.9	6.4	14.3	31.1	65.2
Shipping and warehousing	1.2	2.9	6.8	15.4	32.7	61.6
Food and agriculture	0.3	3.0	6.3	13.1	26.7	53.6
Consumer goods	1.4	2.9	6.1	12.7	26.0	51.9
Total	43.1	109.3	251.1	499.0	842.7	1,330.8

Source: Forrester Research, June 1999.

Limits of direct-order marketing

Convenience is the major benefit for the consumer, but many consumers can be less interested in convenience than in product quality, reliable delivery and in being able to touch, feel and smell the merchandise. In addition, as direct marketing becomes more and more popular, many consumers view the techniques of direct marketing – the unsolicited telephone calls, the junk mail and the trading and renting of mailing lists – as an *invasion of privacy*.

Quelch and Takeuchi (1981, p. 84) questioned the future of non-store marketing by raising the following questions:

● What if postal rates double?
● What if privacy laws prevent direct marketers from selling or buying mailing lists?
● What if a freeze is placed on credit card usage?

These questions are more relevant than ever with the spectacular development of on-line commerce, and the European Commission has issued a directive that prohibits consumer data from being transmitted from member countries to any other country that lacks the EU stringent privacy protections. This directive is hotly opposed by the US Secretary of commerce.

> The EU aims to put consumers in control of their own personal data that circulate in cyber-space by requiring companies to fully disclose the intended uses of the information and by offering consumers the right to reject such uses. An agency or organisation would oversee compliance. The US contends that privacy can be protected as companies agree to abide by a code of conduct for Internet business. But EU members fear that companies given the opportunity to regulate themselves will not comply with a code of conduct. (*International Herald Tribune*, 12 June, 1999)

Cespedes and Smith (1993, p. 16) have proposed rules for fairness use of database marketing. Those rules, which are no so different from those proposed by the EU Commission, are summarised in Exhibit 12.14. Direct marketing is probably less controversial in the field of business-to-business marketing than in the field of consumer marketing.

● ## Entry Strategies in Foreign Markets

The key role of international development was discussed in Chapter 10, in view of the globalisation of the European and of the world economy. One of the critical questions to examine in establishing an international development strategy is to select the entry mode in the target foreign country and the distribution channel. Several alternative entry strategies can be considered as shown in Figure 12.9 from a base of either domestic or foreign production.

Indirect export

The market-entry technique that offers the lowest level of risk and the least market control is indirect export when products are carried abroad by others. The firm is not engaging in international marketing and no special activity is carried on within the firm. The sale is handled like a domestic sales. There are different methods of indirect exporting.

● The simplest method is to treat foreign sales through the domestic sales organisa-tion. For example, if a firm receives an unsolicited order from a customer in Spain

Exhibit 12.14

Rules for Database Marketing Fairness

Rule 1: Data users must have the clear assent of the data subject to use personal data for database marketing (DBM) purposes.

- Companies should avoid deception and secrecy in data collection.
- Targeted consumers should know the marketer's source for information about them.
- Individuals should have the opportunity to opt out of subsequent uses of data.
- A consumer's assent to data use by one company does not automatically transfer to companies sharing that information.

Rule 2: Companies are responsible for the accuracy of the data they use, and the data subjects should have the right to access, verify and change information about themselves.

Rule 3: Categorisations should be based on actual behaviour as well as the more traditional criteria of attitudes, lifestyles and demographics.

Source: Cespedes and Smith (1993, p. 16).

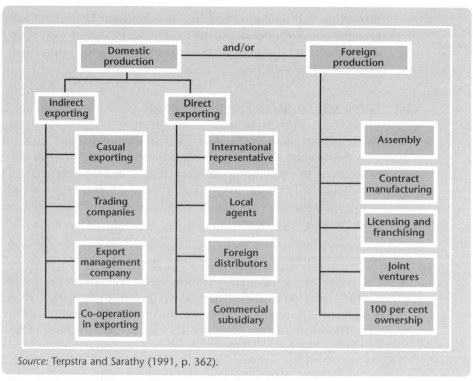

Source: Terpstra and Sarathy (1991, p. 362).

Figure 12.9   Entry strategies in foreign markets

and responds to the request on a one-time basis it is engaging in casual exporting. Or a foreign buyer comes to the firm. Products are sold in the domestic market but used or resold abroad. It is the case of buyers of foreign department stores having buying offices in the firm's home country. If the exporting firm does not follow up the contact with a sustained marketing effort, it is unlikely to gain future sales.

● A second form of indirect exporting is the use of international trading companies with local offices all over the world. Perhaps the best known trading companies are the Sogo Sosha of Japan such as Mitsui or Mitsubishi. The size and market coverage of these trading companies make them attractive distributors, especially with their credit reliability and their information network. The trading companies of European origin are important primarily in trade with former European colonies, particularly Africa and Southeast Asia. The drawback to the use of trading companies is that they are likely to carry competing products and the firm's products might not receive the attention and support the firm desires.

● A third form of indirect exporting is the export management company located in the same country as the producing firm and which plays the role of an export department. That is the firm has the performance of an export department without establishing one in the firm. The economic advantage arises because the export company performs the export function for several firms at the same time. The producer can establish closer relationships and gains instant foreign market contacts and knowledge. The firm is spared the burden of developing in-house expertise in exporting. The method of payment is the commission and the costs are variable. Export management companies handle different but complementary product lines which can often can get better foreign representation than the products of just one manufacturer.

Exporting in this indirect way can open up new markets without special expertise or investment. Both the international know-how and the sales achieved by these indirect approaches are generally limited. In this approach, the commitment to international markets is very weak.

Direct exporting

In direct exporting the firm becomes directly involved in marketing its products in foreign markets. The firm performs the export task rather than delegating it to others. Thus, this implies the creation of an export department responsible for market contact, market research, physical distribution, export documentation pricing, and so on. This approach requires more corporate resources and also entails greater risks. The expected benefits are increased sales, greater control, better market information and development of expertise in international marketing.

To implement a direct exporting strategy, the firm must have representation in the foreign markets. Different solutions can be considered:

● To use *international sales representatives* to be sent into the foreign market to establish contacts and to directly negotiate sales contracts.
● To select *local representatives or agents* to prospect the market, to contact potential customers and to negotiate on behalf of the exporting firm.

- To use *independent local distributors* who will buy the products to resell them in the local market with or without exclusivity.
- To create a fully owned *commercial subsidiary* to have a greater control over foreign operations.

In most cases, the commercial subsidiary will be a joint venture created with a local firm to gain access to local relationships.

Foreign manufacturing

Under certain conditions, the firm may find it either impossible or undesirable to supply foreign markets from domestic production sources. For example, transportation costs may be too high for heavy or bulky products, custom rates or quotas on imports can render products non-competitive, or government preferences for local products can prevent entry in the foreign market (see Table 12.14). Any of these conditions could force the firm to manufacture in foreign markets in order to sell there. Other positive factors can also induce the firm to produce abroad. Among them, the size and the attractiveness of the market, lower production costs, economic incentives given by public authorities, and so on.

Varied approaches can be adopted to foreign manufacturing as shown in Figure 12.9. Each implies a different level of commitment from the firm.

Assembling

Assembling is a compromise between exporting and foreign manufacturing. The firm produces domestically all or most of the components or ingredients of its product and ships them to foreign markets to be put together as a finished product. By shipping CKD (completely knocked down), the firm is saving on transportation costs and also on custom tariffs which are generally lower on unassembled equipment than on finished products. Another benefit is the use of local employment which facilitates the integration of the firm in the foreign market.

Table 12.14   Export price escalation in different channel structures

	Short channel	Long channel	Long channel with importer	Long channel with importer and jobber
Manufacturer's price	95	95	95	95
Transport CIF	–	15	15	15
Tariffs (20%)	–	22	22	22
Importer cost:	–	–	132	132
(25%)			33	33
Wholesaler cost	95	132	165	165
(33.3%)	47	66	83	83
Jobber cost:	–	–	–	248
(33.3%)				124
Retailer cost:	142	198	248	372
(33.3%)	71	99	124	186
Retail price	**213**	**297**	**372**	**558**

Margins are mark-ups.

Notable examples of foreign assembly are the automobile and farm equipment industries. In similar fashion, Coca-Cola ships its syrup to foreign markets where local bottle plants add the water and the container.

Contract manufacturing

The firm's product is produced in the foreign market by local producer under contract with the firm. Because the contract covers only manufacturing, marketing is handled by a sales subsidiary of the firm which keeps the market control. Contract manufacturing obviates the need for plant investment, transportation costs and custom tariffs and the firm gets the advantage of advertising its product as locally made. Contract manufacturing also enables the firm to avoid labour and other problems that may arise from its lack of familiarity with the local economy and culture.

A drawback to contract manufacturing is the loss of the profit margin on production activities, particularly if labour costs are lower in the foreign market. There is also the risk of transferring the technological know-how to a potential foreign competitor. This risk is lessened, however, where brand names and the marketing know-how are the key success factors. A frequent problem is also quality control.

Licensing

Licensing is another way to enter a foreign market with a limited degree of risk. It differs from contract manufacturing in that it is usually for a longer term and involves greater responsibilities for the local producer. Licensing is similar to franchising except that, as described above, the franchising organisation tends to be more directly involved in the development and control of the marketing programme. The international licensing firm gives the licensee patent rights, trademark rights, copyrights or know-how on products and processes. In return, the licensee will (a) produce the licensor's products, (b) market these products in his assigned territory and (c) pay the licensor royalties related to the sales volume of the products.

The benefits of licensing for the two partners are those described above for franchising. This type of agreement is generally welcomed by foreign public authorities because it brings technology into the country.

The major drawback of licensing is the problem of controlling the licensee due to the absence of direct commitment from the international firm granting the licence. After few years, once the know-how is transferred, the risk is real to see the foreign firm to operate on its own and thus the international firm may lose that market.

Joint ventures

Foreign joint ventures have much in common with licensing. The major difference is that in joint ventures, the international firm has an equity position and a management voice in the foreign firm. A partnership between host- and home-country firms is formed, usually resulting in the creation of a third firm. This type of agreement gives the international firm better control over operations and also access to local market knowledge. The international firm has access to the network of relationships of the franchisee and is less exposed to the risk expropriation thanks to the partnership with the local firm.

This type of agreement is very popular in international management. Its popularity stems from the fact that it permits the avoidance of control problems of the other types of foreign market entry strategies. In addition, the presence of the local firm facilitates the integration of the international firm in a foreign environment.

Direct investments

The international firm makes a direct investment in a production unit in a foreign market. It is the greatest commitment since there is a 100 per cent ownership. The international firm can obtain wholly foreign production facilities in two primary ways: (a) it can make a direct acquisition or merger in the host market or (b) it can develop its own facilities from the ground up. In some countries, governments prohibit 100 per cent ownership by the international firm and demand licensing or joint ventures instead.

Foreign market entry strategies are numerous and imply a varying degree of risk and of commitment from the international firm. In general, an international development strategy is a process and is implemented in several steps. Indirect exporting is the starting point. If the results are satisfactory, more committing agreements are made by associating local firms.

Chapter summary

Distribution channels are organised structures performing the tasks necessary to facilitate exchange transactions. The functions of distribution channels are to create time, space and state utilities which constitute the added value of distribution. Distributors (wholesalers, retailers, agents, brokers) are required because manufacturers are unable to assume by themselves, at a reasonable cost, all the tasks implied by a free and competitive exchange process. Distribution channels can be characterised by the number of intermediary levels that separate the supplier from the end-user. The selection of a particular channel design is determined by factors related to market, buyer behaviour and company characteristics. When the channel structure is indirect, some degree of co-operation and co-ordination must be achieved among the participants in the vertical marketing system. Regarding the number of intermediaries necessary, three market coverage strategies are possible: intensive, selective or exclusive distribution. Exclusive distribution through franchising is a popular system present in almost all business fields. The distribution margins, or trade margins, compensate the distribution functions and tasks assumed by the intermediaries in the channel. Significant changes have occurred in the 1990s in the way retailers, and in particular large retailers, perceive their roles in the channel. Today, they are discovering strategic marketing, developing innovative store concepts and sophisticated own brand policies. The development of interactive marketing (that is direct-order and relationship marketing) suggests that the traditional marketing monologue is tending to be replaced by a marketing dialogue, customised marketing being substituted for mass or segment marketing. In designing its international development strategy, the firm can contemplate different foreign market entry strategies, from indirect export to direct local investment.

QUESTIONS AND PROBLEMS

1. You are responsible for the organisation of the distribution of a new chemical compound to be used for the maintenance of water in swimming pools. Suggest alternative distribution channels to be considered to reach the different potential customer groups and describe the functions to be performed by the producer and distributor(s) for each alternative.

2. 'Middlemen are parasites'. This charge has been made by many, and in particular by Marxists. Referring to a market economy system, how would you react to this charge?

3. Godiva chocolates are sold exclusively through company-owned or franchised boutiques. The company wishes to maintain the positioning of Godiva chocolates as a luxury item. What changes in distribution strategy could be contemplated by management in order to increase Godiva's market share?

4. In view of the dynamism and of the growing power of mass merchandisers in the FMCG sector, what type of defence or redeployment strategies can be adopted by brand manufacturers? Analyse the merits and the difficulties of each possibility.

5. A supplier gives a 5 per cent promotional discount to a distributor who already receives a 7 per cent quantity discount. The list price is $4. Calculate the distributor's purchase price with the 7 per cent quantity discount and then with the 5 per cent promotional discount.

6. A distributor's purchase price before taxes is $120. For this product category, VAT is 20.5 per cent and the distribution margin before taxes is 30 per cent. What will the retail price of this product be?

Bibliography

Boyd, H.W. and Walker, O.C. Jr (1990) *Marketing Management: A Strategic Approach*, Homewood IL, R.D. Irwin.

Brown, M.P., Cardozo, R.N., Cunningham, S.M. *et al.* (1968) *Problems in Marketing*, 4th edn, New York, McGraw-Hill.

Business Week (1998) E-Shop Till You Drop, 9 February, pp. 14–15.

Buzzell, R.D. and Ortmeyer, G. (1995) Channel Partnerships Streamline Distribution, *Sloan Management Review*, Spring, pp. 85–9.

Cespedes, F.V. and Smith, H.F. (1993) Database Marketing: New Rules for Policy and Practice, *Sloan Management Review*, Summer, pp. 7–22.

Corstjens, J. and Corstjens, M. (1996) *Store Wars*, New York, John Wiley.

Forsyth, D.P. (1988) Sales Calls Cost More According to McGraw-Hill, *Direct Marketing*, August, p. 67.

Glémet, F. and Mira, R. (1993a) The Brand Leader's Dilemma, *The McKinsey Quarterly*, (2): 3–15.

Glémet, F. and Mira, R. (1993b) Solving The Brand Dilemma, *The McKinsey Quarterly*, (4): 87–98.

Hoch, S.J. (1996) How Should National Brands Think about Private Labels? *Sloan Management Review*, Winter, pp. 89–102.

Hogarth-Scott, S. and Rice, S.P. (1994) The New Food Discounters: Are They a Threat to the Major Multiples? *International Journal of Retail & Distribution Management*, 22(1): 20–8.

IAB/PricewaterhouseCoopers Survey (1999) *1998, Online Advertising in France: Year 1 at Last!*, Internet Advertising Bureau.

Kotler, P. (1997) *Marketing Management*, Englewood Cliifs, NJ, Prentice Hall.

Kuttner, R. (1998) The Net: A Market Too Perfect for Profits, *Business Week*, 11 May, p. 12.

LSA (1996) L'Europe des achats: le nouveau pactole, 29 February, pp. 26–30.

LSA (1997) Marque de distributeurs: les clients les perçoivent mal, No. 1540, 22 May, pp. 30–4.

LSA (1998) Le hard discount en pleine forme, No. 1571, 12 Feb, pp. 28–31.

McGuire, E.P. (1971) Franchised Distribution, New York, The Conference Board, Report No. 523.

Messinger, P.R. and Chakravarthi Narasimhan (1995) Has Power Shifted in the Grocery Channel? *Marketing Science*, **14**(2): 189–223.

Monroe, K.B. (1979) *Pricing: Making Profitable Decisions*, New York, McGraw-Hill.

Nielsen Company Belgium (1997) *L'univers alimentaire en Belgique*, A.C. Nielsen, Belgium.

Palamountain, J.C. (1955) *The Politics of Distribution*, Cambridge MA, Harvard University Press.

Quelch, J.A. and Takeuchi, H. (1981) Non-store Marketing: Fast Track or Slow?, *Harvard Business Review*, **59**, July–August, pp. 75–84.

Quelch, J.A. and Harding, D. (1996) Brand versus Private Labels: Fighting to Win, *Harvard Business Review*, January–February, pp. 99–109.

Sallenave, J.P. (1979) *Expansion de votre commerce par le franchisage*, Gouvernement du Québec, Ministère du Commerce et du Tourisme.

Santi, M. (1997) Marques de distributeurs: six idées fausses, *L'Expansion Management Review*, March, pp. 64–78.

Sheth, J.N., Banwari, M. and Newman, B.I. (1999) *Customer Behavior and Beyond*, Fort Worth, The Dryden Press.

Strauss, J. and Frost, R. (1999) *Marketing on the Internet*, Englewood Cliffs NJ, Prentice Hall.

Terpstra, V. and Sarathy, R. (1991) *International Marketing*, 5th edn, Chicago, Dryden Press.

Vandaele, M. (1998) *Commerce et industrie: le nouveau partenariat*, Paris, Librairie Vuibert.

Watson, R.T., Akselen, S. and Pitt, L.F. (1998) Building Mountains in the Flat Landscape of the World Wide Web, *California Management Review*, **40**(2): 36–56.

Wortzel, L.H. (1987) Retailing Strategies for Today's Mature Market-place, *Journal of Business Strategy*, **7**(4): 45–56.

chapter thirteen

Market-driven pricing decisions

Each product has a price, but each firm is not necessarily in a position to determine the price at which it sells its product. When products are undifferentiated and competitors numerous, the firm has no market power and must take the price level imposed by the market. But when the firm has developed strategic marketing and thus has gained some degree of market power, setting the price is a key decision, which conditions the success of its strategy to a large extent. Until recently, pricing decisions were still considered from a purely financial viewpoint, and largely determined by costs and profitability constraints. This approach changed because of the upheavals in the economic and competitive situation during the crisis years: double-digit inflation, today well under control in Western Europe, costs volatility of raw materials, fast fluctuating interest rates, increased competition, lower purchasing power, consumerism, and so on. All these factors play an important part in making pricing decisions of strategic importance. After describing the strategic role of price in marketing, we will analyse pricing decisions that emphasise costs, competition and demand successively. Figure 13.1 describes the general problem of price setting in a competitive environment.

Chapter learning objectives

When you have read this chapter, you should be able to:

1. understand the buyer's perception of price and its significance for the firm;
2. analyse the cost and profit implications of different pricing alternatives;
3. list and explain the factors affecting the buyer's price sensitivity;
4. describe and compare different methods of pricing in a market-oriented perspective;
5. discuss the impact of the competitive structure on the firm's pricing strategy;
6. describe the way to approach the problem of setting the price for a set of related products;
7. explain the pricing issues facing a firm operating in foreign markets.

⬭ Pricing and the Marketing Mix

From the firm's point of view, the question of price has two aspects: the price is an instrument to stimulate demand, much like advertising for example, and at the same time price is a determinant factor of the firm's long-term profitability. Therefore the choice of a pricing strategy must respect two types of coherence: an *internal coherence*, that is setting a product price respecting constraints of costs and profitability, and an *external coherence*, that is setting the price level keeping in mind the market's purchasing power and the price of competing goods. Furthermore, pricing decisions must remain coherent with decisions regarding product positioning and distribution strategy.

The buyer's perception of price

Price is the *monetary expression of value* and as such occupies a central role in competitive exchange. Purchasing behaviour can be seen as a system of exchange in which searching for satisfaction and monetary sacrifices compensate each other. This behaviour results from forces that balance a need, characterised by the buyer's attitude towards the product and the product's price. From the buyer's point of view, the price he or she is willing to pay measures the intensity of the need and the quantity and nature of satisfaction that is expected. From the seller's point of view, the price at which he or she is willing to sell measures the value of inputs incorporated in the product, to which the seller adds the profit that is hoped to be achieved.

Formally, monetary price can be defined as a ratio indicating the amount of money necessary for acquiring a given quantity of a good or service:

$$\text{Price} = \frac{\text{Amount of money provided by the buyer}}{\text{Quantity of goods provided by the seller}}$$

In fact, the notion of price is wider and goes beyond the simple coincidence of purely objective and quantitative factors. The amount of money paid measures incompletely the sacrifice made, and, in the same way, the quantity of good obtained measures actual satisfaction imperfectly.

The total value of a product

We saw in Chapter 4 that as far as the customer is concerned, a product is a *package of benefits* and the services that are derived from the product are many. The latter not only result from the product's core service, but also from all the objective and perceptual secondary utilities that characterise the product. Therefore the price must reflect the value of all such satisfaction to the buyer.

> Let us compare two watches having the same objective technical quality. Brand A is a prestigious one, with an elegant design, sold exclusively by watchmakers; it carries a five-year guarantee and is advertised using sport and theatre personalities. Brand B is little known, soberly designed, sold in department stores with a 6-month guarantee and advertised as being reliable. Although these two watches provide the same core or functional service (time measurement), we can see that they are two distinct products and their value as perceived by potential buyers will be very different.

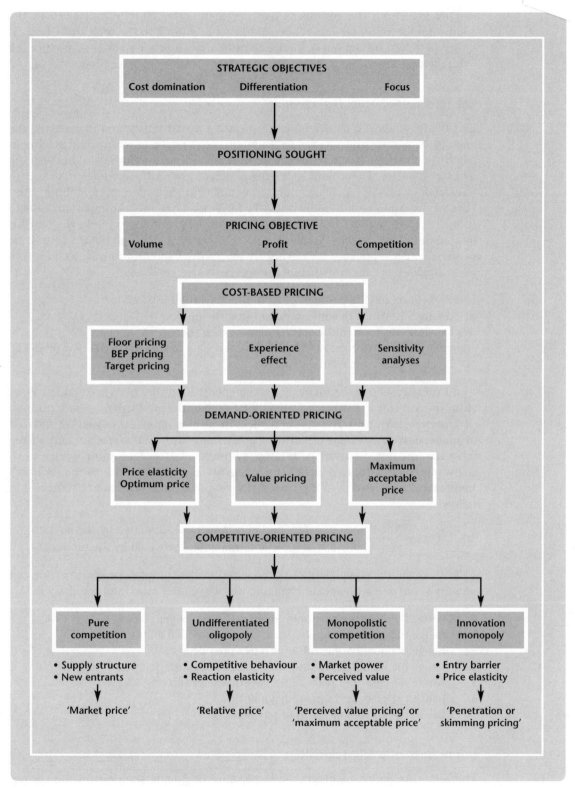

Figure 13.1   Overview of pricing decisions

Therefore, from the customer's point of view, price must be conceived as the compensation for all services rendered and set according to the total value or total utility perceived by the buyer. Hence the importance of a well-defined positioning before setting the selling price.

The total cost of acquiring a product

Just as the obtained quantity of goods measures actual satisfaction imperfectly, the amount of money paid measures the importance of actual sacrifice imperfectly. In fact, the actual cost borne by the buyer not only covers the price paid, but also the *terms of exchange*. These refer to all the concrete practical procedures that lead to transfer of ownership, such as conditions of payment, delivery terms and times, after-sales service, and so on. In some cases, the buyer may have to bear important costs to compare prices, transact and negotiate. This can happen if, for example, the buyer is located in isolated regions. Similarly, the customer may face high *transfer costs*, if he or she changes suppliers after having set the product specifications in relation to a given supplier. The main sources of transfer costs are as follows:

● Costs of modifying products so as to fit a new supplier's product.
● Changes in habits of consuming or using the product.
● Expenditures on training and reorientation of users.
● Investments to acquire new equipment necessary for the use of the new products.
● Psychological costs related to change.

All these costs may be higher for some clients than others. When transfer costs exist, the real cost to the buyer is much higher than the product's monetary price.

Therefore, from the buyer's point of view, the notion of price goes well beyond that of monetary price. It involves all the benefits provided by the product and all the monetary and non-monetary costs borne by the buyer. Hence measures of price sensitivity must take into account all these benefits and costs as well as the product's nominal price. Viewed from the customer's perspective, the price can be redefined as follows:

$$\text{Price} = \frac{\text{Total cost (monetary and non-monetary) supported by the buyer}}{\text{Total benefits (tangible and intangible) provided by the product}}$$

To illustrate the complexity of price viewed in the customer perspective, one can identify seven different ways of changing the above price ratio (Monroe, 1979):

1. Change the quantity of money given up by the buyer.
2. Change the quantity of goods and services provided by the seller.
3. Change the quality of goods or services provided.
4. Change the premiums or discounts to be applied for quantity variations.
5. Change the time and place of transfer of ownership.
6. Change the place and time of payment.
7. Change the acceptable forms of payment.

Importance of pricing decisions

The following points highlight the importance of pricing strategies in the current macro-marketing environment:

- The chosen price directly influences *demand level* and determines the level of activity. A price set too high or too low can endanger the product's development. Therefore, measuring price sensitivity is of crucial importance.

- The selling price directly determines the *profitability of the operation*, not only by the profit margin allowed, but also through quantities sold by fixing the conditions under which fixed costs can be recovered over the appropriate time horizon. Thus, a small price difference may have a major impact on profitability.

- The price set by the firm influences the product or the brand's general perception and contributes to the *brand's positioning* within potential buyers' evoked set. Customers perceive the price as a signal, especially in consumer goods markets. The price quoted invariably creates a notion of quality, and therefore is a component of the brand image.

- More than any other marketing variables, the price is a direct mean for *comparison between competing products or brands*. The slightest change in price is quickly perceived by the market, and because of its visibility it can suddenly overturn the balance of forces. The price is a forced point of contact between competitors.

- Pricing strategy must be compatible with the *other components of operational marketing*. The price must allow for financing of promotional and advertising strategy. Product packaging must reinforce high quality and high price positioning; pricing strategy must respect distribution strategy and allow the granting of necessary distribution margins to ensure that the market coverage objectives can be achieved.

Recent developments in the economic and competitive environment, which were discussed in Chapter 2, have played their part in increasing the importance and complexity of pricing strategies significantly:

- Acceleration of technological progress and *shortening of product life cycles* means that a new activity must be made to pay over a much shorter time span than previously. Given that correction is so much more difficult, a mistake in setting the initial price is that much more serious.

- *Proliferation of brands* or products which are weakly differentiated, the regular appearance of new products and the range of products all reinforce the importance of correct price positioning; yet small differences can sometimes modify the market's perception of a brand quite significantly.

- *Legal constraints*, as well as regulatory and social constraints, such as price controls, setting maximum margins, authorisation for price increases, and so on, limit the firm's autonomy in determining prices.

- *Reduced purchasing power* in most Western economies makes buyers more aware of price differences, and this increased price sensitivity reinforces the role of price as an instrument of stimulating sales and market share.

Given the importance and complexity of these decisions, pricing strategies are often elaborated by the firm's general management.

Alternative pricing objectives

All firms aim to make their activities profitable and to generate the greatest possible economic surplus. This broad objective can in practice take different forms and it is in the firm's interest to clarify from the outset its strategic priorities in setting prices. Generally speaking, possible objectives can be classified in three categories, according to whether they are centred on profits, volumes or competition.

Profit-oriented objectives

Profit-oriented objectives are either profit maximisation or achievement of a sufficient return on invested capital. *Profit maximisation* is the model put forward by economists. In practice, it is difficult to apply this model. Not only does it assume precise knowledge of cost and demand functions for each product; it also assumes a stability that is seldom enjoyed by environmental and competitive factors. The objective of *target return rate on investment* (ROI) is widespread. In practice it takes the form of calculating a target price, or a sufficient price; that is, a price which, for a given level of activity, ensures a fair return on invested capital. This approach, often adopted by large enterprises, has the merit of simplicity, but is incorrect. It ignores the fact that it is the price level that ultimately determines demand level.

Volume-oriented objectives

Volume-oriented objectives aim to maximise current revenue or market share, or simply to ensure sufficient sales growth. Maximising market share implies adopting a *penetration price*, that is a relatively low price, which is lower than competitors' prices, in order to increase volume and consequently market share as fast as possible. Once a dominant position is reached, the objective changes to one of sufficient or 'satisfactory' rate of return. As we saw in Chapter 8, this is a strategy often used by firms having accumulated a high production volume and who expect reduced costs due to learning effects. A totally different strategy is that of *skimming pricing*. The goal here is to achieve high sales revenue, given that some buyers or market segments are prepared to pay a high price because of the product's distinctive (real or perceived) qualities. The objective here is to achieve the highest possible turnover with a high price rather than high volume.

Competition-oriented objectives

Competition-oriented objectives either aim for price stability or to be in line with competitors. In a number of industries dominated by a leading firm, the objective is to establish a stable relationship between prices of various competing products and to avoid wide fluctuations in prices that would undermine customers' confidence. The objective of keeping in line with other firms reveals that the firm is aware of its inability to exercise any influence on the market, especially when there is one dominant firm and products are standardised, as in undifferentiated oligopolies. In this case, the firm prefers to concentrate its efforts on competing on features other than price. Forms of non-price competition will often prevail in this type of market.

To elaborate a pricing strategy, three groups of factors must be taken into consideration: costs, demand and competition. We will now examine successively each of these factors and their implications for price determination.

Cost-based Pricing Procedures

Starting with cost analysis is certainly the most natural way to approach the pricing problem, and it is also the one most familiar to firms. Given that the manufacturer has undergone costs in order to produce and commercialise a product, it is natural that its main preoccupation would be to determine various price levels compatible with constraints such as covering direct and fixed costs and generating a fair profit. Figure 13.2. shows a typical cost structure in which the definitions of the main cost concepts are given.

Cost-based price concepts

Prices, which are based on costs and make no explicit reference to market factors, are called *cost-based prices*. Cost analysis identifies four types of cost-based prices, each responding to specific cost and profit requirements.

The 'floor price'

The *floor price*, or the minimum price, corresponds to direct variable costs (C), also known as 'out-of-pocket costs'. It is the price that only covers the product's replacement value, and therefore implies zero gross profit margins.

Floor price = Direct variable cost

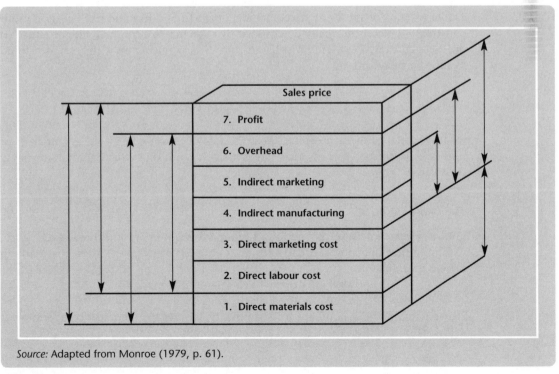

Source: Adapted from Monroe (1979, p. 61).

Figure 13.2   The elements of price

This price concept is useful for negotiating exceptional orders or for second market discounting, when the firm has unused capacity and has the possibility to sell in a new market such that there will be a negligible loss of sales in its main market. Floor prices, also called *marginal price*, are the absolute minimum selling price the firm should accept. Any price above the floor price can allow a firm to use its production capacity to a maximum and still generate extra funds to cover overheads or improve profits. Exceptional orders, generics for large retail chain and foreign markets, provide opportunities for this form of discriminatory pricing strategy.

The 'break-even price'

The *break-even price* (BEP) corresponds to the price where fixed and direct costs are recovered, given the sales volume assumed. It ensures that both the product's replacement value as well as fixed costs (*F*) are recovered.

$$\text{Break-even price} = C + F / E(Q)$$

where $E(Q)$ denotes expected sales volume. The BEP corresponds to the full cost concept, where the level of activity is used as a criterion for allocating the fixed costs.

Break-even prices are usually calculated for different volume levels, as shown in the example of Exhibit 13.1. This defines a range of minimum prices. Note that the break-even price depends on the volume of activity and only coincides with the full cost at that level.

The 'target price'

The *target price*, or sufficient price, includes, apart from direct and fixed costs, a profit constraint, which is normally determined by reference to a 'normal' rate of return (*r*) on invested capital (*K*). This cost-based price is also calculated with reference to an assumed level of activity.

$$\text{Target price} = C + \frac{F}{E(Q)} + \frac{r \cdot K}{E(Q)}$$

where K denotes invested capital and r the rate of return considered as sufficient or normal. Like the break-even price, target price depends on the activity volume being considered.

The 'mark-up price'

The *mark-up price* is set by adding a standard mark-up to the break-even price. Assuming that the firm wants to earn a 20 per cent mark-up on sales, the mark-up price is given by

$$\text{Mark-up price} = \text{BEP} / (1 - \text{desired mark-up})$$

This pricing method, popular for its simplicity, ignores demand and competition. It will work only if the expected sales level is achieved.

The risk of circular logic

Target and mark-up prices are used widely, because of their simplicity and the apparent security arising from the illusory certainty of a margin, since mark-up and target pricing procedures promise to ensure a given return on cost. Their most important shortcoming is the lack of any relationship between price and volume. In fact,

---

Exhibit 13.1

Cost-based Pricing: An Example of Application

*Basic data

Production capacity	180,000 units
Capital invested (K)	$240,000,000
Expected rate of return (r)	10 per cent
Unit direct cost (C)	$1050 per unit
Fixed costs (F)	$90,000,000 per year
Expected sales volume $E(Q)$	120,000 units
Pessimistic estimate	90,000 units
Optimistic estimate	150,000 units

■ **Floor price:**

$$P = C = \$1050 \text{ per unit}$$

■ **Break-even (BE) price:**

$$P = C + \frac{F}{E(Q)} = 1050 + \frac{90,000,000}{E(Q)}$$

$$P_1 = \$2050 \quad P_2 = \$1800 \quad P_3 = \$1650$$

■ **Target price:**

$$P = C + \frac{F}{E(Q)} + \frac{r \cdot K}{E(Q)}$$

$$P = 1050 + \frac{90,000,000}{E(Q)} + \frac{(0.10) \times (240,000,000)}{E(Q)}$$

$$P_1 = \$2317 \quad P_2 = \$2000 \quad P_3 = \$1810$$

■ **Selected target price:**

$$P = \$1950 \text{ per unit}$$

■ **BEV (in volume):**

$$Q_n = \frac{F}{P - C} = \frac{90,000,000}{1950 - 1050} = 100,000 \text{ units}$$

■ **BES (in sales revenue):**

$$SR_n = \frac{F}{\dfrac{P - C}{P}} = \frac{90,000,000}{0.46} = \$195,652,174$$

they implicitly contain a built-in circular logic: volume determines costs, which determine price, which in turn determines the level of demand.

Indeed, there is no guarantee that the adopted target price or mark-up will generate the activity volume on the basis of which it was calculated. Table 13.1 shows what happens to the target price if the firm's sales volume is below the assumed level.

In the example, the expected activity level is 120,000 units and the corresponding target price is £2000. If demand is only 90,000 units, to maintain the desired profitability level the price would have to be increased and the product sold at £2317.

Is raising price the appropriate response in the face of declining demand? Similarly, if the firm's sales exceed expectations, fixed costs are spread over a larger volume and the target price declines. Should management respond to excess demand by cutting prices?

This pricing behaviour runs counter to economic logic and leads to inappropriate recommendations. The firm that sets price from the sole perspective of its own internal needs generally forgoes the profit it seeks.

During the recession of 1974–1975, the automobile industry faced such a dilemma. During 1974–1975, car prices rose on average $1000 while sales fell by 25 per cent. Yet, the automobile industry could not reduce price because of its inflexible, formularised method of pricing. (*Business Week*, 1975)

If all firms within a given industry adopt the same mark-up or target rate of return, prices tend to be similar and price competition is minimised. In practice, cost-based prices are used only as a convenient starting point, because, in general, firms have more reliable information about costs than about demand factors.

Usefulness of cost-based pricing

Cost-orientated prices constitute a starting point for setting a market price. They cannot be the only basis for determining prices because these pricing procedures ignore demand, product perceived value and competition. However, they do have a real *usefulness*, because they provide answers to the following types of questions:

● What is the sales volume or sales revenue required to cover all costs?
● How does the target price or the mark-up price compare with prices of direct competition?
● To what level of market share does the level of sales at the break-even point correspond?
● What is the expected sales increase required to cover a fixed cost increase, such as an advertising campaign, assuming constant price?
● If prices go down, what is the minimum volume increase required to offset the price decrease?
● If prices go up, what is the permissible volume decrease to offset the price increase?
● What is the implied price elasticity necessary to enhance or maintain profitability?
● What is the rate of return on invested capital for different price levels?

Cost analysis is a first necessary step, which helps to identify the problem by focusing attention on the financial implications of various pricing strategies. Armed with this information, the firm is better placed to approach the more qualitative aspects of the problem, namely market sensitivity to prices and competitive reactions.

● Demand-oriented Pricing Procedures

Pricing based exclusively on the firm's own financial needs is inappropriate. In a market economy, it is the buyer who ultimately decides which products will sell. Consequently, in a market-driven organisation an effective pricing procedure *starts with the price the market is most likely to accept*, which in turn determines the target cost. As illustrated in Figure 13.3, it is the market acceptable price that constitutes the constraint for R&D, engineering and purchasing. Thus, price determination in a demand-oriented procedure puts customer sensitivity as the starting point.

The price elasticity concept

An important concept in demand analysis is the *notion of elasticity*. Elasticity directly measures customers' price sensitivity and ideally allows the calculation of quantities demanded at various price levels. Recall the definition of price elasticity:

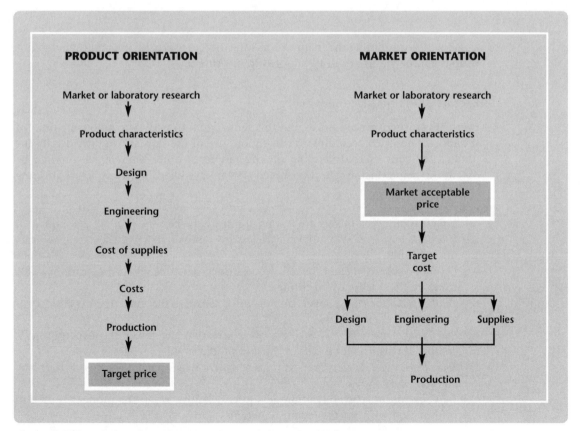

Figure 13.3 Price determination in a market-oriented perspective

it is the percentage change in a product's unit sales resulting from a 1 per cent change in its price.

$$\varepsilon = \frac{\% \text{ of variation of unit sales}}{\% \text{ of variation price}}$$

Price elasticity is negative, since a price increase generally produces a decline in sales while a price cut generally produces an increase in sales. As an illustration, Table 13.1 compares the impact of price elasticity on quantities and on sales revenue for an elastic (– 3.7) and an inelastic (– 0.19) demand.

Table 13.1   Impact of price elasticity on quantity and on sales revenue

Elastic demand curve: $\varepsilon = -3.7$			Inelastic demand curve: $\varepsilon = -0.19$		
Price	Quantity (in 000)	Sales revenue (in 000 F)	Price	Quantity (in 000)	Sales Revenue (in 000 F)
12,000	80	960,000	8.00	300	2400
9000	400	3,600,000	6.00	320	1920
7000	1200	8,400,000	4.00	340	1360

We will first examine the main factors affecting price sensitivity, and then describe various approaches that can be adopted to measure it.

Factors affecting price sensitivity

Every buyer is sensitive to prices, but this sensitivity can vary tremendously from one situation to another, according to the importance of the satisfaction provided by the product, or conversely depending on the sacrifices, other than price, imposed by obtaining the product. Nagle and Holden (1994) have identified nine factors affecting buyers' price sensitivity:

- *Unique-value effect*: buyers are less price sensitive when the product is unique.
- *Substitute awareness effect*: buyers are less price-sensitive when they are less aware of substitutes.
- *Difficult comparison effect*: buyers are less price sensitive when they cannot easily compare the quality of substitutes.
- *Total expenditure effect*: buyers are less price sensitive the lower the expenditure is to a ratio of their income.
- *End benefit effect*: buyers are less price sensitive the lower the expenditure is compared with the total cost of the end product.
- *Shared cost effect*: buyers are less price sensitive when part of the cost is borne by another party.
- *Sunk investment effect*: buyers are less price sensitive when the product is used in conjunction with assets previously bought.

● *Price-quality effect*: buyers are less price sensitive when the product is assumed to have more quality, prestige or exclusiveness.
● *Inventory effect*: buyers are less price sensitive when they cannot store the product.

The questions to examine for assessing buyers' price sensitivity are presented in Exhibit 13.2.

Note that these determinants of price sensitivity apply equally to the decision of buying a particular product category (primary demand price sensitivity) and that of buying a particular brand within a product category (interbrand price sensitivity). In the first case, the question would, for example, be to choose between a laptop computer or a hi-fi; in the second case, the alternatives would be, for example, to buy a Compaq or an IBM laptop computer. Both kinds of decision are affected by the price level of the alternatives.

Price sensitivity of the organisational buyer

We saw in Chapter 3 that in business-to-business markets, buyers' needs are generally well defined and the functions performed by products clearly specified. In these conditions, it is sometimes easier to determine the importance of price to the organisational customer. Porter (1980, pp. 115–18) observed that buyers who are *not price sensitive* tend to have the following behavioural characteristics or motivations:

● The cost of the product is a small part of the buyer's product cost and/or purchasing budget.
● The penalty for product failure is high relative to its cost.
● Effectiveness of the product (or service) can yield major savings or improvement in performance.
● The buyer competes with a high quality strategy to which the purchased product is perceived to contribute.
● The buyer seeks a custom-designed or differentiated variety.
● The buyer is very profitable and/or can readily pass on the cost of inputs.
● The buyer is poorly informed about the product and/or does not purchase from well-defined specifications.
● The motivation of the actual decision-maker is not narrowly defined as minimising the cost of inputs.

Industrial market research studies can help in identifying these behavioural characteristics or requirements. These are useful to know in order to direct pricing policy.

Optimum price based on elasticity

The economic and marketing literature contains many econometric studies on measuring price elasticities, as shown in Table 13.5. For a summary of elasticity studies, see Hanssens *et al.* (1990). Tellis (1988) found a mean price elasticity of –2.5. Broadbent (1980) reported an average price elasticity of –1.6 for major British brands. Lambin, covering a sample of 137 brands, reported an average price elasticity of –1.74 (Lambin, 1976, 1988).

Exhibit 13.2

Factors Affecting Price Sensitivity

1. The Unique Value Effect
- Does the product have any (tangible or intangible) attributes that differentiate it from competing products?
- How much do buyers value those unique, differentiating attributes?

2. The Substitute Awareness Effect
- What alternatives do buyers have (considering both competing brands and competing products)?
- Are buyers aware of alternative suppliers or substitute products?

3. The Difficult Comparison Effect
- How difficult is it for buyers to compare the offers of different suppliers? Can the attributes of a product be determined by observation, or must the product be purchased and consumed to learn what it offers?
- Is the product highly complex, requiring costly specialists to evaluate its differentiating attributes?
- Are the prices of different suppliers easily comparable, or are they stated for different sizes and combinations that make comparisons difficult?

4. The Total Expenditure Effect
- How significant are buyers' expenditures of the product in cash terms and (for a consumer product) as a portion of their incomes?

5. The End Benefit Effect
- What benefit do buyers seek from the product?
- How price-sensitive are buyers to the cost of the end benefit?
- What portion of the benefit does the product's price account for?

6. The Shared Cost Effect
- Do the buyers pay the full cost of the product?
- If not, what portion of the cost do they pay?

7. The Sunk Investment Effect
- Must buyers of the product make complementary expenditures in anticipation of its continued use?
- For how long are buyers locked in by those expenditures?

8. The Price-Quality Effect
- Is a prestige image an important attribute for the product?
- Is the product enhanced in value when its price excludes some consumers?
- Is the product of unknown quality, and are there few reliable cues for ascertaining quality before purchase? If so, how great would the loss to buyers be of low quality relative to the price of the product?

9. The Inventory Effect
- Do buyers hold inventories of the product?
- Do they expect the current price to be temporary?

Source: Nagle and Holden (1994).

Optimal price determination

Economic theory shows that the less elastic (in absolute terms) the demand for a product, the higher the optimal price, that is the price that maximises profit; if we know the elasticity, the optimal price can be calculated as follows:

$$P_{opt} = C^* \frac{\varepsilon}{\varepsilon + 1}$$

Or in words,

$$\text{Optimal Price} = \text{Unit direct cost} \times \text{Cost mark-up}$$

where

$$\text{Cost mark-up} = \frac{\text{Price elasticity}}{\text{Price elasticity} + 1}$$

Thus, the optimal price is obtained by multiplying the unit variable cost (or marginal cost) by a percentage, which depends on the price elasticity and is independent of cost. The derivation of this optimisation rule is presented in Lambin (1994, p. 301).

Table 13.2 shows that the optimal mark-up is higher when price elasticity is lower in absolute value, that is closer to unity and gives some comparisons of mark-up coefficients for a range of elasticities.

One observes that, when price elasticity is high, which is the case in highly competitive markets of undifferentiated products, mark-up is close to unity; the firm's market power is weak and the price accepted by the market is close to unit costs. Conversely, the closer elasticity is to unity, the higher is the price acceptable by the market.

By way of illustration, if $\varepsilon = -2.1$ and $C = 105$, the optimal price is equal to

$$P_{opt} = (105) \cdot \left(\frac{-2.1}{-2.1 + 1} \right) = (105) \cdot (1.9) = 205F$$

The optimal mark-up is here equal to 1.9.

Optimisation rules proposed by economic theory, initially developed in the monopoly case (Dorfman and Steiner, 1954), have been extended to the oligopoly

Table 13.2   Optimal cost mark-up as a function of price elasticity

Price elasticity $\varepsilon_{q,p}$	Optimal cost mark-up $\varepsilon_{q,p}/\varepsilon_{q,p+1}$	Price elasticity $\varepsilon_{q,p}$	Optimal cost mark-up $\varepsilon_{q,p}/\varepsilon_{q,p+1}$
−1.0	–	2.4	1.71
−1.2	6.00	2.6	1.00
−1.4	3.50	–	–
−1.6	2.67	3.0	1.50
−1.8	2.22	4.0	1.33
−2.0	2.00	5.0	1.25
−2.2	1.83	–	–
–	–	15.0	1.07

q = quantity; p = price.

case (Lambin *et al.*, 1975) and also to the dynamic case when market response is distributed over time (Nerlove and Arrow, 1962; Jacquemin, 1973).

Methods of price sensitivity measurement

Several methods exist to estimate customers' price sensitivity. These methods can be grouped into four main categories:

1. *The expert judgement* method consists in asking market experts to provide three estimates or points of the price response curve, successively the lowest realistic, the highest realistic prices and the associated sales volume, plus the expected sales at the medium price.

2. *Customer surveys*, directs or indirects. The most popular is the indirect method through conjoint analysis, presented in Chapter 4 and illustrated with examples of application in Chapter 5.

3. *Price experimentations*, field or laboratory experiments. We are here in the domain of causal research as discussed in Chapter 4.

4. *Econometric studies* based on time series data or on panel data. As underlined above, the availability of scanner data greatly facilitates this type of analysis, particularly in the food sector.

Each of these methods has its own advantage and disadvantages; they are summarised in Table 13.3.

Table 13.3 Evaluation of methods of collecting price response data

Methods/ Criteria	Expert Judgements	Customer Surveys		Price Experiments	Historical Market Data
		Direct	Conjoint Analysis		
Validity	Medium	Low	Medium–High	Medium–Low	High
Reliability	Medium–High	Uncertain	Medium–High	High	Low
Costs	Very low	Medium–Low	Medium	Medium–High	Depends on availability and accessibility
Applicability to new products	Yes	Questionable	Yes	Yes	No
Applicability to established products	Yes	Yes	Yes	Yes	Yes
Overall evaluation	Useful for new products, new situations	Questionable	Very useful	Useful	Useful for established products

Source: Dolan and Simon (1996, p. 75).

Usefulness of elasticity measures

Knowledge of the order of magnitude of an elasticity is on the whole useful in many ways:

● Elasticities provide information about the direction in which prices should change in order to stimulate demand and increase turnover.
● Comparing elasticities of competing brands identifies those that can withstand a price increase better, thus revealing their market power.
● Comparing elasticities of products in the same category helps to adjust prices within the category.
● Cross-elasticities help to predict demand shifts from one brand to another.

To illustrate, Table 13.4 shows estimated price elasticities in the car market and in the market for air transport in the USA. Although the estimates have insufficient precision for the exact calculation of prices, the results are nevertheless very enlightening as far as pricing policy orientation for each product category is concerned.

Table 13.4 Price elasticity estimates: two examples from the US market

Demand for automobiles		Demand for air transport	
Sub-compact	–0.83	First class	–0.75
Compact	–1.20	Economy	–1.40
Intermediate	–1.30	Discount	–2.10
Full-size	–1.54		
Luxury	–2.07		

Source: Automobile data from Carlson (1978); air transport data from Oum and Gillen (1981).

Limitations of price elasticity measures

Despite the relevance of these works, there have been very few practical applications of this highly quantitative approach to the problem of pricing, except maybe in some large enterprises. The reason is that the notion of elasticity presents a number of conceptual and operational difficulties, which reduce its practical usefulness:

● Elasticity measures a relationship based on buying behaviour and is therefore only observable *after the fact*; its predictive value depends on the stability of the conditions that gave rise to the observation; it cannot, for example, be used to determine the price of new products.

● In many situations, the problem is not so much to know how to adapt prices to present market sensitivities, but to know how to change and *act upon this sensitivity* in the direction sought by the firm. From this viewpoint, it is more interesting to know the product's perceived value by the targeted group of buyers.

● Elasticity measures the impact of price on quantity bought, but does not measure the effect of price on the propensity to try the product, on repeat purchases, exclusivity rate, and so on. But these are all important notions for understanding consumers' response mechanisms with respect to prices. Therefore, *other measures*, which are less aggregate, need to be developed for marketing management.

Furthermore, in practice it is often very hard to get sufficiently stable and reliable estimates of price elasticities, which could be used to calculate an optimal selling price.

In an econometric study, an estimate having a Student t-value of 4.0 (rarely obtained) is very satisfactory, because it implies a statistical significance level of 1 per cent for degrees of freedom above 30 (rarely observed). However, at this level of precision, the coefficient of variation, which is the ratio of the standard deviation to the mean, is 25 per cent; this implies that it is highly likely that the true value of the estimated price elasticity falls in an interval of plus or minus 25 per cent, which is operationally a totally unacceptable level of imprecision.

These limitations are inherent in the economic model, which is developed more to help understand economic behaviour than as a decision-making tool. This does not imply, however, that the economic theory of price determination has no relevance to the study of the problem of price determination. Even if imprecise, the order of magnitude of an estimated price elasticity helps in determining the direction of price changes and its impact on sales revenue. A summary of econometric work on marketing variables elasticity is presented in Table 13.5.

Table 13.5 Comparing average elasticity of marketing variables

Published sources	Number of observations	Average value of estimated elasticities			
		Advertising	Price	Quality	Distribution
Lambin (1976, 1988)	127	0.081	−1.735	0.521	1.395
Leone and Shultz (1980)	25	0.003–0.230	–	–	–
Assmus *et al.* (1984)	22	0.221 (0.264)	–	–	–
Hagerty *et al.* (1988)	203	0.003 (0.105)	−0.985 (1.969)	0.344 (0.528)	0.304 (0.255)
Neslin and Shoemaker (1983)	25	–	−1.800	–	–
Tellis (1988)	220	–	−1.760	–	–

Value pricing

Value pricing is a customer-based pricing procedure, which is an outgrowth of the *multi-attribute product concept*. From the customer's viewpoint, a product is the total package of benefits that is received when using the product. Therefore, the customer-oriented company should set its price according to customers' perceptions of product benefits and costs. To determine the price, the marketer needs to understand the customers' perceptions of benefits as well as their perceptions of the costs other than price. Customers balance the benefits of a purchase against its costs. When the product under consideration has the best relationship of benefit to cost, the customer is inclined to buy the product. This customer-based pricing procedure can be implemented in different ways.

The product's perceived value

The basic idea behind this method is the same: it is the product or the brand's perceived value, which should determine the price level. By analysing and measuring the buyers' perception and its determinants using the compositional method, a score of total perceived value can be derived and used to set the price. The notion of perceived value is a direct extension of the multi-attribute attitude model described in Chapter 3.

By way of illustration, let us examine the data of Table 13.6 and the scores given by a sample of potential buyers to brand A and to its direct competitor brand B, over six tangible and intangible attributes. In the example presented, respondents have first evaluated on a 10-point scale the importance of each attribute and then on a 10-point scale also the performance of each brand on each attribute.

Table 13.6 Perceived value analysis: an example

Attributes other than Price	Importance of Attributes	Absolute Performance (scale from 1 to 10)		Relative Performance Brand A
		Brand A	Direct Competitor	
(1)	(2)	(3)	(4)	(5 = 3 + 4)
Tangibles:				
A1	10	8.1	7.2	1.13
A2	20	9.0	7.3	1.23
A3	20	9.2	6.5	1.42
A4	15	8.0	8.0	1.00
Intangibles:				
A5	10	8.0	8.0	1.00
A6	25	9.4	6.4	1.47
Total	100	–	–	–
Absolute performance	–	8.8	7.1	–
Relative performance	–	1.24	0.81	–

The total perceived value of each brand is obtained by multiplying the scores given to each attribute by their respective degree of importance and by summing the weighted scores. The totals obtained are then expressed in index form by reference to the direct competitor. One obtains respectively,

$$Brand\ A = 1.24 \quad Brand\ B = 0.81$$

Thus, one observes that brand A has higher perceived value than brand B, its direct competitor, because brand A performs better on the most important attributes (A6, A2 and A3). If these results can be considered as representative of the target segment perceptions, and assuming that the other marketing factors are equal, the maximum acceptable price for brand A could be determined by reference to the average perceived value (here 7.95), with a brand A's maximum acceptable price 10.7 per cent higher and for brand B a price 11 per cent lower.

> If the average market price is equal to 5000F, brand A could charge a maximum price as high as 5535F while brand B, to be accepted by the market, should charge a price as low as 4450F.

If brand A charges a price lower than its maximum acceptable price, it will have an operational competitive advantage over brand B (better at the same price), which sooner or later will translate into a market share gain. This pricing procedure, based on a compositional approach, is particularly useful when price sensitivity is strongly influenced by qualitative attributes like brand image effect.

The maximum acceptable price

This second pricing procedure is particularly useful for setting the price of industrial products, whose core benefit to the buyer is a cost reduction. To evaluate what the customer is prepared to pay, the procedure followed is to identify and evaluate the different satisfactions or services provided by the product as well as all the costs (other than price) it implies. Thus the procedure is the following:

- Understand the total use of the product from the buyer's point of view.
- Analyse the benefits generated by the product.
- Analyse the costs implied by the acquisition and the use of the product.
- Make cost–benefit trade-offs and determine the maximum acceptable price.

> The highest price that the customer will be willing to pay for the product is given by
>
> Benefits – Costs other than price = Maximum acceptable price (MAP)

The benefits to consider can be functional (the core service), operational, financial or personal. Similarly, the costs implied other than price are just as diverse: acquisition costs, installation, risk of failure, habit modification, and so on.

If the target market is segmented, this analysis should be done for different groups of buyers with non-identical behaviour. Comparing the maximum acceptable price with competitors' prices helps evaluate the firm's margin for manoeuvre. Exhibit 13.3 presents an example of the application of this method. See also Shapiro *et al.* (1978) and Ross (1984).

Contributions of conjoint analysis

The same kind of result can be obtained with a *decompositional approach*, or the conjoint analysis method described in Chapter 4. To illustrate, we refer to a conjoint analysis based on a sample of 200 individuals and made in the blended cigarettes market, in order to compare the price sensitivity of four leading brands: Marlboro, Barclay, Camel and Gauloises Blondes (see Lambin 1994, pp. 150–2). Let us examine here the results obtained for two respondents (no. 17 and no. 86, respectively). As in

Exhibit 13.3

Calculating the Maximum Acceptable Price:

- **Product Description**
  - A chemical compound to be used in conjunction with the regular water-softening chemicals.

- **Uses of the Product**
  - To disperse the water-softening compounds, thus lengthening their economic life.
  - To reduce rust formation in the boiler system.

- **Benefits of the product**
  - Core benefit: reduce the amount of softening chemicals by 35 per cent.
  - Prevent rust formation.
  - Reduction in time and effort required to regenerate the softeners.

- **Costs other than price**
  - Installation of a dispenser and of a storage tank in the plant.
  - Service of the installation and technical assistance.
  - Risk of breakdown.
  - Lack of reference of the supplier.
  - Custom modification.

- **Costs–benefit trade-off analysis**
  - Average use: 40,000 gallons of softening per year.
  - Cost per gallon: 50 cents.
  - Average cost saving: 14,000 gallons (35 per cent), or $7000.
  - Volume of Aqua-Pur: ratio:1/7, or 3715 gallons (26,000/7).
  - Cost of installation: $450, or $90 per year over 5 years.
  - Cost of maintenance: $320 per year.
  - Total maximum acceptable cost: $7000 – ($90 + $320) = $6590.
  - Maximum acceptable unit price: $6590/3715 gallons = $1.77 per gallon.
  - Price of direct competitor: $1.36.

the example presented in Chapter 4, the utilities are expressed in terms of preference ranks lost when the price increases from its lowest level (F57) to a higher one. For respondent no. 17, the following utilities were obtained:

$$(F62; U = -2.5), (F67; U = -3.5) \text{ and } (F72; U = -5.0)$$

We thus have three observations and using ordinary least squares (OLS) average price elasticity was calculated as: $\varepsilon = -3.59$ ($R^2 = 0.958$). For respondent no. 86, we obtained the following pairs of values:

$$(F62: U = -0.25), (F67: U = -1.25), (F72: U = 1.50)$$

The calculated elasticity here is: $\varepsilon = -1.11$ ($R^2 = 0.914$)

Note that the difference in price sensitivity between the two respondents is quite high. Now suppose that we have similar information for a representative sample of 200 buyers. An average price elasticity could be estimated for the whole sample as well as for subgroups of buyers of high or low price sensitivity.

This kind of elasticity coefficient measures price sensitivity in terms of utility rather than in terms of quantity. Although more vague, it is nevertheless useful for comparison of different buyers' relative price sensitivities and to determine the best price level.

Flexible pricing strategies

Firms do not have a single price, but a variety of prices adapted to different market situations. Flexible pricing strategies occur in market situations where the same product is sold to different customers at different prices. Flexible pricing strategies arise primarily because of customers' heterogeneity, showing different price sensitivities, but also because of cost differences or promotional objectives. Price flexibility can be achieved in different ways: by region, period, product form or from one segment to another. We shall examine four different ways of achieving price flexibility. In the economic literature, the term *price discrimination* has been used to designate pricing variations not justified by cost differences.

Second market discounting

This situation occurs when a firm has excess production capacity and has the opportunity to sell in a new market such that there will be a negligible increase in fixed or variable costs and no loss of sales in its first market. The minimum acceptable selling price the firm should accept is the floor price, that is the unit direct cost. Opportunities for this pricing strategy exist in foreign trade, private label brands or special demographic groups, like students, children or senior citizens. The essential requirement for this strategy is that customers of the lower price market cannot resell the product in the higher price market because of the high transaction costs implied.

Periodic discounting

The pricing problem is different here. How to price a product confronted with different price sensitivity among potential buyers at the beginning and at the end of the seasonal period? Some buyers want to buy only at the beginning of the period and are not very price sensitive, while others want to buy the product at any time, but are price sensitive. To exploit the consumers' heterogeneity of demand, the firm will sell at the high price at the beginning of the period and systematically discount the product at the end of the period. This is the principle often involved in the temporal markdowns and periodic discounting of off-season fashion goods, off-season travel fares, matinee tickets and happy hour drinks.

An essential principle underlying this strategy of periodic discounting is the manner of discounting, which is predictable over time and generally known to consumers, who will, therefore, behave accordingly (Tellis, 1986, p. 150).

Random discounting

Which pricing strategy should be adopted in a market where the same product is sold at a low price by some firms and at a high price by others, knowing that some buyers are ready to spend time searching for the low price while others are not ready to do so? In this case, we have heterogeneity of demand with respect to perceived search costs among consumers. The objective of the firm is twofold here: (a) to sell at a high price to the maximum number of 'uninformed' consumers and at the same time (b) to prevent 'informed' consumers from buying at the low price of the competition.

The recommended strategy here is *random discounting*, which involves maintaining a high price and discounting the product periodically 'at random'. The manner of discounting is crucial: it should be indiscernible or random so those uninformed buyers will buy randomly, usually at the high price and the 'informed' will look around or wait until they can buy at the low price (Tellis, 1986, p. 150).

Promotional prices

Companies are often led to temporarily reduce their prices in order to stimulate sales. Promotional prices can take various forms: loss leader pricing as frequently adopted by department stores or supermarkets, special events pricing, low interest financing as often proposed by car dealers, cash rebates, warranties and service contracts, and so on. Every promotion is in fact a *disguised price reduction* having the merit of being temporary and therefore enabling the seller to go back easily to the initial price.

During the last ten years, promotions of all kinds have proliferated with, as the main result, a loss of credibility of the pricing policies adopted by manufacturers and resellers as well. To regain this credibility, two pricing policies are today of current application by resellers in the food sector namely: either *every day fair pricing*, or *every day low pricing* (EDLP), that is slightly reduced price available on a permanent basis. This last pricing policy the one adopted by the supermarket chain Colruyt in Belgium, which has developed a very sophisticated system of price monitoring and who commits itself to the lowest price charged in the market.

One form of promotional pricing regaining popularity among manufacturers is cash rebates, which can be used to stimulate sales without actually cutting prices. Cash rebates are coupons offered to encourage purchase and which have to be mailed back to the manufacturer after the purchase The rebate may be as high as $75 for a Nikon camera or $50 for an image scanner. By comparison with a price cut, this promotional practice has a certain number of advantages for the manufacturer:

● The basic price is not modified and therefore the promotion has no negative effect on the brand image.
● Manufacturers can offer price cuts directly to customers, independently of the retailer who could keep the same price on the shelf and pocket the difference.
● Rebates can be rolled out and shut off quickly, leaving manufacturers to fine tune inventories or respond quickly to competitors without actually cutting the price.
● Cash rebates are inexpensive to the extent that many customers never bother to redeem them, allowing manufacturers to offer phantom discounts.
● Because customers fill out forms with names and addresses and other data, rebates also set off a gusher of information about customers useful in direct marketing.

According to a study published by the *Wall Street Journal* (11 February 1998), Only 5 to 10 per cent of customers redeem cash rebates.

Price administration

Price administration deals with price adjustments for sales made under different conditions, in different quantities, to different types of intermediary in different geographic locations, with different conditions of payment, and so on. These price adjustments or discounts are designed to reward customers whose buying behaviour contributes to cost reductions for the firm. This is the case for quantity discounts, cash payment discounts, seasonal discounts, functional discounts, and so on. For more on this topic, see Monroe (1979, Chapter 11).

Pricing of services and 'yield management'

Differential pricing is of common application in the service sector, and more particularly in sectors with limited and fixed production capacity, like hotels, airlines, media, and so on who have to yield income from perishable assets (see Exhibit 13.4). These sectors have in common the following characteristics:

Exhibit 13.4

Yield Management: Basic Principles

For the majority of seasonal products, the initial launching price is high and then progressively marked down to move the stock. Markdown will continue until the last product is sold. A similar system can be used by services to reach optimal capacity but it will not optimise revenues. Yield management works just the opposite. The lowest-discount items are sold first and the highest priced sold last.

If all the seats on a 200-seat aircraft were priced at a discount fare of $125, the plane would fill quickly with leisure travellers. However, many individuals would be willing to pay more than $125 for a seat. These individuals tend to be business travellers who may not know their schedule until a day or two prior to departure or want more comfort than is offered in the coach section. In fact, these individuals may be willing to pay $300, $400 or more for the seat. Based on historical data and analysis of when passengers made reservations, yield management will build a price schedule and reserve some of the seats for business travellers who are less price sensitive. They will price these seats at $350. Working backward, the airline may price the next 30 at $275, and so on; and the last 60 at $125. To get the $125 price, the airline may have restrictions such at least 30-day advance reservations, no refunds or exchange without a penalty, and a Saturday night Stayfree. Instead of the $25,000 sales revenue earned at the $125 price, $40,500 would be generated. When sales lag behind the schedule, the price is lowered to fill the seats that were allocated. As soon as all seats are sold at one price range, the price is increased to the next level. This increase in price will slow demand.

Source: adapted from Kurtz and Clow (1998, pp. 254–5).

- the proposed service cannot be stocked;
- the service can be booked in advance;
- the production capacity is fixed and its increase would be very costly;
- the market can be segmented on the basis of price and service flexibility criteria.

In the airline market, typically the market can be subdivided into two distinct segments:

- the business travellers who are not price sensitive, very sensitive to schedule flexibility and to comfort; they make their reservations at short notice;
- the vacationers who are very price sensitive, organise their holidays several weeks or months ahead and are ready to accept restrictions reducing their flexibility like advance booking, penalty for change, minimal comfort, and so on.

Using this heterogeneity of demand, airline companies sell their regular tickets at a high price and give high discounts to travellers purchasing their ticket well before their departure date. The problem for these companies is to allocate the production capacity in a dynamic way among different price categories in order to optimise sales revenue.

By combining low tariffs and rigid schedules, airline companies can charge a sufficiently low price to attract vacationers without making price concessions to non-price sensitive travellers. This pricing method initially developed by American Airlines is now in application in numerous service sectors (Smith *et al.* 1992).

Competition-oriented Pricing Procedures

As far as competition is concerned, two kinds of factors greatly influence the firm's autonomy in its pricing strategy: the sector's *competitive structure*, characterised by the number of competing firms, and the importance of *the product's perceived value*:

- *Competitive structures* were described in Chapter 9. Clearly, when the firm is a monopoly, autonomy is great in setting its price; it tends to diminish as the number of competitors increases; we have monopoly and perfect competition at the extremes, and differentiated oligopoly and monopolistic situations as the intermediate positions.

- The *product's perceived value* results from the firm's efforts to differentiate in order to achieve an external competitive advantage; where an element of differentiation exists and is perceived by the buyer as of value, the buyer is usually prepared to pay a price above that of competing products. In this case, the firm has some degree of autonomy over prices.

Table 13.7 presents these two factors, each at two levels of intensity (low or high). We can thus identify four distinct situations, in each of which the question of price determination takes on a different form.

Reality is, of course, more complex and there is a continuum of situations. Nevertheless, it is helpful to place a product in one of these quadrants to understand the problem of price determination:

Table 13.7   Competitive environments of pricing decisions

Perceived value of the product	Number of competitors	
	Low	**High**
High	Monopoly or differentiated oligopoly	Monopolistic competition
Weak	Undifferentiated oligopoly	Pure or perfect competition

- When the number of competitors is low and the product's perceived value is high, we are in structures close to *monopoly or differentiated oligopoly*. Price is a tool for the firm, which has a margin for manoeuvre varying with the buyer's perceived value of the differentiating attribute.

- At the other extreme, where there are many competitors and products are perceived as a commodity, we are close to the *perfect competition* structure where prices are largely determined by the interplay of supply and demand. The firm has practically no autonomy in its pricing strategy.

- The lower-left quadrant, with a low number of competitors and low perceived value, corresponds to an *undifferentiated oligopolistic* structure in which interdependence between competitors is often high, thus limiting their autonomy. Here prices will tend to be aligned with those of the market leader.

- Finally, in the upper-right quadrant we have highly differentiated products offered by a large number of competitors; this corresponds to imperfect or *monopolistic competition* where there is some degree of autonomy, this being limited by the intensity of competition.

These market structures are very different and they can be observed at various stages of a product market's life cycle.

Anticipating competitors' behaviour

In many market situations, competitors' interdependence is high and there is a 'market price', which serves as reference to all. This is usually the case when there is *undifferentiated oligopoly*, where total demand is no longer expanding and the offerings of existing competitors are hardly differentiated. This type of competitive structure tends to prevail during the maturity stage of products' life cycle.

In these markets, the firm can align itself with competitors' prices or those of the industry leader. It can fix its price at a higher level, thus taking the risk of losing some market share. Alternatively, it can fix its price below the market level, thus seeking a competitive advantage that it cannot find from other sources, but also taking the risk of launching a price war. The problem therefore is to determine *relative price*. The outcome of these strategies largely depends on the reactions of competitors.

The objective of analysing competition in pricing strategies is *to evaluate competitors' capabilities to act and react*. In particular, one needs to estimate the reaction elasticity of the most dangerous competitor(s) if prices were to go up or down. We discussed the notion of reaction elasticity in Chapter 8 (see Table 8.3).

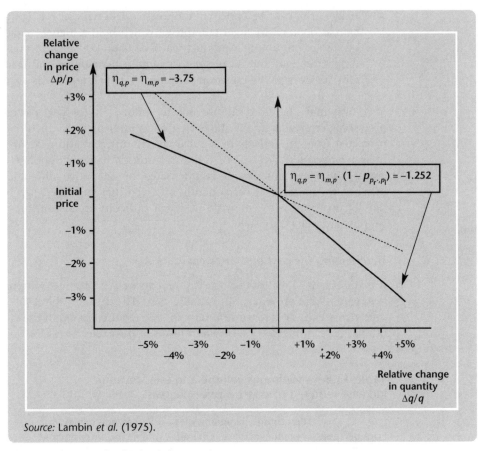

Source: Lambin *et al.* (1975).

Figure 13.4 The kinked demand curve

The direction and intensity of competitors' reactions vary when prices move upwards or downwards. As shown in Figure 13.4, the firm faces a *kinked demand curve*. Elasticity is different on either side of the market price because of different competitive reactions. Some conditions are more favourable to price decreases and some to price increases. These are the conditions that need to be identified.

Initiating price cuts

Initiating a *price cut* with a view to stimulate demand is relevant only when total demand for the product can grow. Otherwise, if the firm reduces its price and if all the competitors react immediately and follow suit, the profits of each will drop and their respective market shares will remain exactly as before in a market that remains the same size, although average price has decreased.

There are, however, some situations, which might be favourable to a price cut in a non-expansible market, without entailing rapid reactions from competitors:

● When competitors' costs are higher and they cannot lower their prices without endangering profitability; not following the price cut implies a loss of market share unless factors of differentiation neutralise the price difference.

● Smaller firms can use a price cut more easily. This represents a lighter investment for them as opposed to larger enterprises, which hold a higher market share, because the cost of promoting a product via price is proportional to sales volume. Larger competitors may indeed prefer to maintain their prices and react on a different front, for example by increasing advertising, which represents a fixed cost.

A firm may therefore choose not to follow a price cut, particularly when its product's perceived value is above that of its immediate competitors. It will then be protected from the effects of a price cut by differentiation factors, such as brand image, range of services or customer relations. Changing suppliers implies transfer costs, which are not always compensated by the price difference. In industrial markets, for example, it is frequently observed that customers accept price differentials of up to 10 per cent without much difficulty if relationships with the usual supplier are well established.

Determining the cost of a price cut

It is important to realise that the *cost of a price cut* is often very high, especially for a firm with a high proportion of variable costs. The data in Table 13.8 define the necessary increases in sales revenue and in volume required to retain the same gross margin (25 per cent in this case) at different levels of price cut.

Table 13.8   Minimum volume and sales revenue increase required to offset a price decrease

Price decrease	Percentage minimum sales revenue increase required	Percentage minimum volume increase required
5%	18	25
10%	50	66
15%	112	150
20%	300	400

(Assuming a gross profit margin of 25 per cent).
Source: Monroe (1979, pp. 70–3).

In this particular case, where the gross margin of 25 per cent before the price cut is to be held, the number of units sold must more than double to compensate for a price cut of 15 per cent. One can imagine that the necessary increase in sales can rapidly be above the impact that can reasonably be expected from a price cut.

Furthermore, it can be shown that a price cut is less favourable to a firm with high variable costs, because the necessary increase in sales to keep the same margin will be higher, the higher the proportion of variable costs (Monroe, 1979, p. 73). In general, for a price decrease, the necessary volume increase to maintain the same level of profitability is given by

$$\text{Volume increase (\%)} = \left(\frac{x}{M^* - x} \right) \times 100$$

where x is the percentage price decrease expressed as a decimal and M^* is the gross profit margin as a percentage of selling price before the price cut.

To illustrate, if a price cut of 9 per cent is envisaged and the gross profit margin is 30 per cent, the required sales volume increase is

$$\text{Volume increase (\%)} = \left(\frac{0.09}{0.30 - 0.09}\right) \times 100 = 42.86 \text{ per cent}$$

If the gross profit margin were to decrease to 25 per cent or 20 per cent the same price cut of 9 per cent would require sales increases of 56.25 per cent and 81.82 per cent, respectively. For the derivation of the break-even formula, see Nagle (1987, pp. 44–6).

Therefore, the firm having the lowest variable costs will be induced to initiate a significant price cut, in the knowledge that other firms could not follow suit.

Computing implied price elasticity

It is also possible to derive an *implied price elasticity* from these figures. This is the price elasticity that should prevail within the targeted group of buyers before profits could be increased.

In the previous example, the price cut of 9 per cent ought to give rise to a 42.86 per cent increase in sales volume in order to retain the gross profit margin at 30 per cent. Therefore, the implied price elasticity is

$$\varepsilon = \frac{+42.86\%}{-9\%} = -4.76$$

A price elasticity of –4.8 per cent is very high and assumes a very price-sensitive demand. If it is considered that the product's market demand is less elastic, and if profit is the only choice criterion, then the price cut is not economically justified.

The risk of a *price war* is always present in an oligopolistic market, which explains why firms are reluctant to initiate price cuts. There are, however, situations where a price cut can improve the competitive position of the firm. As discussed in Chapter 8, reducing the profit margin with price cuts may be compensated for by market share gains, which in the long run mean higher profitability because of cost reductions due to experience effects. Another reason for a price war might be to eliminate a potentially dangerous competitor.

Experience curve pricing

As discussed in Chapter 9, in sectors where the cost of value added represents a large proportion of total unit cost, substantial cost reductions can be obtained as accumulated production increases. If consumers in this market are price sensitive, a good strategy for the firm having the largest experience is to price aggressively, even below current cost, as illustrated in Figure 13.5(a). This strategy presents several advantages. First, competing firms will have to leave the market and the leading company will be confronted with fewer rivals. Second, the firm can benefit from the sales of the other firms and gain experience more rapidly. Also, because of the lower prevailing market price, new buyers will be encouraged to enter the market.

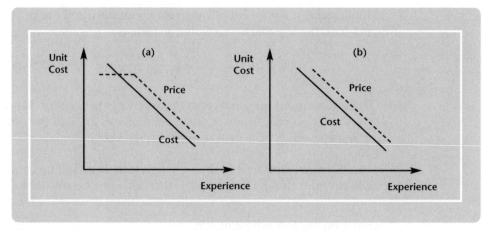

Figure 13.5   Experience curve pricing strategies (logarithmic axes)

However, pricing below cost cannot be maintained for extended periods of time. A less aggressive pricing strategy is the one depicted in Figure 13.5(b) where a parallel is maintained between cost and price reductions.

Initiating price increases

Initiating a *price increase* is also a difficult decision. The firm initiating the increase must be certain that competitors are willing to follow suit. Generally speaking, this willingness depends on the prevailing market conditions at the time, and in particular when production capacity is fully used and demand is growing. As in the case of a price cut, before starting any initiative, it is in the firm's interest to evaluate its margin for manoeuvre.

If price is increased, the permissible volume decrease, that is leaving the previous level of profit unchanged, is determined as follows:

$$\text{Permissible volume decrease (\%)} = \frac{x}{M^* + x} \times 100$$

where x is the percentage price increase expressed as a decimal. If a 9 per cent price increase is contemplated and if the gross profit margin is 30 per cent, the percentage sales volume decrease is

$$\text{Volume decrease (\%)} = \frac{9\%}{30\% + 9\%} \times 100 = 23.08 \text{ per cent}$$

and the implied price elasticity is –2.56. For the price increase to enhance profit, market demand must have a price elasticity below the implied price elasticity of –2.6.

Pricing in an inflationary economy

During inflation, all costs tend to go up, and to maintain profits at an acceptable level, price increases are very often a necessity. The general objective is that price should be increased to such a level that the profits before and after inflation are approximately equal. Decline in sales revenue caused by the price increase should be explicitly taken into account and the market reaction evaluated.

It should be noted that it is not always necessary for a company to increase prices to offset inflationary effects. Non-price measures can be taken as well to reduce the impact of inflationary pressures, namely by improving productivity to offset the rise in costs. Also price increases well above inflationary pressures can be justified to the market if the brand has a competitive advantage over competing brands.

Price leadership

Price leadership strategy prevails in oligopolistic markets. One member of the industry, because of its size or command over the market, emerges as the leader of the industry. The leading company then makes pricing moves, which are duly acknowledged by other members of the reference market.

Initiating a price increase is typically the role of the *industry leader*. The presence of a leader helps to regulate the market and avoid too many price changes. Oligopolistic markets, in which the number of competitors is relatively low, favour the presence of a market leader who adopts an anticipative behaviour and periodically determines prices. Other firms then recognise the leader's role and become followers by accepting prices. The leadership strategy is designed to stave off price wars and 'predatory' competition, which tends to force down prices and hurt all competing firms. There are different types of leadership:

- *Leadership of the dominant firm*, that is the firm with the highest market share. The dominant firm establishes a price and the other producers sell their products at this price. The leader must be powerful and undisputed and must accept maintaining a high price.

- *Barometric leadership* which consists of initiating desirable price cuts or price increases, taking into account changes in production costs or demand growth. In this case the leader must have access to an effective information system providing him or her with reliable information on supply and demand, competition and technological change.

- *Leadership by common accord*, where one firm is tacitly recognised as leader, without there being a formal understanding or accord. The latter would in fact be illegal. Such a leader could be the most visible firm in the sector, for example the firm that leads in technology. It should also have a sensitivity to the price and profit needs of the rest of the industry.

According to Corey (1976, p. 177), the effective exercise of leadership depends on several factors:

- The leader must have a superior market information system for understanding what is going on in the market and reacting in a timely way.
- It should have a clear sense of strategy.
- It should have a broad concern for the health of the industry.
- The price leader should use long-term measures to assess managerial performance.

⬤ It should want to lead and to act responsibly.
⬤ It will tend to behave in a way that preserves short-run market share stability.

On the whole, the presence of a leader acts as a *market stabiliser* and reduces the risk of a price war.

⬤ Pricing New Products

The more a new product is distinct and brings an innovative solution to the satisfaction of a need, the more sensitive it is to price. This price is a fundamental choice upon which depends the commercial and financial success of the operation. Once the firm has analysed costs, demand and competition, it must then choose between two very contradictory strategies: (a) a high initial price strategy to skim the high end of the market, and (b) a strategy of low price from the beginning in order to achieve fast and powerful market penetration.

Skimming pricing strategy

This strategy consists of selling the new product at a high price and thus limiting oneself to the upper end of the demand curve. This would ensure significant financial returns soon after the launch. Many considerations support this strategy; furthermore, a number of conditions need to be met for this strategy to prove successful (Dean, 1950):

⬤ When there are reasons to believe that the new *product life cycle* will be short, or when competition is expected to copy and to market a similar product in the near future, a skimming price strategy may be recommended because a low price strategy would make the innovation unprofitable.

⬤ When a product is so innovative that the market is expected to mature slowly and the buyer has no elements on which to compare it with other products, *demand is inelastic*. It is tempting to exploit this situation by setting a high price and then readjusting it progressively as the market matures.

⬤ Launching a new product at a high price is one way of *segmenting the market*. The segments have different price elasticities. The launching price skims the customers who are insensitive to price. Later price cuts then allow the firm to reach successively more elastic segments. This is a form of time discriminatory pricing.

⬤ When demand is hard to evaluate, it is *risky to anticipate* what kind of demand growth or cost reduction can result from a low price. This is particularly true when the manufacturing process is not yet stabilised and costs are likely to be underestimated.

⬤ To be effective, the introduction of a new product requires heavy expenditure on advertising and promotion. When the firm does not have the *financial means* necessary for a successful introduction, charging high prices is one way of generating the resources.

Price skimming strategy is definitely a cautious strategy, which is more financial than commercial. Its main advantage is that it leaves the door open for a progressive price adjustment, depending on how the market and competition develop. From a commercial point of view, it is always easier to cut a price than to increase it. The importance of the strategy lies mainly in its financial aspect: the fact that some capital, which can be used for alternative activity, is freed early on.

Penetration price strategy

Penetration strategy, on the other hand, consists of setting low prices in order to capture a larger share of the market right from the start. It assumes the adoption of an intensive distribution system, the use of mass advertising to develop market receptivity, and especially an adequate production capacity from the beginning. In this case the outlook is more commercial than financial. The following general conditions must prevail to justify its use:

- Demand must be *price elastic* over the entire demand curve; there are no upper segments to be given priority and the only strategy is to address the whole market at a price low enough to satisfy the greatest number.

- It is possible to achieve *lower unit costs* by increasing volumes significantly, either because of economies of scale or because of potential experience effects.

- Soon after its introduction, the new product is threatened by *strong competition*. This threat of new entrants is a powerful reason for adopting low prices. The penetration strategy is used here to discourage competitors from entering the market. Low prices act as very efficient barriers to entry, as discussed in Chapter 8.

- The top range of the market is *already satisfied*; in this case, penetration policy is the only valid policy to develop the market.

- Potential buyers can easily integrate the new product in their consumption or production; the *transfer costs* of adopting the product other than its price are relatively low and, therefore, a mass market can be developed rapidly.

A penetration price strategy is therefore more risky than a skimming price strategy. If the firm plans to make the new product profitable over a long period, it may face the situation that new entrants might later use new production techniques, which will give them a cost advantage over the innovating firm.

Product Line Pricing

Strategic marketing has led firms to adopt segmentation and diversification strategies which have resulted in the multiplication of the number of products sold by the same firm or under the same brand. Generally a firm has several product lines, and within each product line there are usually some products that are functional substitutes for each other and some that are functionally complementary. This strategy of product development brings about an interdependency between products, which is reflected either by a *substitution effect* (or cannibalism) or by a *complementarity effect*. Since the objective of the firm is to optimise the overall

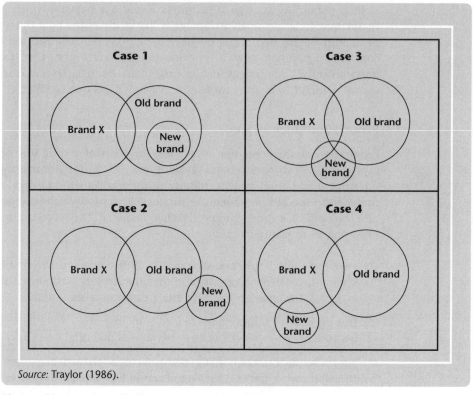

Source: Traylor (1986).

Figure 13.6   Cannibalism in multi-brand firms

outcome of its activities, it is clearly necessary to take this interdependence into account when determining prices (Oxenfeld, 1966).

The risk of a cannibalism effect

Figure 13.6 illustrates the possible scenarios of 'cannibalisation' between two brands of the same firm, the old and the new. The circles represent buyers, with the intersections representing switchers. The total market is defined by the outer boundaries of all circles combined. Brand X denotes the competing brands (Traylor, 1986):

- The first case is the worst; the new brand brings no advantage whatsoever and simply shares sales with the firm's current brand. This situation might still be tolerated if the new brand's gross margin is well above that of the old brand.

- The second case is better, because the new brand has increased the size of the market and also its market share, but without going over the competitor's position. The operation will be globally profitable if the margin obtained on sales to new buyers is greater than that lost on sales of the old brand.

- In the third scenario, the new brand overlaps with the old brand's market as well as with the competing brand's, while extending the size of the market by attracting new customers. As in the previous case, one needs to compare the margins lost and gained to evaluate whether there is a net positive gain.

● The fourth case is the ideal situation, with no cannibalisation. The new brand cuts into competitors' sales and reaches new buyers. Total market share increases and the new brand is bringing in a net cash flow increment. (Traylor, 1986, p. 72)

How can a multi-brand firm eliminate cannibalism? As firms look for finer and subtler definitions of new market segments, the risk of cannibalism goes up. The main objective to pursue is to position the firm's brands against each other as well as against competitors' brands. In addition, some form of cannibalism should be tolerated if the net effect of the multi-brand strategy is in the best strategic interest of the firm as a whole.

Coca-Cola is a good example of a company that has flipped from a very conservative protectionism to an almost reckless use of the Coke name. The intended (Diet Coke, Cherry Coke) and unintended (Coke Classic) brand extensions represent radical departures from the company's traditional reluctance to extend the Coke name (Traylor, 1986, p. 73).

A firm concerned about market power may accept short-term profit losses resulting from cannibalism if it stands to increase its market power overall.

The concept of cross-elasticity

A cross-elasticity measures the degree of interdependence between products sold by the same firm or under the same brand, and identifies the nature of this dependence when it exists: complementarity or substitution.

In the case of two products A and B, their cross-elasticity is defined as follows:

$$\text{Cross-elasticity} = \frac{\text{Percentage change of product A's sales}}{\text{Percentage change of product B's price}}$$

If cross-elasticity is positive, the products are substitutes; if elasticity is negative, then they are complementary. If elasticity is zero or very close to it, then the products are independent.

Contribution analysis in product line pricing

The complexity of product mix pricing is due to the fact that, apart from demand interaction, there is often cost interaction as well. For example, this is true when a change in the manufacturing process of one product affects the cost of other products. In this case, to study the implications of changing the price of one product in a range of products, it is important to take into account the effect of such a change on the overall result.

To illustrate, let us examine the data of an example presented in Table 13.9. A firm is selling *three interdependent products* and has a marketing programme, which it is planning to modify as follows:

By increasing advertising by £50,000, it is expected that sales of product B will increase by 6000 units at a price increased by £20, and increased packaging cost by £5. Sales of product A are expected to decrease by 1000 units because of product interdependence, and sales of product C are expected to decrease by 3000 units because of production capacity constraint. Should this change in the marketing programme for product B be adopted? (Blondé, 1964)

Table 13.9   Product line pricing: an example

	Product A	Product B	Product C
Selling price (£)	200	220	100
Direct cost (£)	150	180	80
Unit profit margin (£)	50	40	20
Volume (units)	20,000	15,000	10,000
Total profit margin (£)	1,000,000	600,000	200,000
Fixed costs (£)	700,000	500,000	100,000
Net profit (£)	300,000	100,000	100,000
Total net profit (£)		500,000	

What would be the impact of such a change on the overall result? A convenient way to proceed is to reason in terms of variations (Δ). The variation in the gross margin (M) of product B is

$$\Delta(M) = \Delta(P) - \Delta(C)$$

which in this case gives

$$\Delta(M) = (+20) - (+5) = +15$$

To determine the effect on the overall result, let us use the following expression, where F denotes fixed costs:

$$\Delta(R) = \Sigma_n \left[\Delta(Q) \cdot M + Q \cdot \Delta(M) + \Delta(Q) \cdot \Delta(M) - \Delta F \right]$$

The summation is over the n products made. In the case of this example, for the three products A, B and C we have

$$\Delta R = (-1000) \cdot (50) + (20,000) \cdot (0) + (-1000) \cdot (0) - 0$$
$$+ (+6000) \cdot (40) + (15,000) \cdot (15) + (+6000) \cdot (15) - 350,000$$
$$+ (-3000) \cdot (20) + (10,000) \cdot (0) + (-3000) \cdot (0) - 0$$
$$\Delta R = -50,000 + 205,000 - 60,000$$

$$\Delta R = + £95,000, \text{ that is an increased profit of 19 per cent.}$$

The new marketing programme is therefore profitable. Total gross margin obtained from the new sales volume for product B with its new unit gross margin is higher than the loss of gross margins on products A and C, due to their lower sales volume and increased fixed costs.

Product line pricing strategies

When a firm is selling a set of related products, the price of each product must be set in such a way as to *maximise the profit of the entire product line* rather than the profit of a single product. The pricing strategy adopted will be different according to whether the related products are complementary to or competitive with each other.

Price bundling

When the products are related but are non-substitutes, that is complementary or independent, one strategic option for the firm is optional price bundling, where the products can be bought separately, but also as a package offered at a much lower price than the sum of the parts. Because the products are not substitutes, it is possible to get consumers to buy the package instead of only one product of the line. This pricing strategy is common practice, for instance, in the automobile and audio-visual markets, where packages of options are offered with the purchase of a car or of stereo equipment. A simple example will illustrate the profit implication of this pricing strategy (Tellis, 1986, p. 155).

Assume a market situation where two related products are offered to two customers, who could buy one product or both. The maximum prices they are ready to pay are presented in Table 13.10.

Table 13.10   Price bundling: an example

Products	Customer 1 ($)	Customer 2 ($)	Total ($)
Product A	12	15	27
Product B	25	24	49
Budgets	37	39	76

What is the best pricing strategy to adopt if tying contracts are excluded?

● Charging each customer the maximum price would yield a total revenue of $76. But this strategy, if not illegal, is difficult to implement if the buyers are sufficiently informed.

● Adopting the lowest price for each product would mean selling product A at $12 and product B at $24 and could induce buyers to buy the two products, since the total cost ($36) for them would compatible with their budget constraints, but the total sales revenue would be only $72.

● Adopting the highest price for each product, that is selling product A at $15 and product B at $25, will generate an even lower total revenue of maximum $49 (if they both buy product B), since the customers will not be able to buy the two products (at a total cost of $40) given their budget constraints.

The best solution is to price product A at $15 and product B at $25 and offer both at $37 for a total revenue of $74. Both customers will accept the package for $37 since this total cost is compatible with their budget constraints (adapted from Tellis, 1986)

This strategy of 'optional bundling', in contrast with *'indivisible bundling'*, leaves the option to the customer to buy only one product or the total package.

Several computer companies have adopted the indivisible bundling strategy. Under this pricing system, not only are costs of hardware and profits covered, but also included are the anticipated expenses for extra technical assistance, design and engineering of the system concept, software and applications to be used on the system, training of personnel and maintenance.

For the customer, this strategy is very attractive because *the manufacturing firm is selling a 'solution' and not simply a product*. To be able to sell a solution, however, the manufacturer has to cover the anticipated expenses for providing services and assistance in use and for keeping the system in working condition. Such a bundling strategy also permits an ongoing relationship with the customer and first-hand knowledge of the customer's needs.

In recent years, however, with the inflationary pressures on costs of services, many companies have begun unbundling their services and charging separately for them.

Premium pricing

This pricing strategy applies to different versions of the same product, a superior version and a basic or standard model. Potential buyers for the standard model are very price sensitive, while buyers of the superior model are not. If economies of scale exist, it is unprofitable for the firm to limit its activity to one of the two market segments. The best solution is to exploit jointly economies of scale and heterogeneity of demand by covering the two segments, the lower end of the market with a low price and the high end with a premium price. The following example illustrates this.

> Consider a firm having the following target prices: $50 at 20 units and $35 at 40 units. The cost of producing a superior version of the same product is $10. Forty consumers per period are on the market for the product. Half of them are price-insensitive and are ready to pay $50 for the superior version. The other half are price-sensitive and will not pay more than $30. In what version and at what price should the firm sell the product? (Tellis, 1986, p. 156).

Costs and profit constraints seem to exceed prices if the firm decides to sell to only one segment at only one price. If the firm targets the low price segment, the market potential is 20 customers and the maximum acceptable price is $30, while the target price at this level of production is $50. Similarly, if the firm targets the high price segment, the market potential is 20 customers willing to pay $50, but the target price is now $60 ($50+$10). This strategy is also unfeasible.

A premium price strategy can solve the problem. The firm should produce 40 units and sell 20 units of the standard product for $30 and 20 units of the superior version for $50, for an average target price of $40. The target prices are respectively $35 and $45, but the market prices will be $30 and $50. Thus, the firm takes a premium on its higher priced version and a loss on its lower priced version, but can profitably produce and sell the product to both segments (Tellis, 1986, p. 156).

This pricing strategy is common practice in many markets, typically durable goods for which several versions differing in price and features cater to different consumer segments.

The same pricing strategy can be applied in the service sector by modifying the service package. For example, airlines have used this pricing strategy very successfully. Their market consists of both a price-insensitive business traveller and a very price-sensitive holiday traveller. Business people place a high value on flexible scheduling. In contrast, holidaymakers generally plan their trips far in advance.

Capitalising on these differences, airlines set regular ticket prices high and offer discounts only to buyers who purchase their tickets well before departure. By offering lower fares only with inflexible schedules, airlines have been able to price low enough to attract price-sensitive buyers without making unnecessary concessions to those who are less price sensitive (Nagle, 1987, p. 169).

Image pricing

A variant of premium pricing is *image pricing*. The objective is the same: to signal quality to uninformed buyers and use the profit made on the higher priced version to subsidise the price on the lower priced version. The difference is that there is no real difference between products or brands, it is only in image or perceptual positioning. This is common practice in markets like cosmetics, dresses, snacks, and so on, where the emotional and/or social value of a product or a brand is important for the consumer.

Complementary pricing

The problem here is to determine the prices of complementary products, such as durable goods and accessories or supplies necessary for the use of the basic product. Examples of complementary products are razors and blades, cars and spare parts, computers and software, and so on. To the extent that buyers are source loyal and want to buy supplies or accessories from the original manufacturer, low prices can be charged for the main product and high prices for the supplies.

> For example, Kodak prices its cameras low because it makes its money on selling film. Those camera makers who do not sell film have to price their cameras higher in order to make the same overall profit. (Kotler, 1991, p. 495)

In evaluating the effect of a price change of complementary products, management must examine the changes in sales revenue and costs not only for the product being priced, but also for the other products affected by the price change. By way of illustration, let us examine the pricing problem of a company selling personal computers and software.

> In this company, the typical buyer of a personal computer also purchases on average three software packages. The gross profit margin on a computer is $1000 or 40 per cent on selling price, while the profit margin on software is $250. If management treated sales of computers and software as independent, the break-even sales quantity for a 10 per cent price cut would be 33.3 per cent (–10%/40% – 10% = 0.333). Thus sales should increase by 33.3 per cent to justify the 10 per cent price cut.

How likely is this sales increase? In fact, the profit contribution for a computer sale is much higher than 40 per cent, since each buyer of a computer also purchases on average three software packages. Thus, the relevant gross profit margin here is $1750 ($1000 + (3 × $250)), or 70 per cent of the selling price. The adjusted break-even sales change is 16.7 per cent (–10%/70% – 10% = 0.167%). Thus, the company could cut its price even if it expects a percentage increase in sales much less than 33.3 per cent.

In retailing, the corresponding strategy is called *loss leadership*. It involves dropping the price on a well-known brand to generate store traffic (Tellis, 1986, p. 157).

International Pricing

The pricing problem in a foreign market should be approached in the same way as in the domestic market. Costs, demand and competition factors should be taken successively into consideration. Specific issues arise, however, for an international firm exporting to foreign markets from a domestic production unit. We shall examine here the main pricing problems to be examined by an exporting firm.

This section relies heavily on Terpstra and Sarathy (1991).

Transfer pricing

Transfer pricing refers to prices placed on goods sold within the corporate family, that is from division to division or to a foreign subsidiary. Transfer pricing is a problem for the large international corporation on at least two levels: (a) pricing from the production division to the international division (b) and from the international division to the foreign subsidiary.

Intracorporate transfer pricing

In setting an intracorporate transfer pricing, the objective should be to optimise corporate rather than divisional profit. More precisely, the two following objectives should be pursued:

- The transfer price should be high enough to motivate the production division. Thus, sales to the international division should be as attractive as sales to other parties and in particular to the domestic market through the traditional distribution network.

- The transfer price should be low enough to enable the international division to be competitive in the foreign market.

Obviously, there is room for divisional conflict here and it is the overall corporate profit which should be the determining factor. Let us take the following example given by Terpstra and Sarathy (1991, p. 429).

Assume that the producing unit makes a product at a full cost of $50. It sells this to outside buyers for $60, but the transfer price to the international division is $58. The producing division may be unhappy because the mark-up is 20 per cent lower to the international division ($8 versus $10). The international division adds its various export-marketing expenses of $10 for an export cost of $68. For competitive reasons, the international division cannot sell the product for more than $72, or a $4 return. Since this is less than 6 per cent sales, the international division is also unhappy. However the return to the corporation is $12 on $72 instead of $10 on $60, or almost 17 per cent ($8 from the producing division plus $4 from the international division).The corporation may find this very attractive, even though both divisions are unhappy with it.

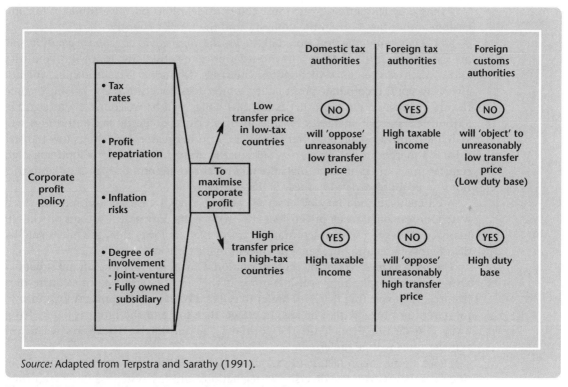

Figure 13.7　Transfer pricing to foreign subsidiaries

Different approaches can be taken to solve this internal transfer-pricing problem. The two extreme solutions would be the *floor price* on the one hand and the *market price* less the distribution margin on the other. The market price would then be the same price as any other buyer outside the firm pays. In general the actual transfer price will be between these two extremes by adopting a *cost plus* transfer price. The 'plus' may be a percentage negotiated between the divisions in an attempt to reconcile the two objectives mentioned above.

Transfer pricing to foreign subsidiaries

This transfer pricing decision is more complex because several new factors must be taken into consideration, namely the foreign tax system, custom rates, exchange rates and also the level of involvement of the international firm in the foreign country.

The main factors interfering with the transfer pricing decision are presented in Figure 13.7. Given that each country has different taxation systems, it is not a matter of indifference to know where the international firm will accumulate profits. The three key questions to examine are the following:

- How do profit tax rates compare from one country to the other?
- What are the rules governing profit repatriation policy?
- What is the risk of inflation?

To these basic questions, one must add considerations on the attitude of tax and custom authorities, both in the domestic and the foreign country.

As a general rule, the firm would like *to use the transfer price to get more profits in low-tax countries*, that is it will use a low transfer price to subsidiaries in low-tax countries and a high transfer price in high-tax countries. Domestic tax authorities will not always accept this corporate profit policy, which does not want to lose taxable income to other countries. On the other hand, this policy will be welcomed by foreign tax authorities, since it increases taxable income. Thus, domestic tax authorities will watch for 'unreasonably low' transfer prices. Another reason for using a low transfer price is a method of financing new subsidiaries abroad. Reasons for adopting a high transfer price, in addition to high tax rate on corporate profits, may also be restrictions on profit repatriation or fear of devaluation.

A different attitude may be observed among foreign customs authorities, which watch for too low transfer prices since they reduce the duty base. Customs officials in many countries refuse to accept transfer prices that are lower than the prices paid by distributors purchasing the same product at market prices.

The *level of involvement* of the international firm and the foreign subsidiary is also a factor to take into consideration. If the subsidiary is a joint venture or a licensee, the exporting firm will prefer to sell at a high transfer price. A low price to joint ventures or licensees means, in effect, that some of the profit is being given away outside the firm. If on the contrary, the subsidiary is fully owned a low transfer price will be preferred.

Those are the main factors to examine when establishing a international transfer pricing policy. Given the diversity of regulations and tax systems among countries, one realises how difficult it may be to have the same international pricing policy. At the European Union level, the elimination of non-tariff barriers and the harmonisation of tax systems will progressively facilitate a standard pricing strategy. However, deep disparities will remain for many years, not only because of the differences between VAT and tax policies, but also because of the different product positioning strategies sought by international firms for their brands.

Export price quotations

Export costs constitute an important part of the price that will be charged in the foreign market. Export price quotations are also important because they spell out the legal responsibilities of each party.

A number of terms covering the conditions of the delivery are commonly used in international trade (see Figure 13.8). Many of these terms have through long use acquired precise meanings. Every commercial transaction is based upon a contract of sale and the trade terms used in that contract have the important function of naming the exact point at which the ownership of merchandise is transferred from the seller to the buyer. Export cost may increase substantially the price of the exported product and undermine its competitiveness abroad. The major trade terms used are defined as follows:

● *Ex Works (ex-factory)*. The buyer takes delivery at the premises of the seller and bears all risks and expenses from that point on. The seller favours this quote since it gives him least liability and responsibility.

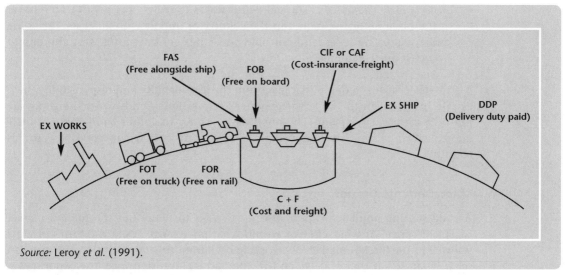

Source: Leroy *et al.* (1991).

Figure 13.8   Description of export costs

- *Free Alongside Ship (FAS)*. The seller must place goods alongside the vessel or other mode of transportation and pay all charges up to that point. The seller's legal responsibility ends once he or she has obtained a clean wharfage receipt.

- *Free on Board (FOB)*. The responsibility and liability of the seller end when the goods have actually been placed on board a ship (ship, aircraft or truck).

- *Cost, Insurance, Freight (CIF)*. The seller, in addition to the FOB obligations, has to pay the expenses of transportation for the goods up to the port of destination, including the expenses of insurance.

Exhibit 13.5

Determination of an FOB Export Price

1. Market price in the foreign market		$7.00
2. Less 40% retail margin on selling price	2.80	
Purchase cost to the retailer		4.20
3. Less 11% wholesaler mark-up on his cost	0.42	
Wholesaler cost		3.78
4. Less 5% importer mark-up on his cost	0.18	
Importer cost		3.60
5. Less 10% VAT on landed value plus duty	0.33	
DDP value of the product		3.27
6. Less 9% duty on landed value CIF	0.27	
Landed or CIF value		3.00
7. Less insurance and shipping costs to market	0.40	
FOB value of the product		$2.60

● *Delivery Duty Paid (DDP)*. The seller undertakes to deliver the goods to the buyer at the place he or she names in the country of import with all costs, including duties, paid. The seller is responsible under this contract for getting the import licence if one is required.

The seller favours a quote that gives him the least liability and responsibility, such as FOB his plant. In this case, the exporter's responsibility ends when the goods are put on a carrier at his plant. The importer-buyer, on the other hand, favours a CIF quote, which means his responsibilities begin only when the goods are in his country.

Market-oriented export pricing

A good starting point for export price analysis is to figure out the foreign market acceptable price. At what price or within what price range could the firm's product sell well in the foreign market? By working back from this market price, the firm can see if it can sell at that price given the international transfer price, the export costs, the taxes and the custom duties.

Assume the firm is selling a consumer product to a foreign country and market research shows that the market acceptable price should be about $7 equivalent (see Exhibit 13.5).

Thus, $2.60 is the FOB plant price, which will allow the firm to meet the foreign market acceptable price of $7.00. Is this price close to the contemplated transfer price? If the domestic FOB plant price does not compare favourably, that is if it is greater than $2.60, export will be difficult and the international firm will have to consider one of the following alternatives (Terpstra and Sarathy, 1991):

● To forget about exporting for lack of sufficient competitiveness.
● To reduce the transfer price and consider marginal cost pricing for exports if there is excess production capacity.
● To adopt a shorter distribution channel, for example by selling directly to whole-salers or to large retailers.
● To design a stripped down and cheaper model for exports.

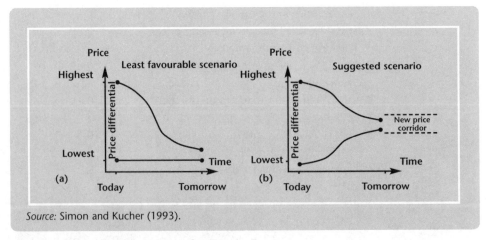

Source: Simon and Kucher (1993).

Figure 13.9   Development of prices in Europe

● To consider foreign manufacturing, assembling or licensing to avoid export and duty costs.

In any case, the market price in the foreign market cannot be inferior to the domestic market price to avoid the charge of dumping by foreign competitors.

Pricing in euros

Comparison of the prices charged for the same product in the international market reveals very significant price disparities among countries, in particular within the EU (see Table 13.11). The causes of these price disparities can be among the following:

● differences between channel structures;
● differences between trade margins for the same product category;
● differences between the VAT rates per country;
● differences between national legislation and price controls or regulations;
● differences in terms of competitive situations;
● differences between the positioning sought within each country.

Table 13.11   Examples of price disparities in Europe ($)

	Belgium	France	Germany	Italy	Spain
Coca-Cola (1.5 litre bottle)	2.05	1.05	1.89	1.65	1.14
Hamburger (Big Mac)	2.86	3.08	2.67	2.48	2.38
VW Golf GL 2-door	13,553	16,317	13,999	17,056	17,356
Unleaded gasoline (1 lt)	0.93	1.03	0.87	0.94	0.73
Dry-cleaned man's shirt	3.68	4.67	2.43	2.75	2.92
Subway or bus ticket	1.32	1.20	2.10	0.83	0.82
Pair of Levi's 501 jeans	71	83	81	69	70
Compaq Presario 2240	1316	1348	917	1208	1267
One-day rental car Mercedes C-Class	154	110	103	243	113
One hour of translation	89	104	78	55	39

Source: Business Week (1998, p. 44).

The creation of the single market and the launching of the euro are contributing to increase market transparency and to greatly facilitate price comparisons. One effect expected from the euro, and sought by the EU, is the reduction of the price gaps between countries of the EU with an alignment to the lowest current level of prices as illustrated in Figure 13.9(a). In effect, if the price differentials remain high (over 15 per cent for instance), arbitrage and *parallel imports* will develop and will contribute to push prices down to their lowest level. This situation can have disastrous consequences on profitability and also undermine the positioning strategy of the firm.

Determination of a European price corridor

To avoid this price erosion towards the lowest level, Simon and Kucher (1993) recommend the creation of a European price corridor just below the arbitrage costs. For that purpose one has to determine the price differential above which parallel imports occur, given the shipping and product adaptation costs and the trade margin required to motivate third parties to start parallel importing.

As shown in the example of Exhibit 13.6, the adoption of a uniform price generates a substantial reduction of total profit. Between these two extreme situations – optimal country-specific prices or optimal uniform price – the objective is to determine the price differential above which parallel imports occur and to adopt the level which neutralises the incentive of parallel imports, while minimising the profit loss.

In the example of Exhibit 13.6, it can be shown that with a 15 per cent price differential, the price corridor is: $P_a = 7.98F$ and $P_b = 9.39F$ with a total profit of 224,2F, a sacrifice of only 2.07 per cent by comparison with the initial optimal solution.

Exhibit 13.6

Country-Specific versus Uniform Optimal Price

Let us consider the case of a manufacturer present in two markets, one (country A) being more price sensitive than the other (country B). Let us suppose that the marginal cost is equal to 5F and that the respective demand functions are:

$$Q_a = 100 - 10.0\ P_a, \text{ with a price elasticity: } \varepsilon = -3$$
$$Q_b = 100 - 6.67\ P_b, \text{ with a price elasticity: } \varepsilon = -2$$

Country-specific optimal prices, independently determined for each country, will be (see Exhibit 13.4):

$$P_a^* = 5\{-3\ /\ (-3) + 1\} = (5) \cdot (1.5) = 7.5F$$
$$P_b^* = 5\{-2\ /\ (-2) + 1\} = (5) \cdot (2.0) = 10.0F$$

The total profit will be 229F, but the price gap between the two countries, calculated by reference to the highest price is very high and equal to 25%.

If the manufacturer adopts a uniform price, the reference demand function becomes

$$Q_{ab} = 200 - 16.67\ P_{ab}, \text{ with a price elasticity: } \varepsilon = -2.43$$

The optimal price becomes

$$P_{ab}^* = 5\{-2.43\ /\ (-2.43) + 1\} = 8.5F \text{ and the profit: } 204F$$

The price gap between the two countries is closed, but the profit is 10.9 per cent lower than the previous one

Source: adapted from Simon and Kucher (1993).

This solution proposed by Simon and Kucher is interesting and implies both price increases and decreases. It is not of general application to neutralise parallel imports, however, since the single incentive is the price differential between countries. Parallel imports can also occur under other circumstances, namely when the parallel importer is 'free riding' on the strategy of the main importer (see Tan *et al.*, 1997).

Chapter summary

The choice of a pricing strategy must respect two types of coherence: an internal coherence, that is setting a price respecting constraints of costs and profitability, and an external coherence, that is setting a price compatible with the buyer's price sensitivity and with the price of competing goods. Cost-based pricing (break-even, target and mark-up pricing) is a first and necessary step, which helps to identify the financial implications of various pricing strategies. Pricing based exclusively on the firm's own financial needs is inappropriate, however, since in a market economy it is the buyer who ultimately decides which product will sell. In demand-oriented pricing, the notion of price elasticity is central although difficult to estimate empirically with sufficient precision. The factors affecting buyers' price sensitivity are useful to help estimate price elasticity in qualitative terms. Value pricing is a customer-based pricing procedure, which is an outgrowth of the multi-attribute product concept. Flexible pricing strategies (second market, periodic or random discounting) arise primarily because buyers' heterogeneity shows different price sensitivities. Two kinds of factors influence competition-oriented pricing: the competitive structure of the market and the product's perceived value. One objective of analysing competition in pricing is to evaluate competitors' capacity to act and react. Special issues in pricing are pricing new products (skimming versus penetration pricing), product line pricing (price bundling, premium pricing, image and complementary pricing) and international pricing (transfer price and export costs).

QUESTIONS AND PROBLEMS

1. A distributor sells an average of 300 units per week of a particular product whose purchase cost is $2.50 and sales price $3. If the distributor gives a 10 per cent price reduction during one week, how many units should the firm sell in order to keep its gross profit margin unchanged?

2. Company Alpha distributes a product in a market, which is price inelastic. Sales are 30,000 units per year. The operating data of the product are as follows:

Direct unit cost	$9.90
Fixed unit cost	$3.30
Total	$13.20
Sales price	$19.80
Net profit per unit	$6.60

The firm wants to increase its sales volume by 3000 units and, for that purpose, has adopted an $39,600 advertising budget per year. What minimum price increase should the firm should adopt in order to leave its profit unchanged?

3. The Elix Company produces and distributes a product, which is differentiated from competing products by a better design. The average market price is $50 and the total market amounts to 1,000,000 units; Elix market share is 10%. The price elasticity for this product category is in the range –1.7 to –2.0. The operating data for Elix are as follows:

Direct unit cost	$20
Fixed costs	$2,000,000
Expected rate of return	10%
Invested capital	$10,000,000

The market research department has conducted a brand image study for Elix and for its priority competitor, the brand Lumina. The attributes' importance scores for the product category are respectively: 0.50 / 0.25 / 0.25; and the performance scores are: 10 / 6 / 9 for Elix; 8 / 7 / 9 for Lumina. Calculate the target price, the value price and the optimum price. What pricing strategy do you recommend?

4. X and Y are two divisions of the New Style Company. Division X manufactures the product Alpha. The operating data are:

Direct costs raw materials	$6
Labour	$4
Fixed costs	$2
Total	$12

The Alpha market is a perfect competition market and the market price is 16. Alpha is also sold to Division Y. Market sales imply a selling cost of $2 per unit. Given that demand for Alpha is sufficiently large in order to permit Division X to work at full capacity, at what transfer price should Division X sell the Alpha product to Division Y?

Bibliography

Assmus, G., Farley, J.V. and Lehmann, D.R. (1984) How Advertising Affects Sales Meta-Analysis of Econometric Results, *Journal of Marketing Research*, **21**, February, pp. 65–74.

Blondé, D. (1964) *La gestion programmée*, Paris, Dunod.

Broadbent, S. (1980) Price and Advertising: Volume and Profits, *Admap*, **16**, pp. 532–40.

Business Week (1975) Detroit Dilemma on Prices, 20 January, pp. 82–3.

Business Week (1977) Flexible Pricing, 12 December, pp. 78–88.

Business Week (1998) Let the Shopping Spree Begin, 27 April, pp. 44–5.

Carlson, R.L. (1978) Seemingly Unrelated Regression and the Demand for Automobiles of Different Sizes: A Disaggregate Approach, *The Journal of Business*, **51**, April, pp. 243–62.

Corey, E.R. (1976) *Industrial Marketing: Cases and Concepts*, Englewood Cliffs NJ, Prentice Hall.

Dean, J. (1950) Pricing Policies for New Products, *Harvard Business Review*, November–December, **28**, pp. 28–36.

Dolan, R.J. and Simon, H. (1996) *Power Pricing*, New York, The Free Press.

Dorfman, R. and Steiner P.O. (1954) Optimal Advertising and Optimal Quality, *American Economic Review*, December, pp. 826–33.

Hagerty, M.R., Carman, J.M. and Russel, G.J. (1988) Estimating Elasticities with PIMS Data: Methodological Issues and Substantive Implications, *Journal of Marketing Research*, **25**, February, pp. 1–19.

Hanssens, D.M., Parsons, L.L., and Schultz, R.L. (1990) *Market Response Models: Econometric and Time Series Analysis*, Boston MA, Kluwer.

Jacquemin, A. (1973) Optimal Control and Advertising Policy, *Metroeconomica*, May, **25**, pp. 200–07.

Kotler, P. (1997) *Marketing Management*, Englewood Cliffs NJ, Prentice Hall.

Kurtz, D.L. and Clow, K.E. (1998) *Services Marketing*, New York, John Wiley & Sons.

Lambin, J.J. (1976) *Advertising, Competition and Market Conduct in Oligopoly over Time*, Amsterdam, North-Holland.

Lambin, J.J. (1988) Synthèse des études récentes sur l'efficacité économique de la publicité, CESAM, unpublished working paper, Louvain-la-Neuve, Belgium.

Lambin, J.J. (1998) *Le marketing stratégique*, 4th edn, Paris, Ediscience international.

Lambin, J.J., Naert, P.A. and Bultez, A. (1975) Optimal Marketing Behavior in Oligopoly, *European Economic Review*, **6**, pp. 105–28.

Leone, R.P. and Schultz, R. (1980) A Study in Marketing Generalisations, *Journal of Marketing*, **44**, pp. 10–18.

Leroy, G., Richard G. and Sallenave, J.P. (1991) *La conquête des marchés extérieurs*, Paris, Les Editions d'Organisation.

Monroe, K.B. (1979) *Pricing: Making Profitable Decisions*, New York, McGraw-Hill.

Nagle, T.T. and Holden, R.K. (1994) *The Strategy and Tactics of Pricing*, 2nd edn, Englewood Cliffs NJ, Prentice Hall.

Nerlove, M. and Arrow, K.J. (1962) Optimal Advertising Policy under Dynamic Conditions, *Economica*, **29**, pp. 129–42.

Neslin, S.A. and Shoemaker, R.W. (1983) Using a Natural Experiment to Estimate Price Elasticity, *Journal of Marketing*, **47**, pp. 44–57.

Oum, T.H. and Gillen, D.W. (1981) *Demand for Fareclasses and Pricing in Airline Markets*, Queen's University School of Business, Working Paper No. 80-12.

Oxenfeldt, A.R. (1966) Product Line Pricing, *Harvard Business Review*, 44, July–August, pp. 137–44.

Porter, M.E. (1980) *Competitive Strategy*, New York, The Free Press.

Ross, E.B. (1984) Making Money with Proactive Pricing, *Harvard Business Review*, **62**, November–December, pp. 145–55.

Shapiro, B.P. and Jackson, B.B. (1978) Industrial Pricing to Meet Customers 'Needs', *Harvard-Business Review*, **56**, November–December, pp. 119–27.

Simon, H. and Kucher, E. (1993) The European Pricing Time Bomb and How to Cope with It, *Marketing and Research Today*, February, pp. 25–36.

Smith, B.C., Leimkuhler, J.F. and Darrow, R.M. (1992) Yield Management at American Airlines, *Interfaces*, **22**(1): 8–31.

Tan, S.J., Lim, G.H. and Lee, K.S. (1997) Strategic Responses to Parallel Importing, *Journal of Global Marketing*, **10**(4): 45–66.

Tellis, G.J. (1986) Beyond the Many Faces of Price: An Integration of Pricing Strategies, *Journal of Marketing*, **50**, October, pp. 146–60.

Tellis, G.J. (1988) The Price Elasticity of Selective Demand: a Meta-Analysis of Econometric Models of Sales, *Journal of Marketing Research*, **25**, November, pp. 331–41.

Terpstra, V. and Sarathy, R. (1991) *International Marketing*, 5th edn, Chicago IL, Dryden Press.

Traylor, M.B. (1986) Cannibalism in Multibrand Firms, *The Journal of Consumer Marketing*, **3**(2): 69–75.

Wall Street Journal (1998) Manufacturer's Boon: Few Consumers Redeem Rebates, 11 February.

chapter fourteen

Market-driven communication decisions

We saw in Chapter 1 that marketing is an action-oriented process as well as a business philosophy. To be effectively implemented, the firm's strategic choices must be supported by dynamic action programmes, without which there is very little hope for commercial success. To sell, it is not enough to have a competitively priced product made available to target potential buyers through a well-structured distribution network. It is also necessary to advertise the product's distinctive features to the target segment, and to stimulate the demand through selling and promotional activities. An effective marketing strategy requires the development of a communication programme having the two interrelated objectives of *informing* potential buyers about products and services and *persuading* them to buy. Such a programme is based on various means of communication; the most important of which are personal selling, advertising, promotion and public relations. The objective of this chapter is to examine the major strategic decisions facing a firm when developing its communication programme (see Figure 14.1).

Chapter learning objectives

When you have read this chapter, you should be able to know and/or understand:

1. the nature of the different modes of marketing communication;
2. the steps in designing an effective communication programme;
3. the tasks and objectives of relationship selling;
4. the different objectives of advertising communication;
5. the roles and impact of sales promotions;
6. the objectives of public relations and of sponsoring.

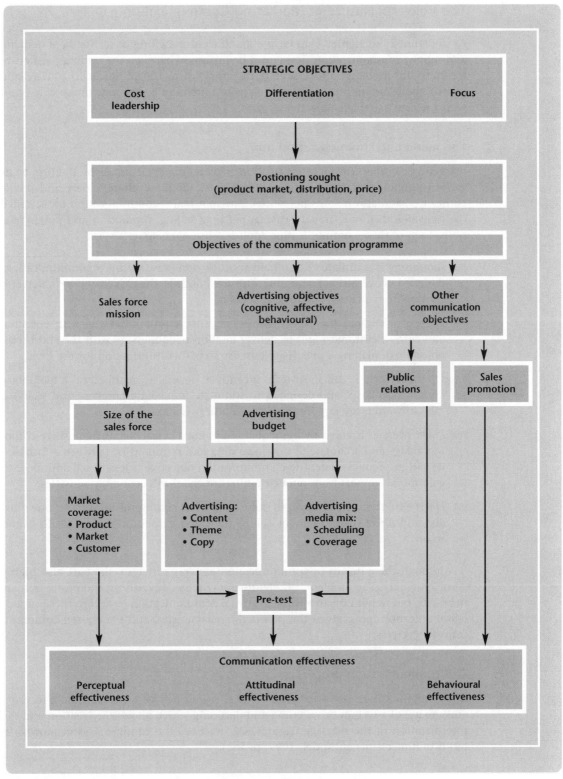

Figure 14.1   Overview of communication decisions

⬤ The Role and Nature of Marketing Communication

As underlined in Chapter 1, to ensure an efficient matching of segments of demand and supply, communication flows must be organised between the trading partners to facilitate the exchange process. It is therefore up to the producer to initiate and control these communication flows to create a brand or a corporate image consistent with the firm's strategic objectives.

The marketing communication mix

Marketing communication refers to all *the signals or messages* made by the firm to its various publics, that is customers, distributors, suppliers, shareholders and public authorities, and also its own personnel. The four major communication tools, called the *communication mix*, are advertising, personal selling, promotion and public relations. Each of these communication tools has its own characteristics:

- ⬤ *Advertising* is a unilateral and paid form of non-personal mass communication, designed to create a favourable attitude towards the advertised product and coming from a clearly identified sponsor.

- ⬤ *Personal selling* has the objective of organising a verbal dialogue with potential and current customers and to deliver a tailor-made message with the short-term objective of making a sale. Its role is also to gather information for the firm.

- ⬤ *Promotion* includes all short-term incentives, generally organised on a temporary and/or local basis, and designed to stimulate immediate purchase and to move sales forward more rapidly than would otherwise occur.

- ⬤ *Public relations* involve a variety of actions aimed at establishing a positive corporate image and a climate of understanding and mutual trust between a firm and its various publics. Here, the communication objective is less to sell and more to gain moral support from public opinion for the firm's economic activities.

- ⬤ *Direct advertising*. In addition to these traditional communication tools, one must also add direct mail, catalogue selling, fairs and exhibitions, telemarketing, and so on.

Although these means of communication are very different, they are also highly complementary. The problem is therefore not whether advertising and promotion are necessary, but rather how to allocate the total communication budget to these various communication tools, given the product's characteristics and the chosen communication objectives.

The communication process

Any communication involves an *exchange of signals* between a sender and a receiver, and the use of a system of encoding and decoding which allows the creation and the interpretation of the message. Figure 14.2 describes the communication process in terms of nine elements (Kotler, 1997, p. 568).

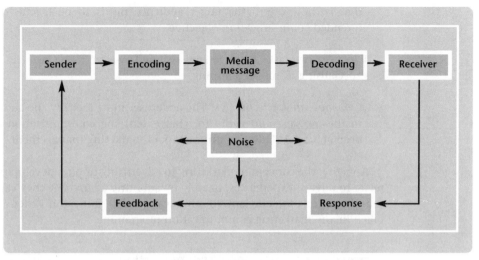

Figure 14.2 The communication process

● *Sender:* the party sending the message to another party.
● *Encoding:* the process of transforming the intended message into images, language, signs, symbols, and so on.
● *Message:* the information or the claim to be communicated to the receiver by the sender.
● *Media:* the communication channel through which the message moves from the sender to the receiver.
● *Decoding:* the process through which the receiver assigns meaning to the symbols transmitted.
● *Receiver:* the target audience.
● *Response:* the set of reactions that the receiver has after exposure to the message.
● *Feedback:* the part of the target audience's response that the receiver communicates to the sender.
● *Noise:* the distortions that occur during the communication process.

Figure 14.2 describes the relationship between these nine factors and helps to determine the *conditions for effective communication*. Four conditions can be identified:

● *Communication objectives.* Senders must know what audiences they want to reach and what type of response they want. This implies the choice of a target audience and the determination of specific communication objectives. These tasks are typically the responsibilities of strategic marketing people.

● *Message execution.* Communicators must be skilful in encoding messages and able to understand how the target audience tends to process messages. This involves designing advertisements and ensuring, through testing, that the target group processes them in the intended manner to produce the desired communication effect.

● *Media planning.* Two decisions are involved here. First, media selection, that is 'where' to reach the target audience most efficiently; second, media scheduling, that is 'how often' the target audience needs to be reached to produce the intended communication objective.

These last two tasks are in general assumed by advertising agencies and/or by agencies specialising in media planning.

● *Communication effectiveness.* The advertiser must identify the audience's response to the message and verify to what extent the communication objectives have been achieved. This is again the task of marketing management.

Applying the concept of marketing to advertising implies developing messages that relate to buyers' experiences, namely by adopting a language they can decode. These four conditions for efficient communication determine the various decisions to be taken in any marketing communication programme.

Personal versus impersonal communication

The two most important tools of marketing communication are personal communication, assumed by the sales force, and impersonal communication, achieved through media advertising. The problem is to know when direct intervention by a sales representative is more effective than advertising. A comparison of the main features of each of these two means of communication is shown in Table 14.1.

Table 14.1   Comparing personal and impersonal communication

Elements of the communication process	Personal communication	Impersonal communication
Target	■ Very well identified target	■ Average profile of the target
Message	■ Tailor-made message ■ Many arguments ■ Weak control of form and content	■ Standard message ■ Few arguments ■ Strong control of form and content
Media	■ Personalised and human contact ■ Few contacts	■ Unpersonalised contact ■ Several contacts
Receiver	■ Continued attention ■ Weak consequence of encoding error	■ Volatile attention ■ Strong effect of encoding error
Response	■ Immediate behavioural response possible	■ Immediate behavioural response difficult

Source: Adapted from Darmon *et al.* (1982, p. 398).

This comparison suggests the following:

● Personal selling is by far the most efficient and powerful communication tool. But it costs almost a hundred times more to contact a prospect with a sales person's visit than with an advertising message.

⬤ Media advertising, however, has the advantage over personal selling in that it can reach a large number of people in a short period of time, while a sales representative can only visit a limited number of customers within a day.

⬤ When a product is complex and difficult to use and is targeted to a limited number of people, a sales representative is clearly much more effective than an advertising message, which is necessarily too general and too simplistic.

⬤ A sales person acts directly and can obtain an immediate order from the customer, whereas advertising works through brand awareness and through attitude formation. These are often long-term effects.

Consequently, whenever the personal factor is not essential to communication, advertising is more economical both in terms of costs and of time. Recent developments in the field of advertising tend to reconcile the advantages of these two communication means, which is indeed the objective of interactive or response advertising.

It is therefore not surprising to observe that firms selling industrial goods devote a larger proportion of their communication budget to personal selling than firms operating in the field of consumer goods.

Costs of communication activities

It is difficult to evaluate the *costs of communication activities* because available information is sketchy. Furthermore, orders of magnitude vary tremendously with the field of activity. It is nevertheless generally accepted that personal communication expenses

Table 14.2 Marketing communication expenditures in Europe (Germany, United Kingdom, France, Italy, Spain, the Netherlands, Belgium, Switzerland)

| | 1996 | | 1997 | | 1997/96 |
	Million USD	Per cent	Million USD	Per cent	Per cent
Press	25,355	19.5	26,324	19.2	3.8
– dailies	10,070	7.7	10,463	7.6	3.9
– free press	3584	2.8	3679	2.7	2.6
– magazines	7423	5.7	7756	5.7	4.5
– professional	4277	3.3	4426	3.2	3.5
Television	19,556	15.0	20,941	15.3	7.1
Radio	3029	2.3	3191	2.3	5.3
Posters	3558	2.7	3782	2.8	6.3
Cinema	503	0.4	555	0.4	10.2
Total Mass Media	52,001	40.0	54,792	40.0	5.4
Direct Marketing	26,063	20.1	28,219	20.6	8.3
Directories	5014	3.9	5212	3.8	3.9
Promotions	23,698	18.2	24,839	18.1	4.8
Sponsoring	4805	3.7	4975	3.6	3.5
Fairs, Exhibitions	11,422	8.8	11,831	8.6	3.6
Others	7548	5.8	7824	5.7	3.7
Total Non-Media	77,950	60.0	82,282	60.0	5.6
Internet	5		33	n.s.	n.s.
TOTAL	129,956	100.0	137,108	100.0	5.5

Source: Havas (1998).

devoted to the sales force are greater by far than advertising expenditure; they are also more significant in industrial markets as compared to consumer goods markets.

Data from Table 14.2 provide evaluation of the relative importance of advertising expenditures in the eight European countries and also compare the relative weight of above and below the line advertising outlays. Inspection of this data suggests the following comments:

● Below the line communication expenditures account for 60 per cent of total advertising communication expenditures.

● Direct marketing (20.6 per cent) is the most important medium followed by press advertising (19.2 per cent), sales promotions (18.1 per cent) and television (15.3 per cent).

● The strongest growth is observed for direct marketing (after cinema advertising, which remains marginal).

● Total advertising communication expenditures are growing at an average 5 per cent rate during recent years.

These data are aggregate data for the eight European countries; the same data are available on a country-by-country basis in the Havas monograph.

The cost of personal selling keeps on increasing, mainly in the industrial markets, while the cost per advertising contact is decreasing as the result of better media selectivity.

A survey made on 'Fortune 1000' (Lucas, 1995) has revealed that the average cost of a call, estimated at $100 dollars in 1970, was more than $500 dollars in 1995, five times higher within a period of fifteen years. Another survey has shown that, on average, three calls were necessary to conclude sales with an existing customer versus seven calls for a new customer (O'Connell and Keenan, 1990). These costs of a sales call should be compared with the cost of an advertising contact made through a printed ad in a magazine and estimated at 17 cents in 1987. (Forsyth, 1987)

Table 14.3   Cost of the sales force in the industry

Industry sectors	Cost of the sales force in % of turnover	Industry sectors	Cost of the sales force in % of turnover
Agriculture	13.8	Instruments	9.3
Leisure services	2.3	Machine tools	3.9
Chemicals	14.3	Fabrication	6.8
Communications	9.0	Office equipment	3.3
Construction	6.8	Papers and others	1.5
Electronic components	19.0	Basic metallurgy	4.1
Electronic	21.0	Printing/publication	10.8
Metallic products	2.7	Gum/plastic	7.7
Food	3.4	Wholesalers	7.4
Mean	**6.2**		

Source: Dartnell Corporation (1994).

This cost comparison has generated a general reassessment of the respective roles of advertising and of personal selling, in view of the development of new media such as on-line communication. In Table 14.3, data are presented on the cost of the sales force observed in the US in selected industrial sectors.

From this table, as expected, one verifies that the share of the sales force is higher in business-to-business than in consumer markets.

Selling or Personal Communication

Personal selling is the most effective means of communication at certain stages of the buying process, especially when preferences need to be developed and the decision to buy spurred on. Due to the developments in communication technology, the role of salespersons is now undergoing a major transformation. Their role in strategic marketing is on the increase and the more routine tasks are increasingly being assumed by cheaper impersonal means of communication.

Sales force tasks and objectives

The first step in developing a personal communication strategy is to define the role of the sales force in the overall marketing strategy. This can only be done by clearly defining the kind of relationship the firm wants to establish with its customers in each product market.

As illustrated in Figure 14.3, one can identify three types of activity that any sales force exercises:

● *Selling*, which implies prospecting and approaching potential buyers, negotiating sales conditions and closing sales.
● *Servicing*, which implies delivery, technical assistance, after-sales service, merchandising, and so on.

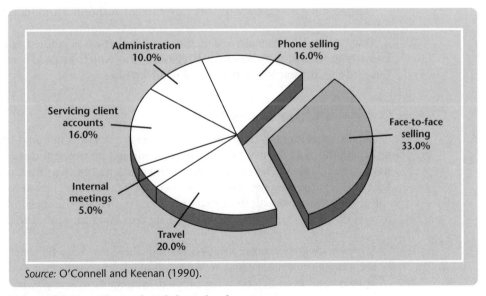

Source: O'Connell and Keenan (1990).

Figure 14.3   The tasks of the sales force

- *Information gathering*, which involves market research, business intelligence, monitoring of competitors' activities, needs analysis, and so on.

Thus, the salesperson is not only the firm's commercial arm, but also an important element in its marketing information system.

In practice, the terms 'salesperson' and 'sales representative' can cover very different missions, depending on the emphasis placed on one or other of the three functions above. The following categories of sales person can be identified:

- *The delivery person's* function is to ensure the physical delivery of the product.

- *The sales clerk's* role is to assist customers in their choice and to take orders. Sales clerks operate at the point of sale or stand behind the counter.

- *The travelling salesperson* visits the retailers or the distributors, takes their orders and performs non-selling activities such as checking inventory, handling retailers' complaints, and so on.

- *The merchandiser's* role is not to sell but rather to organise promotional activities at the sales point and to arrange point-of-purchase displays.

- *The missionary delegate* is not permitted to take an order, but has a role to inform and educate potential users. This is typically the role played by the medical representatives in the pharmaceutical industry.

- *The sales engineer* has a technical competence and operates as a consultant *vis-à-vis* the customer, providing assistance and advice. It is the role played by IBM sales engineers.

- *The sales representative* is an independent salesperson selling durable goods like cars and vacuum cleaners, or services like insurance, where creative selling is very important.

- *The negotiator* is in charge of the financial engineering of vast industrial projects and responsible for negotiations with government authorities and industrial partners.

Once the type of mission assigned to the salesperson is defined, the problem is to know how to organise commercial relations and which tasks to assign to the sales force, to the distribution network and to advertising.

Personal selling in the marketing mix

Generally speaking, the true role of a sales person remains first and foremost tied to satisfying the need for two-way communication felt by well-informed customers who have demands about how the product can be adapted to their own needs. From the firm's viewpoint, the sales force's new effectiveness is mainly linked to their ability in collecting and transmitting information so as to increase the speed of adjustment to market changes. This is how a Japanese firm conceives the role of the sales force:

> Salesmen are irreplaceable canvassers of information; they must be trained: (a) to listen to the customer, much more than to know seductive sales speech of the kind: 'the ten secrets of selling'; (b) to be humble when criticised, much more than display militant pride of the

kind: 'the products of firm X are the best'; (c) to be in solidarity with other salesmen and with his firm to facilitate cross-checking and return of information, much more than pursue the superficial solitude of the sales person who only tries to reach his quota in order to improve his own performance. (Xardel, 1982, pp. 59–75)

This evolution in the notion of the role of the sales force therefore tends to increase its direct participation in strategic marketing. In addition to operational marketing functions, the sales force now exercises various strategic functions. The typical *functions of the sales force* are:

- Winning acceptance for new products.
- Developing new customers.
- Maintaining customer loyalty.
- Providing technical service to facilitate sales.
- Communicating product information.
- Gathering information.

Several of these selling objectives, such as winning acceptance for new products, developing new customers and gathering information, are typically related to strategic marketing. The sales person can therefore play an important role in strategic marketing, in so far as he or she participates in elaborating product policy through the information they supply regarding buyers' needs.

The commercial negotiation

Selling is the end result of the whole marketing process. It is the central point of the free and competitive exchange, which itself is at the core of the market economy system. Commercial exchange is based upon a negotiation process, which, in industrialised economies at least, has almost disappeared as a formalised process in the field of consumer goods. It remains, however, discreetly present as consumers become better informed, smarter and able to make trade-off between brands and store brands, between consumption situations, and so on. Whatever the selling situation, sales are always based upon a process of negotiation whose mechanisms have to be well understood.

Foundations of negotiation

When considered as an instrument, negotiation is a system for decision making where the actors decide to agree to act by common assent rather than separately. Although there are many, diverse, examples of negotiation, Dupont (1994, p. 11) proposes the following definition:

An activity where two or more actors are face to face, and, when confronted with differences and interdependency, chose to, or think it advisable to, voluntarily look for a mutually acceptable solution which would allow them to initiate, maintain or develop, perhaps temporarily, a relationship.

There are six elements to this definition:

1. Being face to face, either directly or indirectly, implies communication, which can assume various forms (verbal, written, formal, secret). Because it is face to face, negotiation requires contact, a certain ritual, a special process, and so on. It is important to realise that these rituals and procedures can vary from one country or culture to another.

2. There are *conflicting interests* at stake for all parties. These differences are the actual reason for negotiation and can be extremely different. They can vary from just a matter of interpretation, to a financial problem or to a fundamental conflict of values.

3. The *parties share certain concerns* because of their interdependence. Each actor can only act (undertake a project, sign a contract, resolve a conflict) in agreement with his or her partner.

4. The *agreement is mutually acceptable*. The fact that each party recognises the acceptability of the solution incorporated in the agreement does not exclude the instability of such a solution. Moreover, an agreement does not mean compromise or equilibrium or even an equal share of resources and costs.

5. *Parties are bound, at least temporarily, by a voluntary relationship.* An actor chooses to start, remain in or leave negotiations. Negotiations involve the parties concerned in a spirit of conciliation or of agreement so as to overcome divergences. This presupposes that each party hopes to reach an agreement. If it is true that you may have to participate in negotiations, this does not mean that you have to negotiate.

6. This is a *relational procedure*. The relationship of negotiation is an activity of sharing out or of exchange of resources among parties. Negotiation implies a move towards the other party and is spurred by the desire to come to an agreement. These partners have both conflicting and common interests but prefer a relationship, which is not based upon opposing strengths, imposing one's authority or calling upon a third party.

Negotiation is, as such, at the heart of the business philosophy prevailing in a market-oriented strategy.

Negotiation, this relationship of a fundamentally egalitarian exchange where each actor tries to persuade or convince but does not attempt to dominate the other, summarises the whole concept of marketing. We can consider this to be a major axis in the development of a global civilisation where the merchant tends to replace the warrior. (de Maricourt *et al.*, 1997, p. 417)

Characteristics of commercial negotiation

Negotiation in marketing covers a large area (it includes all the steps in obtaining a present or future market linking two or more parties) and has a certain number of characteristics which distinguish it from other types of negotiation:

● It covers many situations and, as Dupont suggests (1994, p. 216), it is important to differentiate *major* and *minor* commercial negotiations. The former concerns big contracts and *business to business*; the latter refers to day-to-day buying of lesser importance.

● As a rule, one of the parties in a commercial negotiation, the seller, will be *more active than the other*. This is the one to make propositions and counter-propositions or concessions so as to reach a transaction.

● Commercial negotiation is dominated by the product or service and its attributes (price, quality, and delays, purchasing conditions) and *by reference to the market and competition* in particular. This explains why negotiation involves both objective aspects defined in terms of the market and relational arguments based on interpersonal aspects.

● Commercial negotiation shows up the tension between the need to come to an agreement which is to one's advantage and the desire to establish a long-term relationship. The tendency is to *share satisfaction*. A balance is reached when a need is satisfied on one side and a benefit on the other. Integration will be clear in so far as the seller shows an attempt to satisfy the customer's real needs, which is of course the best way to ascertain his loyalty.

● *The actors in a commercial negotiation*, and this is not necessarily true in other types of negotiations, share certain references, principles, values, and so on.

● Lastly, a commercial negotiation is an intermediate or final link in an *economic chain*. This explains why interdependence binds all the participants in such a chain. The supplier and the subcontractor alike know that their buyer also has to meet certain costs and is himself, somewhere along the chain, faced with sellers and buyers.

These characteristics, which differentiate commercial negotiation from other forms of negotiation, appear in varying degrees in both selling and buying negotiations.

Opposition between transaction and relationship marketing

Commercial negotiation and selling techniques are often thought to be the same. These are, however, two completely different procedures.

> Selling is convincing someone – the customer – that a proposed product or service best answers his or her needs; 'negotiating' is jointly analysing a situation where there is some common interest, even though diverging interests are apparent and each party has something to sell or conditions to impose, so as to come to a mutually satisfying agreement. (Guérin *et al.*, 1979, quoted by Dupont, 1994, p. 247)

Selling techniques are indubitably efficient *to close the sale* and are often associated with various aggressive selling methods: hard sell or manipulative marketing. These techniques were popular in the 1960s in operational marketing when the *sales orientation* was predominant (see Chapter 1). They have been challenged over the past ten years, under the influence of all the changes in customer behaviour and in the competitive environment, as mentioned previously.

The differences between single transaction and relationship marketing are many. Transaction marketing focuses on a discrete, individual sale. The relationships end once the sale is consummated. Relationship marketing is oriented towards a strong and lasting relationship. Maintaining and cultivating the customer base is the key objective, in order to create a mutually profitable relationship. Relationship marketing presupposes the opportunity for shared benefits, while transaction marketing works on a model of contradictory needs: the buyer wants a good price; the seller wants a high profit.

> Single transaction sellers are sometimes part of the seedier side of marketing. New York City electronic retailers, for example, often run afoul of the authorities for advertising unrealistically low prices, then once the consumer is in the store, engaging in 'bait-and-switch' and other less savoury sales tactics. They can get away with it because of the steady flow of tourists and the almost complete lack of repeat business. Their goal is not to build lasting relationships with customers but to make a continuous series of first-time purchases. Other merchants, with a greater incidence of repeat business, would not last long with such practices. (Schnaars, 1998, p. 190)

Relationship marketing differs from transaction marketing in other respects as well. While the latter focuses almost solely on price, the former shifts the emphasis to non-economic benefits, such as services, delivery time and the certainty of continued supply.

Traditional selling techniques had to evolve towards relationship selling for three reasons:

1. In traditional selling (based on the systematic application of selling techniques), it is rarely understood that selling is above all an act of communication, a mutual discovery of questions and answers and not a unilateral act of manipulation.

2. If traditional selling techniques seem less efficient today and often come up against resistance and scepticism from well-informed prospects (partially due to consumerism), this is because the decision to buy depends more upon *complex mechanisms of social influence* and less upon elementary psychological mechanisms.

3. Third, traditional selling techniques do not consider the fact that the *practice of relationship marketing*, that is helping a customer find the solution to a problem, has become the core principle of a market-oriented strategy, where selling is *customer problem solving*, not merely selling available products.

Characteristics of relationship marketing

The practice of relationship or counselling selling – as opposed to the 'impose–convince–suggest–please' system – is characterised by the importance accorded (a) to true and non-manipulative exploration of the customer's motivations and motives and

(b) to the search for a long-lasting mutually satisfactory relationship between buyers and sellers. Relationship selling has shifted attention from 'closing' the singular sale to creating the necessary conditions for a long-term relationship between the firm and its customers that in the long run breeds successful sales encounters:

> Relationship selling is customer-oriented, as opposed to traditional selling which is product-oriented. Selling is customer problem-solving, not merely selling available products. (Donaldson, 1998, p. 79)

In market-oriented firms, there is a tendency to change the vocabulary from sales force to *sales counsellors, professional representatives* or *sales consultants*.

In a company having chosen to develop a market-oriented strategy, commercial negotiation has received a mission, which is capital for the firm's survival: to build a sustainable relationship with customers. This means a relationship which is profitable for both parties. In relationship marketing, *the profit centre is the customer* and not the product or the brand. Attracting new customers is viewed as an intermediate objective; maintaining the existing customer base is a major objective for a long-term mutually profitable relationship. In this context, the monitoring of the customer's portfolio composition and of the quality of the market share (see Table 5.6) are of primary importance. Read Slymotsky and Shapiro (1993) on this subject.

Pitfalls of relationship marketing

As pointed out by Schnaars (1998, p. 190), sometimes relationships are forced, namely when the sellers engineer switching costs into their transactions that tie the customer in a way that denies the buyer a real choice and makes him a captive customer. Firms that rely on proprietary technologies and patented parts also forced lasting relationships. Long-term contracts do the same. In each of these cases the seller may bolt given the opportunity to do so. There are other limitations to relationship marketing:

● The firm that builds a relationship usually charges a premium price and is therefore vulnerable to price competition from low price sellers.
● Some customers may refuse to become dependent on a single supplier.
● Customers may place their easy-to-fill orders to lower-price competitors and leave the more difficult orders to the high service firm.
● In other cases, there may be no mutual benefit for buyer and seller.

Relationship selling is particularly useful in *business-to-business* marketing where this supplier–customer link is especially close, lasting and important for both parties. This is also the philosophy underlying trade marketing, in the relationship binding manufacturers and distributors. In general, relationship selling is the irreplaceable complement to a strategy based on the *solution-to-a-problem approach* as described earlier. To go further on the subject of relationship marketing, see Dwyer *et al.* (1987), Jackson (1985) and Payne (1995).

Setting up a relationship selling process

Approaching customers in relationship selling is different from traditional selling because of the emphasis on pre-sales and post-sales activities. There are five different phases in relationship selling:

1. *Systematic search for information*. This means identifying prospects, potential customers who might need the product and who might buy it. This is a permanent activity.

2. *Selecting a target*. Here the purpose is to analyse the objective reasons why a prospect could become a prospective customer and have reasons for becoming a buyer. The real question is to find out to what extent our firm can be useful to this customer.

3. *Convincing good customers*. It is essential that the salesperson attract customers whose value and potential justify the time and effort which will be devoted to them. This is the beginning of the selling phase itself, which includes the sales presentation, negotiation, answers to objections and the conclusion of the agreement.

4. *Building the relationship*. A relationship of trust must be built up and, once the relationship is established, the follow-up must be organised. The salesperson is the problem-solver, who sells, not a product, but the service (or the solution) provided by the product.

5. *Maintaining and reinforcing the relationship*. Maintaining a relationship is particularly based on personalised service achieved through better understanding of customers' needs. The objective is to maintain close contact with the customer and to build up customer loyalty. The firm can thus construct a barrier to competition, as changing suppliers would imply switching costs.

Relationship selling implies giving the role of advisor to the salesperson, as a seller of solutions. In a company which has opted for market orientation, a salesperson is a partner working towards the customer's long-term performance, even if he or she cannot see the possibility of an immediate sale. Relationship selling has developed substantially in the business-to-business context and is progressively gaining a foothold in consumer marketing through the possibilities offered by direct and interactive marketing. For an analysis of the difficulties in relationship marketing in consumer goods, read Fournier *et al.* (1998).

Organisation of the sales force

A firm can organise its sales force in different ways. The organisation can be by territory, by product, by customer or even a combination of these:

● *Territory-based organisation*. This is the most common structure and also the simplest organisation. The salesperson is the firm's exclusive representative for its full product line for all current and potential customers. This structure has several advantages: first, it defines clearly the sales representative's responsibilities; second, it motivates the salesperson, who has the full exclusivity on the territory; and finally, it minimises costs and travel expenses.

This structure is only appropriate when products are few in number or similar and when customers have the same kind of needs. A firm producing paints and varnishes, whose customers are wholesalers, retailers and industrial users (building painters, car bodies, and so on) clearly cannot use the same salesperson to cultivate these different customer groups.

● *Product-based organisation*. This second structure is preferable when products are very different, technically complex and require appropriate technical competence. In this case, the salesperson is more specialised and better equipped to meet clients' needs and also to counter rivals.

The problem with this structure is that costs may increase manifold, since several salespersons from the same firm may visit the same customer. For example, Rank Xerox uses different salespersons for photocopying machines and for word-processing units.

● *Customer-based organisation*. Organisation by customer categories is adopted when clients' needs are very different and require specific abilities. Customers may be classified by industrial sector, by size or by their method of buying. We find here the same criteria as those of segmentation presented in Chapter 7.

The advantage of a customer-based structure is that each sales force is specialised and becomes very knowledgeable about specific customer needs. But if customers are dispersed geographically, this organisation can be very costly. Most computer firms organise their sales force by customer groups: banks and insurance, industrial customers, retailers, and so on.

Other more complex forms of organisation combining pairs of criteria also exist. Salespersons can be specialised by product–territory, customer–territory or even by territory–customer–product. This normally happens in very large enterprises with many products and varied clients.

Deciding on the size of the sales force

Determining the number of salespeople is a problem logically similar to the advertising budget. In practice, however, it can be resolved more simply because market response is easier to measure. Different approaches are possible. The simplest no doubt is the one based on the salesperson's *work load*. An example of its application was shown in Chapter 11 (see Table 11.6). The procedure is as follows:

● The underlying philosophy in the call-load approach is that large customers should be serviced differently from medium-sized customers, and medium-sized customers differently from small customers. Thus, the first step is to have a *breakdown of customer by class*.

● The next step is to develop a theoretical *call frequency for each class*. Experience shows that as customer grows larger, the number of sales calls does not grow in direct proportion to the increase in sales. Churchill *et al*. (1997) suggested that the relationship between customer size and sales calls can be clearly seen when these two factors are plotted on semi-log paper, which reflects the presence of diminishing returns. For every customer class, multiplying the call frequency times the number of account in any class provides a specific call frequency.

⬤ In the third step, the *number of calls* made by an average salesperson during one year must be determined. The factors to consider here are: number of working days after deducting holidays, weekends, vacations, and so on; percentage of non-selling time devoted to sales meetings, sick leave, laboratory training, and so on; number of calls made per day by salesperson and by territory; and variation in call capacity between urban and rural territories.

Given the number of visits that a salesperson can make in a given customer class, it is then possible to determine the size of the necessary sales force from the following expression:

$$\text{Size of sales force} = \frac{(\text{Number of customers for class}) \times (\text{Call frequency})}{\text{Average number of calls for salesperson}}$$

The calculation is repeated for each customer class. This approach is valid for current customers and must be extended to prospective customers as well. For other methods of setting the size of the sales force, see Semlow (1959) and Lambert (1968).

Other methods are based on direct or indirect measures of market response to an increase of the frequency of calls through the sales force. The method developed by Semlow is based on several indicators of buying power within each sales territory. A successful application of this method to the insurance sector is presented by Lambin (1965).

In business-to-business markets, direct sales measures of visit frequency are more easily obtainable. An econometric study conducted by Lambert (1968) in the hospitals market has contributed to improve in a significant way the overall allocation of selling efforts among sales territories.

⬤ Advertising Communication

Advertising is a means of communication by which a firm can deliver a message to potential buyers with whom it is not in direct contact. When a firm resorts to advertising, it is effectively following a *pull communication strategy*. Its main objective is to create a brand image and brand equity, and to ensure co-operation from distributors. Just as the sales force is the best tool for a push strategy, advertising is the best means for a pull strategy.

In Chapter 3, we described what advertising represents for the advertiser and its utility to the buyer. Recall briefly that:

⬤ For the *firm*, the function of advertising is to produce knowledge for consumers and to generate interest among them in order to create demand for its product.

⬤ For *consumers*, advertising allows them to learn about the distinctive characteristics claimed by the manufacturer. Advertising also helps them to save personal time, since the information reaches them directly without their having to collect it.

The different forms of advertising communication

Since the advent of the early form of advertising, advertising communication objectives have diversified considerably, and different forms of advertising can be identified while using the same media.

Concept advertising

This is a media-advertising message with a mainly 'attitudinal' communication objective: to influence the buyer's attitude towards the brand. Its role can be defined as follows:

> The creative efforts of many national advertisers are designed, not to induce immediate action, but to build favourable attitudes that will lead to eventual purchase. (Dhalla, 1978)

This definition implies that the effectiveness of this type of advertising can only be viewed from a long-term perspective. The notion of attitude holds a central position here. The objective is mainly to create an image based on communicating a concept.

Promotional advertising

This is a media-advertising message with a mainly 'behavioural' communication objective: to influence the buyers' purchasing behaviour rather than their attitudes. The objective is to trigger the act of purchase. Its effectiveness is evaluated directly in terms of actual sales. This is the most aggressive type of communication, although it is not incompatible with image creation. However, its immediate purpose is to achieve short-term results.

Response advertising

This is a personalised message of an offer, having the objective of generating a 'relationship' with the prospect by encouraging a response from the latter on the basis of which a commercial relation can be built.

This type of advertising tries to reconcile the characteristics of the two previous ones: building an image, but also encouraging a measurable response allowing an immediate appraisal of the effectiveness of the communication. This type of media advertising is expanding rapidly now, and is directly linked to interactive marketing, discussed in Chapter 12.

Prerequisites of concept advertising

There are still too many firms that tend to assimilate advertising with marketing and to approach marketing by advertising. In fact, advertising is only a complement, which is sometimes, but not always, indispensable to a more fundamental process of strategic marketing. For advertising to be effective, a number of prerequisites should ideally prevail:

● Advertising is one element of the *marketing mix* and its role cannot be separated from the roles of the other marketing instruments. As a general rule, advertising will be effective only when the other marketing factors have been chosen: a differentiated and clearly positioned product sold at a competitive price through a well-adapted distribution network.

● Advertising is useful to the consumer mainly for complex products having *internal* qualities that cannot be discovered by inspection. For *experience goods* (such as food products or shampoos) and for *credence goods* (such as motor oil and medical services) consumers have lots to gain from truthful advertising.

⬤ To be effective, advertising should promote a *distinctive characteristic* to clearly position the brand in the minds of consumers as being different from competing brands. The distinctive characteristic can be the promise of the brand, but also its personality, its look or its symbolic value.

⬤ Advertising is particularly effective in markets or segments where *primary demand is expansible*. Its role is then to stimulate the need for the product category as a whole. In non-expansible markets, the main role of advertising is to stimulate selective demand and to create communication effects at the brand level.

⬤ The size of the reference market must be large enough to absorb the cost of an advertising campaign, and the firm must have enough financial resources to reach the *threshold levels* of the advertising response function.

Thus, the advertising communication platform is the complement of a strategic marketing programme. The advertising positioning sought must be in line with the marketing positioning adopted and based on a sound strategic thinking, without which advertising cannot be effective.

Alternative advertising objectives

To determine the objectives of advertising communication, it is useful to refer back to the three levels of market response analysed in Chapter 5:

⬤ *Cognitive response*, which relates to awareness and to knowledge of the product characteristics. At this level, the advertiser can set objectives of information, recall, recognition or familiarity.

⬤ *Affective response*, which relates to the overall evaluation of the brand in terms of feelings, favourable or unfavourable judgements and preferences. The objectives will be to influence attitude and to create purchase intention.

⬤ *Behavioural response*, which refers to buying behaviour and to post-purchase behaviour, but also to all other forms of behavioural response observed as the result of a communication, such as visiting a showroom, requesting a catalogue, sending a reply coupon.

It is common practice to consider these three levels as a sequence, as potential buyers pass successively through the three stages: cognitive, affective and behavioural (Lavidge and Steiner, 1961). This sequence of reactions is known as the *learning model*. As noted in Chapter 5, this model needs to be adjusted in terms of the buyer's degree of involvement (see Figure 5.1). Although not generally applicable, the learning response model nevertheless remains a useful tool for defining the priority objectives of communication.

Keeping this hierarchy of objectives in mind, Rossiter and Percy (1987, p. 132) have identified *five different communication effects* that can be caused, in whole or in part, by advertising. These effects reconstitute the process followed by the buyer when confronted with a purchasing decision; there can therefore be as many possible objectives for communication.

Development of primary demand

Existence of need is a prerequisite that determines the effectiveness of any act of communication. Every product satisfies a product category need. Perception of this need by potential buyers can be stimulated by advertising. Advertising thus helps develop total demand in the market. Three distinct situations can exist:

● The category need is *present and well perceived* by potential buyers. In this case, generic advertising is not justified. This is the case for many low-involvement, frequently purchased products, where purchasing is done on a routine basis.

● The category need is *perceived but neglected or forgotte*n and the role of generic advertising is to remind the prospective buyer of previously established need. This is the case for infrequently purchased or infrequently used products like pain remedies.

● The perception of the category need is *weak or not established* in the target group of potential users. In this case, generic advertising can sell the benefits of the product category. The typical example is the campaign in favour of the use of condoms to fight against the spread of AIDS. Selling category need is a communication objective for all new products, and in particular for new-to-the-world products.

In generic advertising campaigns, the advertising content places the emphasis on the core service of the product and/or on the product benefits (see Exhibit 14.1). This type of communication message will not only benefit the advertiser but also the competing firms.

Creating brand awareness

This is the first level of cognitive response. In Chapter 6, we defined brand awareness as the buyer's ability to identify a brand in sufficient detail to propose, choose or use a brand. Three kinds of advertising objective, based on awareness, can be identified:

● To create or maintain *brand recognition* so those buyers identify the brand at the point of sale and are induced to check the existence of a category need.
● To create or maintain *brand recall* to induce buyers to select the brand once the category need has been experienced.
● To emphasise both *brand recognition and brand recall*.

These communication objectives imply different advertising contents. For brand recognition, the advertising content will emphasise the visual elements (logo, colours and packaging), while for brand recall the advertising will seek to repeat the brand name in audio and visual media and in headlines and to associate the brand name with the core service.

Creating a favourable brand attitude

The objective is to create, improve, maintain and modify buyers' attitudes towards the brand. It is therefore affective response which intervenes here (see Exhibit 14.2). Chapter 5 describes the components of attitude. The following communication strategies are open to the advertiser:

Exhibit 14.1

Is Advertising of Prescription Drugs Different?

In the US, since the Food and Drug Administration (FDA) relaxed its guidelines on televi-sion advertising in August 1997, spending on direct-to-consumer advertising has taken off. Spending in America on ads for prescription drugs, estimated at more than $1 billion in 1998, now exceeds that on beer advertising. A study published in 1998 by *Prevention* magazine and supported by the FDA found that 90 per cent of the 1200 people ques-tioned had seen a drug advertisement and a third had visited their doctors as a result. Remarkably, 80 per cent of doctors agreed to prescribe the drug.

In Europe, a 1992 ruling from the European Commission prohibits prescription-drug companies from selling their wares directly to Europe's consumers. This means they cannot advertise their products in the popular press or on television. They can pitch them to doctors and pharmacists only in medical journals and other professional publications. At the same time the European Commission and many European governments talk loftily of the need for 'patient empowerment', greater public awareness and understanding about diseases and their therapies. Many advocates for patients' rights raise the following ques-tion: can patients simultaneously be asked to take more responsibility for their health and denied access to some of the information that may help them to do so?

It remains that it is right to treat advertising of prescription drugs differently from adver-tising of baked beans. Drugs have side effects and patients may ignore them more readily than their doctor would. Drug firms are also tempted to make misleading claims. In addi-tion, in Europe, patients pay far less of the drugs bill than those in the United States. So advertising may encourage patients to put pressure on their doctors to dispense something that appears almost free to them, but raises the bill to the taxpayer.

However, consumer advertising is also a powerful way to stimulate public interest in health. It need not become a tough sell. Indeed in Europe, people still think of themselves as patients rather than health-care consumers. As a first step, it would be reasonable to insist that advertising gives information about diseases and alternative treatments rather than merely pushing a single product. For, if patients are to take more responsibility for their health, they do deserve reliable information on available treatments.

Source: Adapted from *The Economist*, 8 August, 1998, pp. 57–8.

- To convince the target audience to give *more importance* to a particular product attribute on which the brand is well placed in comparison to rival brands.
- To convince the target audience of the firm's *technological superiority* in the product category.
- To *reinforce beliefs* and the conviction of the target audience on the presence of a determining attribute in the brand.
- To *reposition the brand* by associating its use with another set of needs or purchase motivations.
- To eliminate a *negative attitude* by associating the brand with a set of positive values.

Exhibit 14.2

Kodak Focuses on Teen-Girls Consumers

Eastman Kodak Co. has seen the future: it is female and barely adolescent. In an attempt to boost sales in what it regards as a lucrative demographic group, the US Company is launching its first youth marketing campaign, one that targets so-called tween girls – generally defined as those 9 to 15 years old. Kodak's internal marketing presentations proclaim that this is an era of 'girl power' in which females 13 to 15 are 'hyper consumers' and the 'key drivers' of today's trends and pop culture. Kodak says it will spend $75 million over 5 years to reach tweens through television, radio, print and Internet banner ads created by the ad agency Saatchi & Saatchi PLC. A company study shows that tween girls are more likely than boys to own a camera, 75 per cent to 49 per cent. An independent study used by Kodak shows that tween girls consider taking pictures as popular as dating. And pictures, they say, are more important possessions than their own pets. In its print ads, Kodak beckons to tween girls by saying that its disposable cameras 'get guys to smile at you with the touch of a button' and that the camera 'attracts a crowd like flies to the school cafeteria'.

Source: *The Wall Street Journal Europe*, 17 June, 1999.

- To call attention to *neglected attributes* by consumers in their decision-making process.
- To alter the beliefs of the target audience about *competing brands*.

The last strategy can only be adopted in countries where comparative advertising is authorised, as in the UK. The European Commission has recently published a directive for comparative advertising in the EU.

It is important to identify clearly the implicit assumptions of a communication strategy based on brand attitude. They can be summarised as follows:

- The advertiser must emphasise the features or characteristics in which it has the strongest competitive advantage.
- It is useless to try to modify buyers' perceptions when the brand does not really have the claimed characteristic.
- The major criticism directed against advertising is the adoption of arguments or themes, which are totally unrelated to product attributes important to the buyer.

In other words, a *market-driven communication strategy* is based on the idea that advertising is mainly designed to help the buyer buy and not simply to praise the advertiser. This vision of a communication strategy falls well in line with the market orientation concept.

Stimulate brand purchase intention

Purchase intention is halfway between the affective and the behavioural response. Two kinds of situation may arise:

⬤ The buyer is weakly or not at all involved in the purchasing decision and there is *no conscious, prior intention to buy* until the last minute at the point of purchase. This is the case for low perceived-risk products and also for routinely purchased products. In this type of situation, to stimulate brand purchase intention is not an advertising objective.

⬤ The buyer has a *conscious purchase intention* during advertising exposure.

In the latter case, promotional advertising can play a role by using incentives (price reductions, special offers, and so on) that precipitate the buying decision or encourage repurchase.

Recall that the intention to buy is only expressed when there is also a *state of shortage that is when the category need is felt*. Thus, the two states, need and intention, are closely associated. Yet intention to buy is not a frequently recurring event in any particular consumer.

Markets that are huge in their annual volume are made up of buying decisions made by very small numbers of people in a given period of time. For example, in a typical week in 1982, American retailers sold over $365 million worth of shoes. But during that week (as shown in our study that year) only six persons in 100 bought shoes for themselves or their children. Similarly, only 28 adults in 1000 bought any kinds of women's slacks, jeans, or shorts in the course of a week, and only 21 bought a dress. Fourteen in 1000 bought a small appliance; 18 in 1000 bought furniture; 3 in 1000 bought an article of luggage. (Bogart, 1986, p. 267)

Hence, many markets with very high turnovers, such as those mentioned in the examples above depend each week on the buying decisions of a small number of people. It is not surprising to find that advertising messages give rise to relatively few immediate purchase intentions, since in most cases the prerequisite is not there: namely the existence of a state of need.

Purchase facilitation

This last objective of advertising communication deals with the *other marketing factors* (the four Ps), without which there can be no purchase: a product that keeps its promise, retail availability of the product, acceptable price, and competence and availability of the sales force. When these conditions are not all met, advertising can sometimes help to reduce or minimise problems by, for example, defending the market price, or by working as a substitute to distribution through direct marketing.

The advertising objectives are numerous and very diversified and it is important to define them clearly before the organisation of an advertising campaign. As already indicated above, it is up to strategic marketing people, generally brand managers, to propose the advertising communication objective.

⬤ Sales Promotion

Sales promotion includes all the incentive tools which, often locally and in a non-permanent way, are used by the firm to complement and reinforce advertising and the sales force action, and to stimulate quicker and/or larger purchase of a good or service. Sales promotion is part of the overall marketing strategy as suggested by the following definition:

> Sales promotion is a process combining a set of communication tools and techniques, implemented within the framework of the marketing plan designed by the firm, in order to induce among the target groups, in the short or in the long term, the adoption or the modification of a consuming or purchase behaviour. (Ingold, 1995, p. 25)

During the last decade, promotion has gained in importance and sales promotion expenditures have been increasing annually as a percentage of the total communication budget.

> According to the Havas study (1998), promotion expenditures in the UK amounted to 17,210 Mln GBP in 1997, against 15,917 Mln in 1996, or a 8.1 per cent increase. Direct marketing expenditures amounted to 2890 Mln GBP in 1997. In per cent of total marketing communication expenditures, promotion amounted to 17.2 per cent and direct marketing to 16.8 per cent. (Havas 1998, p. 26)

The share of promotion expenditures in the total marketing communiocation budget observed in each European country is shown in Table 14.4.

Table 14.4 Share of sales promotion expenditures in the total marketing communication budget

Countries	Share of promotion expenditures in the communication budget in 1997 (%)	Expenditures in local currencies
Germany	15.7	22,054 million DM
United Kingdom	17.2	2965 million GBP
France	15.9	25,109 million FRF
Italy	22.2	7735 billion ITL
Spain	16.6	212,217 million ESP
The Netherlands	19.7	3096 million NLG
Belgium	35.2	60,694 million BEF
Switzerland	19.5	1664 million CHF

Source: Havas (1998).

Several factors, both internal and external, have contributed to the rapid growth of sales promotion:

- Consumers, confronted with a decline of their purchasing power, are more price sensitive and react positively to promotional activities.
- Distributors, more concentrated and powerful, demand from manufacturers more promotions to help them build store traffic.
- Competition intensifies and competitors use consumer and trade promotions more frequently.

● Effectiveness of mass media advertising has declined because of rising costs, media clutter and similarity among competing brands.
● Companies confronted with a slowing down of sales are more concerned by short-term results.
● Any promotion is in fact a disguised price reduction, but which is limited in time and scope. This flexibility is highly praised by marketing people.

To these factors, one must also add the development of direct marketing, which by nature often has a promotional content.

Objectives of sales promotion

The objectives of sales promotion vary with the type of promotions; it is common practice to make a distinction according to the sender of the promotion (manufacturer or distributor) and according to the target (consumer, distributor, sales force). Following Ingold's classification (1995, p. 26), we will make a distinction between four types of promotions:

● *In consumer promotions* a direct, indirect or hypothetical benefit (samples, coupons, rebates, cash refund offer, and so on) is proposed to consumers to stimulate the purchase of a product. Manufacturers generally offer consumer promotions through the distribution channel.

● *Trade promotions* are proposed to retailers or wholesalers, generally taking the form of money allowances, to persuade them (a) to carry the brand, (b) to carry more units than the normal amount, (c) to promote the brand by featuring display or price reductions or (d) to push the products in their stores.

● *Commercial promotions* are promotional activities organised by distributors and targeting their own customers' base, generally using the financial support given by manufacturers.

● *Sales force or network promotion*, where the objective is to stimulate all the partners involved in the selling activities (sales force, wholesalers, retailers) through individual incentives.

These distinctions are sometimes artificial to the extent where a specific promotion can take simultaneously one of these forms. The distinction remains useful, however, to define as clearly as possible the promotion objective. Examples of promotion objectives are presented in Table 14.5. For a more detailed description of these objectives, see Ingold (1995, pp. 63–70).

The different promotion tools

There are many different sales-promotion tools which can be divided, as proposed by *LSA* (1982), into four main groups:

● *Price reductions*. Essentially this is selling something for less money; several methods exist.

Table 14.5 Objectives by types of promotion

CONSUMER PROMOTIONS	COMMERCIAL PROMOTIONS
Trial	Visit to new outlets
First purchase	Customer retention
Repurchase	Visit frequency increase
Loyalty	First purchase
Retention	Purchase in new store facings
Reduced prices	Increase of the average basket
Increase of quantity purchased	
Increase of quantity consumed	
Purchase frequency increase	
Trial of a new variety	

DISTRIBUTOR PROMOTIONS	NETWORK PROMOTION
List of new products	Increase of quantity sold
Stock	Gain in distribution presence
Facing increase	Introduction of new products
Point of purchase display	Increase in size or range
Participation to advertising	Reselling actions

Source: Ingold (1995, p. 63).

● *Selling with premiums or gifts*. Small items are given to buyers either at the time of purchase or afterwards.
● *Samples and trials*. Free distribution, trials or tasting allow consumers to test the product.
● *Games and contests*. These games give buyers a chance to win a big prize.

There are many ways of applying each group as shown in Table 14.6.

New sales-promotion tools have appeared over the last few years based upon information obtained from bar codes, via, for instance, customer loyalty cards and coupons (see Exhibit 14.3). Electronic coupons are immediately distributed to customers targeted through their purchases electronically recorded when they pay.

The system developed by Catalina Marketing is based on reading bar codes by an intelligent scanner and thus avoids giving out coupons to customers who would not be interested in the product. The scanner instructs the computer to print out a coupon for Fanta for someone who had just bought Orangina. Or a customer who had just bought baby products receives a coupon for Pampers.

This has just been brought before the courts in France by Orangina as unfair competition. A decision has not yet been made (*LSA*, 27 November, 1997, pp. 18–19). It is the misappropriation of clientele which is at stake here.

In other words, Orangina would accept that customers buying Coca-Cola get a coupon for Fanta (which belongs to the same group) or that those buying Mars get a Coca-Cola coupon (complementary product) but not a coupon from a competitor for the same product category.

Table 14.6   Description of promotion tools

1. PREMIUMS	3. PRICE REDUCTIONS
With-pack premium: an extra product accompanies the product inside (in-pack) or on pack (outside)	*Coupons*: certificates entitling the bearer to a stated saving on the purchase of a specific product
Recipe: recipe files offered with purchased product	*Special offer*: a reduced price for a limited period of time
Differed premium: an advantage, which is offered at a later date	*Extra-pack*: 3 products for the price of 2, 4 products for the price of 3, and so on
Sample: a sample is included	*Banded pack*: two related products banded together
Package: a reusable container, which can be used after consuming the product	*Cash refund*: provide a price reduction after the purchase with proof of full payment
Premium (gifts): merchandise offered at a relatively low cost or free	*Buy back*: the manufacturer buys back obsolete model of the brand
Self-liquidating premium: item sold below its normal retail price at no cost for the brand	
2. GAMES AND CONTESTS	**4. TRIALS AND SAMPLES**
Contests: possibility of winning a big prize in a contest based on consumer's observation, knowledge or suggestion	*Free sample*: offer on a limited base of a free amount of product or service
Sweepstakes: diverse forms of games based on chance with a lottery draw	*Gifts*: merchandise offered as an incentive to purchase a product, to visit a store
Winner per store: (or patronage award): a lottery where a client may win even without purchasing	*Free trials*: invite prospective buyers to try the product without cost and without obligation to buy
	Demonstrations: point of purchases (POP) displays and commercial presentations, sometimes with trials or tastings

Source: Adapted from: *LSA*, No. 869–70, December 1982.

The issue at stake is important: do distributors have the right to orient customers to any products they choose? May a distributor dispose of his clientele as he wishes?

This explosion of sales-promotion tools and actions has of course a negative side in that they present a high cost both for the manufacturer and for the distributor. At the same time the positive effect of promotions is assailed by competitors who counterattack a successful sales-promotion action with a 'reaction' sales promotion. While such an escalation of promotions benefits the consumer, it ends up by providing neverending promotions, weakening their effect and provoking speculation and a state of expectancy from consumers.

This explains the *Every Day Low Price* strategy that Procter & Gamble launched with Wal-Mart in the US where P&G promises to deliver its products without sales promotion but at the lowest possible cost. This is part of a trade marketing strategy as seen earlier in Chapter 12.

Exhibit 14.3

Catalina Electronic Couponing

Catalina printers are installed in over 12,000 outlets, mainly in the United States, Great Britain, Japan and France. Over 700 French stores give out coupons called Eco-bo (Géant, Hyper U, Casino, Champion, Super U, Cora, Match and Intermarché). More than 400 brands are in the system and over 165 million coupons have been distributed. Over 15 million coupons have been returned by customers, which means a response rate of 8 to 10 per cent, compared to 2.4 per cent for coupons in mailboxes.

Source: LSA, 27 November, 1997, p. 19.

Impact of promotions on sales

The effects of sales promotion are complex and go beyond just affecting sales even if that is the main objective. We can distinguish between effects on consumers and effects on distributors. Along with such immediate effects there are long-term consequences which can sometimes be negative for a brand. A distinction must be made between the impact on consumers and on distributors.

Impact of promotions on consumers

These effects are many and varied as illustrated in Figure 14.4. They can be felt before, during and after the promotion action itself:

- *Internal transfer effect.* Loyal buyers take advantage of an offer but would have bought the brand in any case.

- *Anticipation effect.* Sales go down just before a promotion comes into effect because consumers wait for the promotion to buy. This is particularly true when the periodicity for sales promotions is regular.

- *Decay effect.* Sales go down after a special promotion because consumers have stocked up on the product.

- *Cannibalisation effect.* There are purchasing transfers among different sizes and varieties within a range of products during sales promotions.

- *Brand switching effect.* This is what was intended. Additional sales through a switch from some other brand to the brand under promotion.

- *Trial effect.* Whatever the tool, it induces consumers to use the product. This is especially important for new products.

- *Retention effect.* Here we have the positive effects that survive the period of promotion and can keep the product at a superior level of sales after the promotion.

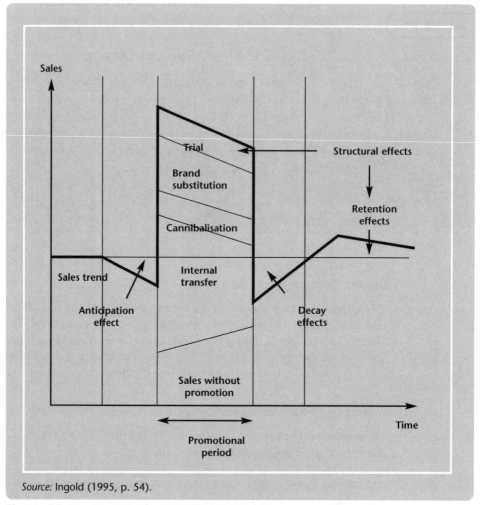

Source: Ingold (1995, p. 54).

Figure 14.4   Impact of promotions on sales

These promotion effects vary according to the phase of product life cycle (PLC) reached by the reference market. During the introduction and growth phases, sales promotion has an accelerator effect in the development of primary demand, by inducing consumers to try out the product. In contrast, during the maturity phase of the PLC, the benefits obtained through promotion are made at the expense of competition, and this can trigger a chain reaction of sales promotion.

Impact of promotions on distributors

Sales promotions organised at the point of sales always have an impact on distributor behaviour. Three major effects can be identified:

● *Postponement effect.* Distributors know, and demand to know, the operational marketing programme of their suppliers and tend to defer purchases in order to stock up for sales promotions.

● *Overstocking effect.* When ordering at times of sales promotions, distributors tend to order as a function of their storage space, which decreases post-promotion orders.

● *Deviant ordering.* Some distributors only order when the products are on promotions and refuse to purchase the product at full price. This is the attitude adopted systematically by hard discounters who can then charge very competitive prices.

Promotions have an important role to play in creating traffic flow in the store and in stimulating shelf rotation. As mentioned earlier, sales promotions also add to logistic and administrative costs for distributors. This means that it is important to check that the proposed promotions are compatible with distributors operating mode.

Negative side-effects of promotions

Overly frequent sales promotions can produce a certain number of negative side effects on buying behaviour and brand image. There are four types of negative effects:

● *Escalation of promotions.* As already mentioned, because of the very success of a first sales promotion, promotion after promotion may be launched. This is desirable neither for the manufacturer nor for the distributor.

● *Brand confusion.* If there are too many promotions the brand image is weakened and promotions can conflict with the brand positioning strategy.

● *Speculation.* If a growing number of purchases are made during sales promotions, consumers may change their buying behaviour by postponing their purchases. This of course is counterproductive, as the purpose of promotions is to increase sales in normal periods. The anticipation effect is then prevalent. It is however important to distinguish between consumers who wait for sales promotion periods and the very particular group that waits for sales-promotion actions.

● *Difficulty in price comparison.* The multiplication of sales promotions increases the difficulty of evaluating a 'fair price' and of comparing prices. This can reduce a consumer's sensitivity to prices, as Chapter 13 showed (see Exhibit 13.2).

Several authors, one of whom is Froloff (1992), can be consulted on the sensitivity of consumers to sales promotions.

Table 14.7   Cost and profit impact of promotions

Distributors	Cost of promotions in % of turnover	Increase of turnover (in %)	Net income per franc spent
GB	5	13	1.79 F
Delhaize	4	9	1.26 F
Cora	9	19	2.73 F
Match	7	6	0.68 B
Mestdagh	8	11	1.46 F

Source: Tendances, 19 February, 1998, p. 59.

Profitability of sales promotions

Measuring the effectiveness and profitability of sales promotions can often be done by direct observation when detailed sales figures are available, as is usually the case for consumer goods. The development of new measuring techniques based on scanning panels, mentioned earlier in Chapter 5, has revolutionised this. The Nielsen Company, in particular, has developed several tools, among which are Sabine and Scanpro, for directly measuring the impact of sales promotions.

> The Accuris group in Belgium has developed a measuring system helping company's optimise expenditures in sales promotions. Table 14.7 gives some of the results published recently which can explain why sales promotions are so popular.

Pan-European promotions

With the globalisation of markets, and particularly of the European economy, marketers are striving for a consistent and international message. Apart from the economies of scale to be gained, a consistent pan-European promotion message can help strengthen a brand. But setting up an effective pan-European promotion to run in 12 languages across a dozen countries sounds like the ultimate marketing nightmare. For companies having global brands – like Kodak, Mars, Swatch, British Airways, American Express, and so on – the tools at their disposal for promoting them through retail channels around Europe are far from harmonious. Table 14.8 summarises some of the tactics allowed in a few key European markets.

Table 14.8   Cross-border conflicts of European sales promotions

Tactic	Germany	France	UK	Netherlands	Belgium
Onpack price reductions	Yes	Yes	Yes	Yes	Yes
In-pack gifts	??	??	Yes	??	??
Extra product	??	Yes	Yes	??	??
Money-off vouchers	No	Yes	Yes	Yes	Yes
Free prize contest	No	Yes	Yes	No	No

Key: Yes: legally allowed; ??: under review; No: not legally allowed.
Source: UK Institute of Sales Promotion: in: *Marketing News*, 26 April, 1999, p. 10.

The European Commission is working to find agreement between member states on all forms of cross-border communications. They even form an expert group to advise and recommend on the issues. What is likely to emerge is a system of 'mutual recognition', in which companies can carry out sales promotion activities in the target country as long as they are legal in the company's country of origin. The fact that on-pack, in-pack, vouchers and prize giveaways can be run in many European countries simultaneouly will mean economies of scale in managing such campaigns. It also means that brand owners can print the same message – granted a multilanguage one – on all European products rather than distinguishing which will be on some and not on others, as is required today. The issue of local adaptation will remain however.

A sales promotion is trying to prompt changes in consumer behaviour, not attitudes, and people's behaviour differs from one market to another. You are never going to succeed if you try to homogenise the mechanics of a pan-European promotion. Even if the laws regarding sales promotion were the same in different countries, you probably wouldn't want to do it. (Kiernan, 1992)

For example, recently Pepsi ran an on-pack promotion across nine countries that offered exclusive Spice Girls prizes, with a menu of different tactics available in each of the countries where the promotion ran to ensure that the campaign was tailored to each market's needs and legal environment (Stewart-Allen, 1999, p. 10).

Public Relations and Non-media Communication

In the first three styles of communication, the product or brand is at the heart of the advertising message. Institutional advertising does not talk about the product, but aims to create or reinforce a positive attitude towards the firm. The objective is therefore to create an image, but that of the firm: to describe the firm's profile and stress its personality in order to create a climate of confidence and understanding. The purpose is to *communicate differently* in a saturated advertising world and to fight against the fatigue of product advertising with a softer approach, by drawing attention to the firm itself, its merits, its values and talents. Clearly, the effectiveness of this kind of advertising can only be evaluated in the long term and can essentially work on attitudes.

Objectives of public relations

Public relations group the communications tools developed by the firm to promote the corporate activities, goals and value and create a positive corporate image in the general public and more particularly among the key market actors, distributors, prescribers, and institutional, financial and commercial partners. Public relations differ from other forms of marketing communication in three ways:

- *Objectives* are different. It is not a matter of selling but rather of gaining moral support from public opinion to pursue its economic activity.
- Targets are more diversified. The target is broader than just customers, covering all *market stakeholders* who, directly or indirectly, are active players in the market, including public opinion.
- *Tools* are varied. Along with the house journal and press releases, they include sponsoring and patronage. The objective is to use an intermediary (a journalist, an event) to convey the information with greater credibility.

In research conducted by des Thwaites *et al.* (1998) in Canada to identify the objectives of sponsoring sport events, the following objectives emerge as presented in Table 14.9.

The tools of public relations

There are many tools in public relations, which can be grouped under four headings:

Table 14.9 Sports sponsorship objectives

Objectives	Number	Mean	Std. Dev.
Community involvement	43	5.60	1.55
Enhance company image	44	5.32	1.39
Increase public awareness of the company	44	5.18	1.24
Corporate hospitality	41	4.88	1.40
Build business/trade relations and goodwill	40	4.82	1.55
Increase media attention	42	4.79	1.57
Reinforce market perception of product	41	4.56	1.90
Increase sales	40	4.55	1.69
Increase current product awareness	40	4.48	1.87
Identify product with a particular market segment	40	4.40	2.02
Enhance staff/employee's relations and motivation	41	4.37	1.88
Alter public perception of the company	41	4.07	1.77
Increase new product awareness	40	3.97	2.02
Alter market perception of product	39	3.90	1.90
Block competition	41	3.68	2.11
Personal objectives of senior managers	41	2.95	1.83
Counter adverse publicity	41	2.66	1.77

Mean scores based on a seven-point scale: 1 = not important; 7 = very important.
Source: des Thwaites *et al.* (1998, p. 41).

⬤ *Information on the company*, such as launching of new products, signing a major contract, R&D results, a merger or an acquisition, and so on. Once the information is chosen, PR specialists organise press releases or press conference.

⬤ *Publications*, such as annual reports, house journals, catalogues, and so on, which now are often directly available on CD-ROM or on the Internet.

⬤ *Events or special occasions* or communication through events such as sport competitions, concerts, exhibitions sponsored by the company or through events specially organised by the company, such open house days, factory visits, training sessions for dealers combined with leisure activities, and so on.

⬤ *Patronage*, where the company supports a particular cause of general interest, humanitarian, scientific or cultural.

The last two PR tools belong to what is called *institutional advertising* where the company tries to position itself in public opinion as a good corporate citizen. This type of communication can be very effective as illustrated by the data of Table 14.10 where the attitude scores of companies users and non-users of institutional advertising are presented (de Jaham, 1979).

Table 14.10   Measuring the effectiveness of institutional advertising

Indicators of attitude	Types of advertisers	
	Non-users of institutional advertising (%)	Users of institutional advertising (%)
Awareness of company name and activities	82	93
Familiarity with company name and activities	63	77
Overall positive image of company	38	51

Source: de Jaham (1979).

Sponsoring and patronage

These are two specific ways of institutional advertising. The latter runs the risk of tiring the public, which can become irritated and view these campaigns as attempts at self-satisfaction. Hence new forms of communication have developed, based on the idea that 'there is more splendour in being virtuous than taking credit for it' (Van Hecke, 1988).

> A typical example of one of these media stunts is the financing by American Express of the restoration of Van Eyck's masterpiece *L'agneau mystique*, which considerably increased its prestige in a way that no other campaign could have done.

The objective is to increase awareness of the firm's brand and to improve its image by association with positive values. The event being supported, which often unfolds in an unpredictable manner, thus reinforcing the credibility of the message, must have a testimony value, in the sense that a link should exist between the sponsored event and the sponsoring organisation, even if the link is indirect.

> Whether the firm is sponsoring an expedition in the Himalayas or a transatlantic race, it is emphasising its adherence to moral values such as team spirit and courage. On the one hand it proves its open-mindedness and its harmonious integration in society, and on the other hand, with regards to internal communication, it increases support from its personnel and develops a favourable climate within the firm. (Van Hecke, 1988)

It should be noted that sponsorship is a commercial operation, implying a two-way relation of rights and obligations: on the one hand material or financial support for the sponsored event, and on the other direct and methodical exploitation of the event by the firm. Thus sponsorship is distinct from patronage, in which generosity and lack of interest in profit are dominant.

It is clear that forms of advertising, pursued objectives and the means used to achieve them are very different. Before launching the advertising, it is therefore important to have a clear view of the role that advertising is to play in the marketing programme.

Worldwide sponsorships expenditures

The figures of Table 14.11 give an idea of the importance of sponsorship in the world as marketing communication tool. There are several interesting observations that can be drawn from this table:

Table 14.11   Worldwide sponsorship expenditures in 1996

Continent/country	Sponsorship rights value in $m	Continent/country as % of world sponsorship total	Sponsorship as % of advertising expenditure continent/country
Austria	95	0.6	6.0
Belgium	97	0.6	6.0
Denmark	80	0.5	6.1
Finland	81	0.5	7.1
France	630	3.8	6.0
Germany	1648	9.9	7.2
Greece	110	0.7	8.0
Ireland	28	0.2	6.0
Italy	791	4.8	13.6
Netherlands	213	1.3	6.0
Portugal	89	0.5	8.0
Spain	391	2.4	8.0
Sweden	154	0.9	8.1
UK	792	4.8	4.8
Switzerland	187	1.1	6.0
Others	114	0.7	5.8
EUROPE	**5500**	**33.2**	**7.0**
USA	5525	33.3	5.5
Canada	375	2.3	5.3
C. and S. America	700	4.2	3.7
AMERICA	**6600**	**39.8**	**5.2**
South Africa	194	1.2	13.2
Others	55	0.3	3.1
AFRICA	**249**	**1.5**	**7.6**
Japan	2200	13.3	4.8
Korea	400	2.4	5.7
Others	800	4.8	4.3
ASIA	**3400**	**20.5**	**4.8**
Middle East	110	0.7	4.7
Australia	650	3.9	13.8
New Zealand	58	0.3	6.6
Others	5	0.0	10.0
PACIFIC	**713**	**4.3**	**12.7**
WORLD TOTAL	**16,572**	**100.0**	**5.7**

Source: Meenaghan (1998, p. 8).

● First of all, the table clearly shows that sponsorship is indeed a worldwide phenomenon in terms of the number of countries reporting substantial sponsorship activity.

● A closer examination of these figures indicates that six countries (Germany, Italy, UK, US, Japan and Australia) account for 70 per cent of total global expenditures,

Exhibit 14.4

Ambush Marketing

In a survey conducted a month after the 1996 Olympics in Atlanta, consumers were asked to name the official sponsors of the Summer Games. For credit cards, 72 per cent named Visa while only 54 per cent named American Express. Those results were almost identical to a similar survey conducted after the 1994 Winter Olympics, in which 68 per cent named Visa and 52 per cent named American Express. One might conclude from these surveys that Visa does a better job than American Express in promoting its association with the Olympic Games – except Visa paid $40 million for the exclusive rights to be an official sponsor in the credit card category, while American Express was not an official sponsor of the Olympic Games. How did American Express achieve such a high level of recognition as an official sponsor without being one? It engaged in what is known as 'ambush marketing', a strategy aimed at creating the false impression of being associated with an event to gain some of the benefits and recognition of official sponsors.

Source: Shani and Sandler (1999).

a fact which clearly associates large-scale sponsorship activity with mature consumer economies.

● However, it is also important to note that even where sponsorship expenditure is minuscule in world terms, this medium still accounts for 5 or 6 per cent of advertising expenditures in the local domestic market, a share very close to that observed at world market level.

A special form of sponsorship, which is growing in popularity, is *cause-related marketing* which is gradually replacing philanthropy or charity. In this type of promotion, the firm commits itself to donate a part of the sales revenue generated to a cause or to a non-profit organisation. The promotion organised by American Express to help finance the restoration of the Statue of Liberty in New York is an excellent example.

> There were three goals in the promotion: (1) increase the use of the Amex card by current holders; (2) encourage distributors to accept payment with the card; and (3) improve company image and profile. American Express promised to give 1 cent for every transaction in the US and 1 dollar for every new card issued during the last quarter of the year. The campaign was a success both for the sponsor and the cause. Close to 1.7 million dollars went to the renovation project and the rate of use of the Amex card increased by 2.8 per cent over the preceding year and was accepted more readily by distributors. (Meenaghan, 1998, p. 14)

Except for promotion activities directly linked to such a cause, it is difficult to measure the real impact of sponsoring and patronage activities (see Exhibit 14.4). Analysis of this kind of action for the Olympic Games shows that there are positive results for the companies involved. On this topic, see Stipp (1998).

Chapter summary

Marketing communication refers to all the signals and messages made by the firm to its various publics. The four major communication tools, called the communication mix, are personal selling, advertising, sales promotion and public relations. The four tasks in designing a communication programme are; communication objective, message execution, media planning and communication effectiveness. Due to developments in communication technology, the role of the sales force is undergoing a major transformation and relationship selling and commercial negotiation are tending to replace traditional selling techniques. This evolution gives salespeople an important new role to play in strategic marketing. When a firm resorts to advertising, it is effectively following a pull communication strategy. Its main objective is to create a brand image and brand equity and to ensure co-operation from distributors. Advertising objectives can be defined by reference to the three levels of market response; cognitive, affective and behavioural. The share of sales promotion expenditure is growing in the total marketing communication budget as a result of the development of direct marketing. There are a large variety of promotion tools whose effects are complex and which can sometimes have a negative impact on the brand image. Public relations is a form of softer communication, which is gaining in popularity as one observes a decrease in the communication effectiveness of media advertising. Sponsorship and patronage are two special forms of institutional advertising, which are more frequently observed in industrialised economies.

QUESTIONS AND PROBLEMS

1. Compare traditional selling techniques with relationship selling. Show how and why relationship selling is well in line with the market-orientation business philosophy and the theory of the problem–solution approach?

2. Sales representatives of an FMCG company visit hypermarkets once every fortnight and supermarkets once a month. The company is rethinking the organisation of its sales force for an area with 200 supermarkets and 30 hypermarkets. Knowing that a visit to a hypermarket takes an average of one and a half hours for a sales rep and one hour to a supermarket, how many sales reps will the company need for this area? (A representative works 8 hours a day and 5 days a week.)

3. Compare the goals of product advertising, institutional advertising, response advertising and publicity.

4. Can one expect some long-term sales or market share effects of a sales promotion?

5. Why are sponsorship and patronage as communication forms gaining in popularity in industrialised economies?

6. Under which conditions can a firm contemplate basing a communication campaign on a cause of general interest?

7. Is ambush marketing unethical?

Bibliography

Bogart, L. (1986) *Strategy in Advertising*, Lincolnwood Hill, NTC Business Book.

Churchill, G.A., Ford, N.M. and Walker, O.C. (1997) *Sales Force Management*, 5th edn, Chicago IL, Irwin.

Darmon, R.Y., Laroche, M. and Petrov, J.V. (1982) *Le Marketing, Fondements et Applications*, 2nd edn, Montreal, McGraw-Hill.

Dartnell Corporation (1994) *28th Survey of Sales Force Compensation*, Chicago, IL, Dartnell Corporation.

De Jaham, M.R. (1979) Le défi de la publicité institutionnelle, *Revue Française du Marketing*, **77**: pp. 33–41.

de Maricourt, R., Andréani, J.C., Bloch, A. *et al.* (1997) *Marketing Européen, Stratégies et Actions*, Paris, Publi-Union.

des Thwaites, D., Anguilar-Manjarrez, R. and Kidd, C. (1998) Sports Sponsorship Development in Leading Canadian Companies: Issues and Trends, *International Journal of Advertising*, **17**(1): 29–49.

Dhalla, N.K. (1978) Assessing the Long Term Value of Advertising, *Harvard Business Review*, **56**, January–February, pp. 87–95.

Dupont, C. (1994) *La négociation: conduite, théorie et applications*, Paris, Editions Dalloz.

Donaldson, B. (1998) *Sales Management: Theory and Practice*, 2nd edn, London, Macmillan.

Dwyer, F.R., Schurr, P.H. and Sejo, O.H. (1987) Developing Buyer–Seller Relationships, *Journal of Marketing*, **51**, April, pp. 11–27.

Forsyth, D.P. (1987) Cost of a Business-to-Business Sales Call, McGraw-Hill Research, *Laboratory of Advertising Performance*, LAP Report 8013.9.

Fournier, S., Dobscha, S. and Mick, D.G. (1998) Preventing the Premature Death of Relationship Marketing, *Harvard Business Review*, January–February, pp. 43–51.

Froloff, L. (1992) La sensibilité du consommateur à la promotion des ventes: de la naissance à la maturité, *Recherche et Applications en Marketing*, **7**(3): 69–88.

Havas (1998) *Europub; le marché publicitaire Européen*, Paris, Havas.

Ingold, P. (1995) *Promotion des ventes et action commerciale*, Paris, Vuibert.

Jackson, B.B. (1985) *Winning and Keeping Industrial Customers*, Lexington MA, Lexington Books.

Kiernan, P. 1992) The Euro Promo Comes of Age, *Marketing Week Sales Promotion*, 18 September.

Kotler, P. (1997) *Marketing Management*, 9th edn, Englewood Cliffs NJ, Prentice Hall.

Lambert, Z.V. (1968) *Setting the Size of the Sales Force*, Philadelphia, Pennsylvania University Press.

Lambin, J-J. (1965) *La décision commerciale face à l'incertain*, Paris, Dunod.

Lavidge, R.J. and Steiner, G.A. (1961) A Model of Predictive Measurement of Advertising Effectiveness, *Journal of Marketing*, **25**, October, pp. 59–62.

Libre Service Actualité (LSA) (1997) La justice veut moraliser le couponing électronique, 27 November, pp. 18–19.

Meenaghan, T. (1998) Current Developments and Future Directions in Sponsorship, *International Journal of Advertising*, **17**(1): 3–28.

O'Connell, W.A. and Keenan, W. (1990) The Shape of Things to Come, *Sales & Marketing Management*, January, pp. 36–41.

Payne, A. (ed.) (1995) *Advances in Relationship Marketing*, London, Kogan Page.

Rossiter, J.R. and Percy, L. (1997) *Advertising and Promotion Management*, 2nd edn, New York, McGraw-Hill.

Schnaars, S.P. (1998) *Marketing Strategy*, New York, The Free Press.

Shani, D. and Sandler, D. (1999) Counter-attack: Heading off Ambush Marketing, *Marketing News*, 18 January, p. 10.

Slymotsky, A. and Shapiro B.P. (1993) Leveraging to Beat the Odds: the New Marketing Mind Set, *Harvard Business Review*, **71**, September–October, pp. 75–987.

Stipp, H. (1998) The Impact of Olympic Sponsorship on Corporate Image, *International Journal of Advertising*, **17**(1): 75–87.

Stewart-Allen, A.L. (1999) Cross-border Conflicts of European Sales Promotions, *Marketing News*, 26 April.

Van Hecke, T. (1988) Avis aux mécènes: la brique est porteuse, *La Libre Belgique*, 11 June.

Xardel, D. (1982) Vendeurs: nouveaux rôles, nouveaux comportements, *Harvard-l'Expansion*, **25**, Summer, pp. 59–75.

chapter fifteen

Market-driven advertising decisions

To be effective, an advertising campaign must be designed and programmed within the framework of a well-defined marketing strategy supported by a well-thought-out general communication policy. The objective of this chapter is to review the different steps to follow in the preparation of an advertising campaign. One of the difficulties in advertising programming is the sharing of responsibilities that exist between, on the one hand, advertisers' marketing and advertising staff and, on the other, advertising agency and media people. The organisation of an advertising campaign implies a clear sharing of tasks between these two groups. The advertiser has to monitor the work done by the creative people who must receive a clear brief but who should remain in charge of the design and execution of the advertising message itself. One can identify four phases in the organisation of an advertising campaign: message selection and design, media planning, advertising budget decision and measuring advertising effectiveness. These four decisions do not always come in that order, but they are always present in any advertising campaign.

Chapter learning objectives

After reading this chapter, you should be able to:

1. understand the role and the methods of advertising creativity;
2. explain the objectives and methods of media planning;
3. recognise the potential presented by electronic communication;
4. understand the methods of advertising budgeting;
5. define the different levels of advertising effectiveness;
6. be aware of the characteristics and limitations of global advertising.

Designing the Advertising Message

The very first task in the organisation of an advertising campaign is to determine and to design the message to be communicated to the target audience. Usually, the general platform of the campaign is already agreed upon and is the outgrowth of the strategic positioning adopted for the brand. It is important to keep in mind that it is up to strategic marketing people to prepare the briefing for the advertising team. It is then within the framework of this brief that advertising people will have to translate the communication platform into a message taking the form of a slogan, an image or a story.

The role of creativity in concept advertising

Once the communication objective is well defined and understood by advertising people, their role is to encode the message in ideas, symbols, shapes, sounds, language, situations, and so on, which can be easily decoded by the target audience and which are communicated in a creative way in order to break the wall of indifference of the target group daily bombarded by all kind of messages. This challenge is non-negligible since the quality of the message determines the overall effectiveness of the communication process. In fact, the relevance of the message and the quality of its expression are factors which directly determine the productivity of the advertising investment. Advertisers can adopt various creative approaches in their choice of the message design and execution.

The copy strategy

The most conventional approach, called *copy strategy* in advertising jargon, is based on four components:

- *Target*: What is the target group to reach?
- *Promise*: What is the distinctive proposal made to the target?
- *Argument*: What is the support of the promise?
- *Tone*: What style or format should be adopted for executing the message?

The *copy strategy statement* is a blueprint for creative people: it defines what must be communicated by advertising. Its strength lies in the fact that it forces marketing managers to choose an axis of communication that will be maintained over many years. As a result, the brand becomes endowed with a specific image and a positioning.

Kapferer (1985) underlines in particular the effectiveness of this strategy in the case of predominantly functional products for which there exist elements of differentiation based on technical features.

> For example, during the 1960s, when Ariel was being launched, housewives in large families (target) were promised unparalleled washing (promise) thanks to the biological agents in the powder (argument); the communication had a resolutely serious style (tone) so as to give the message credibility. (Kapferer, 1985, p. 102)

Yet in many fields brands have proliferated, and it is difficult to find specific promises which are not already 'occupied' by competing brands. To differentiate at any

price, the manufacturer might run the risk of putting out details that might be significant to it, but derisory to the buyer.

The star strategy

This trend has led advertisers, in France in particular, to adopt another creative approach called the *star-strategy*, developed by Séguéla (1982), which emphasises the 'tone' of the communication and the personality of the brand's character.

> No properly respected copy strategy would have allowed TBWA to launch the pen Pentel in France with its campaign based on the three following slogans referring to the green colour of the Pentel pens: 'Mettez-vous au vert' (reference to ecology), 'Allez les verts' (reference to a football team wearing green shirts), 'Envers et contre tout' (reference to the word 'vert'). Here, there is no promise. But what does Pentel exactly promise? Nothing, or nothing distinctive. On the other hand, the advertising has managed to create an attractive brand personality, which drives people to try Pentel. Its actual properties will only be discovered once the pen is in the hand (Kapferer, 1985, p. 103).

'Star strategy' determines the axis of communication on the basis of three elements: the brand's physical characteristics (its function), its character or personality, and the style of expression. This kind of creative approach is particularly effective when the product has no significant factor of differentiation.

Other creative notions have also been proposed. Variot (1985) extends Séguéla's approach and suggests that a brand's identity can be decomposed into six facets: its physical function and its personality, but also the uses to which it is associated, its cultural facet, its buyers' image (others' viewpoint) and its self-image. For example, the identity of the brand Porsche in France can be described as follows (example quoted in Kapferer, 1985, p. 104):

1. *Physical*: Performance.
2. *Personality*: Perfectionist.
3. *Use*: Personal rather than family oriented.
4. *Cultural*: German technology.
5. *Buyer's image*: Winners' car.
6. *Self-image*: Surpassing oneself.

This advertising approach is very demanding because it requires great coherence of expression. The reason is that form, style and tone are more important than substance in constructing the image. Good examples of this creative approach are the different advertising campaigns launched by Perrier in Western Europe.

Searching for a good advertising idea

To build the advertising campaign on a good advertising idea is essential. Several methods can be adopted to help discover good advertising ideas.

The Maloney grid

In the USA, Maloney (1961) has developed a model, which continues to be relevant today, and which helps to generate ideas for advertising themes. Table 15.1 classifies on

Table 15.1 Searching for advertising appeal

Type of potentially rewarding experiences	Potential type of reward			
	Rational	Sensory	Social	Ego satisfaction
Results of use experience	(1)	(2)	(3)	(4)
Product-in-use experience	(5)	(6)	(7)	(8)
Incidental-to-use experience	(9)	(10)	(11)	(12)

Source: Maloney (1961, pp. 595–618).

the one hand the kinds of rewards buyers seek in a product, and on the other the source of those rewards in the use of the product. This classification identifies 12 possible axes of advertising communication and creative people can put forward a theme for each.

As underlined above, the choice of the advertising message (theme, appeal, and copy) is part of the product positioning decision, since it expresses the major benefits that the brand offers to the buyer. Yet within the adopted positioning concept, there are several possible messages and creative people have latitude to change the message without changing the product-positioning concept. Consistency and continuity in advertising communication are important factors for building brand image and brand equity.

Creative styles

The impact of a particular advertisement does not depend only on the message content but also on the quality of the message execution. Advertising creation must have some degree of originality and there are clearly many ways to express the same idea. Different creative styles exist and these are grouped in nine categories in Table 15.2.

In creating an advertisement, creative people should keep in mind a golden rule, already stated several times in this book. *You are not selling the product, you are selling the benefits of the product.* Too many advertisements suffer from the same kind of egotism. They assume that the reader or the viewer is as interested in the product as is the advertiser. In reality, most individuals do not readily enter the advertiser's realm of reality. They do so only when convinced that the product will do something for them. If an advertiser does not answer the prospect's implicit question – *What's in it for me?* – the ad is unlikely to attract any real interest.

Another useful and somewhat related guideline is the *KISS principle* (Keep It Simple, Stupid). The argument here is simplicity. In most cases, advertising is not a sought out message. Advertising needs to catch the eye quickly and to deliver its message quickly. Good ads are simply descriptive and directly address the problems that the product or service solves and suggest how that solution makes life better for the potential consumer.

The dilemma: quality versus quantity

Which is more important in an advertising campaign: the creativity factor or the amount of money spent? At least one thing is clear. Only after gaining attention can an advertising message help to generate sales. Gross (1972) has shown the economic value of creative advertising and several empirical studies have confirmed his observations.

Table 15.2 Typology of creative leverages

Rational argumentation	Call to feelings and emotions	Stimulation and trial
The rational message (reference to values)	Reference to a symbolic person or to a myth (affective transfer effect)	Perceived risk or psychological cost reduction (facilitation effect)
The argumentation message, technical expertise (call to logic)	Reference to an emotional situation, a lifestyle (call to emotion)	Event creation of collective ambience (group effect)
The demonstration (proof effect)	Reference to sex or to sensuality (call to libido)	Financial gain (premium effect)

Source: Adapted from de Maricourt *et al.* (1997, p. 497).

An interesting argument has been put forward in the USA by Nelson (1974) and confirmed in the UK by Davis *et al.* (1991). For experience and credence goods, that is for goods that consumers cannot discover the quality or usefulness of without buying them repeatedly over a long time period (for example motor oil or shampoo), the mere fact of advertising heavily is more important than the advertising content. For this type of goods, the advertiser should not simply tell consumers that its product is better than its rivals; everyone says that. Rather, it should signal that it believes the product will be around for a long time by spending more than its rivals on advertising. Consumers will decode the message in this sense and therefore the cost or volume of advertising can be just as important as any direct or creative message the advertising contains. For good discussions of this question, see Nelson (1974) and Davis *et al.* (1991).

● Media Planning

Having defined the target, message content and the expected response, the advertiser must choose the best combination of media support that will allow it to achieve the desired number of exposures to the target audience, within the limits imposed by the advertising budget. Table 15.3 shows the definition of the most important concepts and terms used in the field of media planning.

Alternative media strategies

Different strategies of how to use the media can be envisaged (Chandon, 1976, pp. 19–23). The choice will vary with the communication objectives, the message complexity or the competitive situation.

Reach versus frequency

The *first alternative* opposes the two objectives of 'reach' and 'frequency'.

> Adopting an extensive campaign with a view to reaching the greatest number of people through maximum reach, or, on the contrary, adopting an intensive campaign to reach, as emphatically as possible, a restricted target through maximum frequency or repetition.

Table 15.3 International comparison of advertising expenditure per media, 1997

	Total media Expenditure (Min. US$)	Per capita Expenditure (US$)	Dailies (%)	Magazines (%)	TV (%)	Radio (%)	Cinema (%)	Outdoor (%)
Austria	1,593	165.5	44.6	16.9	22.7	8.9	0.2	6.6
Belgium	1,627	158.9	24.6	22.7	34.4	8.5	1.5	8.2
Finland	1,058	205.3	57.0	16.2	20.3	3.3	0.1	3.1
France	9,258	158.8	24.0	23.1	34.0	6.6	0.6	11.7
Germany	19,169	233.3	48.2	18.6	24.9	3.9	1.0	3.4
Ireland	697	193.6	63.1	3.0	21.5	6.3	0.7	5.3
Italy	5,875	102.2	20.5	16.0	57.5	3.5	–	2.5
Netherlands	3,522	226.9	49.8	22.3	18.9	4.9	0.4	3.7
Portugal	884	89.6	15.3	18.1	47.6	7.0	0.3	11.5
Spain	4,418	112.3	31.3	15.3	38.3	9.7	0.8	4.6
Sweden	1,855	209.7	58.9	13.0	20.1	2.9	0.6	4.5
Switzerland	2,722	383.9	55.0	18.4	9.4	2.8	1.1	13.3
UK	15,719	271.0	40.5	18.4	32.5	3.7	0.8	4.2
USA	105,016	384.3	37.7	12.6	36.9	11.7	–	1.1

Source: The European Advertising and Media Forecast (1997).

Generally, a high degree of reach is necessary when launching a new product or starting an ambitious programme of promotion. On the other hand, a high degree of frequency is required when the message is complex, the product frequently bought and brand loyalty low. However, too much repetition is useless, as it may cause boredom or irritation. Krugman (1975, p. 98) for example, considers that three 'perceived' exposures' are often sufficient.

Continuity versus intermittence

The *second strategic option* is between 'continuity' as opposed to 'intermittence' in advertising:

> Seeking continuity of advertising efforts over time to overcome the forgetting rate, stimulate repeated purchases, oppose rivals' efforts, and so on or, on the contrary, seeking intermittence (pulsing) so as to optimise consumer learning or reinforcement, or to 'stretch budgets' to coincide with consumption patterns.

The problem is to decide how to schedule advertising. But there is no clear answer to the dilemma. It is important to take into account the nature of the product, its purchase frequency, seasonality in sales, rivals' strategies and the distribution of memory over time. The fact that the life of a message is a function of its communication quality renders the problem even more complicated.

Concentration versus diversification

Finally, the *third strategic choice* is between media 'concentration' or media 'diversification'.

> Seeking diversification in various types of media so as to enjoy complementarity between them, obtain a better net reach, a better geographical allocation, and so on, or, on the contrary, concentration on a single media, so as to dominate the medium best suited to the target, to personalise the campaign and the product and to benefit from economies of scale and discounts.

> All depends on the adopted segmentation strategy. Diversification is desirable if the firm follows undifferentiated marketing; if, on the contrary, it follows a market nicher strategy, then it is probably more effective to concentrate on a single medium.

Criteria for media selection

Media selection is guided by quantitative and qualitative criteria that are listed below. Among *quantitative criteria*, the following are important:

- ● *Target-audience* media habits, that is the proportion of the target group that can be reached through the medium.
- ● The *stability* of the reach over time, for instance from one week to another or from one season to another.
- ● The possibility of having *frequent exposures* to the message.
- ● The medium *selectivity* in terms of socio-demographic or lifestyle profiles.

Exhibit 15.1

Definition of the Parameters Used in Media Planning

- ■ Target: the specific group of prospects to be reached.
- ■ Circulation: the number of physical units through which advertising is distributed.
- ■ Audience: the number of people who are exposed to a particular vehicle.
- ■ Effective audience: the number of people with the target's characteristics who are exposed to the vehicle.
- ■ Exposure: the 'opportunity to see' (OTS) or opportunity to hear (OTH) the message, which does not imply that the person actually sees or hears the advertisement.
- ■ Reach: the number of different persons or households exposed to a particular medium vehicle at least once during a specified period of time.
- ■ Frequency: the number of times within a specified period of time that a prospect is exposed to the message.
- ■ Gross Rating Point (GRP): equal to reach multiplied by frequency and measures the total number of exposures (weight).
- ■ Impact: the qualitative value of an exposure through a given medium.

- The *cost per thousand* persons reached, which is a function of the vehicle audience and of the medium cost.

These data are provided by the media themselves, by the media sales houses or by organisations responsible for the control of media circulation or diffusion.

Qualitative criteria of media selection must complement the quantitative ones. The following can be noted in particular:

- *Audience attention* probability, which is, for instance, very high for cinemas and very low for outdoor advertising.
- The duration of the *message's life*, that is the period during which the message can be perceived.
- The perceptual *environment* of the message.
- The *editorial quality* of the vehicle, that is its prestige and credibility.
- The *technical quality* of the medium, for instance, the use of colour, the quality of sound or of images, and so on.
- The degree of *advertising saturation* of the vehicle and the presence of competitive advertising.

The final choice is summarised in a *media plan* describing budget allocation between the different media. Once one has chosen the media, the next decision is to select the *specific vehicles* to advertise in within the media. Although the choices are complex and numerous, a number of paid research services in media and vehicle selection provide data to help the decision-maker. The latter choice is now increasingly made using computer models of vehicle selection.

The Web, a new advertising medium?

Every Internet user has been exposed to electronic advertising taking the form of banner advertisements generally placed at the top of the computer screen. These banner adverts are exploited as a conventional advertising space to attract the user's attention and interest, and are generally (full banner) single 480×60 pixel graphics, either animated or static. The graphic usually links the user to the advertising company's Web site when clicked on. The design of an effective banner advert is a real challenge given its limited size. The objective is to induce the user to click-through. The more interactivity and involvement created by banners, the higher the click-through rates (see Exhibit 15.2).

The Web's distinctive strength lies in its ability to provide extensive product information unlike traditional advertising media, which are not suitable for carrying large amounts of product information. Think how little a firm can say about a product on an advertising billboard. On a Web site, the advertiser can offer all the information the user asks and then leave it to the reader what information he or she wants to see about products or services and even propose to the user an order form to make a purchase on the spot.

Characteristics of on-line advertising

One of the most interesting features of on-line advertising is its capacity to use *selective targeting* thereby improving greatly banner effectiveness and creating opportuni-

> **Exhibit 15.2**
>
> ## Procter & Gamble Makes Debut with On-line Mouthwash Advertising
>
> Procter & Gamble made its long-anticipated splash on the Internet with a Valentine's Day campaign for scope mouthwash. The ads reprise the Send-a-kiss campaign that debuted last year. The first advertising venture for P&G with America On Line Inc. (AOL), which serves more than 15 million Internet users, involves a pop-up box that users can click on to send a kiss by e-mail. The message appears along with animated lips that dance across the receiver's screen. P&G disclosed last year that in April and June quarter it had increased spending on Internet advertising to $3 million. But the company said opportunities on the Internet were limited.
>
> *Source: Marketing News*, 1 March, 1999, p. 10.

ties for immediate interaction with, and feedback from, consumers. Selective targeting consists in distributing banner ads to Web site users according to their profile or expressed interests. To assist advertisers in this task, many search engines (for example Yahoo!) allow advertisers to buy keywords so that their banner appears only when a user enters those words. Another way to increase relevance is to use an ad network. These firms store banner ads on their servers and distribute them to Web site users according to their expressed interest or socio-demographic profile.

> For example, users who visit a site about dogs may receive a pet food banner ad the next time they stop by one of the ad network's client Web sites.

The interaction potential of the Internet goes well beyond simple communication. The Internet can be used to complete all activities in the traditional sales cycle, from providing information about products and services and the organisation, through purchase ordering and payment, to distribution of certain products and customer support.

An advertiser's dream is to be able to efficiently target products and ads to a market segment of one: *one-to-one*. A Web technology called *cookies* makes that dream at least partially possible today. Cookies are small data files that are written while a user browses or when a user completes a Web form. Cookies help companies to personalise Web pages by applying user's name or by listing previous purchases, thus building relationships with users, one at a time.

> As an example, consider Amazon, which uses cookies to identify repeat visitors, greet them by name and call up their billing and shipping information. This is also how Amazon can make recommendations to users based on purchases of other similar customers. They gather information on one user's tastes and compare it with aggregated data on similar users. (Strauss and Frost, 1999, p. 272)

To go further on this topic, see Strauss and Frost (1999, Chapter 7) and Kassaye (1999).

Through the cookies technology, marketers have access to lots of information about every consumer and business and that information can be easily stored in a database for direct marketing communication. In this context, guarding consumer privacy becomes a sensitive issue and, as explained in Chapter 12, there is an ongoing debate between the EU and the USA on the best way to provide effective consumer protection (see also *Business Week*, 16 March, 1998).

Table 15.4   The Internet finds a welcoming audience at the top of the world (Internet users per 1000 people in 1998)

Iceland	320.3	Denmark	178.6
Finland	305.4	Singapore	140.0
Norway	304.1	Switzerland	138.2
Sweden	289.8	UK	137.3
US	283.0	Netherlands	124.8
Australia	234.1	Hong Kong	98.7
Canada	211.5	Israel	95.7
New Zealand	190.1		

Source: *Computer Industry Almanac* (1999).

Benefits of advertising on the Internet

Advertising on the Internet has a relatively short track record and as such has had little time to prove itself. As discussed in Chapter 12 in the section on electronic commerce, the number of direct sales attributable to Internet advertising is still low and on-line commerce has yet to prove that it can achieve satisfactory returns on investments. Nevertheless, the potential benefits of on-line advertising are numerous (Ollier, 1998, pp. 44–6):

1. The Internet is *gaining in popularity* in the entertainment and information stakes and winning customers away from traditional media such as magazines and TV (see Table 15.4).

2. Advertising on the Internet is an *inexpensive method* of advertising compared with traditional print and broadcast options.

3. Advertising on the Internet is *measurable*. It is easy to monitor the number of hits and click-throughs an advert receives.

4. On-line advertising creates the opportunity for *immediate interaction* with and feedback from consumers, while traditional media do not.

5. The Web forte lies in its ability to provide *extensive product information* unlike traditional advertising media.

6. It is possible to deliver messages over the Web to a very *narrowly defined target group*.

7. Internet advertisements are not necessarily time-based. In the case of a Web site, it can be accessed *24 hours a day*.

8.   The Internet is suitable for advertising products and services to both *local and global audiences.*

9.   *Competitors* may already be ahead of the game and using the Internet to advertise their products and services. By being left behind the firm may be sending the wrong signals to consumers.

However, advertisers should not misunderstand the medium and there are some specific properties that should not be overlooked:

1.   Web users are seeking information as well as *entertainment.* Advertisers should address these needs in their on-line campaigns.

2.   The medium is entirely *self-selecting.* It is unlike other forms of advertising in that users must seek out the advertising rather than have the advertising brought to them as it is on TV.

3.   Web advertising does not sell itself. Once a brand site exists, it must then be *promoted.*

4.   On-line adverts must be appealing to users and make them want to return by providing added value content. Advertising on the Internet must be content-driven. It must be entertaining and functional and above all *it must change.*

5.   Measuring the *success of an on-line advertising* campaign is not straightforward; response will be a mix of on-line and off-line reactions, which is less quantifiable.

6.   When developing a media plan, advertisers should always consider whether the message *content is appropriate* for the Internet.

Impact of electronic communication

As a result of the impetus from developments in the Internet, cable television, pay TV, satellite communication, interactive videotext terminals, personal computers, and so on, electronic communication is at present in full development. These new possibilities influence our way of life as well as the communication strategies of firms. As put by Daniel Bell (1979):

> telecommunications constitute for humanity as big a revolution as did the advent of printing, writing and language.

The development of electronic communication not only modifies the respective roles of personal selling and of advertising, but also changes the objectives and the content of advertising communication. Many significant changes are already observable in our society:

●   To begin with, the new means of communication tend to be more *interactive*, that is two-way rather than one-way as in the past. Today, a visitor to an Internet site has the possibility of asking for, choosing and sending back information rather than simply being passively subjected to a bombardment of irrelevant messages. We are moving in fact towards 'advertising on demand'.

⬤ Furthermore, it is now possible to have access to huge data banks, in the most varied fields, on available products, their comparative performance, their prices, and so on. The firm will therefore face a more and better-informed public. Such facts will further reinforce the *informative and factual character* of communication, which will increasingly be set up as an aid to the buyer rather than as a sales instrument.

⬤ Another consequence of the development of electronic communication is its *greater selectivity*. The combination of possibilities offered by the telephone, the computer and the television means that very well-defined targets can be reached with personalised messages. We are therefore moving towards personalised electronic mail systems, which improve communication effectiveness and favour the development of interactive marketing.

⬤ The Web is a very *egalitarian medium*. Since customers intentionally seek the message, access opportunities are essentially equal for all players regardless of size. Shares of voice are essentially uniform and no advertiser can drown out others. Given that initial set-up costs are relatively low and that there is no barrier to entry, small companies have easy access to the Web. With a well-designed home page, a small company can look as professional and credible as a large multinational company. The biggest challenge facing on-line advertisers is to attract and interact with a relatively large number of visitors on the first visit and thereafter. The paradox is that advertisers are trying to achieve this objective through traditional advertising media, as Amazon does.

⬤ Regionalisation of radio and television programmes also favours *selectivity of communication*. The introduction of local channels will allow local firms and local advertisers to have access to radio and television. Media plans could allocate different degrees of pressure from region to region and thus better adapt the brand situation from one region to another.

⬤ Finally, a last consequence is that the considerable increase in geographic zones covered by a transmitting station, thanks to the use of satellites and cable, will *reinforce the internationalisation* of brands and advertising campaigns.

Thanks to these developments in the means of communication, a whole series of tasks once exercised by salespersons could henceforth be achieved by impersonal means of communication at a lower cost. Well-addressed direct mail, the telephone, a catalogue that can be consulted on a TV screen or a computer can all bring more extensive and more precise information and faster than a sales person's sales speech. This is why we are now observing a spectacular development in direct marketing systems.

⬤ Advertising Budget Decisions

Conceptually, advertising budget decisions can be analysed using marginal rules of economic theory. Expenditure on each method of communication is increased until any further increase reduces profits. Similarly, the allocation of total budget between different methods is such that each instrument is used to the level where all marginal revenues are equal. Economists have developed optimisation rules based on elasticities (Dorfman and Steiner, 1954), also extended to situations of oligopoly (Lambin *et al.*, 1975), as well as dynamic models to allow for lagged response to advertising (Palda, 1963; Jacquemin, 1973). The derivation of the optimisation rule for the advertising budget is illustrated on Appendix 15.1.

As for the selling price, this approach is rarely operational in practice because of all the problems of estimating response functions. It is therefore necessary to use other more general methods, and only to use marginal rules as guidelines. When available, the analysis of elasticities can be useful *a posteriori* to evaluate the effectiveness of advertising and of the sales force. In this section we will examine different methods of determining the advertising budget.

Cost-oriented advertising budgets

As for cost-oriented prices discussed in the previous chapter, cost-oriented budgets are calculated on the basis of cost considerations, without explicitly taking demand reactions into account. There are three types of cost-oriented budget: affordable, break-even and percentage of sales budgeting methods.

Affordable budget

The budget is directly linked to the short-term financial possibilities of the company. Advertising will be appropriated after all other unavoidable investments and expenses have been allocated. As soon as things go badly, this budget can be eliminated, and if cash is abundant then it can be spent. The fiscal system also encourages this type of practice, since increased advertising expenditure reduces taxable profit. This is not a method as such, but rather a state of mind reflecting an absence of definite advertising objectives.

Break-even budget

The break-even budget method is based on the analysis of advertising's profitability threshold. The absolute increase in unit sales and in turnover necessary to recoup the incremental increase in advertising expenditure is simply obtained by dividing advertising expenditure (S) by the absolute gross profit margin or by the percentage of gross profit margin:

$$\text{Break-even volume} = S/P - C$$

and

$$\text{Break-even turnover} = S/(P - C/P)$$

For instance, if the gross profit margin is £60, or 30 per cent of the unit price, the absolute increase in unit sales to recoup a £1.5 million advertising budget will be

$$1,500,000/60 = 25,000 \text{ units}$$

and the break-even turnover

$$1,500,000/0.30 = £5,000,000$$

To determine the percentage increase of sales volume or turnover necessary to maintain the previous level of profit, one can use the following expression:

$$\text{Percentage sales increase} = \Delta Q/Q = 100 \times \Delta S/(F + S + \text{Profit})$$

where ΔS is the proposed change in budget. The advertiser can determine by how much sales must increase to retain the same level of profit, and also calculate the implicit demand elasticity to advertising, by comparing expected sales levels 'with advertising' to expected volume 'without advertising'.

Using these data, the advertiser can verify whether the proposed budget implies an unrealistic increase in market share given the state of the market, competitors' power, and so on. The weakness of the method is that it is strictly an accounting exercise. But clearly some advertising objectives are not necessarily reflected in higher sales in the short run, even if they have been reached completely. Nevertheless, this type of analysis is useful because the advertiser is encouraged to view advertising as an investment rather than overhead costs.

Percentage of sales budget

The percentage of sales budget method is used frequently and treats advertising as a cost. In its simplest form the method is based on a fixed percentage of the previous year's sales. One advantage of this procedure is that expenditures are directly related to funds available. Another advantage is its relative simplicity.

Although this method is quite popular, it can easily be criticised from a logical point of view, because it inverts the direction of causality between advertising and sales. Relating advertising appropriation to *anticipate sales* makes more sense, because it recognises that advertising precedes rather than follows sales. Nevertheless, this approach can lead to absurd situations: reducing the advertising budget when a downturn in sales is predicted, and increasing it when turnover is growing, with the risk of overshooting the saturation threshold.

In practice, however, it seems that this method is mainly used by management with the objective of controlling total advertising expenditure at the consolidated level of turnover, in order to keep an eye on total marketing expenditure or to compare with competitors. More refined methods are used when deciding on advertising at the brand level.

Cost-oriented advertising budgets are only the first stage of the process of determining the advertising budget. They enable the firm to define the problem in terms of financial resources, production capacity and profitability. As for the determination of prices, these methods must be completed with an analysis of market attitudinal and behavioural responses.

Communication-oriented advertising budgets

This approach, also called the 'task and objective' method, is the one most widely used. It emphasises communication objectives and the means necessary to reach them. Two methods can be adopted: one based on 'contact', defined in terms of reach and frequency, and one based on 'perception'.

Task and objective budgeting

The method starts either with an objective of reach and frequency for which a budget is calculated, or with a budget constraint for which the best combination of reach and frequency is sought to maximise total exposure. By trying to maximise exposure, this approach places the emphasis on the first level of advertising effectiveness, that is communication effectiveness, while clearly linking the communication objectives to costs.

As defined in Exhibit 15.1 above. the term 'exposure' here has a very precise meaning, because it only refers to opportunity to see (OTS) or to hear (OTH), which does not imply perception. Newspapers only sell OTS to advertisers: a certain number of readers (maybe) will have the paper in their hands, but this does not imply that they will see the advertisement, or that they will familiarise themselves with it or assimilate it. The method ensures the productivity of the budget by searching for the best way to spend the money in the media given the target audience and given an expected creative level of the campaign. This is why the task and objective method is widely used by advertising agency people. By way of illustration, let us consider the following example.

> A company wants to reach women in the 25–49 age group. The socio-professional profile is determined by the following criteria: business, middle management, or owners of small-medium sized companies. The size of the target population is 3,332,000 women, or 16.7 per cent of women of 15 years old and more. The vehicles are magazines selected for their affinity with the target. The budget is 650,000 francs.

The advertising agency has proposed the three media plans presented in Table 15.5. In the table are reported for each plan: the number of ads per magazine, the reach, the frequency, the *GRP* and the budget. Logically plan 2 will be preferred because it has the highest GRP.

Table 15.5 Comparing three media plans

Media Plans	Plan 1	Plan 2	Plan 3
Magazine 1	3(1 + 2)	4(1 + 3)	-
Magazine 2	2(2)	–	3(1 + 2)
Magazine 3	3(1 + 2)	4(1 + 3)	(1 + 3)
Magazine 4	3(1 + 2)	4(1 + 3)	4(1 + 3)
Magazine 5	3(1 + 2)	4(1 + 3)	–
Magazine 6	3(1 + 2)	4(1 + 3)	4(1 + 3)
Budget (in FF)	660,500	652,120	650,130
Reach	67.07%	66.3%	65.4%
Frequency	3.7	4.1	3.7
Gross rating point	248.2	271.8	242.0

3(1+2) = 1 double page quadrichrome + 2 pages quadrichrome.
Source: Troadec and Troadec (1984, p. 47).

The value of this budgeting method is its attempt to search for the best possible allocation of the budget given the profile of the target group and the structure of the audience of each media or vehicle. Another advantage is its simplicity. The major drawback is its systematic overestimation of the number of people reached by the ad. The gap between the number of people 'exposed' and the number of people having 'perceived' the message may be very high.

Perceptual impact budgeting

Perceptual impact budget is based on psycho-sociological communication objectives. To achieve these objectives, conditions are defined in terms of the means used (media, reach, repetitions, perceptions, and so on). Next, the cost of the various activities is calculated and the total determines the necessary budget. What is sought here is an impact on one of the three components of attitude (cognitive, affective or behavioural).

This is a much more fundamental approach, based on the learning process (Lavidge and Steiner, 1961) and the resulting hypothesis about the hierarchy of advertising effects (Colley, 1961). The difficulty with it is that the advertiser must be able to link the communication impact to the perceptual impact and the perceptual impact to the attitudinal impact and finally to the behavioural response. Typically, the budgeting problem is stated in the following terms:

> How many OTS or exposures to the message in a given medium are necessary to achieve, among 60 per cent of the potential buyers within the target group, the cognitive objective of 'knowing product characteristics', the attitudinal objective 'being convinced of product superiority' and the behavioural objective 'intention-to-buy'?

In the task and objective budget example given above, all the women belonging to the target were simply supposed to be exposed to the vehicle. This number should be corrected by two factors: first, the probability of reading which is in general specific to each magazine and second an estimate of the ad's perception probability. This perception probability will be determined by the creativity of the message, its relevance for the target group, its capacity to get attention, and so on.

This method is much more demanding, but it has the advantage of requiring management and advertising people to spell out their assumptions about the relationships between money spent, exposure, perceptions, trial and repeat purchase.

Communication-oriented advertising budgets constitute the second stage of the process of determining the advertising budget. They are in fact an initial way of explicitly taking into account market response. Because it is mainly based on intermediary objectives of communication, the advantage of the method is the emphasis it places on results directly attributable to advertising, and the fact that it allows the advertiser to control the advertising agency's effectiveness.

The limitations of these methods are that there is not necessarily any link between achieving the intermediate communicational objective and the final goal of improving sales. One cannot therefore view measures of communicational effectiveness as substitutes for direct measures linking advertising to sales or market share.

Sales-oriented advertising budgets

Determining a sales or market share-oriented advertising budget requires knowledge of the parameters of the response function. In some market situations, in particular where advertising is the most active marketing variable, it is possible to establish this relationship and then use it to analyse the effects of various levels of expenditure on market share and profits.

Various models of determination of advertising budget exist in the literature. The most operational among them are the model by Vidale and Wolfe (1957) and the model ADBUDG by Little (1970). Both models have some strong and some weak points that we shall consider briefly. The contribution of economic analysis will also be reviewed.

Budgeting to maximise profit

The advertising optimisation rules are presented in Appendix 15.1. These rules can be used to verify whether the current level of advertising spending is about right or whether the firm is over-advertising. As for the price optimisation problem, these rules can be used as a guide for the budgeting decision.

The normative value of this type of economic analysis is reduced, not only because of the always present uncertainty about the true value of the response coefficients, but also because the advertiser faces multiple objectives other than profit maximisation. Also, the advertising quality (copy and media) is taken at its average value, while large differences may exist from one campaign to another. For these reasons, the output of economic analysis should be used as a guideline for advertising budget decisions and be complemented by other approaches.

The Vidale and Wolfe advertising model

The model developed by Vidale and Wolfe expresses the following relationship between sales (in units or value) and advertising expenditure:

$$\frac{ds}{dt} = \left[(\beta) \cdot (A) \cdot \frac{S-s}{S} \right] - (1-\lambda) \cdot (s)$$

where

ds/dt = rate of increase of sales at any time t
β = sales response constant when $q = 0$
A = rate of advertising
s = company or brand sales
S = product category saturation level
λ = sales retention rate

In words, within a given period, the increase in sales (ds/dt) due to advertising is equal to:

- The product of the sales response constant per dollar of advertising when sales are zero and of the rate of advertising during the period (response effect)

- adjusted by the proportion of the untapped market potential (saturation effect)

- reduced by the fraction of current sales that will decrease in the absence of advertising because of product obsolescence, competing advertising, and so on (depreciation effect).

This is an interesting model because it takes into account the main features of advertising response functions while explicitly setting out the key parameters to be estimated. By way of illustration, let us consider the following example.

Sales of brand X are $40,000 and the saturation level is $100,000; the response constant is $4 and the brand loses 10 per cent of its sales per period when advertising is stopped. By adopting a $10,000 advertising budget, the brand could expect a $20,000 sales increase.

$$ds/dt = 4\,(10,000)\,(100,000 - 40,000/100,000) - 0.10(40,000) = 20,000$$

One can also state the problem in terms of the advertising budget required to achieve a given sales objective. Referring to Table 15.6, the equation has to be solved for A, the advertising budget.

Table 15.6   Comparing two advertising budget models

*The Vidale and Wolfe model

$$ds/dt = (\beta) \cdot (A) \cdot (S - s/S) - (1 - \lambda) \cdot (s)$$

where

ds/dt	= sales increase per period
β	= sales response constant when $s = 0$
A	= advertising expenditures
s	= company or brand sales
S	= saturation level of sales
λ	= sales retention rate

*The ADBUDG model of Little

$$MS(t) = MS(min) + [MS(max) - MS(min)] \cdot \frac{Adv^{\gamma}}{\delta + Adv^{\gamma}}$$

where

MS(t)	= initial market share
MS(min)	= minimum market share with zero advertising
MS(max)	= maximum market share with saturation advertising
Adv	= effective advertising (adjusted for media and copy effectiveness)
γ	= advertising sensitivity coefficient
δ	= constant

Sources: Vidale and Wolfe (1957) and Little (1970).

The Vidale and Wolfe model does, however, have some weak points:

● The model does not allow explicit consideration of marketing variables other than advertising, such as price, distribution, and so on.

- The model does not integrate competitive advertising and is therefore implementable only in monopolistic situations.

- The model assumes that advertising merely obtains new customers and increased customer usage is neglected.

- The model does not explicitly consider possible variations in advertising quality, unless one could assume different sales constants per medium or per advertising theme.

- In some markets, it is difficult to estimate the absolute market potential.

Vidale and Wolfe's model has an interesting conceptual structure, but its range of application is limited.

The ADBUDG model of Little

The ADBUDG model, developed by Little (1970), can be applied to a market where primary demand is non-expansible and where advertising is a determinant factor in sales and market share development. The model establishes a relationship between market share and advertising and assumes that managers are able to provide answers to the following five questions:

- What is the current level of advertising expenditure for the brand?
- What would market share be if advertising were cut to zero?
- What would maximum market share be if advertising were increased a great deal, say to saturation (saturation advertising)?
- What would market share be if the current level of advertising were halved?
- What would market share be if the current level of advertising were increased half as much?

The market share level estimates in response to these five questions can be represented as five points on a market share response to advertising curve, as illustrated in Figure 15.1.

The ADBUDG model has the following mathematical expression:

$$MS(t) = MS(min) + \{MS(max) - MS(min)\} \cdot \frac{Adv^\varepsilon}{\delta + Adv^\varepsilon}$$

where

$MS(t)$	= initial market share
$MS(min)$	= minimum market share with zero advertising
$MS(max)$	= maximum market share with saturation advertising
Adv	= effective advertising (adjusted for media and copy effectiveness)
γ	= advertising sensitivity coefficient
δ	= constant

The expected market share in any given period is then equal to:

- The *minimum market share* (min) expected at the end of the period if advertising is cut to zero (depreciation effect)...

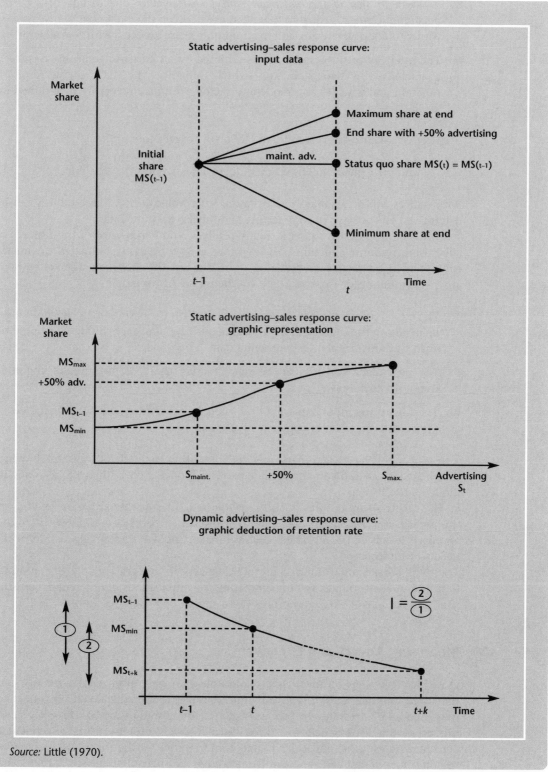

Static advertising–sales response curve:
input data

Market
share

Initial
share
MS(t-1)

maint. adv.

Maximum share at end

End share with +50% advertising

Status quo share MS(t) = MS(t-1)

Minimum share at end

t-1

t

Time

Static advertising–sales response curve:
graphic representation

Market
share

MS_max

+50% adv.

MS_t-1
MS_min

S_maint.

+50%

S_max.

Advertising
S_t

Dynamic advertising–sales response curve:
graphic deduction of retention rate

MS_t-1

MS_min

MS_t+k

$I = \dfrac{②}{①}$

t-1

t

t+k

Time

Source: Little (1970).

Figure 15.1   The ADBUDG model

- ...plus a *fraction of the maximum market share change* due to advertising; this maximum change is equal to the difference between the maximum share expected with saturation advertising and the minimum share expected with zero advertising.

- The intensity of the response is determined by an *advertising intensity coefficient* characterised by two parameters: which influences the shape of the response function and γ, which is a moderator factor. Both parameters are determined by input data.

Effective advertising is given by the following expression:

$$\text{Adv}(t) = \{\text{medium efficiency}(t)\}.\{\text{copy effectiveness}(t)\}.\{\text{Adv. dollars}\}$$

Both indices will be assumed to have a reference value of 1.0. These indices can be determined on the basis of copy testing and media exposure data.

This is an interesting model in many respects, and it has most of the features of advertising response functions. Furthermore, it can be easily estimated on microcomputers in interactive mode. Thus, users can test the model themselves without any help from outside experts. These are the model's strong points:

- The model parameters can be estimated either on the basis of management judgements using the five-question procedure outlined above, or through econometric analysis of historical or experimental data.

- The dependent variable can be sales, market share or measures of cognitive response, such as awareness.

- The advertising input data can be adjusted for advertising quality using indices of media efficiency and of copy effectiveness.

It is also possible to add marketing variables other than advertising, which makes the models more difficult to manipulate. The model used is then the BRANDAID model (Little, 1979).

The ADBUDG model was initially made essentially for interactive use relying on the *decision-maker's subjective judgements*. However, experience has shown that this approach is elusive because most decision-makers hold only a small fraction of the necessary information.

On the other hand, it forms a useful framework for integrating objective information from various sources and for simulating the implications of different advertising strategies on market share and profits (for a similar approach, see Lambin, 1972).

Measuring Advertising Effectiveness

Once the objectives of advertising communication have been clearly defined and translated into messages, it is already much simpler to measure advertising effectiveness. Figure 15.2 describes the process of advertising communication. Three key stages can be distinguished, defining three distinct levels of advertising effectiveness: perceptual, attitudinal and behavioural, corresponding to the three levels of market response mentioned earlier (cognitive, affective and behavioural) (see Exhibit 15.3) For a review of the methods used at each level, see Franzen *et al.* (1999).

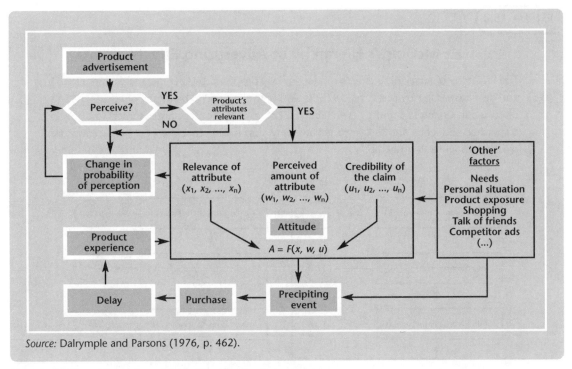

Source: Dalrymple and Parsons (1976, p. 462).

Figure 15.2 The advertising communication process

Perceptual effectiveness of advertising

Effectiveness at this stage means the ability to overcome potential buyers' indifference or perceptual defences and to be seen, read, heard and memorised by the target group. Clearly, the first quality of an advertisement is to be noticed (see Table 15.7). Without it, nothing can happen to attitudes or behaviours. One can thus better understand advertisers' preoccupation – sometimes irritating to the outside observer – with 'getting across' and their willingness to achieve it using means such as humour, dreams, the unseemly, stars, and so on. Also, the *proliferation of advertising messages* aggravates their worry, because it leads inevitably to reduced levels of attention from a public that rejects boring or undesirable elements.

> In the USA, the number of advertising messages had doubled between 1967 and 1982. Most experts believe that the number of messages will double again before 1997. (Bogart, 1986, p. 220)

Table 15.7 Comparing the perceptual effectiveness of different media

Media	Attention	Recall
Cinema	85%	70%
Television	40%	15%
Press	30%	10%
Radio	20%	5%

Source: Morgensztern (1983).

Exhibit 15.3

McGuire's Hierarchy of Advertising Effects

The hierarchy of advertising effects model, initially proposed by Lavidge and Steiner (1961) and developed later by McGuire (1978) is similar to the general hierarchy of effects models discussed in Chapters 4 and 11 (see Table 11.12), in that the steps are assumed to occur in a specified sequence and failure to achieve any step means that the next step cannot be reached, as illustrated below.

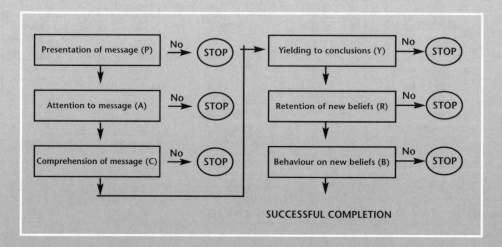

In brief, the model requires that (1) the ad be *presented* to a consumer, (2) she or he then pay *attention* to it, (3) it be *comprehended* or understood, (4) it leads to the consumer *yielding* or being persuaded as to the ad's conclusions and recommendations, (5) the persuasion or influence be *retained* over some time span, finally (6) the overt *purchase behaviour* the ad desires is actually taken by the consumer. The system is based upon the notion of probabilistic linkages between the stages. For example, to simplify, if each stage probablity (*p*) is 0.50, the overall impact of the advertisement will be

$$\text{Purchase probability} = p(P) + p(A) + p(C) + p(Y) = p(R) + p(B)$$

$$= 0.50 \times 0.50 \times 0.50 \times 0.50 \times 0.50 \times 0.50 = 0.0156$$

In this example, the ad would have a probability of 1.6 per cent of leading to the desired behaviour. Before coming to conlusions, the following comments are in order:

- Our initial assumption of a 0.5 probability at each stage is too high and the final probability will be lower than 1.6 per cent

- The probabilities for the system's stages are almost certainly not equal. It is much easier for an advertiser to obtain consumer exposure than consumer attention and/or comprehension.

Exhibit 15.3 *(continued)*

■ The probabilities will differ by product category. The impact of advertising for a box of chocolates or for a car is of course very different.

■ Finally, these probabilities need to be applied to the huge consumer market comprising millions of potential buyers. Thus, even a small purchase probability can lead to large sales volume.

As discussed above in Chapter 5 this hierarchy model is based on the assumption of a learning process which is not of general application, namely for the product categories with low involvement.

Source: Adapted from Wilkie (1994, p. 452).

The consequence for communication effectiveness can easily be imagined.

In 1965, 18 per cent of TV viewers were able to remember one of the last advertising spots to which they had been exposed the previous day. In 1987, this percentage had fallen to 7 per cent. (Bogart, 1986, p. 240)

This first level of 'advertising quality' – the perceptual effectiveness – determines the *productivity of advertising communication*. Important differences between advertising campaigns of the same intensity are observed in practice. Indicators of effectiveness used are tests of brand recognition, of unaided awareness, brand recall (Beta factor), and so on, described in Chapter 6.

Overemphasising the perceptual stage, however, runs the risk of leading to unbridled advertising creations, which lose sight of the fact that advertising is only to complement and support a marketing position. Some advertising critics even go as far as suggest that advertising is too important to be left in the hands of creative or agency people, who are often tempted to emphasise the communicational impact of advertising at the expense of the marketing positioning objective. The copy strategy approach has precisely the merit of refraining from creative outbursts, as opposed to the star strategy where the risk is less well contained.

Attitudinal effectiveness of advertising

The second level of effectiveness concerns the psycho-sociological aspect, which calls into question the affective response and the impact of the perceived message on attitudes towards the product or brand. The fact that a message has been properly perceived by the targeted group of buyers does not imply effectiveness in terms of attitude change. A message, which is perfectly received, understood and digested, may be totally inoperative because of being maladapted, not credible or simply irrelevant. It is why knowledge of the target group's components of attitude is required to define the advertising appeal.

Twedt (1969) suggests that the proposition or promise made must have the following characteristics:

● *Desirability*: the message must first say something desirable or interesting about the product.
● *Exclusiveness*: the message must say something exclusive that does not apply to every brand in the product category.
● *Believability*: the message must be believable or provable; at stake here is the credibility of the message sender.

There is no recipe in the field of creative advertising, even if there are many advertisers who claim to have one. In addition to the criteria already suggested, the following questions can also be addressed regarding the quality of effective advertising:

● Is the advertising positioning in line with the *marketing positioning* sought for the brand?
● Is the *benefit* brought to the buyer clearly evidenced, simple to understand and, if possible, provable?
● To what extent is the promise *unique* as compared to the promises made by competing brands?
● To what extent is there *consistency and continuity* in the adopted advertising theme across media and over time?
● Is the message based on a *creative* idea easy to memorise for the target audience?
● Does the advertisement succeed in gaining *attention* from the reader or the viewer?
● Is there a clear and simple *link* between the product, the benefit, the advertising appeal and the advertisement's execution?

Generally speaking, one should beware of too original ideas in advertising. They run the risk of obscuring the message to be put across, and the public remembering the advertisement but not the brand name. Some agencies tend to make the advertisement the centrepiece, forgetting that the centrepiece is the product.

If these conditions are met, advertising has achieved its objectives regarding attitudes and the target group is in a state of positive receptiveness towards the product or brand. This state of receptiveness will either be reinforced by repeated exposure to the message, or, on the contrary, modified by competing messages. Exhibit 15.4 shows one example of measuring the effectiveness of the attitudinal stage of a concept advertising campaign.

Behavioural effectiveness of advertising

The third level of the process is the *effectiveness of the behavioural stage*, that is purchasing behaviour directly caused by advertising, which is the ultimate objective being pursued. Indicators used are then trial purchases, sales or market share, decomposed into penetration intensity, exclusivity or loyalty rates as shown in Chapter 5.

> ### Exhibit 15.4
>
> ## Example of Attitudinal Measure of Advertising Effectiveness: Texas Gulf Phosphoric Acids and Fertilizer Manufacturers
>
> ■ **Advertising objective**
> To increase by 10 per cent within 1 year the knowledge and conviction about the product's distinctive characteristics among fertiliser manufacturers.
>
> ■ **Advertising theme**
> To gain conviction about the product's superiority. It contains fewer impurities and has a distinctive green colour: 'clean and green'.
>
> ■ **Results of the advertising effectiveness study**
>
> | | Before advertising | After advertising |
> |---|---|---|
> | – Identification of the message | 3.6% | 16.3% |
> | – Knowledge of the claimed distinctive characteristics | 15.3% | 35.1% |
> | – Conviction of product superiority over competing products | 9.4% | 24.3% |
>
> *Source*: Bryk and Davis (1973).

Characteristics of advertising response functions

Advertising response curves have important characteristics, which must be taken into account in advertising budget decisions:

● Advertising response functions are typically *non-linear* and subject to the law of diminishing returns, as illustrated in Figure 15.3(a). Thresholds exist reflecting inertia, perceptual resistance or fatigue effects.

● The slope of the response curve is determined by the *communication quality of the message*. For an identical level of advertising expenditure, very different response curves can be observed as a function of the medium used, the relevance of the message, the creativity of the advertisement, and so on.

● The advertising response is *dynamic* and its effects are distributed over time. The structure of the lagged effects also varies with media, products and advertising themes. In a way, advertising can be viewed as an investment, which creates for the brand a lasting demand over time.

● Last, but not least, the advertising effect does not exist independently of *other marketing factors,* such as distribution and price. The interaction effect between these factors is multiplicative, which means that the sum of their isolated effects is different from their joint effects.

The presence of such characteristics simply reflects the complexity of buyers' behaviour. But it also seriously complicates the problem of quantitative estimation both for

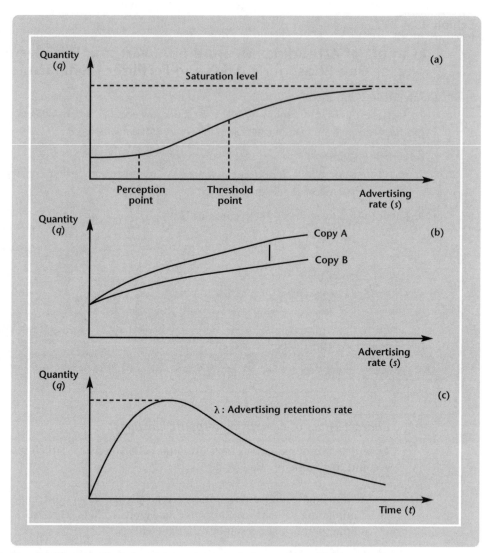

Figure 15.3   Characteristics of advertising response functions

advertising and the sales force. For a fuller discussion of the characteristics of sales and market share response functions, see Hanssens *et al.* (1990, Chapters 6 and 7).

The development of response advertising and of direct marketing leads to the use of intermediate measures of behavioural response such as mailing back a coupon, visiting a showroom, requesting a catalogue or a flyer, and so on; these are typical active expressions of interest triggered by an advertising message and therefore reflect its effectiveness. In reality, these indicators reflect the communication effectiveness as well, since it is difficult to distinguish between reactions motivated by the attractiveness of the incentive provided in the advert from those which are really motivated by the product or service proposed.

Advertising-sales effectiveness research

There are four groups of methods that can be used to measure the sales effectiveness of advertising.

1. Direct observation

A first method is *direct observation* when sales and advertising data are available on a weekly, monthly or even quarterly basis. This is more and more frequently the case with the development of scanning systems in supermarkets. An example was presented in Chapter 5 (see Figure 5.9), where the observations were presented successively on a bimonthly, monthly and weekly base. In the case presented in Figure 15.4, market share data are available on a quarterly base and it is rather straightforward to measure the impact of a promotional advertising campaign by simply comparing the observed average market share 'before' and 'after' the campaign.

> In this particular case, one observes a short-term gain (that is within the quarter) of 6.3 market share points, and a longer term gain (lagged effects) of 3.6 and 1.1 market share points after two and three quarters respectively. The added cumulative volume due to the advertising campaign was estimated at 44,342 cubic metres.

On this basis, it is not difficult to calculate the long-term profitability of each dollar spent on advertising.

2. Test market

A *test market* is another method, which can be used in markets where the competitive climate is not too aggressive. This method belongs to the domain of controlled experimentation described in Chapter 5 (see Chapter 4). The experiment conducted in the

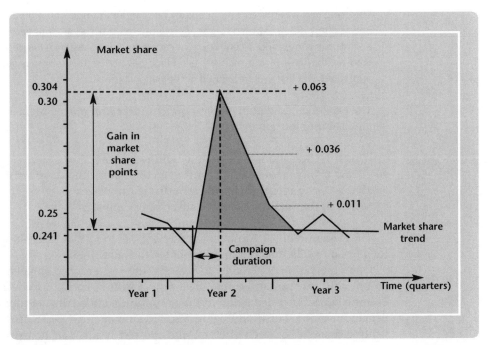

Figure 15.4   Impact of a promotional advertising campaign on market share

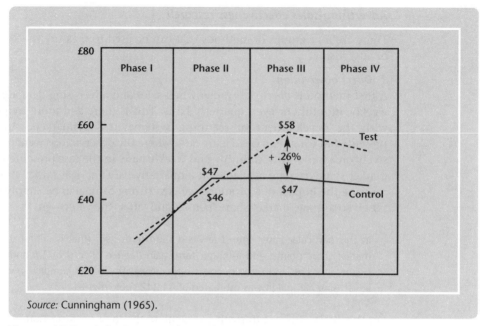

Source: Cunningham (1965).

Figure 15.5 Sales impact of an advertising campaign

USA by AT&T is a good example of application of this method. The objective of the advertising campaign was to promote lower tariffs for long-distance calls after 9 p.m. The design of the experiment was as follows:

> The campaign was spread over one year. Two random samples of 5000 users were selected, one as a test group exposed to the advertising, the other as a controlled group, and this in a single city comprising 20,000 users. In each group, long-distance telephone use was measured on the basis of the monthly telephone bills. Users of the test group received seven printed adverts that would be used in the national press.

The experimental design is a *before-after-with control group* design. The test period is subdivided into four phases:

- Phase 1, three months before the tariff reduction;
- Phase 2, three months with tariff reduction, but without advertising;
- Phase 3, two months with the advertising campaign;
- Phase 4, four months after the advertising campaign.

The evolution of the turnover per user and per month at each phase of the test for long-distance calls after 9 p.m. is presented in Figure 15.5.

One observes a 25 per cent increase in the test group compared to the control group. This increase can be due however to a shift of demand from regular hours to evening hours. After deduction of this substitution effect, the net increase of primary demand remains statistically significant and amounts to 4 per cent. Thus, the advertising campaign has been effective and the test results can be extrapolated to the national market to assess the expected profitability of the advertising investment.

Exhibit 15.5

The BehaviorScan System

In Europe, Marketing Scan, a joint subsidiary of Médiamétrie (a firm specialising in audience measurement) and the German group GFK, has developed *BehaviorScan*, an instrument to measure the impact of TV spots which establishes correlations between consumers' TV exposure and purchase behaviour. The basic principle is the unique source of information. Since 1994, in France, Marketing Scan has equipped the TV sets of 3000 households in the city of Angers with a control device; each household also received an ID card. Thanks to these control devices, different advertising messages can be diffused through the different French national television chains. The purchases made in the regional retail chains are then recorded and analysed thanks to the ID cards.

These experimental techniques are gaining in popularity with the development of consumer panels collecting scanner data, such as Consoscan (SECODIP), Scan 9000 (Nielsen) or BehaviorScan (GFK).

Information collected through scanned panels can provide answers to very sensitive questions to advertisers. What is the impact on brand sales of different advertising weights? Should the advertising campaign be concentrated or spread over time? How do consumers react to different advertising copies, and so on. The work of Lodish *et al.* (1995) on the impact of television advertising is particularly interesting.

Lodish *et al.* (1995) analyse results of 389 BehaviorScan matched household, consumer panel, split cable, real world tests that were completed between June 1992 and December 1988. The only difference between the matched panels is their exposure to different TV advertising treatments. Sales results of the various treatments are available unobtrusively from individual level household scanner data for the matched panels. Two types of advertising treatment were adopted: (1) copy tests, consisting of two cells with different copy and equal weight, and (2) weight tests, consisting of two cells having the same copy but different level of exposure.

For the weight tests, the results observed were the following:

- For 85 weight tests out of the 141 tests (or 60 per cent), the increase advertising weight had no significant impact on sales or market share; for 56 tests, the impact was significant.

- TV advertising weight tests were more effective for new products than for established products, with 55 per cent of these tests showing significant positive effects versus 33 per cent for established products.

- The average advertising elasticity observed is very weak, a result already evidenced by Lambin (1975), and equal to 0.13 for the entire sample of 141 tests, equal to 0.05 for the established products ($N = 89$) and equal to 0.26 (five times higher) for new products ($N = 52$).

For the advertising copy tests, the results were the following:

- A total of 96 copy tests were made, of which 86 (or 90 per cent) were for established products.
- For new brands ($N = 10$), 6 (or 60 per cent) tests showed significant effects versus 25 per cent (or 21) for established products.

On the whole, these experiments show that advertising, be it copy or weight, cannot by themselves alone influence sales or market share in a very significant way.

3. Econometric analysis

A third method or group of methods is econometric analysis, whenever times series or cross-sectional data are available on sales or market share and the key marketing variable. The objective is then to build a dynamic econometric model relating sales or market shares to the main variables of marketing. An example of application is presented in Figure 15.6.

The development of information technology and the availability of mega data banks combined with the new powerful analysis techniques briefly presented in Chapter 4 greatly expand the domain of application of this method.

4. Marketing engineering

A last method or group of methods is based on the use of computer-assisted expert systems like the ADBUDG model described above which use expert judgements as input data. This is the domain of *marketing engineering* which integrates concepts, analytic marketing techniques and operational software to help managers to make marketing decisions (see Lilien and Rangaswamy, 1998).

International Advertising

The debate about whether to customise or to standardise the marketing mix (see Chapter 2) is particularly acute in the field of international advertising. Academicians and practitioners alike are still divided on the advisability of using standardised (universal) or localised (individualised) advertising approaches in international campaigns. Advertisers who use the standardised approach argue that consumers anywhere in the world have the same basic needs and desires and can therefore be persuaded by universal appeals. On the other hand, advertisers who follow the localised approach assert that the success of an advertising campaign in a global environment requires *cultural empathy* (the ability to identify with different cultures) and that consumers differ from country to country and must accordingly be reached by advertising tailored to their respective countries. In this section, we shall first briefly review the limitations and obstacles to global advertising and then examine the alternative international advertising strategies.

Limitations on global advertising

In the communication theory it is well established that an individual's cultural environment significantly affects the way he or she perceives information. Consequently, if a sender of a message lives in a cultural environment different from his or her intended receiver and wishes to communicate effectively, a knowledge of the culture

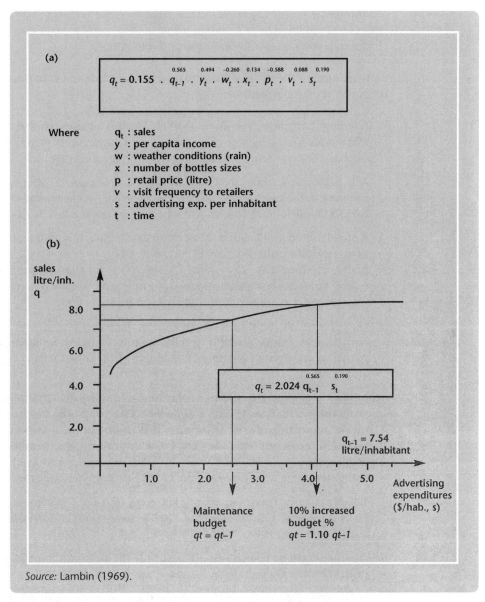

(a)

$$q_t = 0.155 \cdot q_{t-1}^{0.565} \cdot y_t^{0.494} \cdot w_t^{-0.260} \cdot x_t^{0.134} \cdot p_t^{-0.588} \cdot v_t^{0.088} \cdot s_t^{0.190}$$

Where

q_t : sales
y : per capita income
w : weather conditions (rain)
x : number of bottles sizes
p : retail price (litre)
v : visit frequency to retailers
s : advertising exp. per inhabitant
t : time

(b)

$$q_t = 2.024 \, q_{t-1}^{0.565} \, s_t^{0.190}$$

$q_{t-1} = 7.54$ litre/inhabitant

Maintenance budget
$q_t = q_{t-1}$

10% increased budget %
$q_t = 1.10 \, q_{t-1}$

Advertising expenditures ($/hab., s)

Source: Lambin (1969).

Figure 15.6 Example of econometric demand function

of the receiver is necessary (Schramm, 1954). To test the above argument different empirical studies have attempted to measure to what extent advertising practitioners are standardising their offerings.

The most recent research results reveal that the majority of the studied firms are guided by the localised approach (Kanso, 1992; Shao *et al.*, 1992). The findings of these studies suggest that, if human wants and needs are in effect more or less universal, the way to address these wants and needs is not.

Although the story of Boy meets Girl is as old as time, the 'body language' of how Boy meets Girl varies considerably for culture to culture. If we get the language even subtly wrong, the local consumer rejects the whole concept (Perry, 1992).

In addition to the cultural issue, many other obstacles exist to discourage attempts at advertising standardisation:

● *Language.* Language diversity in world markets is a major issue in communication. Difficulties with language can arise through carelessness in translation, but also because of the capability of languages to convey meaning.

Also some brand names may have strong resemblance to a word not used in polite company in another country. Examples in French are Pet milk products and toothpaste called 'Cue'. Similarly in Spanish with the Chevrolet brand called 'Nova'.

A standardised global advertising campaign is therefore vulnerable to distortion, as a result not only of language but local slang, or regional dialect. For a global brand, the ideal is to search out a nonsense word that is pronounceable everywhere but has no specific meaning anywhere; *Kodak* is a famous example. Another good example, with a positive meaning, is *Visa*.

● *Use of foreign language.* In several countries the use of foreign words in prohibited. For example, France prohibits totally the use of English words that have already passed in the French language like 'jumbo jet', 'supermarket', 'cash-and carry', and so on.

● *Media availability.* The ability to standardise a campaign internationally presupposes the international media availability. Television is by far the most important media internationally. Yet two-thirds of Western Europe may be said to be underserved in terms of programme choice, with government controlling the number of television channels, amount of broadcasting hours and availability of advertising. There are also wide differences in television viewing rates.

Television viewing habits vary broadly in Europe, with 230.6 minutes yesterday in the UK, 202.9 in Portugal, 198.2 in Spain and 126.0 in Switzerland, 137.6 in Denmark, and so on. (Euro Time Survey, 1994)

Similar differences or restrictions also exist for the press and for radio. See the European Planning Guide (Media & Marketing Europe, 1995–96).

● *Legal considerations.* In most countries, there are restrictions on the use of advertising for certain product categories.

For example, alcohol advertising is banned in Austria, Denmark, Finland, France, Norway and Switzerland. It is restricted by law in Ireland, Italy, Luxembourg, Portugal and Spain. It is restricted voluntarily in Germany and Holland. It is permitted in Belgium and Greece. (Carat, 1994)

● *Symbols.* Symbols are abstract characters that represents ideas, feelings and other aspects of culture. The way symbols are perceived varies among countries.

For example, snakes symbolise 'danger' in Sweden and 'wisdom' in Korea.

● *Colours.* The significance of colours can vary from culture to culture. In Western European countries we use colours to identify emotions: We 'see red', we are 'green with envy' or we 'feel blue'.

Black signifies mourning in Western countries, whereas white is often the colour of mourning in Eastern nations. Green is popular in Muslim countries, while red and black are negative in several African countries.

The marketer needs to know these patterns in planning products, packages and advertising. Some international firms were obliged to change their logos.

● *Family structure.* In Europe, what constitutes a household is the nuclear family: two parents and children; while in Africa the extended family includes: grandparents, uncles, aunts, and so on. Thus, even the target group may be different from one country to the other.

● *Consuming habits.* In the USA orange juice is consumed at breakfast but not in France. Thus, an orange juice's brand should be positioned as breakfast drink in the USA and as refreshment in France. Similarly, toothpaste is a cosmetic product in Italy and Greece, but in Holland is a household cleaning product.

● *Social roles.* Gender roles are sometimes very different from one country to the other. In Arabian countries, shopping is always done by women and never by men.

● *Tradition.* What is viewed as 'appropriate' behaviour may be very different from one country to the other.

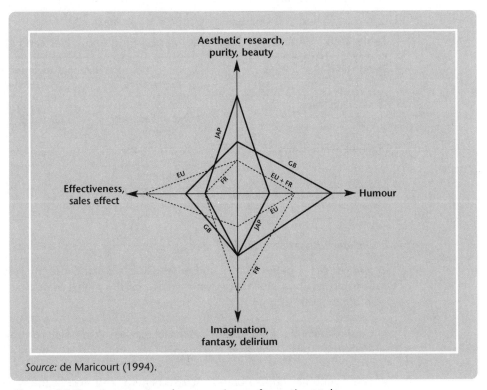

Source: de Maricourt (1994).

Figure 15.7   International comparison of creative styles

Advertisers should not underestimate the difficulties of designing an effective global advertising campaign. Critical questions have to be examined in detail:

● Are the needs really similar across the target countries?
● Is the message compatible with the traditions and the culture of each country?
● Is the message compatible with the laws and regulations of each country?
● Is the text of the message properly translated or transposed in each country language?
● What is the impact of the *made in* effect, that is, the impact of the country of origin on the perception of the message?

Given the large cultural differences observed among countries, it is not surprising to observe large differences also in the creative styles of different countries, as illustrated in Figure 15.7.

Alternative international advertising strategies

As already underlined in Chapter 2, too often the standardisation versus customisation issue is presented in terms of an *all or nothing* question. In reality, intermediate solutions exist and the real question is to know how to reconcile the two approaches.

For example, in most cases brand and advertising standardisation are implicitly considered as interdependent decisions. Thus two basic options are available: to standardise both or not standardise both. Following Sandler and Shani (1992), we support the idea that branding and advertising are two independent decisions, which can occur in varying combinations as shown in Table 15.8.

Table 15.8　Alternative international branding and advertising strategies

Brand name	International advertising	
	Standardised	Non-standardised
Same brand name	Strategy No. 1: Brand and advertise globally	Strategy No. 2: Brand globally and advertise locally
Different brand names	Strategy No. 3: Brand locally and harmonise advertising	Strategy No. 4: Brand and advertise locally

Source: Adapted from Sandler and Shani (1992).

Brand and advertise globally

In *Strategy No. 1* brand names and advertising are standardised. This situation will tend to prevail in a global environment where the global forces are strong and the local forces weak.

Classical examples of this strategy are Marlboro, Coca-Cola, Gillette Sensor, Sony Walkman, McDonald's, Levi, Gucci, Ariel, and so on.

These genuinely global brands deliver benefits to the consumers who value them in all countries: Coke for the convenience and the appeal of American young imagery; Sony for the attraction of 'music on the move'; Hermès for fashion and romance. These benefits can be hard-to-copy innovations like Pampers or Polaroid instant cameras, or emotional benefits like Dunhill or Cartier.

> An especially strong kind of positioning to be exploited globally involves national stereo-types: German quality in cars, for example, or French style and romance in perfume, or English conservatism in men's tailoring, or American youth and fun in fast food (Riesenbeck and Freeling, 1991).

Procter & Gamble seems to have adopted this policy regarding brand names since 70 per cent of its turnover comes from brands sold all over the world, such as Ariel, Pampers, Clearasil and Vick. One exception: the P&G shampoo Wash & Go was launched in 60 different countries, but under 6 different brand names. The concept 'two in one' is the same in each market, however. Slight variations in the advertising expressions also exist. This last example illustrates the fact that complete standardis-ation will probably never be possible. To illustrate the benefits and the shortcomings of globalisation, see Exhibits 15.6 and 15.7.

Brand globally but advertise locally

Strategy No. 2 standardises brand names but localises advertising campaigns. This situ-ation will probably prevail in transnational environments where both global and local forces are strong.

Exhibit 15.6

A Global Marketplace Means Global Vulnerability: The Coca-Cola Case in Europe

Coca-Cola Co., one of the world's most powerful corporations, discovered in June 1999 what it feels like to be on the losing end of globalisation. The soft-drink giant was rocked by a health scare in Europe that spread faster than a computer virus. Regulators in Belgium, France, Luxembourg and the Netherlands pulled the company's soft drinks from shelves after reports of contaminated Coke. And Coca-Cola spokesmen, after curtly insisting there wasn't any danger, began scrambling to offer assurance and apologies.

The Coca-Cola flap shows that just as capital and technology move instantaneously in the global economy, so does bad news. Consumer problems that start in Belgium can race around the globe – tarnishing the world's most powerful brand name and even affecting its stock price on Wall Street. For America's hard-charging corporate executives, this is the flip side of globalisation. For even as the technology revolution is empowering corpora-tions, it also is giving new leverage to regulators and consumer groups. They're no such things as a 'local problem' anymore, as Coca-Cola's experience shows. 'Global brand name recognition has an Achilles heel of vulnerability', says the consumer advocate Ralph Nader. The events last week show that the value of Coca-Cola's brand, built up over more than a century, can be shaken as suddenly and capriciously as the Thai baht or the Indonesian ringgit.

Source: International Herald Tribune, 22 June, 1999.

Exhibit 15.7

McDonald's, a Case Study in Successful Globalisation

The folks at McDonald's like to tell the story about the young Japanese girl who arrived in Los Angeles, looked around and said to her mother: 'look, mom, they have McDonald's here too'. You could excuse her for being surprised that this was an American company. With 2000 restaurants in Japan, McDonald's Japan is the biggest McDonald's franchise outside the United States. 'You don't have 2000 stores in Japan by being seen as an American company', said James Cantalupo, head of McDonald's International.

The way McDonald's has packaged itself is to be a 'multi-local' company. By insisting on a high degree of local ownership, and by tailoring its products just enough for local cultures, it has avoided the worst cultural backlashes that some other US companies have encountered. Not only the localities now feel a stake in McDonald's success but also, more important, countries do. Poland, for instance, has emerged as one of the largest regional suppliers of meat, potatoes and bread for McDonald's in central Europe. That is real power. McDonald's is gradually moving from local sourcing of its raw materials to regional sourcing to global sourcing. One day soon, all McDonald's meat in Asia will come from Australia, all its potatoes from China. Already, every sesame seed on every McDonald's bun in the world comes from Mexico. That's as good as a country discovering oil.

Source: T.L. Friedman, *International Herald Tribune*, 12 December, 1996.

Examples of this strategy are given by Bacardi and Volvo and also to a lesser degree by P&G with the shampoo Wash & Go. These firms use the same brand name worldwide but the advertising themes and/or expressions are adjusted in each country.

In instances where brand standardisation tends to be high, localised advertising gives the firm the opportunity to take into account local culture and sensitivity and to position the brand in the local market.

Brand locally and harmonise advertising globally

Strategy No. 3 harmonises advertising but keeps local brand names. This is a strategy adopted by European firms, like Unilever and Kraft, having developed their portfolio of brands through acquisitions. Unilever management, for example, seems to believe (see Fraser, 1990) that as long as core brand values can be harmonised, the name does not really matter. Unilever tends to draw the line in its harmonising policy at changing names.

Unless the original name is meaningless, it would be very dangerous to drop it. Names that have been built up over years and years are an essential part of brand's franchise or equity. (in Fraser)

This is the justification of the approach taken with a Unilever fabric softener called Cajoline in France, Coccolino in Italy, Kuschelweich in Germany, Mimosin in Spain and Snuggle in the USA. Although the name is different in every country, it suggests cuddly softness everywhere. And the product benefits are always presented by a talking teddy bear, a universally understood symbol of softness. Far from being a disadvantage, the different names actually bring the brand closer to the hearts of local consumers.

> The 'same advertising–different name' approach has also been used for the fish fingers of Unilever. The well-known salty sea captain has appeared in commercials throughout Europe even though he is variously known as Bird's Eye, Findus or Iglo. All he has to do is change his cap and speak a different language in each country, which leads to significant cost savings in the production of television commercials.

Kraft General Food also manages to combine centralised European marketing with local brand sensitivity. It does not, for example, market a multinational ground coffee brand, but it does own over a dozen such brands in various European countries where it is the uncontested number one.

> Because of the way the company grew, mainly via acquisitions, we control many local brands. There was a tentative effort by Klaus Jacobs (the former proprietor of Jacobs Suchard which was bought by General Foods) to internationalise them. But it has been abandoned. Discouraged by the costs of such an alignment, management also recognised the gigantic waste that killing off the local brands, rich in capital and heritage, would represent. (Subramanian, 1993)

This attitude is very different from the one adopted by Mars. Has Mars carried things too far by investing major sums in the name changes of successful brands: Raider to Twix, Marathon to Snickers, Kal-Kan to Whiskas? Too much centralisation leads naturally to excessive standardisation.

In Europe, the dominant concept seems to be 'brand locally, harmonise advertising globally', taken as a way to manage European diversity. For Americans, in contrast, the natural concept seems to be 'brand globally, advertise locally'.

Brand and advertise locally

Strategy No. 4 will be adopted in environments where the local forces are strong and the global forces weak. In general, it is considered that this situation prevails in the food sector where tastes, flavours and colours are important factors.

This was typically the strategy adopted by Unilever until recently as explained above (Omo, All, Persil, Skip, Via). This strategy of complete decentralisation seems more and more difficult to maintain for an international firm, because *speed and scale* are and will be more and more crucial success factors in the newly integrated European market.

> We were at trouble competing well with companies like P&G because we needed speed and scale – and we didn't have that when we had to go through 16 or 17 countries', explains Alfred Jung, one of Lever's first Euromanagers (Dalgic,1992).

At Unilever, two types of difference can exist: (a) same product but different brand names or (b) same brand name but different products.

> Iced sparkling tea is sold under the brand name Liptonic in France, Lipton Ice Tea in Belgium and Lipton Ice in the UK. On the other hand, under the same brand name Lipton Ice Tea,

the drink is sparkling in France and non-sparkling in Belgium. Similarly, Calvé is a salty mayonnaise in Belgium and a sweet one in Holland.

It is clear that with the development of cross-border purchases, this diversity of brand names and content is very confusing for the consumer and that some degree of standardisation is required. In the European context, the word *harmonisation* of branding policies rather than 'standardisation' is probably more appropriate.

Chapter summary

When a firm resorts to advertising, it is effectively following a pull communication strategy. Its main objective is to create brand image and brand equity and to ensure co-operation from distributors. Advertising objectives can be defined by reference to the three levels of market response; cognitive, affective and behavioural response. The creative design of the advertising message and the selection of the most appropriate media mix are two key factors which determine the productivity (or quality) of the advertising investment. The selection of media is based on a set of criteria, quantitative and qualitative. Different methods of setting the advertising budgets are used in practice, the most popular one being the task and objective method. Two mathematical models, Vidale and Wolfe and ADBUDG, can be used when the key parameters of the advertising response function are known. There are three types of measures of advertising effectiveness; perceptual, attitudinal and behavioural effectiveness. One of the key issues in international advertising is the standardisation versus customisation question. In reality several alternative solutions exist to this problem, among others the strategy of 'harmonised advertising' probably better suited to the European situation.

QUESTIONS AND PROBLEMS

1. Re-examine the five objectives of advertising communication described in this chapter. Look for examples of advertising messages, which illustrate these objectives in two different vehicles or media.
2. Pick a brand of a consumer good you know well and use the Maloney grid to identify three communication platforms to suggest to your advertising agency.
3. Compare the goals of product advertising, institutional advertising, response advertising and publicity.
4. The advertising manager of a large consumer goods company proposes to the management committee a FF1 million advertising budget increase that should generate a FF5 million increase in sales revenue. The general manager asks you to prepare a memo and to formulate a recommendation to the committee. How would you proceed to prepare this recommendation?
5. A manufacturer wishes to determine the level of advertising which will maintain his current sales growth rate at 4 per cent. Current sales are $50,000 and it is estimated

that sales could reach a level of $150,000 at saturation. Sales response to advertising dollars is estimated at 1.1, and it has been determined that the company would lose 0.2 of its sales per period if no advertising were made. How much advertising is needed to maintain the desired growth rate? What rate of growth would be sustained if $20,000 were spent per period for advertising?

6. The ABC Company has been selling its highly rated line of System X colour TV sets for $700, $500 and $300 respectively. These prices have been relatively uncompetitive in the market. After some study the company substitutes several cheaper components (which engineering says may reduce the quality of performance slightly) and passes on the savings to the consumer in the form of a $100 price reduction on each model. Company ABC institutes a price-oriented promotional campaign that neglects to mention that the second-generation System X sets are different from the first. Is the company's competitive strategy ethical?

Bibliography

Bell, D. (1979) L'avenir: la société de communication, *Harvard-L'Expansion*, **57**, pp. 9–19.

Bogart, L. (1986) *Strategy in Advertising*, Lincolnwood IL, NTC Business Book.

Bryk, C.S. and Davis, R. (1973) Ads Work: Texasgulf Proves in Positioning Campaigns for Acids, *Industrial Marketing*, **58**, August, pp. 52–62.

Carat (1994) *European Television Minibook*, London, NTC Publications.

Chandon, J.L. (1976) L'état de l'art en matière de planification publicitaire, unpublished paper, University of Nice.

Colley, R.H. (1961) *Defining Advertising Goals for Measured Advertising Results*, New York, Association of National Advertisers.

Cunningham, R. (1965) *Some Attempts to Measure the Sale Effects of Advertising*, New York, The Association of National Advertisers.

Dalgic, T. (1992) Euromarketing: Charting the Map for Globalization, *International Marketing Review*, **9**(5): 31–42.

Dalrymple, D.J. and Parsons, L.J. (1976) *Marketing Management: Text and Cases*, New York, John Wiley & Sons.

Davis, E., Kay, J.O. and Star, J. (1991) Is Advertising Rational?, *Business Strategy Review*, **2**.

de Maricourt, R. (1994) La société de haute communication, *Revue Française du Marketing*, No. 149, pp. 5–23.

de Maricourt, R., Andréani, J.C., Bloch, A. *et al.* (1997) *Marketing Européen, stratégies et actions*, Paris, PubliUnion.

Dorfman, P. and Steiner, P.O. (1954) Optimal Advertising and Optimal Quality, *American Economic Review*, **44**, pp. 826–33.

Franzen, G. *et al.* (1999) *Brands and Advertising*, London, Admap Publications.

Fraser, I. (1990) Now only the Name's not the Same, *Eurobusiness*, April, pp. 22–5.

Gross, I. (1972) The Creative Aspects of Advertising, *Sloan Management Review*, **14**, pp. 83–109.

Jacquemin, A. (1973) Optimal Control and Advertising Policy, *Metroeconomica*, **25**, May, pp. 200–7.

Kanso A. (1992) International Advertising Strategies: Global Commitment to Local Vision, *Journal of Advertising Research*, January–February, pp. 10–14.

Kapferer, J.N. (1985) Publicité: une révolution des méthodes de travail, *Revue Française de Gestion*, September–December, pp. 102–11.

Kassaye, W.W. (1999) Sorting out the practical concerns on World Wide Web advertising, *International Journal of Advertising*, **18**(3): 339–361.

Krugman, H.E. (1975) The Impact of Television Advertising: Learning without Involvement, *Public Opinion Quarterly*, Autumn, pp. 349–56.

Lambin, J-J. (1969) Measuring the Profitability of Advertising: An Empirical Study, *Journal of Industrial Economics*, **17**, pp. 86–103.

Lambin, J-J. (1972) A Computer On-Line Marketing Mix Model, *Journal of Marketing Research*, pp. 119–26.

Lambin, J-J., Naert, P.A. and Bultez, A. (1975) Optimal Advertising Behavior in Oligopoly, *European Economic Review*, **6**, pp. 105–28.

Lambin, J-J. (1975) What is the Real Impact of Advertising? *Harvard Business Review*, May–June, pp. 139–47.

Lavidge, R.J. and Steiner, G.A. (1961) A Model of Predictive Measurement of Advertising Effectiveness, *Journal of Marketing*, **25**, pp. 59–62.

Lilien, G.L. and Rangaswamy, A. (1998) *Marketing Engineering, Computer-assisted Marketing Analysis and Planning*, Reading MA: Addison Wesley.

Lilien, G.L., Kotler, P. and Moorthy, S. (1992) *Marketing Models*, Englewood Cliffs NJ: Prentice Hall.

Little, J.D.C. (1970) Models and Managers, the Concept of a Decision Calculus, *Management Science*, **16**, pp. 466–85.

Little, J.D.C. (1979) Decision Support for Marketing Managers, *Journal of Marketing*, **43**, pp. 9–26.

Lodish, L.M., Abraham, M., Kalmenson, S. Livelsberger, J., Lubetkin, B., Richardson, B. and Stevens M.E. (1995) How TV Advertising Works: Meta-Analysis of 289 Real World Split Cable TV Advertising Experiments, *Journal of Marketing Research*, **32**.

Maloney, J.C. (1961) Marketing Decisions and Attitude Research, in Baker, G.L. (ed.), *Effective Marketing Coordination*, Chicago IL, American Marketing Association.

McGuire, W.J. (1978) An Information Processing Model of Advertising Effectiveness, in Davis, H. and Silk, A. (eds), *Behavioural and Management Sciences in Marketing*, New York, Ronald Press/John Wiley.

Morgensztern, A. (1983) Une synthèse des travaux sur la mémorisation des messages publicitaires, in Piquet, S., *La publicité, nerf de la communication*, Paris, les Editions d'Organisation.

Nelson, D. (1974) Advertising as Information, *Journal of Political Economy*, **82**, pp. 729–54.

Ollier, A.(1998) *Guide to Marketing on the Internet*, London: Aurelian Information UK.

Palda, K.S. (1963) *The Measurement of Cumulative Advertising Effects*, Englewood Cliffs, NJ, Prentice Hall.

Perry, M. (1992) *Investing in Brands*, Barcelona, IAA 33rd World Congress, 29 September.

Riesenbeck, H. and Freeling, A. (1991) How Global are Global Brands?, *The McKinsey Quarterly*, No. 4, pp. 3–18.

Sandler, D.M. and Shani, D. (1992) Brand Globally but Advertise Locally, An Empirical Investigation, *International Marketing Review*, **9**(4): 18–31.

Schramm, W. (1954) *The Process and Effects of Mass Communication*, 1st edn, Urbana IL, University of Illinois Press.

Séguéla, J. (1982) *Hollywood lave plus blanc*, Paris, Flammarion.

Shao, A.T. Shao, L.P. and Shao, D.H. (1992) Are Global Markets with Standardized Advertising Campaigns Feasible?, *Journal of International Consumer Marketing*, **4**(3): pp. 5–16.

Subraminian, D. (1993) In Search of Eurobrands, *Media & Marketing*, pp. 22–3.

Strauss, J. and Frost, R. (1999) *Marketing on the Internet*, Englewood Cliffs NJ, Prentice Hall.

The European Advertising and Media Forecast, in *Marketing Pocket Book 1999*, The Advertising Association, NTC Publication, pp. 164–5.

Troadec, L. and Troadec, A. (1984) *Exercices de marketing*, Paris, Les Editions d'Organisation.

Twedt, D.W. (1969) How To Plan New Product, Improve Old Ones and Create Better Advertising, *Journal of Marketing*, **33**, pp. 53–7.

Variot, J.F. (1985) *L'identité de marque*, Paris, Institut de recherches et d'études publicitaires, *Journées d'études de l'IREP*, June.

Vidale, M.L. and Wolfe, H.B. (1957) An Operation Research Study of Sales Response to Advertising, *Operations Research*, June, pp. 370–81.

Wilkie, W.L. (1994) *Consumer Behavior*, New York, John Wiley and Sons, p. 452.

Appendix 15.1

Derivation of the Advertising Optimising Rule

In a monopolistic market, where primary demand is non-expansible, the brand demand function can be written as

$$Q(S) = K_s \cdot S^\varepsilon$$

and the profit function

$$\pi = (P - C) \cdot Q(S) - S - F$$

where S denotes advertising expenditures, ε advertising-sales elasticity, C variable costs and F fixed costs. The optimum is reached when

$$\frac{\delta\pi}{\delta S} = (P - C) \cdot \frac{\delta Q}{\delta S} - 1 = 0$$

Multiplying by S/PQ, we obtain the advertising optimisation rule expressed by reference to advertising-sales elasticity,

$$\frac{P - C}{P} \times \frac{\delta Q}{\delta S} \times \frac{S}{Q} - \frac{S}{PQ} = 0$$

Rearranging terms, we obtain the following decision rules:

$$\text{Optimal advertising sales ratio} = \frac{S}{PQ} = (\varepsilon_{q,\,s})\,\frac{(P - C)}{P}$$

and the optimal advertising budget is given by

$$\text{Optimum budget} = S^* = \{\varepsilon_{q,\,s} \cdot (P - C) \cdot K\}^{1/1-\varepsilon}$$

The second-order condition stipulates that $0 \le \varepsilon \le 1$.

part five

Ten Case Studies in Market-driven Management

STRUCTURE OF THE BOOK

PART ONE The Changing Role of Marketing

The role of marketing in the firm and in a marketing economy
CHAPTER ONE

From marketing to market-driven management
CHAPTER TWO

PART TWO Understanding Customer Behaviour

The customer choice behaviour
CHAPTER THREE

The marketing information system
CHAPTER FOUR

The customer's response behaviour
CHAPTER FIVE

PART THREE Market-driven Strategy Development

Needs analysis through market segmentation
CHAPTER SIX

Market attractiveness analysis
CHAPTER SEVEN

Competitiveness analysis
CHAPTER EIGHT

Formulating a market strategy
CHAPTER NINE

The strategic marketing plan
CHAPTER TEN

PART FOUR Market-driven Management Decisions

Market-driven new product decisions
CHAPTER ELEVEN

Market-driven distribution decisions
CHAPTER TWELVE

Market-driven pricing decisions
CHAPTER THIRTEEN

Market-driven communication decisions
CHAPTER FOURTEEN

Market-driven advertising decisions
CHAPTER FIFTEEN

PART FIVE Ten Case Studies in Market-driven Management

1. The Lander Company *W.J. Stanton*
2. The WILO Corporation *R. Köhler*
3. TV: Cold Bath for French Cinema *A. Riding*
4. Ecover *D. Develter*
5. Volvo Truck Belgium *J.J. Lambin*
6. The Petro-equipment Company *J.J. Lambin*
7. Sierra Plastics Company *W.J. Stanton*
8. Tissex *G. Marion*
9. Newfood *G.S. Day et al.*
10. SAS: Meeting Customer Expectations *D.L. Kurtz and K.E. Clow*

case study one

The Lander Company

This case study was prepared by W.J. Stanton in *Fundamentals of Marketing*,
McGraw-Hill. Reproduced with permission.

In the autumn of 1970, Luis Lander, president and majority stockholder of Lander Ltd
returned from a business trip to the United States. While there, he had visited extensively with a number of former business associates one of whom was a marketing executive with a large US oil company. His discussions with this particular individual had
raised some doubts in his mind as to whether or not his company was sufficiently
conscious of the value of marketing.

Lander's father, a prominent South American businessman, had founded Lander Ltd
in 1927 to weave cotton cloth. The company remained a family-held enterprise until
1940 when the public was invited to subscribe to the new capital required financing
the company's expansion.

Immediately following the Second World War, the company experienced a remarkable growth. By 1970, the number of employees had risen to 4000, the number of spin-
dles to over 100,000, and the number of looms to over 4200. Investment in plant and
equipment increased tenfold during this 15-year period.

In the late 1940s and early 1950s, Lander widened the scope of the company's activities through both backward and forward integration and, also, by diversifying its
product line. Backward integration was accomplished by Lander's entry into the spin-
ning business so as to supply its own yarn. Forward integration was undertaken
through the introduction of printing, finishing and dyeing processes which enabled
the company to control the entire production cycle of its products.

Lander sold its products through a network of 46 independent distributors. Cloth
was shipped to these distributors who held it on consignment until sold to retailers
and to small manufacturers who produced limited lines of ready-to-wear apparel.
Consigned goods were usually sold within 30 days of delivery to distributors. Another
group of customers consisted of some 72 large garment manufacturers who were
served directly from the company's plant.

Lander's oil company friend had surprised him considerably with his views on the
marketing concept. 'In essence', his friend told him, 'this concept holds that
marketing is literally the most important part of a business. You're in business to make
a sale, and you can best do this by understanding the wants and needs of the ultimate
consumer of your products. Once this much is understood, all of your actions – and
certainly all of your decisions – must be geared to finding ways to satisfy these wants.
Everybody in the organisation must focus on the consumer and must strive constantly
to find new and better ways of serving him or her.'

While Lander thought that he understood what his friend was saying, he was not too sure of how this concept should be implemented within his own organisation. His friend had pointed out that Lander Ltd really had no marketing organisation and that its product line was made up largely by designers and colour experts who had very little contact with the housewives or the male consumers who ultimately purchased the fabrics in one form or another produced by the company. It was also pointed out that Lander Ltd had no marketing research department, did no consumer advertising, and did little or nothing to help its customers to sell the merchandise in which their products were incorporated.

In attempting to apply the concept to his company, Lander considered setting up a separate company which could be likened to a sales agent. Essentially, this new company would serve solely as a marketing agency and would be responsible for 'ordering out' all production. It would be responsible for selling all company products, researching the market to determine what new patterns to produce and in what quantities and advertising the various company products to the consumer – often in co-operation with the larger garment manufacturers and retailers. Under such an arrangement, the company's present sales force of five men and the entire staff of designers would be transferred to the new organisation. The present organisation – minus those personnel shifted – would literally function solely as a production unit.

The sales agency would be a wholly owned subsidiary. It would include the company's name in its title and would establish separate offices in the heart of a nearby city. It would buy all merchandise from the plant at cost plus 10 per cent. Its responsibilities would include, however, the setting of all prices – including quantity discounts. It would be responsible for making profits – in fact, its profits would be an important part of the company's overall profits.

Lander recognised that this type of organisational change would meet considerable resistance within the company, and yet the more he thought about it, the more he was convinced that it was a good idea.

Questions

1. Do you believe that the Lander Company has a problem?
2. What do you think of the new organisational structure proposed by Lander?
   Analyse the merits and the disadvantages of the proposed structure.
3. Suggest other possible organisational structure(s) aiming at reinforcing the level of market orientation of the firm.
4. How would you proceed to implement such an organisational change.

The WILO Company

This case study was prepared by Professor R. Köhler from Cologne University. Used with permission of the author.

WILO is an internationally leading manufacturer of pumps for heating systems. The corporation's business spreads over the whole of Europe with 14 subsidiaries and several agencies abroad. WILO's activities are divided into four business units, defined mainly by customer groups and partly by product features:

- Domestic (private one- or two-family houses)
- Commercial (commercial or public builders)
- OEM (Original Equipment Manufacturer = industrial customers)
- Customer Service and Maintenance (including recycling).

Recently, the new business unit 'Systems' was created; it includes pressure-intensifying installations, transfer stations for district heating, filters for private swimming pools and collectors for the use of rainwater. However, after having shifted the entire OEM production to France, there are still four business units remaining in Germany.

Until 1990 WILO was organised in the 'classical' functional structure, as indicated in Figure CS2.1. The functional division 'Marketing/Sales' included departments for sales in Germany, sales abroad and export. The central Marketing Department (Marketing Services) was in charge of market research, advertising and sales promotion as well as the corporation's representation at trade fairs. Additional marketing specialists were working for the business units 'Domestic' and 'Commercial', just as 'OEM' and 'Customer Service' were supported by special marketing and sales units. Figure CS2.1 shows this structure valid until 1990.

The functional structure shown in Figures CS2.1 and CS2.2 was suffering a significant disadvantage: too many organisational levels between workbench and customer caused co-ordination problems and time delays. For that reason a fundamental reorganisation was implemented in 1991.

The new structure was aiming for the following improvements:

- priority for market and customer orientation;
- short distances between market and production;
- comprehensive process orientation instead of functional departments;
- delegation of responsibilities to small co-operative groups within the company;
- higher motivation of the staff.

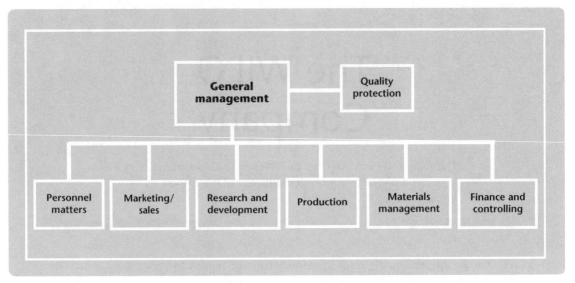

Figure CS2.1   Functional organisation at WILO until 1990

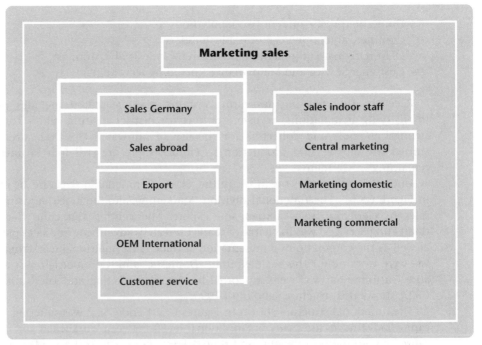

Figure CS2.2   The organisation of marketing sales at WILO until 1990

As the main element of the reorganisation, the so-called *CIF-Teams* were created ('CIF' standing for 'Customer in the Focus'; German: *Kunde im Mittelpunkt* = KIM). Each of the above-mentioned business units was assigned its own CIF-Team, led by an expert in Marketing/Sales or Customer Service. The rest of the team members were recruited from Research and Development, Materials Management, Production and Controlling, to ensure that experts from all relevant business functions contribute to the creation of customer benefit throughout the whole value chain of the corporation.

The CIF-Teams' work is mainly strategy oriented: designing marketing strategies taking into consideration the competitive situation and market development. However, they are also supposed to supervise the implementation of these strategies (for example by introducing new products to the market). In addition, the CIF-Teams are responsible for establishing long- and short-term objectives and the supervision of their realisation.

The immediate closeness to customers is provided by the external organisation of WILO, which consists of 16 Sales and Service Teams, 3 Regional Managers and one Key Account Management. Since the leaders of the CIF-Teams are part of the external organisation, strategy development on the basis of the newest information about the market and customer needs is ensured.

The so-called 'Round Table' is a further committee, which works as a link between the CIF-Teams and the modularly designed production. Members of the 'Round Table' are: one delegate from the Sales Department (indoor staff), one expert of the Purchasing Department, one manager from the Production Department and one Controller. They have to ensure that production reacts in a flexible way to market needs and considers the strategic priorities marked by the CIF-Teams. The field staff passes customers' orders immediately on to the competent production unit.

Figure CS2.3 offers an overview of the new CIF organisation.

The 'classical' Marketing Department, to be seen in Figures CS2.1 and CS2.2, was given up at WILO. Merely Market Research and Advertising are still centralised.

Market	Optimising closeness to customers	Strategy development and implementation	Improved reactions to the market	Higher flexibility
	External organisation	CIF-Teams*	'Round table' as a link between sales and production	Factories
C U S T O M E R	Key account management	4 CIF areas with team members from:	1 delegate from the sales indoor staff	Production planning
	3 regional managers	Sales	1 member of the purchasing department	Production (motor production, installation, mechanical processing)
	16 sales and service teams	Research and development	1 production manager	
		Materials management	1 controller	Quality control
		Production		
		Controlling		

* CIF = 'Customer in the Focus' (German: *Kunde im Mittelpunkt* = KIM)

Figure CS2.3 Customer and process-oriented CIF organisation at WILO since 1991

Otherwise, the process organisation, which overcomes traditional department limits, provides the framework for market orientation. The reorganisation was combined with an intensive 'internal marketing' with the goal to create a customer-oriented mentality among the staff. This new pattern of organisation has proved its worth over the last four years.

The current plan is to group the 14 European subsidiaries into four larger regions: Central Europe, Northern Europe, Southern Europe and Eastern Europe. The managers of these regions will have a seat and a vote on the CIF-Teams, whenever their regions are involved or adjustment to local particularities (for example of product innovations) is concerned. The CIF-Teams shall guarantee a balance between central control and local adjustments, corresponding to the 'transnational marketing' approach (suggested by Bartlett and Ghoshal/Nohria).

Question

1. Compare the advantages and disadvantages of a functional organisation over a cross-functional organisation similar to the one adopted by the WILO Company.

TV: Cold Bath for French Cinema

Article written by Alan Riding and published in the *International Herald Tribune*, January 10, 1996. Reproduced with permission.

France's troubled movie industry has long resisted change because change would mean abandoning its artistic tradition and surrendering to the commercialism of Hollywood. But change may be coming anyway, not from Hollywood but from the television companies that are fast emerging as leading financiers of French films. In truth, television companies have already 'saved' the industry because they are required by law to invest in French movies and to broadcast a quota of French films each year. 'French cinema would have died 10 or 15 years ago without television', said Ronan Girre, who runs the movie branch of the government-owned France 3 television channel. But, tiring of handing out money for intellectual 'auteur' movies with minimal box-office appeal, the TV companies have begun using their financial leverage to press producers and directors into making more commercial and popular films that have a chance of winning back lost audiences. 'If movie attendance in France has fallen from 200 million to 130 million per year since 1980, it's not because American films are better but because ours are worse', said Guillaume de Verg's, head of the movie department at TF1, the country's largest television network. 'We should have some self-criticism and recognise that we don't make films people want to see'.

The television companies, which last year accounted for one-third of the $575.8 million invested in new French movies and often act as a first step in getting other financing, have a clear interest in shaking up the movie industry. Led by the pay-TV channel Canal Plus, they need viewers to watch French movies if they are to draw advertisers. And where the companies are involved in co-productions, they want a better return on their money. But they are also couching their message to the industry in 'for-your-own-good' terms. Sooner or later, they warn, the artificial world of quotas and government subsidies will be swept away by European Union deregulation and by satellite broadcasting outside French government control. So, they say, the movie industry must learn to compete or face extinction.

Alain Sarde, who produces films for Studio Canal Plus, the channel's movie production company, said he found it irritating to hear French directors constantly griping that Hollywood is 'stealing' their audiences. 'Let's make good films', he said. 'Of 120 French films in a good year, 20 to 25 are interesting. In the 1970s, there'd be 50 interesting ones. It's a question of talent'. Still, under pressure mainly from Canal Plus and TF1, change is slowly coming. 'We work with name directors who now include box-office in their plans', said Brahim Chioua, who runs Studio Canal Plus and co-produces

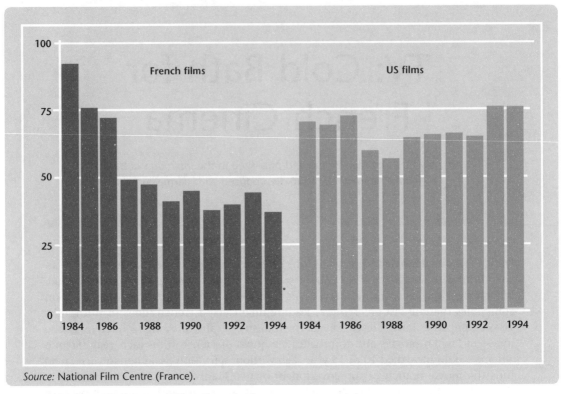

Source: National Film Centre (France).

Figure CS3.1   The type of films French cinema-goers watch

films. De Verg's said television's influence was already significant. 'Producers are beginning to see that people want commercial films', he said. 'The auteur world will not last because of television. Television and television fiction have produced a lot of new talent that sees cinema in a different way'. But resistance to change also runs deep.

French auteurs, for example, have always viewed television with hostility, not only because its arrival undermined French moviegoing habits, but also because it is regarded as vulgar. 'The difference between cinema and television', Jean-Luc Godard, one of France's New Wave directors of the 1960s, once noted, 'is that you raise your eyes for cinema and lower your eyes for television'. Claude Miller, a respected director who is now preparing an adaptation of Emile Zola's novel *Nana*, said that television companies preferred to back more conventional productions because they want films that can draw huge prime-time audiences. 'The negative, even perverse, effect of television is that it aims overwhelmingly for family entertainment', he said. 'But prime-time appeal is not what characterises the best of French cinema'. Further, for many French directors, any hint of adopting Hollywood's commercial approach is a potential threat. After all, under the current system, there is no easier place than France for a young director to make a first or second film, while known directors can find finance for a new film every year or two – notwithstanding whether their previous movie lost money. The justification is that their work is art and not entertainment.

In 1994, France won exclusion of the audio-visual industry from new international free-trade rules, and it is now fighting to preserve the European Union regulation that

European productions constitute at least half of movies shown on television in the region. Yet, despite protection and subsidies, there is no disguising that the French movie industry is in crisis. From 1984 to 1994, the annual number of moviegoers in France fell from 190 million to 126 million, the number of new French films each year fell from 134 to 89 and their share of the French market fell from 49.3 per cent to 27.8 per cent. Further, while the industry routinely complains that France is being flooded with Hollywood 'trash', in the last decade annual attendance at American movies has risen only from 70 million to 75 million. In that period, tickets sold for French films have fallen from 94 million to 35 million. Put differently, the French industry has lost its edge.

But it lives on, thanks to the government – and television. Under French law, which goes further than European Union regulations, 60 per cent of movies shown on television must be European, including 40 per cent French, which means that television is now the principal market for French films, with 639 French films (old and new) bought and broadcast by the five non-pay channels and Canal Plus in 1994. Because Canal Plus, which has 4 million subscribers, is largely a movie and sports channel, showing no fewer than 195 French films in 1994, it has emerged as the pivotal force in the movie industry. And because it is obliged to spend 20 per cent of its annual revenue on film purchases, its pre-purchase policy means it can virtually decide what films are made. René Bonnell, who as Canal Plus's director of cinema last year spent $150 million purchasing new French films, said producers and directors turn first to the channel for support. 'We see about 500 screenplays a year and pick around 100', he said. 'Because we represent 30, 40 or even 50 per cent of a film's budget, if you don't have Canal Plus, you can't make your film or else you take a tremendous risk.' For de Verg's of TF1, intellectual snobbery is still a problem. 'We're not there to make art, we're there to get people into movie theatres', he said, noting that the most successful post-war French film, Jean-Marie Poiré's *Les Visiteurs*, was dismissed by intellectuals because it was a slapstick comedy. 'Do you think', he asked, 'it's nice for those who succeed to be told their work is rubbish because it isn't art?'

Questions

1. What would imply the adoption of a market orientation by the French film industry?
2. Should the French film industry be market oriented, or is cinema too different? Explain your answer.

Ecover

Case study prepared by D. Develter and published in
The Ecological Factory Manual (1992), Ecover publications.
Reproduced with permission from the author.

Ecover, the manufacturer of green cleaners and detergents based in Belgium, grew out of the green washing products marketing and distribution business set up by entrepreneur Frans Bogaerts in 1979. In 1982 the business became Ecover, and in 1988 it began manufacturing its own liquid cleaners. Ecover has an explicit aim of striving towards 'minimum environmental impact' during each stage of product manufacture and use. When it comes to raw materials the company, whenever possible, sources natural raw materials and avoids the synthetic petrochemical products, which have become the mainstay of the cleaning products industry. For example, surfactants based on sugar and soap are used which use renewable sources and quickly biodegrade unlike their more modern petrochemical counterparts. To keep pollution and waste during usage down to a minimum, the company uses minimum packaging, modular packaging of washing powder bleach (to allow it to be used in white washes but not in coloured washes) and even warns its customers against using too much of its product.

The Ecover vision went far beyond the usual concept of green products. The company saw its product range as:

Far more than a series of ecological products. It is a symbol, a statement, a point of view: we can no longer continue like this. We want to be able to swim again in our rivers, drink water from the tap without being afraid, and look forward to our children's future with confidence.

The only difficulty with developing a strategy of minimal environmental harm, which went beyond the product itself, was those conventional production processes and facilities could not provide the sort of green production performance that the Ecover vision entailed.

The company therefore set about creating the world's first 'ecological factory' based on a number of green principles. It aims for 'closed-loop processes' and has neither a chimney nor a polluting discharge pipe. The 1.5 million litres of water used each year is purified and recycled using a reed bed. Energy consumption is kept to a minimum through the use of solar power and heat recovery. Solid waste is sorted to maximise recycling opportunities. The building itself is a product of 'organic architecture'. It is made from entirely biodegradable materials including an insulating and aesthetically pleasing lawn roof garden supported by wooden rafters (sustainably sourced), and exterior walls made from recycled coal slag. In the choice of building materials, criteria for environmental quality pioneered by the Technical University of Eindhoven were used in addition to conventional technical parameters. The building was also designed to cater for the health and welfare of its inhabitants through good thermal and acoustic insulation, and good natural ventilation and lighting.

Company policies include car-pooling, the provision of company bicycles and allowances for using public transport or switching to a fuel-efficient car. (Although it might seem inappropriate that any workers at a factory like Ecover's should contribute to global warming by commuting to work, the company has calculated that the volume of carbon released into the atmosphere by the journeys of their staff will equate to the annual atmospheric carbon absorbed by the grass roof.) Office staff are networked on computers to reduce consumption of recycled stationery, and can take advantage of flexible hours and working from home via their portable computers.

Building the ecological factory involved a premium of 30 per cent additional cost compared to a conventional plant. However, due to its choice of materials for reuse, recycling or easy disposal, decommissioning the plant will cost only one-tenth of that for a conventional plant.

Questions

1. Is Ecover really better for the environment?
2. How can the firm communicate its superiority?
3. How do you get the consumer to pay for the product superiority?

Volvo Trucks Belgium

Adapted from the case study Volvo Trucks Europe, J.-J. Lambin
and T.B. Hiller (1994) in J.-J. Lambin *Problèmes de Marketing*,
Paris, Ediscience International

During the last decade, there was a considerable increase in the quantities of goods transported by road and one result of this has been a significant growth in sales of trucks. This state of affairs must surely be due in part to the major improvement in the Western Europe road network, but was equally the result of the advantages that road transport has over other means of haulage (water, rail, air). These can be summed up as flexibility, cost saving, just-in-time delivery and product integrity. Since 1985, total sales figures for trucks in Belgium have evened out with something in the order of 5500 new truck registrations being recorded each year.

Current practice within the truck industry is to describe the truck market by refer-ring to the figure of maximum permitted cargo weight (gross vehicle weight or GVW) and to make a distinction between light trucks (under 7 tons), medium weight trucks (from 7 to 16 tons) and heavy trucks (over 16 tons). The light and medium segment comprises 51 per cent of the whole market based on registrations and is contested by four main manufacturers: Mercedes, Daf, Scania and Renault. In the heavy truck cate-gory, which comprises 49 per cent of the total market, the main competitors are Volvo, Daf, Scania and Mercedes.

A second method of dividing up the market which is in current use is the size of the fleets owned by truck customers: 57.3 per cent of all haulers have a fleet of 3 vehicles or less; 18.3 per cent own between 4 and 10 vehicles and 24.4 per cent own more than 10 trucks.

The advantage of these two segmentation criteria, GVW and fleet size, is that devel-opments within the market place can be easily monitored as the registration statistics include this information and these are published at regular intervals.

An analysis of the truck buyer profile according to the use to which the vehicles are put suggests they can be divided up into three types of business: leasing companies (of minor importance in Belgium), own-account carriers (65.6 per cent) and professional carriers (34.4 per cent). Own-account carriers consist of businesses which transport their own products as part of their manufacturing (for example, a brewery) or commer-cial (for example a supermarket chain) activity. Whereas professional carriers perform transport of goods on behalf of others over regional, national or international distances. Some of these are specialists in transporting particular types of goods.

According to a recent survey among hauliers, 11.5 per cent are own-account haulers having a fleet of ten trucks or more, while 14.7 per cent are professional transporters with a fleet of maximum 3 trucks. In each of these categories, there are three types of haulage based on distance: regional haulage (almost entirely composed of retail distributors and building materials transport), national haulage and international freight.

Question

1. How would you proceed to segment this market from the customer's perspective?

The Petro-Equipment Company

Case study prepared by J.-J. Lambin, on the basis of an example presented by M. Porter (1989) in *Competitive Advantage*, New York, The Free Press.

Bill Spencer is the marketing manager of the Petro-Equipment Company specialising in the development and manufacturing of oil drilling equipment. The oil field equipment industry offers two types of drilling equipment to its customers: standard electro-mechanical equipment and sophisticated electronic and computer-based equipment. Electro-mechanical equipment is highly versatile and can be used for both deep and shallow drilling, whereas the electronic systems are used for deep drilling only. The Petro-Equipment Company specialises in advanced electronic systems and has a world-wide market organisation.

Spencer is currently developing a strategic plan for its line of oil drilling equipment and has to decide the type of market coverage to adopt. For that purpose, he is trying to segment the market in a meaningful way.

In a first step, Spencer tries to identify the main characteristics of potential customers and he realises that there are several ways in which buyers can be classified. The type of end-buyers that purchase the company's products are oil companies which are geographically located in both developed and developing countries. It is common practice in the petroleum industry to classify oil companies by size and to adopt three categories: major oil companies, large independent and small independent. A further complication comes from the fact that the ownership status also differs: some companies are private, others are state-owned. Finally, the technological sophistication of the end-buyers is also a relevant criterion to consider when segmenting the market. Some oil companies clearly have the required know-how, while others do not.

Spencer is convinced that all these criteria are useful to describe the purchasing behaviour of potential customers, but he also realises that some combinations of these segmentation criteria are infeasible combinations. For instance, all independent oil companies are by definition private-owned and state-owned companies are generally large companies. Similarly, he is aware that it is very unrealistic to propose sophisticated technologies to oil companies operating in developing countries. The company has an excellent reputation, not only for the quality of the equipment sold, but also the technical assistance provided to its customers, a service highly appreciated mainly by small oil companies.

Questions

1. Using the three-dimensional macro-segmentation procedures, define the market in terms of functions, technologies and buyers.
2. Build a segmentation grid describing the market of oil drilling equipment and presenting all the 'existing' potential segments.
3. Propose a market coverage strategy adapted to the distinctive characteristics of the Petro-Equipment Company.

Sierra Plastics Company

This case study was prepared by W.J. Stanton and published in
Fundamentals of Marketing, McGraw-Hill.
Reproduced with permission.

Over a period of two years, the price of polyethylene pipe had dropped steadily and significantly. This fact, coupled with the recognition that his company was operating in an industry chronically faced with excess capacity, made Walter Riley, the marketing manager of Sierra Plastics Company, realise that his company might have to alter its pricing policy. Located in San Francisco, the Sierra Plastics Company was a relatively small manufacturer of polyethylene and other plastic products. The company's main product, accounting for 60 to 70 per cent of annual sales, was polyethylene pipe, which was manufactured in a variety of sizes ranging from ½ inch to 6 inches in diameter. About 30 to 40 per cent of the company's sales came from a variety of plastic compounds intended for industrial uses such as wall panels, electrical installations and soundproofing. Polyethylene is also widely used by other manufacturers in the production of sheeting, bottles, toys, appliance components and automotive parts, but the Sierra Plastics Company had not entered these markets.

Compared with metal pipe, the plastic product was lighter, easier to install, non-corrosive and less expensive. Polyethylene pipe was an excellent product for farm irrigation, wells, lawn sprinklers and other uses where the liquid pressure requirements were relatively low – up to 100 pounds per square inch. For the transmission of potable water, the only polyethylene pipe used was made from virgin materials and carried the National Sanitation Foundation (NSF) seal. Pipe not made from virgin material was considered the 'second-grade line'. About 60 to 80 per cent of the polyethylene pipe produced were of the second-grade, non-NSF, lower-priced variety intended for consumer and industrial market uses other than transmitting drinking water.

Since the end of the Second World War, the growth of the plastic pipe industry had been phenomenal, as many new uses for the product were quickly developed. Because of the attractiveness of this market, many new firms entered the industry and generated a production capacity well in excess of the level which even the expanding market could absorb. A major factor enabling this over-capacity to develop was the ease of entry into the industry. Initial investment requirements were low, and the basic technical knowledge could be easily acquired. The raw-materials producers and the manufacturers of the extrusion machines used in making the pipe eagerly supplied the engineering and production information. The extrusion rates on a mixed basis of pipe ½ to 6 inches in diameter were such that one machine operating twenty-four hours a day, seven days a week, could produce in excess of 1 million pounds of finished pipe per year. Two major producers alone had more than fifty machines, each capable of producing 1 million pounds of finished polyethylene pipe per year.

There were about sixty manufacturers of polyethylene pipe located over the entire United States, but only a small number marketed their products nationally. Most of the manufacturers were regional extruders, making only a limited line of polyethylene pipe. The Sierra Plastics Company fell in this category, operating twelve machines and marketing in California, Oregon and Arizona. The machine used by the Sierra Plastics Company for extruding polyethylene pipe could also be used for the production of other plastic products. By marketing in a limited geographic area, the Sierra Company could fill orders faster and give better service generally than the large, national firms.

The company's financial position was strong. However, its profit margins, while adequate, were endangered by the price-cutting in the industry. Sierra Plastics had a sales force of ten men. They reached the consumer market by selling to sprinkler installation firms, to lawn equipment dealers and distributors, and to landscape contractor-gardeners. In the industrial market the salesmen sold to agricultural co-operatives, agricultural equipment dealers, and plumbing and heating wholesalers. In many cases, Sierra sold directly to large farms and to businesses which wanted to install a lawn sprinkling system, and to manufacturers with industrial watering systems.

The conditions of excess capacity in the plastic pipe industry had induced many firms to cut their prices in an attempt to broaden their market share and thus utilise some of the excess production capacity in their plants. Because it was difficult, if not impossible, to differentiate its products from those of its competitors, the Sierra Plastics Company had been forced to cut its prices to meet competition. Over the past two years Sierra's price for non-virgin polyethylene pipe had dropped from 52 cents a pound to 38 cents a pound. During the most recent year, unit sales remained relatively constant, so the potentially depressing effect on profits was evident. Currently, the cost of raw materials was 40 to 50 per cent of the selling price. High-quality pipe meeting NSF standards sold for proportionately more than the second-grade product line.

Riley was studying several alternative courses of action in an attempt to stimulate sales and to stem the profit decline. His first thought was to reduce prices further and try to do a better job of promoting the Sierra brand. He hoped to bring the product into a price range which would attract a new market, not previously users of polyethylene pipe. He believed that these actions would increase unit sales volume enough to more than compensate for the unit price reductions. Riley realised that competitors would undoubtedly retaliate if Sierra's prices were reduced. The speed and effectiveness of this price retaliation would be a function of Sierra's ability to differentiate its product, the ability of the customer to judge product quality, and the importance of price in the consumer's buying decisions. Another unknown was the extent to which prices, once cut, could ever be restored to their former levels. Riley was also considering the alternative of reducing product quality and thus reducing costs enough so that unit prices could be cut without any loss of unit gross or net profit.

Pope, the production manager, had recommended an almost polar-opposite plan. He suggested that Sierra produce and market a new high-quality line made from superior resins. This new pipe would be sold at a price above even that of the premium pipe now produced to NSF standards. The intention would be to break away entirely from the 'price-football' image of the second-grade and the virgin product line. Pope believed that the company's distributors and ultimate users could be convinced that this new product was truly of higher quality and thus warranted a higher price. To help convince both the distributors and the users, Pope would institute a distinctive warranty programme. Under it, Sierra Plastics would pay for all labour and materials charges incurred in replacing or repairing defective pipe.

Questions

1. What course of action should the company follow to counter the problems of price reductions and excess capacity?

The Tissex Company

Case prepared by Gilles Marion from ESC Lyon. Translated and reproduced
with the permission of the author.

Tissex is a French company whose sole activity is the production and sales of fabrics composed of artificial and synthetic fibres. In spite of a turnover of FF536 million and a gross profit margin of 17 per cent in 1983, the net result was not very high. Its know-how in production processes (gluing, weaving, dying, finishing) combined with advanced technical collaboration with manufacturers of fibres have so far been sufficient to maintain its position in comparison with both French, European or Japanese competitors. A turnover of FF200 million from exports, mainly to the Common Market but also to the USA, gives the group an international dimension.

Tissex offers a large range of products which includes fabrics for clothing (polyester silks), linings, sportswear (anoraks, clothes, and so on) and household linen (quilts, bedspreads, and so on) as well as safety fabrics (technical fabrics for the army, the police, the chemical and oil industries, and so on), printing ribbons (ready to be inked) for typewriters and computers. Over the past three years Tissex has invested in modern equipment and machinery. This policy should be sustained if Tissex wants to maintain its position in the international market.

Henry Bonnet, the new CEO, must evaluate the company's overall performance and develop a strategy for the next three years. This is what he says about the situation of his company:

> We have five factories, mainly in the Lyon area. However, by acquiring St. Renard in 1980, we now have two other plants in Roubaix, in the North of France.
>
> This acquisition brought us a turnover of FF123 million in 1983, mainly from linings, but we are, however, more interested in St. Renard's technical fabrics. Up until then our activity in this area has been secondary, let's say from FF4 million to FF5 million in 1980. We have concentrated all of this activity in Roubaix so that today we have 30 per cent of the market with a turnover of FF33 million. This is really good for a market with an average annual growth rate of 9 per cent, especially as the gross margin for this activity is over twice that of the group's average.
>
> Competition rose quickly! Particularly textile companies of northern France and among them Guillez with a turnover of FF20 million in 1983. They followed our example and started to export their goods. The other competitors are smaller, companies with a 5 to 10 per cent market share each. Most of them are French. So far, however, we are well protected because of the highly specialised demands of our customers. Exporting is slow to get off the ground but we're not in a hurry; we are confident in our know-how. The Germans and English cannot

catch up with us right away. Furthermore, each country still has its own standards. There are approximately 100 potential clients in all of Europe and what they are looking for is 'service'.

As for linings, the situation is completely different: this is a depressed market, as is the case for the traditional garment industry. It will decline from 2 to 3 per cent next year, as it did in previous years. Womenswear was in a somewhat better position, but as a whole the sector is doing poorly. We have over 2000 clients in this activity but every year there are several bankruptcies. Our sales representatives have standing orders not to deliver unless they have the go ahead from Sales Information Service. The price war is fierce and when you're the leader in the European market, with only 12 per cent of the market, you have a hard time maintaining your position. Belgian companies are the toughest to compete with: they have invested a lot over the past few years. For example, Deckerman who has only 7 per cent of the market earned more money than we did. Up until now we have tried to hold on even if the gross margin for linings is largely inferior to that of the group average: 10 per cent, this is worrying. Luckily the Japanese can't come in on this market, as the price per metre is too low.

Our objective is clear: slightly increase prices to maintain the same level of turnover (FF160 million) without affecting the volume of production and without losing our French clients who represent 45 per cent of our turnover. We will also reach some new markets because our weaker competitors will have disappeared – in France, Germany, England and maybe outside the Common Market as well. We have 12 multicard agents in France and our headquarters are in charge of foreign markets. The Roubaix plant delivers to Paris, northern France, the Benelux and Great Britain. Roanne sends goods out to southern France and to all other countries. Germany receives special treatment because an own sales subsidiary was created in 1977 for some obscure reason. Results there are very poor and we now plan on dealing directly from France for large orders.

Roanne is a real headache. Last year we had to lay off 90 people, mostly working on polyester. Globally Roanne had a 1983 turnover of FF256 million with FF70 million for linings and the rest for clothing. Moreover, weaving of polyester fabric is divided between two workshops equipped with different weaving machinery. One-third of production comes from very modern and rapid machines and two thirds are produced traditionally. With a gross margin of 7 per cent the polyester activity is the worst of our group and the market has not increased for the past few years.

The Japanese have hurt us in this area. They now have over 5 per cent of the European market with good quality products they can sell at a higher price than we can. We are far behind with just 1 per cent of the market. However we do export 40 per cent of our production thanks to the quality of our sales network but at very low prices. And we can't ask our clients to pay more. However we can observe that this market is also being concentrated: many clients have disappeared. Five years ago we had 2500 clients; today there are 800 in France and 600 in the other European countries. These numbers will still decrease until we will only have the most interesting companies as clients.

Luckily there is the Lyon factory: a FF157 million turnover in 1983 and 6 to 7 per cent of growth in value every year. The sportswear activity is advancing rapidly, 8 per cent per year as compared to 6 per cent for printing ribbons for computers and typewriters (but ribbons in the USA are increasing by 20 per cent annually). As a matter of fact, the Lyon factory has two really distinct activities and I wonder if we shouldn't separate them completely. The factory manager has a real problem with his production planning.

We keep very little stock on hand for printing ribbons. Whatever is produced is delivered immediately and we have three eight-hour shifts. The looms are rapid, with air or water jets, and, most important, high quality is constant. Our clients know us very well; there are only

90 throughout the world including 10 in France. We export 60 per cent of our production. In 1980, the Japanese were the first to drastically reduce their prices by 30 per cent but in this activity we were able to follow their lead and we invested in very modern Swiss equipment. We have 5 per cent of the market, just a bit lower than the two world leaders who are Japanese and German. The Spaniards and English are now beginning to invest. This is going to be a running battle. We just hope that the market can be maintained long enough for us to write off our investments over the next 2 or 3 years. In 5 years the market will have changed and we'll have to readapt but a 30 per cent gross margin is acceptable today.

The sportswear fabric is less risky. Profit is still to be made, mainly for the special quality features we propose, and our clients seem to maintain their positions. The FF67 million turnover is spread evenly over 30 customers and, even if we do have a low export profile here, our clients export their goods pretty well. The Sporting Company is the top competitor with 20 per cent of the French market, but 2 or 3 of us are close behind. We must pass the others and I believe we can catch up with Sporting as they have had a problem with deliveries and quality when there was a strike at their fibre suppliers. We always have several supply sources so as to avoid this kind of problem. Thanks to Sporting's difficulties we have been able to reach customers who, up until now, were out of reach. If we can develop these contacts we'll go from 15 per cent to 20 per cent of the market next year or the following year.

The Italians of course have tried to compete with us but this market fluctuates too fast for them; you really have to be on the spot to anticipate demand and to manage your stock correctly. Most clients are located around Lyon or Paris and we know them very well. Our sales network is excellent and we work well with each of its members.

Our sales director will retire at the end of this year and I think that we will then no longer call upon the two multicard agents who now work for us. The gross margin is even higher than for technical fabrics (36 per cent) and I am planning on maintaining the same level of sales.

Questions

1. Define the strategic segments that are relevant for Tissex's activities.
2. Make a strategic analysis of Tissex's portfolio of activities according to whatever method is, to your mind, the most appropriate (BCG matrix, multi-factors portfolio matrix, and so on). According to this method, is there a problem facing Tissex? If so, what is this problem?
3. Identify the various strategies which could be developed for each of Tissex's activities. Choose the ones you think are the most appropriate.

Newfood

Case prepared by G.S. Day *et al.* (1983) in *Cases in Computer and Model Assisted Marketing Planning*. The Scientific Press. Used with permission.

Davies, newly appointed new products marketing director, is considering the possibility of marketing a new highly nutritional food product which has widely varied uses. This product can be used as a snack, a camping food, or as a diet food. The product is to be generically labelled Newf.

Because of this wide range of possible uses, the company has had great difficulty in defining the market. The product is viewed as having no direct competitors. Early product and concept tests have been very encouraging. These tests have led Davies to believe that the product could easily sell 2 million cases (24 packages in a case) under the proposed marketing programme involving a 24c package price and an advertising programme involving $3 million in expenditure per year. The projected P&L for the first year national is:

Sales	2.00 million cases
Revenue	$8.06 million (assumes 70 per cent of the retail price is revenue to the manufacturer)
Manufacturing costs	$3.00 million ($1 million fixed manufacturing costs plus $1 per case variable)
Advertising	$3.00 million
Net margin	$2.06 million

There will be no capital expenditures required to go national, since manufacturing is to be done on a contract pack basis. These costs have been included in the projected P&L. Concorn has an agreement with the contract packer requiring that once a decision to go national is made, Concorn is obligated to pay fixed production costs ($1 million per year) for three years even if the product is withdrawn from the market at a later time. Even though there are no capital requirements, it is the company's policy not to introduce new products with profit expectations of less than $0.5 million per year (a three-year planning horizon is usually considered).

Mr Davies is quite confident of his sales estimates (and hence his profit estimate) although he does admit that they contain some uncertainty. When pressed, he will admit that sales could be as low as 1 million cases in the first year, but points out those sales might also exceed the estimate by as much as 1 million cases. His operational definition of these extremes is that each has no more than a 1 in 10 chance of occurring. He is more concerned about sales after the first year. Historically, most new products with which he is familiar have had sales that decayed over time. After some effort, he summarised his feelings about the sales for the new product in Table CS9.1.

Table CS9.1 First year sales estimates

First year's sales	Probability	Decay rates per year (%)	Probability
0.5–1.0	0.10	+10 to –10	0.25
1.0–1.5	0.20	–10 to –30	0.50
1.5–2.0	0.25	–30 to –50	0.25
2.0–2.5	0.25		
2.5–3.0	0.10		
3.0–3.5	0.10		

There are also other marketing plans under consideration. A second alternative involves a 10c price increase (34c retail) to be used to finance higher advertising expenditures ($6 million) in the first year. The advantage of this second plan is that higher advertising could bring as many people into the market as the lower price and that in subsequent years advertising expenditures could then be cut back to the $4 million level. There is some concern that the higher price would affect repeat sales, hence sales might decay even faster over time under this plan. A casual estimate is that the decay rate might increase by 50 per cent due to the higher price. There is also some discussion of coupling the lower price with high advertising ($6 million) or using a middle price (29c) and a middle level of advertising expenditure ($4.5). These alternatives have not as yet been fully explored.

Davies believes that the potential of the product is so high that national introduction should be started as soon as possible. His primary concern is the choice of a strategy.

Rank, the director of market research, suggests that a market test be performed. Although he agrees that the project looks good, his sales estimates are somewhat lower than Davies'. He agrees to the sales range of 0.5 to 3.5 but, based on the history of new product failures, assigns the probabilities shown in Table CS9.2.

Table CS9.2 Alternative first year's sales estimates

First year's sales (million cases)	Probability
0.5–1.0	0.15
1.0–1.5	0.25
1.5–2.0	0.35
2.0–2.5	0.20
2.5–3.0	0.05
3.0–3.5	0.00

Rank argues that not only would the market test reduce the uncertainty in the sales estimate, but it would also provide an opportunity to find out more about how prices and advertising affect sales. He has not as yet worked out a test plan, but believes he could conduct a 6-month test that would cost no more than $75,000 in which it would be possible to estimate national first year sales within a quarter million cases (the estimated sampling error of his instrument).

Davies is hesitant to accept the proposal, not only because of costs and time delays but also because he is concerned about the usefulness of the results. He notes that the proposed test could at best give him information on first year sales while he is most concerned about future sales. He also questions Rank's ability to test within the stated error range.

Questions

1. If Davies has to decide whether to introduce Newfood without the aid of a market test, how should he decide; if his planning horizon is 1 year or if his planning horizon is 3 years?
2. How would you use Davies' probability estimates in the analysis?
3. Should a market test be conducted? How much would a 'perfect' market test be worth?

SAS: Meeting Customer Expectations

Case study prepared by D.L. Kurtz and K.E. Clow (1998)
and published in *Services Marketing*, New York, John Wiley.
Reproduced with permission.

Flying has become a lot lighter on the wallet than it used to be. In the last 20 years, airline ticket prices have dropped by as much as 60 per cent – as have airline profits. With more airlines and service alternatives available to consumers than ever before, competition among carriers has become fierce, and meeting customer expectations crucial. Despite budget crunches and airline ticket price slashing by the competition, Scandinavian Airlines remains committed to meeting passenger expectations.

'Our goal is that 100 per cent of our customers must want to travel with SAS again', says Jan Stenberg, president and CEO of Scandinavian Airlines System. 'Ninety-five per cent of them do today, so there is some room for improvement, says Stenberg, confirming that customers' past experiences are critical to his company.

Scandinavian Airlines System (SAS), the third largest carrier in Europe, is one of a number of airlines struggling to stay aloft. A deregulated European market, a recession, and the fact that 7 of its 20 competitors are either government owned or subsidised has not made the 1990s an easy decade for the company. However, after suffering four consecutive years of operating losses, in 1994, SAS made a U-turn, posting a profit.

What created the winds of change for SAS? While some of its competitors slashed prices in order to fill seats, SAS took another approach. Instead of selling cheap seats, the company expanded a marketing strategy initiated in the mid-1980s: it became 'The business traveller's airline'. More recently SAS increased its number of flights and connections, offered free one-day stopovers in Copenhagen and Stockholm for business travellers wishing to sightsee, and revamped its planes with ergonomically designed seats, airphones and fax capabilities. Travellers can also check in for their flights at SAS-affiliated hotels or even from their car phones, eliminating pre-service waiting.

SAS also boasts the best on-time flight record of any European airline, which is important to business people traveling on tight schedules. 'Care is about how our product makes people feel. It includes personal and professional service, friendly and respectful attention at every stage of the trip, and understanding of the customer's situation and the willingness and ability to provide comfort and solve problems,' says Stenberg.

Part of solving problems involves admitting flights can sometimes be delayed and assisting passengers affected by them. All passengers who are delayed more than four hours are given a 'customer message card' upon which they can fill in messages to be forwarded by phone or fax by SAS. The approach seems to be working. The company now transports more business-class flyers than any of its European competitors.

> At SAS we used to think of ourselves as the sum total of our aircraft, our maintenance bases, our offices, and our administrative procedures. But if you ask our customers about SAS, they won't tell you about our planes, or our offices, or the way we finance our capital investments. Instead, they'll talk about their experiences with the people at SAS,

commented SAS's former CEO, Jan Carlzon, who envisioned and implemented expanded business-class services in the mid-1980s.

In his book, *Moments of Truth*, in which he detailed his formula for SAS's successes in the 1980s, Carlzon estimated that 10 million SAS customers every year came in contact with five SAS employees for 15 seconds per encounter – amounting to what he called '50 million moments of truth'. 'SAS is not a collection of material assets but the quality of the contact between an individual customer and the SAS employees who serve the customer directly,' he said.

Still, *Moments of Truth* must be sustained from decade to decade and from CEO to CEO. Despite SAS's best efforts on a continuing basis, it is still possible to fall short. Said Helle Katholm Invardsen, a public relations manager from Denmark: 'I travel with SAS very often. SAS used to be better than other airlines. But several times recently I've felt that they didn't bother to apologise for delays. And the other advantages, such as the lounges, cabin service, and so on, are the same all over no matter what company in Europe you travel with. I used to think I was almost home when I boarded a SAS plane, but I don't feel that way anymore.'

Questions

1. To improve profitability, SAS was forced to reduce its workforce by over 1000 employees. How might such reductions affect the ideal, desired, predicted and adequate levels of service? Can the company adjust consumers' zones of tolerance in order to cope with staff reductions?

2. Identify the antecedent expectations of people intending to book airline flights. What factors play a part in their decisions? How can SAS improve its firm-induced factors in order to attract customers?

Sources: Edvaldo Pereira Lima, 'Pioneering in People', *Air Transport World*, Vol. 32 (April, 1995), pp. 51–4; 'Scandinavian Airlines Takes Austerity Steps to Cut Costs by 10%', *Wall Street Journal* (12 November, 1993), p. A7B; George Newman, 'The Morning After', *Across the Board*, Vol. 29 (September, 1992), pp. 11–12; John Marcom, Jr, 'Moment of Truth', *Forbes*, Vol. 148 (8 July, 1991), pp. 83–8; Kenneth Labich, 'An Airline That Soars on Service', *Fortune*, Vol. 122 (31 December, 1990), pp. 94–6; Jan Carlzon, *Moments of Truth* (Cambridge, MA: Ballinger, 1987).

Index

NAME INDEX

SUBJECT INDEX